Melvin Mencher's News Reporting and Writing

Eleventh Edition

Melvin Mencher

Columbia University

**McGraw-Hill
Higher Education**

Boston   Burr Ridge, IL   Dubuque, IA   New York   San Francisco   St. Louis
Bangkok   Bogotá   Caracas   Kuala Lumpur   Lisbon   London   Madrid   Mexico City
Milan   Montreal   New Delhi   Santiago   Seoul   Singapore   Sydney   Taipei   Toronto

The McGraw-Hill Companies

McGraw-Hill
Higher Education

Published by McGraw-Hill, an imprint of The McGraw-Hill Companies, Inc., 1221 Avenue of the Americas, New York, NY 10020. Copyright © 2008, 2006, 2003, 2000, 1997, 1994, 1991, 1987, 1984, 1981, 1977 by Melvin Mencher. All rights reserved. No part of this publication may be reproduced or distributed in any form or by any means, or stored in a database or retrieval system, without the prior written consent of The McGraw-Hill Companies, Inc., including, but not limited to, in any network or other electronic storage or transmission, or broadcast for distance learning.

This book is printed on acid-free paper.

1 2 3 4 5 6 7 8 9 0 DOC/DOC 0 9 8 7

ISBN: 978-0-07-351193-1

MHID: 0-07-351193-5

Editor in Chief: *Michael Ryan*
Publisher: *Frank Mortimer*
Sponsoring Editor: *Suzanne Earth*
Marketing Manager: *Leslie Oberhuber*
Developmental Editor: *Craig Leonard*
Production Editor: *Regina Ernst*
Manuscript Editor: *Leslie Ann Weber*
Design Manager: *Andrei Pasternak*
Cover Designer: *Andrei Pasternak*
Art Editor: *Ayelet Arbel*
Manager, Photo Research: *Brian J. Pecko*
Production Supervisor: *Dennis Fitzgerald*
Composition: *10/12 Text Font by Laserwords Private Limited*
Printing: *PMS 562, 45# New Era Matte, R. R. Donnelley & Sons/Crawfordsville, IN*

Cover: The cover credits section for this book begins on page xx and is considered an extension of the copyright page.

Credits: The credits section for this book begins on page 597 and is considered an extension of the copyright page.

Library of Congress Cataloging-in-Publication Data

Mencher, Melvin.
    Melvin Mencher's news reporting and writing / Melvin Mencher.
        p. cm.
    Includes index.
    ISBN-13: 978-0-07-351193-1 (alk. paper)
    ISBN-10: 0-07-351193-5 (alk. paper)
    1. Reporters and reporting. 2. Journalism—Authorship. I. Title.
PN4781.M4 2008
070.4'3—dc22

                                    2007035879

The Internet addresses listed in the text were accurate at the time of publication. The inclusion of a Web site does not indicate an endorsement by the authors or McGraw-Hill, and McGraw-Hill does not guarantee the accuracy of the information presented at these sites.

www.mhhe.com

Contents

Preface

This is the eleventh edition of *News Reporting and Writing* and though much has changed in the classroom and in the media since the first edition, the fundamentals remain, as does the purpose of *NRW:*

1. To teach the skills necessary for a variety of media work.

2. To provide the background knowledge essential to accurate and informed reporting and writing.

3. To suggest the values that direct the practice of journalism.

Learning to report accurately and to write precisely and vigorously is no simple task. Digging through the clusters of events and the torrent of verbiage to find useful, relevant information and then capturing these nuggets in purposeful language require mastery of a demanding discipline.

This may seem a daunting task. Don't worry. The guidelines in *NRW* provide ample help. They have shown the way for successful news writers over the years. Here are some of the journalists who will help you on your way:

Guides We will accompany a young reporter as she conducts her first interview, and we will watch an experienced reporter dig through court records to reveal a shameful part of our past.

We will look over the shoulder of a reporter as she makes her way over the Internet for the background essential to her story. We will venture into newsrooms where multimedia news workers write for online, broadcast and print media.

We will sit in the press box with reporters covering high school football and major league baseball games. We will join a police reporter as she races to cover a triple murder.

We will watch a reporter labor over his story until "little beads of blood form on his forehead," as Red Smith described the agony of the journalist's search for the words that will accurately portray the event. And we will share in the reporter's joy when the story is finished and is given a byline and placed on the front page or makes the evening network newscast.

We will stand at the side of newsletter and magazine writers, alternative and special-interest journalists, and we will watch how a news release is prepared.

In other words, we will be concerned with the processes of reporting and writing—how reporters gather information from sources and from their observations, how they verify the material, and how they put it together in news stories and features.

The journalists we will be watching work for small newspapers in Iowa, South Dakota and Oregon, and they are on the staffs of metropolitan dailies in Chicago, Los Angeles and New York. Some serve online news services. One reporter writes for a network television station in New York; another covers local events for a television station in San Francisco. We will see how general assignment reporters and the men and women assigned to cover politics, sports, business, the police, city hall, education and other beats do their jobs.

The Basics

Whether covering a college basketball game, writing an obituary or reporting the president's State of the Union address, the journalist follows the same basic process. The sports reporter, the entertainment writer, the general assignment reporter in a town of 25,000 and the Associated Press's White House correspondent all share a way of thinking and a similar set of techniques that have guided journalists through the years, whatever the changes in technology.

In their reporting, journalists seek out the new, the significant, the material they decide will inform their readers, viewers and listeners. And they find a suitable form for this information in a story that satisfies the public's need to know.

The journalists we will be following not only show a mastery of the basics. We will see that they share an ethic that directs and gives meaning to their work.

The Morality of Journalism

Power of Knowing

"Knowledge will govern ignorance, and a people who mean to be their own governors must arm themselves with the power knowledge gives. A popular government without popular information or the means of acquiring it is but a prologue to a farce or a tragedy or perhaps both."
—*James Madison*

The literary critic Northrop Frye could have been describing journalistic morality: "The persistence of keeping the mind in a state of disciplined sanity, the courage of facing results that may deny or contradict everything that one had hoped to achieve—these are obviously moral qualities, if the phrase means anything at all."

James O. Freedman, former president of Dartmouth, might have been speaking of the practice of journalism when he described his experience as a law clerk to Thurgood Marshall: "In that year, I learned from a great advocate that law must be practiced not only with craft and passion but also with a tenacious commitment to ideals."

Mary McGrory, the Washington columnist, described an aspect of how journalists approach their work in comments she made after interviewing 45 journalists who had applied for Nieman Fellowships at Harvard. She said she found these journalists to have a "great deal of commitment and compassion." Most had a trait in common, she said: "They knew a great deal about what they were doing. They did not think it enough."

McGrory was a role model for generations of journalists. At a time when too many reporters seem umbilically attached to their computers and rarely venture from their office chairs, McGrory prided herself on being a shoe-leather journalist.

"I have to see," she said. "I have to hear. I don't want anyone doing my listening or watching for me."

McGrory understood the morality of journalism. "No great men call me," she said. "You know who calls me? Losers. I am their mark. If you want to abolish lead mines. If you want to save children from abuse or stupid laws or thickheaded judges, you have my telephone number."

McGrory's spirit animates this edition, as does the work of the reporters whose work I have borrowed to provide instructional material . . . reporters like Clifford Levy, whose series on the abuse of the mentally ill won a Pulitzer Prize. "Of all the praise I got for the series, the most meaningful was from other reporters at the paper (*The New York Times*) who said it made them proud to work there because it was a classic case of looking out for those who can't look out for themselves."

The journalists I know—my former colleagues and students, from whom I have shamelessly taken time and borrowed ideas—would shrink at being described as moralists. Yet they consider their work to have a large moral component. Most of them worry about the abuse of power.

Adversary Journalism   Although adversary journalism is often criticized and sometimes ignored, it is as old as the Republic. Today's journalists are descended from a press described by the historian Robert A. Ruthland as "obstreperous newspapers (that) signalled the rise of a new kind of journalism in America that would not truckle long to any officialdom."

The journalist knows that democracy is healthiest when the public is informed about the activities of captains of industry and chieftains in public office. Only with adequate information can people check those in power. Jack Fuller of the *Chicago Tribune* put this simply: "To me, the central purpose of journalism is to tell the truth so that people will have the information to be sovereign."

Walt Whitman, journalist and poet, described the fragility of democracy and its source of strength this way: "There is no week nor day nor hour when tyranny may not enter upon this country, if the people lose their supreme confidence in themselves—and lose their roughness and spirit of defiance."

Confident, rough and defiant. An apt description of the journalist at work—but also characteristics that have aroused anger and animosity. In its role as watchdog for the public, the press has been relentlessly scrutinized and sometimes attacked for its revelations. Journalists understand that the path of the truth teller is not always smooth, that people are sometimes disturbed by what the journalist tells them.

This eleventh edition is offered to students with a commitment to and a belief in the traditional role of the press as a means of enabling people to improve their lot and to govern themselves intelligently. *News Reporting and Writing* takes seriously the observation in the Book of Proverbs: "The instruments of both life and death are contained within the power of the tongue."

Public Service Journalism

The kind of journalism that underlies this textbook can be described as public service journalism, a journalism that meets the needs of people by supplying them with the information essential to rational decision making. Public service journalism has a long and glorious history. It has attracted writers like Charles Dickens, whose crusading newspaper *Household Words* carried stories that revealed his indignation at the indecencies visited on the young, the poor and the powerless—themes current today.

Dickens visited orphanages, saw for himself the conditions under which homeless women lived. He walked the streets teeming with the uneducated young. He described what he saw.

Dickens said his ambition as an editor was that his newspaper "be admitted into many homes with confidence and affection," and it was. His biographer says the result of Dickens' revelations was a "huge and steadily growing audience ranging in both directions from the middle and upper middle classes."

Today's journalists are worthy inheritors of this tradition of public service journalism, and we will be looking at their work. We'll watch a reporter handle a news release from angry parents who charge the local schools with exposing students to racist books.

Journalism intends to entertain us as well as to inform us, and we will also follow reporters as they show us the zany side of life. We'll eavesdrop on a truck-diner waitress as she trades quips and barbs with her burly customers.

Journalism's Tradition

Journalism has always had its down periods, and there has been no shortage of nostrums offered for a quick cure. Its survival, however, has rested on the bedrock of its tradition. Albert Camus, the French journalist and author, was sustained by that sense of his calling during the Nazi occupation of France when he wrote from the underground. Accepting the Nobel Prize for literature, Camus said, "Whatever our personal frailties may be, the nobility of our calling will always be rooted in two commitments difficult to observe: refusal to lie about what we know and resistance to oppression."

Journalism "is something more than a craft, something other than an industry, something between an art and a ministry," says Wickham Steed, an editor of *The Times* of London. "Journalists proper are unofficial public servants whose purpose is to serve the community."

Mentor   My model for this amalgam of artist, sentry, public servant and town crier is Ralph M. Blagden, who taught a generation of journalists their duty and introduced them to the power and splendor of their native language. Ralph's classrooms were the newsrooms of newspapers from New Hampshire to California, where he worked as reporter and editor.

Ralph was my competitor as a state capitol correspondent, and never was there such a mismatch. As a beginning reporter, I reported what people said and did and stopped there. Ralph generously took the youngster in tow and showed him that a good reporter never settles for the surface of the news, that the compelling commandment of the journalist is to dig. He refused to make reporting divisible: All good reporting is investigative reporting, he insisted.

Long before investigative reporting became the fashion, Ralph was digging out documents and records to disclose truths. His journalism was in the tradition of Joseph Pulitzer and that publisher's crusading editor, O.K. Bovard. Those of us who were fortunate to work with Ralph feel ourselves to be members of a journalistic family whose roots are embedded in a noble tradition.

Benjamin C. Bradlee, who directed *The Washington Post* Watergate investigation that led to the resignation of President Richard M. Nixon, recalls the first story he wrote for Blagden when he was a young reporter.

"It had to do with the post-war housing mess," Bradlee said, "and he made me rewrite it 16 times. I've never done that to a reporter, but I suspect I should have. He had a great dollop of righteous indignation, which I learned to admire enormously.

"And of course he wrote with style and punch and clarity."

Bradlee says this of Blagden:

> Ralph taught me to be dissatisfied with answers and to be exhaustive in questions. He taught me to stand up against powers that be. He taught me to spot bullies and resist them. He taught me about patience and round-the-clock work. He taught me about ideas and freedom and rights—all of this with his own mixture of wit and sarcasm and articulate grace. He could also throw a stone farther than I could, which annoys me to this day.

I recall the first story I covered with Ralph. He had heard that patients in a state hospital for the mentally ill were being mistreated. Some had mysteriously died. We interviewed doctors, nurses, attendants and former patients, and we walked through the wards and corridors of the institution. I learned that secondhand accounts are just a starting point, that direct observation and other techniques of verification are essential, and when we wrote the story I learned the power of the simple declarative sentence. I also learned that journalists can be useful members of society, for after the story appeared and both of us had moved on, the state built a modern hospital to replace that aging snake pit.

New to the Eleventh Edition

This edition is accompanied by four free online supplements. You can find them at www.mhhe.com/mencher11.

1. The *Student Workbook:* Now online and in an interactive format. Each chapter begins with "Check It," a section of writing exercises and journalism quizzes with suggested stories and answers to the quizzes in pop-up boxes so that students can check their work. Also, each chapter offers reporting and writing exercises and assignments on such current topics as student cheating, anorexia, the decline of civility and increasing juvenile crime. (Mencher)

2. *NRW Plus:* Now online and interactive, *NRW Plus* contains entire stories accompanied by the comments from the reporters who wrote them; interactive, self-teaching exercises; and audio and video clips. (Mencher)

3. *Brush Up:* Now online and interactive, *Brush Up* offers basic instruction in language use and mathematics. Self-teaching exercises relieve instructors of

the onerous task of teaching grammar, punctuation, style, percentages, fractions, averages and rates—all essential knowledge for the journalist in training. (Mencher and Wendy P. Shilton)

4. *New Reporting Simulation: A Fire Scenario:* Developed by Columbia University, this interactive simulation puts students on the scene of a five-alarm fire, as it rages late at night in a high-rise apartment in Freeport, a fictional Midwest city. Students act the role of the reporter on the police beat and are given a two-hour deadline to write the story. To access this interactive simulation:

A. Go to the URL http://cero.columbia.edu/full/melvin_mencher.html

B. Click on "News Reporting Simulation: A Fire Scenario."

C. Click on "Click here to begin" in the next browser.

D. Click on the link "Unregistered users of Columbia Educational Resources Online" below "Non-Columbia User."

E. On the next screen, enter your information in the form to register for a 60-day free trial subscription to Columbia Educational Resources online. Click the "Submit" button to send your information.

F. You will receive an e-mail confirmation from Columbia University Digital Knowledge Venture with your username and password.

G. You may use your username and password provided in the e-mail to access the simulation exercise, available at http://cero.columbia.edu/full/melvin_ mencher.html

H. Follow steps B and C to get to the login screen.

I. Click on "Registered Users of Columbia Educational Resources Online" and enter your username and password provided in the e-mail to access *A Fire Scenario.*

(Mencher and John V. Pavlik)

Instructor Resources

The instructor's manual is available online at www.mhhe.com/mencher11 and contains sample stories for the *Workbook* and a wealth of anecdotes and incidents that instructors can use in class lectures, as well as many useful pedagogical aids. (Mencher)

Also Available

Reporter's Checklist and Notebook, a handy guide to handling beats and covering a variety of stories. Checklists for 15 story types are included, as is "Useful Math for Reporters." Sold independently. (Mencher)

Acknowledgments

Many have contributed to *NRW*—my first city editor, George Baldwin, whose patience with a beginner lifted me from days of dark despair; former students whose journalism I have included here; academic colleagues whose suggestions have helped make *NRW* classroom-useful.

I learned from my student who stormed out of the classroom when I said I would not assign her to the story she said she wanted to cover because I was worried about her safety, and I am in debt to my bureau chief at the United Press who had worn down a pencil putting thick, black lines through my copy. "Just show us what the guy did," he told me. "Let the reader draw the conclusions."

The following list acknowledges some of those who shared in the preparation of the eleven editions of *News Reporting and Writing*. Only I bear responsibility for the contents.

Marjorie Arnold
The Fresno (Calif.) *Bee*

Steven K. Bagwell
Oregon State University

Brian Barrett
Office of the New York County
District Attorney

Frank Barrows
Managing Editor, *The Charlotte*
(N.C.) *Observer*

Joan Bieder
Columbia University

Mervin Block
Broadcast writing coach

Paul Byers
Marymount University

Art Carey
Bucks County (Pa.) *Courier Times* and
The Philadelphia Inquirer

Debbie Cenziper
The Miami Herald

Marcia Chambers
The New York Times

Sherry Chisenhall
The Wichita Eagle

Susan Clark
Associated Press

Kenneth Conboy
Coordinator of the New York City
Criminal Justice System

Claude Cookman
The Miami Herald

Sharon Dennehy
Paris Junior College

Jere Downs
The Philadelphia Inquirer

Robert A. Dubill
Executive Editor, *USA Today*

Jack Dvorak
Indiana University

Coke Ellington
Alabama State University

Julie Ellis
Freelance writer

Fred Endres
Kent State University

Heidi Evans
Daily News, New York City

Ellen Fleysher
WCBS-TV, New York City

Mike Foley
University of Florida

Thomas French
St. Petersburg Times

Joseph Galloway
UPI, *U.S. News and World Report*

Mary Ann Giordano
Daily News, New York City

Joel M. Gora
American Civil Liberties Union

Sara Grimes
University of Massachusetts, Amherst

Susan Hands
The Charlotte Observer

Donna Hanover
WTVN-TV, Columbus, Ohio

Jena Heath
The News & Observer, Raleigh, N.C.,
Austin American–Statesman

Frank Herron
The Post-Standard, Syracuse, N.Y.

Michael Hiltzik
Courier-Express, Buffalo, N.Y., and
Los Angeles Times

Anne Hull
St. Petersburg Times

Louis E. Ingelhart
Ball State University

Tommy Jackson
University of Central Arkansas

Melissa Jordan
Associated Press

Rachele Kanigel
San Francisco University

Jeff Klinkenberg
St. Petersburg Times

Eric Lawlor
The Houston Chronicle

John Leach
The Arizona Republic

Elizabeth Leland
The Charlotte Observer

Lynn Ludlow
San Francisco Examiner

Jack Marsh
Argus Leader, Sioux Falls, S.D.

Paul S. Mason
ABC News

Tony Mauro
Gannett News Service

John McCormally
The Hawk Eye, Burlington, Iowa

Frank McCulloch
The Sacramento Bee

Bill Mertens
The Hawk Eye, Burlington, Iowa

Eric Newhouse
Great Falls Tribune

Merrill Perlman
The New York Times

Lew Powell
The Charlotte Observer

Bruce L. Plopper
University of Arkansas, Little Rock

Roy Rampal
Central Missouri State University

Ron Rapoport
Los Angeles Times, Chicago Sun-Times and Los Angeles *Daily News*

Elizabeth Rhodes
The Charlotte (N.C.) *Observer* and *Seattle Times*

Ronald Robinson
Augustana College, Sioux Falls, S.D.

Sam Roe
The Blade, Toledo, Ohio

Geanne Rosenberg
Baruch College, City University of New York

Chris S. Roush
University of North Carolina

Bill Ruehlmann
Virginia Wesleyan College

Mort Saltzman
The Sacramento Bee

Sydney Schanberg
The New York Times

Wendy Shilton
University of Southern Maine, University of Prince Edward Island

Allan M. Siegal
The New York Times

Rex Smith
Editor *Times Union,* Albany, N.Y.

Jeff C. South
Virginia Commonwealth University

Peter Spielmann
Associated Press

Laura Sessions Stepp
The Washington Post

Herbert Strentz
Drake University

Diana K. Sugg
The Sacramento Bee

Lena H. Sun
The Washington Post

Mike Sweet
The Hawk Eye, Burlington, Iowa

Jeffrey A. Tannenbaum
The Wall Street Journal

Bob Thayer
The Providence Journal

Jim Toland
San Francisco Chronicle

Carolyn Tuft
Belleville (Ill.) *News-Democrat*

Howard Weinberg
Executive producer, "Bill Moyers' Journal"

Elizabeth Weise
USA Today

Jan Wong
The Globe and Mail, Toronto

Molly Wright
Burson-Marsteller

Emerald Yeh
KRON-TV, San Francisco

Phoebe Zerwick
Winston-Salem Journal

The affiliations of the contributors are given as of the time of their assistance.

A Personal Word

Some of you are probably thinking of the kind of journalism you want to be doing and the best place to launch your career. Fortunately, the field is wide open. Journalism is the gateway to a variety of careers.

You may choose the path to newspaper, magazine or broadcast work. You may have an interest that leads you to one of the several thousand special publications and newsletters. Or you may choose to report and write online or work for an ethnic or alternative publication.

Journalism training opens many doors. But you will find that you have to push hard. "Work harder than anyone else," Ben Bradlee advises those starting out. Not that it's all work. Deborah Howell of the Newhouse News Service says, "Work hard. But have fun and do good."

The first job is important. Howard Gardner, a professor of psychology at Harvard who has studied journalists, says of the first job, "It's like an inoculation. If you don't have examples of good workers, it's difficult to know what good work is."

 For tips on how to prepare a job résumé, see Appendix G **The Journalism Job Hunt** in *NRW Plus*.

—Melvin Mencher

Part Opener Photos

Part One

Chris Keating of *The Hartford Courant* takes notes as the governor discusses her plans for legislation.

—Photo by Lori Golias

Part Two

Police surround a fleeing robbery suspect.

—Photo by Richard Green, *The Californian*

Part Three

On deadline.

—Photo by *The Wichita Eagle*

Part Four

A reporter asks for the names and addresses of the accident victims.

—Photo by Wayne Miller

Part Five

Reporters cover a variety of events—from her first day of school to a flood.

—Photos: Left column, top to bottom: Mark Welsh, *Daily Herald;* David McDermand, *The Eagle;* Michael Rafferty, *Asbury Park Press.* Right Column: top: Spencer Tulis, *The Leader-Herald;* bottom: Rick Musacchio, *The Tennessean*

Part Six

Decision-making on controversial issues—intruding on privacy, photos of bodies and nudity.

—Photos: left column, top: Charlie Riedel, *Hays Daily News;* bottom: Joel Sartore, *The Wichita Eagle;* right column, top: David C. Neilsen, II, *Oroville Mercury Register;* bottom, The Library of Congress.

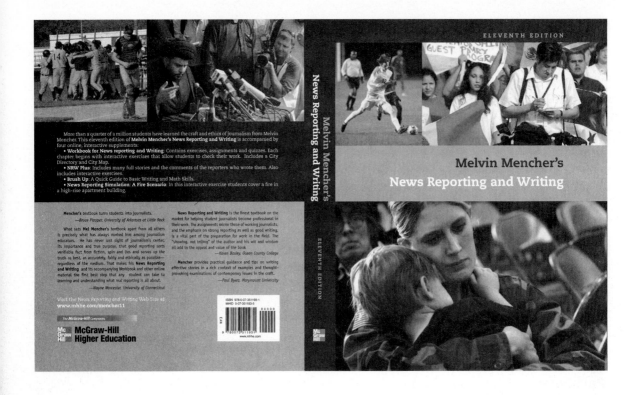

Cover Photos
Winners and Losers, Protest, Deployment

Front Cover

(A) A soccer player begins his move toward the winning goal. Nill Toulme took this photo during a game for the league title.

(B) A staffer for *The Wichita Eagle* takes notes during a rally protesting restrictive immigration laws. Photo by Mike Hutmacher of the *Eagle.*

(C) Specialist Tammi Jasmine Messick, 22, hugs her 2-year-old son before being deployed to the Middle East in this photo by Renee C. Byer of *The Sacramento Bee.*

Back Cover

(D) Spencer Tulis of *The Leader-Herald* captured the joy of victory and the despair of defeat at a local baseball game.

(E) Travis Heying of *The Wichita Eagle* photographs a fiery speech by an Iraqi cleric who heads a powerful militia.

1   On the Job

R.L. Chambers

Details from the crime scene.

Climb the stairs.
Knock on doors.

Preview

Watching journalists at work we see that they respond quickly to events that interest and affect people. They are tenacious in their search for relevant information. They have a passion for accuracy and a determination to be fair.

- The caller was furious. His wife had been airlifted out of Iraq where she was serving in the Army and sent to a hospital at Fort Stewart, Ga. He had visited her and saw that hospitalized soldiers were in barracks with no running water, no air conditioning; showers and toilets were in an adjacent building that was filthy and buggy. Can you do something? he asked a reporter.
- A man wanted by the police barricades himself in his home in central Phoenix. Two women and a child are believed inside. A SWAT team responds.
- The farm labor recruiter has an enticing offer. He tells the homeless men at a Florida shelter he has a good job for them, and he promises hot meals, a solid roof over their heads and all the crack they want.
- Ray Charles, the pianist-singer known over the world for his soul and rhythm and blues music, dies of liver failure.
- A killer tornado strikes Spencer, a small South Dakota community.
- Plane crashes into World Trade Center.
- Eating disorders—anorexia and bulimia—kill a fifth of their long-term victims.
- A serial killer stalked a Wichita, Kan., suburb from 1974 to 1991. The investigation goes cold, but years later a letter arrives in the newsroom of *The Wichita Eagle* whose return address bears the name Bill Thomas Killman. When the *Eagle* was covering the killings, it named the killer the "BTK strangler" because he would bind, torture and kill his victims. Was the letter a hoax?
- A Houston lawyer discovers problems in the way the police department's laboratory is doing forensic testing.

- A shooting breaks out at a high school in northeastern Arkansas.
- A 2-year-old Denver boy dies after his father throws him on the bathroom floor.
- A college newspaper tracks on its Web site shootings that take 33 lives on campus.
- TV reporter covers fatal fire.
- Drive-by shooting takes life of two-year-old.
- A $30,400 highway sinkhole repair costs $8.5 million...so far.
- Sleep deprivation among teenagers. Deadly consequences.
- Tales of courage and despair among the aged.
- Health department endangers the lives of women.
- Dangerous drugs remain on market.
- Online journalists break stories.
- Going behind a press release about banning books.

Journalists at Work

We learn about these events because journalists tell us about them. These journalists, some just out of college and some 20-year newsroom veterans, are our link to the world beyond our direct experience. Using their judgment, experience and a set of journalistic guidelines, they decide what is worth calling to our attention.

The Guidelines

The journalist's job begins with selecting what is newsworthy from the multitude of events that occur every day. By newsworthy, the journalist means what's important to readers and viewers, what will interest, affect and entertain them.

Hospital Conditions   The husband of the hospitalized soldier called Mark Benjamin of United Press International because he had read Benjamin's stories about strange illnesses afflicting some of those returning from service in Iraq. He told Benjamin that the treatment and the conditions at the Georgia service hospital were deplorable. He said his wife had to wait six weeks before a doctor saw her.

Benjamin knew at once that the situation was *important,* that if he could verify the caller's assertions the story would have *impact.* Shabby treatment of those who serve their country is clearly newsworthy. He immediately flew to the base in Georgia to see for himself. Here is the beginning of his story:

> FORT STEWART, Ga. Oct. 17 (UPI)—Hundreds of sick and wounded U.S. soldiers including many who served in the Iraq war are languishing in hot cement barracks here while they wait—sometimes for months—to see doctors.

Barricaded Man The police call came in around noon: An armed man had barricaded himself in his home. He was wanted by the police on a probation violation. Two women and a child were believed to be with the man. Within minutes, Christopher Kline of *The Phoenix Republic* posted a story on azcentral.com, the newspaper's Web site:

> An armed man barricaded himself inside a central Phoenix house on Friday morning, according to police.
>
> Officials believe two females and a child were also inside the home near 12th and Roosevelt Streets.
>
> Police said the suspect is wanted on a violation of probation warrant but that they have not been able to communicate with him.
>
> A 12News photographer on the scene said police were using a loudspeaker, telling the suspect, "Come out and no harm will come to you or your child, or anyone else who is inside."
>
> A SWAT team is standing outside the home. . . .

Kline is based in the KPNX-TV newsroom to draw on the station's expertise in covering breaking news. Kline's job is to write such news for azcentral.

Seven minutes after Kline sent out the first story, he wrote another:

> Two women and a child were freed by a SWAT team on Friday afternoon from an alleged barricade situation at a home in central Phoenix, according to officials.
>
> Police said they believe an armed man was still inside the house near 12th and Roosevelt Streets. . . .

Thirty minutes later, the newspaper's Web site carried this story by Kline:

> A SWAT team stormed a central Phoenix home on Friday afternoon, arresting an armed man who had barricaded himself inside, and freeing two women and a child held with the suspect, according to police. . . .

Within the next hour, Kline wrote two more stories. The longest story, the wrap-up at 1:22 P.M., ran around 150 words.

By its nature, online journalism emphasizes *timeliness*. Unlike the newspaper's one or two deadlines, there is a deadline every minute for the online journalist.

Labor Recruiting Ronnie Greene of *The Miami Herald* had noticed a number of cases brought by the federal government against labor contractors seeking Mexican and African-American workers to pick oranges, tomatoes and other crops in Florida. The government called the conditions under which the men and women worked "servitude." The workers called their housing "slave camps."

The laborers sank into debt for rent and meals and could barely pay the 100 percent interest the contractors charged. At some camps, liquor and drugs were supplied at exorbitant prices. Not only was the story *important,* but all this was happening in Greene's backyard. Its *proximity* gave the situation added news value.

Greene was also guided in his decision to dig into the migrant labor market by another of our guidelines, *necessity.* Greene felt compelled to reveal the deplorable conditions in which those who pick our fruit and vegetables work. He felt it necessary to do the story. Perhaps exposure would lead to reform.

It did. Greene's series, "Fields of Despair," led the state legislature to increase the penalties for farmworker abuse.

Death of an Entertainer   The obituary of Ray Charles was news over the country. At the same time, the death of a local band leader was noted in an obituary that ran only in his hometown newspaper. Why the difference? Charles was well-known, and *prominence* is one of our guidelines. The band leader was known in and around Topeka. His death was newsworthy there only.

Spencer Tornado   The tornado was big news in South Dakota, but the farther from that state the less newsworthy it was to news editors. *Proximity* played a role in determining newsworthiness.

Some events transcend borders. The Sept. 11 World Trade Center bombing was a momentous event, one of enormous *impact. USA Today* sold a record 3,368,600 copies of its report the day after the twin towers collapsed in searing flame and jumbled metal. Much of the world has been living in the shadow of the event since.

Before we continue with the events outlined at the start of this chapter, let's go back to the day terrorists struck the World Trade Center and the Pentagon and watch how some journalists reacted to the event.

Spencer Tulis,
The Leader-Herald
Ray Charles

The Bombings

ABC news correspondent Don Dahler was looking out his window at home when the first airliner hit one of the World Trade Center towers. He watched a huge plume of smoke envelop the upper stories. He saw people jumping out of windows in a frantic attempt to escape the inferno.

Dahler grabbed his telephone and called ABC. "The whole building has collapsed," he reported. Then he ran downstairs to what became known as Ground Zero, the scene of twisted metal girders, smoke and fire and futile rescue attempts. He stayed there, on camera, for 18 straight hours.

Three weeks later, Dahler was sent to Pakistan to cover the war against the Taliban.

In Washington, several staffers of *USA Today* were on their way to work driving past the Pentagon when a third plane struck. Mike Waller said, "Time stood still as I watched the plane descend and then head for the building. There was a gigantic fireball and then sheer terror.

"I don't know how I am going to sleep after this," he thought. But he went on to the office to help put out the newspaper.

To see how the paper was put out under pressure, see *USA Today* in *NRW Plus.*

David Handschuh, a photographer for the *Daily News,* was nearby when the terrorists struck the World Trade Center. The force of the explosion threw him more than a hundred feet. He lost his glasses, his cellphone and his pager. But his digital camera was intact and despite broken bones and the loss of his eyeglasses, he stayed to record the continuing horror. As he scrambled through the ruins, he tripped, fell, lost his bearings.

Emergency crews pulled him from the rubble three times that day. "They saved my life," he said.

In the four hours following the terrorists' strike, the Associated Press moved on its wires 40 flashes, NewsAlerts and bulletins. See **Terror Bombings** and **The Associated Press** in *NRW Plus* for a rundown of this coverage.

Dieters Anorexia is a "serious medical problem," says Jayne Garrison, senior projects director for *WebMD,* an online medical news service. To put the rapidly increasing medical problem in human terms, staff reporters sought out a variety of women with anorexia who were willing to describe their experiences as severe dieters. The result was a nine-part series that reported the disease is spreading up and down the age brackets, from the college-aged to 9- and 10-year-olds and the middle-aged. One article was written by a 19-year-old who runs a "pro-anexoria" Web site. Another reported the personality traits for "people at highest risk for anorexia or bulimia":

Obsessive

Perfectionist

Anxious

Novelty-seeking

Impulsive

Serial Killer

Dennis Rader went to the post office once too often. Although he had sent many letters and packets, some to *The Wichita Eagle,* during the decade following a series of grisly murders, police were baffled. The murders had faded from community memory and had been placed in the police cold case file.

One letter contained a photocopy of three blurred Polaroid pictures of what appeared to be a woman's body. A woman's driver's license was on the photocopy. The envelope bore a return address with the name "Bill Thomas Killman." Those initials—BTK—rang a bell for veteran police reporter Hurst Laviana to whom the letter was addressed. The newspaper had named the unknown killer the "BTK strangler" because he would bind, torture and kill his victims. But had the killer decided to reclaim his notoriety? "Most people believed that BTK was probably dead or in prison," said Sherry Chisenhall, the editor of the *Eagle.*

Laviana decided to take the letter to police headquarters where it was carefully examined. A few days later, a police lieutenant told Laviana, "I'm 100

The Wichita Eagle
He murdered ten.

percent certain it's BTK." The closed file was reopened. The FBI stepped in and the search for BTK intensified.

Newsroom Mobilized   The *Eagle* broke the news of the reopened case on its Web site, Kansas.com. Chisenhall put every reporter she could spare on the story. Story after story moved on the newspaper's Web site. "The news rocked Wichita," she said, and "it showed the *Eagle*'s news staff how different it was to cover this story in the age of the Internet and 24/7 TV news coverage. The Web made our news coverage vastly more interactive with readers," Chisenhall said.

The town also swung into action. "Residents armed themselves, installed security systems, and took other steps to safeguard their security," Chisenhall said. Meanwhile, the police investigated the tips that were pouring in, including one that named Laviana. Police asked him to provide a DNA sample.

The story went national. Tips abounded, and although the competition was too ready to use unconfirmed material, Chisenhall said, "Our challenge was sticking to standards of confirmation and attribution."

Tracing the Disk   The police held news conferences designed to communicate to BTK, and he responded. He included a computer disk in one of his responses which police and the FBI tracked to a church in a Wichita suburb. Eleven months after Bill Thomas Killman's letter arrived in the *Eagle*'s newsroom the case broke open.

Dennis Rader, the president of the church congregation, a married man with two grown children and a former Boy Scout leader, was arrested and charged with 10 counts of first degree murder. Within two minutes of Rader being named, Kansas.com had the news online. "We updated that story about 25 times that day," Chisenhall said.

Rader pleaded guilty and is serving 10 consecutive life terms in the state penitentiary.

In all, the *Eagle* published nearly 800 stories, online and in print.

More on the Guidelines

The Houston lawyer who was disturbed by reports of incompetent forensic testing in the local police department laboratory called KHOU–Houston. An alert sounded in the station newsroom. Lab work, reporters knew, is the key evidence in thousands of criminal cases. The lab tests can send a woman to prison for 20 years, a man to death row. If the lab work is tainted, innocents suffer, and trust in the police and the courts is eroded. The lawyer's tip was *important*.

Harris County, in which Houston is located, sends more men and women to death row than any county in the nation. So when David Raziq and Anna Werner of KHOU learned of the possibility of flawed lab tests, they investigated.

Flawed Tests   They sent some of the lab's DNA test results to forensic experts. The findings confirmed the reporters' concern: The experts reported "egregious errors . . . repeated gross incompetence . . . errors that seem to favor the prosecution. . . ." One report said that the lab work done in a rape case was "the equivalent of a scientific train wreck."

The result of the TV station's digging: A thousand cases were reopened and new tests ordered. Among the victims of the lab's work was a prisoner convicted of rape at 16. He was freed after serving four years in a state prison.

Doped Athletes   One of sports' ongoing stories is the suspicion that several of its star athletes have been taking banned substances to improve their performance. Superfast sprinters, home-run hitting outfielders, aquatic marvels—all have been suspect. The story simmered for years until authorities raided a drug laboratory in California. Among its customers were several headline athletes who had set world records.

Suddenly, athletes and banned substances became big news. We call this news guideline *currency* . . . a simmering situation boils to the top of the news, becomes current.

Next, let's look at the coverage of a school shooting. The reporting of this event illustrates another of our guidelines, *timeliness.* An event that happens today is more newsworthy than the event had it happened yesterday or last week. The school shooting also illuminates the relationship of the reporter and the public.

The Agreement

An implicit understanding exists between the reporter and the public.

1. **The reporter** will do his or her best to give the public a complete and accurate account of the event as soon as possible. After the AP learned of a school shooting in Jonesboro, Ark., the Little Rock bureau immediately put the information on its wire:

> a0662 11:41 AM
> BC—APNewsAlert, 0021 <
> Shooting at Jonesboro, Ark., middle school; school office reports one dead, at least 13 hurt.

Then it informed news editors:

> An AP reporter and photographer are heading to the scene of the school shootings in Jonesboro, Ark.

Within 15 minutes of moving its NewsAlert, the AP had this story on its wires:

> JONESBORO, Ark. (AP)—Two youths wearing camouflage opened fire on middle school students Tuesday as they assembled outside during a fire alarm. At least one person was killed and other injured.

2. **The public** presumes that the reporter's account is honestly and accurately reported and written. Although pollsters tell us that people are wary of the news

they see and read, the reality is that people act on the information they obtain from their newspapers and broadcast stations:

The mother of three children in Little Rock schools who is disturbed by the Jonesboro shootings asks her state senator to press for stringent gun-control laws.

When newspapers and broadcast stations carried the proposal to do away with the study of evolution in Georgia public schools, public pressure forced the head of the state department of education to back off. A similarly aroused public spoke up when *Denver Post* reporters found that child abuse was a systemic problem, that the state's foster care system was failing in its responsibilities to children.

In West Virginia, *The Charleston Gazette* has been less successful in its long campaign to force coal operators to abide by the law that requires them to rebuild what they have destroyed. State and federal authorities, says reporter Ken Ward, Jr., look the other way, and the public has not mustered the strength to cope with the powerful political presence of the operators. But Ward continues to write about the destruction of the environment.

Continuous Coverage

Some of the events we have been looking at were breaking news stories—the killer tornado, Ray Charles' death, the terror bombings in New York, the Arkansas school shooting. Others were what journalists call enterprisers, stories the reporters developed themselves—the terrible conditions Iraq war wounded encountered in a Georgia Army hospital, the Florida slave camps, the incompetent Houston police lab, Colorado's poor foster care system.

Reporters covering breaking stories keep a steady stream of stories flowing. Broadcast reporters send frequent pulses of news. Print journalists who in the past wrote for two or three editions now are on an accelerated pace to meet the demands of the readers of their newspaper's Web site. Not only do these reporters post "everything we can as soon as we can," as the executive editor of *The Miami Herald* instructs his reporters, but they supply audio and video along with the text.

Let's move closer to some of these reporters as they cover a couple of breaking news stories, first to Sioux Falls, S.D., where reporters for the *Argus Leader* hear ominous reports about an approaching storm. Then we will return to the AP Little Rock bureau for a closer look at how the school shooting was covered. Later, we will watch a TV reporter and other journalists at work.

First to Sioux Falls.

A Tornado Hits Spencer

The skies are darkening over southeastern South Dakota. In the *Argus Leader* newsroom, the small Saturday night staff is alerted to the possibility of worsening weather. Assistant City Editor Rosemary McCoy calls reporter Rob Swenson at home to tell him he may have to return to the newsroom to help with coverage.

David Kranz, another reporter, has Saturday off but decides to go in when he hears of the gathering storm. He shows up at 9 P.M., just as a weather bureau warning of a tornado rushing toward Sioux Falls sends everyone into basements from 9 to 9:30 P.M., not the place to be with a 10:10 P.M. deadline for the first edition.

As the Sioux Falls alert is ended the newsroom hears that the tornado has hit the small town of Spencer, 50 miles west of Sioux Falls. The tornado struck the town with its full fury.

McCoy sends Swenson and a photographer to Spencer. "Our mission was to get there quickly and call back with observations in time for the Sunday edition," Swenson says. "The deadline was a major factor the moment we left the parking lot."

Blocked But police had cordoned off the town and Swenson had to park about a quarter of a mile outside town. "The town was dark except for a slow-moving parade of flashing lights from ambulances, fire trucks and other emergency vehicles, which stretched from where we stood to the center of town," Swenson said.

In the Newsroom

Knowing that Swenson and photographer Ken Klotzbach were unable to get into Spencer, Kranz started to work the phones. He had good contacts, having been the editor of *The Daily Republic* in Mitchell, which serves the Spencer area. "I was fairly familiar with the town," Kranz says, "but I only knew a handful of people. I began calling them and got no answer. I then worked the phones in the area, thinking some rural Spencer people may have been in the town to check on things. No answer anywhere."

Enterprise "At that point, I shifted my attention to law enforcement types. I called the wives of two law enforcement or emergency people that I knew would be there. First, I called the Minnehaha County Emergency Management director's wife. I asked for his cell phone number."

He continued to call and hit paydirt by finding the Davison County sheriff's cell phone number.

"The sheriff saved our day. He stood in the middle of the debris and described the situation to me. He pointed out areas familiar to me. He then handed the phone to the U.S. Marshal who gave us a vivid description of the way Spencer was and what he was now seeing.

"As deadline neared, the sheriff told us he knew there were fatalities. He saw one for sure, but expected there were others."

With 10 minutes before the deadline for the last Sunday edition, Kranz asked the sheriff if the governor were anywhere near. "He told me he was standing five feet away. I asked him to hand the governor the phone and I asked the governor how many people were dead. He put the number at four."

With the minute hand sweeping toward deadline, Kranz made one more call, this one to a woman in an area outside Spencer. Again, he was lucky. She had

Ken Klotzbach, *Argus Leader*

The Morning After

driven into Spencer to check on her mother. Her observations of the devastation in the town added a "real people" voice to the story, Kranz says.

Continued Coverage   Within minutes of putting the Sunday paper to bed, the staff began planning further coverage of the disaster. Jill Callison, the religion writer, was to cover church services. Six other reporters would go to Spencer. In the Sioux Falls newsroom, several reporters would write obituaries and gather information on how people could help the town.

Under a banner headline were two stories. One was about the tornado's effects. Written by Kranz and Swenson, it begins:

SPENCER—Shocked survivors wandered their ripped-apart community Sunday searching for tornado-scattered belongings and mourning six neighbors who died.

The whole community reeled from the devastation that Saturday's vicious storm left behind.

"It's just like a bomb hit us," Tom Simmons said. "Just like a bomb hit."

Most of the homes had been reduced to rubble.

"This whole town is gone," said Gov. Bill Janklow.

The other story began:

> Here are ways people may help victims
> of the Spencer tornado:

Summing Up the Coverage

Managing Editor Peter Ellis says, "We covered every angle of this story we could think of. We told about the heroes, the 8,000 volunteers who showed up to help, the governor who camped out there for a week, the prisoners who were happy to help, the minister who was spared while his wife died a few feet away from him.

"The main lesson from Spencer, I think, is that nothing beats good reporting, and lead reporter Dave Kranz is one of the best. He is always working his beat, including keeping up with former sources from years ago. It was because of this that we were able to get the sensational coverage, especially on the first day, that we did."

School Shooting

Next to the AP bureau in Little Rock. It is getting on to noon and Kelly Kissel, the bureau's news editor, is about to have his chicken sandwich when he hears that the state police have been asked to set up a perimeter outside Westside Middle School. There has been a shooting at the school in Jonesboro. A person has been killed. Kissel shoves his lunch aside, tells reporter Jenny Price to take off for Jonesboro.

He wants her to call him every half hour. During her first calls, Kissel, who knows northeastern Arkansas from having spent summers at his grandparents' farm there, gives Price shortcuts: Take a left a mile past the grain elevator, another left, then right just past the railroad tracks. But even with these instructions, it will take Price two hours to reach Jonesboro and Kissel must put something on the AP wire quickly.

Early Stories

Kissel calls state police, local reporters in Jonesboro, the school superintendent's office. It isn't until he has the superintendent's secretary on the line that he has something good enough for the wire. He writes these three paragraphs:

> JONESBORO, Ark. (AP)—Two men wearing camouflage opened fire on middle school students Tuesday as they assembled outside during a fire alarm. At least one person was killed.
>
> Connie Tolbert, secretary to the school district superintendent, said eight to 13 people, mostly students, were injured. Other reports put the number of injured at up to 16.

Student Newspaper Tracks Campus Mass Murder

The Virginia Tech student newspaper, *The Collegiate Times,* tracked the shootings on its Web site:

9:47 a.m.: Shots were fired on campus in West Ambler Johnston Hall in the early morning hours.

The Collegiate Times is currently investigating the story. More information will be posted as it is made available.

10:00 a.m.: A gunman is confirmed loose on campus.

10:04 a.m.: The university is encouraging everyone to stay indoors and away from windows.

10:20 a.m.: All classes are cancelled.

10:32 a.m.: At this time, one death and one injury have been confirmed. More information will be made available as it breaks.

10:36 a.m.: Due to serious wind helicopters cannot be used to transfer the injured. According to the police scanner, ambulances are being used to transport the victims to Montgomery Regional Hospital.

11:36 a.m.: At this time, University Relations is reporting one individual in custody and is searching for a second shooter.

11:50 a.m.: The Associated Press has reported at least one death and seven injuries stemming from two shooting incidents on the Virginia Tech campus.

11:57 a.m.: Three people were escorted out of Norris Hall in handcuffs by police. The three were then unhandcuffed and canine teams were sent into Norris Hall.

12:23 p.m.: Virginia Tech police have confirmed 22 fatalities resulting from the campus shootings today. The gunman has also been confirmed dead.

1:16 p.m.: Multiple shootings occurred on campus this morning. There have been 20 fatalities in a shooting that occurred in Norris Hall. There was one fatality in

West Ambler Johnston and the other fatality was the shooter, who has not yet been identified, said Virginia Tech President Charles Steger at a press conference. . . .

2:13 p.m.: As of now, 32 people are confirmed dead. One person from West Ambler Johnston Hall and at least 20 people from Norris Hall have been killed. The shooter as well has been killed, but it is uncertain whether he is a student or not.

2:37 p.m.: Fox News is reporting that the police have recovered two 9 mm handguns.

4:44 p.m.: University Relations has confirmed 31 deaths at Norris Hall, in addition to two deaths at West Ambler Johnston. The identity of the shooter is currently unknown as no identification was present with the suspect.

4:54 p.m.: Police have confirmed that the shooter took his own life.

5:01 p.m.: Parents are advised to call 1-540-231-3787.

The killer was identified as a student, Cho Seung-Hui, who underwent a federal instant check at the two gun stores where he bought the .22 caliber and .9 millimeter handguns he used to kill himself and 32 students and faculty members.

COLLEGIATE**TIMES**

THE DEADLIEST SHOOTING SPREE IN U.S. HISTORY DEVASTATES THE VIRGINIA TECH COMMUNITY

HEARTACHE

OUR SORROW, OUR RESOLVE

Jonesboro is a city of 46,000 about 130 miles northeast of Little Rock.

Kissel calls the AP general desk in New York to discuss coverage. He is given the green light to send another reporter, Peggy Harris, to the scene. Over the next week, seven AP staff members will be rotated in and out of Jonesboro.

As Price is making her way to Jonesboro, Kissel and other staffers gather more information to try to flesh out the story.

Escalating Deaths   Bulletins, more NewsAlerts, new leads follow in rapid order through the day. At 12:07, a NewsAlert reports a second death. At 12:11, the second lead has 15 injured. In a few minutes, a third lead corrected the 15 to 13. Then, at 12:31, the AP reports two suspects, ages 11 and 13, have been taken into custody. Then a story with background about other school shootings and the figure of 13 injured is reduced to 12. At 13:03 (1:03 P.M.), a NewsAlert reports a third death. At 13:37, a NewsAlert goes out about a fourth death.

Price has now reached the scene, and it is time to collect the bits and pieces for a definitive story. Price will write this, and it will be followed for the next six and a half hours by 10 Writethrus, each with new information. To read how this coverage unfolded, see **Jonesboro School Shooting** in *NRW Plus.*

An Announcement and a Fire

We are in the newsroom of a midwestern newspaper with a circulation of 25,000. The telephone on the city editor's desk rings and, after listening for a moment, the city editor calls out to a young reporter. "Bob, the publicity director of the Lions Club has a story."

The caller tells the reporter his club intends to donate some equipment to a city playground next Saturday at 10 A.M. at a ceremony the governor will attend.

The reporter calls the governor's press secretary to check the governor's itinerary in case he is making other local stops. In 15 minutes, he has written a short piece, putting the governor in the lead. He again checks the date, time and location of the ceremony against his notes.

A few minutes later, he is told to cover a fire with a photographer.

An hour later, Bob returns to the newsroom.

Human Interest   "It was a small fire, about $7,500 in damage, but there's some good human interest in it," Bob tells the city editor.

"Don't tell me you've got three columns on a three-paragraph fire, Bob," the city editor replies. "What's it about?"

Without looking at his notes, he answers. "The story isn't the fire but the background. I found out the family bought the house a few months ago. They had just remodeled it, and this week the wife went to work to help pay for it. She leaves their 10-year-old boy home with his 12-year-old brother for a few hours every day.

"Well, the 12-year-old wanted to make some money cutting grass. He knows they're short of money. He was filling the lawn mower with gasoline in the garage when the tank tipped over against the water heater. Woosh. Lucky he wasn't hurt."

The city editor thinks a moment.

"Got any good quotes from the older boy?" he asks.

"Yes."

"Well, it sounds as though it's worth more than a couple of paragraphs. But don't make it a chapter in the book, Bob."

At his desk, Bob pauses before writing. He can start his story like most accounts of fires he has read:

> A fire of accidental origin caused $7,500 in damage to a house at 1315 New Hampshire St. today.
>
> No one was injured in the blaze that started in the garage when the 12-year-old son of the owners, Mr. and Mrs. Earl Ruman . . .

Direct Lead He has put a direct news lead on the story, which he knows his newspaper prefers for stories of this sort. But he is unhappy with this start. This is not the way he described the fire to the editor, he recalls. Then he remembers advice he was given by a reporter: "Every story demands to be told a certain way. Don't impose a form or style on it. The way you write it has to flow from the nature of the event."

The nature of his story was the youngster's good intentions gone awry. So he starts again:

> Two months ago, Mr. and Mrs. Earl Ruman moved into a three bedroom house at 1315 New Hampshire St. It was their dream house.
>
> After years of skimping and saving . . .

At this rate, he will write the book his editor warned him against, he thinks. Although he wants a dramatic story—one that will build to a climax—he cannot take forever to develop the point. Readers will drift away.

Feature Lead His editor has been telling his reporters to try for feature-type leads when the event makes it possible. Perhaps this is one of those events. The youngster is the heart of the story, Bob reasons, and the boy must go into the lead. He tries again:

> Teddy Ruman knew his father and mother had skimped and saved to put aside enough money to buy their dream house at 1315 New Hampshire St.
>
> This morning, he decided to help, too. But his well-intentioned efforts turned to tragedy.
>
> The 12-year-old . . .

That seems to be more like it. In 40 minutes, he has the story in good shape, he thinks.

The city editor reads through the copy.

"Yes, it's a sad story," he tells his cub reporter. "It's hardly a tragedy, but it would be sadder if they didn't have insurance to cover their loss."

Bob makes for the telephone on his desk. He remembers another bit of advice: "Don't leave unanswered any questions the reader may have. Don't leave any holes in your story."

Next, to another fire, this one far more serious, that is covered by a TV reporter.

TV Covers a Fire

It is Christmas Day in the newsroom of a New York City television station. A teletype clicks off a story about a fire in a small town in New Jersey. The AP reports that while a family was asleep, a fire broke out and flames raced through their house. Four died. Only two boys escaped.

The news editor calls to a reporter, "Elaine, take this one on."

On the way to the fire, Elaine thinks of questions to ask and the locations in which to shoot the story.

"When I go out on an assignment I am conscious of the need for pictures," she said later. "I look for things that have an immediate impact, because I have a short time to tell the story—maybe two-and-a-half minutes.

"So I look for the strongest statement in a talk, the most emotionally appealing part of the running story. When I arrive at a story, I want to be the first one to interview the eyewitness, so that the person is still experiencing the event. The emotional facts have to tell the story."

On the scene, Elaine learns from the fire chief that the surviving youngsters had run to a neighbor's house during the fire. As crews from competing stations arrive, she and her crew approach the neighbor's house through the backyard to avoid being spotted.

"When I spoke to the woman next door, I asked her what happened when the boys burst into her home. She became tense and distraught as she described one boy's face, burned and blackened by the fire," Elaine recalled.

"On a breaking story, a broadcast journalist usually asks fewer questions than the print journalist. On this story all I needed to ask the neighbor was two or three questions and let her tell the story."

On the return drive, Elaine structures the script in her mind. She has pictures of the fire scenes and interviews of the neighbor and the fire chief. She works the script around these, the most dramatic shots.

A Child's Death

It was a drive-by shooting. The victim: 2-year-old Heather Brown. The family had been to church and stopped on the way home at McDonald's for ice cream.

At home, Heather was fidgety and wouldn't go to sleep, so her father took her into the living room and began to rock her to sleep on the couch.

Suddenly, 60 high-caliber slugs tore into the house. One struck Heather in the head and she died in her father's arms.

For Diane Sugg of *The Sacramento Bee* the story was not so much the shooting death but the story of a lovable little girl. She found that story by driving out to the Valley Christian Church and waiting for its pastor, A.D. Olivan. He was close to Heather's parents and had spoken to them since the shooting.

Sugg had telephoned the minister but he didn't want to talk, so she drove to the church and waited. One hour. Two. After three hours, he arrived and Sugg persuaded him to talk to her about the child who used to run around the church singing to herself and hugging everyone she saw. There was something special about Heather, and everyone knew it.

"I would never have gotten Heather's story if I hadn't waited in a dark parking lot for three hours, hoping the family's pastor would come back to the church," Sugg says. "He did, and he could see I was sincere."

Longer Stories

Let's look at stories that took time to develop, report and write, stories that are important but are not immediate.

First, to Jere Downs who covers transportation for *The Philadelphia Inquirer*. Essential to her coverage, she says, is her "habit of scooping up all paper from an agency whenever I have the chance: operating budgets, capital budgets, requests for proposals, studies, board meeting minutes." She organizes the material, after carefully reading it all, even the inch-thick operating budget of the local transit agency.

"This is going to be boring," she thought. But she kept reading and underlining budget items that seemed unusual. One jumped at her—$32 million for paying lawsuit claims. That turned into a story.

The Big Hole

Sources are essential for reporters, and Downs has lunch with one on Monday, visits the office of another Tuesday. Wednesday she was shooting the breeze with a highway construction engineer.

"In the course of our chat about the Route 202 construction project, he mentioned that construction was bogged down by a troublesome sinkhole that had so far swallowed $4 million in concrete," Downs said. Sinkhole repairs had been budgeted at far less, $30,400. But a warren of limestone caverns was discovered directly beneath the location of the $224 million interchange. Downs knew at once she had a story, and after her chat with the engineer she set out to gather information.

Her story begins this way:

> The long-awaited solution to one of the state's worst highway traffic nightmares—King of Prussia's congestion of cloverleafs—will take longer and cost more money because of unexpected and huge sinkholes in the construction zone.
>
> "There is no bottom to it," said Carmine Fiscina, the Federal Highway Administration engineer overseeing the Route 202 project. "We all knew there were sinkholes, but this is an unbelievable turn of events.
>
> "This is a Pandora's box."

That was just the beginning. "PennDot is still pumping cement into the ground—$8.5 million to date," Downs says. The agency exhausted the region's supply of cement. "So it is building a cement plant on the construction site." More holes, more cement, more stories.

Children and Families

"Readers devour issues presented up close and personal," says Laura Sessions Stepp of *The Washington Post.* One, she found, is adolescence, its perils and its promises. She wrote about the growing confidence of Josh, a 12-year-old she watched dig fence poles and stretch wire on his parents' farm in southwestern Kansas.

Josh told Stepp that if he "stretched the wire too tightly it might snap, and the herd of Hereford crossbreeds would wander onto the highway, perhaps into the path of an 18-wheeler."

Sleep Problems   Stepp discovered that sleep deprivation is prevalent among many young people. "Beginning at age 15, kids need more sleep than younger children," she quotes a sleep researcher. They need nine hours of sleep but are getting only six, Stepp was told.

"This three-hour debt accumulates over a couple of days," her source told Stepp, "until their bodies take over and fall asleep regardless of what they're doing." When that happens, disaster can be moments away, and this is how Stepp begins her story about sleep deprivation among teen-agers:

> There wasn't a day when Erik Utterman, a junior at Sidwell Friends School, didn't leave school a little tired. But on this particular March evening two years ago, he felt a little drowsier than usual. He had been up all night, finishing an English composition. He had skipped lunch, then spent two hours after school at baseball practice.
>
> He was two miles from home as he steered the family van east down Westmoreland Street in Falls Church about 6 P.M. Edward Lee Rogers, an environmental lawyer who lived in nearby McLean, was driving west on the other side. . . .

Utterman dozed off and his van struck Rogers' Volvo on the driver's side, killing him almost instantly. Rogers' seat belt was of no avail.

Utterman, also belted, escaped without serious physical injury but with a vision he will carry always.

As he whispered to his mother when she arrived at the scene, "Mom, I know I killed him. I know what his head looked like."

Christmas Fund

When Cailin Brown took over the Christmas Fund stories for the *Times Union* in Albany, N.Y., the newspaper had been running brief pieces taken from material submitted by local social service agencies. Pseudonyms were used for the people briefly profiled. The reporters handling the Fund drive never interviewed those whose stories they told.

Brown decided to change everything. She believed that the "same tenets of journalism" that work for other stories should be applied to the fund-raising drive.

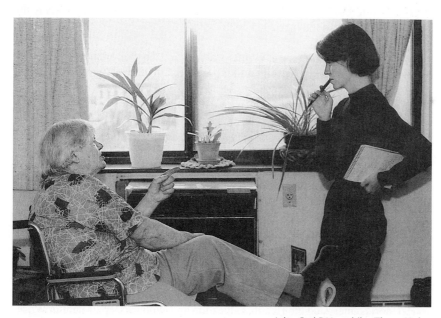

John Carl D'Annabile, *Times Union*

Downed, But Still Feisty

Stella Jabonaski makes her point emphatically to reporter Cailin Brown, who covers the Christmas fund drive for the *Times Union*. The drive is devoted to aiding the elderly needy in the Albany, N.Y., area. During the holiday season, Brown profiles 25 men and women for front-page stories of courage and perseverance despite debilitating physical conditions and, too often, forgetful families. Brown's stories have led to a steady increase in donations to the Christmas fund.

"After countless meetings and some heated disagreements, the newspaper, social service workers and I came to terms on my plan," she says. She would interview the elderly the newspaper profiled and the paper would run their photographs.

The stories, which appear on page 1 of the *Times Union,* are tales of courage and despair, devotion and loneliness. Brown, a general assignment reporter during the year, says that the people she interviews "are usually forgotten by their families, something unthinkable to our readers.

"I have covered my share of crime, both violent and white collar. I have written the story of a vibrant 3-year-old waiting for the death knell of leukemia. Yet never in 13 years as a reporter have I been so moved by the human condition as I have been listening to these people talk about getting old."

Investigative Stories

We expect the media to do more than keep us informed of the day's news. While that's important enough, we also want the media to keep track of those in power, to tell us how well and how honestly they are performing. This is the watchdog function of the journalist.

With the Disabled　A few weeks after Cammy Wilson took a reporting job with the *Minneapolis Tribune,* her city editor gave her a feature assignment: Spend a day with a woman in a wheelchair to see how disabled people get around in the city. Wilson accompanied the woman as she went about her chores, shopped and had lunch. At the end of the day, the woman remarked to Wilson, "Isn't it awful how much we have to pay to be taken to the doctor?" "How much?" Wilson asked. "Forty to fifty dollars," she replied.

Wilson sensed a story of greater impact than the feature she was assigned to write. Wilson asked the woman if she had a receipt for a trip to the doctor. The woman did.

An Ethic
"Making a living is nothing; the great difficulty is making a point, making a difference—with words."
—*Elizabeth Hardwick*

Overbilling　By the time she finished her reporting, Wilson had a major scandal laid out: The transportation of the disabled was a multi-million-dollar operation in which people were being billed $40 to $120 for a round-trip to a medical facility. Companies were billing at an individual rate even when they took groups from a nursing home or a senior citizen center to a clinic.

Her stories interested the Health, Education and Welfare Department in Washington D.C., and, because Medicaid money was involved, HEW investigated. The Minnesota legislature held hearings and enacted several laws to regulate the transportation firms.

Exploitation　A couple of weeks later, Wilson was house hunting. In one house, she noticed that every item was for sale. From worn-out washcloths to underwear, everything had a price tag. "Has the owner died?" she asked the realtor. "No," he said, "the owner is in a nursing home." "Why is he selling?" "He's not selling. The conservator is," the realtor replied.

Once again, Wilson had a story. She learned that the owner, Ludvig Hagen, 86, suffered a fall and was taken to a nursing home to recover. While there, the church that he had named in his will marked the house and all of Hagen's possessions for sale. Wilson began her story this way:

> "4415 17th Ave. S."
> "4415 17th Ave. S."
> The old man in his wheelchair repeated the address, tears beginning to well.
> "I don't have to sell my house. It's paid for."
> But his house is for sale. It and all his possessions are part of an estate valued at $140,000. . . .

As a result of the story, the county attorney launched an investigation.

Wilson then looked at probate, the handling of wills and estates by the courts. She learned that the county probate court had appointed a management firm to handle the estates of various people and that the firm had sold their homes for well under the market price to the same buyer, who within six months resold the houses for 50 to 100 percent more than the purchase price.

A Tip and an Exposé

"The message on my answering machine was straightforward: 'I have a story that may be of interest to you.'

"Although reporters often get calls like this, many of which lead nowhere, I was intrigued, given the source, someone I had interviewed from time to time during the three years I covered the health, hospital and AIDS beat for the New York *Daily News* . . . someone who had never called me before . . . someone who sounded troubled."

Heidi Evans returned the call. The caller told her that the city health department had quietly stopped giving Pap smear tests to thousands of low-income women who depended on its clinics for free gynecological care.

"Since many of the clients of these clinics fit the profile of women most at risk of developing cervical cancer—sexually active women who have had several partners and little access to medical care—I knew I had the start of an important story," she said.

She dug into the records, interviewed people and found an even bigger story—the health department had endangered the lives of many women.

Here is how Evans began her story:

> More than 2,000 Pap smears languished in a city health department laboratory for as long as a year, leaving hundreds of women at high risk of developing cervical cancer without knowing it.

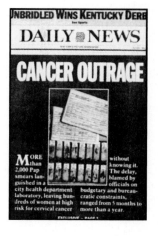

Heidi Evans

She continued to dig and learned that 93 of the test smears indicated health problems, women who needed to be told to seek immediate medical attention. Evans found that instead of being informed quickly, the women received notices nine and ten months after their tests. When these women were finally notified and took further tests, some were fortunate. Some were not:

> When Mary Pollack got the Mailgram it was Friday evening, too late to call the Health Department to have someone explain the message that read, "Urgent!! Concerning Your Health! Medical Emergency!"
>
> On Monday morning, as Pollack held the Mailgram in her shaking hands, the doctor at the city's Jamaica, Queens, clinic gave her the scare of her life.
>
> "You have cancer," he told her.

Gang Rape

Loretta Tofani went face-to-face with her editors at *The Washington Post* about a discovery she had made while covering the Prince George's County Courts. During a sentencing, a lawyer told the judge, "Your honor, my client was gang raped in the county jail." The assertion shook Tofani. "I asked the judge how often he heard about the rapes. 'Oh, it happens all the time,' he said."

Tofani decided to check. She continued to cover her beat, but on her days off and when she finished work, she went to see jail guards at their homes, and she interviewed rape victims. After six weeks, she went to her editor. About a dozen men a week were being raped, most of them held in jail because they lacked bail money.

"They were gang raped because the jail failed to enforce its rules and permitted prisoners to block the view of guards with black trash bags," she told her editor. "Jail policies actually promoted the gang rapes because the jail failed to separate the weak from the strong, to separate those charged with drunk driving, shoplifting and trespassing, who became rape victims, from convicted murderers and armed robbers, the typical rapists."

Her editor replied: "Let's put it on the back burner." She went over his head to another editor. He turned her down. "Spend your time on daily stories," he told her. Her third try was successful, and the metropolitan editor ordered her immediate editor to give Tofani time to do the story.

The stories about gang rapes in the county jail won a Pulitzer Prize.

Using the Internet

Reporters use the vast resources of the Internet to gather information for their stories. In Cleveland, *The Plain Dealer* used the tools of computer-assisted reporting to find that a widening racial health gap exists across the country.

Two Tracks

The staff checked the records of the Centers for Disease Control and Prevention to discover racial health disparities in such areas as Essex County, N.J., where thousands of HIV-infected drug addicts live on the streets of Newark. In Bacon County, Ga., black families "are being destroyed by an epidemic of heart disease and diabetes—diseases that are usually discovered and treated in white residents," Dave Davis wrote.

The series described individual stories of pain and heartbreak. John Holley, a 47-year-old, Lima, Ohio, resident, tried to have a doctor treat him for chest pain. The doctor refused to see him. Days later, Holley died.

Davis wrote that Holley's wife was certain the couple's lack of health insurance was the reason for the doctor's action. She told Davis: "When we got there, the doctor said, 'I don't understand why they sent you here. I'm not going to touch you.' I was so shocked, I just said, 'Thank you.'"

Davis's conclusions: Poverty, lack of health insurance and a racial factor are involved. "African Americans admitted to hospitals receive less medical care than whites who are the same age, same gender and about as sick," he wrote.

Foster Care

It took reporters for *The Denver Post* seven months to answer the question they asked themselves: Was the death of a 2-year-old an isolated instance of anger, or did it reveal a deeper pattern?

The reporters had a hunch that the foster child system was at fault, that some, perhaps many, of the foster parents were unfit for the task, that some had criminal records. To verify their hunch, they crunched 1.8 million computer records, created computer tables to track inspection reports and looked over a database of Colorado criminals and matched it with a database of foster parents.

They found matches: A foster father had spent more than half his adult life in prison, a foster mother had pleaded guilty to solicitation for prostitution, a woman who operated a daycare center had been charged with selling drugs out of the center. The state legislature took action.

It's a short hop from Denver to Las Vegas, Nev., where Brendan Riley of the Associated Press has been working on a story about crime in the fastest-growing city in the United States. Riley is especially interested in the effectiveness of the Las Vegas Metro Police Department in solving crimes.

Online Journalism

Corpus Christi, Texas, is home to many Navy families, and when the USS Inchon, an aircraft carrier, and four sister ships were making their way to home port, the *Corpus Christi Caller-Times* provided readers with stories on the newspaper's Web site. The stories were filed by the newspaper's on-board reporter, Stephanie Jordan.

"My kids rush to the computer every night to see where Daddy is," a Navy wife told the newspaper. "I would like to thank the *Caller-Times* for this wonderful Web page."

When Hurricame Bret threatened the Gulf Coast, the newspaper put its staff to work filing frequent stories on the site, www.caller.com. One story quoted Omar Garza, "I wasn't scared. The wind was only 120 mph."

Web Writing

"When I say 'the paper' I also think of the Web site," said Dean Baquet, when managing editor of the *Los Angeles Times.* "It's very different. It should be different. It should look different." The site, latimes.com, runs fewer stories than the print version, and it emphasizes what one editor described as "splashy" features, stories about celebrities, conspiracies and sex.

At www.projo.com, the Web site of *The Providence Journal,* the stories that print reporters write are rewritten "radio/TV style," says the online editor, Andrea Panciera.

At the *Times-Record News* in Wichita Falls, Texas, Carroll Wilson advises writers for www.trnonline.com: Write short. Keep as close to one computer screen as possible. People scan and surf the Web, Wilson says. "This is different from reading a newspaper. When you go to the Web for information you go for quick bites, quick hits."

The Characteristics of the Reporter

Different as these journalists may appear at first glance, they share certain characteristics, and there are many similarities in the way they handle their assignments.

One characteristic we notice is the reporter's attitude. He or she is curious. The reporter wants to know what is happening—firsthand. This curiosity is not born of nosiness. Journalists learn early that seeing and hearing for themselves is better than secondhand accounts. The firsthand account rings with authenticity.

Persistent

The journalist knows how important persistence is in getting to the truth. Persistence allowed Lisa Newman to tell the story of how a Chicago police officer was transferred as punishment for giving the daughter of the police superintendent a traffic ticket. Newman heard about the incident from an officer, but when she talked to the officer who issued the ticket he refused to confirm her tip.

Newman, a reporter for *The Daily Calumet and Pointer,* gradually lessened the police officer's resistance, and he finally gave her the details. She also learned that the ticket was dismissed in traffic court.

With the information, Newman wrote several stories that led to an investigation.

GOYA/KOD

When *The Washington Post* was digging up exclusives in its Watergate coverage, the national editor of *The Los Angeles Times* was disturbed by the failure of the *Times'* Washington bureau to match the coverage. The *Times'* reporters were trying to cover the scandal by telephone, the editor learned.

"Tell them to get off their asses and knock on doors," the editor shouted to the Washington news editor. The demand went out with increasing frequency and ferocity, until the Washington editor decided to post a sign in the office:

GOYA/KOD
Get Off Your Asses
and
Knock On Doors

Asking Questions   Persistence also means asking question after question until the issue is clarified, the situation made understandable for the reader or viewer. The columnist Dave Barry says, "I was a pretty good writer and I thought that was all that mattered. But journalism isn't about writing. You learned that what it's really about is asking hard questions, being persistent."

Dangerous Drug   David Willman of *The Los Angeles Times* Washington bureau learned that a drug to treat diabetes had been removed from the market in Great Britain but was still being sold in the United States. A year's investigation led to his two-part series on the deaths the drug Rezulin had caused. But the Food and Drug Administration took no action. For the next 14 months he wrote about the mounting death toll and the growing concern of physicians in 25 follow-up stories. The FDA finally removed the drug from the market. An editor described Willman as "the most tenacious guy I ever met as far as grabbing something and never letting it go." Willman won a Pulitzer Prize for investigative reporting for his stories.

Number One
    At *USA Today* an editor set as the First Commandment for his staff: "Break stories. Investigate. Spot the trends."

Fair

In journalism's younger days there was a newsroom saying, "Never check out a good story." Today's journalist always looks for the rejoinder, the defense, the reply, the other side of the story. A survey of working journalists found near unanimous agreement on two reporting necessities—getting the facts right and getting both sides of the story. Later in this chapter we will watch a reporter as he tries to steer a middle course in a conflict over school reading material.

Knowledgeable

Stanley Walker, one of the great city editors, was once asked, "What makes a good reporter?"

"The answer is easy," he replied, with a show of a smile around his eyes. "He knows everything. He is aware not only of what goes on in the world today, but his brain is a repository of the accumulated wisdom of the ages." Walker, who helped make *The New York Herald Tribune* admired for its fine writing, continued: "He hates lies and meanness and sham, but keeps his temper. He is loyal to his paper and to what he looks upon as his profession; whether it is a profession, or merely a craft, he resents attempts to debase it."

The wider the reporter's knowledge base, the quicker the reporter can bring the story into focus. As soon as the reporter heard the speaker say that the country's politics had gone wrong with Franklin Roosevelt's New Deal, he knew his story was about a conservative's approach to politics. Reporters always try to get a jump on their stories, given the short time they have to do their reporting and writing. The more they know, the faster they can find the theme of the event.

Multi-Skilled

In addition to this knowledge base, journalists are equipped with an array of skills to meet the needs of media users. These skills, says Thomas Curley, president of the Associated Press, allow reporters to pace themselves to what Curley calls "consumption-on-demand." Today's journalist is multi-skilled to meet multi-media demands.

Along with the written text, journalists may shoot still photos and full-color video as well as provide audio material for their stories that go online.

Feeding the Web   Tom Priddy, online content producer at the *Herald-Journal* in Spartanburg, S.C., went to an open house to celebrate the new ballpark for the local Class A baseball team. "I covered the story, took photos, interviewed the principals and gathered some natural sound with my new toy, an Olympus DS-2 digital recorder," he says. "I wrote the story for print, passed along one photo to the sports editor, then edited the audio and photos and created an audio slideshow for our Web site, GoUpstate.com."

When the newspaper's statehouse reporter accompanied church volunteers who spent their spring vacation repairing Katrina-damaged houses, he took photos and recorded interviews with the volunteers. He passed the material to Priddy for the Web site.

News 24/7   Reporters are asked "to get the news online almost instantly," reports *Editor&Publisher*. This means filing stories on breaking news events "several times a day—in addition to the eventual print version. Add to that requests for audio and video components, podcasts, blogs and chats. . . . "

An *Indianapolis Star* reporter says reflection time is cut down in the rush to put stories online. She is asked to have a story within 15 minutes of a news conference for posting on the paper's Web site. Updates must also be filed quickly.

Beneath the technology, underlying the new skills, journalism is unchanged. Quality reporting remains the basis of all journalism. "Content," says Curley, "is more important than container."

Let's look at three components of quality journalism.

Enterprise

News conferences, interviews and ball games present few problems. But for every easily accessible situation there is a tougher assignment, a less accessible source. The lore of journalism includes tales of enterprising reporters such as the one about the Chicago reporter who was blocked from a crime scene. He noticed doctors being waved into the building. He sprinted down the street to a pawn shop, pointed to a small suitcase, handed over a few dollars and raced back. Holding the case in his most professional manner, the reporter was allowed to pass.

Finding the Casualties   When Chinese troops shot down hundreds of students demonstrating in Tiananmen Square for democratic reforms, reporters were prevented from entering the area. Officials denied that any of the young men and women were killed. Jan Wong realized she could learn about casualties by going to local hospitals. She found the front doors were barred to outsiders.

"But no one guards the back door," and she went in. "Dozens of corpses, mostly unrefrigerated, decompose on the fifth day after Chinese troops slaughtered unarmed demonstrators near Tiananmen Square," she wrote for her newspaper, *The Globe and Mail* of Toronto.

A week later, the authorities decided Wong was finding out too much. As she was walking down a street, a car with no license plate cut her off, secret servicemen grabbed her and tried to shove her in the car. She kicked and screamed, attracting passersby who protested. The police released her.

Naming the Coach   In the days of intense competition between the United Press International and the Associated Press, reporters knew that a beat would result in a major play in newspapers and on stations. Sources did not want to show preference, so they would hold news conferences which allowed all the media an even shot. The trick was to break down the wall of silence before the scheduled conference, and the UPI did just that when a new football coach was to be announced at Rice University.

The Houston UPI bureau called around the country to the coaches who had been mentioned as candidates. No luck. The only one left was the assistant coach at Rice, and a call went out to his home. The maid answered. No, the coach wasn't in. Nor his wife.

"Is she going to go to the news conference this afternoon?" the UPI reporter asked.

"Yes, sir. She wouldn't miss that for the world," the maid answered.

In seconds, the bureau put out a story about the assistant coach's new job.

You might say that was risky. But would the assistant coach's wife be going to a news conference to hear someone else named coach?

Courage

For Ian Stewart of the Associated Press, the question was simple: Rely on people to tell him what was happening, or see for himself? Should he and an

Reporting Is Central

"Reporting is the essential ingredient in good journalism. Everything else is dressing. Whether covering the White House or the school board, the reporter is the engine that drives the newspaper, the contributor who makes the newscast worthwhile. Forget the fancy packaging. The news organizations that are the most successful—the ones audiences consider essential—are those that care most about good reporting."

—*Sid Bedingfield, president, Fault Line Productions*

AP cameraman and an AP television cameraman venture to Freetown in Sierra Leone, which was being threatened by rebel gunmen? For 10 months, the rebels had rampaged across the countryside, earning a fearsome reputation by hacking off the hands and feet of villagers in a campaign of intimidation.

"The choice was simple," Stewart said. "We had to go to give the people of Sierra Leone a voice and to tell their story."

They went and they met with disaster. Myles Tierney, the TV cameraman, was killed, and Stewart suffered a bullet to his brain that left an arm and hand useless.

Given the disastrous outcome, was his choice wise? "I could not in clear conscience ignore the plight of an innocent people," Stewart said. Not go? "That is not why I entered journalism, nor is that what I was trained to do."

The same ethic motivated Ellen Whitford of *The Norfolk Virginian-Pilot* to go into an abortion clinic and allow herself to be examined and prepared for an abortion. Whitford wanted to prove what she had learned secondhand, that abortions were being performed on women who were not pregnant.

"Murderous Resistance"   In the journalism quarterly, *Nieman Reports,* Gene Roberts and Hank Klibanoff write about the "small group of liberal and moderate Southern editors, probably no more than 20 at any one time, who risked the anger of their readers as well as circulation and advertiser boycotts to urge compliance with the Supreme Court's school desegregation decisions of 1954 and 1955." This was a period of "murderous Southern resistance to the civil rights movement," the historian Sean Wilentz says.

> Roberts and Klibanoff write:
> There may never have been a time in our nation's history when more journalistic courage was shown than in the civil rights era in the 1950's, 60's and 70's. The presence of Southern editors willing to display dissent against rising mob madness emboldened national leaders—presidents, congresses, religious figures, corporate executives and, especially, black civil rights leaders—to press for change. The bravery of reporters and photographers drove them to penetrate the South to see firsthand—and, more importantly, to show—the raw grip of white supremacy on an entire region of the country.

This is the journalistic legacy you inherit.

At the Square   One of the standard stories from China is the visit to Tiananmen Square on the anniversary of the massacre. Although protests are banned by the authorities, some Chinese manage to register their desire for democracy. This is dangerous for the protesters and for journalists. It proved a disaster for Todd Carrel, an ABC news correspondent who was interviewing a lone protester as he unfurled a banner of complaint.

"Undercover Chinese policemen attacked me," Carrel says. "And that beating changed my life." The Chinese police beat him so severely that Carrel is disabled. The protester, Carrel learned, had his life changed as well. He was confined to a mental institution.

Reporters are "a cross between a bootlegger and a whore . . . a lot of lousy, daffy buttinskis, swelling around with holes in their pants, borrowing nickels from office boys. And for what? So a million hired girls and motormen's wives'll know what's going on."
—*Ben Hecht and Charles MacArthur, "Front Page"*

". . . reporters tend to be dilettantes who know a little bit about a lot of things and not very much about any one thing. And the nature of the game, the dailiness of it, never gives them very much opportunity to learn very much about any one thing."
—*Victor Navsky, editor of* The Nation

". . . I see a pale-skinned man in his early forties . . . at two in the morning. He's divorced, his wife has taken his children to another town and when he goes home in the morning there's nothing in the ice box."
—*Thomas Powers, former United Press International reporter*

Reporters and photographers have died covering wars and disasters. Mark Kellogg, a correspondent for the *Bismarck* (Dakota Territory) *Tribune,* fell while riding with Custer and the 7th Cavalry at Little Big Horn in 1876. Ernie Pyle, the legendary war correspondent, was shot by a sniper in the closing days of World War II. More than 40 journalists were killed covering the war in Iraq.

Compassion

James Fallows, national correspondent for *The Atlantic Monthly,* describes as "the highest achievement" of journalism making "people care about and understand events or subjects they had not previously been interested in."

Increasingly, journalists have turned their attention to the defenseless, the poor, those without a voice.

Children Eric Newhouse found that growing numbers of children in Montana were suffering from depression, bipolar disorder and attention deficit hyperactivity. Teen-age suicides had increased seven-fold since the 1950s. He wondered why and he set out to find the answers for his series in the *Great Falls Tribune.* He interviewed mental health experts, and he talked to many troubled teen-agers.

Let's follow a reporter who exhibits some of these characteristics as he tries to background a press release that challenged his values and assumptions.

A News Release That Needs Backgrounding

In the newsroom of a daily newspaper in Maryland, the editor calls the education reporter over to his desk. "Dick, here's something pretty important. Overnight took these notes from a fellow who said he is the publicity chairman of an organization called the Black Parents Association. See if the outfit amounts to anything and, if it does, let's have some comments. Write it down the middle. It's a touchy issue."

Pressure
The Vietnam War followed what the United States charged was an attack on an American warship in the Gulf of Tonkin, an allegation some journalists found dubious. When the CBS news show "60 Minutes" alleged the attack was fabricated to justify U.S. intervention, President Lyndon Johnson called the president of CBS in the middle of the night to tell him, "Your boys shat on the American flag."

The notes read as follows:

The association has just sent a complaint to the state board of education. We are disturbed by the use of certain books our children are being given in the city's schools and school libraries.

Some of this reading gives the children—black or white—a stereotyped view of minority people. At a time when we are in danger of becoming two societies, every effort must be made to understand each other. Some of the books our children are being asked to read do not accomplish this. They portray black people as ignorant, lacking in culture, child-like, sexually loose, etc.

We are asking that certain books be removed from the library and the classroom—<u>Huck Finn, Manchild in the Promised Land</u> and <u>Down These Mean Streets.</u> We intend to add to the list.

"The picture of Jim in the Twain book is that of the stereotyped black man of slave days," says James Alberts, association president. "Impressionable children are led to think of black people as senseless, head-scratching, comic figures. We object to that portrayal of Nigger Jim."

Alberts said that in 1957 the Finn book was banned from elementary and junior high schools in New York City by the city board at the request of the NAACP. Later, he said, black students at Brandeis University picketed a school near the university that used the book. In recent years, some cities have removed the book from reading lists. In Waukegan, Ill., it was removed on the ground that it was offensive to blacks. Dr. John H. Wallace, an educator on the Chicago School Board, calls it "the most grotesque example of racist trash ever written."

"If it is to be read, it should be read at home under the direction of their parents," Alberts said.

The group met in Freedom Hall of the Mt. Zion Baptist Church tonight.

Background Check

Dick checks his newspaper's files to see if there are any stories about the association. He finds a 1990 story that says that the association was formed in 1955, one year after the U.S. Supreme Court ruling on school desegregation, and that it has been active in local school affairs.

He telephones the president of the association to ask if any particular incident provoked the action. The president tells him a parent brought up the issue at a meeting last month. Dick asks for the name of the parent, but the president has forgotten it.

For reaction from the schools, he looks up the telephone numbers of the city school superintendent, some high school principals and the head of the board of education. He asks for their comments. If he has time, he thinks he will try to go over to a high school. He would like to interview black students, he decides. But that may have to wait for a folo (follow-up story).

He rereads the release. Many readers will know *Huckleberry Finn,* but what about the other books? He will have to find out something about them.

Balance   He remembers that, when he took a course in American literature, one of his textbooks described *Huckleberry Finn* as the greatest of all American novels. Maybe he will work that in to give the story some balance. He read the book for the course and remembers Jim as a man of dignity. But his reactions certainly are not those a black high school student might have, he concedes. Yes, he will have to talk to students and to their parents as well. He also will have to guard against putting his opinions into the story.

Dick looks up *Twain* on the Internet and, to his surprise, he finds that the book is properly titled, *The Adventures of Huckleberry Finn.* He had better check the other titles.

Censored Writers

Dick admits to himself he does not like what the association is doing. It is too close to censorship, he thinks. After all, Mark Twain is a great writer. And people are always objecting that some authors are dangerous reading for the young—Hemingway, Salinger, Vonnegut, Steinbeck. But Mark Twain?

Can a great writer be prejudiced? There's a running debate about Shakespeare's *The Merchant of Venice* and Dickens' *Oliver Twist.* He recalls reading a wire story about some parents asking that *The Merchant of Venice* be restricted to high school seniors on the ground that younger students are vulnerable to the anti-Semitic stereotypes in the play.

He also recalls reading that when Twain was a young reporter in San Francisco, he wrote an account of an attack by a gang of young whites on a Chinese man. Several policemen stood by and watched, Twain had written. Twain's story, a straightforward account of the incident, never ran in the newspaper. Even so, it's possible Twain could have been a racist by today's definition.

Dick has a vague recollection of reading a story about Twain helping a black student at Yale. Better look into that, too. He will need time to check out all these recollections, he decides. He will not trust his memory.

Also, he will need to look into the whole issue of book censorship, which, he knows, has been in the news for some time. He knows that battles are being waged across the country over appropriate material for the school curriculum. He will have to use the Internet to obtain a lot of background material for his story, and he will have to interview parents, school officials and teachers—and students.

Censored Books
"Cumulative findings since 1982 show that the most frequently attacked books are American classics. The top three targets since we began our monitoring have been John Steinbeck's *Of Mice and Men,* J. D. Salinger's *The Catcher in the Rye* and Mark Twain's *The Adventures of Huckleberry Finn.*"
—*People for the American Way, a constitutional liberties group*

To follow Dick as he gathers information for his story, see **Huckleberry Finn** in *NRW Plus.*

What Motivates Reporters?

The public editor or ombudsman of *The New York Times,* Byron Calame, sought to answer this question. "Based on the hundreds of reporters with whom I've worked and competed," he said he came up with seven motivations. They are:

Being First With New Facts or Fresh Insights

The drive to be first with the basic facts of a newsworthy development remains embedded in the culture of newsrooms and in the minds of reporters. . . . The obvious signal to reporters: Old-fashioned scoops still count.

Pursuing Stories That Can Have Impact

All reporters want to write articles that people talk about—but some are driven to journalism that produces corrective action or beneficial changes. Two major goals of these reporters are to hold the powerful accountable and to right wrongs.

Winning Prizes

Reporters are most reluctant to acknowledge that their journalism is driven by the desire to win a prize. The criteria for many journalism contests, however, favor stories that cause change or make waves.

Impressing Sources

The better reporters assigned to cover a beat or specialized area of coverage are likely to cultivate the better sources, including experts on the subject. Such reporters will write certain articles that will be viewed as unfavorable by some sources. Yet many of the journalists remain highly motivated to impress their sources with the accuracy, fairness and depth of their work.

Finding Out What's Really Happening

A fundamental motivation of reporters is the curiosity that drives them to get to the bottom of a confusing or complicated situation and find patterns that help explain it to readers. Making sense out of chaos—especially when you can do it first—is something many reporters find very rewarding.

Telling Stories in a Compelling Way

There are two motivations (and often fairly strong egos) at work here. One is the desire of almost all reporters to tell an important story so that it will be read to the end. The other is the satisfaction, or even the delight, that many reporters derive from good writing of the kind that can move readers to laugh or cry.

Getting on the Front Page

While it's no longer a dominant motivation, the hope of turning up a really big story that will make the front page never seems that far from the minds of many reporters.

Summing Up

Journalists live in a world of confusion and complexity. Nevertheless, they manage through enterprise, wit, energy and intelligence to move close to the truth of the event and to shape their understanding into language and a form that can be understood by all. The task ahead of us in this book is to help you develop the journalist's craft and to find a personal credo to work by. A reporter who worked her way from small newspapers in New Mexico, Pennsylvania and New Jersey to the AP and then to *The New York Times* says her motto is "Keep cool but care." This philosophy seems to describe the reporters we will be following in the rest of this book.

Journalists make mistakes. It is important to learn from mistakes and not to be discouraged. Although mistakes can be embarrassing and humiliating, they are unavoidable. Look at the Corrections box on page two of any issue of *The New York Times,* which is staffed by some of the best journalists in the business. Day after day, two to five admissions of error are published—wrong names, wrong addresses, wrong figures. Don't live in fear of making a mistake; that will cut down your range. Do the best you can. That's all anyone can ask of you.

Further Reading

At the end of each chapter, suggested supplementary reading is listed. The listed books have been recommended by journalists and by authorities in the fields discussed in the chapter.

This list includes, for example, the autobiography of a major figure in American journalism, Lincoln Steffens. It also includes Vincent Sheean's recollections of his life as a foreign correspondent, a book that persuaded many young men and women that journalism is for them. Also listed is a biography of Edward R. Murrow, the eminent broadcast journalist. One book describes the women journalists who broke through barriers at *The New York Times.* Finally, no journalism bibliography would be complete without the book that describes how two young reporters, Bob Woodward and Carl Bernstein, toppled a president.

Frankel, Max. *The Times of My Life and My Life with The Times.* New York: Random House, 1999.

Kendrick, Alexander. *Prime Time: The Life of Edward Murrow.* Boston: Little, Brown, 1969.

Kroeger, Brooke. *Nellie Bly: Daredevil, Reporter, Feminist.* New York: Times Books, 1994.

Robertson, Nan. *The Girls in the Balcony: Women, Men, and The New York Times.* New York: Random House, 1992.

Serrin, Judith and William. *Muckraking: The Journalism That Changed America.* New York: The New Press, 2003.

   The 121 articles from colonial days to the present display the work of crusading and investigative reporters. The great names are all here—Steffens, Tarbell, Riis, Wells, Woodward and Bernstein—along with the worthy work of lesser-known journalists of conscience.

Sheean, Vincent. *Personal History.* Boston: Houghton Mifflin, 1969.

Steffens, Lincoln. *The Autobiography of Lincoln Steffens.* New York: Harcourt Brace, 1931.

Waldron, Ann. *Hodding Carter: The Reconstruction of a Racist.* Chapel Hill, N.C.: Algonquin Books of Chapel Hill, 1993.

Woodward, Bob, and Carl Bernstein. *All the President's Men.* New York: Simon & Schuster, 1974.

Part 2: The Basics

Marooned truck driver rescued—a breaking news story.

Preview

News stories must be:

- **Accurate.** All information is verified before it is used. Direct observation is the surest way to obtain accurate information.
- **Properly attributed.** The reporter identifies all sources of information.
- **Complete.** The story contains the specifics that illustrate, prove and document the main point of the story.
- **Balanced and fair.** All sides in a controversy are presented.
- **Objective.** The writer does not inject his or her feelings or opinions.
- **Brief and focused.** The news story gets to the point quickly and keeps to the point.
- **Well-written.** Stories are clear, direct, interesting.

Adhere to the A, B, Cs—accuracy, brevity, clarity.

If we were to generalize from the work of the reporters we have been watching, we might conclude that the reporter:

1. Attempts to report accurately the truth or reality of the event through:
   A. Direct observation.
   B. The use of (a) authoritative, knowledgeable and reliable human sources and (b) relevant and reliable physical sources.
2. Tries to write an interesting, timely and clear story. Quotations, anecdotes, examples and human interest enliven the story.

If journalism needs rules, these would be the starting points.

Accuracy

The highest praise A. J. Liebling, a master reporter for newspapers and *The New Yorker* magazine, could pay a colleague was, "He is a careful reporter," by which

Liebling meant that the reporter took great care to be accurate. Although reporters often work under severe space and time limitations, they make every effort to check the accuracy of information through verification and documentation.

Joseph Pulitzer, a towering figure in U.S. journalism, had a cardinal rule for his staff: "Accuracy, accuracy, accuracy." There may be arguments in newsrooms about writing style, about the best way to interview a reluctant source, but there is no debate about errors. A journalist may be tolerated if his or her writing does not sparkle, but reporters won't last if they are error-prone.

Check and Check Again

Mistakes occur when the reporter fails to check an assumption or a source's assertion.

When she was the public editor at *The Oregonian,* Michele McLellan recalls, "The newspaper featured a local high-school band member in a photo on the local news cover. The picture was tailor-made to brighten the family scrapbook. And it might have been the only time Julia Carr would see herself in her local newspaper.

"But we misspelled her name in the caption. I cringed that we had failed a young person in such a basic way. The bandleader provided the wrong spelling, but our photographer accepted responsibility. I was proud we didn't just shrug, blame the source and move on."

When the news editor of *The New York Times* spotted a line in a story that described the Canadian city of Sudbury as a "suburb of Toronto," he checked an atlas. Sudbury, he found, is 250 miles north of Toronto. The reporter blamed the source, an FBI agent, but the editor said that was no excuse. "It should have been second nature to check," he said.

And These

The headline writer put the famous mountain peak El Capitan in Yellowstone National Park.

In one story, *The New York Times* writer wrote of "the University of Wisconsin at Ann Arbor" and Los Alamos in "the desert sands of New Mexico."

A *Times* story refers to the "Ida P. Wells housing project in Chicago."

In another *Times* story, a westward train makes several stops "before arriving in Santa Fe." The writer also describes Santa Fe as being "in New Mexico's desert."

The caption in a midwestern newspaper refers to 22 women in the Washington State Senate. The picture shows 23 women.

***Newsweek* recommends parents let their 5-month-olds feed themselves raw carrot sticks and zweiback.**

No, El Capitan isn't where the headline put it, but west in Yosemite National Park. And we all know where the University of Wisconsin is located. It's Ida B. Wells. No trains stop in Santa Fe, which is hardly in the desert being some 7,000 feet high, as is Los Alamos. As for *Newsweek*'s recommendation for feeding children, the magazine had to call back several hundred thousand copies of the issue. Its recommendation of carrots and zweiback could cause 5-month-olds to choke.

Costly Difference

The recipe in *Gourmet* magazine called for a dash of wintergreen oil. While the magazine was on the press, someone discovered that wintergreen *extract* was called for. Wintergreen oil is poisonous. Oops. The magazine printed the proper ingredients on a sticker and put it on the 750,000 copies of the magazine.

Fear

"The best newsrooms are places where people live in fear of being wrong. Good journalists can't stand errors."
—*Caesar Andrews, editor, Gannett News Service*

Unanimous

A poll of 550 journalists on journalistic values ranked highest (1) getting the facts right and (2) getting both sides on record.

Hold It   Speed, the essential ingredient of much journalism, is accuracy's enemy. Consulting the dictionary for the proper shade of a word's meaning takes time. That extra 30 seconds may mean the story won't make the 6 o'clock broadcast or the first edition. But check we must.

Corrections

When mistakes are made, corrections follow so that the record is accurate.

Correction

In last week's edition of the Michigan Chronicle, the story "Fauntroy stirs breakfast crowd," Congressman Walter Fauntroy's grandmother was misidentified. The matriarch was known to Fauntroy family members as "Big Ma," not "Big Mouth" as reported.

Past Due

In 1961, *The Columbia Journalism Review* criticized *The Daily News* for suggesting that medication taken by John F. Kennedy might affect his judgment. In 2003, the *Review* published a correction and apology. A book that investigated Kennedy's illnesses stated that medication Kennedy took for Addison's disease did affect his judgment.

Language, Too

Accuracy also applies to the use of language. Words are chosen carefully to match the situation, event or individual. The writer who settles for the imprecise rather than the exact word lives dangerously, teetering on the brink of being misunderstood or misleading readers and listeners.

Precision   We don't say she was "unusually tall." We write she was "an inch over six feet tall." No matter how concise our broadcast news item is, we don't write that "the ship damaged the pier." We write, "the tanker (freighter, battleship, ferry) caused $500,000 in damage to the pier."

Firsthand Observation

The reporter knows that a story based on direct observation is superior in accuracy and reader interest to one based on secondhand information.

As Bertrand Russell, the British philosopher, advised his students:

> Make the observation yourself. Aristotle could have avoided the mistake of thinking that women have fewer teeth than men by the simple device of asking Mrs. Aristotle to keep her mouth open while he counted. Thinking you know, when in fact you don't, is a fatal mistake to which we are all prone.

Despite the air of certainty in the tone of news stories, many are not based on the reporter's direct observation. The reporter rarely sees the burglar breaking in, the policy being drafted, the automobile hitting the telephone pole. The reporter obtains information about these events from authoritative sources such as documents and records (police files for the burglary and the accident) and from reliable individuals (policy makers and participants and witnesses).

News Filters

When the reporter bases his or her story on direct observation, the story is a *firsthand* account. But when the reporter is not on the scene and information is obtained from those who were present, the reporter's story is a *secondhand* account. It has been filtered through the source.

Some stories are based on accounts that have been filtered twice before reaching the reporter, a *thirdhand* account. For example, an official agency holds a meeting at which the participants are sworn to secrecy. The reporter learns that one of those attending the meeting described it to a member of his staff, who happens to be a good source of news for the reporter. The reporter manages to obtain the staff member's account of the executive's account of what occurred.

Here are examples of stories based on direct observation and on secondary sources:

SHREWSBURY—About 250 anti-abortion demonstrators were arrested yesterday and charged with trespassing and violating a court order after they blocked the doors to the Planned Parenthood clinic for several hours.

The protesters, who prayed and sang as they were dragged and carried to police vans and a rented bus, were part of a new national group, called Operation Rescue, which has targeted abortion clinics. The group takes its name from a Bible passage in the Book of Proverbs: "Rescue those who are being drawn away to death."

> **Firsthand Account**
> Elaine Silvestrini and Sherry Figdore saw the protest and watched the protesters being dragged into the waiting police vans.

WASHINGTON, Oct. 7—Striking at night from aircraft carriers and distant bases, the United States and Britain launched a barrage of cruise missiles and long-range bombers against Afghanistan today. Their aim was the destruction of the terrorist training camps of Osama bin Laden and the Taliban government that has protected it.

The president ordered the strike. "These carefully targeted actions are designed to disrupt the use of Afghanistan as a terrorist base of operations and to attack the military capability of the Taliban regime," President Bush said in a televised statement from the White House at 1 P.M., half an hour after the attack began.

> **Secondhand Account**
> The reporter learned about the launching of the attack from a White House briefing.

FBI agents have established that the Watergate bugging incident stemmed from a massive campaign of political spying and sabotage conducted on behalf of President Nixon's re-election and directed by officials of the White House and the Committee for the re-election of the President.

The activities, according to information in FBI and Department of Justice files, were aimed at all the major Democratic presidential contenders and—since 1971— represented a basic strategy of the Nixon re-election effort.

During their Watergate investigation federal agents established that hundreds of thousands of dollars in Nixon campaign contributions had been set aside to pay for an extensive undercover campaign aimed at discrediting individual and Democratic presidential candidates and disrupting their campaigns. . . .

—*The Washington Post*

> **Thirdhand Account**
> Carl Bernstein and Bob Woodward said that they based their story "on strains of evidence, statements from numerous sources, deduction, a partial understanding of what the White House was doing, the reporters' familiarity with the 'switchblade mentality' of the President's men and disparate pieces of information the reporters had been accumulating for months."

Attribution

The farther the reporter is from direct observation, the more concerned he or she is about the accuracy of the information. Accurate and comprehensive direct observation is difficult enough. After the information has been filtered once or twice,

How the News Is Filtered

Firsthand Account
The story is based on direct observation of the event by the reporter.

Secondhand Account
The story is based on the account passed on by a participant or witness.

Thirdhand Account
The story is based on information supplied by a source who was informed by a participant.

only the most foolhardy journalist would stake his or her reputation on the accuracy of the material. To make clear that secondhand and thirdhand accounts are not based on the reporter's direct observation of the event, the reporter attributes the information about the event to a source.

Here are the first two paragraphs from a story in *The Detroit News:*

> For six minutes, a Detroit police operator listened on the telephone as 24 bullets were fired into the bodies of an East Side couple.
>
> But, according to the police, the civilian mistook the shots for "someone hammering or building something" and dispatched the call as a routine burglary.

Bill Carter, *The Norman Transcript*

Attribute?

Not necessary. No reporter from *The Norman Transcript* was on hand when this tractor plowed into this house at lunchtime, but the evidence speaks for itself.

The lead may give the reader the impression the reporter was at the phone operator's elbow. But the second paragraph attributes the information to the police.

Attribution refers to two concepts:

1. **Statements** are attributed to the person making them.

2. **Information** about the events not witnessed by the reporter is attributed to the source of the information.

Here is a story that contains both types of attribution:

(1) Mayor Stanley Kretchmer said yesterday the city probably could balance its budget this year and next without laying off any workers.

(1) The decision, he said, "depends on a number of factors—the passage of a new tax package, the cooperation of municipal labor unions, general prosperity that keeps revenues high."

(2) At a meeting last week, the mayor told department heads they should consider the possibility of layoffs of about 10 percent of their workforce, according to city officials who attended the meeting.

(2) Police and fire department personnel would be exempt from the cuts, sources reported.

Generally, we attribute what we do not observe or know to be factual. Although the reporter may take the information from a police record, the document does not necessarily attest to the truth of the information, only that some source—the police, a victim, the suspect, a witness—said that such-and-such occurred. The reporter attributes the information to this source.

Some news organizations such as the AP demand rigid adherence to the following policy: Always attribute what you do not see unless it is common knowledge.

Let us examine three stories to see how this policy is carried out. Under each story are the comments of an experienced reporter about the reasons attribution was or was not used. (Her direct quotes follow each story.)

Mike Roemer

Attribute?

Of course. We attribute statements to those making them.

YMCA

(1) NEW YORK AP—Dr. Jesse L. Steinfeld, former Surgeon General of the U.S. Public Health Service, has been appointed chairman of the National YMCA Health and Physical Education Advisory Council.

(2) Steinfeld is professor of medicine at the University of California at Irvine, Calif., and chief of medical services for the Veterans Hospital in Long Beach, Calif.

(3) The advisory council will play an important role in the setting of future directions of the Y's nationwide programs, national board chairman Stanley Enlund said today in announcing Steinfeld's appointment to the nonsalaried post.

(1) There is no need for attribution of the appointment because the action is obviously on the record.

(2) Steinfeld's background is taken from records and needs no attribution.

(3) The role of the council is an opinion offered by the chairman of the board and must be attributed to him.

Hotel Fire

(1) BRANFORD, Conn. AP—The Waverly Hotel, popular earlier in the century, was destroyed by a two-alarm fire today.

(2) The roof collapsed into the heart of the building. At daylight the burned-out hotel was still smoldering.

(3) Myrtle Braxton, 73, who lived alone in the massive three-story building, was reported in fair condition at Yale-New Haven Hospital suffering from smoke inhalation.

(4) Officials said the fire was reported by Mrs. Braxton at 3:41 A.M. They said it apparently started in the kitchen area where Mrs. Braxton was living after having closed off most of the rest of the building. She was living there without central heating or electricity, officials said.

(5) A neighbor said that a large number of antiques on the third floor were destroyed. Also lost was a huge ship's wheel from a sailing ship, a centerpiece in the dining room.

(6) The bank that holds the mortgage said the land and hotel were worth $40,000 to $50,000.

(1)(2) The condition of the hotel is a physical fact about which the reporter has no doubt.

(3) The attribution is implied as coming from the hospital.

(4) "Officials," presumably fire department officials, are cited as the authority because only they could have known this. In the second sentence, the location of the fire's origin is attributed.

(5)(6) Attribution gives the information credibility.

CBC

(1) The Citizen's Budget Commission, a private taxpayer's organization, said today that the proposed city budget of $185 million is more than the city can afford.

(2) The budget was submitted two weeks ago.

(3) Mayor Sam Parnass described it as an austerity budget.

(4) The Commission said it concluded after studying the budget that "significant cuts can be made."

(5) The $185 million spending plan is up 12 percent from the current year.

(6) When he submitted the budget, Mayor Parnass said anticipated revenues would cover the increase. The Commission is supported by the city's business community.

(1) A charge, allegation or opinion is always attributed, usually at the beginning of the lead. Here, the Commission is immediately identified as the source of the allegation.

(2) Background need not be attributed because it is part of the record.

(3) Attribute the mayor's opinion to him.

(4) Attribution to the source of the material.

(5) Background needing no attribution.

(6) Attribute the mayor's statement. (The last sentence is the reporter's attempt to give the reader the why of the Commission's opposition—it's a taxpayer's group that likes austerity budgets because it means lower taxes. Nice touch.)

"Remember," the reporter cautioned, "attribution does not guarantee the accuracy or truth of the material. All it does is place responsibility for the material with a source.

"If it turns out the information is inaccurate, the publication or station isn't responsible for the misinformation. The source is.

"If you don't identify the source, the reader or listener is going to assume that you stand behind the statements because you know they are true."

Types of Attribution

Generally, reporters presume that those who speak to them can be named as the source of the information. Occasionally, a source will request he or she not be named. The reporter then has to determine whether the source can be referred to in a general way, as a "city hall official" or a "state legislator" or a "bank executive," for example.

The source may say the information is for *background* only or *off the record*. These terms have specific meanings to reporters but may not have the same meanings to sources. The reporter must clarify with the source whether the material can be used without direct attribution or not used at all but is being provided solely for the reporter's information, or somewhere in between.

Four Types

On the Record:
All statements are directly quotable and attributable, by name and title, to the person who is making the statement.

On Background:
All statements are directly quotable, but they cannot be attributed by name or specific title to the person commenting. The type of attribution to be used should be spelled out in advance: "A White House official," "an Administration spokesman."

On Deep Background:
Anything that is said in the interview is usable but not in direct quotation and not for attribution. The reporter writes it on his or her own.

Off the Record:
Information is for the reporter's knowledge only and is not to be printed or made public in any way. The information also is not to be taken to another source in hopes of getting confirmation.

Some reporters refuse to accept material if there is a condition that it may not be used in any form. They may bargain with the source, asking if they can go to another source to obtain confirmation. Or they may ask if the material can be used without using the source's name.

Caution: Many editors refuse to accept copy that contains charges or accusations with no named source. They will not accept attribution to "an official in city hall," "a company spokesperson."

Background and off-the-record information pose problems for conscientious reporters because they know that backgrounders can be used to float *trial balloons.* These stories are designed by the source to test public reaction without subjecting the source to responsibility for the material. Reporters, eager to obtain news of importance and sometimes motivated by the desire for exclusives, may become the conduits for misleading or self-serving information.

When a reporter attributes assertions to a source, the reader can assess the accuracy and truth of the information on the basis of the general reliability of the source and his or her stake in the information.

The lesson for reporters is clear: Avoid commitments not to use names of sources.

Anonymous Sources

The reporter's job is to put sources on record, by name. Readers and listeners trust such a report. "When we write 'sources say,' they're convinced we're making it up," writes David Shaw, media critic of the *Los Angeles Times.*

Some publications and stations insist that all material be attributed to a named source, but others will use nonattributed information when the reporter is sure the material is reliable. In these cases, the editor usually wants to know the name of the source.

Special care must be exercised when an anonymous source makes a charge of wrongdoing. *The New York Times* tells its staff:

> We do not want to let unidentified sources (like "law enforcement officials") use us to circulate charges against identifiable people when they provide no named complainants or other verifiable evidence.

Here is the policy of the Associated Press:

> We do not routinely accede to requests for anonymity. We want information on the record. When a news source insists that he or she not be identified by name, we say so. If we accept the condition of anonymity, we keep our word. But within the rule set by the newsmaker, we do everything possible to tell readers the source's connections, motivations and viewpoints.

The Reporter as Source

When reporters dig out the information for their stories, the material can be attributed to the publication or station:

Credibility

A study found that quotes attributed to named sources have high credibility, whereas there is less belief in stories without a named source. S. Shyam Sundar of Pennsylvania State University found that even online news tidbits are "attended to as deliberately as news stories printed in a newspaper" when material is attributed to sources.

> Austin police used force against African-Americans and Hispanics at significantly higher rates than they did against whites during the past six months, according to an Austin American-Statesman analysis of police statistics.

Some editors are more conservative than those at this Texas newspaper. Jason Riley and R. G. Dunlop of *The Courier-Journal* in Louisville developed a series on dysfunctional county courts that lost and buried hundreds of felony cases. Riley wrote a lead that said the court system was flawed. His editor sent back Riley's draft with the comment, "Says who?"

Riley's response: "I didn't think it needed attribution because it was the conclusion I had drawn after six months of investigation." Riley held out and won out. Here is his lead:

> FRANKFORT, Ky.—Justice in Kentucky is dispensed unequally because of differences among judges and prosecutors and a lack of state oversight that has allowed thousands of felony cases to stall, to disappear or to be dismissed for lack of prosecution.

The third paragraph begins with this attribution:

> An eight-month investigation of the state's criminal justice system by *The Courier-Journal* found that some criminal cases took up to two decades to complete. . . .

Warning

Attributing information to sources does not absolve reporters of responsibility for libelous statements in their stories. A reporter for a Florida newspaper reported that a county employee smoked marijuana, and the worker brought suit. "The reporter's own testimony indicated she had relied on second- and thirdhand accounts when writing the story," *Editor&Publisher* reported. A jury awarded the employee $70,000. (See Chapter 25 for further discussion of libel.)

See for Yourself   Journalists sometimes go astray when they neglect to ask for proof of assertions their sources make. Records, documents, reports are more reliable than a source's version of them. But these must be examined by the reporter.

A cornerstone of a journalist's allegation about Hillary Clinton's honesty was that she had vastly overstated the value of the Clintons' real estate holdings in a loan application.

The allegation was given widespread attention. Then a reporter who checked the document found that at the bottom of the front page was the notation: "Both sides of this document must be complete." On reading the other side, the reporter found that Mrs. Clinton had accurately stated the value.

The journalist who had attacked Mrs. Clinton defended his story by stating that his source had not provided the back of the page.

Verification

Attributing material to a source does not prove its truth. All a reporter does when attributing information is to place responsibility for it with the source named in the story. Attribution says only: It is true that the source said this.

The reporter who cares about truth is reluctant to settle for this half step but often is prevented from moving on by deadline pressures and the difficulty of verifying material. If a reporter tried to check every bit of information, most stories would never be written. There are, of course, certain routine verifications a reporter must make:

- Names, addresses and telephone numbers are checked in the newspaper's or station's library, the telephone directory and the city directory.

- Background information is taken from the files.

- Dubious information is checked against records, with other sources.

Check the Farm   Harlyn Riekena was worried, he told *New York Times* reporter David Cay Johnston. He had heard all this talk about how the federal estate tax would hurt farmers like him. His 950 acres planted in soybeans and corn in central Iowa was valuable, worth about $2.5 million. Riekena "fretted that estate taxes would take a big chunk of his three grown daughters' inheritance," Johnston wrote.

President George W. Bush had made the point repeatedly: "To keep farms in the family, we are going to get rid of the death tax," the president said. (Opponents of the estate tax had taken to calling it the death tax, a more ominous title.) Bush had rounded up enough votes in the House to reduce the tax and then abolish it. But how true was the administration's dire prediction of the death of the family farm unless the tax was repealed?

Johnston went to farm country to check, and he did find fear of loss. But was the fear justified? Johnston asked Neil Harl, an Iowa State University economist whose tax advice "has made him a household name among Midwest farmers," Johnston wrote.

Harl told Johnston: "It's a myth." Harl said "he had searched far and wide but had never found a case in which a farm was lost because of estate taxes," Johnston wrote.

Johnston checked with the American Farm Bureau Federation, a supporter of the repeal. But, Johnston wrote, "It could not cite a single example of a farm lost because of estate taxes."

Johnston's guiding journalism philosophy is to "examine not what politicians say, but what they have done." This kind of reporting, he says, is "what readers want. . . . they want facts that are rounded and even-handed so they can apply their own lens of perception and draw their own conclusions."

Nonverifiable Information

The reporter can verify this statement: "The mayor submitted a $150 million budget to the city council today." All the reporter needs to do is examine the minutes of the meeting or the budget. But he or she cannot verify the truth of this statement: "The budget is too large (or too small)." A city councilman might have indeed stated that he would oppose the budget because it was too large, whereas the head of the Municipal League might have declared her organization's distress at the "paltry budget that endangers health and welfare projects." We can determine that the statements were made, but we cannot determine the truth of opinions and judgments. All we can do is to quote the source accurately, seek countering opinions and let the reader or viewer decide.

The Techniques of Verification

Verification is not the use of another opinion to counter the view of a source. Journalists should offer several views on controversial matters, and they should seek out the victims of charges. But that is balance, not verification.

Sen. Trent Lott said that in 1991 when President George Bush asked for authorization to use force against Iraq, "I don't believe there was a single Democrat that voted for that."

David E. Rosenbaum of *The New York Times* checked the files rather than allow an accusation to appear in print without verification.

Then Rosenbaum inserted in his story: "In fact, 86 Democrats in the House and 10 in the Senate, including Al Gore, voted for the authorization."

Not all charges and accusation can be verified, of course, and when this happens and the source has not offered proof, the news writer says so.

During wartime, journalists depend on official sources because so much happens out of their sight and hearing. Sometimes, however, a reporter will try to verify material released by an official source. The result can be illuminating.

In Vietnam When the United States announced its planes had accidentally bombed the Cambodian village of Neak Luong, the U.S. Embassy told correspondents that the damage was minimal. Sydney H. Schanberg, a *New York Times* correspondent, decided to see for himself and sought air transportation to the village. The Embassy intervened to keep him from flying there, but Schanberg managed to find a boat.

Schanberg stayed in Neak Luong long enough to interview villagers and to see for himself whether the damage was minimal. It wasn't.

To see more about Schanberg's coverage, see **In Neak Luong** in *NRW Plus*.

In Iraq Early in the Iraq war, the military—sensitive to charges it had kept reporters from the front lines in previous engagements—allowed reporters to travel with the troops. Reporters were "embedded" with units and were able to file firsthand, graphic accounts of the action. But some reporters complained that

Avoiding the VP

When Vice President Dick Cheney spoke at a dinner fund-raiser for the Republican candidate for the U.S. Senate there was a missing guest, the candidate himself, Thomas H. Kean Jr. Actually, Kean did show . . . 15 minutes after Cheney left.

Reporters sensed a purposeful tardiness, given Cheney's dismal ratings in public opinion polls. So when Kean did show they asked him why he was late. Busy, busy with his duties in the state senate, he said. He went north as soon as he finished "as quickly as I could." But there were traffic delays on Route 1, which he told his driver to take because the Turnpike is usually crowded in the afternoon.

David Chen of *The New York Times* wondered. Traffic delays on Route 1, the Turnpike? Chen called Shadow Traffic and was told that Route 1 was "relatively traffic free" that afternoon. He then checked the Turnpike Web site and found: ". . . no traffic delays." Chen had his story.

their activities were still limited to the troops to which they were assigned and that they were not free to see and hear as they pleased and had to rely on service briefings.

Complete

Here is a brief story that ran in the business section of a major newspaper:

The United States' highest-paid chief executive officer resigned his post as Computer Associates International Inc., the world's largest independent software company, reshuffled its senior ranks and announced plans to spin off key divisions in an attempt to bolster its lackluster stock.

Company founder Charles Wang handed the CEO's reins to chief operating officer Sanjay Kumar, but will stay on as chairman and play an active role in the company with the responsibility of developing news initiatives.

Complete? Does the story leave unanswered any questions the reader might have? If you noticed that the story does not follow up the generality "highest-paid chief executive officer" with the amount Wang is paid, go to the head of the class.

There isn't a reader of this piece who isn't wondering how high in the stratosphere of executive salaries Wang's ascends.

Complete stories are written by reporters who anticipate and answer the questions their readers, viewers and listeners will ask.

Missing Prices The radio reporter began her 60-second piece about summer rentals in an exclusive area this way:

> Once, renters fought for space at the Hamptons. Now, there are dozens of listings and few takers. The prices have gone way down. Still, there are long lists of available rentals.

After this beginning, what do you expect to hear? You want to know just how high those rentals were and how low they descended. But our reporter forgot to follow her generality with a specific. Her piece was not complete because she never gave us a single specific price.

Try These How would you follow these lines taken from some stories?

1. The temperature reached an all-time high yesterday at noon.

2. While in college, she set records in 100- and 200-meter races.

3. He said that today's rap stars will join yesterday's "in the dustbin of forgotten groups."

You would expect:

1. The temperature hit 102 degrees, breaking the record of 98 degrees set on April 10, 1999.

2. Her times of 11.2 in the 100-meter dash and 22.03 in the 200-meter race remain standing at the college to this day.

3. "Who remembers 'Four Hot Dogs' today? Or 'The Malignants'?"

The complete story is also fair and balanced.

Fairness

When Walter Anderson, the editor in chief of *Parade,* was a young reporter he interviewed a woman whom he described as the "unmarried mother of five." After the story appeared, the woman's son called to ask Anderson, "Why did you write that? Why is that anyone's business?"

On reflection two decades later, Anderson said, "The article I wrote was accurate, but I don't think it was fair. I had gotten the facts right, but I was not right."

Bias

The media are caught in the crosshairs of those aiming charges of bias. Conservatives find a liberal bias, and liberals find a conservative bias. "Our paper is under constant criticism by people alleging various forms of bias," says Eric Black of the *Star Tribune* in Minneapolis. "And there is a daily effort to perform in ways that will make it harder to criticize. Some are reasonable, but there is a line you can cross after which you're avoiding your duties to truth-telling."

The Essentials

The *Washington Post* "Deskbook of Style" makes these points:

- No story is fair if it omits facts of major importance or significance. So fairness includes completeness.

- No story is fair if it includes essentially irrelevant information at the expense of significant facts. So fairness includes relevance.

- No story is fair if it consciously or unconsciously misleads or deceives the reader. So fairness includes honesty—leveling with the reader.

- No story is fair if reporters hide their biases or emotions behind such subtly pejorative words as "refused," "despite," "admit." So fairness requires straightforwardness ahead of flashiness.

- No story is fair if innocent people are hurt.

Balance

During political campaigns, editors try to balance—in some cases down to the second of air time or the inch of copy—candidate A and candidate B.

Edward Reed

Self-Discipline?

Whatever the reporter feels about a candidate for office, the account of his campaign is written objectively. The reporter quotes the candidate on his positions, on issues, asks him questions and describes his appearances at street rallies. The reporter allows the reader to make judgments.

Balance is important. But balance does not require journalists to station themselves precisely at the midpoint of an issue. If candidate A makes an important speech today, the speech may be worth page 1 play. If, on the same day, opponent B repeats what he said yesterday or utters nonsense, the newspaper or station is under no obligation to balance something with nothing. A journalism of absolute balance can add up to zero. Balance is a moral commitment and cannot be measured by the stopwatch or the ruler.

The same common sense is applied to matters that require fair play. Should candidate A make a serious accusation against opponent B, the reporter seeks out B for a reply. The targets of charges and accusations are always given their say, and the reply is placed as closely to the allegation as possible.

Here is the AP's policy on balance:

> We make every reasonable effort to get comment from someone who has a stake in a story we're reporting—especially if the person is the target of an attack or allegations. . . . If someone declines comment, we say so. If we can't get comment from someone whose side of a story should be told, we spell out in our copy the steps we took to try to get that comment. . . . Whenever possible we also check our files to see what, if anything, the person has said in the past relating to the allegations. Including past comment may provide needed balance and context.

Objectivity

The Standard—

"My business is to communicate facts; my instructions do not allow me to make any comment upon the facts which I communicate. . . . I therefore confine myself to what I consider legitimate news."
—*Lawrence Gobright, first AP correspondent in Washington, D.C., 1861*

Lack of balance and the absence of fairness are often inadvertent. Because writing is as much an act of the unconscious as it is the conscious use of controlled and disciplined intelligence, the feelings of reporters can crop up now and then.

In describing an official the reporter dislikes, a reporter might write, "C. Harrison Gold, an ambitious young politician, said today. . . ."

Or, writing about an official the reporter admires, that reporter might write, "Gerald Silver, the dynamic young state controller, said today. . . ."

It is acceptable for a young man or woman to be "ambitious," but when the word is used to describe a politician, it has a negative connotation. On the other hand, the "dynamic" politician conjures up an image of a young man or woman hard at work serving the public. Maybe the reporter is accurate in these perceptions. Maybe not. The reporter's job is to let the reader draw conclusions by describing what the politician says and does.

In other words, the reporter straddles the middle line. We say the careful reporter is objective. If the reporter feels that Gold is overly ambitious to the point of sacrificing principles, then it is the reporter's job to prove it through meticulous reporting. The reporter must verify his or her suspicions, feelings or hunches.

Unfair and unbalanced journalism might be described as a failure in objectivity. When journalists talk about objectivity, they mean that the news story is free of the reporter's opinion or feelings, that it contains facts and that the account is written by an impartial and independent observer. Stories are objective when they can be checked against some kind of record—the text of a speech, the minutes of a meeting, a police report, a purchase voucher, a payroll, or vital statistics.

If readers want to weep or laugh, write angry letters to their senators or send money to the Red Cross for tornado victims, that is their business. The reporter is content to lay out the facts. Objective journalism is the reporting of the visible and the verifiable.

Objectivity's Limitations

In the 1950s, social and political problems that had been proliferating since the end of World War II began to cause cleavages in society, and reporters found their methodology of objective reporting inadequate in finding causes and fixing responsibility.

Journalists were concerned about the attention they had given Joseph McCarthy, the Wisconsin senator whose charges of Communist conspiracies had been given front-page play over the country. Their tortured self-analysis led them to assume collective responsibility for the senator's rise to power. They realized it was not enough to report what McCarthy had said—which was objective reporting. McCarthy had indeed made the charges, but many of the charges were later found to be false.

Frustrated Journalists   Elmer Davis, a radio journalist, pointed to the limitations of objective journalism during the McCarthy period. He described the frustrations of reporters who knew officials were lying but were unable to say so in their stories.

Davis said that the principle of objectivity holds that a newspaper or station will run "everything that is said on both sides of a controversial issue and let the reader make up his mind. A noble theory; but suppose that the men who talk on one side (or on both) are known to be lying to serve their own personal interest, or suppose they don't know what they are talking about. To call attention to these facts, except on the editorial page, would not, according to most newspaper practice, be objective."

Davis wondered whether readers have enough background on many subjects and he asked, "Can they distinguish fact from fiction, ignorance from knowledge, interest from impartiality?"

The newspaper is unworthy of the reader's trust, Davis continued in his book *But We Were Born Free,* "if it tells him only what somebody says is the truth, which is known to be false." The reporter has no choice, he wrote, but to put into "the one-dimensional story the other dimensions that will make it approximate the truth." The reporter's obligation is to the person who goes to the news "expecting it to give him so far as humanly possible not only the truth and nothing but the truth, but the whole truth." Then, in a paragraph that influenced many journalists, Davis wrote:

> The good newspaper, the good news broadcaster, must walk a tightrope between two great gulfs—on one side the false objectivity that takes everything at face value and lets the public be imposed on by the charlatan with the most brazen front; on the other, the "interpretive" reporting which fails to draw the line between objective and subjective, between a reasonably well-established fact and what the reporter or editor wishes were the fact. To say that is easy; to do it is hard. No wonder that too many fall

back on the incontrovertible objective fact that the Honorable John P. Hoozis said, colon quote—and never mind whether he was lying or not.

Adjustments

Another broadcast journalist, Edward R. Murrow, who had moved from radio to television, pioneered in-depth reporting. He sought to make television journalism more than a bulletin board with news for the middle class. In his work in the 1950s, Murrow demonstrated a passion to get at underlying truths along with curiosity and journalistic discipline.

Davis, Murrow and a few other journalists gave a broader scope to objective reporting. Journalists—with their unique nonpartisan perspective and their commitment to democratic values, accurate observation and truth—began to see how they could provide insights for the public and for policy-makers. To do so more effectively, they knew they had to change some of their traditional practices. Underlying their conviction that changes in the practice of journalism were needed was their assumption that journalists are publicly useful men and women.

Providing Context Some of these journalists found support and justification for their attempt to widen journalism's scope in their discovery of a report that had been issued in 1947 by a group of academicians, *A Free and Responsible Press. A General Report on Mass Communications: Newspapers, Radio, Motion Pictures, Magazines, and Books.* The report told journalists that they are most useful when they give "a truthful, comprehensive, and intelligent account of the day's events in a context which gives them meaning. . . . It is no longer enough to report *fact* truthfully. It is now necessary to report the *truth about the fact.*"

Journalists began to find ways to go beyond just reporting assertions and claims. They sought to give an added dimension to their stenographic function by checking statements and by looking for causes and consequences of actions. This kind of journalism takes the public closer to the truth.

Such reporting is now commonplace. It is expected of all reporters that they will report the *truth about the fact.* In Elizabeth Rosenthal's report from China about Chinese officials wooing the International Olympic Committee for the 2008 games, she quotes a Chinese Foreign Ministry spokesman, "Most Chinese believe that the human rights situation in China is the best ever."

That satisfied the stenographic function. Then she placed the statement in context, "But that was not true for all Chinese this week," she wrote. She described the detention of members of a human rights group and the imprisonment of a woman for signing a petition urging the Olympic Committee to call on China to release jailed human rights advocates. Rosenthal also reported the stepped-up surveillance of demonstrators at Tiananmen Square where human-rights advocates try to speak out.

Personal Involvement

How close can a reporter move to the event before he or she loses objectivity and risks becoming part of the story? The easy answer is that the reporter must maintain a distance, keep an objective detachment. Sometimes? Always?

When Ron Martz, a reporter for the *Atlanta Journal-Constitution,* was embedded with the Army in Iraq he had to decide whether to help out in a medical emergency. An Iraqi civilian had been wounded and medics who were treating him needed help. Martz dropped his reporter's notebook and held an intravenous drip bag as the medics worked.

Was that right? Martz wondered when he filed his war diary entry on National Public Radio. Ethicists, Martz said, consider this kind of situation cloudy territory. Martz's decision, he reported on NPR, was that he is a human being first, a reporter second.

Brevity

In our generalization about the reporter's job at the outset of this chapter, we pointed out that the news story is succinct. Here is a two-paragraph story that says a great deal although it contains only four sentences:

JOHANNESBURG, South Africa, Nov. 8—The bodies of 60 victims of an accidental dynamite explosion a mile and a half down a gold mine 100 miles southwest of Johannesburg were brought to the surface today.

Of the dead, 58 were Basuto tribesmen from Lesotho, chosen for the dangerous job of shaft-sinking, or blasting a way down to the gold-bearing reef. The two others were white supervisors. The black Africans will be buried in a communal grave tomorrow.

—*The New York Time*

Creative work is based on the art of omission. When Beethoven was struggling with the music to his opera "Fidelio," he realized that the leisurely pace of the music did not meet the demands of the theater, and for years he pared down his work. David Hamilton, the music critic, describes Beethoven's effort as a "ruthless piece of self criticism . . . Beethoven expunged balancing phrases, trimmed decorative expansions, excised anything that did not move forward, eventually achieving the terse urgency that now marks the opera's crucial scenes."

In eliminating large sections of his music, Beethoven rejected three overtures he had written. One, "Leonore No. 3," became one of the most popular pieces in the orchestral repertory. Despite its obvious beauty and power, Beethoven found it unsuited to his opera.

Joseph G. Herzberg, an editor on several New York City newspapers, said, "Newspapering is knowing what to leave out and condensing the rest." But stories can be so condensed they are misleading, as is this obituary from *The Hartford Courant:*

Robert "Bob" E. Welch, 56, of Enfield, passed away, Saturday (January 29, 2005) at the West Haven Veterans Hospital after a long battle with his family at his bedside.

The Ultimate Art
". . . there is but one art: to omit! O if I knew how to omit, I would ask no other knowledge. A man who knew how to omit would make an *Iliad* of a daily newspaper."
—*Robert Louis Stevenson*

Too Brief
Headline writers are the brevity experts. But sometimes their tightening misdirects meaning:

Kids Make Nutritious Snacks

Squad Helps Dog Bite Victim

Eye Drops off Shelf

Stud Tires Out

Still True
From the 1931 movie, *Dance, Fools, Dance:* City Editor to reporter Bonnie Jordan, played by Joan Bennett, "Is this all of it?" Jordan answers, "Yes, but I could write some more." City Editor, "There's your story in the first three paragraphs. You can have the rest of it."

Selectivity

The way out of the dilemma of being brief but not writing telegrams is through Herzberg's advice, which can be summed up in one word—selectivity. Brevity is a function of selectivity—knowing what to leave out.

Edna Buchanan, the police reporter for *The Miami Herald,* began her account of a record-breaking week of violence in Dade County this way:

> Dade's murder rate hit new heights this week as a wave of violence left 14 people dead and five critically hurt within five days.

A couple of paragraphs compared these figures with murder figures of previous years, and then Buchanan summarized most of the deaths:

In the latest wave of violence, a teenager's throat was cut and her body dumped into a canal. A former airline stewardess was garroted and left with a pair of scissors stuck between her shoulder blades. Four innocent bystanders were shot in a barroom gun battle. An 80-year-old man surprised a burglar who battered him fatally with a hammer. An angry young woman who "felt used" beat her date to death with the dumbbells he used to keep fit. And an apparent robbery victim was shot dead as he ran away from the robbers.

Guideline   The test for selectivity is to put yourself in the chair of the reader, listener, viewer. Is he or she satisfied with the account? Have I answered the questions he or she would ask? **What** happened? **Who** was involved? **Where** did it happen? **When** did it happen? **How** and **Why** did it happen?

Strain   A natural tension exists between the editor and the reporter. The editor, confronted with ever-decreasing space and time, wants shorter stories. The reporter, excited by the event and driven by a compulsion to tell the full story, wants more time and more space. Online journalists are even more pressed to compress their work.

Some editors contend that if Genesis can describe the earth's creation in a thousand words, then no reporter needs any more for any event of human dimension. But some events are so complex that only an extended account will do. Important stories often require scene setting and background that consume time and space. The guide for the length of stories is: Make it brief but clear and complete.

Clarity

The executives of 40 daily newspapers in Iowa and journalism instructors at the state's three journalism schools were asked to rank characteristics considered most important for beginning reporters. Both groups put the ability to write clearly and interestingly first.

Clear prose follows comprehension. That is, the reporter must be able to understand the event before he or she can explain it clearly and succinctly. You cannot clarify what you do not understand.

Clarity is enhanced by simplicity of expression, which generally means short sentences, everyday language, coherence and logical story structure. We shall be looking at these in detail in Chapter 7.

Human Interest

To make certain the story interests people, the journalist recounts events in ways that substitute for the drama of the personal encounter. One of the ways the journalist does this is to tell the story in human terms.

A change in city zoning regulations is dramatized by pointing out that now low-income families can move into an area that had been effectively sealed off to them by the previous two-acre zoning rule. A factory shutdown is personalized by talking to workers who must line up at the unemployment office instead of at a workbench.

Polluting In a story about chemicals polluting the Hudson River and ruining the fishing industry, Barry Newman of *The Wall Street Journal* begins:

Grassy Point, N.Y.—In the gray-shingled shack at water's edge, four fishermen sit playing cards around an old kitchen table, ignoring the ebb tide laden with the spring run of shad. The wall is hung with foul-weather gear; rubber boots are piled in the corner. On the refrigerator door somebody has taped up a newspaper clipping about the awful chemicals in the fish of the Hudson River.

"I do my fishing from the window here," an old man says, looking off to the quiet hills on the east bank, three miles across the river from this small valley town.

"No nets for me this year," another man says. "No pay," says the third. And the fourth: "A lot of trouble, this."

Localizing In Washington, the talk was of budget cutting. Members of Congress used the podium as a pulpit to expound on the morality of frugality.

Back home in Minneapolis, the *Star Tribune* decided to see just what role federal spending played in Anoka County. "This was an attempt to bring down to a personal level the debate in Washington over extremely intricate financial and policy issues," said Mike Kaszuba, suburban affairs reporter. He teamed with the newspaper's Washington bureau chief Sharon Schmickle to do the reporting and writing.

The reporters found that billions of dollars had flowed into the county since the New Deal built the Anoka high school stadium. Federal money "built the bridge that carries traffic over the Rum River into downtown. Now it pays Mary Wellman, hired last year as Anoka's only female police officer."

The series gave faces and names to those helped by federal funds—students eating school lunches, students attending the local technical college, people using the Anoka ambulance, people who need help with their heating bills, salaries for teachers who help special education students.

Responsibility

Ted Williams was one of baseball's greatest players. The Boston Red Sox outfielder won six batting titles over a span of 17 years and was one of the few to win the Triple Crown twice, leading the league in 1942 and in 1947 in batting, runs batted in and home runs. To many baseball fans, he was heroic. To some sports writers, he was, as Roger Kahn put it, "a pill."

It was possible for readers to know the real Williams because, Kahn says, when nine writers covered Red Sox games "it was impossible to conceal" the truth about Williams. "If one writer courted The Thumper by refusing to report a tantrum as news, another inevitably seized the tantrum as news. Regardless of each reporter's skill, an essential, imperfect system of checks and balances worked. If you cared enough about Williams, and I did, you could find a portrait that was honest by consensus."

But most of the Boston newspapers that covered Williams are gone, as are others in many cities. There are fewer than 30 cities with competing daily newspapers. This means that the responsibility for truth-telling falls on fewer shoulders. It falls, in most U.S. cities, in fact, on a single reporter, for most local news beats are covered by only one journalist.

Responsibility is not a visible part of a news story. It is an attitude that the reporter carries to the job. It encompasses all the components we have discussed in this chapter.

Responsibility is the reporter's commitment to the story, to journalism and to the public. Responsibility demands of the reporter that the story be accurate, complete, fair and balanced, that it be so clear anyone can understand it.

> **"Irresponsible Journalists"**
>
> "I wish I could remember how many times when I was Ambassador to Yugoslavia I was officially requested to persuade, convince, or direct *The New York Times* and *The Washington Post* to behave 'responsibly.' I doubt whether there is, in truth, any objective standard of responsible journalism. We tend to think papers are responsible when we agree with them and irresponsible when we object to their content."
>
> —*Laurence Silberman, Judge of the District of Columbia Circuit of the U.S. Court of Appeals*

Summing Up

Editors tell their new news writers that journalism begins with the ABCs—accuracy, brevity and clarity. Of course, there is more required of the journalist, but these are good for starters.

Accuracy of fact and language.

Brevity in making the point succinctly.

Clarity so there is no doubt about what happened.

These can be seen as moral requirements as well as necessities for the practice of the craft. Journalists take on the responsibility of telling people about the world around them so that they can act on what they read, see and hear. But action depends on clear, understandable and accurate information. Without reliable information, action may be misdirected or, just as bad, never taken.

Polls tell us that much of the public is suspicious of journalists. Public distrust can begin with such simple mistakes as leaving the event before it's over as a *Boston Globe* music reviewer did. He praised the Allman Brothers Band's "show-climaxing" song "Revival." Trouble is, "Revival" was not the last piece the band played. The *Globe*'s critic had relied on the planned song list and left early to beat the traffic.

Misspelled Name

Further Reading

Bensman, Joseph, and Robert Lilienfield. *Craft and Consciousness*. New York: Wiley, 1973.

Commission on Freedom of the Press. *A Free and Responsible Press*. Chicago: University of Chicago Press, 1947.

Edwards, Julia. *Women of the World: The Great Foreign Correspondents*. Boston: Houghton Mifflin, 1988.

Liebling, A. J. *The Press*. New York: Ballantine Books, 1964.

Morris, James McGrath. *The Rose Man of Sing Sing: A True Tale of Life, Murder, and Redemption in the Age of Yellow Journalism*. New York: Fordham University Press, 2004.

   The Rose Man was Charles E. Chapin, city editor of Pulitzer's *New York Evening World*. Chapin's life "spanned the birth and adolescence of the modern mass media," writes Morris. His story is as lurid as the tales he relentlessly drove his reporters to provide.

Siebert, Fred S., et al. *Four Theories of the Press*. Urbana: University of Illinois Press, 1956.

Preview

We look closely at the news values that guide journalists in determining the newsworthiness of events. These values are

- **Impact, importance.** Most stories fall into this category.
- **Timeliness.**
- **Prominence** of the people involved.
- **Proximity** to the audience.
- **Conflict.**
- **Currency.** The sudden interest people have in an ongoing situation.
- **Necessity.** A situation the journalist feels compelled to reveal.

Karl Mondon, *Contra Costa Times*
He missed a left turn: Impact . . . Timeliness . . . Proximity.

Some Answers Past and Present

We know that some subjects draw people to the media. The weather is one of these. Parents want to know how to dress their children for school and themselves for work and for the trip to the shopping mall. The result: Radio gives us the forecast every 10 minutes and some newspapers devote as much as a full page to the weather report.

We know something about the people who look at TV, listen to the radio, read newspapers and magazines and use the Internet for the news. Women over the age of 50, for example, are avid followers of news about health. The result: daytime TV, day and nighttime radio and cable feature news about illness and remedies. Men under 40 make up, almost exclusively, the sports followers. The morning newspaper has a large sports section and morning radio and TV are heavy on sports before men leave for work and in the evening when they are at home.

Journalism isn't stenography. Dig.

We know something about the news habits of those 18 to 34. More than half of them use the Internet to read the news online. We know they want their news presented in tightly written sections.

Wars, Dragons and Business

The first printed newsbook, published in 1513 and titled *The trewe encounter,* described the Battle of Flodden Field in which James IV of Scotland was killed during his invasion of England. The Anglo-Scottish wars that followed provided printers with material for more newsbooks. The elements of our modern-day journalism were featured in these accounts—names of officers in the wars and their deeds. Adventure, travel and crime were reported, along with accounts of disasters.

As one printer-pamphleteer put it, people are interested in "and most earnestly moved with strange novelties and marvelous things." These early day journalists favored stories of monsters and dragons, not unlike our own day's tales of the Abominable Snowman and the Loch Ness monster.

During the 17th century, news sheets spread to the business centers of Europe, reporting news of commerce. In this country, as historian Bernard Weisberger has pointed out, the newspaper "served as a handmaiden of commerce by emphasizing news of trade and business."

Day and Bennett

The newspaper editors of the 19th century understood that to stay in business they had to appeal to a large audience, and this realization led to definitions of news that hold to this day. The papers in the large cities were printing news for the newly literate working class. One of the first penny papers—inexpensive enough for working people—contained the ingredients of popular journalism. In 1833, the first issue of Benjamin H. Day's *New York Sun* included a summary of police court cases and stories about fires, burglaries and a suicide. Other stories contained humor and human interest.

Several years later, James Gordon Bennett—described by historians as the originator of the art, science and industry of news gathering—used the recently developed telegraph to give the readers of his *Herald* commercial and political news to go along with his reports of the everyday life of New York City, its sins and scandals. His formula of news for "the merchant and man of learning, as well as the mechanic and man of labor" guides many editors today.

Pulitzer

Day and Bennett followed the tastes and appetites of their readers, but they also directed and taught their readers by publishing stories they deemed important.

This blend of entertainment, information and public service was stressed by Joseph Pulitzer, who owned newspapers in St. Louis and New York. He, too, gave his readers what he thought they wanted—sensational news and features. But Pulitzer also used his news staff for his campaigns to curb business monopolies and to seek heavy taxes on income and inheritance. In 1883, Pulitzer charged the staff of his New York *World* with this command:

> Always fight for progress and reform, never tolerate injustice or corruption, always fight demagogues of all parties, never belong to any party, always oppose privileged classes and public plunderers, never lack sympathy with the poor, always remain devoted to the public welfare, never be satisfied with merely printing news, always be drastically independent, never be afraid to attack wrong, whether by predatory plutocracy or predatory poverty.

The Library of Congress

Joseph Pulitzer

Hearst

Pulitzer and William Randolph Hearst were locked in a circulation war for New York readers when Cuba rebelled against its Spanish rulers. Spain was severe in repressing the insurrection and the New York newspapers seized on the story of helpless Cubans trying to free themselves from ruthless oppressors.

Hearst's *Journal* was particularly imaginative. After the United States declared war in 1898 and the troops were slow in making it to Cuba, Hearst urged them on with inventive news stories.

"Over the next week," writes Arthur Lubow in *The Reporter Who Would Be King,* "the *Journal* reported an exciting sequence of landings, bombardments and fleet battles, all admirably detailed, all entirely fictitious. The *Journal* was selling so well thanks to its apocryphal scoops that its rivals began to play the same game, often rewriting the accounts of the creative *Journal* writers."

Today's Editors

Modern mass media editors overseeing newsrooms humming with the latest electronic wonders apply many 19th-century concepts of news. They would define their news menu as did Pulitzer—a mixture of information, entertainment and public service. They would also agree with the definition of news offered by Charles A. Dana, who ran the *New York Sun* from 1869 to 1897. Dana said news is "anything that interests a large part of the community and has never been brought to its attention before."

One of Dana's editors, John B. Bogart, contributed the classic definition, "When a dog bites a man, that is not news, because it happens so often. But if a man bites a dog, it's news."

Another enduring definition of news was offered by Stanley Walker, a Texan gone East to succeed as city editor of *The New York Herald Tribune* in the early 1930s. He said news was based on the three W's, "women, wampum, and wrongdoing." By this he meant that news was concerned with sex, money and crime—the topics people desired to know about. Actually, Walker's formula is as old as the contents of Caesar's *Acta Diurna* 2,000 years ago, which, along with information about public affairs, offered news of sports, crime and sensational events.

Definition Changes   By the mid-1970s, the United States had been through three crises: a war in Vietnam that wound down with guilt and defeat for many Americans; the Watergate scandals; and the failure of some political, social and economic experiments of the 1950s and 1960s that had been hailed as solutions to international conflict, racial tension and poverty.

It was not surprising, then, to see a shift in the criteria used to determine the news. Av Westin, the executive producer of the American Broadcasting Company's "Evening News" program, said Americans wanted their news to answer the following questions: Is the world safe? Are my home and family safe? If they are

Pioneer
In response to criticism of the *Journal's* fabrications, Hearst ran a front-page editorial about its so-called news from Cuba: "The *Journal* realized what is frequently forgotten in journalism, that if news is wanted, it often has to be sent for . . . the public is even more fond of entertainment than it is of information."

Three Views of News
"A news sense is really a sense of what is important, what is vital, what has color and life—what people are interested in. That's journalism."
—*Burton Rascoe,* Chicago Tribune, *1920s*

"Marketing should be the king of all editors. They should forget what university professors stuffed into their heads, find out what readers really want and give it to them."
—*Stuart Garner,* Thomson Newspapers, *1980s*

"News is truth that matters."
—*Gerry Goldstein,* The Providence Journal, *1990s*

This Is News?

safe, then what has happened in the last 24 hours to make them better off? Is my pocketbook safe?

People not only wanted more pocketbook stories but escape stories as well. Editors asked for more entertainment in the form of copy about lifestyles, leisure subjects and personalities.

In the 1990s, editors devised the "reader-friendly" story. Readers, they argued, want to learn how to diet, how to raise their children, where to invest their money. The news agenda was being shaped to conform to the interests of middle-class readers and viewers who bought the products of media advertisers.

News in the New Century   The 21st century opened with proof of Walker's wampum and Westin's pocketbook theories of news. Stories abounded of the high-flying economy and its new dot-com millionaires. In short order, the news focus shifted to an economy in retreat, dot-coms collapsing, jobs lost, corporate crime, pensions disappearing. Pessimism replaced optimism. Wars in Afghanistan and Iraq sent amputees and body bags home. People lost confidence in their leaders.

Subjects once given major play no longer held the public's attention, and those usually ignored made it to the top of the news. A study by the Project for Excellence in Journalism found a significant decline in crime news. Religion-related issues became big news: the disclosure that in many dioceses of the Catholic Church pedophiles were protected and the controversy over gay marriage. The political muscle exercised by the religious right became a persistent news subject.

Definitions of news may change, but two general guidelines remain constant:

- News is information about a break from the normal flow of events, an interruption in the expected, a deviation from the norm.

- News is information people can use to help them make sound decisions about their lives.

How does a reporter or editor determine what events are so unusual and what information is so necessary that the public should be informed of them? Journalists have established some guides, called news values, for answering these questions.

Alert

"Never, never neglect an extraordinary appearance or happening. It may be a false alarm and lead to nothing. But it may, on the other hand, be the clue provided by fate to lead you to some important advance."

—*Alexander Fleming, discoverer of penicillin*

News Values

The following eight factors determine the newsworthiness of events, personalities and ideas:

1. Timeliness

Events that are immediate, recent. The daily newspaper, cable TV, the online news services and the hourly newscast seek to keep readers and listeners abreast of events. Thus, broadcast news is written in the present tense, and most leads on newspaper stories contain the word *today.* No matter how significant the event, how important the people involved, news value diminishes with time. André Gide, the French novelist, defined journalism as "everything that will be less interesting tomorrow than today."

The media are commercial enterprises that sell space and time on the basis of their ability to reach people quickly with a perishable commodity. The marketplace rewards a fast news carrier. Most newspapers created Web sites to meet the demand for news NOW. They ask their reporters to file running stories online and then write for the printed newspaper. Radio, which was being prepared for its funeral when television captured a large segment of the listening audience, staged a comeback with the all-news station.

Timely Information Essential   There is another side to our need to know quickly. Timeliness is important in a democracy. People need to know about the activities of their officials as soon as possible so they can assess the directions in which their leaders are moving. Told where they are being led, citizens can react before actions become irreversible. In extreme cases, the public can rid itself of an inefficient or corrupt official. Officials also want quick distribution of information so that they can have feedback from the public. This interaction is one of the reasons the Constitution protects the press. Without the give-and-take of ideas, democracy could not work.

Timeliness is also the consequence of advertising necessities. Because most businesses are based on the quick turnover of goods, advertisements must appear soon after goods are shipped to stores. The news that attracts readers to the advertisements must be constantly renewed.

2. Impact

Events that are likely to affect many people. Journalists talk about events that are significant, important. They talk about giving high priority in their coverage to situations that people need to know about to be well informed. The more people that are affected by the event, the bigger the story. An increase in the postal rates will be given major attention because so many are affected. An increase in a town's property tax will receive considerable play in that town and nowhere else, but a change in the federal income tax rate will receive national attention.

Journalists may take the initiative in digging up situations that have considerable impact. David Willman, a reporter in the Washington bureau of the

Juan Carlos,
Ventura County Star

Flooded Out

Sudden changes in weather affect large numbers of people and are given major play by journalists.

Los Angeles Times, suspected that the federal Food and Drug Administration had lost its effectiveness as the guardian of public health. He spent two years examining the FDA's work and discovered it had approved seven prescription drugs that were believed to have caused the deaths of more than 1,000 people. Despite warnings from its own specialists about the drugs—among them a painkiller, a diet pill and a heartburn medicine—approval had been granted.

In Chapter 1, we saw how reporters for KHOU-Houston found repeated gross incompetence in the police department's lab tests. The impact of the station's reporting was considerable—cases were retried, prisoners freed, the lab system replaced.

3. Prominence

Events involving well-known people or institutions. When the president trips disembarking from an airplane, it is front-page news; when a city councilmember missteps, it is not worth a line of print or a moment of air time. A local banker's embezzlement is more newsworthy than a clerk's thievery, even when the clerk has stolen more. The more prominent the person, the bigger the story. Names make news, goes the old adage, even when the event is of little consequence.

Two events that probably received the most massive media coverage of the 1990s were the result of prominence—the pursuit, arrest and trials of O.J. Simpson and the sexual affair of President Clinton with a young White House intern. Never mind that the economies of several large countries were crumbling, that the Middle East and Northern Ireland saw carnage amidst peace efforts, that nuclear proliferation arose and that ethnic warfare killed hundreds of thousands and made refugees of many more. Names made news, big and bigger news.

Prominence applies to organizations as well, and even to some physical objects. The repair of a major bridge in Akron is given coverage in that city and not elsewhere. But when the Golden Gate Bridge shuts down that action merits national coverage.

The American poet and journalist Eugene Field was moved by the journalism of personalities to write:

> *Now the Ahkoond of Swat is a vague sort of man*
> *Who lives in a country far over the sea;*
> *Pray tell me, good reader, if tell me you can,*
> *What's the Ahkoond of Swat to you folks or me?*

Despite Field's gentle poke, journalists continue to cater to what they perceive as the public's appetite for newsworthy names.

4. Proximity

Events that are geographically or emotionally close to people interest them. In Chapter 1, we read about the tornado that ripped apart the small town of Spencer, S.D. The *Argus Leader,* the state's major newspaper, sent reporters and photographers

50 miles west to cover the storm and used 1½-inch type on page 1 over its story. In Lubbock, Texas, the newspaper did not carry the story, but a radio station in Minneapolis, 300 miles away, gave it 60 seconds airtime.

If 42 people die in an airplane crash in the Andes and one of the passengers is a resident of Little Rock, the news story in Little Rock will emphasize the death of the local person. This is known as *localizing* the news. When two tour buses collided in Wales, injuring 75 people, *USA Today* began its account this way:

> Teen-agers from Lancaster, Pa., Houston and St. Louis were among 75 people hurt when two tour buses returning from Ireland collided in Wales.

Emotional Closeness   People are interested in events and individuals that seem close to them. The tie may be religious, ethnic, racial. Newspapers and stations with large Catholic or Jewish populations give considerable space and time to news from the Vatican or the Middle East. After the space shuttle Challenger exploded and sent seven crew members to their deaths, the *Amsterdam News,* a weekly in New York with a predominantly black readership, headlined on page 1 the death of the black astronaut who was aboard.

5. Conflict

Strife, antagonism, warfare have provided the basis of stories since early peoples drew pictures on their cave walls of their confrontations with the beasts that surrounded them. People and their tribes and their countries have been at war with each other, and with themselves, since history has been kept, and the tales that resulted have been the basis of saga, drama, story and news.

To journalists today, conflict has a more nuanced meaning. "The most effective stories I've read," says Peter St. Onge, a staff writer for *The Charlotte Observer,* "involved ordinary people confronting the challenges of daily life."

Although critics of the press condemn what they consider to be an overemphasis on conflict, the advance of civilization can be seen as an adventure in conflict and turmoil. Indeed, one way to define, and to defend, journalism is that it provides a forum for discussion of the conflicts that divide people and groups, and that this peaceful debate makes conflict resolution possible.

6. The Unusual

Events that deviate sharply from the expected, that depart considerably from the experiences of everyday life make news. We know that. But here we are talking about the truly different, the bizarre, strange and wondrous.

When a dog bites a man, it isn't news. But when a police dog, a tried and true member of the K-9 Corps, sinks his teeth into the arm of his police handler, that's unusual, and it's news. We've all seen big watermelons in the supermarket, but

Mike Roemer

Political Conflict

The opponents of abortion do battle with placards, parades and politics. This long-running conflict sometimes becomes violent.

the 165-pound monster makes page 1 of the B section of *The Freeport News* when the farmer offers it to the First Baptist Church for its annual picnic.

Domestic Violence Domestic spats are not news, unless they are so violent murder is committed. But when Lorena Bobbitt tired of her husband's mental and physical attacks and cut off his penis. . . . Yes, that was news for a week or two.

The wide coverage of the Bobbitt family surgery led Peter Kann, publisher of *The Wall Street Journal,* to condemn "media fascination with the bizarre, the perverse and pathological—Lorena Bobbitt journalism."

Today, few people can identify Lorena Bobbitt or recall the reason for her fleeting media attention. The bizarre has the lifespan of a firefly's momentary flash.

To some, though, the attention was important and worthwhile, for the incident made people think about domestic violence and its victims, and in its wake some governors pardoned women imprisoned for killing husbands who had for years tormented and beaten them. Cause and effect? Possibly.

A Symbol The young man who stood alone before a column of tanks on their way to bloody Tiananmen Square struck everyone who saw the photograph and read the accompanying story as so amazing, so wondrous that the act quickly became a symbol. (See next page.) To some, the act showed defiance of tyranny. To others, it was, as the writer and critic Ian Buruma wrote, a symbol "of the futility of empty-handed opposition to brute force."

7. Currency

Occasionally, a situation long simmering will suddenly emerge as the subject of discussion and attention. Historians might describe the situation as an idea whose time has come. When it does, the media catch up.

In the early 1960s, President Kennedy called attention to the plight of the poor. Then President Johnson declared a "war on poverty." Newspapers responded by covering health and welfare agencies and by going into poor areas of their cities in search of news. Television produced documentaries on the blighted lives of the poor. More than 40 years later, poverty, although as pervasive, receives less attention.

The plight of women and members of minority groups in achieving recognition for their talents was long ignored. Victims of the glass ceiling and discrimination in the executive suites, they finally broke through to the media and became the subject of coverage.

Generally, journalists have not been in the vanguard of these discoveries. Sometimes though, journalists will decide that a situation needs attention and will make it newsworthy. We saw a few pages back how a *Los Angeles Times* reporter, David Willman, revealed that a federal agency had approved the sale of prescription drugs that were killing people. He stayed with the story for two years before the agency pulled the drugs from the market.

The work of Willman also falls in an eighth category, a category that stems from the reporter's feelings that he or she must act.

A Religious Nation

For decades, news about religion consisted of stories about forthcoming services and summaries of the sermons of prominent preachers. Suddenly, journalists realized that Americans are deeply religious, and religion became an important beat for many newspapers.

Asked, "How important is religion in your life?" 59 percent of Americans answered "Very important." In other countries, the percentages were United Kingdom, 33; Canada, 30; Italy, 27; Germany, 21; Japan, 12; France, 11.

AP Photo by Jeff Widener

A Lone Man's Plea

As the tanks headed down Cangan Boulevard in the government's show of strength in Beijing, a young man darted in front of the column. The tanks stopped. The man looked up and called out to the soldiers to stop the killing. The tanks tried to weave around him, easing him aside. He cried out again, pleading for no more violence. Bystanders finally pulled him away, fearing he would be crushed under the treads.

8. Necessity

The seven previous categories of newsworthiness involve people, events and situations that call out for coverage—meetings, speeches, accidents, deaths, games and the like. This final category is of the journalist's making. That is, *the journalist has discovered something he or she feels it is necessary to disclose.* The situation or event, the person or idea may or may not come under any of the previous seven categories of newsworthiness. The essential element is that the journalist considers the situation to be something everyone should know about, and usually it is a situation that needs to be exposed and remedied.

This is journalism of conscience. The journalists who report and write these stories are on the staffs of small and large publications, network and local stations, specialized publications and magazines, and some convey their work online.

Here are some examples of their work:

Pensacola News Journal—Exposure of a culture of corruption that led to the indictment of four of the five county commissioners.

The Atlanta Business Chronicle—Sarah Rubenstein and Walter Woods found questionable connections between state officials and landowners whose property was needed for right-of-way acquisitions for a $2.2 billion highway project. After publication, the project was put on hold.

National Public Radio—"We're the only industrialized nation that can't see fit to insure everyone though we spend one-third more per capita on health than the next biggest spender," reported Susan Dentzer, health correspondent for "The NewsHour with Jim Lehrer." Dentzer interviewed several of the uninsured among the 40 million who, she said, are receiving "second-rate, third-rate and even zero care."

The Boston Globe—Despite a veil of secrecy, the newspaper uncovered sexual abuse by Roman Catholic priests in many parishes. Priests were transferred rather than dismissed. The *Globe* disclosures led other media around the country to investigate their parishes.

WMAQ, Chicago—The TV station revealed that U.S. Customs officers at O'Hare International Airport were using racial and gender profiling to target black women for invasive strip searches. The story led to a class-action suit and an investigation by the Customs Service of procedures at all international airports.

60 Minutes—American soldiers in Iraq had to scavenge Iraqi dumps for scrap metal to protect their lightly armored Humvees that had become death traps, reporters Steve Kroft and Leslie Cocburn reported.

Westwind—To check on military recruiting practices, 17-year-old J. David McSwane, a reporter on the Arvada, Colo., high school newspaper, told an army recruiter he was a high school dropout addicted to marijuana. Was he army material? he asked. Not to worry, the recruiter told McSwane: He would be given a fake general education diploma and instructed to take a fluid that would help him pass the urinalysis. McSwane's story was headlined: ARMY DESPERATION LEADS TO RECRUITING FRAUD.

South Florida Sun-Sentinel—In the wake of Hurricane Katrina, staffers found widespread mismanagement by the federal government of hurricane aid. Indictments resulted.

Portland Press-Herald—Barbara Walsh examined Maine's care for mentally ill children and found the system was chaotic. After hundreds of interviews, and an examination of thousands of documents, Walsh wrote that children had to wait months and years for help, that some children were placed in juvenile lockup for lack of an adequate placement program. The governor and legislators vowed reform.

WTVF-TV—Despite a budget crisis and the largest tax increase in the state's history, Tennessee was awarding contracts to firms without competitive bidding—and the companies had close ties to the governor. Bryan Staples and Phil Williams of the Nashville station also learned that companies had overcharged the state. The governor retaliated, impeding the reporters from checking records and pulling $160,000 in highway safety advertising from the station. Despite attacks on the reporters' credibility, the FBI and IRS decided to investigate.

Labor of Love

Investigative reporting isn't glamorous, says Phil Williams. "There are long hours of tedium—whether it's dissecting computer databases, combing through records and hiding in the back of a van for hours on surveillance without a bathroom break. If that sounds like a great job to you, then it can be."

The Overlooked   For many of these stories, reporters dug into situations that one reporter described as affecting "the least of them," the men, women and children that journalism usually overlooks. Noreen Turyn, an anchor at WSET in Lynchburg, Va., heard about an old state law still on the books that allowed the forced sterilization of men and women. The law had been adopted during the heyday of eugenics, a social movement that used pseudo-science to bring about what it called the "improvement of the race." Under the law, youngsters who had minor offenses and those whose parents said they could not control them were shipped off to Lynchburg Colony where they were forced into sterilization "without any understanding of what was happening to them," Turyn reported. Turyn interviewed the victims, among them a World War II Bronze Medal winner. The state acted to repeal the law after Turyn's series was aired.

Katherine Boo of *The Washington Post* describes this reporting as traveling through "the shadowlands of the disadvantaged and disenfranchised." In two separate series, Boo disclosed the horrible conditions in which the city's retarded lived—and died. She documented beatings, robberies, rapes and the use of the retarded for slave labor in so-called training programs.

Abortions for All When Heidi Evans of the *Daily News* was told by a caller that every woman who went to a cash-only abortion clinic was informed that she was pregnant, Evans raced over to the clinic the next day with a urine sample of her own.

"The owner, who did the tests himself, told me I was pregnant and tugged at my arm to have the procedure right then," Evans said.

"The following day, I sent another reporter with a sample from one of our male colleagues. The urine also tested positive." After two more weeks of reporting, in which she showed how poor, mostly immigrant women were herded by the clinic owner to a back room where a fly-by-night doctor operated, the state shut down the clinic.

Hog Heaven In Raleigh, *The News & Observer* examined an unlikely source of environmental degradation—hog lagoons.

Raising hogs is big business, and the bigger the hog farm the better the business because the slaughterhouse can be next door, eliminating the expense of hauling the hogs to the meat cutters. But the big hog farms—some have a million animals—do the following, the newspaper revealed:

Contaminate Ground Water

Through the emission of ammonia gas into the atmosphere that is returned with rain, streams are being choked with algae.

Waste from the hogs—which produce as much as four times as much waste per hog as do humans—is piling up in open fields.

The series on the hog farms contamination won a Pulitzer Prize.

Questionable Deaths In North Carolina, disability advocates had complained about the state's mental health system. The governor didn't listen. Parents complained about the lack of services for their children. Legislators weren't interested. Debbie Cenziper of *The Charlotte Observer* listened and became interested. The result: More than 30 stories beginning with a five-part series that revealed that 34 people with mental disabilities—many of them young—died under questionable circumstances while in the care of the state's mental health facilities. "They died from suicide, murder, scalding, falls," Cenziper says. "They suffocated, starved, choked, drowned." Most of the deaths were never investigated because the state had not been told of them.

Chris Seward, *The News & Observer*

Hazard

When Hurricane Floyd hit North Carolina, thousands of hogs were drowned. Officials estimated 28,000 hogs were killed. The decaying carcasses became a health hazard and had to be incinerated.

The stories led to increased mental health funding, money for hiring 27 inspectors for mental health facilities and two laws to correct the dangerous flaws Cenziper had described.

See **Broken Trust** in *NRW Plus.*

Does It Work? In all these stories the common element is that something was not functioning properly, that something was wrong with the system. David Burnham, a former *New York Times* reporter, says the increased bureaucratization of public life calls for a new approach to news. The media need to spend more time asking: How are the bureaucracies that affect our lives working? Are they deviating from our expectation that they are there to serve us?

Is the police department engaged in crime prevention; is the power company delivering sufficient energy at a reasonable price; are the high schools graduating college-entry seniors?

Dying Lakes The *Times Union* in Albany, N.Y., felt it necessary to track the progress, if any, being made to cope with the effects of acid rain in the nearby Adirondacks Park, the largest wilderness area east of the Rockies. What it found did not make for optimism.

Reporter Dina Cappiello found that 500 of the 6-million-acre park's 2,800 lakes are dead. Unless something is done, she wrote, within 40 years a thousand more lakes will be lost to acid rain, lakes empty of plant and animal life.

See **Dying Lakes** in *NRW Plus.*

News Is Relative

These eight news values do not exist in a vacuum. Their application depends on those who are deciding what is news, where the event and the news medium are located, the tradition of the newspaper or station, its audience and a host of other factors.

Economic Pressures

The media are a business, a profit-seeking enterprise. Most stations and newspapers are no different from General Motors, Microsoft and Home Depot. Their operations are designed to maximize profits.

Advertising is the engine that drives the media. This can be seen quickly enough when the newspaper has 48 pages because the department stores are advertising white sales. The result is a large news hole, with plenty of space for stories. On days when the advertising is slim, the newspaper may run to 32 pages and stories are cut to the bone, or not run at all.

More broadly, when times are good and advertisers clamor for space and time, staffs are large, coverage deep. When there is a hitch in the economy, foreign bureaus are closed, staffs are cut. Some events are not covered.

Increasingly, media outlets are owned by large companies whose stock is traded on the stock market. The result: "The pressure to maximize stockholder return has

All-Out Coverage
When terrorists struck New York City and Washington, newspapers turned away from the bottom line and ordered robust coverage. Arthur O. Sulzberger Jr., publisher of *The New York Times,* said that although cancellations of advertising during September, when the hijacked planes struck, would cost the *Times* "millions of dollars," coverage would be all out.

Mike Roemer

Changing Times . . . Changing Beats

A century ago, 50 percent of the workforce in the United States made a living from agriculture. Farm news was big news. Today, with 2.5 percent so employed, farm news is important outside agricultural areas only when the cost of food goes up. At the beginning of the 20th century, fewer than 115,000 students attended college and journalists paid little attention to them. Today, more than 50 times as many are enrolled and higher education is a major beat.

become ever more intense," says Larry Jinks, for more than 40 years an executive with Knight-Ridder. "That affects how news is gathered and presented."

A Wall Street analyst put the matter bluntly: "Some reporters don't understand that they work for a company that sells advertising. They're in the advertising business, not in the journalism business. They don't get it. Without the bottom line, they don't have jobs. They're in a business and the business is to sell ads and make money. The people that own the company are the shareholders, not the reporters."

Advertisers Muscle the Media   Hardly a month goes by without the report of some advertiser or commercial group deciding to hold back on advertising because of news coverage.

In New York, a series of articles in the *Daily News* reported that "more than half the city's supermarkets fail inspections because of vermin, filth and rotting food." The reaction of the markets was swift. All but one pulled their advertising. The *News,* battling declining revenue and serious circulation losses,

Conflicting Goals: Sales vs. Truth

Advertising is the principal source of revenues that supports our media system. That dependence creates an incongruity between the public's preferences and the criteria employed by the people in charge. As consumers of communication, we judge it by its value and meaning for us; advertisers judge it by its efficiency in disseminating what they call "exposure opportunities."

Media content has been driven primarily by the need to maximize audiences for sale rather than by the desire to communicate the truth about our world or express deep thoughts and feelings. To this end, broadcasting and film have vied with each other in pursuit of violence and vulgarity. The largest of our mass media, the daily press, traditionally the forum for contention and irreverence, has undergone a steady attrition of competition and a general retreat to the safety of the middle ground. Left to its own devices, the public persistently drifts toward amusement rather than enlightenment, avoiding confrontation with the pressing, perhaps overwhelming, problems that confront the nation and the world.

—**Leo Bogart**

apologized in a four-page advertorial designed by the business department of the newspaper. The material, *The New York Times* reported, was "effusively complimentary."

Asked if the section righted matters, the manager of one of the market chains replied, "I'll go back if they fire the reporter and the editor." That, said the *News*'s executive editor, was not going to happen.

At *The Washington Post,* Leonard Downie had been looking into an arrangement between corrupt real estate speculators and local savings and loan institutions to gouge inner-city residents. The bankers got wind of Downie's checking and told the managing editor that if the *Post* ran the series, they would pull their advertising.

Downie, who later became the *Post*'s executive editor, recalls Benjamin C. Bradlee, his editor, telling him about the visit and the threat. Bradlee looked at Downie and said simply, "Just get it right."

The reporting continued, the series ran and the banks pulled their advertising, costing the newspaper $750,000 in lost advertising revenue.

The Influence of Owners

In addition to putting their imprint on their products by deciding how much money to take out of the enterprise, media owners can exert a powerful tonal influence. Some are cautious, unwilling to dig into news that might stir controversy. Their papers and stations cover the surface of the news, what we describe in Chapter 11 as Layer 1 news, the stenographic report of what people say and do. Some go further, imposing a particular political point of view and slant on the news. And some combine avarice and political slant.

Cave In   When the Chinese government was upset by the British Broadcasting Corporation's news coverage of human rights abuses in China, it made its displeasure known to Rupert Murdoch, the owner of a massive global media conglomerate that includes large holdings in China. Murdoch's Hong Kong broadcast operation had been airing the BBC newscasts that irritated Chinese Communist Party leaders.

Murdoch acted quickly. He eliminated BBC news. He said that using the BBC, considered the provider of the finest broadcast journalism in the world, would jeopardize his business in China.

Murdoch again made the news with a move motivated by his business interests in China. HarperCollins, a book publisher owned by Murdoch, planned to publish a book by Chris Patten, the last British governor of Hong Kong. Patten was an outspoken critic of China's authoritarianism and miserable human rights record.

U.S. Cities with Competing Daily Newspapers

■ Two separate newspapers
● Newspapers under joint operating arrgements

● Tucson Arizona Daily Star
● Tucson Citizen
● Tucson Territorial

● Denver Post
● Denver Rocky Mountain News

■ Washington Post
■ Washington Times

■ Honolulu Advertiser
■ Honolulu Star-Bulletin

■ Chicago Defender
■ Chicago Daily Herald
■ Chicago Southtown
■ Chicago Sun-Times
■ Chicago Tribune

● Salt Lake City Desert News
● Salt Lake City Tribune

● Fort Wayne (Ind.) News-Sentinel
● Fort Wayne Journal Gazette

■ Boston Globe
■ Boston Herald

● Detroit Free Press
● Detroit News

■ Columbia (Mo.) Missourian
■ Columbia Daily Tribune

■ Trenton (N.J.) Times
■ Trenton Trentonian

● Albuquerque (N.M.) Journal
● Albuquerque Tribune

■ New York Daily News
■ New York Post
■ New York Times
■ Staten Island (N.Y.) Advance

● Wilkes-Barre (Pa.) Times Leader
● Wilkes-Barre Citizens' Voice

● York (Pa.) Dispatch
● York Daily Record

■ Kingsport (Tenn.) News
■ Kingsport Times-News

● Seattle Post-Intelligencer
● Seattle Times

● Charleston (W. Va.) Gazette
● Charleston Daily Mail

■ Green Bay (Wis.) Press-Gazette
■ Green Bay News-Chronicle

● Madison (Wis.) Capital Times
● Madison Wisconsin State Journal

Dying Competition

The number of cities with competing newspapers has steadily declined, and the number of chain-owned newspapers has spiraled over the past three decades, the result of declining advertising income and a decrease in the circulation of afternoon newspapers. Thirty-four states have no competing newspapers.

Cause and Effect

The news article quoted producers as saying that the new Brad Pitt movie was "loathsome," "absolutely indefensible," "deplorable on every level." The movie review in the same newspaper, *The Hollywood Reporter,* said the movie "is exactly the kind of product that lawmakers should target for being socially irresponsible. . . ." The production company, 20th Century Fox, stopped all its movie advertising in an obvious attempt, *The New York Times* reported, "to damage the trade paper financially."

Murdoch's Empire

"Murdoch uses his diverse holdings, which include newspapers, magazines, sports teams, a movie studio and a book publisher, to promote his own financial interests at the expense of real news-gathering, legal and regulatory rules and journalistic ethics. He wields his media as instruments of influence with politicians who can aid him, and savages his competitors in his news columns. If ever someone demonstrated the dangers of mass power being concentrated in few hands, it would be Murdoch."

—*Russ Baker, "Murdoch's Mean Machine," Columbia Journalism Review*

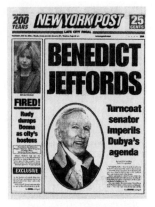

Murdoch Buys Wall Street Journal

When Rupert Murdoch offered $5 billion to buy Dow Jones & Co., publisher of *The Wall Street Journal,* the amount surprised many in the media. His offer amounted to almost twice the price of a share of the company's stock. Staffers at the *Journal* launched a searcher for a buyer who they felt would be less likely to use the newspaper for political and financial purposes.

The *Journal* staffers said Murdoch had lowered the journalistic standards of the media outlets he already owned, and that the columns of his newspapers were infiltrated by a conservative slant. To appease editorial staffers, Murdoch agreed to submit hires to an independent board. The sale went through.

Maxim

"Freedom of the press is guaranteed only to those who own one."

—Joe Liebling

When Murdoch learned of the publication plans he ordered HarperCollins to drop the book.

Owners' Politics Murdoch is politically conservative, and his politics impose a deep imprint on his media properties. When Sen. James Jeffords of Vermont changed his party membership from Republican to Independent, thus giving control of the U.S. Senate to the Democrats, the front page of Murdoch's *New York Post* put a photo of Jeffords on page 1 that was doctored to portray him as a traitorous Benedict Arnold.

Courageous In contrast, to the bottom-line journalism of many publishers, some put the public welfare before the dollar sign. In the darkest days of *The Washington Post*'s coverage of Watergate, when President Nixon threatened economic reprisals to *Post* properties, publisher Katherine Graham stood steadfast. In a tribute to Graham on her death, Hendrik Hertzberg wrote in *The New Yorker:*

> The courage she summoned in the face
> of serious, and at that time frightening,
> abuses of power put democracy in her debt
> in a way that few other American publish-
> ers, perhaps none, have ever equaled.

Fearful Some newspapers duck controversy in an attempt to be all things to all their readers. After the governor of South Dakota signed the most stringent anti-abortion bill any state had adopted, a national controversy erupted. Even many right-to-life supporters opposed the law. But the state's major newspaper, the *Argus Leader,* was mute. Taking a position, wrote the editor of the Gannett paper, "could well jeopardize the credibility we have worked long and hard to establish."

Contrast the mute South Dakota newspaper with the work of Ira B. Harkey, the editor and publisher of the newspaper in Pascagoula, Miss., during the South's furious resistance to court-ordered school desegregation. When Harkey editorialized in support of the 1954 Supreme Court decision *Brown v. Board of Education,* a cross was burned in front of his home. Worse was yet to come.

During the desegregation crisis at the University of Mississippi, Harkey urged the peaceful admission of James Meredith, who would become the first black student at Ole Miss. Federal troops had to be called out to quell the rioting protesters.

Harkey's life was threatened, a cross was burned in front of his newspaper office and rifle and shotgun blasts rattled his home. Yet Harkey was steadfast in his support of desegregated schools.

Chains

The media are spiraling toward a concentration of ownership in fewer and fewer large corporations. Fifty years ago, families owned almost all the daily newspapers.

Today, four of five newspapers are owned by groups, known as chains. "The family-owned newspaper is an endangered species," says H. Brandt Ayers, whose family has owned *The Anniston Star* in Alabama for parts of three centuries.

The *Star*'s ownership is happy if it can make 10 percent profit, Ayers says. Chain owners want twice as much and more to placate dividend-hungry stockholders.

Most media commentators find the concentration worrisome. "The pressure on them is to produce dollars," says Ben Bagdikian. Profits come before good journalism, he says.

Group ownership has its defenders. Their large resources enable local editors to take on the community power structure without fear of economic retaliation, the defenders say.

The reality is mixed. Some group-owned media provide minimal coverage. A radio chain with hundreds of stations has no news staff in most of its stations. Some newspapers and stations continue to dig and provide their readers and viewers with illuminating journalism. The difference often lies with the tradition of the newspaper or station and its ownership.

The Charleston (W.Va.) *Gazette* has long spoken for protection of its environment. This Scripps Howard paper has encouraged reporter Ken Ward, Jr., to take a strong point of view to his work. "The area is economically depressed and controlled by a few large companies that rape and pillage and don't leave much for the people," he says. "If there is any place in the United States that needs good investigative reporting that comes at things with a good set of values, it's here."

Tradition

Some publications and broadcast stations have a history of public service journalism that guides them in their selection of what is worthy of their reporters' time and the owners' funds.

The Charlotte Observer has challenged the tobacco industry. More recently it took on the home builders. Reporters Ames Alexander and Rick Rothacker accompanied building inspectors on their rounds, watched houses being built, pored through public records and interviewed more than 400 homeowners, builders, inspectors and others. The paper's database editor, Ted Mellnick, helped them examine "4 million computer records on all building inspections conducted in Mecklenburg County since the 1970s," says Alexander.

The project took eight months. The reporters concluded that "North Carolina's laws favor builders over buyers."

See **Home Buyer Beware** in *NRW Plus.*

The Audience

When the TV actress Ellen DeGeneres announced that she is a lesbian, the *San Francisco Chronicle* put the story on page 1 alongside a four-column photo of a crowd in town watching the show on a big screen. *The New York Times* national edition put the story on page 17A. The reason for the difference in play: San Francisco has a large percentage of gay men and women in its population.

Everything media writers do is aimed at an audience, and the nature of that audience may well be the most important influence in media performance.

Network TV Once king of the media hill, network television is now struggling for footing on a downward slope. Viewership has eroded, and the networks have been engaged in a search to match the news to its different audience. Their advisers have suggested that the morning audience wants less news of government and domestic and foreign affairs and more of crime, celebrities and lifestyle. Nothing too heavy. That's for the evening newscasts and for the "PBS NewsHour." Why the difference? Demographics. The morning viewers are younger.

Demographics Age, race, gender, geography, income, ethnicity—these are factored in when news managers make their decisions on what is printed and put on the screen.

If we look at the audience for National Public Radio, the content of its news becomes understandable. The audience, reports the Project for Excellence in Journalism, "falls between 25 and 54 years of age, has college degrees, and votes, and half have household incomes of over $75,000. This has created a situation in which NPR is a media resource used by a young, culturally elite group."

Ethnic publications, along with the alternative press, are two of the few media that have growing audiences. While English language newspapers have lost 11

Corporate Journalism

". . . one can argue that considering there are nearly 1,500 daily papers in the United States, and considering that most of these are handsomely profitable, the percentage of excellence is abysmally low. Today's typical daily is mediocre, with a strong overlay of provincialism. And industry trends are only making matters worse."

—Leaving Readers Behind: The Age of Corporate Journalism *by Thomas Kunkel and Gene Roberts*

Five Packs a Day

Although *The Charlotte Observer* circulates among farmers who grow two-thirds of the tobacco used to make cigarettes, the newspaper published a 20-page special report "Our Tobacco Dilemma" that called attention to the health hazards of smoking. On the front page of the section was this photograph of James McManus, 62, who has, the newspaper reported, "smoking-caused emphysema" and requires an "oxygen tank to survive." The tobacco industry spends more than $1 billion a year on advertising.

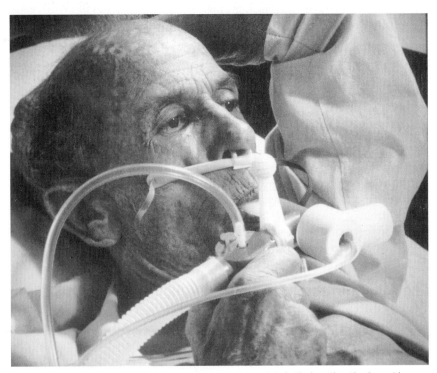

Mark Sluder, *The Charlotte Observer*

percent of their circulation in the past 15 years, the circulation of Spanish language dailies has tripled to 1.7 million. The Spanish-speaking population in the
United States has more than doubled, whereas the black population has increased
only by a third.

The standard media are reaching out to non-whites and various ethnic groups.
News is no longer confined to the activities and assertions of the white middle class.
The days when news of blacks, Asians and Hispanics was not news are gone.

The Reporter

Despite the many media changes, it remains true today what has been opera-
tive through the years: For the most part the reporter, the man or woman on the
beat, makes the news. The court reporter who looks through a dozen court filings
chooses the one or two that she will write about. The police reporter, whose daily
rounds begin with the examination of the dozen arrests made overnight, decides
which two or three he will report. The feature writers with a dozen ideas swirling
through their heads have time for a couple.

Yes, the guidelines do help, the news values that we have discussed—
timeliness, prominence, impact and the others. But there is wide latitude within
these categories. For example: Just who is prominent? To Karen Garloch, a medical writer for *The Charlotte Observer,* a local building contractor named Vernon
Nantz may not have been prominent, but his situation qualified him for her attention. Nantz was dying of cancer and had decided to forgo chemotherapy. He
wanted to die at home, close to his family.

"The idea for this story was born out of my interest, as a medical writer, in
the end of life care," Garloch says. "I had written many stories about living wills
and advance directives, the forms people sign to declare their expectations about
extraordinary medical care. I had also written about the growth of the hospice
movement and discussions among ethicists and doctors when to stop treatment
that appears to be futile.

Dying with Dignity   "With millions of Americans facing these choices, I wanted
to tell the story of the end of life through a real person who made the choice to
reject extraordinary medical care and die with dignity at home."

Garloch's series about Vernon Nantz began this way:

> When Vernon Nantz was diagnosed with
> a recurrence of cancer, his doctor told him:
> "We can treat it, but we're not gonna beat
> it." Vernon had just months. He decided
> to use Hospice at Charlotte, stay at home
> with his wife and be around his family and
> friends.
>
> More and more we want a choice about
> how and where we die.
>
> This is the story of one man's choice.

The Affluent
   USA Today devotes
plenty of space to its
"Money" section. A third
of the newspaper's readers
have incomes of more than
$100,000, the readers that
advertisers are anxious to
reach.

Garloch was with Nantz when he decided not to get out of bed to dress for the visit of the hospice nurse. She was there when the family gathered around his bed, sure he was dying, and she was there when he rallied and ate an entire fried fish dinner with french fries and hush puppies. And she arrived at the Nantz home shortly after he died at 2 A.M.

Reader response was overwhelming, said Garloch's editor, Frank Barrows.

Like many of the reporters we have seen at work, Garloch could be said to have made the news with this story of Vernon Nantz. She and the others could be described as activist journalists.

For Garloch's story, see **Vernon's Goodbye** and **Readers Respond** in *NRW Plus.*

Activist Journalists   To some journalists, news consists of overt events—an automobile accident, a city council meeting, a court document, the State of the Union Address. Their journalism is denotative, pointing to what has happened. Necessary as this reporting is, some journalists would complement denotative journalism with a more active, seeking-out journalism.

Activist journalists seek to place on the public agenda matters that they believe require consideration, civic discussion that could lead to some kind of action. The action could be an awareness of another way to end one's days, as the Garloch feature demonstrated. Or it could lead to remedial action, as Willman's stories about deadly prescription drugs accomplished. The sociologist Herbert Blumer says that issues come to public attention, not because of the "intrinsic gravity of the social problem," but because they have been given status by some respected group that has called attention to the problem. These groups can legitimatize an issue as a matter of concern requiring action, Blumer says.

Among those that can legitimatize situations Blumer lists educational organizations, religious leaders, legislators, civic groups and the press. Once legitimatized, the issue can be acted upon quickly, Blumer says.

Summing Up

Impersonal and objective as journalists would like to make the determinants of news, journalism is based on selection, and choice is a highly personal affair. It derives from the journalist's professional background, his or her education and the intangible influences of family, friends and colleagues.

The professional decisions are framed by other considerations as well: the need to entertain to keep readers and viewers who are constantly being seduced by entertainment media; the pressures of the business of journalism such as budgeting restrictions, meeting the competition, considering the needs of advertisers.

Further Reading

Bagdikian, Ben H. *The New Media Monopoly.* Boston: Beacon Press. 2004.

> In the first edition of his book, in 1983, Bagdikian warned that media concentration in the hands of some 50 corporations endangered democracy and threatened to control the marketplace of ideas. Since then, ownership has become even more concentrated, and the dangers even greater.

Gelb, Arthur. *City Room.* New York: G.P. Putnam's Sons, 2004.

> Gelb tells his story of his rise from copyboy to managing editor of *The New York Times* with anecdotes that enliven the estimable *Times.*

Kunkel, Thomas, and Gene Roberts. *Leaving Readers Behind: The Age of Corporate Journalism.* Little Rock: The University of Arkansas Press, 2001.

Roberts, Gene, and Hank Kilbanoff. *The Race Beat: The Press, the Civil Rights Struggle and the Awakening of a Nation.* New York: Alfred A. Knopf, 2006.

> "At no other time in U.S. history were the news media more influential than they were in the 1950s and 1960s," the authors say in this examination of how reporters covered the civil rights movement. They find that most of the white journalists who covered the story "simply didn't recognize racism in America as a story" until the trial of the two killers in the 1955 murder of the black teen-ager Emmett Till in Mississippi. The book was awarded the 2007 Pulitzer Prize in History.

Sloan, Bill. *"I Watched a Wild Hog Eat My Baby"—A Colorful History of Tabloids and Their Cultural Impact.* Amherst, N.Y.: Prometheus Books, 2001.

Photograph by Ron Martz, *Atlanta Journal-Constitution*

Sending news from the Iraq battlefront.

Preview

Journalists rely on a variety of tools, including the computer, audio recorder and telephone. They use these tools, especially the Internet, to find people, official documents, reliable data and other sources of information. The journalist:

- Understands how to use basic references and digital resources.
- Knows public-record laws.
- Uses the computer to gather and analyze information and to write stories and transmit them to an editor.
- Can evaluate the credibility of online and other information.
- Understands math and statistics and can interpret a public opinion poll.

Question your assumptions.

When *The Charlotte Observer* wanted to know how many people died in auto-racing accidents, the answer was elusive: No government agency or industry group collected such statistics. So Liz Chandler and other reporters had to ferret out the information themselves, using a combination of traditional and high-tech research methods that demonstrate how newsrooms have changed over the past decade.

They scoured the Internet, including Web sites and chat rooms about racing. They searched the online archives of newspapers and magazines for stories about track-related deaths. The results of their search: they found that at least 260 people, including 29 spectators, had been killed at racetracks between 1990 and 2001. Using digital phone books, the reporters located and interviewed relatives, witnesses, drivers, track officials and safety experts, supplementing and often correcting information reported or posted elsewhere.

*This chapter was written with the assistance of Jeff C. South of Virginia Commonwealth University.

The Observer built a computer database with details about each death, enabling reporters to reveal patterns with authoritative precision. The newspaper reported that fences and barriers failed regularly and that drivers were rarely screened for experience, health problems or drunken-driving convictions. For a 16-page special section called "Death at the Track: Racing's Human Toll," Chandler wrote the lead story that began: "When someone dies in auto racing, it's often called a freak thing or a fluke—so isolated and rare it can't happen again. But deaths aren't as rare or isolated as the racing world believes."

The project, which won an investigative award from the Associated Press Sports Editors, demonstrates the importance of online research and data analysis to complement shoe-leather reporting. In today's competitive news environment, journalists are as comfortable with digital tools as they are with pencils and notebooks. *The Observer*'s investigation couldn't have been done without computer-assisted reporting techniques, Chandler said.

"We used computers at every step of the project: to find deaths at the racetracks; to find people who could tell us about those deaths; and to examine why the deaths occurred," she said.

Computer skills alone aren't enough. *The Observer*'s team, supervised by project editor Gary Schwab, relied on police reports and other documents and interviewed more than 400 people. The result was groundbreaking journalism that spurred safety reforms in auto racing.

"Pointing out the human toll increased the pressure on racing to address safety issues like equipment and soft walls," Schwab said.

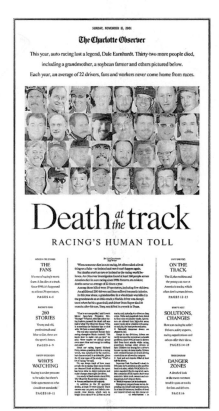

Tools for Today's New Media Journalist

With the expansion of multimedia ownership has come the multimedia journalist, also known as the new media journalist. This reporter must gather material that can be used for print, online and broadcast news media. That means carrying into the field an array of equipment, such as:

1. A digital camera that can take high-resolution still photos and video.

2. A laptop computer with wireless Internet access.

3. A handheld computer, such as a Palm personal digital assistant. When attached to a collapsible keyboard, a PDA is "not only a personal organizer with calendar and address book but also increasingly a fully functional computer," notes John Pavlik, chairman of the Department of Journalism and Mass Media at Rutgers University. PDAs also can connect wirelessly to the Internet, enabling reporters to do online research and submit stories by e-mail.

4. A digital audio recorder for recording interviews. Recordings can be stored on a computer and can even be converted into editable documents with voice-to-text software.

5. A digital cell phone, not only for making and receiving phone calls but also for accessing e-mail and surfing the Web. Such "smart phones" include Black-Berry devices, the Palm Treo and Motorola Q.

6. A mobile Global Positioning Satellite (GPS) receiver for location finding. GPS coordinates can be stamped directly on photos and video as a digital water-mark to protect copyright and to authenticate time and date.

7. A high-capacity "flash drive," a portable device that can fit in a pocket and store gigabytes of information.

8. A variety of software packages installed on the laptop. The programs would include software to edit video, audio, photos, images and graphics; a word processor and spreadsheet; and e-mail software and a Web browser with various plug-ins.

9. Instant Messenger and Voice over IP (VoIP) software for real-time, no-cost communications (including text, voice and images) over the Internet. When used with a "Web cam," such software allows reporters to hold video conferences with editors and sources.

10. A handheld scanner for digitizing documents on the spot.

11. A satellite telephone for making calls when cell phone service is unavailable. Reporters also use videophones, a combination of digital video camera and satellite phone, to provide video for breaking stories too difficult to reach with satellite uplink facilities. Videophones are small enough to fit in a briefcase and be carried on an airplane as hand luggage.

Covering the "War on Terror."   To cover the wars in Afghanistan and Iraq, reporters used various high-tech tools, including satellite phones, for talking to editors and transmitting stories and digital photos. With a lightweight video-phone, a lone TV journalist could deliver live reports from remote locations.

Basic Newsroom References

Every reporter has several reference works handy—including the news organization's stylebook, a dictionary, and telephone directories.

The stylebook ensures consistency in spelling, capitalization, punctuation and abbreviation. Is it 18 Fifth Ave. or 18 Fifth Avenue? The stylebook tells us. Do newspapers use postal abbreviations for states? The stylebook tells us to use Calif., not CA. (You'll find a stylebook in this textbook, beginning on p. S-1.)

Reporters use the dictionary to verify spellings and to make certain that the words they want have the shades of meaning they intend.

Steven Feiner

Mobile Workstation

The reporter-photographer-videographer of the future sets out to cover a story for his multimedia employer. He is carrying the tools he requires as a new media journalist.

Besides the regular phone book, reporters rely on city directories containing details about people living in the community. A typical entry will include a resident's name, occupation and employer; the street address, including apartment number; spouse's name; and whether the person owns or rents, is retired or is a student. Other directories list phone numbers and residents' names by address—so you can look up who lives on a particular street. That is invaluable on a late-breaking story when the office-bound reporter needs details from the scene.

Every reporter should know how to use these reference materials:

- *The World Almanac and Book of Facts.*
- *Statistical Abstract of the United States.*

ALPHABETICAL DIRECTORY WHITE PAGES

Ⓗ HOUSEHOLDER   Ⓡ RESIDENT OR ROOMER

correct full name —————————— Landon Edw G & Charlotte D; servmn B F Goodrich
h1215 Oak Dr

occupation and employer ————— Landon Fred M & Mary E; supvr Reliance Elec h60
Norman Av

complete street address
including apartment number ———— Landon Kenneth A & Carol L; clk First Natl Bk
h1400 E Main St Apt 14

student 18 years of age or older ——— Landon Kenneth A Jr studt r1400 E Main St Apt 14
Landon Virginia E r1641 W 4th St

cross reference of surnames ———— Lane See Also Layne
Lane Allen M & Joan M (Allen's Bakery) h1234
Grand Blvd
Lane Avenue Restaurant (Ernest G Long) 216
Lane Av

out-of-town resident employed
in area ——————————————— Lane James M & Betty B; brkmn Penn Central
r Rt 1 Jefferson O

armed force member and
branch of service ———————— Lane Marvin L USA r1234 Grand Blvd
Lane Root B & Margt E; retd h1402 N High St
Lane Walter M r1234 Grand Blvd
Layne See Also Lane

wife's name and initial ————————— Layne Agnes E Mrs v-pres Layne Co h2325
Eureka Rd
Layne Albert M & Minnie B; slsmn Hoover Co h19
Bellows Av

corporation showing officers and
nature of business ————————— Layne Co Inc Thos E Layne Pres Mrs Agnes E
Layne V-Pres Edw T Layne Sec-Treas bldg
contrs 100 N High St
Layne Edw T & Diane E; sec-treas Layne Co h140
Oakwood Dr
Layne Ralph P & Gladys M; formn Layne Co h1687
Maple Dr

suburban designation ——————— Layne Thos E & Agnes E; pres Layne Co h2325
Eureka Rd
Leach See Also Leech

retiree ———————————————— Leach Wm E USMC r1209 Ravenscroft Rd (EF)
Lee Alf M & Celia J; retd h2106 Oakwood Dr

business partnership showing
partners in parenthesis —————— Lee Bros (Louis J And Harry M Lee) plmbs 151
Abbott St
Lee Harry M & Karen L (Lee Bros) h2023 Stone Rd

husband and wife employed ———— Lee Louis J & Martha B (Lee Bros) h1616 Fulton
Lee Martha B Mrs ofc sec Lee Bros h1616 Fulton

"r" resident or roomer ——————— Lee Minnie M Mrs h87 Eastview Dr
Lee Muriel E r810 LaForge St

"h" householders ————————— Lee Sterling T & Nadine S; mtcemn Eastview Apts
h202 Wilson St Apt 1

owner of business showing name
of business in parenthesis ———— Lee Thos W & Effie M (Tom's Men's Wear) r Rt 23

bold type denotes paid listing ——— **LEE'S PHARMACY (Lee A Shaw) Prescriptions
Carefully Compounded, Complete Line Of
Toiletries And Cosmetics, Fountain Service,
Greeting Cards, 1705 N High St (21505) Tel**

business firm showing name of
owner in parenthesis ——————— Leech See Also Leach
Leech Doris E tchr North High Sch
h1323 W McLean St
Leech Joseph B & Lucy V; slsmn Metropolitan Dept
Store h824 Wilson St

unmarried and unemployed
resident ————————————— Leech Joseph B Jr studt r824 Wilson St
Leech Marcia M clk Community Hosp r1323 W
McLean St

more than one adult in household — Lewis Anne M Mrs clk County Hwy Dept h914
Wilson Av
Lewis Ernest W studt r914 Wilson Av
Lewis Harold G & Anne M; mgr Cooper Paint Store
h914 Wilson Av
Lewis Robt B lab County Hwy Dept r1410 Union
Hwy Rt 2

church showing name of pastor —— Lewistown Methodist Church Rev John R Allen
Pastor 515 Maple Valley Rd

- An encyclopedia.

- State and local history books.

- Maps (especially local) and an atlas.

- *Bartlett's Familiar Quotations.*

- *National Five-Digit Zip Code and Post Office Directory.*

- *Who's Who in America,* containing biographical information on about 100,000 leaders in social, economic, cultural and political affairs. Other biographical directories published by the same firm, Marquis Who's Who Inc., include regional directories and directories of people in particular professions.

Many of those reference materials are available on CD-ROM and the Web for faster and more efficient searches, notes Liz Donovan, who was research editor at *The Miami Herald,* where the newsroom stylebook is available only online.

For example, the Marquis Who's Who Web site has a database of more than 1 million biographies. And reporters often go online to find the phone number assigned to a particular address or the name assigned to a particular phone number.

In the past, many newspapers subscribed to the *Reader's Guide to Periodical Literature* and *The New York Times Index.* Today, newsrooms subscribe to Encyclopedia Britannica Online (http://www.eb.com) and to Lexis-Nexis or Factiva, searchable databases of full-text articles, says Linda Henderson, the library director for *The Providence Journal* in Rhode Island.

For more about resources recommended by news librarians, see **"Sources Online,"** *NRW Plus.*

Using the Computer

Precision journalism. Analytic reporting. Data-driven journalism. Computer-assisted reporting. Those are all terms for the ways personal computers have revolutionized the reporting process.

It's no longer enough for a journalist to be a nimble wordsmith. In today's information society, "a journalist has to be a database manager, a data processor and a data analyst," says Philip Meyer, of the University of North Carolina and a pioneer in applying social science methods to journalism.

Derek Willis, who has won national awards as a writer and data specialist for the Center for Public Integrity, agrees. "Increasingly, the people and institutions that we cover as journalists use computers to perform their jobs and make sense of the world. Organizations from governments to baseball teams make sophisticated use of computers to analyze their strengths and weaknesses," says Willis, now at *The Washington Post.*

The computer has put a vast amount and variety of information at the fingertips of journalists, and it has helped them process information—crunch the

Using the Internet Every Day

A survey of 500 journalists throughout the country showed that more than 98 percent check their e-mail daily. They use the Internet to correspond, to find story ideas, develop new sources and check for news releases that could lead to stories. The average reporter spends three hours a day reading or sending e-mail, the *Middleberg/Ross Survey of Media in the Wired World* reports.

"I can find out if a person has been sued, or divorced, or whether he or she has a criminal record. I can locate within five minutes any person in the United States who uses a credit card or has a bank account, and I can probably locate his or her family members and address history in less than 30 minutes," says Bob Port of the *New York Daily News.*

data—with speed and accuracy. Let's take a deeper look at these two indispensable tasks the computer performs for the reporter: first, locating information; second, processing information.

Locating Information

The Internet contains millions of Web sites with vast quantities of documents, reference materials, images, data and other information helpful to journalists. It also contains a lot of bogus and obsolete information. For reporters, the challenge is to separate the useful from the junk.

Starting Points

Several journalists and journalism organizations have assembled collections of reliable Web sites, often categorized by beat or function. For example, Bill Dedman, the managing editor of *The Telegraph* in Nashua, N. H., maintains PowerReporting .com; Duff Wilson, a *New York Times* reporter, created the Reporter's Desktop (www.reporter.org/desktop/); the Foundation for American Communications provides FACSNET (www.facsnet.org); the National Institute for Computer-Assisted Reporting (www.nicar.org) offers a "Net Tour" for investigative reporters; and *The New York Times* allows access to its CyberTimes Navigator (www.nytimes.com/navigator). These hyperlink collections can point you to the best Web sites for covering politics, health and many other topics.

Sarah Cohen, a Pulitzer-winning database expert at *The Washington Post,* urges reporters to explore such hotlists and surf the Web in advance. "Good Internet reporters are like good shoppers: They've looked around, and know where to go for the best deal when they decide to buy."

Web Search Tools

When you don't know where to look for information, a search tool can help. Google (www.google.com), the most popular search engine, is a computerized index of more than 4 billion Web pages. Use it to find pages with the keywords you're interested in. The Librarians' Index to the Internet (http://lii.org) is a much smaller directory in which librarians have categorized entire Web sites. Use it to find a site about a particular subject. Some tools, such as Yahoo! (www.yahoo.com), offer both Web-page search engines and Web-site directories. Others, like Dogpile (www.dogpile.com), search several Web-page indexes simultaneously.

The challenge for reporters is to narrow the search to produce the most relevant "hits." Some rules are the same for all major search tools: When searching for a phrase, for instance, put it in quotation marks. But other rules vary from tool to tool. Before using a search tool, look on the site for a "Help" page. That may tell you how to limit your search to only government Web pages or to the most recently posted material.

Several online resources evaluate search tools and offer tutorials and other search tips. These resources include Search Engine Watch (http://searchengine watch.com) and Research Buzz! (www.researchbuzz.com). Those sites also link to specialized search engines such as MedHunt (www.hon.ch/MedHunt/) for medical and health information and LawCrawler (http://lawcrawler.findlaw.com/) for legal information.

The "Deep Web" or "Invisible Web"

These terms refer to online databases, often of government records, such as census data, political contributions and school test scores. Most search tools don't penetrate these databases, and so reporters must know where to find them.

One way is to explore the Direct Search Web site (www.freepint.com/gary/direct.htm) created by Gary Price, director of online information resources at ask.com. The site provides a map of the "invisible web." For example, under "Business/Economics," the directory lists online databases with documents that publicly owned companies must file with the U.S. Securities and Exchange Commission. (You can search www.sec.gov/edgar.shtml for a company's annual report, which is called a 10-K. It shows revenues and other financial information. You can also obtain a proxy statement, or DEF 14A, which lists executive salaries and other compensation.)

Finding Sources

The Internet offers numerous ways for reporters to find experts and "real people" to interview for stories. ProfNet (www.profnet.com) is a collaborative of public relations professionals at 800 colleges and universities and 3,500 companies, PR agencies, nonprofit organizations, government agencies and think tanks. A reporter can search Profnet's database of experts or e-mail a query to info@ profnet.com for help with a story.

Journalists also can search for sources at AllExperts.com, Experts.com and the Yearbook of Experts (www.yearbook.com). The National Press Club maintains an experts database (http://npc.press.org/newssources/searchdirectory.cfm); and the Special Libraries Association, which represents news librarians, has an extensive list (www.ibiblio.org/slanews/internet/experts.html).

Beware, though, that some people list themselves as experts mostly for self-promotion—and they may have little expertise. A 1993 cartoon in *The New Yorker* said it best: It shows a dog sitting at a computer and telling a fellow canine, "On the Internet, nobody knows you're a dog."

Besides experts, the Internet can help you find everyday people to talk to. The Ultimate White Pages Web site (www.theultimates.com/white/) lets you search several Internet telephone directories at once. It's easy to find a phone number if you have only a person's name and city, or even just the state. Or for a feature story you can find area residents who share a celebrity's name.

You can also look up the names and phone numbers of residents on a particular street—important for contacting people in a neighborhood where news is breaking. And if you have a phone number, you can find out to whom it belongs. That would come in handy if you obtained a public official's telephone records and wanted to know whom the official was calling.

Listservs, Discussion Boards and Online Forums

You can find sources and help for your stories by subscribing to listservs, or e-mail discussion lists, or by monitoring message boards, chat rooms and other online forums. The Web site www.tile.net has a searchable directory of e-mail lists; Google has a tool for searching message boards (called Usenet newsgroups); and many Web sites, especially those hosted by news organizations and community groups, include online forums.

So if you are doing a story about Attention Deficit Disorder, you might subscribe to one of several listservs for parents of children with ADD; browse the postings on the Usenet newsgroup called "alt.support.attn-deficit"; or read the messages on the Attention Deficit Disorder Forums Web site (www.addforums .com/forums/). However, it is unethical to quote from a posting without the author's permission.

Reporters also use listservs to get advice from their peers. Investigative Reporters and Editors Inc. (www.ire.org), the National Institute for Computer-Assisted Reporting (www.nicar.org) and other groups have e-mail lists for discussing journalistic methods and other issues.

Julie Poppen, a reporter for the *Rocky Mountain News* in Denver, once sent an e-mail to the listserv of the Education Writers Association (www.ewa.org) asking about school districts that require students to attend summer school if they score low on standardized tests. She received responses from reporters in Greenville, S.C., Richmond and Chicago.

Commercial Information Services   Until now, we have been talking about the free part of the Internet. Many newspapers and magazines offer free access for a limited period, then place the material in a paid archive service. You can search these archives if your organization subscribes to a commercial information service such as Lexis-Nexis or Factiva, formerly called Dow Jones News Retrieval.

Not Just a Search Engine but a Verb

Google handles more than 200 million searches a day from people all over the world. It's so popular that "Google" has now become a verb meaning to search the Web. The word's new application got a boost from an episode of the TV show "Sex and the City," in which a character suggested "Googling the Russian" to get more information about him.

Google has expanded its features in hopes of providing "one-stop shopping" for Web searchers. The site allows users to search recent news headlines, phone books (including reverse lookups), street maps, stock quotes and even tracking numbers for Federal Express, UPS and the U.S. Postal Service.

Locating Information, in *NRW Plus,* has links to helpful Web sites and tip-sheets on search strategies, e-mail etiquette and other topics.

Cautions and Warnings

Journalists have a saying: If your mother says she loves you, check it out. That caveat applies to online information, too. If your mother's Web site says she loves you, check it out.

It's easy to post false information on the Internet; Stephen Glass, the disgraced journalist who fabricated stories for *The New Republic,* created bogus Web sites to cover his deception. While the information might not be a hoax, it can still be wrong or outdated. In this regard, search engines don't help: Google displays its results based on Web-page popularity, not factual reliability.

Neil Reisner, a former training director for the National Institute for Computer Assisted Reporting, says the Internet is "just another tool for journalists. Use the same methods you use to verify any other source."

Examine the Domain

One way to assess an online source is to examine the "top-level domain"—the ".com" or ".edu" in the Web address. Apply the Miller Internet Data Integrity Scale, created by Stephen Miller, a technology expert at *The New York Times.* MIDIS is a hierarchy of trust, and at the top are government Web sites, which end in ".gov" (such as the Census Bureau's www.census.gov site) or ".state.XX.us" (in which the XX is a state's postal abbreviation, such as ".state.va.us"). Next come studies by universities (".edu") and nonprofit groups (".org").

"While we are all caught up in terms like cyberspace and virtual reality, the reality is that real people, not pixels, created the information displayed on your computer screen. Those people are no different from the ones we interview in person or over the phone," Miller says. "There are good people who tell you the truth. There are bad people who lie to you. And there are the rest of us somewhere in the middle. Too much faith has been placed in information generated by computers. Just because it's digital doesn't make it true."

The University of California–Berkeley has an excellent guide for evaluating Web pages (http://www.lib.berkeley.edu/Teaching Lib/Guides/Internet/Evaluate .html). It suggests looking for a date, the author's name and the author's credentials. By truncating the Web address, you often can find what organization operates the site that hosts a particular Web page. Moreover, by searching the InterNic domain registry (www.internic.net/whois.html), you can identify who owns and administers the site.

See **Verifying Online Information** in *NRW Plus.*

Now on the faculty of Florida International University, Reisner bemoans "the evil wrought on journalism by such wonders as Google." He says that journalism students "seem to believe that if it ain't on Google, it ain't. They make search engines their first stop rather than their last. And that can be real, real misleading."

The Internet, Reisner says, is the "best thing that ever happened to good reporters—and the worst thing that ever happened to lazy ones (though the lazy probably think it's the best)." Before resorting to Google, he says, "use the tried-and-true sources—real people, documents, Web sites that you know and trust."

Crunching the Numbers

Truncating

Truncating refers to a process of shortening the Web address so that you can back up to the so-called mother page. For example, you have done a Google search for information about juveniles and the death penalty on this page: http://www.abanet.org/crimjust/juvjus/jubcases.html. If you are uncertain about who has posted this page—who "owns" the Web site—you would truncate the address to: http://www.abanet.org. You would see that this is the Web site for the American Bar Association.

The computer is an organizing tool. Fed information, it can perform these functions:

• **Alphabetizing:** Similar jobs, similar names can be placed in a series. Reporters at the *Dayton Daily News* in Ohio, for example, analyzed payroll data for county workers and found that several employees held two jobs and were receiving two paychecks.

• **Rank ordering:** Instructed to put any list in some kind of order, the computer will rank lowest to highest, best to worst or biggest to smallest. That's how the Dayton reporters also learned which county workers were receiving unusually large amounts of overtime pay.

• **Correlating or matching:** The computer will compare two different lists. For instance, *The Providence Journal* took a list of bus drivers and matched it with a list of traffic violators. It found some drivers had been ticketed as many as 20 times.

Using All the Functions   Debbie Cenziper, a reporter for *The Miami Herald,* once thought that "database reporting was a skill only specialists needed." She now says computer-assisted reporting methods are an essential part of her work, that they are important for all journalists.

Cenziper has used CAR to do an award-winning investigation into Miami's crumbling schools. Earlier, at *The Charlotte Observer,* she analyzed a database

The Library of Congress, *Newsday*

The Old . . . and the New Newsrooms

Before the computer revolutionized the newsroom, paper, pencils, glue pots and spikes were the tools of the trade for copy editors. Under the harsh light of bright bulbs overhead, the editors slashed at the stories on their desks. In today's newsrooms, stories are edited on the screen, and no one jams a hand on the copy desk spike. And women are slowly taking over.

of 600,000 deaths to expose abuses in North Carolina's mental health system, as described in Chapter 3. She used the data every day while working on the mental health series. "I've learned that without these skills, I cannot complete my work."

At *The Miami Herald,* Cenziper spent three months checking hundreds of county housing department files. She found favoritism, waste and lack of oversight. One developer was paid $1.7 million of taxpayer's money to build 54 homes. Instead, he used the money to build an estate for his family. Cenziper received the 2007 Pulitzer Prize for Local Reporting for her investigation.

Here are other stories that used computer-assisted research:

Smoke and Drink   Bob Sanders had heard that alcohol and cigarette distributors target minority neighborhoods. To check, he obtained billboard locations from the city planning commission and the minority population concentrations for area census tracts from the Census Bureau. After correlating the data, Sanders wrote a story for *The Post-Standard* in Syracuse, N.Y., that began:

> Jeff Scruggs has a blue ribbon on his
> front door on Seymour Street proclaiming
> his opposition to drugs.

Smarts
   "Tools and technology are important only in reference to their application. A baboon with a computer is a baboon."
   —*Ed Miller, former editor and publisher,* The Morning Call, *Allentown, Pa.*

Not Just for Geeks

"The phrase 'computer-assisted journalism' has been an anachronism for a long time. It's a description beloved by its practitioners because it sets us apart from the unwashed masses of the newsroom—colleagues who wouldn't know a function from a fraction to save their careers and who still puzzle over listserv commands. But, in truth, every successful journalist—not just the geek experts—should have a good understanding of technology employed in a modern newsroom and how to use it: spreadsheets, databases, intra-nets, scanners, servers, etc.

—*Ted Bridis, staff writer, The Associated Press*

But when he opens that door each day, he is confronted by a different message: a long, smoldering cigarette gracing a 12-by-25 foot billboard, providing a backdrop on a corner neighbors say is a hot spot for drug dealers. . . .

All up and down Salina Street and Erie Boulevard, outside the mom-and-pop stores on South Avenue and on the near west side, more than half the city's 247 street-level billboards give residents two major messages: smoke and drink.

Court Racism   *The Los Angeles Times* analyzed criminal court sentences and found that black first-offenders were much more likely to be jailed than white first-offenders for the same crimes.

"Super-Speeders"   The *St. Paul Pioneer Press* analyzed speeding tickets issued by the Minnesota State Patrol between 1990 and 2004. Reporters found "the number of drivers caught hurtling more than 100 mph has quadrupled over the past decade to nearly 400 last year. More than one in four super-speeders ticketed in 2003 were nabbed during rush hour."

Money in Politics   Ted Bridis, an AP staff writer, designed a database that tracked every campaign contribution to Indiana lawmakers during the election cycle in 1996, when the state maintained only paper records of donations. The AP photocopied thousands of pages of documents, manually keypunched the records and then categorized each contribution. "We found influence-peddling and illegal contributions common in Indiana, where its reliance on paper records made meaningful oversight nearly impossible," Bridis recalls. "The project led to legislative reforms, including appropriations for a new computerized state system to do what AP accomplished."

For more examples of data-driven journalism, see **Deadly Nursing and Other CAR Stories** in *NRW Plus*.

Spreadsheets   A spreadsheet is a computer program that stores information in columns and rows. Such software makes it easy for reporters to sort, summarize, combine and do calculations with the information. For example, with just a few clicks, you can add up a column of thousands of numbers or alphabetize a list of thousands of names. For a demonstration of how to use a spreadsheet, see **CAR Spreadsheet** in *NRW Plus*.

Public Records

Reporters know what records are available to them on their beats. Among the many online records usually accessible to the public are:

- Assessment and tax records, deeds and property transfers.

- Licenses, including restaurant, dog, liquor, tavern and other business and professional licenses.

- City engineer's records showing streets, alleys, property lines and highways.

- City building permits, variances, unpaid taxes, liens and violations.

- Election returns.

- Articles of incorporation and partnerships. Most states require officers to file their names and holdings in the corporation.

- Bills and vouchers for all governmental purchases, as well as copies of the checks (warrants) paid out for goods and services.

- Minutes of city council and county commission meetings, plus all appropriations and budgets.

- Most judicial records, such as indictments, trials, sentences and court transcripts.

- Wills, receiverships and bankruptcies.

- Most police records.

Sunshine Laws

All states have "sunshine laws" or Freedom of Information acts that require records to be available for public examination. Several Web sites can help reporters with such issues. They include the Reporters Committee for Freedom of the Press (http://rcfp.org), IRE's FOI page (www.ire.org/foi/), the Society of Professional Journalists site (www.spj.org) and the Freedom Forum First Amendment center (www.firstamendmentcenter.org).

Government agencies now put many public records on the Internet. A Web site called Search Systems (http://searchsystems.net/) has a state-by-state directory of online records. Moreover, if public records are kept in a database, reporters have a right to obtain it.

Reporters combine the use of public records with computer-assisted techniques to break blockbuster stories. In one of the earliest uses of computer-assisted reporting, Bill Dedman, then of *The Atlanta Journal-Constitution,* exposed racial discrimination by banks and other mortgage lenders. He won a Pulitzer Prize for Investigative Reporting in 1989 for his series of articles.

Freedom of Information Act

Access to federal records was limited until Congress enacted the Freedom of Information Act in 1966. The act, and important amendments in 1975, unlocked millions of pages of federal documents. The FOIA states that the public has the right to inspect any document that the executive branch possesses, with nine exceptions. These exceptions prevent reporters, or anyone else, from examining income tax returns, secret documents vital to national defense or foreign policy, intra-agency letters and other sensitive material.

The 1975 amendments gave the federal courts the power to review classified documents to make sure that they are properly classified, and they put a limit on the time an agency can take to reply to a request.

Still FOIA battles can drag on. It took the *San Francisco Chronicle* 17 years to obtain records about the FBI's covert operations at the University of California–Berkeley in the 1950s and '60s. In 2002, the paper received more than 200,000 pages of documents from the bureau. They showed that the FBI schemed to fire the university president, oust liberal professors, harass Vietnam War protesters and boost the political career of then-Gov. Ronald Reagan, who went on to become president.

The most recent changes in the federal open-records law were approved by Congress in 1996. The amendments, called the Electronic Freedom of Information Act, or E-FOIA, require agencies to post frequently requested documents on their Web sites.

See **How to Use the FOIA-Freedom of Information Act,** in *NRW Plus.*

Useful Data

Journalists have always used numbers to enlighten us. Economic data can warn us that inflation may be getting out of hand. Alcohol-related traffic deaths may indicate that governments should crack down on drunken driving. An increase in childhood diseases may be a sign that immigrant children are not getting immunization shots.

Not long ago, reporters had to dig such data out of printed reports. Now the information is stored in easily accessible databases. Let's start with one of the more useful sets of data.

Census Data

Reporters who want to track social change in their community will find census data essential. Working mothers, children in nursery school, shifts in family patterns and demographic changes—data on all this are available. Reporters have used census data to find pockets of elderly residents or ethnic groups and to chart changes in the racial makeup of neighborhoods.

Civic Profiles   For a story about housing stock, reporters can find the number of houses that lack toilets, private baths and hot water. They also can determine housing density—the population per square mile. By analyzing who lives in a political district, it is possible to predict how the legislator might vote or what pressures the representative will face regarding public housing, Social Security and other issues. The data also can be used to document the need for daycare centers, low-cost housing, senior citizen facilities and other services.

Printed census reports are available at public and university libraries and at many local, state and federal agencies. Each state has a State Data Center, where experts can help interpret the data and make comparisons with previous censuses. Census data are available from the centers and through the bureau's Web site, www.census.gov.

The Census Bureau takes more than 250 sample surveys a year to monitor trends in employment, population growth, fertility, living arrangements and marriage. It makes surveys of a number of activities every five years, including housing, agriculture, business, construction, government, manufacturing, mineral industry and transportation. (Indeed, the bureau is replacing the decennial "long form" census questionnaire with a rolling survey of households to provide more current demographic data.)

Disease and Death Data

Some of the best-kept official records are those for disease and death. Doctors, clinics and hospitals are required to keep scrupulous records. These are sent to city and county health offices, which relay them to state and federal agencies.

Because this information has been kept for many years, it can provide the journalist with an insight into changing community health standards. Infant mortality rates are sometimes described as the measure of the civilization of a society. These rates show how many children out of 1,000 live births die before age 1.

The U.S. Census Bureau compiles health statistics on 227 countries around the world. Forty nations—including 19 industrialized countries—have lower infant mortality rates than the United States, according to the bureau's 2004 International Data Base. The rates in some U.S. cities are higher than in some developing countries.

Infant mortality is highest in urban areas and poor rural areas and among minority, teen-age and unwed mothers. Reporters can make geographic comparisons because most local health agencies break the city into health districts. Thus, you can compare low-income districts with middle-income districts, or predominantly white districts with nonwhite districts.

Such data show stark differences. Here are the infant mortality rates for a recent year, according to the National Vital Statistics Reports, which are issued in October:

	Black	White
Infant Mortality Rate	14.01	5.72

Data on death and disease are available from the state health department; from the Centers for Disease Control and Prevention (www.cdc.gov); and from the National Center for Health Statistics (www.cdc.gov/nchs). The report on infant mortality, for example, is available at www.cdc.gov/nchs/fastats/infmort.htm.

You can see that a lot of the material reporters gather is in the form of numbers—quantitative data. This takes us to another useful tool, but one that makes some journalism students shudder.

For more material on how to access and analyze health statistics, see **Useful Data** in *NRW Plus*.

Mathematics for the Reporter

The wire service dispatch reads:

> The average American who lives to the age of 70 consumes in that lifetime the equivalent of 150 cattle, 24,000 chickens, 225 lambs, 26 sheep, 310 hogs, 26 acres of grain and 50 acres of fruits and vegetables.

A Nevada newspaper reader who saw the story was puzzled. That seemed like a lot of meat to consume in a lifetime, he thought. He consulted his butcher who estimated the dressed weights of the various animals listed in the story. They came up with a total of 222,695 pounds of meat. The reader wrote the wire service that he had done some figuring. He multiplied 70 years by 365 days to find the total number of days in the average person's lifetime. The figure was 25,500 days. He divided the total meat consumption of 222,695 pounds by 25,500 days. "That figures out to a whopping 8.7 pounds of meat a day," he wrote.

The wire service retired the reference work from which the item was gleaned.

The reporter who handled the story would have avoided embarrassing the wire service had he observed Rule No. 1 for numbers: Always check them.

Tangled Numbers   A CBS newscast cited a poll that asked whether the United States should send its troops into battle in Afghanistan. "Women were more in favor than men," the newscaster read. "Three of ten women approved, whereas <u>only</u> two of three men approved sending in U.S. troops."

Hold everything. A CBS spokesman clarified the mess his mathematically challenged newswriter had created. "The number three seemed larger than two, so the writer got his numbers and sexes jumbled." There's more to it than that. Even if the newswriter had written that two of three men approved and <u>only</u> three of ten women approved, the listener would be left trying to compare thirds and tenths. Obviously, the newswriter could not do the simple mathematics that would have enabled him to write:

> Men were more in favor than women. Almost 70 percent of the men approved sending in U.S. troops, but only 30 percent of the women polled approved.

Or he could have used fractions:

> Two-thirds of the men approved, but less than a third of the women supported sending in U.S. troops.

Or used a ratio:

> Twice as many men as women approved sending in U.S. troops.

Go Figure

"He had a generous new Warner Bros. contract in his pocket, guaranteeing him $150,000 annually for the next seven years. . . . At thirty-four, Ronald Reagan was by his own standard, 'well fixed,' with a beautiful wife, two pretty children, and more than one and a half million dollars coming in."

—*Dutch, a biography of Reagan,* by Edmund Morris

Basic Calculations

To avoid embarrassing errors, reporters must be able to handle three fairly simple calculations—how to figure a percentage, an average and a rate.

Percentages

This is probably the most useful calculation in the journalist's toolbox. We use percentages to make comparisons rather than raw numbers because the percentage is more easily understood. Percentages are used to compare this year's traffic deaths with last year's; the increase or decrease in crimes; population shifts. The list is endless. Let's start with the growing population of the United States:

2000 Census	2006 Estimated
281,421,906	296,410,404

The increase is 14,988,498, an unwieldy figure. But if we derive a percentage, the increase is better understood.

To find the percentage increase we subtract the older figure from the new and divide the result by the older figure:

$$\frac{14,988,498}{281,421,906}$$

The result is **5.3** percent increase.

We've been reading about the increasing number of Spanish-speaking people in the United States, that they constitute a greater percentage of the population than people of African descent. True? Let's check the percentages:

	2000 Census	2006 Estimated
Black	34,658,190	37,909,341
Hispanic	35,305,018	42,687,224

We can derive percentages for both black and Hispanic groups using the total population for 2000 and 2006 and we find:

	% of Total Population	
	2000	2006
Black	12.3	12.8
Hispanic	12.5	14.4

Using percentages, we can see at a glance that the Hispanic population is growing at a faster pace than the black population.

Averages

We're all familiar with averages, such as a grade point average, average household income and the average temperature for last month. You compute an average by totaling all the numbers (say, the high temperature each day during January) and dividing by the number of incidents (in this case, 31 days).

$$\frac{807}{31} = 26.03$$

So you can write that the average high temperature in January was a frigid 26 degrees. You can compare that with previous months and with Januarys of previous years.

In the same way, average household income is the total income for all households divided by the number of households.

Averages can get tricky. A baseball player's batting average, for example, is a bit of a misnomer: It's really a fraction of the whole—the number of hits divided by the number of at-bats. Take the first baseman who is in a batting slump. The sportswriter says the player has had only nine hits in his last 45 appearances at the plate. The sports fan wants to know: What's that mean in terms of his batting average? And so the reporter calculates: Hits divided by plate appearances:

$$\frac{9}{45} = \frac{1}{5} \text{ or } .2 \text{ or } .200$$

We drop the decimal point. Our star first baseman is batting a dismal 200. He'd better improve or his $4 million salary will go down the drain next year when he renegotiates his contract.

Averages are important. But as we will see later in this chapter, they aren't always the best way to describe a group of numbers.

Numbers vs. Rates

Number of Murders	
Los Angeles	1,119
New Orleans	338

Murder Rate	
Los Angeles	8.6
New Orleans	25.5

In numbers, Los Angeles ranked first, New Orleans 13th in the country. In rates, New Orleans ranked first, Los Angeles 34th.

Rates

Reporters work with rates all the time—murder rates, death rates, divorce rates, infant mortality rates. Rates tell us more than raw numbers because they take factors like the population into consideration.

In a recent year, Ohio State University reported to the U.S. Department of Education 765 campus incidents of liquor law violations involving disciplinary actions or judicial referrals. That same year, the University of South Carolina reported 553 such incidents. Seems as though Ohio State students are hard drinking guys and dolls, more so than the temperate South Carolinians.

Hold it. Let's look at the size of the two schools. Ohio State reported a student population of 50,995, the University of South Carolina 25,596. Let's apply the number of liquor law violations to the student population of both universities:

	Ohio State	South Carolina
Violations	765	553
Population	50,995	25,596

Let's calculate the number of violations per student:

$$\frac{765}{50,995} = .0150 \qquad \frac{553}{25,596} = .0216$$

These decimals are hard to read, so in most rate calculations we use a multiplier. We can multiply by 100 so that we can say that for every 100 students at Ohio State, 1.5 were involved with a liquor violation, and at South Carolina the figure was 2.16. But those decimals are silly. Who's heard of .5 of a student or, worse, .16 of a student? If we multiply by 1,000 we'll get these figures:

For every 1,000 students at Ohio State, 15 were involved with a liquor violation, and at South Carolina, 22 students were involved. (We rounded off the .6.)

So you can see that by using rates we have a more accurate, more truthful picture of one aspect of the campus scene.

We can apply the same sort of analysis to crimes such as murder or to infant mortality. You'll find that the states with the largest number of infant deaths are not among the states with the highest rates.

The bottom line: Rates are a better indicator than raw numbers.

See **Campus Crime** in *NRW Plus* for more material about FBI crime data.

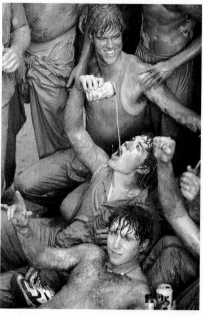

Thomas E. Carver,
Spartanburg Herald-Journal

Chug-a-Lug

Fraternity members enjoy themselves in the mud pit.

Ratios

A couple of pages back we showed the infant mortality rates of black (14.01) and white (5.72) children. The figures are a stunning indication of a serious health problem in the United States. But the figures would have even greater impact if a ratio (the comparison between numbers) were used.

To calculate a ratio, we take the larger number and divide it by the smaller:

$$\frac{14.01}{5.72} = 2.45$$

That's more than two to one, which allows us to write that black babies died at a rate almost two and a half times greater than white infants.

Means, Modes and Medians

How would you describe the average salary at J.C. Walnut and Co., an upholstery shop whose employees are on strike? Walnut says it is $31,140, and he has put a sign in his window saying so and telling his customers that the employees are ungrateful.

You Get a Zero

A recent posting on an e-mail list for journalists asked: "If there were 0 individuals who carpooled in 1990, and 7 who carpooled in 2000, that's a 700% change, right?"

"No, it's not. To calculate change over time, you take the most recent number (7), subtract the old number (0), and divide by the old number. But it's impossible to divide by 0—so in this case, you can't compute percentage change."

Here is how the annual salaries for the company break down:

- 72,500 (1) Mr. Walnut
- 59,600 (1) Son Theodore
- 30,500 (4) Master craftsmen
- 25,200 (6) Upholsterers
- 20,600 (3) Laborers

If we add up the salaries, being careful to multiply by the number of workers in each category, we reach a total payroll of $467,100. To find the average Walnut reached, we divide by 15, the total number of people on the payroll. The average is $31,140. So Walnut is right, right? Wrong.

Darrell Huff, the author of books about mathematics says, "When you are told something is an 'average,' you still don't know very much about it unless you can find out what kind of average it is: mean, median, or mode."

Mean: This is the average Walnut used. To derive it, we add up all the figures in our set and divide by the total number of individual components.

Mode: The component occurring most often in a listing of components.

Median: The midpoint in a grouping.

The mean distorts when there are unusually high or low components. Here, Walnut and son Theodore make far more than anyone else, and so the average salary tilts toward the high end.

The mode here is $25,200, which is the most frequently occurring salary.

The median, which is often used in describing a set of numbers, requires you list all the salaries to find the midpoint:

	72,500	
	59,600	
	30,500	
	30,500	
	30,500	
	30,500	
Mode	25,200	
	25,200	← **Median**
	25,200	
	25,200	
	25,200	
	25,200	
	20,600	
	20,600	
	20,600	

Look at this list of 15 numbers. The midpoint is the eighth on the list because there are seven salaries above it and seven below it. The eighth salary on the list is $25,200, which is the same as the mode.

Our figure of $25,200 is considerably less than Walnut's average of $31,140. And if we use some common sense, we realize that only the employees are on strike, so what is Walnut doing putting his and his son's salaries in the computation?

Take out the top two on the list and we get 13 salaries. The mode and the median are still $25,200. The mean is $25,769.

An important note about computer skills: If you have spreadsheet software, you don't have to manually list all of the numbers in a set to calculate the median or do painstaking addition and division to calculate the average. Programs such as Microsoft Excel have built-in formulas that will instantly compute the mean, median and mode.

Let's take this a step further before we leave the delightful realm of mathematics. Let's look behind the median. There's more here than meets the eye.

Analyzing Averages

The Census Bureau recently announced that the median household income was $46,326. But wait a minute. Common sense, based on our reading and experience, tells us that income varies widely by race, ethnicity and gender. We want a breakdown of the median. Look at what we find:

Median Household Income	
Asian	$60,367
White	50,622
Hispanic	36,278
Black	30,939

These figures tell us something about the nature of our society: The median household income of blacks is 61 percent that of whites; for Hispanics, it's 71 percent.

We also can see that men make more than women:

Median Individual Income	
Men	$43,317
Women	33,421

In other words, for every $1 a man earned, a woman earned about 77 cents.

For more on how to access and analyze income statistics, see **Income Data** in *NRW Plus.*

Selling a Tax Cut

When President George W. Bush proposed a tax cut, critics said it would benefit the rich mostly. The Republican Senate majority leader responded on *Fox News Sunday,* "When you say that there are 92 million people who are going to be handed a check for $1,000 this year, your viewers right now, is that a tax cut for the rich?" The media swallowed the $1,000 figure.

The $1,000 was the *mean.* When the mean is applied to such matters as income, the figure is usually weighted toward the high or low ends.

In this case, the benefits to taxpayers at the highest end weighted the figure significantly: 1 percent of those filing their income would receive an average check of $24,000, and those earning $1 million or more would be sent a refund of $90,200. Taxpayers in the middle fifth of all those paying income tax—those in the *median* group—would be sent a check for $256.

Personalizing Numbers

Numbers tell us a great deal about the way we live. But for journalists, numbers are the starting point. Behind the percentages, rates and averages are human beings, and it is their story that the journalist is obliged to tell.

That's what Phoebe Zerwick of the *Winston-Salem Journal* did after learning that the infant mortality rate in North Carolina was among the highest in the nation and that the death rate of black infants in the *Journal*'s home county was more than twice the state average. Zerwick gave the figures a human dimension. One of her stories calling attention to the toll begins this way:

Stealth Candidates

When the former grand wizard of the Ku Klux Klan, David Duke, ran for governor of Louisiana, polls consistently underestimated his actual vote. Why? Voters are unwilling to admit their true feelings when race is an issue, says pollster Paul Maslin. To correct for this, pollsters divide the undecided white vote 4:1 for the white candidate in a race of a white versus a black candidate. Some interviewers will ask general questions to gauge whether interviewees have racist sentiments.

Yvette Johnson took her punishment for smoking crack day after day as she watched her 3-pound son struggle to live.

"Even today, after being clean for four years, I still remember those months," Johnson said.

"Seeing this baby suffer, seeing those needles and tubes and seizures, I really felt it was my fault," she said. "The only way I could say I was sorry was to go there every day and stay clean.

"Basically my son died about 10 times in the hospital. That was the worst punishment that I could actually say a person could have given me. Jail wouldn't have done no good. A whipping would have done no good.

"For the first three-and-a-half months I didn't do nothing. I just sat there and looked at my baby and cried."

Personalizing the Smoker

"An estimated 50 million Americans smoked 600 billion cigarettes last year," the story about a local anti-smoking proposal said. The city editor calls you, the reporter handling the story, to the desk.

"Let's put this and a lot of the other figures into some understandable terms," he tells you. "In this case, why not follow the sentence with one that says, 'This means the average smoker lit up so many cigarettes a day.' "

Back at your desk, you make a few simple calculations: 600 billion cigarettes smoked a year ÷ 50 million smokers = 12,000 cigarettes per smoker a year.

You want average daily use, so you make the next calculation: 12,000 cigarettes a year ÷ 365 days = 32.87 cigarettes per smoker a day.

You round that off to 33—a pack and a half a day. A reader can see the smoker crumpling up a pack and smoking halfway through a second pack for his or her daily dose. This is more graphic than the millions and billions, which depersonalize the story.

For more about the use of mathematics, see **More Math** in *NRW Plus*.

Public Opinion Polling

Abortion. Prayer in school. Gun control. Tax increases. Voting for the president, the mayor. How do we stand on these issues; how will we vote? In the past, the answers were hardly convincing. Reporters would chat with politicians, those supposedly perceptive insiders with delicate olfactory organs attuned to the mildest breezes. The result might be interesting reading, but it had no predictive value whatsoever.

Now, the science of surveying gives the journalist a surer hand to reach into areas of coverage that before had been handled with impressions and conjecture.

Polls are used for a variety of stories. The well-designed poll can tell with a fair degree of accuracy not only what people think of a president's performance, but also whether a proposed school bond issue is popular in a middle-class section of the community or what types of daycare are favored by working mothers. Polls have been used to determine whether Catholics approve of abortion, how people feel about the death penalty, what African Americans think of affirmative action. *The New York Times* even ran a survey that established that 87 percent of 3- to 10-year-olds believe in Santa Claus.

Recognizing the value of polls and surveys, many newspapers and television stations have hired pollsters and polling organizations. The reporter is still essential, for the poll can supply only the information. Journalists must make the poll into news. To do this, they must understand how polls work and their possibilities and limits.

Use with Care The poll is a systematic way of finding out what people are thinking at a given time by questioning a sample population. It can provide a fairly accurate snapshot of a situation at that time.

> ### Language Barrier
> With the increasing numbers of Latinos and Asians in the population, pollsters who use English only in asking questions of these people will not get an accurate result. In California, Latinos asked questions in English favored a proposition 52 to 42 percent. Asked in Spanish, 15 percent supported the measure, and 69 percent were opposed.

Poll results have to be read carefully. Some are designed and interpreted in ways to favor a product, a point of view, a candidate. How would you read the following poll results to a proposition about gay marriage?

Proposition

Gays and lesbians should be able to marry legally.

Answer Choices and Results

1. Yes—25 percent.
2. No legal recognition of gay marriages—37 percent.
3. Civil unions for gay partners are OK—35 percent yes.

Interpretations

1. 72 percent oppose gay marriage.
2. 60 percent favor gay marriage or civil unions.

Political Polls

There are hundreds of polling organizations and firms. Most are local groups that conduct marketing surveys. The big firms—Gallup and Harris—handle commercial clients, too, but are best known for their political polls and surveys. It is this political polling that so often finds its way into newspapers and news broadcasts. Unfortunately, the news media often dwell on the "horse race"—obsessing over who's ahead—instead of using polling data to write about people and the issues they care about.

Many journalists also ignore the limitations of polls. They fail to consider or report the margin of error, the number of people surveyed, how respondents were chosen, when the poll was conducted and how the questions were worded and ordered.

Although reputable pollsters pretest their questions, ambiguities do creep in. Reporters always should examine the questions behind the polling data to make sure that they are clear and, for polls conducted for private clients, to ascertain whether they are loaded.

Reporting
"There is no substitute for what you see and hear. This is as true in the age of the Internet as before it, perhaps more so, because the temptations to shortcuts and the means to take them have multiplied beyond measure."

—*Roger Cohen,*
international writer at large,
The New York Times

Winners and Losers

Journalists must be careful about their tendency to heed the demands of readers and listeners for definitive opinions and for winners and losers. A poll can only state what people say they are thinking or how voters say they will vote at the time they are polled, and sometimes even then the contests are too close to call.

Journalists should remember this: People change their minds; polls cannot guarantee that behavior will be consistent with intentions.

Reputable pollsters know just how far they can take their data. But they are often under pressure to pick winners in election contests. When pre-election polls indicate a 60–40 percent breakdown, a pollster feels at ease in choosing the winner. But when an editor, reflecting the desire of readers and listeners, asks for a choice in a 44–42 race with 14 percent undecided, then trouble lies ahead.

For a more detailed explanation of polling, see **More about Polls** in *NRW Plus.*

Summing Up

Journalists have an array of research and reporting tools that, if used with intelligence and care, can lead to accurate, thorough and high-impact stories. The tools enable reporters to access a range of reference material, find sources and other resources for their stories, and obtain and analyze a vast amount of information.

Further Reading

Aueletta, Ken. *The Highwaymen: Warriors of the Information Super-highway.* New York: Random House, 1997.

Calishain, Tara. *Web Search Garage.* Upper Saddle River, N.J.: Prentice Hall, 2004.

Cohn, Victor, and Lewis Cope. *News & Numbers: A Guide to Reporting Statistical Claims and Controversies in Health and Other Fields,* 2nd ed. Ames, Iowa: Blackwell Professional, 2001.

Houston, Brant, Len Bruzzese and Steve Weinberg. *The Investigative Reporter's Handbook: A Guide to Documents, Databases and Techniques.* Boston: Bedford/St. Martin's, 2002.

Huff, Darrell, and Irving E. Gers. *How to Lie with Statistics.* New York: Norton, 1993.

Meyer, Philip. *Precision Journalism: A Reporter's Introduction to Social Science Methods,* 4th ed. Lanham, Md.: Rowman & Littlefield Publishers, 2002.

Paulos, John Allen. *A Mathematician Reads the Newspaper.* New York: Anchor Books/Doubleday, 1996.

Pavlik, John. *Journalism and New Media.* New York: Columbia University Press, 2001.

5 The Lead

Bill Miskiewicz,
Times/Record, Fort Worth, Texas

"Fire Takes the Lives of Three Firefighters"—
Direct lead.

Preview

The lead gives the reader the sense of the story to follow. There are two basic types of leads:

- **Direct:** This lead tells the reader or listener the most important aspect of the story at once. It is usually used on breaking news events.
- **Delayed:** This lead entices the reader or listener into the story by hinting at its contents. It usually is used for features.

The lead sentence usually contains one idea and follows the subject-verb-object sentence structure for clarity. It should not exceed 35 words.

The effective story lead meets two requirements. It captures the essence of the event, and it cajoles the reader or listener into staying awhile.

Follow the facts,
wherever they take you.

We slept last night in the enemy's camp.
—By a correspondent for the *Memphis Daily Appeal,* after the first day of the Civil War Battle of Shiloh

Millionaire Harold F. McCormick today bought a poor man's youth.
—Carl Victor Little, UP, following McCormick's male gland transplant operation in the early 1920s. UP's New York Office quickly killed the lead and sent out a sub (substitute lead)

The million-to-one shot came in. Hell froze over. A month of Sundays hit the calendar.

Don Larsen today pitched a no-hit, no-run, no-man-reach-first game in a World Series.

—Shirley Povich, *The Washington Post & Times Herald,* on the perfect game the Yankee pitcher hurled against the Brooklyn Dodgers in 1956

"I feel as if I had been pawed by dirty hands," said Martha Graham.

—Walter Terry, dance critic of *The New York Herald Tribune,* after two members of Congress denounced Graham's dancing as "erotic"

What price Glory? Two eyes, two legs, an arm—$12 a month.

—St. Clair McKelway, *Washington Herald,* in a story about a disabled World War I veteran living in poverty

Snow, followed by small boys on sleds.

—H. Allen Smith, *New York World-Telegram,* in the weather forecast

Rule Breakers, but Memorable

These leads defy almost every canon decreed by those who prescribe standards of journalistic writing. The first lead violates the rule demanding the reporter's anonymity. The UP lead is in questionable taste. Povich's lead has four sentences and three clichés. Terry's lead is a quote lead and McKelway's asks a question—both violations of the standards. Smith's weather forecast is a little joke.

Yet, the leads are memorable.

They work because they meet the two requirements of lead writing: They symbolize in graphic fashion the heart of the event, and they entice the reader to read on. Here are two leads from New York City newspapers that appeared the morning after the mayor announced his new budget. Which is better?

Mayor Lindsay listed facilities for public safety yesterday as his top spending priority for next year, shifting from his pledge of a year ago to make clean streets his first objective in capital expenditures.

—*The New York Times*

Mayor Lindsay dropped his broom and picked up the nightstick yesterday, setting law enforcement facilities as the top priority in the city's construction plans for the coming fiscal year.

—*Daily News*

Great Beginnings

The business of luring the reader into a story is hardly confined to journalistic writing. Andrew E. Svenson, the prolific author of many of the Nancy Drew,

---

More Fiction Than Fact

McKelway's lead, used in several editions of this textbook, has been cited in books and articles to illustrate a nation's callousness to those who have made sacrifices in its wars. But the lead and most of the story McKelway wrote is a fabrication, McKelway later admitted.

Frank Herron of *The Post-Standard* in Syracuse, N.Y., did the sleuthing and came up with a *New Yorker* article McKelway wrote in 1957, 35 years after his piece, written as a young and imaginative reporter, appeared. In his article, McKelway said the veteran's original injury was not war-connected but the result of a training accident in the Philippines.

His major injuries were the result of his contracting "two diseases of the kind I recognized as being unmentionable," McKelway wrote. The serviceman had been treated for them and discharged from the Army. He was advised to continue treatments, but failed to do so.

Three years later, he was arrested in San Francisco as a street beggar and turned over to an Army hospital, which found his diseases had progressed to cost the ex-soldier his eyesight and the amputation of both legs and an arm, McKelway wrote—35 years later.

Classic Lead

It was called "the crime of the century," the thrill murder in 1924 of 14-year-old Bobby Franks by Nathan F. Leopold and Richard A. Loeb, two well-educated young men. The trial brought out the eloquence of Clarence Darrow in defending the pair, who were spared execution but were sentenced to life plus 99 years.

In 1936 in Joliet Penitentiary, Loeb made what a fellow prisoner described as improper advances, and the convict slashed Loeb with a straight-edge razor, killing him. Edwin A. Lahey wrote this lead for *The Chicago Daily News,* a lead some consider unequaled in the annals of leads:

Despite his fine college education, Richard Loeb today ended his sentence with a proposition.

Bobbsey Twins and Hardy Boys juvenile books, said that the trick in writing is to set up danger, mystery and excitement on page 1 to convince the child to turn the page. He said he had rewritten page 1 as many as 20 times.

The great Russian writer Leo Tolstoy said the idea behind good writing is jumping "straight into the action."

The Old Testament begins with simple words in a short sentence: "In the beginning God created the heavens and the earth."

Everyone remembers great beginnings:

> It was the best of times, it was the worst of times, it was the age of wisdom, it was the age of foolishness, it was the epoch of belief, it was the epoch of incredulity, it was the season of Light, it was the season of Darkness, it was the spring of hope, it was the winter of despair.

As most high school students know, that is how Charles Dickens began *A Tale of Two Cities.* Another book, written 92 years later, is also familiar to high school readers, probably because the beginning trapped them into reading further:

> If you really want to hear about it, the first thing you'll probably want to know is where I was born, and what my lousy childhood was like, and how my parents were occupied, and all that David Copperfield kind of crap, but I don't feel like going into it, if you want to know the truth.

The writer—J. D. Salinger. The book—*The Catcher in the Rye.*

Importance of the Lead

The writer Henry Fairlie says, "Every journalist who has ever struggled with [a lead] knows why it can take so much effort. It is as important to him as to the reader. Writing it concentrates the mind wonderfully, forcing him to decide what in the story is important, what he wants to emphasize, and can eventually give the shape to the rest of the story as he writes it."

Thomas Boswell of *The Washington Post* says of the lead that "once you find that idea or thread, all the other anecdotes, illustrations and quotes are pearls that hang on this thread. The thread may seem very humble, the pearls may seem very flashy, but it's still the thread that makes the necklace."

John McPhee, a *New Yorker* writer who has written a dozen books and scores of articles, says, "I've often heard writers say that if you have written your lead you have 90 percent of your story."

Finding the Lead

Leads emerge from the reporting. Much of the time, the idea for the lead is clear during the reporting: a speeding car goes through a stop sign and kills a motorcyclist . . . the city council adopts a record $450 million budget . . . the Pistons defeat the Lakers on a last-minute basket . . . Ray Charles dies . . . Renee Menton wins a Merit Scholarship.

Veteran reporters John W. Chancellor and Walter R. Mears say that the best way to write good leads "is to think of them in advance—to frame the lead while the story is unfolding." Experienced journalists do this. As they report, they ask themselves, "What's this story really about?" Thinking the lead during the reporting guides the reporting.

If you know what the heart of the story is—the lead idea—then you are able to direct your reporting toward gathering the buttressing and explanatory information necessary to document the lead. You can ask the right questions, look for the specifics, search out the anecdotes and graphic detail that make the story come alive.

Writing the Lead

Framing the lead puts ideas into words. Easier said than done, even for experienced writers. If you see a reporter perspiring heavily despite the air conditioning, you'll know why. McPhee says, "The first part—the lead, the beginning—is the hardest part of all to write. You have tens of thousands of words to choose from, after all—and only one can start the story, then one after that, and so forth. What will you choose?"

Stumped?   Editors, experienced reporters, novelists and essayists offer all sorts of advice. Look out the window. Walk around for a bit.

Some writing coaches say, "Just start writing the body of the story. As you go along, the lead will come to you." Bad advice. In the first place, most news stories are written under deadline pressure—the 6 o'clock newscast, the 10 p.m. first edition, the insatiable demands of the Web site. Even monthly magazine writers talk of deadline pressure. There's no time to fiddle while the editor twiddles her thumbs waiting for copy. You're expected to churn out the story *NOW*. Just as important, unfocused writing can become a habit, a bad one.

Finding the Thread

Let's walk through some scenarios. We'll watch reporters search for their leads, sometimes successfully, sometimes not.

A thief broke into an auto parts store and stole a batch of batteries. Here's how a reporter for *The Charlotte Observer* wrote the story along with an analysis provided by her editor:

Thieves Get 36 Batteries

Thieves who entered a Charlotte auto parts store stole 36 Delco batteries, police were told yesterday.

Crowell Erskine, 49, manager of the Piedmont Auto Exchange at 410 Atando Ave., told officers the store was broken into between 5 p.m. Tuesday and 8 a.m. Wednesday by thieves knocking a hole in the rear wall of the one-story brick building.

Erskine said the batteries were valued at $539.18.

—The Charlotte Observer

Analysis

1. The lead focuses on the basic idea, the theft of a batch of batteries. The reporter knows the reader opens the newspaper each day with the question, "*What* happened today?"

2. The reporter answers what he or she thinks will be the logical questions a reader might ask, "*Where* did the break-in occur? *When* did it happen? *How* was it done?" The answers to those questions explain and amplify the lead.

3. Background is provided. The reporter knows the reader will want to be told the value of the goods stolen.

Other Scenarios   Let's say that the thief had somehow managed to bring off the job in broad daylight. Then *when* the theft occurred and *how* it was managed would be the main elements in the lead, the thread along which the story would be written.

Had the thief scaled a 15-foot wall to gain entry, *how* the theft was managed would be placed in the lead.

If the thief left a note in the store apologizing for his act and saying he needed the money to pay medical bills for his sick wife, *why* the theft occurred—according to the thief—would be put into the lead.

The Five W's and an H   The most important element always forms the basic idea for the lead. To find that basic element, the reporter anticipates the questions the reader will ask and then answers them. These questions have been summarized as *who, what, when, where, why,* and *how*—the Five W's and an H.

The question and the answer that come closest to the nature of the event provide the building blocks for the lead, which almost always begins the story. When this happens, when the lead idea starts the story, we have a *direct* lead. For feature stories, the lead idea may be placed further down in the story, in which case we say we have a *delayed* lead.

More about these two types of leads later. For now, two more scenarios of reporters searching for leads for their stories.

Burying the Lead

The most common mistake young reporters make is burying the lead. That is, the main idea is swimming somewhere in the body of the story instead of being placed in the lead. Here are a couple of examples taken from student news stories:

> The Student Council met last night to discuss and adopt next year's budget.

> The university has changed its stand on admissions policies and will put them into effect in two years.

The reader has to wade through a few paragraphs before getting to the point: that the budget for next year includes $4,500 to bring "diverse speakers" to the campus; that the university adopted a "need-blind admission policy" that should make for a more diverse student body. These belong in the lead.

Frank's Struggle   Let's watch a student write a story about the local United Way Campaign, which was in the middle of a fund drive. Frank thought that the midpoint of the drive might be a good time to check progress. Here is the story he turned in:

> The local United Way Campaign today issued its second weekly report in its current campaign to raise $750,000 for next year's activities.
> Tony Davis, the campaign chairman, said that donations in the first two weeks had exceeded last year's fund-raising at a similar time.
> "We've collected $350,000, and that's about $25,000 ahead of last year," Davis said. "Thanks to the work of our downtown volunteers, the local merchants have been canvassed more thoroughly than ever before, and their gifts have been very generous."
> The month-long drive seeks funds for 28 local organizations, including the Big Brothers, Senior Citizens House and a new program to aid crippled children.

The Problem   The story is clear but it has a glaring fault: The basic idea or theme was placed in the second paragraph. Occasionally, a reporter will intentionally delay the lead, usually for dramatic effect. This was no such instance. The most significant fact Frank gleaned from his reporting was that the campaign was running ahead of last year's receipts. And because this is a straightforward or spot news story, the progress report should have been placed in the lead. Given this advice by his instructor, Frank rewrote the story:

> The United Way Campaign to raise $750,000 is running ahead of last year's drive at the midway point.
> Tony Davis, the campaign chairman, said today that in the first two weeks of the month-long fund drive, $350,000 had been collected. That is $25,000 ahead of last year's collections at this time.

> "Thanks to the work of our downtown volunteers, the
> local merchants have been . . ."

The same set of facts was given to a reporting and writing class. Here are some of the leads that emerged:

> Tony Davis, the chairman of the United Way Campaign,
> reported today that the fund drive is running ahead of
> schedule.
>
> The United Way Campaign has collected $350,000, which
> is $25,000 ahead of last year's drive at this time.
>
> Local merchants were credited today with helping to push
> the United Way Campaign closer and faster toward its goal
> of $750,000.

In each of these leads, the basic idea is the same: Collections are ahead of those of last year. This is the most important element and it must be the basis of the lead.

Pregnant Teen-Agers

Let's accompany Sarah as she works on a story about a talk she has just covered. A Harvard sociologist spoke about teen-age pregnancy to a campus audience. He said that the bill for social services, special schools, lost work hours and hospital care for the infants, who are often born prematurely, adds up to several billion dollars a year.

"Last year," he said, "about 375,000 unmarried teen-agers gave birth, and almost as many teen-agers had abortions. The dollar costs have been enormous, to say nothing of the social costs."

Sarah is writing for the campus newspaper. She has a couple of hours before deadline. If she were working for a newspaper with a Web site, or a radio or TV station, she would not have the luxury of time to think about her lead and story. As Chancellor and Mears state in their book *The News Business:*

> When you've got to run to a telephone to start dictating, or when you've got to go on camera and start talking, the one thing you really need is to have a lead in your head. It doesn't have to be fancy, but if you frame it properly, the rest of the story will flow from it in a natural and graceful way.

Sarah knows that if she can identify the heart of the talk, her story will just about organize itself because the next several paragraphs after the lead will consist of quotes that buttress and amplify the lead material she has selected. Easier said than done, she muses.

Well, what's her lead? She had better start writing, and she does:

> A Harvard sociologist studying teen-age pregnancy gave
> a speech last night to more than 200 students and faculty
> members in Hall Auditorium.

No Good   Sarah isn't happy with her lead. She talks to herself:

> **Trouble. That's called burying or backing into the lead. All this kind
> of lead tells the reader is that the speaker spoke to an audience, which
> is hardly interesting or important enough to merit anyone's attention.
> He did say something interesting—in fact, he made several interesting
> points.**

Sarah had been surprised by the large number of teen-agers who gave birth and
the number of abortions among these young women. Lead material?

Not really, she reasons, because the speaker devoted most of his talk to the
cost of teen-age pregnancy. This information was clearly the most important. She
could work the figures into the second and third paragraphs to explain the reasons
for the high cost. Sarah writes:

> A Harvard sociologist said last night that teen-age pregnancy
> is costing the country billions of dollars a year.
> Gerald Cantor told 200 students and faculty members in
> Hall Auditorium that the annual costs associated with the
> pregnancies of almost 750,000 unmarried women under the
> age of 20 "are vastly greater than we had thought."
> He attributed the costs to social services. . . .

Almost There   Sarah pauses to read what she has written. She is satisfied that she
has found the most important part of the talk for her lead, that she has identified the
speaker properly and placed the talk, that she has kept the Five W's and an H in
mind. . . . Wait. She isn't happy with the word *said* in her lead. Not very exciting.

> **Should I make it *warned?* Or is that too strong? He really didn't
> warn. I'll leave it as is.**

Sarah has answered the first three of our four questions for lead writing:

1. **What:** The high cost.

2. **Who:** Harvard sociologist.

3. **Direct or delayed:** Direct.

We take leave of Sarah as she ponders the fourth question. If you wish, lend
her a hand.

A Race for Congress

Here is a lead a reporter wrote about a congressional race. He thought he had
answered the first two questions writers ask themselves when writing a lead:

> Replies of Rep. Ronald A. Sarasin and William R. Ratchford,
> candidates in the Fifth Congressional race, to a Connecticut
> League of Women Voters questionnaire were released today.

Reporters ask themselves four questions in their search for suitable leads to their stories:

1. *What* was unique or the most important or unusual thing that happened?

2. *Who* was involved—who did it or who said it?

After answering these questions, the reporter seeks words and a form that will give shape to the responses by asking three more questions:

3. Is a direct or a delayed lead best? (Does the theme of the story go in the first sentence or somewhere within the first six paragraphs?)

4. Is there a colorful word or dramatic phrase I can work into the lead?

He did include *what* had happened and *who* was involved. But he did not make his answer to the first question sufficiently specific. What did they say in their replies? The reporter reached this answer down in the story, but his editor pointed out that voters want to know the opinions and positions of their candidates quickly in stories about politics. Such events do not lend themselves to delayed leads.

A better lead for the political story might have been:

> Ronald A. Sarasin and William R. Ratchford, candidates for Congress in the Fifth District, agree that financing Social Security is the major domestic issue facing the nation.

The next paragraph might have included the background information that the reporter had mistakenly put into his lead:

> Their positions on Social Security and on other issues were released today by the Connecticut League of Women Voters. The League had sent its questionnaires to all major candidates for office.

The subsequent paragraphs would expand the Social Security theme and introduce additional material from the replies of the candidates.

Types of Leads

If you look back at the leads we have been discussing—the United Way Campaign, pregnant teen-agers and a race for Congress—you will see that they took the reader and the listener directly to the main idea or theme of the story. They are appropriately called *direct leads.* Although young journalists are offered long lists of lead types, there are really only two types, the *direct* and the *delayed* lead. The *who* and the *what* leads, the *anecdotal, contrast* and *shotgun* leads, the *question, quote* and *gag* leads—they all fall into these two categories.

Let's look more closely at the direct lead, and then we will examine the delayed lead.

Direct Lead

The direct lead is the workhorse of journalism. It is used on most stories. As we have seen, the direct lead focuses on the theme of the event in the first paragraph. The surest way to test a reporter's competence, editors say, is to see whether his or her leads on spot news events move directly to the point. Here are some direct leads:

The temperature reached 102 degrees at noon yesterday and set a record high for the city.

On a day of unspeakable horror for New York and the nation, terrorists crashed planes into the World Trade Center and the Pentagon yesterday in the deadliest assault on the United States in its history.

WASHINGTON—The House of Representatives voted today to impeach President Clinton.

A local couple was awarded $150,000 yesterday in Butte County Court for injuries they suffered in a traffic accident last March.

Another in a series of snowstorms is expected to hit the Sierra today.

SAN FRANCISCO—The California Supreme Court ruled today that newspapers and television stations can be held liable for news-gathering techniques that intrude on privacy.

WASHINGTON—The U.S. Senate this afternoon acquitted President Clinton of the two impeachment charges brought against him by the House of Representatives. The vote on both charges fell far short of the two-thirds required for conviction.

NEW ORLEANS—Rescuers along the hurricane-ravaged Gulf Coast pushed aside the dead to reach the living Tuesday in a race against time and rising flood waters.

NEW YORK—Oprah Winfrey says her lawyers shouldn't have gone after the man who is trying to promote her as a candidate for president.

For more leads on the terror bombing story see **Terror Bombings** in *NRW Plus.*

Lead Essentials

Direct leads usually contain:

* Specific information about what happened or what was said.

* When the event occurred.

* The location of the event.

* The source of the information.

Lively Leads   Direct leads need not be dry and dull. Here's a direct lead by Aljean Harmetz of *The New York Times* for a business story, which we usually think of as a dry subject with prose to match:

Retribution
When *The Washington Times* began publication, many of its staffers were members of the Rev. Sun Myung Moon's Unification Church. One of them turned in this lead for a fire story:

A 39-year-old Fairfax man was punished by God Thursday night for smoking in bed by burning to death.

Two veteran motion picture industry executives were chosen today by the board of Walt Disney Productions to head the troubled company a mouse built.

When a fire struck a high-rise apartment building in Queens, New York, here's how the *Daily News* began its story:

Strong winds combined lethally with a fire in a Queens high-rise building yesterday, creating a "blowtorch" that roared through an apartment building and into a hallway, killing three people and injuring 22.

The image of a blowtorch searing its way through the building is powerful. A battalion fire chief used that word in an interview and the reporter had the good sense to put it in the lead. Good reporting makes for good writing.

Online Leads The direct lead is the mainstay of stories on the Web sites of newspapers and online news services. Studies have shown that online readers want their news in capsule form. They want to know quickly what happened and to whom.

Online editors tell their writers to try to answer the Five W's and an H in the leads of their stories.

Delayed Lead

If the direct lead is the workhorse of journalism, the delayed lead is the showhorse. Used for feature stories and increasingly for news features, the delayed lead intentionally buries or delays the theme of the story. Some reporters call the delayed lead, when it appears in the story, a *kicker* because of the jolt it can sometimes present, as it does in this piece by Edna Buchanan of *The Miami Herald:*

Bad things happen to the husbands of the Widow Elkin.
Someone murdered husband No. 4, Cecil Elkin, apparently smashing his head with a frying pan as he watched "Family Feud" on TV.
Husband No. 3, Samuel Smilich, drowned in a weedy South Dade canal.
Husband No. 2, Lawrence Myers, cannot be found. . . .

Anyone out there who isn't hanging on every word? Notice the detail, the visual images Buchanan supplies: It was not just any pan but a frying pan with which No. 4 was dispatched. And he wasn't just watching television but "Family Feud." The canal where No. 3 was found was "weedy."

Buchanan goes on to write about Widow Elkin and then concludes the piece:

> It is the murder of her fourth husband
> that got Margaret Elkin in trouble. She is
> accused of trying to hire a beekeeper to
> kill him. The trial is set for Sept. 9.

The prosaic way to have started this story would have put the date set for the trial in the lead. But Buchanan's reporting turned up a remarkable series of events, and she gave us a modern morality tale with a climax.

The delayed lead is intended to pique our interest, to lure us into the story.

> Jack Loizeaux is a dentist of urban decay,
> a Mozart of dynamite, a guru of gravity.
> Like Joshua, he blows and the walls come
> tumbling down.

What does Loizeaux do? Our interest is aroused. The delayed lead purposely does not provide essential information to the reader or listener. This suspense is part of the attraction of the delayed lead. (Loizeaux runs a demolition company, revealed to us a few paragraphs later.)

"Children of Fire"   Delayed leads are often used on narratives. Here is how Thomas French of the *St. Petersburg Times* began the first of four articles about the children of Southeast Asian refugee families and their adjustment to life in the United States:

Quietly, she weaves among the other children. She stands at the edge of the playground and waits her turn at the swings. She runs with the other girls, all of them holding hands and laughing, their black hair blowing in the wind, their bodies forming a line that ripples and curves. When it is time to go inside and rest, she lies on her towel and stares out the classroom window, gazing at the ocean of blue sky where her mother will soon be going to live.

Mari Truong is in her first year at preschool. Her teachers keep close tabs on her and her situation at home. They worry in the way of all mothers, and they watch in the way of all teachers, and they make sure she knows she is not alone. In the middle of class, one of them pulls her onto her lap and brushes her hand across the child's cheek.

"You have to stay little," the teacher tells her. "Or else I'll miss you, and I'll cry."

Mari smiles, returns the hug, then slips away. She is only 4 and still shines with the radiance of the very young. Yet there is something elusive about her, something fierce that refuses to be pinned down, captured, categorized. Already she looks at the world with the eyes of someone who will never surrender.

They are astonishing, Mari's eyes. Impossibly big and round, sharp and piercing, so dark brown they almost blossom into black. Despite her age, they seem to be charged with decades of emotion and experience. What have her eyes seen that

Cherie Diez, *St. Petersburg Times*

Mari

Mari does not yet have words to explain? Do they carry memories, passed along in stories, of what her parents witnessed on the other side of the globe? Do they open at night, in her bed, and replay scenes from the refugee camp in Thailand where she was born? Does she see visions of her mother, like she used to be, before the doctors and the hospital and the wasting away?

For more about Mari and her friends, see **The Girl Whose Mother Lives in the Sky** in *NRW Plus.*

News Magazines   The delayed lead is a favorite approach of the news magazines for events that readers are already familiar with through online reports and newspaper and broadcast coverage. Here is how *U.S. News & World Report* began its long piece on the week's big story:

He had a temper so combustible that he once ejected Lana Turner and Ava Gardner from his Palm Springs house, screaming "Out, out, out!" and then hurling Gardner's cosmetics, clothes and records into the driveway. His buddies included mobsters and thugs, and he divided the world, Sicilian style, into friends—recipients of lavish gifts—and enemies. Face to face, the blue eyes could drill through you, and he could be unpredictable, foul-mouthed and crude, taking swings at anyone who got in his way.

Compare this beginning with the AP's direct lead on the same event:

LOS ANGELES (AP)—Frank Sinatra, the dashing teen idol who matured into the premier romantic balladeer of American popular music and the "Chairman of the Board" to his millions of fans, died Thursday night of a heart attack. He was 82.

On Track   Just any incident or anecdote will not do for the beginning. It must be consistent with the news point, the theme of the story. John Rebchook of the *El Paso Herald-Post* illustrates his point about a drive to collect unpaid traffic warrants by beginning with a specific driver who has avoided paying:

In less than three miles, Joseph L. Jody III ran six stop signs, changed lanes improperly four times, ran one red light, and drove 60 mph in a 30 mph zone—all without a driver's license. Two days later, he again drove without a driver's license. This time he ran a stop sign and drove 80 mph in a 45 mph zone. For his 16 moving violations Jody was fined $1,795.

He never paid. Police say that Jody has moved to Houston. Of the estimated 30,000 to 40,000 outstanding traffic warrants in

Example

police files, Jody owes the largest single amount.

Still, Jody's fines account for a small part of $500,000 owed to the city in unpaid traffic warrants.

In February, Mayor Jonathan Rogers began a crackdown on scofflaws in order to retrieve some $838,000 in unpaid warrants. As of mid-March, some $368,465 had been paid.   **Delayed Lead**

Leads on News Features

As the movement of news and information speeded up with all-day, all-news radio and TV stations and then online news, print publications with a much slower access to readers turned to writing techniques to attract readers who already had some idea of the event. One of the techniques is the news feature. The writer "featurizes" the breaking news event by putting a delayed lead on the story.

Custody   By the time *The New York Times* was on newsstands and doorsteps, everyone knew the end to a legal battle over custody of 2½-year-old Jessica. The Supreme Court had dashed the hopes of Jessica's adoptive parents to keep her. This meant the child would have to be turned over to her biological mother, who had given her up for adoption shortly after Jessica was born.

Don Terry put this lead on his news feature:

> BLAIRSTOWN, Iowa, Aug. 2—When she is grown up, maybe Jessica DeBoer will understand why the adults in her young but complicated life have caused so much hurt in the name of love.
>
> But starting today, the 2½-year-old has more immediate lessons to learn, namely how to live without the only people she has ever known as Mommy and Daddy, Roberta and Jan DeBoer of Ann Arbor, Mich.

Slaying   The Associated Press, which traditionally had taken a conservative approach to newswriting, put this beginning on a murder story:

> DECATUR, Ga., Jan. 26 (AP)—Aster Haile, an Ethiopian immigrant, was delighted when her cousin arranged a marriage for her—so excited that she bought clothes for her first date with the man and showed them off.
>
> But the day after the date, Ms. Haile called a friend and said that the man was too old and that she could not marry him. A day later, she was found dead along an Atlanta highway, shot in her head.

In the third paragraph is the arrest, which in times past would have been the lead to this story.

> The police have charged the man who set up the date, Arega Abraha, with murder. Mr. Abraha was arrested on Friday at the Cincinnati–Northern Kentucky International Airport on a Federal charge of unlawful flight to avoid prosecution.

Dr. Ruth's Blooper   In her story for *USA Today,* Barbara S. Rothschild describes a sex therapist's boo-boo with this delayed lead:

> There may finally be a question that embarrasses Dr. Ruth Westheimer. It's about the accuracy of her book.
>
> Teens who read the new sex book co-authored by the USA's best-known sex therapist could get more than they asked for.
>
> A baby, perhaps.
>
> *First Love: A Young People's Guide to Sexual Information,* by Dr. Ruth and education professor Nathan Kravetz, has a major error on page 195.
>
> In a chapter on contraception, the $3.50 book says it's "safe" to have sex the week before and the week of ovulation.
>
> It should read "unsafe"—since those are the times a woman is *most* likely to become pregnant. . . .

The Combo Lead

Some reporters have mastered a technique that combines the direct and delayed leads. The story begins with a few general sentences. Then the reporter hits the reader with a karate chop at the end of the first paragraph. Buchanan, the Pulitzer Prize–winning police reporter for *The Miami Herald,* is master of this kind of lead. Here are two typical Buchanan leads:

> The man she loved slapped her face. Furious, she says she told him never, ever to do that again. "What are you going to do, kill me?" he asked, and handed her a gun. "Here, kill me," he challenged. She did.
>
> On New Year's Eve, Charles Curzio stayed later than planned at his small TV repair shop to make sure customers would have their sets in time to watch the King Orange Jamboree Parade. His kindness cost his life.

Direct, with a Difference   Buchanan covered a story about an ex-convict, Gary Robinson, who pushed his way past a line at a fried-chicken outlet. He was persuaded to take his place in line, but when he reached the counter there was no fried chicken, only nuggets, whereupon he slugged the woman at the counter. In the ensuing fracas, a security guard shot Robinson. Buchanan's lead was:

> Gary Robinson died hungry.

Jim Hughes, *Daily News*

Adrift

The storm was expected, but it seemed to catch everyone by surprise. Direct or delayed lead on the story? Here's how the *Daily News* began its story:

Didn't anyone see this coming? And were emergency officials caught napping?

These questions surged to the top in the wake of the raging storm that caught most New Yorkers by surprise and produced startling scenes of motorists nearly drifting into the East River.

City officials were warned and should have passed their alert on to the public, the National Weather Service said last night.

Buchanan says her idea of a successful lead is one that could cause a reader who is breakfasting with his wife to "spit out his coffee, clutch his chest, and say, 'My god, Martha. Did you read this?' "

For her lead on a story about a drug smuggler who died when some of the cocaine-filled condoms that he had swallowed began to leak in his stomach, Buchanan wrote:

> His last meal was worth $30,000 and it
> killed him.

A Difficult Choice

Let us listen to Margaret as she mulls over the notes she has taken at a city council meeting:

There were 13 items on the agenda. Well, which were the important ones? I'll circle them in my notes—

- **General traffic program to route heavy trucks to Stanley Street and keep Main for lighter traffic.**
- **56 stop signs to be bought.**
- **Paving program for Kentucky Street that will later fit into the bypass.**
- **OK'd contract to White Painting Co. to paint City Hall, $28,000.**
- **Hired consulting firm for traffic study.**

Clearly, I need a direct lead here. Four of them seem to deal with traffic. Should I summarize them or should I pick out the truck route or the

traffic study? They seem equally important, so maybe I'll summarize the four. I'll drop the stop signs way down and then go into the painting contract.

She writes:

The City Council today took three significant actions to cope with the city's downtown traffic congestion.

The Council:

1. Approved the employment of Rande Associates, a consulting firm from Burbank, Calif., to make a study of traffic patterns.
2. Called for bids on paving 12 blocks of Kentucky Street, which is planned as part of a downtown bypass.
3. Endorsed the city traffic department's proposal to route heavy vehicles to Stanley Street away from Main Street.

Doubts   At this point, second thoughts assail Margaret. She remembers that the truck traffic issue has been argued for several months. Downtown merchants complained to the mayor about the truck traffic, and Stanley Street home owners petitioned the Council to keep the trucks away. Her newspaper and the local radio station have editorialized about it. In her haste to structure a complicated story, her news judgment went awry, she thinks. She writes:

The City Council today decided to route truck traffic to Stanley Street and away from downtown Freeport.

She is pleased with the lead she has written. But then more doubts. Maybe the overall pattern is more important than the single item about Stanley Street. After all, she thinks, the Council's three major actions will affect more people than those involved in the Stanley Street situation. Margaret decides that she needs some advice and she shows the city editor both leads.

"That's a tough one," he tells her. "Sometimes you flip a coin. Why don't you use your first lead and move up the third item, the one on Stanley Street, and put it first in the list?"

If we look closely at the two leads Margaret prepared, we notice that the single-element lead about the routing of truck traffic to Stanley Street denotes a specific action the council took. The summary lead about the council taking three "significant" actions to "cope with" traffic congestion is the reporter's conclusion or interpretation. Editors allow experienced reporters to interpret the news.

Good Reporting Makes for Good Leads

Many weak leads are the result of inadequate reporting. Consider this lead:

Barbara Elizabeth Foster, 19, St. Mary's University sophomore, will be queen of the city's Rose Festival.

Immediately, the city editor knows he is in for a tedious trek through the copy. The reporter failed to single out an interesting characteristic of the new queen to add to her age and year in school. Glancing through the copy, the editor notices that her mother was named Maid of Cotton 25 years ago. At the end of the story, there is a fleeting mention that her father enjoys gardening.

The editor runs his fingers through thinning hair. Masking his exasperation, he circles two sections and suggests to the reporter that there just might be a lead in the mother–daughter relationship and that a logical question to have asked the new queen was whether her father grew roses. Without good reporting no story can shine, much less be complete.

Color

Next, to the fourth of our four guides to writing leads: "Is there a colorful word or dramatic phrase that I can work into the lead?"

When Florida conducted the first execution in the United States in a dozen years, many reporters were assigned to the event. The nation had engaged in a debate about the morality of the death penalty. How best to put the Florida execution into words? Here is the lead Wayne King wrote for *The New York Times:*

> STARKE, Fla., May 25—The state of Florida trussed Arthur Spenkelink immobile in the electric chair this morning, dropped a black leather mask over his face and electrocuted him.

The choice of the verb "trussed" is inspired. Not only does it mean to secure tightly; its second definition is "to arrange for cooking by binding close the wings or legs of a fowl."

S-V-O

The basic construction of the lead should be subject-verb-object, S-V-O. That is, the lead should begin with the subject, should be closely followed by an active verb and should conclude with the object of the verb.

The S-V-O structure has an internal imperative: It directs the reporter to write simple sentences, sentences with one main clause. This kind of construction keeps leads short, another major requirement for a readable beginning.

Here is a direct lead using the S-V-O structure:

> SAN FRANCISCO—A federal judge has ordered the City of San Francisco to

---

Actors and Writers

Actors are told, "Act the verb." Writers are told, "Write the verb." Gerry Goldstein of *The Providence Journal* says, "We have the verb, and everything else is plaster."

A Poet's Perception

"Reduced to its essence, a good English sentence is a statement that an agent (the subject of the sentence) performed an action (the verb) upon something (the object)."

—*John Ciardi*

> hire 60 women patrol officers within the
> next 32 weeks.

S = judge   V = has ordered   O = San Francisco

Here is a delayed lead using the S-V-O structure:

> BALTIMORE—The Baltimore Orioles dared
> Barry Bonds to beat them.

S = Baltimore Orioles   V = dared   O = Barry Bonds

Most Used   Three-fourths or more of the sentences reporters write follow the S-V-O pattern. It parallels discourse, conforms to the command, "Write the way you talk." Also, it is the most direct way to answer the first two questions the reporter asks when trying to find the lead: What happened? Who was involved?

Lead Length

Reporters navigate between two divergent currents when they write their leads. One pulls them toward writing long as the reporter tries to include significant information. The other pushes them toward writing short because they know a short sentence is easier to understand than a long one.

Whatever their preference, reporters write short. The AP tells its reporters: "When a lead moves beyond 20–25 words it's time to start trimming." Some of the extra baggage that can be jettisoned:

- Unnecessary attribution.

- Compound sentences joined by *but* and *and.*

- Exact dates and times unless essential.

Momentous Events   When an event is compellingly important, all rules and guidelines are tossed aside and the writer is allowed to jam the facts into the first paragraph. Here's the lead in *The New York Times* after the Sept. 11, 2001, terror bombings in New York and Washington:

> Hijackers rammed jetliners into each of New York's World Trade Center towers yesterday, toppling both in a hellish storm of ash, glass, smoke and leaping victims, while a third jetliner crashed into the Pentagon in Virginia. There was no official count, but President Bush said thousands had perished, and in the immediate aftermath the calamity was already being ranked the worst and most audacious terror attack in American history.

Look at this lead in *The Washington Post* that runs 39 words long:

> Five men, one of whom said he is a former employee of the Central Intelligence Agency, were arrested at 2:30 a.m. yesterday in what authorities described as an elaborate plot to bug the office of the Democratic National Committee.

Not much artistry here, just the facts. But what facts. This was the opening salvo in the *Post*'s exposure of the Watergate scandal that led to the resignation of Richard Nixon from the presidency.

Readability

A reporter handed in this lead:

> The city planning office today recommended adding a section to the zoning code regulations on classification for residential use of property.

The editor puzzled over it and then instructed the reporter to say specifically what the proposed section would do. The reporter tried again:

> The city planning office today recommended that property zoned for two-acre, one-family dwellings be rezoned to allow the construction of cooperative apartment houses for middle- and low-income families.

The city editor suggested, "Let's take it a step further." "What's the point of the recommendation?" He answered his own question. "To change the code so ordinary people, not only the rich, can move into that wooded area north of town near the Greenwich Estates section. Let's try to get people into the lead." The reporter returned in 10 minutes with these two paragraphs:

> Low- and middle-income families may be able to buy apartments in suburban areas north of the city.
> This is the intention of a proposal made today by the city planning office. The recommendation to the city council would rezone property in the area from the present restrictions that permit only single-family dwellings on two-acre lots.

In this process of writing and rewriting, the reporter went from a jargon-loaded, impenetrable lead to one that stated succinctly and clearly what the proposed regulation was intended to bring about. Accuracy was not sacrificed for simplicity and readability.

> **Roundups**
> A *roundup* is a story that joins two or more events with a common theme. Roundups usually take multiple-element direct leads. They are often used for stories on traffic accidents, weather, crime. When the events are in different cities and are wrapped up in one story, the story is known as an "undated roundup." Here's an example:
> Torrential rains in Missouri and Kansas left five persons dead, hundreds homeless and crop losses of more than $1 million.

Readability Components

Readability stems from the ideas that make up the sentence, the order in which they are written and the words and phrases chosen to give the ideas expression:

Ideas: When possible, the lead should contain one idea. "The sentence is a single cry," says Sir Herbert Read, the British critic and author, in his *English Prose Style*. Too many ideas in a sentence make for heavy going. Also, the idea selected should be easy to grasp; complexities should be simplified.

Sentence order: The subject-verb-object construction is the most easily understood.

Word choice: Because the lead moves on its subject and verb, the choice of nouns and verbs is essential for readability. Whenever possible, the subject should be a concrete noun that the reader can hear, see, taste, feel or smell. It should stand for a name or a thing. The verb should be a colorful action verb that accelerates the reader to the object or makes the reader pause and think.

Summing Up

Good leads are based on the writer's clear understanding of the theme of the story. All else follows. This is why finding the theme is no.1 in our list of guidelines for writing readable leads:

1. Find the essential element(s) of the event.

2. Decide whether a direct or a delayed lead better suits the event.

3. If one element is outstanding, use a single-element lead. If more than one is, use a multiple-element lead.

4. Use the S-V-O construction.

5. Use concrete nouns and colorful action verbs.

6. Keep the lead short, under 30 or 35 words.

7. Make the lead readable, but do not sacrifice truthful and accurate reporting for readability.

Further Reading

Howarth, W. L. *The John McPhee Reader*. New York: Vintage Books, 1977.

Mills, Eleanor, with Kira Cochrane, eds. *Journalistas: 100 Years of the Best Reporting by Women Journalists*. New York: Carroll & Graf, 2005.

Women, long absent from newsrooms, have been flooding the media over the past two decades. This anthology reminds us of the great women reporters before the flood—Martha Gellhorn, Rebecca West, Susan Sontag, Mary McCarthy. Gellhorn reports from the Dachau concentration camp she visited at the end of World War II:

> We have all seen a great deal now; we have seen too many wars and too much violent dying; we have seen hospitals, bloody and messy as butcher shops; we have seen the dead like bundles lying on all the roads of half the earth. But nowhere was there anything like this. Nothing about war was ever as insanely wicked as these starved and outraged, naked, nameless dead.

Murray, Donald. *Writing for Your Readers*. Chester, Conn.: The Globe Pequot Press, 1983.

6 Story Structure

Preview

Planning precedes writing. Each sentence, every paragraph is purposely placed. Even while reporting, reporters try to visualize the shape and content of their stories.

Most news stories have a linear structure:

- The beginning includes a summary of the most important material.
- The remainder of the story amplifies, buttresses, gives examples and explains the beginning. It also contains background and secondary material.

Kevin Hann, *The Toronto Sun*

An infant is given life-saving breath—a single-element story.

Writing must move.
Provide the momentum.

First the idea. Then the words.

As the young reporter struggled with his story, he recalled this advice that his city editor gave him the day before. Having written the obituary of a banker in 45 minutes, he was proud of his speed. But the editor said that the story was disorganized, without a focus. "Think the story through before you write," he told the reporter. The reporter read his story carefully, keeping in mind his editor's comment. Yes, he was writing without a firm idea of what he wanted to say and how it would fit together.

Suddenly, he was struck by what he had just told himself: "What do I want to say? Where do I put it?" That was the key to putting his notes into some kind of structured shape.

- What do I want to say?
- Where does it go?

This reporter's discovery is made all the time by young journalists. Usually, it is followed by another revelation: The news story form or structure is simple:

- The lead.
- The material that explains and amplifies the lead.
- The necessary background.
- The secondary or less important material.

The Main Idea

The city editor's advice about thinking before writing has been offered to generations of students. As an essay by Edward Everett Hale in the *Fifth Reader,* a grade school textbook of the 1880s, puts it, "In learning to write, our first rule is: '*Know what you want to say.*'" Hale had a second rule: "*Say it.* That is, do not begin by saying something else which you think will lead up to what you want to say."

Every writer who has written about the writer's craft—whether journalist, poet or novelist—has understood these first principles of writing. George Orwell, the British journalist and novelist, wrote that the first question scrupulous writers ask themselves before writing is, "What am I trying to say?" The next step is to find the appropriate form or structure for what you want to say.

The Structure

In *The Elements of Style,* the "little book" that generations of college students have used, authors William Strunk Jr. and E.B. White begin their section on writing this way: "Choose a suitable design and hold to it." They continue: "A basic structural design underlies every kind of writing. . . . The first principle of composition, therefore, is to foresee or determine the shape of what is to come, and pursue that shape."

Too often reporters start to write without a plan in mind. As a result, their stories lack focus. Henry Fairlie, a British journalist, calls this deficiency "shapelessness." He attributes it to "an intellectual inability, on the part both of the reporter and copy editor, to master the story," which must be put to use "before writing."

Eight Steps to the Organized Story

1. Identify the focus or main idea from notes.

2. Locate the material that supports, explains, amplifies the main idea.

3. Organize the secondary material in order of importance.

4. As you write, make sure the separate elements are linked with transitions.

5. Read the completed copy to make sure you have buttressed, documented, explained the lead high in the story.

The inability to fix on the point causes writers to go on and on and on. They believe that as long as they keep going, they will hit on something newsworthy. They are like Lewis Carroll's Alice in her conversation with the Cheshire Cat:

"Would you tell me, please, which way I ought to go from here?"

"That depends a good deal on where you want to get to," said the Cat.

"I don't much care where—" said Alice.

"Then it doesn't matter which way you go," said the Cat.

"—so long as I get somewhere," Alice added as an explanation.

"Oh, you're sure to do that," said the Cat, "if you only walk long enough."

No editor will permit a writer to wander aimlessly through a story on the way to *somewhere*.

6. Read the completed copy for accuracy, brevity, clarity.

7. Read the completed copy for grammar, style, word usage.

8. If steps 5 through 7 indicate problems—and they usually do turn up—rewrite.

The Single-Element Story

A story that consists of one important action or is based on one major fact or idea is a single-element story. Also known as the single-incident story, it is probably the story form most often used. The story requires:

- Lead.

- Explanatory and amplifying material.

- Background (if necessary).

- Secondary material (if any).

For broadcast and online stories, the background and secondary material may be ignored or mentioned briefly.

Here's the lead to a newspaper story:

ST. LOUIS—A picturesque lake in a nearby suburb has vanished in a matter of days, leaving behind a 50-yard smelly sinkhole and thousands of flopping fish among pop cans and other garbage.

The story continued for eight paragraphs. The online version consisted of two sentences:

A sinkhole has swallowed what was once a picturesque lake near St. Louis. Left behind were thousands of dying fish and trash that had littered the lake bottom.

Every so often, a reporter finds that the lead needs to include two or three themes. An election results in two major rebuffs to a governor (two-element lead);

a study finds three causes of death and disability from heart disease (three-element lead). Complicated as these may sound, they are handled with the same approach as the single-element story. Watch.

Two-Element Story

Here are 11 paragraphs from an election story in the *Daily News*. The story is based on two major themes: (A) rejection of the bond issue and (B) Republican control of the legislature. The reporter uses the effect of the voting on Gov. Hughes to attract readers to the story of the balloting:

Gov. Hughes Loses Bonds & Legislature

by Joseph McNamara

(1) New Jersey Gov. Richard J. Hughes took a shellacking all around in yesterday's statewide election. The voters rejected the $750 million bond issue proposal on which he had hung much of his political prestige, and the Republicans gained control of both houses of the Legislature.

(2) Hughes, who had warned during the campaign that if the bond issue were defeated he would ask the Legislature in January for a state income tax and sales tax to meet the state's financial needs, announced early today that he "may have to do some rethinking" about the size of the need. And he made it clear that the "rethinking" would increase his estimate of the amount required.

(3) "I accept the verdict rendered by the people," he said in a written statement.

Behind from the Start

(4) The bond issue proposal, which was broken into two questions—one on institutions and the other on roads—trailed from the time the polls closed at 8 p.m. With the count in from 4,238 of the state's 4,533 districts, the tally early today was:

(5) Institutions: No, 868,586; Yes, 736,967.

(6) Highways: No, 866,204; Yes, 681,059.

(7) As a measure of Hughes' defeat, in the Democrats' Hudson County stronghold—

where the Governor had hoped for a plurality of 150,000—he got only a 100,501 to 64,752 vote in favor of the institutional bonds and 93,654 to 66,099 in favor of the highway bonds.

(8) Four other referendums had no great opposition, and passed easily. They were on voter residency requirements, a tax break on farm land and a change in exemptions from the ratables to the finished tax for both veterans and the elderly.

(9) The Republicans have controlled the State Senate for the last half century, and smashing victories yesterday in crucial Essex, Burlington and Camden Counties increased their majority—which had shrunk to a hairsbreadth 11–10—to two-thirds.

(10) Democrats swamped in the avalanche included Gov. Hughes' brother-in-law Sen. Edward J. Hulse of Burlington County. He was unseated by Republican Edwin B. Forsythe who ran up a convincing 6,000-vote majority.

(11) In populous Essex County, Republican C. Robert Sarcone defeated Democrat Elmer M. Matthews—who conceded shortly after 11 p.m. without waiting for the final count. And in Camden County, Republican Frederick J. Scholz unseated incumbent Joseph W. Cowgill. . . .

Analysis: 2 Elements

(1) The lead contains a colloquial phrase in the first sentence to emphasize the effect of the voting. The second sentence summarizes the two themes, A and B.

(2–7) These six paragraphs refer to theme A. In 2, the reporter gives a possible consequence of the loss of the bond issue.

In any election, vote tallies are essential, and the reporter supplies them in 5 and 6, which set up a good example in 7 of the extent of the governor's shellacking.

(8) Secondary information about other items on the ballot.

(9–11) Elaboration of theme B. Examples of specific races are given.

Three-Element Story

The following is an example of a story that begins with a three-element lead. The reporter would have singled out one element had she thought that one was the most important of the three. She decided the three were of equal importance.

Analysis: 3 Elements

(1) The lead has a three-part theme: A study concludes that smoking, A, overweight, B, and physical inactivity, C, increase risk of heart disease.

(2) Brody tells the reader the source of the material and where it came from and then gives more information about theme A.

(3) More detail on A.

(4) Here she jumps to C, physical inactivity. It might have been better to have followed the A, B, C order.

(5) More on physical inactivity.

(6) Brody moves on to theme B, overweight.

(7) More on B; its relationship to A and C.

(8) Brody considered this secondary information.

A less cluttered lead might have put the attribution in the second paragraph. The lead would begin: "Smoking, an overweight condition and physical inactivity. . . ."

Study Links 3 Factors to Heart Ills

By Jane E. Brody

(1) A new study conducted among 110,000 adult members of the Health Insurance Plan of Greater New York has once again demonstrated that smoking, an overweight condition and physical inactivity are associated with a greatly increased risk of death and disability from heart disease.

(2) The study, published yesterday in the June issue of The American Journal of Public Health, reported that men and women who smoke cigarettes face twice the risk of suffering a first heart attack as do non-smokers.

(3) The annual incidence of first heart attacks among pipe and cigar smokers was also found to be higher than among non-smokers, but not as high as among cigarette smokers.

(4) Men who are "least active," both on and off the job, are twice as likely as "moderately active" men to suffer a first heart attack and four times as likely to suffer a fatal heart attack.

(5) Men who were classified as "most active" showed no advantage in terms of heart attack rate over men considered "moderately active." The authors reported that other differences between active and inactive men, such as the amount they smoked, could not account for their different heart attack rates.

(6) The heavier men in the study had a 50 percent greater risk of suffering a first heart attack than the lighter-weight men. An increased risk was also found among women who had gained a lot of weight since age 25.

(7) None of the differences in risk associated with weight could be explained on the basis of variations in smoking and exercise habits, the authors stated.

(8) The incidence of heart attacks was also found to be higher among white men than among non-whites and among Jewish men than among white Protestants and Catholics. But the heart attack rate among Jewish women was not markedly different from that among non-Jewish women.

—The New York Times

Some reporters might have found a lead in the information Brody places in the last paragraph. Although most events have obvious leads, a number do not. News judgment is essential on multiple-element stories, and judgments differ. Brody was on target. The last paragraph is secondary.

Brody's story also illustrates another basic guideline for structuring a story: Put related material together.

Story Units

In organizing their stories, news writers move from one theme to another in the order of the importance of the subjects or themes. The lead is elaborated first, and then the next-most-important theme is stated and then elaborated and explained. The rule is: Put everything about the same subject in the same place.

When his editor explained the rule "like things together" to the journalist Dwight Macdonald, his first reaction was, "Obviously." His second, he said, was, "But why didn't it ever occur to me?" His third was, "It was one of those profound banalities 'everybody knows'—after they've been told. It was the climax of my journalistic education."

The Inverted Pyramid

The story structure explained in this chapter—important elements at the beginning, less important at the end—has for decades been taught to students as the "inverted pyramid" form. The term can be misleading. An inverted pyramid is an unbalanced monolith, a huge top teetering on a pinpoint base. It is a monstrous image for journalists, for the top of a story should be deft and pointed. Discard the picture of this precariously balanced chunk and remember that all it means is that the most important material is usually placed at the beginning of the story and the less important material is placed at the end.

The news story takes its shape from the requirements and limitations of the craft as measured by the clock—a silent but overwhelming presence—and the available space and time for copy. Given these realities, most stories must be written in such a way that they can be handled quickly and efficiently. If the 10 inches of available space suddenly shrinks to 8 and the 40 seconds of airtime to 20, no problem. The story structure makes it possible to cut the bottom two paragraphs without losing key information.

Meets Needs If the only justification for the standard news story form were its utility to the people writing and editing the news, it would not have stood up over the years, even for as modern a media outlet as online journalism. The form has persisted because it meets the needs of media users. People usually want to know what happened as soon as the story begins to unfold. If it is important and interesting, they will pay attention. Otherwise, they turn elsewhere. People are too busy to tarry without reward.

Sometimes the pleasure may come from suspense, a holding of the breath until the climax is revealed deep in the story. When the reporter senses that this kind of structure is appropriate for the event, a delayed lead will be used.

News forms may be said to be utilitarian or pragmatic, in the tradition of the hustle and bustle of American life. But there is also an aesthetic component in the standard news form that its detractors sometimes fail to detect. If the expression "form follows function" implies beauty in the finished work, then the news story is a work of art, minor as it may be. The news story meets the demands of art: It reveals a harmony of design.

Occasionally, the delight in the story's design may come from suspense, the deliberate withholding of key information. Everyone loves a good story,

Here is a story structure the *Journal* uses:

Anecdote: Begin with an example or illustration of the theme.

Explicit statement of theme: The lead. It should be no lower than the sixth paragraph. Sometimes this paragraph is called the *nut graph*.

Statement of the significance of the theme: Answers the reader's question, "Why should I be reading this?"

Details: Proof, elaboration of the theme.

Answers to reader's questions: Why is this happening? What is being done about it?

and journalists are happy to provide one—when the event makes storytelling appropriate.

Storytelling

The storytelling form—also known as narrative writing—is simple enough: Invite the reader, listener, viewer into the piece with an interesting tidbit:

Driving to Easter services yesterday about 1:45 p.m., James Freeman saw a man standing on the South Street bridge.

"I knew he wanted to jump," said Freeman. "I made a U-turn right on the bridge and stopped traffic."

Freeman left his wife, his granddaughter and four foster children—all dressed in their Easter finery—watching from their minivan. Then, Freeman walked toward the lone figure staring down into the Schuykill 60 feet below.

This is how Jere Downs of *The Philadelphia Inquirer* began a story. The reader is hooked. Will Freeman talk the would-be suicide into backing off? She follows Freeman as he approaches and talks to the man:

"I've been where you want to go," Freeman said he told the man. "Whatever it is, it's not worth it."

Freeman said the man, in his mid-40s, looked at him with a pinched face lined with tears.

Then the man looked back across the river toward the University of Pennsylvania campus.

"I gotta do it," Freeman recalled saying. "Nobody loves me. I'm a Vietnam vet. My being here is like a burden on everybody."

Downs has used a column of type to this point, and she goes on to describe how others stopped their cars to help. A minister approached the distraught man and said to him, "You're looking down when you should be looking up to God."

The Climax   Finally, in the 24th paragraph, the man climbs down from the concrete abutment.

(Postscript: A few days later, Downs received a handwritten note in the mail. "I enclose a check which I made out to you. Would you possibly be able to funnel this money in some way to allow Mr. X to receive some quality psychotherapy.

I must remain anonymous. My reasons for doing this are (1) I was once where Mr. X was. (2) I have come back and am a successful businessman. Thank you for writing a terrific article." The check was for $1,000.)

Structure Essential

Beginners love the storytelling form. *Free at last,* they shout. *Free of that dull and boring inverted pyramid. Free to express myself.*

Sorry to throw cold water on the flames of creativity, but the storytelling form is as demanding in its structure as is the straight news story.

Both forms require the writer to select the major theme, and both demand that the writer be scrupulous in writing the lead. We know that the major theme goes in the lead of the straight news story. In the narrative form, the incident or example selected to begin the piece must fit neatly into the theme. And woe to the writer who decides to put a delayed lead on a straight news story.

Unexpected Columnists are fond of storytelling. But even with the freedom columnists are granted, they follow the rule that the beginning of the column must lead directly to the point of the piece. Look at how John Kass of the *Chicago Tribune* begins this column:

> The tiny old man had lived into his 90s. Even when he was alive, he was barely 5 feet tall, and when I saw him in his coffin, he looked tinier still.
>
> He was shriveled, like a gnome, the size of a boy, with wispy old man's hair and those folded, wrinkled hands. A silver crucifix was pinned to the satin of his coffin. Another larger crucifix on the wall looked down on the peaceful old guy who died naturally.

These two paragraphs seem an elegy for a decent fellow who has lived a life as quiet as the mortuary parlor in which his coffin lay.

But then Kass counterpunches, telling us what we least expected:

> And that's odd to think Marshall Caifano would get to die a natural death.
>
> Because in life he was said to favor the shotgun and the car bomb, as one of the most notorious hit men in the history of the Chicago outfit.

Online Writing

Mark Fitzgerald of *Editor&Publisher* says, "The computer screen is notoriously inhospitable to long stories. Even a story that amounts to just 10 inches on the newspaper page seems endless on a computer screen."

Studies of online news readers indicate that they are attracted by headlines and brief summaries and will read a short piece. "Web readers tend to be impatient and tend to skim," says John Leach, online editor for *The Arizona Republic.* Leach says that studies of the readership of azcentral.co, his newspaper's Web site, have shown that readers will spend no more than two minutes on an online story. "Brevity is essential," he says.

The story form preferred by Web writers is our old friend the inverted pyramid style in which the key elements of the event are placed at the beginning of the story. "Our readers want to get straight to the heart of the story," says Leach. "An 18-year-old reader describes what he wants from an online news site as 'the straight dump,' which an older reader might describe as 'just the facts ma'am.'"

MSNBC.com uses a story form it calls the Model T. The top of the T is a summary lead that gives the reader the point of the story at once. The vertical part of the T, the body of the story, can be told in any fashion the writer finds appropriate—straight news story, feature or narrative.

Ruth Gersh, editor of multimedia services at the AP, says the screen "seems to beg for a simpler writing style." Here's an example of the style Gersh is talking about. We saw the lead to this story in Chapter 5 under the heading **Direct Lead.** Here is the lead again and several paragraphs. Note the informal, colloquial style of writing:

> NEW YORK—Oprah Winfrey says her lawyers shouldn't have gone after the man who is trying to promote her as a candidate for president.
>
> Not because she's running, mind you.
>
> "I feel flattered by it," the 52-year-old talk-show host told the Associated Press on Monday. "My lawyers overreacted, I think, by sending him a cease-and-desist order because it really is a flattering thing."
>
> It should have been handled in a telephone call, said Winfrey, who said she's thinking of calling Patrick Crowe of Kansas City, Mo, herself.

The General, Then the Specific

The best advice she received from an editor, a reporter remarked, was "Follow every generality with a specific."

Every story has a logical structure, the editor told her, of general to specific. For example, when a council member says that next year's budget will set a record high, the reporter asks how high that will be, what the amount will be:

> Riggio said next year's budget will set "a record high." He estimated it would amount to $725 million.

Here's another example:

Miles said, "Vince Lombardi was wrong when he said that winning is everything." It's more important, Miles said, to develop an athlete's sense of fair play and his or her love of sport.

Specific-to-General

The reverse story structure is also used when the specific highlights the generality. This structure is often used for news features.

> Antoinette Trotter couldn't figure out what was wrong with her boy. Shawn seemed so clumsy, the way he dropped dishes and sent cups clattering to the floor. He was restless, always squirming at the dinner table, unable to sit still.

This is the way Stephanie Armour began her story about workers who bring toxins from the job into their homes, putting family members in danger. Here is how the *USA Today* story continued:

Concerned, the mother brought the 6-year-old to doctors, who ran tests and told her that Shawn's blood contained nearly four times the acceptable level of lead for children, according to a lawsuit filed by the family.

Antoinette was surprised, but she was even more stunned when investigators told her why.

The boy, they told her, was being poisoned by her husband's job.

Shawn's father, Lashla, repaired and rebuilt batteries, work that brought him into contact with lead dust. . . .

After seven paragraphs of the specifics of the Trotter family's problem, Armour presents her generality:

In a health risk that is often overlooked and undocumented, people of all ages are being exposed to workplace hazards so potent that they can change cell structures, slow mental development and unleash life-threatening tumors. But these are people who have never set foot in the workplaces that are poisoning them. All have been exposed to toxins that their family members unknowingly brought home from the job.

DAD: Dialogue, Action, Description

To the news writer, form and content are one. Each reinforces the other. No matter how well-reported a story is, if it zigs here and zags there, the reader or viewer will not bother to try to make sense out of the chaos. And if the story lacks dialogue, action or description, the bored reader will move on.

Dialogue, action, description: DAD. Let's look at a story that contains these essential elements, a religion story. This story by Jena Heath that appeared in *The Charlotte Observer* stirred a tempest.

Letters showered down on the newspaper for a month, and Heath received calls of support and outrage from Virginia and the District of Columbia as well as from North Carolina after the piece was put on the Knight-Ridder wire and run on the front page of the religion section of *The Washington Post.*

Women Priests

Heath thought it was time to write something about the role of women in the Catholic Church, and her editor suggested she talk to women who want to be priests. Newsroom colleagues came up with the names of people Heath could interview.

Heath worked on the story for two weeks. The story ran at the top of page 1 of the Sunday newspaper. Look at how Heath blends description, action and dialogue in these opening paragraphs:

Robert Lahser, *The Charlotte Observer*

Sister Carol Symons

It was seven winters ago, but Sister Carol Symons hasn't forgotten.

She was ministering to the sick in Boone. The day the call came, the town's only priest was away. Sister Carol raced the seven minutes from her home to the hospital, where she found anguish. A Mexican migrant worker had given birth to a stillborn girl.

As she entered the dimly lit recovery room, the nun murmured to the woman's husband, tears glistening on his face. She walked across the room and took the woman's hand. Looking up from her stretcher, the woman choked out the words in Spanish.

Quiero confesar mis pecados, she pleaded. I want to confess my sins.

Sister Carol couldn't help. In the Roman Catholic Church, only priests can offer the peace of absolution.

"For me, the heart of the story is that there I was, a person in ministry and I couldn't help her," Sister Carol said.

Change is coming for Catholic women, not fast enough for some, too fast for others. One door, though, remains firmly shut: the door to the priesthood.

The image of a female priest at the altar is an emotional one for Catholics. Traditionalists say Jesus chose 12 men as his disciples, that Jesus himself was a man and that the church's long history of an all-male clergy means the priesthood was never intended for women.

Many Catholic women, meanwhile, have seen female priests in the Episcopalian Church since 1976, when it began ordaining women. They've seen female rabbis since 1972 and a host of female ministers, including Southern Baptists, since 1964.

Yet Catholic women who feel called to the priesthood say they must live with the pain of knowing they cannot serve God as their hearts dictate.

Mission

"My job is to amplify the voices of those who often go unheard. It is vital that everyone understands how our laws and policies actually affect people's lives, so a large part of my work as a journalist has been to help people voice concerns and express fears about circumstances they confront."

—*Eric Newhouse*

Alcoholism

Eric Newhouse's yearlong series in the *Great Falls* (Mont.) *Tribune,* "Alcohol, Cradle to Grave," begins with a scene at the Great Falls Rescue Mission, "which has been called the final pit stop before the graveyard for those unable to handle their addictions," Newhouse writes.

Breakfast is at 6 a.m. Today it's grits and eggs, and clients are expected to clean up the cafeteria and sweep out the dayroom before they head out. . . .

Tom Jerome, a former ranch hand from Miles City, is sitting on a bench in the Rescue Mission, already drunk and waiting for coffee at 9 a.m. Considering the Mission's rules, how did he spend the night there?

"I didn't," he says. "I usually spend the nights out."

But the gray-tiled dayroom can be a dry place, so Jerome periodically slips out into the alley where he has a cache of beer waiting for him.

When the reporter is conscious—as Newhouse was—of the need to organize the story around dialogue, action and description, the story tends to write itself. Newhouse's series won a Pulitzer Prize.

For more stories from Newhouse's series and his explanation of how the series came about and how he did his reporting, see **Alcohol: Cradle to Grave** in *NRW Plus*.

Physical Description   Let's walk into Langan's, an Irish bar in New York City, with John Cassidy, who is doing a profile for *The New Yorker* of journalist Steve Dunleavy, at 62 a veteran of decades of opinion-laced journalism. Cassidy describes Dunleavy's face: "creased like an old pair of leather shoes." Cassidy approaches Dunleavy:

> He was smartly dressed, in a gray three-piece suit, white monogrammed shirt with French cuffs, gold cufflinks, red silk tie, and shiny black shoes. His pallor was that of a rotting cod. His silver pompadour, which makes him resemble an aging Elvis, shot from his crown in glorious defiance of taste and gravity

We've been discussing writing. As you know, writing and reporting are interlocked. Journalists have a saying that a story cannot be any better than the reporting behind it, by which they mean that no amount of classy and clever writing can disguise a poorly reported story. Readers and viewers want relevant, timely information. It's time we looked at some basics about reporting.

Story Necessities

Take any event and play the reporter's game. What are the necessary facts for an automobile accident story, a fire story, an obituary? Let us say an automobile hits a child. What must the story include? It will have to contain the child's name, age and address; the driver's name, age, address and occupation; the circumstances and location of the accident; the extent of the child's injuries; the action, if any, taken against the motorist.

Description
"I am a great believer in description. I try to make the reader feel that he can see and taste and smell and touch and hear whatever the incident is. I've just listed the five senses."
—*Everett Allen*, The Standard Times

Given an assignment, the reporter has in mind a list of necessities for the story. The necessities guide the reporter's observations and direct the questions he or she will ask of sources. But there can be a problem.

Seeing the Differences Unless the reporter can spot the significant differences between stories of a similar type, one accident story will be like another, one obituary like a dozen others. The reporter on the "automobile hits child" story tries to discover the unusual or unique aspects of the event that should be given priority: Was the youngster playing? If so, was he or she running after a ball, playing hide-and-seek? Was the child looking for a dog, cat, younger brother? Was the child crossing the street to go to school? How seriously was the child injured? Will the youngster be able to walk normally?

Once the reporter has (a) thought about the necessities of stories he or she is assigned and (b) sought out the facts that differentiate this story from others like it, the story is on its way to being written. The final step is to construct a lead around the important or unique element. There is no simple formula for determining what should go into the lead. The criteria for news we developed in Chapter 2 are helpful.

News Judgment Basically, news judgment is an exercise in logical thinking. When a fire destroys a hotel worth $30 million and takes 14 lives, the reporter focuses the lead and structures the story around the lives lost, not the destruction of the hotel, no matter how costly. The reporter reasons that life cannot be equated with money. If no one was killed or hurt in the fire, then the significance may well be that it was a costly structure, not a three-story hotel for transients that had seen better times. If there were no injuries and the hotel had some historical interest, the lead might be that a landmark in town was destroyed by fire. Finally, if no one was hurt and the hotel was a small, old building like many others in town, the fire would rate only two or three paragraphs and a single sentence, maybe two, on the 11 p.m. newscast.

Covering a Strike Threat

Let's watch a reporter assigned to the education beat. Told to check a report that public school teachers might not report for work next fall, she thinks of several essential questions that will guide her reporting:

- Is the report true?
- How many teachers and children are involved?
- What are the reasons for the strike?
- When will the decision be made about whether to strike?
- What are the responses of authorities to the threat?
- What plans are being made for the students should there be a strike?

The answers to these questions and other observations made during her reporting are the building blocks for the story. The reporter knows what her lead will be from the minute she receives the assignment—the possibility of a teacher strike and schools not opening.

These are the first few paragraphs of the story she writes:

> Teachers in all 15 public schools in the city today threatened to strike next September unless they are given an 8 percent wage increase in next year's contract.
>
> Spokesmen for the local unit of the American Federation of Teachers, which represents 780 Freeport school teachers, said the strike threat will be presented to the City Board of Education at Thursday's negotiating session.
>
> More than 15,000 school children would be affected by a strike.

Notice that our reporter answered several of her questions in the first few paragraphs of her story.

When the Thursday session led to no resolution of the issue, the reporter's story about this development began this way:

> The possibility of a strike of public school teachers next September loomed larger today when six hours of contract talks failed to settle the wage issue.
>
> The teachers' union seeks an 8 percent pay increase over the current pay levels for next year's contract. The school board has offered 4 percent.
>
> More than 15,000 school children would be affected by a strike.
>
> The nonstop discussion between the union and the city school board failed to produce a settlement, said Herbert Wechsler, the president of the local unit of the American Federation of Teachers. The union, which represents the city's 780 public school teachers, issued its strike threat Tuesday and presented it formally at today's session.
>
> Joseph Foremen, the state superintendent of education, who is attending the contract talks at the invitation of both sides, said:
>
> "The two groups are widely separated. We need a cooling-off period. Unless one side or the other makes some kind of concession, we may have no teachers in the schools Sept. 9. And a concession is the last thing on their minds now."

Summing Up

A reporter with more than 30 years of experience on California newspapers told a beginner, "Those of us who survive work on our stories from the minute we get the assignment." The work the reporter is talking about takes the form of projecting at each level of reporting and writing the story as it will appear in its final form.

Reporters try to visualize and structure their stories at these stages:

• Immediately on receiving the assignment.

• While gathering material at the event.

• Before writing.

• During writing.

Further Reading

Bellows, Jim. *The Last Editor: How I Saved The New York Times, The Washington Post, and the Los Angeles Times from Dullness and Complacency.* Kansas City: Andrews McPeel Publishing, 2002.

> Anecdotes tumble over each other as Bellows recalls his half a century of "kamikaze journalism" that included guiding some of the nation's major newspapers.

Snyder, Louis L., and Richard B. Morris. *A Treasury of Great Reporting.* New York: Simon & Schuster, 1949.

Wilson, Ellen. *The Purple Decades: A Reader.* New York: Farrar, Straus and Giroux, 1982.

Preview

The well-written story:

- Makes its point clearly.
- Engages the reader, viewer or listener with human-interest material, quotations, incidents and examples.
- Sets a pace and has a style appropriate to the event or personality being described.
- Satisfies the viewer, listener or reader that the story is complete and is truthful.

Mike Roemer
Sentences clear and crisp as a winter's morn.

Journalists write to be read and to be heard. They know that unless their stories are clear, interesting and well written their readers, viewers and listeners will move on to something else. To attract, keep and satisfy this fickle public, journalists have developed ways of telling stories that make their stories compelling.

Journalists know that good writing helps people visualize the event, the personality being profiled, that good writing moves people to the scene. George Orwell, whose writing influenced and inspired many journalists, said, "Good prose is like a window pane." The window pane, unlike the stained glass window, does not call attention to itself. Good writing calls attention to the people in the story, the event, the information.

Writers Write . . . and Read, Too

The men and women who write for a living—whether journalists, poets, novelists or essayists—work at learning and mastering their trade. They have an "idea of craft," as the writer-teacher Frank Kermode puts it, a drive toward "doing things right, making them accurate and shapely, like a pot or a chair."

Every writer who is familiar with the agony of chasing elusive words knows that words can be brought to life only by strenuous and continued effort. The aim

Don't tell us when you can show us.

Love Affair
"Reading usually precedes writing. And the impulse to write is almost always fired by reading. Reading, the love of reading, is what makes you dream of becoming a writer."
—*Susan Sontag*

is perfection of expression, the absolute fit of words to the event. Walt Whitman, journalist and poet, described the writer's goal this way:

> A perfect writer would make words sing, dance, kiss, do the male and female act, bear children, weep, bleed, rage, stab, steal, fire cannon, steer ships, sack cities. . . .

Poet or police reporter, the writer is engaged in a struggle to find words and phrases to match his or her observations. When Ernest Hemingway covered the police court for the *Kansas City Star,* he would take his notes home and work over them to simplify the testimony of witnesses until he had captured in a few words the essence of the evidence. He would use the language he had heard in court.

This style is evident in the ending to *A Farewell to Arms.* Frederic has just pushed the nurses out of the room where Catherine has died so that he can be alone with her:

> But after I had got them out and shut the door and turned off the light it wasn't any good. It was like saying good-bye to a statue. After a while I went out and left the hospital and walked back to the hotel in the rain.

Writers Teach Writers   Journalists read widely to master style and technique, to learn the tricks of the writer's trade. Stephen King, the prolific writer of best-selling horror stories, says, "Writing is a matter of exercise . . . if you write for an hour and a half a day for ten years you're gonna turn into a good writer." In his book *On Writing, A Memoir of the Craft,* King lists first in his suggestions for aspiring writers, "Read a lot of books."

"You can't write well if you don't read," says veteran reporter Joe Galloway. "Don't show me your resumé," he says of job applicants. "Show me your library card." The writing coach Don Murray says, "Professional writers never learn to write; they continue to learn writing all their professional lives. The good writer is forever a student of writing."

Doing It Right—in a Hurry

Novelist or journalist, said Hal Boyle, for years one of the AP's top reporters, the writer has the same task: "The recognition of truth and the clear statement of it are the first duties of an able and honest writer."

Unlike the novelist, the journalist cannot spend hours in the search for the right word, a couple of days to devise a beguiling beginning. The journalist is asked to write—and to write well—now, quickly, before the clock's hands sweep to the inexorable deadline. No other writer is asked to perform with such speed. Yet journalists manage to do the job, creating stories that are, in Kermode's words, "accurate and shapely."

Preliminaries

It is impossible to write for the public unless you understand what you are writing about. Comprehension precedes clarity. You cannot "be wholly clear about something you don't understand," says John Kenneth Galbraith, the Harvard economist whose books and articles about what is called "the dismal science" of economics are models of clarity.

Reach the Reader
"The key questions are: Is this stuff interesting? Does it move, touch, anger, tickle, surprise, sadden or inform? If it does you are in for a treat, a good read."
—*Thomasine Berg*, The Providence Journal

With a firm grip on writing mechanics and the theme clearly in mind, the story will spin out of the computer. Well, almost.

A reminder: Don't write writing. Don't make clever prose the purpose of your writing. Your job is to communicate information. "I never heard a reader praise the quality of writing," says Henry McNulty, for many years the ombudsman for *The Hartford Courant.* "They are only interested in the facts in a story and their accuracy." Write well, the best you can to attract and retain readers, listeners and viewers. But never at the expense of a truthful telling of the story.

Writers who try to write well are always asking themselves whether the words they are using make their stories clear and direct. When they are dissatisfied with the answer, they revise and rewrite. An interviewer asked Hemingway what the problem was that caused him to rewrite the last paragraph of *A Farewell to Arms* 39 times. Hemingway replied, "Getting the words right."

Show, Don't Tell

In our effort to find some guides to help us write well, we might start with Leo Tolstoy who, in describing the strength of his masterwork *War and Peace,* said, "I don't tell; I don't explain. I show; I let my characters talk for me."

Journalists rediscover Tolstoy's maxim in newsrooms everywhere. Rick Bragg recalls that as a new reporter in Birmingham a senior editor would take him aside and tell him his "one basic rule of good writing: Show me, don't tell me. Let me see what you see. Paint me a picture. Then I'll follow you anywhere, even past the jump."

Make Pictures

Picture-painting helps the writer make his or her point. Look at how *Daily News* reporter Dave Goldiner puts the reader at the scene of the Sept. 11 World Trade Center terror bombing:

Tears streaming down his face, Fire Lt. Vincent Boura stumbled yesterday out of The Pit—and wondered if anything would ever be the same.

Along with thousands of other soot-covered firefighters, Boura spent hour after exhausting hour climbing in and out of a huge hole rescuers carved into the World Trade Center rubble.

They rappelled down 30-foot ropes as bright sunshine glinted off their helmets amid smoke.

They stumbled through the debris-choked blackness that once housed stores on the concourse. They searched—mostly in vain—for any signs of life.

"I'm going to go home and kiss my daughter," said Boura, who lurched down the street, soot covering him from head to toe. "She's just starting to say 'Daddy.' Unfortunately, a lot of kids are not going to be able to say 'Daddy' anymore."

Action Verbs
   In Goldiner's story, the verbs propel the reader into the scene of destruction and death—*stumbled, carved, rappelled, glinted, searched, lurched.*

We don't have to be told how terrible the scene of death and devastation is. We are shown, and the effect is greater than if we were told.

Enduring Lesson Louis Lyons, a Boston newspaperman and later curator of the Nieman Foundation for journalists at Harvard, never forgot the lesson his night editor taught him. "When I was a cub reporter I had a story to do on the quarterly report of the old Boston Elevated system, whose history then as now was a nearly unbroken record of deficits," Lyons recalled. "This time they were in the black. I knew just enough to know how extraordinary that was.

"I wrote: 'The Boston Elevated had a remarkable record for January—it showed a profit. . . . '

"The old night editor brought my copy back to my typewriter. He knew I was green. In a kindly way, quite uncharacteristic of him, he spelled out the trouble.

"He pointed out that the word *remarkable* 'is not a reporting word. That is an editorial word.' " Then he advised Lyons to write the story so that the reader would say, "That's remarkable."

Human Interest Essential

The Department of Health and Human Services reported that 1.1 million minors run away or are thrown out of their homes every year. Most runaways are physically or sexually abused by a parent. About a third have an alcoholic parent, and many are from foster homes.

Critical

"Literature is not read and journalism is unreadable."
—*Oscar Wilde*

Troubled Teens To give the report life and meaning, Sonia L. Nazario of *The Wall Street Journal* found some troubled teenagers in California. Her account begins:

HOLLYWOOD—Five teen-agers crouch over a candle in a dark, fetid cavern under a busy roadway. Around them, the dirt floor seems to move as rats look for food. As the teen-agers pass around a half-gallon bottle of Riesling, they talk about their latest sexual scores. This is the place the teens call, simply, the Hole. "This is my home," reads a graffito scrawled on a concrete wall.

Here at the Hole, an ever-changing group of about 30 teen-agers, who have run away from home or been thrown out, have banded together to form a grotesquely modern kind of family. Predominantly white, middle-class and from troubled backgrounds, the "Trolls," as they call themselves, come to the Hole to find empathy and love. They have adopted a street father, a charismatic ex-con named John Soaring Eagle, or "Pops" to his flock. In return for his affection and discipline, the Trolls support Pops—and themselves—by panhandling, prostitution and mugging.

Teen Priorities In a three-sentence paragraph, Sam Blackwell of the Eureka, Calif., *Times-Standard* shows us a lot about teenage romance:

They had met cruising the loop between Fourth and Fifth Streets in Eureka. She fell in love with Wes' pickup truck, then fell in love with Wes. Wes gave her an engagement ring the day she graduated from high school.

Mencken on Writing

H.L. Mencken was a master of invective. A columnist for *The Baltimore Sun,* he was never so masterfully abusive as when skewering writing he considered contemptible. Here is perhaps the most famous bashing on record. Mencken is commenting on the writing of President Warren G. Harding:

> I rise to pay my small tribute to Dr. Harding. Setting aside a college professor or two and a half a dozen dipsomaniacal newspaper reporters, he takes the first place in my Valhalla of literati. That is to say, he writes the worst English that I have ever encountered. It reminds me of a string of wet sponges; it reminds me of tattered washing on the line; it reminds me of stale bean-soup, of college yells, of dogs barking idiotically through endless nights. It is so bad that a sort of grandeur creeps into it. It drags itself out of the dark abysm (I was about to write abscess!) of pish, and crawls insanely up to the topmost pinnacle of posh. It is rumble and bumble. It is balder and dash.

Visualize   Showing can be accomplished even within the confines of a single sentence. Consider the science reporter who wanted to describe the size of a small worm. She wrote, "Although they strongly caution against inferring too much about human life spans from worms no bigger than a comma at the end of this clause, they say that evolution. . . . "

If one of the writer's most compelling directives is to make the reader see, then the science writer did just that. Telling not only makes for dull reading, it makes readers passive. Showing engages readers by making them visualize, draw conclusions, experience insights.

Let Them Talk, Act

"Isn't anybody in this town can beat me. I'm invincible." This is Bella Stumbo of *The Los Angeles Times* quoting a politician. She doesn't have to tell us the man has a gigantic ego.

Good writers let the words and the actions of their subjects do the work. John Ciardi says, "Make it happen; don't talk about its happening."

When the reporter makes it happen, the reader moves into the story. The writer disappears as intermediary between the event and the reader.

To show the effects of the disappearance of dairy farms in the northeast, the reporter wrote of the farmers who stick around after selling their farms and can be seen "in the general store buying their morning beer."

Details show us more than generalities do. A story about a former Minnesota beauty queen pleading guilty to shoplifting described her loot as "several items." When the story reached an AP editor, she found out what had been stolen and put the items in the story—a swimsuit, silk scarves and hairpieces.

Frank Sinatra Has a Cold   Here's the beginning of the article *Esquire* says is the best story it ever published:

> Frank Sinatra, holding a glass of bourbon in one hand and a cigarette in the other, stood in a dark corner of the bar between two attractive but fading blondes waiting for

32,000 Times Better
Henry James, the writer, advised young writers that "an ounce of example is worth a ton of generalities."

People the Sentence
Frederick C. Othman, a veteran reporter for UPI, advised young reporters to put as many personal references as possible into each sentence, "he, she, uncle, boy, girl or any such word describing a human being. The more such words, the more interesting the story."

him to say something. But he said nothing; he had been silent during much of the evening, except now in his private club in Beverly Hills he seemed even more distant, staring out through the smoke and semidarkness into a large room beyond the bar where dozens of young couples sat huddled around small tables or twisted in the center of the floor to the clamorous clang of folk-rock music blaring from the stereo. The two blondes knew, as did Sinatra's four male friends who stood nearby, that it was a bad idea to force conversation upon him when he was in this mood of sullen silence, a mood that had hardly been uncommon during this first week of November, a month before his fiftieth birthday.

Then a second blockbuster paragraph about some of the reasons for his sullen mood—publicity about his dating a 20-year-old; a CBS TV documentary that speculated on "his possible friendship with Mafia leaders." And at the end of the second paragraph: "Frank Sinatra has a cold."

The third paragraph begins:

> Sinatra with a cold is Picasso without paint, Ferrari without fuel—only worse. For the common cold robs Sinatra of that uninsurable jewel, his voice, cutting into the core of his confidence. . . ."

Whew. A writer is at work here. A study of Gay Talese's *Esquire* article from 1966 is worth a week of a journalism student's time. The Sinatra article and others by Tom Wolfe, Norman Mailer, John Sack and Richard Ben Cramer are available at www.esquire.com.

Star Trek and Wimpy   When a television reporter returned with a feature about a local store that was selling books, posters, pictures and other material based on television's "Star Trek," his editor praised his enterprise. But the tape concentrated on the material sold. There was little about the customers, the "Star Trek" fans.

"We missed," the editor said. "We should have followed a customer around and used him as the center of the story."

Sometimes reporters fail to personalize events that easily lend themselves to human interest. When a puppy fell into the shaft of an abandoned well in Carlsbad, N.M., the rescue operation became a front-page story in many newspapers. One press service story that used the name of the puppy, Wimpy, was widely preferred to the competition's story that lacked the pup's name.

Poison Center   Compare these two stories:

I

All doctors hope their patients never have occasion to use the Poison Control Center recently established in the emergency room of the Community General Hospital. However, it should be reassuring to citizens, particularly parents, to know the center exists for use in an emergency.

Ten Guides to Good Writing

1. Make sure you understand the event.

2. When you have found the focus for your story—when you know what you want to say—start writing.

3. Show, don't tell.

4. Put good quotes and human interest high in the story.

5. Put relevant incidents and anecdotes high in the story.

6. Use concrete nouns and colorful action verbs.

7. Avoid adjectival exuberance and resist propping up verbs with adverbs.

8. Avoid judgments and inferences. Let the facts talk.

9. Don't raise questions you cannot answer in your copy.

10. Write simply, succinctly, honestly and quickly.

Springfield is one of only eight cities in the state which have official "recognized" centers to handle poisoning cases. The other seven cities are. . . .

II

A frantic mother called her physician and cried that her two-year-old had been at the oven cleaner. The child's lips were smudged with the liquid.

The label said poison. What should she do?

Her call set in motion a series of checks and other calls. In a short time her physician knew precisely what chemicals were in the cleaner, which were poisonous, and what should be done.

The child was treated and beyond a few small burns on the lips and tongue the toddler is doing well.

This was the first case for the Freeport Poison Information Center in the Community General Hospital.

The journalist who wrote the second piece did a better job of writing because his reporting was superior. Incidentally, he contributed a greater public service because the picture he painted of a "frantic mother" is etched in the minds of parents. The second story is also more appropriate to the event—it *shows* what the Center does.

The style of the second piece is consistent with the event. The average sentence length of the first five sentences, which describe the poisoning incident, is around 11 words. The next three average 21 words because the reporter was seeking to give an air of calm after the frenzy of the incident.

Human Interest Up High

We try to place as close to the lead as possible the human-interest example, incident or anecdote that spotlights the theme of the story:

The steady increase in tuition is driving some students away from the colleges of their choice and keeping them in schools close to home.

Life

William Maxwell, one of the great editors and a writer, said: "After 40 years, what I came to care about most was not style, but the breath of life."

Interesting   **Dull**

> Ralph Cramer, a high school senior, was admitted to an Ivy League college, but the $25,000-plus tuition was out of his family's reach. . . .

As you see, the example amplifies and humanizes the story theme. When delayed leads are used, the human interest incident usually begins the story. With direct leads—which often stress the formal aspect of the event—the human-impact illustration or example should be close to the lead.

We are all a little like Alice (of *Alice's Adventures in Wonderland*). "'What is the use of a book,' thought Alice, 'without pictures or conversations?'" The print reporter lets the anecdotes serve as pictures, and the quotations as conversations.

Quotations Are Essential

Wallace Stevens, the insurance company executive who wrote poetry that influenced a generation of poets, commented with some incredulity on events that were swirling around him: "In the presence of extraordinary actuality, consciousness takes the place of imagination." Fact has supplanted fiction.

Why, then, is so much journalism dull and unconvincing? Possibly because writers do not use in their stories what they see and hear. They paraphrase good quotes. They explain instead of letting the incident show the reader.

Here are two paragraphs from a book by Studs Terkel, *Working: People Talk About What They Do All Day and What They Think of While They Do It.* Terkel, a radio reporter based in Chicago, interviewed a 14-year-old newsboy, Terry Pickens:

> I don't see where being a newsboy and learning that people are pretty mean or that people don't have enough money to buy things with is gonna make you a better person or anything. If anything, it's gonna make a worse person out of you, 'cause you're not gonna like people that don't pay you. And you're not gonna like people who act like

Listening Pays Off

Reporters develop an ear sensitive to the revealing statement. The actress Farrah Fawcett was quoted, "The reason that the all-American boy prefers beauty to brains is that he can see better than he can think."

The astronomer James Jeans provided a reporter with this image of the universe, "Put three grains of sand inside a vast cathedral and the cathedral will be more closely packed with sand than space is with stars."

they're doing you a big favor paying you. Yeah, it sort of molds your character, but I don't think for the better. If anybody told me being a newsboy builds character, I'd know he was a liar.

I don't see where people get all this bull about the kid who's gonna be president and being a newsboy made a president out of him. It taught him how to handle his money and this bull. You know what it did? It taught him how to hate the people on his route. And the printers. And dogs. . . .

No paraphrase or summary would have the impact of Terry Pickens' own words. For that matter, few psychologists with their understanding of the problems of adolescence can express so succinctly and convincingly—and with such emotion—the realities of growing up.

When the Virginia State Bar Association voted to admit its first black member despite a determined effort by some senior members to block the move, a news story quoted a Richmond lawyer as praising the applicant as a "commendable person with a high standing as a lawyer." Then the story quoted him as adding, "But he is a Negro and therefore I am opposed to accepting him as a member of this association. . . . I have a good many Negro friends, but I don't invite any of them to my home or club to socialize with me."

In two quotations, the reporter crystallized an aspect of racism.

Slaughter's Witness   Let people talk and you are bound to hear a vivid image, a colorful phrase, a passionate vehemence, a deep sadness. After a riot at the New Mexico State Penitentiary during which 33 prisoners were beaten, burned and hacked to death by fellow inmates, a reporter asked what it had been like inside as prisoners wielded blowtorches, hammers and hacksaws. An inmate replied:

> Man, what can I tell you? It was like
> the devil had his own butcher shop and you
> could get any cut you wanted.

In her story in *The Washington Post* about depression among youngsters, Laura Sessions Stepp balances the statements of authorities with the comments of adolescents like Darrell.

"Right over there," she quotes Darrell as he points across the street, "some boy got shot. I was at the skate rink across the street when it happened. You never know when it's going to be pointing your way. You shouldn't have to worry about getting shot when you're a kid."

Good Quotes Up High

Here's how Colleen Krantz began her story about sexual predators for the *Des Moines Sunday Register:*

> CEDAR RAPIDS, IA—The growing
> number of computer-savvy teens are at

Mark Henle, *The Phoenix Gazette*

'Magical Door'

"With envy, I listen to my grandchildren and great-grandchildren speak the beautiful language. Speaking English is like a magical door to anywhere for them."

—Irene Begody, 77, Navajo Reservation

Words

"Don't go for ordinary words. Pick something else. Look at each word and use another word, especially when it comes to verbs. That's something we all should do, but reporters don't have the confidence to try a new word. Some words don't work and are forced and clichéd. But take a risk."

—*Anne Hull,* The Washington Post

© Greg Lovett

Taking the Gospel to College Students

The careful reporter listens closely to the message of this young evangelist as she proclaims the gospel at the University of Arkansas. The writer quotes her, describes her intensity, watches students' reactions. The reporter also interviews the students to whom she is preaching and talks to the evangelist about her successes and failures.

increasing risk of being targeted online by sexual predators, federal authorities said.

"The danger zone used to be the playground," said Rod Jensen, U.S. postal inspector who was among the federal officials who raised the issue at a news conference last week at the U.S. attorney's office in Cedar Rapids. "Now, the danger zones are Web sites, news groups and the private chat rooms."

Quotes like those Krantz used sum up the event. Quotations also help achieve conviction, that the reporter was there.

Styling the Story

Every event has its own tone, texture and pace that writers try to reflect in their stories. The way a story is written is known as its *style.* An understanding of style might start with Cicero, the Roman statesman and orator: "Whatever his theme he will speak it as becomes it; neither meagerly where it is copious, nor meanly where it is ample, not in this way where it demands that; but keeping his speech level with the actual subject and adequate to it."

In the following story of a murder, the short sentences reflect the starkness of the event:

Fight for Hat Cited as Motive in Boy's Slaying

Sixteen-year-old Kenneth Richardson was killed Thursday over a floppy brown hat, police said.

"It was just a plain old hat," Metro Homicide Detective Hugo Gomez said.

Richardson was wearing it. Someone tried to take it. Richardson refused.

Others entered the fray. The youth ran. They chased him.

"It was a running and shooting type thing. They were shooting directly at him," Gomez said.

Richardson still had the hat when taken to International Hospital, where he died in surgery. Dade's 554th homicide this year.

He was shot in the parking lot of the Miami Gardens Shopping Plaza at 12:15 a.m., soon after the nearby Gardens Shopping Skating Center closed for the night, police said.

No arrests have been made.

"They were all Carol City kids," Gomez said. "There was talk of several guns."

About 25 youths were in the area at the time, police say. "But there was nothing but the dust settling when we got there," Gomez said.

—*The Miami Herald*

Making Words Fit the Event

Because journalists are obliged to tell their stories briefly, they must choose words that count, words that quickly and efficiently paint pictures. The story is most effective when the journalist selects words in which the denotative and connotative meanings, the explicit and implicit meanings, mesh.

When New York City was close to bankruptcy, the city appealed for federal aid. President Ford brusquely said no, that the city's profligacy and incompetence had caused its fiscal misery and that it had to put its house in order itself. Pondering the story on the president's refusal, William Brink, the managing editor of the *Daily News,* cast about for the five or six words he could fit into the *News'* page 1 headline for the story. He tried:

```
FORD REFUSES
AID TO CITY
```

Quote Them

"Realistic dialogue involves the reader more completely than any other single device. It also defines character more quickly and effectively than any other single device. (Dickens has a way of fixing character in your mind so that you have the feeling he has described every inch of his appearance—only you go back and discover that he actually took care of his physical description in two or three sentences; the rest he has accomplished with dialogue.)"

—*Tom Wolfe*

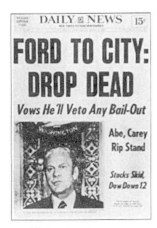

Historic Headline

The *Daily News* headline is recognized as the height of the art. Contrast it with this headline from a competing morning newspaper:
Ford, Castigating City, Asserts He'd Veto Fund Guarantee
This headline was in *The New York Times*.

Too Much

Columnists are allowed more leeway than news writers, but sometimes they are checked, even when their reputations are based on colorful writing. Molly Ivins, whose column was written from Texas, wrote of a local politician that "if his IQ slips any lower, we'll have to water him twice a day." But when she wrote of "a fella . . . havin' a beer-gut that belongs in the Smithsonian," her editors made it read, "a man with a protuberant abdomen."

The headline was dull, and the top line was half a unit too long. He tried again:

FORD SAYS NO
TO CITY AID

This fit, but it was as dull as the first. Brink recalls that in the back of his mind was the idea that "Ford hadn't just declined to help us. He had, in effect, consigned us to the scrap heap." He then wrote two words on a piece of copy paper. After a few moments, he put three other words above them.

The headline in the margin here was instantly famous. Television news stations displayed it that night, and *Time* and *Newsweek* ran it in their summaries of the city's plight. It not only presented the information succinctly (denotative), it also suggested the president's disdain for New York (connotative) in language New Yorkers understand. The headline was appropriate to the subject.

Ford said that the headline cost him the election in his race against Jimmy Carter for the presidency. Carter had 297 electoral votes to Ford's 240. Ford lost New York's 41 electoral votes by 300,000 votes out of a total of 6.5 million.

Vocabulary Helps The key to stylistic excellence is a wide vocabulary and a sensitivity to language that guides word choice. For instance, when the treasurer of a large utility is convicted of stealing $25,000 in company funds, a reporter can write:

- The *employee* was xxx.

- The *official* was xxx.

- The *executive* was xxx.

Each noun has a different connotation. *Employee* would be appropriate for a lower-ranking worker. Although he is an *official* of the company, the word usually is used in connection with public officials. *Executive* seems most appropriate.

Next some verbs:

- He *pilfered* $25,000 xxx.

- He *took* $25,000 xxx.

- He *appropriated* $25,000 for his own use.

- He *embezzled* $25,000 xxx.

- He *stole* $25,000 xxx.

Pilfered seems to trivialize the event. *Took* is prosaic: We *take* a rest, *take* cream in our coffee. *Appropriated* suggests an official action: Congress *appropriates* funds. *Embezzled* and *stole* are strong words and probably the best to use.

Good writing is anchored in control, but sometimes the words take off on their own:

Thoughts flew like spaghetti in his brain.
"Marvin," she hissed.

The muscles on his arms rose slowly, like a loaf of bread taking shape.

The Stylist

The stylist is prized in every newsroom, just as an individual style is valued in every field. Yet reporters often are unimaginative in their selection of facts, and too often their writing is uninspired. A vapid writing style begets stereotyped observations and vice versa. Compare the beginnings of these two stories about Memorial Day. Which one is more appropriate to the event?

Topeka Reminded of Debts to Dead

An Army general officer and a Navy lieutenant commander reminded Topekans of their debt and responsibility to America's war dead in two Memorial Day services Tuesday morning.

Brig. Gen. John A. Berry, commanding general of Fort Riley, spoke to representatives of 18 veterans organizations at ceremonies at Mount Hope Cemetery.

Earlier, Lt. Cmdr. John G. Tilghman, U.S. Navy Reserve, talked briefly at services on the Topeka Avenue Bridge.

"It is good for us to gather this morning to think of—and thank—those men and women who gave their lives in wars past that you and I may have the full benefits and privileges and responsibilities of our American heritage," said Cmdr. Tilghman.

"Many men in our wars did not always understand all the causes behind the war in which they fought, but they were sure they wanted those of us at home to continue to enjoy the birthright and heritage which is ours, and gave their lives that we might do so.

—*The State Journal*

Fresno Rites Honor Fallen War Heroes

Walk with me early this Memorial Day through the Liberty Cemetery before the ceremonies begin and a thousand feet scatter the dust over these quiet gravestones.

Here are the dead of many of our nation's wars.

A Flag flutters beside each grave and flowers grace them all. No one is forgotten.

Some died in uniform. Others, like Sergeant William J. Dallas of the 2nd Tennessee Infantry in the Spanish-American War, went to war and returned to live a long life—80 years long.

Many stones stand upright, their marble veined with the passage of time. What stories lie behind some of these stones? The passerby cannot tell. The inscriptions simply say:

Michael O'Connor, US Navy, Spanish-American War.

Or, in the Civil War section: Isaac N. Ulsh, Company B, 13th Kansas infantry.

Other markers tell more:

Jack T. Martin, Jr., 1922–1942, USS Langley, Lost At Sea.

James S. Waggoner, CEM, USN, USS Kete, 1917–1945, Lost at Sea. . . .

—*The Fresno Bee*

The first story is like dozens of Memorial Day stories. The oratory, although perhaps passionately uttered, has little emotional impact because it ignores those the event commemorates—the victims of war. The second story teeters on the edge of sentimentality in the lead, but soon settles into understated narrative that seeks to match the solemn nature of the event.

Changing Styles

Journalistic writing is an evolving, changing form of writing. It has been at times lush and imaginative, then spare and direct. Print writers are searching for ways to tell stories that will grab and hold the attention of people increasingly distracted by the clamor of everyday life and the enticements of an entertainment culture. Online writers are told to keep their stories short to hold readers too busy to tarry.

Tom Wolfe Over the past 45 years, journalistic style embraced the New Journalism of Tom Wolfe and other rule-breakers. In a review of an anthology of Wolfe's journalism, *The Purple Decades: A Reader,* Ellen Wilson describes Wolfe's inspiration for this new way of writing:

In the early Sixties, Tom Wolfe went to the New York Coliseum to cover a Hot Rod and Custom Car show, and came back with the New Journalism. As he tells it in the introduction to "The Kandy-Kolored Tangerine-Flake Streamline Baby," he felt frustrated by his inability to recreate the atmosphere of the show, with its "nutty-looking, crazy baroque custom cars, sitting in little nests of pink angora angels hair," in standard journalese. He needed a style flexible and uninhibited enough to capture everything a straight news story would miss: the carnival atmosphere and the thoughts and emotions of the participants.

He came up with a style incorporating slang and contemporary speech patterns, stream of consciousness and abrupt switches in perspective. The first step was painstaking research and close attention to detail. After that, he was free to select from the novelist's whole bag of tricks.

Technique
"Sometimes the eye too narrowed on technique misses the point of purpose and content."
—*William Safire*

"Technique holds a reader from sentence to sentence, but only content will stay in his mind."
—*Joyce Carol Oates*

Storytelling The New Journalism has been succeeded by narrative writing, storytelling that takes some of its components from the techniques of fiction writers, as Wolfe recommended. These tools include emphasis on individuals through whom the action is advanced, dialogue, scene-setting, suspense. It takes to the outer limit the injunction "show me, don't tell me."

The storytelling form, some critics argue, tends to overstate the dramatic and the colorful, sometimes at the expense of nuance and ambiguity, the irritating details that complicate the story line. Others, such as Jack Lule in his book *Daily News, Eternal Stories: The Mythological Role of Journalism,* counter that the news media are in trouble because they have strayed from storytelling. The result, says Lule, is that "news has become less valuable, less central."

Clearly, some events are best told using the standard news form of direct lead and then the body of the story that buttresses the lead. Some events lend themselves to the storytelling form.

When the police finally solved a triple murder in Florida and put the killer on trial, Tom French of the *St. Petersburg Times* knew that he had the makings of a narrative.

French spent three years on and off to gather information about the disappearance and death of a woman and her two daughters while they were on vacation in Florida. His work led to a seven-part series and the Pulitzer Prize. For excerpts from French's narratives, see **Angels & Demons** in *NRW Plus*.

Writing for the Medium

Much of what we have been discussing seems to be print-centered. Actually, the concepts are applicable to all the media. But reporting and writing for broadcasting and Web sites do have special requirements.

Broadcast writing, which we will discuss in detail in Chapter 9, is more condensed than print writing. The reader can always go back to reread unclear print material. The radio listener and the TV viewer have to grasp meaning now. This means broadcast writing does not have much detail, few complications. Online writers know their readers want stories boiled down to the essence.

Convergence   A growing number of media companies have been using a one-style-fits-all form of writing in their converged newsrooms. The same story is supposed to be used for print, broadcast and online outlets. More common, however, in the converged newsroom is the requirement that the reporter write separate versions of the story for each of the media.

This means that present-day news writers must be familiar with all forms of newswriting. In some newsrooms, print reporters also go on air to discuss their stories.

Before we go on, a reminder and a qualifier.

The reminder: A great deal of work is done before the reporter writes. Good journalistic writing is the result of good reporting and clear thinking. Clever writing cannot conceal a paucity of facts, stale observations or insensitive reactions to people. But bad writing can nullify superior reporting.

The qualifier: In the rest of this chapter—and in other chapters, too—rules, formulas and injunctions are presented. They are offered as guidelines, as ways to get going. They should not be considered inviolate laws. But it is best for the beginner to accept them for the time being, until his or her competence is proved. After this apprenticeship has been served, the experienced journalist can heed Anton Chekhov's comments about writing in his play *The Seagull.* "I'm coming more and more to believe that it isn't old or new forms that matter. What matters is that one should write without thinking about forms at all. Whatever one has to say should come straight from the heart."

Reporting

The journalist uses details to build a picture that shows us what is going on and that convinces us of the truth of the account. The journalist's eye catches the tears of the child whose puppy takes third place instead of first at the dog show.

Tribute
"His writing always sparkled. He liked concrete nouns and active verbs, and each paragraph was solid as a brick."
—*Pete Hamill, an obituary of Lars-Erik Nelson of the* Daily News *and* Newsday

Plain Talk
"If any man were to ask me what I would suppose to be a perfect style of language, I would answer, that in which a man speaking to five hundred people, of all common and various capacities, idiots or lunatics excepted, should be understood by them all, and in the same sense which the speaker intended to be understood."
—*Daniel Defoe*

"If language is not correct, then what is said is not what is meant; if what is said is not what is meant, then what ought to be done remains undone."
—*Confucius*

Such specific observations convince the reader that the reporter's account can be trusted.

Details, Specifics

In his series about the shooting of a policeman, Robert L. Kaiser of the *Chicago Tribune* put his readers on the scene with these details:

As they prepared for their shift, one of the officers put his "9 mm SIG-Sauer P22—black and silver with a 13-shot magazine" in his holster. They rode in a "Ford Crown Victoria." The radio "crackled with news of a shooting near 43rd and State Streets" and the driver "mashed the accelerator with his size 9 boot and headed north." A gang member in a housing project notorious for drug dealing fired his gun, "a .357 can travel up to 1,350 feet per second—faster than the speed of sound. This one seared at least 60 feet in less than a heartbeat. With a muffled thump it tore into Ceriale. The bullet had a copper jacket and a core of lead. It opened a half inch hole in the lower left abdomen just below the protective vest, flattening as it burrowed down below the pubic bone toward the hip."

A victim of sniper shootings in the Washington, D.C., area was given individuality by the reporter's use of detail. Premuwar Walekar, a taxi driver from Pune, India, was shot while pumping gas "moments after buying a newspaper, a lottery ticket and a pack of gum," the reporter wrote.

Authoritative Sources

Readers and listeners find some news unconvincing because the sources that journalists use are officials or so-called experts who have not experienced the situations they are describing. A local story about unemployment that quotes only officials and data is inadequate. Unemployment is more than figures released by an official sitting at a desk. It is men and women standing idle on street corners or waiting anxiously in offices day after day for job interviews.

In his article "Nobodies" about the exploitation of Mexican immigrant farm labor that appeared in *The New Yorker,* John Bowe asks Adan Ortiz if he had ever owned any land. Ortiz answers, "I don't even own the dirt under my fingernails."

Conviction

Some people find the news they read, hear and see unconvincing.

"What's the real story?" reporters are asked, as though they were prevented from revealing the truth by powerful advertisers or friends of the publisher or station manager. These pressures rarely influence reporters. More often, the pressures of time and the inaccessibility of documents and sources impede truth telling, and just as often, reporting and writing failures get in the way of the real story. Here are the components of a story that is accurate, complete and credible:

Reporting:

1. Relevant factual material from personal observation and physical sources. Details, specifics.

2. Authoritative and knowledgeable human sources for additional information.

3. Significant and complete background information.

Writing:

1. Simple language.

2. Incidents, examples and quotes that document the lead.

3. Human interest.

4. Appropriate style.

Next, let's look at how journalists use—and misuse—their basic tool, words.

Accuracy of Language

The city editor of a medium-size Iowa daily stared at the lead in disbelief. A reporter who had covered a city commission meeting the night before had written that the commission adopted a controversial resolution "with one descending vote." The proper word is *dissenting,* the city editor informed his errant reporter.

Without accuracy of language, the journalist cannot make the story match the event. The obvious way to check words for accuracy is to use the dictionary.

Ernest Hemingway's writing was simple, but it was not simplistic. He shaved language to the bone, but at no sacrifice to meaning. This required hard work. Reaching for a baseball metaphor, Hemingway said of the writer that "he has to go the full nine even if it kills him."

Use Words with Referents

A reporter's vocabulary comes from a feel for words, for the way people use language, which sometimes differs from dictionary usage. "The true meaning of a term is to be found by observing what a man does with it, not by what he says about it," says the scientist P.W. Bridgeman.

Journalists use words that correspond to specific objects. When the journalist writes about the state treasurer's annual report, she is describing a specific person who has issued a document that can be examined. But when the reporter takes it upon herself to describe the report as *sketchy* or *optimistic,* she is moving into an area in which there are no physical referents. She may use such words in an interpretative story, but only if she anchors them to specific facts and figures.

Words such as *progress, freedom, liberal, conservative, patriotism, big business* cause trouble because they float off in space without being anchored to anything specific, concrete or identifiable. Reporters do quote sources who use these words and phrases, but they make sure to ask sources to explain just how they are using these vague terms.

No Farm   Unwary reporters can become <u>accomplices in brainwashing</u> by using vague language. When an oil company distributed a press release announcing the

Journalism
"See a thing clearly and describe it simply. That is the essence of good newspaper work."
—*Arthur Brisbane*

The Right Word
Here are Mark Twain's observations about word usage:
A powerful agent is the right word. Whenever we come upon one of those intensely right words . . . the resulting effect is physical as well as spiritual, and electrically prompt.
The difference between the right word and the almost right word is really a large matter—the difference between lightning and the lightning bug.

construction of an "oil farm" outside a Massachusetts town and the reporter dutifully wrote in her lead that the "oil farm will occupy a tract southeast of the city," the reporter was not only using language inaccurately, but helping the oil firm obscure reality. The so-called farm was to be used for oil storage tanks, which have a grimy image. A farm, with visions of white barns and green pastures, is what the oil company wanted readers to imagine so that potential opposition would be diverted. *Farm* as used by the oil company and the reporter is a euphemism.

Euphemisms

Cloaking Reality

The use of euphemisms can lead to absurdity as in this lead to an obituary in the journal *Journalism and Mass Communication Educator:*

George Gerbner, 86, Annenberg School for Communications at the University of Pennsylvania dean emeritus, passed Christmas Eve in Philadelphia.

The fact is that Gerbner *died.* The journal heads its obituary column *Passages,* another euphemism.

When Congress was discussing *taxes,* it sought to soften the impact of that dread word by substituting the words *revenue enhancement.* In Northern California, where marijuana is a major agricultural product, the polite term for its cultivation is *cash-intensive horticulture.* A company does not demote an employee; it hands him or her a *negative advancement.* When the *Challenger* shuttle exploded, the bodies were placed not in coffins but in *crew transfer containers.* In obituaries, people do not *die,* they *pass away.*

When a pleasant word or phrase is used in place of one that may be grim, the substitute is called a *euphemism.*

Some journalists may consider themselves compassionate for letting euphemisms slip by. After all, what is the harm in permitting people who work with convicts to describe prisoners as the *consumers of criminal justice services?* What, for that matter, is wrong with *senior citizens* for older people or *sight deprived* for the blind? Surely, these euphemisms hurt no one.

Actually, they do damage us because they turn us away from reality. If the journalist's task can be reduced to a single idea, it is to point to reality. Words should describe the real, not blunt, blur or distort it.

Said

Use the Senses

"Generally speaking, if he can't see it, hear it, feel it and smell it, he can't write it."

—*William Burroughs*

These misuses of language are dangerous shoals on which many reporters have run aground. If we could mark the reefs that threaten writers, the most dangerous would be where reporters have gone under while fishing for synonyms for the verb *to say.*

Michael Gartner, editor of *The Daily Tribune* in Ames, Iowa, tells of his experiences with his editor as a young reporter. Bill Kreger, a news editor at *The Wall Street Journal,* would spot a "he laughed," "he sputtered," "he grimaced" in the attribution. He would call Gartner, or the other miscreant, to his desk.

"Laugh me this sentence," he would say. "Sputter me this sentence." Or: "Grimace me this sentence."

Then he would make the copy read, "he said."

In Stephen King's five suggestions to aspiring writers, he says, "Use *said* and *says* for attributing in dialogue."

Let it be said at once, loud and clear, the word *said* cannot be overused for attribution. If tempted to replace it with *affirmed, alleged, asserted, contended, declared, pointed out, shouted, stated* or *whispered,* see the dictionary first. Better still, recall Ring Lardner's line: "Shut up he explained."

Facts First, Words Second

To some writers, style is an end in itself. An article in *The New York Times Magazine* about the terror bombing of the World Trade Center led the writer Wyatt Mason to ask, "Is there a style in which the truth cannot be told?" He cited these two sentences from the magazine article:

And then Tower 2 sighed. The top floors buckled out, spraying tiny white shards, and the building sank into itself, crouching beneath the trees and out of frame.

Mason comments:

A sigh, that gentlest and most trivial of exhalations, reserved for moments when we are placidly tired or mildly disappointed turns the collapse of one hundred thousand tons of steel and glass—which made a cloud visible from space and a sound audible forty miles away—into a mild human wind.

As a "nice touch," however idyllic, Whitehead's use of the word "sighed" is as clear an instance as I have encountered of a stylistic choice, an aesthetic shaping, that distracts us instead to the description.

Whether it is words, the zoom lens or tape splicer, technical brilliance and technique have their place, second to truth telling.

Spelling

A few words about the bane of the copy editor, the misspelled word. A word incorrectly spelled is a gross inaccuracy. It is like a flaw in a crystal bowl. No matter how handsome the bowl, the eye and mind drift from the sweeping curves to the crack. A spelling error screams for attention, almost as loudly as an obscenity in print.

Maybe not. These days we read *its* for it's, *cemetary* for cemetery. Even *The New York Times,* surely one of the most scrupulously edited newspapers, has its share of misspellings. A story about nuns who support the ordination of women stated, "They want nuns to have a visible role at the *alter.*"

Spell-Check Limited   Some reporters put their trust in computer programs that check spelling. But such programs will not flag correctly spelled words that are misused, such as *alter* for *altar.* The program was of no use to the student journalists who wrote these headlines for the Columbia University daily student newspaper:

Baker Field Sight of Football Triumph

Soccer Hopes for Tourney Birth after 2–1 Win

Spell-Check didn't help the reporter for *The Napa Valley Register* whose story about the plans of Google to enlarge its information base included this sentence:

It wants us to feel free to load all the information we want into Google Base to create the largest suppository of information on the planet.

So There
When Harvard awarded Andrew Jackson an honorary degree, John Quincy Adams boycotted the ceremonies, describing Jackson, known as the people's president, as "a barbarian who could not write a sentence of grammar." Jackson replied, "It is a damn poor mind indeed which can't think of at least two ways to spell any word."

R. L. Chambers
Oops
The city parks department needs to invest in a dictionary, and learn how to use it.

Check the Spell-Check
The campus newspaper heard that the midterm for Psych I consisted of a short-answer quiz and an essay question and was a killer. But most students interviewed felt they had done OK. The reporter wrote:

Most students said the testes were very hard but that they managed to pass them.

Nor did the computer catch this misspelling in *Quill*'s interview with Kai Ryssdal of the American Public Media's "Marketplace" program: "We all know that we bare the burden of making this entertaining and interesting."

Intelligent reporters—good spellers or bad spellers—use the dictionary. Many editors associate intelligence with spelling ability because they consider the persistent poor speller to be stupid for not consulting the dictionary—whatever his or her native intelligence.

Clarity

The words and phrases the journalist selects must be put into a setting, into sentences and paragraphs that make sense to readers. "If you're going to be a newspaper writer you've got to put the hay down where the mules can reach it," said Ralph McGill of the *Atlanta Constitution.* Although his reporting ranged over subjects as complex as race relations and foreign affairs, McGill's writing was clear to all the paper's readers. A reader of the King James version of the Bible, he learned early the strength, vigor and clarity of the precise word in the simple declarative sentence.

"A word fitly spoken is like apples of gold in pictures of silver," McGill said of the journalist's craft, quoting from Proverbs in the Old Testament. We know several ways to make these pictures—these sentences and paragraphs—clear to our readers.

Grammar

First, there are the essentials of grammar and punctuation. In our grandparents' day, students stood at the blackboard and diagrammed sentences. They broke sentences down into nouns, verbs, pronouns, adjectives, adverbs, prepositions, conjunctions and interjections. Then they examined clauses—main and subordinate. This is how they learned sentence construction. In most schools today, the only grammar students learn is taught in foreign language classes. For a journalist, this is inadequate training.

One way the beginning journalist can cope with this inadequacy is to invest in a handbook of grammar.

Punctuation

Punctuation is the writer's substitute for the storyteller's pauses, stops and changes in voice level. The proper use of punctuation is essential to clarity. Misuse can change emphasis or meaning:

"Let's eat, Grandma."

"Let's eat Grandma."

Sentence Length

Spurred by an anxiety to cram facts into sentences, some inexperienced reporters write blockbuster sentences. When you have a sentence running three lines or more,

Five Fatal Flaws

After reading through dozens of freshman compositions, Loretta M. Shpunt, an English teacher at Trinity College in Washington, D.C., said she considered buying a red ink pad and a set of rubber stamps that read:

Not a Sentence
"It's" Equals "It Is"
"Its" Is Possessive
Dangling Participle
"I" Before "E" Except After "C"

think of the self-editing of Isaac Babel, a Russian writer whose short stories are highly polished gems:

> I go over each sentence, time and again. I start by cutting all the words it can do without. You have to keep your eye on the job because words are very sly. The rubbishy ones go into hiding and you have to dig them out—repetitions, synonyms, things that simply don't mean anything.
>
> Before I take out the rubbish, I break up the text into shorter sentences. The more full stops the better. I'd like to have that passed as a law. Not more than one idea and one image to a sentence.
>
> A paragraph is a wonderful thing. It lets you quietly change the rhythm, and it can be like a flash of lightning that shows the landscape from a different perspective. There are writers, even good ones, who scatter paragraphs and punctuation marks all over the place.

The maxim that each sentence should, if possible, carry only one idea has been assumed to be an injunction limited to journalism. Not so, as we see from Babel's comment. Good journalistic writing is based upon the principles of good writing. Journalism is a part of the world of letters.

Guide   The press associations have concluded after a number of studies that one of the keys to readable stories is the short sentence. Here is a readability chart:

Average Sentence Length	Readability
8 words or less	Very easy to read
11 words	Easy to read
14 words	Fairly easy to read
17 words	Standard
21 words	Fairly difficult to read
25 words	Difficult to read
29 words or more	Very difficult to read

One sentence after another under 17 words would make readers and listeners feel as though they were being peppered with bird shot. The key to good writing is variety, rhythm, balance. Short and long sentences are balanced.

For an example of how sentence story length is varied for effect, see **A Pulitzer Prize Story: Workings of the Brain** in *NRW plus*.

Transitions

Some reporters have trouble writing short sentences because they cannot handle transitions, the links between sentences and paragraphs. Because these reporters have no mastery of the device that enables a writer to move smoothly from sentence to sentence, their tendency is to think in large clots of words. The journalist with control of transitions thinks in smaller sentence clusters.

There are four major types of transitions:

1. **Pronouns:** Use pronouns to refer to nouns in previous sentences and paragraphs:

   Dr. Braun began teaching history in 1977. *He* took *his* Ph.D. that year. *His* dissertation subject was the French Impressionists.

2. **Key words and ideas:** Repeat words and ideas in preceding sentences and paragraphs:

   He has been accused of being an *academic purist. Those words* make him shudder. "*Academic purist* is made to sound like an epithet," he said.

3. **Transitional expressions:** Use connecting words that link sentences. A large array of expressions function as connectors. Here are most of the major categories of conjunctions and some of the words in each category that can be used as transitions:

   Additives: again, also, and, finally, furthermore, in addition, next, thus, so, moreover, as well.

   Contrasts: but, however, nevertheless, instead, on the other hand, otherwise, yet, nonetheless, farther.

   Comparisons: likewise, similarly.

   Place: adjacent to, beyond, here, near, opposite.

   Time: afterward, in the meantime, later, meanwhile, soon.

   He tried twice to obtain permission to see the paintings in the private museum. *Finally,* he gave up.

   Dr. Braun's *next* project centered on the music of Berlioz. *But* his luck remained bad. An attempt to locate a missing manuscript proved a *similar* failure.

   In the meantime, he continued his study of Spanish so that he would be able to do research in Spain.

4. **Parallel structure.** Sentences and paragraphs are linked by repeating the sentence pattern:

> *No one* dared speak in his classes. *No one* ventured to address him in any but the most formal manner. *No one,* for that matter, had the courage to ask questions in class. His lectures were nonstop monologues.

Logical Order

A news story should move smoothly. When natural sequence is disrupted, the story loses clarity. Here are two paragraphs from a story in an Oklahoma daily newspaper:

> "There is nothing new in the allegations," Bartlett said. "We've heard them all before."
>
> "When we first heard them we thought there was nothing to it, but then we had a second look," Tillman said.

Although the first paragraph is closed by quotation marks, which means that the speaker (Bartlett) is finished, most readers jump ahead to the next quote and presume that Bartlett is still talking. They are jolted when they find that Tillman is speaking. The solution is simple: When you introduce a new speaker, begin the sentence or paragraph with his or her name.

Also, jumps in time and place must be handled carefully to avoid confusion:

NEW YORK (April 13)—A criminal court judge who last month ruled that a waiter had seduced but not raped a college student sent the man to jail for a year **yesterday** on a charge of escaping from the police after his arrest.

On March 19, Justice Albert S. Hess acquitted Phillip Blau of raping a 20-year-old Pembroke College student. The judge said a man could use guile, scheme, and be deceitful, but so long as he did not use violence, rape did not occur.

At that time, women's groups protested the decision.

"Despite the protests of outraged feminists who demand your head, or other and possibly more appropriate parts of your anatomy," the judge told Blau **yesterday,** "I shall punish you only for crimes of which you have been found guilty."

The changes in time are clearly indicated at the start of the second and third paragraphs. From "yesterday" in the lead, the reader is taken to "March 19" in the second paragraph and is kept there in the third paragraph by the transition "At that time" beginning the paragraph. When the quote begins the fourth paragraph, the reader is still back in March with the women. Midway through the paragraph the reader suddenly realizes the judge is speaking and that he spoke yesterday.

> **Painful**
> "Writing is so difficult that I often feel that writers, having had their hell on earth, will escape punishment thereafter."
> —*Jessamyn West*

The jolts in time and place could have been avoided with a transition at the beginning of the fourth paragraph:

> In sentencing Blau **yesterday,** Justice Hess
> commented on the protests. He said: . . .

This may seem to be nitpicking. It is not. The journalist knows that every sentence, every word, even every punctuation mark must be carefully selected. Readers read from word to word, and are maneuvered, teased, pushed, sped and slowed through the story by the way it is written. Major disturbances of logic and order in the story confuse readers, just as a quick jump cut on television can destroy the continuity of the story for the viewer.

Chronological Order   The most common organizing principle is chronology. The chronological approach has two forms. The writer can use the storytelling approach by beginning sometime before the climax:

Two Mallory College sophomores began the day yesterday in a hurry.

Judy Abrams had studied late the night before and had slept late. She gulped her breakfast of coffee and jumped into her car, five minutes before her 9 a.m. class.

Franklin Starrett did not have time for breakfast before he, too, sped off in his car for the campus. He had an appointment with his English instructor at 9 a.m.

Within minutes of their departures, the cars they were driving collided on Stanford Avenue south of the campus. . . .

Or the writer can put a direct news lead on the story and then, a few paragraphs down in the story, begin the chronological account:

Two Mallory College students were critically injured when the cars they were driving collided head-on yesterday morning on Stanford Avenue south of the campus.

Community Hospital officials said the students suffered multiple fractures and internal injuries. They called on students to volunteer blood for transfusions.

The students began the day in a hurry. . . .

Now that we are clear about word usage and how to string these words together with appropriate punctuation and transitions, let's step back and look at the story as a whole. The first and most important requirement is that the piece flows smoothly.

Movement

Stories must move along, and the nature of the event determines the pace at which the story progresses. A story about a tornado or hurricane striking a community will move at the speed of the wind, but the piece about the burial service for the victims will follow the deliberate cadence of the prayers of the minister as he speaks.

Here is an excerpt from a frontline dispatch by Ernie Pyle, who covered World War II for Scripps Howard:

Then a soldier came and stood beside the officer, and bent over, and he too spoke to his dead captain, not in a whisper but awfully tenderly, and he said:

"I sure am sorry, sir."

Then the first man squatted down, and he reached down, took the dead hand, and sat there for a full five minutes, holding the dead hand in his own and looking intently into the dead face, and he never uttered a sound all the time he sat there.

And finally he put the hand down, and then reached up and gently straightened the points of the captain's shirt collar, and then he sort of rearranged the tattered edges of his uniform around the wound. And then he got up and walked away down the road in the moonlight, all alone.

Reach the Reader
"The key questions are: Is this stuff interesting? Does it move, touch, anger, tickle, surprise, sadden or inform? If it does, you are in for a treat, a good read."
—*Thomasine Berg,* The Providence Journal

The Army Signal Corps operator who sent Pyle's dispatch over shortwave radio to United Press headquarters in New York told Pyle's biographer, "I had to struggle through that piece to make my voice override my tears." (*Ernie Pyle's War: America's Eyewitness to World War II,* James Tobin.)

For the full story, see **Captain Waskow** in *NRW Plus.*

With the Troops   Murray Kempton, the reporter and columnist admired by many journalists for his dogged reporting and distinct writing style, paid homage to Pyle who, Kempton wrote, "stands above the rest because he most fully incarnated what a reporter ought to be. Pyle went again and again wherever the worst extremes waited, the unconscripted man bound by conscience to the comradeship of the conscripted and enduring by free will what they were compelled to endure by necessity."

Pyle understood the use of understatement. Reread the four paragraphs about Captain Waskow's death. The emotion comes from you, the reader. When he went ashore with the troops on D-Day, Pyle wrote of what he saw strewn on Omaha Beach as men were mowed down—socks, sewing kits, family pictures. The details gave a personal cast to the body counts.

Jack Foisie, also a World War II combat correspondent, said of Pyle that he "seldom injected himself into his writings. He never mentioned his own close calls with death, although he had a number of them."

Scripps Howard Foundation
Ernie Pyle

With the Navy   When the war in Europe ended, Pyle went to the Pacific to cover the sea war against Japan. There, Pyle felt uncomfortable about what he saw as the Navy caste system.

Soon after he was aboard a ship he found that his dispatches were being censored. The names of the sailors he had written about were deleted and only the names of high-ranking officers were left untouched. He also balked at the system that relegated black sailors to the food services. Pyle was able to change the first by threatening to abandon Navy coverage for the Marine and Army GIs, and the Navy gave in and stopped censoring his stories.

Intrepid

". . . the never-ending tension of deadlines and the piles upon piles of corpses rendered him almost continually sick, sleepless . . . to millions of Americans he was their eyes and ears on the war . . . thousands wrote to him to look up their sons as he made his way through Europe."
—Raymond A. Schroth

But he could not change the discrimination against black servicemen. That took three more years and the action of President Truman in 1948.

The End   The death of good men haunted Pyle, and when he was shot by a sniper on Ie Shima in 1945, the soldiers who had risked their lives to bring back his body found in his pocket a column he had written for the end of the fighting in Europe. Here is some of it:

> Those who are gone would not wish themselves to be a millstone of gloom around our necks.
>
> But there are many of the living who have had burned into their brains forever the unnatural sight of cold dead men scattered over the hillsides and in the ditches along the high rows of hedge throughout the world.
>
> Dead men by mass production—in one country after another—month after month and year after year. Dead men in winter and dead men in summer.
>
> Dead men in such familiar promiscuity that they become monotonous.
>
> Dead men in such monstrous infinity that you come almost to hate them.

For the entire column Pyle wrote, see **Cold Dead Men** in *NRW Plus.*
Pyle is buried beside GIs in the Punchbowl Cemetery in Hawaii.

Let's see if we can wrap up this long chapter with a few conclusions about the art of writing.

Word Choice

Here is some practical advice from John Ciardi, poet, essayist and writer on writing:

> Count the adjectives and verbs; good writing (active writing) will almost invariably have more verbs. . . . A diction in which every noun is propped up by an adjective may be almost flatly said to be a bad one.

Mark Twain advised, "Whenever you see an adjective, kill it." And that vast source of material, Anonymous, is quoted on writing as saying, "The adjective is the enemy of the noun."

As for verbs, the action verb is our object. Mervin Block, the television writing coach, received a script with this lead: "The Dow was down more than 62 points." Block commented: "The verb *was* doesn't convey any action. The writer needs a vigorous verb like *fell.* Or *sank.* Or *slid.* Or *skidded.* Or *dropped.* Or *plunged.* Or *tumbled.* But *was* doesn't move."

Sentences

Red Smith's teacher at Notre Dame, John Michael Cooney, wanted sentences from his students that were "so definite they would cast a shadow." He was an enemy of vague writing and began class by intoning, "Let us pray for sense."

Sense for whom? Harold Ross, the founder and longtime editor of *The New Yorker* wanted his magazine never to contain "a sentence that would puzzle an intelligent 14-year-old."

The sentences should be put to good use, and that means using them for quotations, anecdotes and illustrations. Donald Murray, the writer and writing coach, comments on the use of examples, illustrations and anecdotes:

> You tell them the anecdote and they say, "Boy, this is a bad situation." That's the art in it—not to tell the reader how to think, how to feel, but to give the reader the old Mark Twain thing, "Don't say the old lady screamed. Drag her on stage and make her scream."

> **Two Essentials**
> Writers talk about "concrete nouns and action verbs," by which they mean nouns that represent something physical that can be pointed to, something specific and action verbs that move.
> *The 6-year-old sprinted home* is better than *The boy went home.*
> *She wept* is better than *She is sad.*

Summing Up

Those who write for a living strive to blend a bit of artistry with information-giving. Here is some advice from a writer who wrote well and thought a lot about the writing craft, Robert Louis Stevenson:

• **Accuracy:** ". . . there is only one way to be clever and that is to be exact. To be vivid is a secondary quality which must presuppose the first; for vividly to convey a wrong impression is only to make failure conspicuous. . . ."

• **Brevity:** ". . . the artist has one main and necessary resource which he must, in every case and upon any theory, employ. He must, that is, suppress much and omit more. He must omit what is tedious or irrelevant. . . ." But he must retain the material essential to the "main design."

• **Language:** The words with which the writer works should be from "the dialect of life."

• **Structure:** ". . . every word, phrase, sentence and paragraph must move in a logical procession." No word or phrase is selected unless it is "what is wanted to forward and illustrate" the work.

Further Reading

Lule, Jack. *Daily News, Eternal Stories: The Mythological Role of Journalism.* New York: The Guilford Press, 2001.

Nichols, David, ed. *Ernie's War: The Best of Ernie Pyle's World War II Dispatches.* New York: Random House, 1986.

Ross, Lillian. *Reporting.* New York: Dodd Mead & Co., 1981.

Ross, a *New Yorker* writer, is a practitioner of fly-on-the-wall journalism. Her articles are studied by beginners and professionals for her discerning eye, receptive ear and a style that allows us to draw our conclusions. Her piece on Hemingway, one of several classics in this collection, is still debated: Is this a portrait of a monumental bore and braggart or of a man desperately trying to be one of the he-men he wrote about?

Terkel, Studs. *Working: People Talk About What They Do All Day and What They Think While They Do It.* New York: Pantheon, 1972.

Terkel, Studs. *The Good War: An Oral History of World War Two.* New York: Pantheon, 1984.

Tobin, James. *Ernie Pyle's War: America's Eyewitness to World War II.* New York: Free Press, 1997.

Features, Long Stories and Series 8

Preview

Features are written to entertain and/or inform. The writer lets the actions and comments of the personalities carry the story.

Long stories are written to provide readers with information about a complicated idea or situation.

Series are written when the subject is too complex for the long story format. Each article has a major theme; sidebars may be used to develop subthemes.

Anita Henderson, *Beloit* (Wis.) *Daily News*
Features make us laugh and cry.

The Feature

The feature has had a reputation much like penny stocks, slightly suspect. Although it has worthy antecedents in the satire and parody of poets and essayists who used the pen to attack individuals in public and private life, the feature was approached gingerly by editors. Many editors subscribed to the philosophy of Richard Draper, who wrote in his Boston *News-Letter* in the 18th century that he would use features only when "there happens to be a scarcity of news."

Conservative editors of the 19th century found the features published by the penny press from the 1830s to the Civil War distasteful. Directed to the working class, which had been enlarged by the country's industrial revolution, these inexpensive newspapers ran stories about domestic tragedy and illicit sex, stories that editors such as Horace Greeley found unworthy of journalism. When he established the *Tribune* in New York in 1841, Greeley announced that his

The greatest story is how we live now.

newspaper would avoid the "immoral and degrading Police Reports, Advertisements and other matters which have been allowed to disgrace the columns of our leading Penny Papers." But Greeley was soon running the kind of material he had condemned.

Embroidered Stories

The feature story was a weapon in the great circulation wars between Pulitzer and Hearst in New York at the turn of the 20th century. Crime stories, sports, society news, science news—all of it embroidered with sensational details often as much invented as factual—were used to attract readers. This type of feature became synonymous with Yellow Journalism.

The Hearst newspapers were perhaps the most successful of the sensational and flamboyant papers of their day. W. A. Swanberg, in his biography *Citizen Hearst,* describes them:

> They were printed entertainment and excitement—the equivalent in newsprint of bombs exploding, bands blaring, firecrackers popping, victims screaming, flags waving, cannons roaring, houris dancing and smoke rising from the singed flesh of executed criminals.

A reporter for a Hearst newspaper described a typical Hearst paper as "a screaming woman running down the street with her throat cut." The Chief, as Hearst was known to his employees, had the man fired.

In the days of Front Page Journalism, the feature writer's job was to wring tears from the bartender, smiles from the policeman and gasps of wonderment from the tenement dwellers. The tales of the city, as spun out by the feature writers of the day, were long on drama, short on fact.

Tale of the Cat   During the circulation war between the Hearst and Pulitzer papers, a reporter for Pulitzer's *New York World* who covered shipping described what happened when reporters tried to make features of straight news:

> One of those wrecked ships had a cat, and the crew went back to save it. I made the cat a feature of my story, while the other reporters failed to mention the cat and were called down by their city editors for being beaten. The next time there was a shipwreck, there was no cat but the other ship news reporters did not wish to take chances and put the cat in. I wrote the report, leaving out the cat, and then I was severely chided for being beaten. Now when there is a shipwreck, all of us always put in a cat.

The Decline   As the United States grew into a world power and its citizens had to confront the consequences of World War I and then a pervasive depression, some of the press graduated to more serious pursuits. The feature came to be seen as too frivolous for the responsible newspaper. Newspapers that held on to the old formulas declined in popularity. The Hearst chain dwindled from 22 newspapers to 8.

In 1947, when Joseph G. Herzberg, city editor of *The New York Herald Tribune,* put together a series of essays by *Tribune* staffers for the book *Late City Edition,* not one of the 29 chapters was devoted to the feature story.

Now Thriving

Today, the feature thrives. First, editors discovered that serious journalism does not have to be dry. They rediscovered the fact known to Greek playwrights 2,300 years ago—events have a human dimension. Indeed, it is the human aspect of the event that makes it worth communicating. In his play *The Frogs,* Aristophanes has the playwright Euripedes say, "I made the drama democratic. I staged the life of every day, the way we live." This is an excellent description of our approach to the feature today.

The contemporary journalist tries to present the full dimension of how we live now: how we make a living, raise a family and spend our money; the ways we entertain ourselves and make our way through the trials and triumphs life holds for us. The feature proved a useful tool to tell many of these stories. So useful, in fact, that in 1979, after many years of ignoring the feature, the Pulitzer Prize board established a category for a distinguished example of feature writing, "giving prime consideration to high literary quality and originality."

The Somber   The first Prize in the new category went to Jon Franklin for his story about brain surgery. The Prize has gone to Lisa Pollak of *The Baltimore Sun* for her "compelling portrait of a baseball umpire who endured the death of a son while knowing that another son suffers from the same deadly genetic disease." The Prize has honored features about inner-city youngsters' determination to succeed despite barriers.

The Cheerful   An unvarying diet of the serious does not tell the full story of how we live now. Also, any mass medium given over to a steady diet of the somber will be rejected by the audience. So the media offer a variety, and one of the offerings is the entertaining feature.

The news story might be a piece from Washington, D.C., about a sudden rise in the cost of living. The feature writer will use that as a takeoff for a feature about how the candy bar her dad says he bought for a nickel now costs 10 times as much. Where, she wonders, do kids these days get the money for a Mars bar? She lurks around candy counters to find out.

What she learns astounds her. Some youngsters are rolling in dough. Even poor kids are sporting $150 athletic shoes, she notices. One story begets another. But first, for the candy bars. It won't be nominated for a Pulitzer Prize, but that's all right. It's a fun story to write. . . . and, she hopes, for people to read.

Caution: Some young reporters say they prefer to write features rather than hard news because the feature is easier to handle. This is the blather of the uninformed. The momentum of the news event carries most spot news stories. The feature is an exception to some of the writing rules, and this imposes on the writer the task of pioneering in each piece, beginning anew to find a form, a story tone, the appropriate quotations and the telling scenes for this particular story. Readers demand more of feature writers than of straight news writers and so do editors.

The Difference

"The news writer tells you the bridge fell in and how many cars fell off. The feature writer tells you what it was like to have been there: 'When Joe Smith began to walk across the bridge, it began to tremble, and he grabbed the railing'—that sort of detail."

—Jules Loh, AP feature writer

R.L. Chambers

R.L. Chambers

Story Ideas

Go behind the signs. There's probably a feature there.

Guidelines

- Show people doing things.
- Let them talk.
- Underwrite. Let the action and the dialogue carry the piece.
- Keep the piece moving.

Making the individuals carry the action requires a discerning eye to see the telling action and a discriminating ear to catch the illuminating quote.

Arm Wrestlers   When David Stacks was sent to cover an arm-wrestling tournament, he knew that his story for *The Anniston Star* would be a feature, which meant he would have to watch for an incident or a situation with which to begin his piece. Here's how he handled the assignment:

Sweat beaded on Bruce Jernigan's forehead. His biceps swelled as blood rushed through his strong chest and into his right arm. His face grimaced with exertion.

Bruce's opponent, Claude Bradford, smiled in seeming defiance as the two boys' fists—locked in an arm-wrestler's grip— teetered slowly back and forth over the tabletop.

Then, with a burst of energy, 14-year-old Claude overcame his opponent's balanced show of strength. Both boys fell from near exhaustion as the referee declared the match concluded.

Elbow Grease

Contests, games and rivalries far from the big playing fields and the fieldhouses can make for interesting features. There is drama in the playoffs of the boys' and girls' soccer leagues, the bowling alleys and the school tennis courts.

An arm-wrestling tournament provided a writer–photographer team from *The Anniston Star* with a feature story about an ancient sporting tradition.

Ken Elkins, *The Anniston Star*

Theirs was a test of strength, endurance and will. In the end, Claude managed to wear down his friend and adversary Bruce, 14, in the Anniston Park and Recreation Department's first arm-wrestling tournament Saturday morning at Carver Community Center on West 14th Street.

"It's all in the way you move," Claude said afterwards.

Arm wrestling is an ancient contest of power in which two opponents grasp each other's hands with their elbows resting on a flat surface. The one who forces the other's arm down to the surface wins . . .

Conforming Kids Lena H. Sun, *The Washington Post* Beijing bureau chief, took her readers into a kindergarten to show how Chinese children are made into conforming, obedient citizens:

> BEIJING—It is a playtime at the Tongren Kindergarten. As 3-year-olds run relay races in the schoolyard, the teacher suddenly calls out to one girl.
>
> "You didn't run on the dotted line," the teacher says disapprovingly. The girl, pigtails bobbing, immediately retraces her steps on faded red spots painted on the concrete. The teacher smiles and nods. No one else makes the same mistake.

"Show people doing things," our first guideline, is the thrust of Sun's lead.

Sometimes, the feature writer looks back. Elizabeth Leland did that in her feature for *The Charlotte Observer* that put a shaft of light on a dismal chapter in U.S. history.

An American Tragedy

Here is how Leland began her story of a family tragedy:

Gene Cheek was 12 when a judge took him from his mother.

It was a Monday morning, Nov. 18, 1963, and Gene remembers being excited because he didn't have to go to school. He put on his best clothes—a white shirt and his Sunday coat, a size too small—and rode with his mother on a city bus to the courthouse in downtown Winston-Salem. They were going to get the $413 in child support his father owed them. They'd go shopping afterward.

His mother sat up front in the courtroom to the right of the judge. His father and an uncle sat to the left. Gene remembers goofing off by himself on a bench a few rows back, not paying attention to what anyone was saying, when he heard his mother crying. He walked up front.

The gray-haired judge in the black robe was telling her something, and as Gene listened he realized it was not about money. It was about her boyfriend.

The judge said it wasn't good for Gene to live with her because she was seeing a Negro man and had a Negro baby.

Gene's mother pleaded. I'm a good mother, she said, her voice breaking, tears wetting her cheeks.

The judge gave her a choice: Give up the baby or give up the boy.

Before the Separation

Gene Cheek holds his brother Randy. Next to him are his mother Sally and her boyfriend Cornelius Tucker. Seventeen months after this family portrait was made, a judge gave Gene's mother a choice: Give up Randy or give up Gene. For years, Gene wanted the story told, and when Elizabeth Leland did so, Gene Cheek said, "It's a cleansing to tell this story."

When Gene Cheek told Leland about the separation, she was skeptical. She said she found it "incredible" that a judge would issue such an order. Even when relatives verified the story, she was uneasy.

Leland knew that only documentation—a court file—would be persuasive to readers. Without it, it was just a tale told by upset people.

For Leland's complete story and how she managed to find the documentation she needed, see **An American Tragedy** and **The Legacy of the Gene Cheek Case** in *NRW Plus.*

Planning

Frank Barrows, Leland's managing editor at *The Charlotte Observer,* says careful planning of the feature is essential. "Simply because a feature is not written to be cut from the bottom—as a news story might be—does not mean that the material can be randomly set down on paper.

"For a feature to be something other than puffery, you must do the type of serious preparation and thinking that lead to organization. For instance, you might not want to put all the straight biographic data in one place."

Barrows knows that such material is usually tedious. Beginners tend to bunch up background. More experienced hands break up background such as biographical material and place bits and pieces into the moving narrative. For example, he says, when a reporter comes to a place in the story where she is showing how the subject's hometown influenced his life, that is the place to put something about his birthplace and a few other routine details. In other words, the necessary background is spotted or blended into the ongoing story.

Another fault of beginners is the leisurely pace they set at the outset of the piece, as though they are feeling their way toward the theme of the story.

"Too often in features the writer does not tell his reader soon enough what he is writing about," Barrows says.

Truck Stop   Look at how Eric Lawlor of the *Houston Chronicle* slides the reader right into his piece about what goes on at a truck stop outside town. He sets a scene in the first paragraph, pulls us into the restaurant in the second and in the third we meet Tina and then listen in on the chatter:

The truck stop on the North Freeway is ringed with rigs. Trucks glide past one another with the grandeur of sailing ships: 16-wheel galleons bearing—not spices from the Indies or gold from the New World—but auto parts and refrigerators.

Truckers weave as they enter the restaurant; like sailors on shore leave, they are still finding their legs.

Tina Hernandez, an 18-year-old waitress here, serves an order of ham and eggs.

"Where are my grits?" asks the recipient.

"You don't get grits unless you ask for them," she tells him. "If you want grits, you gotta say, 'I want grits.'"

If this sounds unnecessarily acerbic, it's not, in fact: Tina and her customers are actually fond of one another. An affection that masquerades as good-natured abuse.

"Give me a bowl of split-pea soup," says a man whose face looks curiously flat. Perhaps

someone sat on it. "Is there any meat in there?"

"There's meat in there all right," says Tina. "The problem is finding it."

"How are you and Billy (not his real name) doin'?" he wants to know.

"We don't talk anymore," says the waitress. "He got scared. Just checked out."

"Oh, I don't believe that. I'll bet you are goin' out and just don't want anyone to know about it."

"I'm tellin' ya: that man is scared of women."

"Maybe he just doesn't like YOU," offers Myrtle, another waitress.

At a nearby table, a driver is telling a colleague about a recent fling.

"I had to leave her finally because she was so cold-blooded. You could get pneumonia sitting next to a woman like that."

Techniques

Feature writers call on all sorts of approaches to their writing. When the occasion calls for it, a writer may compose an all-quotation story, letting the characters carry the action with their words.

Cinematic Approach   One way to look at feature writing style is through the lens of a movie camera. If we did that, we would first focus through the telescopic lens on a small part of the scene and magnify it, then use the wide angle lens to show the big picture. Here is how Ellen Graham handled an assignment for *The*

Tribute to a Tree

When Elizabeth Leland learned that an old tree was being spared, she decided to write her story "in the style of a children's book, yet making sure it would appeal to young and old readers." She began her story this way:

A long time ago, there lived a boy who loved a little tree.

He was about 10 when he dug a hole and planted the white oak in his family's yard near the center of town.

He grew up and started his own family and grew old and died, but the tree kept growing and growing and growing and growing.

One morning in March of this year, the Town Manager looked out of his office window . . . the track hoe had flexed its long hydraulic arm and was attacking the tree. Already, the teeth of the shovel had ripped off the lower limbs. . . .

Sigma Delta Chi gave Leland its feature writing award. "The story was conceived brilliantly, solidly reported and sourced, and beautifully executed. The tone of the piece made it an incredibly enjoyable read."

Wall Street Journal to see how the Girl Scout cookie crumbles. Let's zoom in on her work:

> Eleven-year-old Kathleen Totz is a small but important cog in a sales effort unique in the annals of American enterprise. This year, the slim, bespectacled Girl Scout was the top cookie seller in Wallingford, Conn.'s Troop 265, toting up $498 in receipts for 266 boxes.

Then Graham takes a step back for the big picture:

> By dribs and drabs, the door-to-door earnings of volunteers like Kathleen add up: The annual cookie sale—the Girl Scouts' main funding source—generates an estimated $400 million in revenue.

And still another step back to deliver in the fourth paragraph the point Graham is leading up to:

> But many in this volunteer cadre—the Scouts, troop leaders and parents who provide the free labor—are starting to question the annual cookie drive, saying the troops simply don't see enough of the profits. Tax-free cookie proceeds mainly support the Girl Scouts' sprawling bureaucracy, critics say, while the girls themselves are left with the crumbs.

Tone and Style

In any discussion with feature writers, the words *tone* and *style* usually come up. A feature writer uses one tone—one kind of voice—for a piece about a classical guitarist, another for a guitarist with a rock group. Tone is established by selection of facts, quotes, illustrations, by word choice, length of sentences, even by the length of paragraphs. The rock musician may be quoted in one- or two-sentence paragraphs to match the rock beat, whereas the classical musician's quotes may run in longer paragraphs to give the reader the sonority of classical music.

The News Feature

The news feature usually has its origins in some news event. When Carl Hiassen of *The Miami Herald* dug into the court case involving a doctor and his millionaire wife, he came up with a tale of greed preying on loneliness. His story begins:

To Dr. Edward Gordon, love meant never having to say he was out of money.

Six years ago, the solicitous Miami Beach physician married a patient who was worth more than $8 million. Her name was Elizabeth Buffum, and she was a lonely alcoholic.

With Gordon, she stayed lonely and she often stayed drunk. She just barely stayed wealthy.

Today, as lawyers doggedly try to retrieve her scattered fortune from all over the globe, the former Mrs. Gordon lies in a Fort Lauderdale nursing home, permanently brain-damaged. Relatives say her life was destroyed by four ruinous years as the doctor's wife. They say it wasn't a marriage, it was a matrimonial Brink's job.

"Unbelievable," says one son, Peter Beaumont. "It's sort of a classic: elderly lady with lots of bucks heads down to Retirement City and gets fleeced by local doctor."

It began as a September love affair. He was 62, silver-haired and single, with a new medical practice in Florida. She was 60, a bit overweight and twice divorced, given to irascibility and depression. . . .

The lead is inviting. Nobody, every writer knows, ever tires of reading about love, money and violence. The second and third paragraphs are like the coming attractions at a movie, or the come-on advertising of television. The fourth paragraph drives home the theme: A woman ruined by her marriage. And in the fifth paragraph, a quote is used to sum up the theme. The sixth paragraph introduces us to the chronological narrative the writer will spin.

Ideas for Features

The advertisement read:

HEARTBROKEN

Anyone who purchased (at my Garage Sale last week) a small white canister with blue flowers, please call me. It contains remains of a dearly departed family member.

There's a story in that canister. How did it find its way into the garage sale? Who bought it? Was it returned? And if so, where will the dearly departed be placed now?

Just look around. Notice that group sitting in the cafeteria, those high school students? One is griping. About what? Listen in: His mother doesn't like his girlfriend: "She thinks I'm too young to be going steady. She thinks I should spend my time on school work. But me and my girl were meant for each other."

A young woman says to no one in particular, "I don't fit in, not even here. I don't think I look good enough. I don't like the way my body is. Everyone else is popular. Not me."

James J. Malloy, *The Providence Journal*

Saying Goodbye to a Good Buddy

The story by W. Zachary Malinowski of *The Providence Journal* about the burial of a teenager killed in a drive-by shooting begins this way:

Tears streamed down Wayne Tucker's face as he led the funeral procession down the center aisle at St. Teresa's Church yesterday. Behind Tucker stood eight teenage pallbearers in black sweat-shirts and loose-fitting jeans, bearing the silver casket holding their friend, Tommy DeGrafft, who died in a barrage of gun-fire last weekend. In Tucker's hands was a basketball covered with the scrawled signatures of DeGrafft's former team-mates. One said simply, "To Tommy from All of Us."

Another teenager says he just had some news that has relieved him after a couple of weeks of stress: "I thought that my girlfriend was pregnant. Lost a lot of sleep, and weight. I just found out she isn't."

Ideas are everywhere. A letter writer to Ann Landers says that college students consume an average of 34 gallons of alcoholic beverages a year and quotes the chancellor of the University of Wisconsin as saying that the biggest problem on campus today is alcoholism.

Avoiding the Pitfalls

The following suggestions are from a dozen feature writers:

• "Good stories come from good material. Good material comes from good reporting—and that is just as true if not more so with feature writing as with news writing," says Sheryl James of the *St. Petersburg Times.* As Tom Wolfe puts it, "Style can't carry a story if you haven't done the reporting."

• Do not have such a love affair with quotes that you fail to paraphrase routine material. Worse: Do not use quotes chronologically from the interview as a prop for failing to organize the piece.

• Know what you are going to say and the tone in which it is to be said before starting. Otherwise, the story will never get off the ground.

• Develop an enthusiasm for the piece. Features can be marred by an objectivity that keeps the reader at a distance. "The idea of a feature is to involve the reader," a reporter said. "This is often taken to mean good craftsmanship through colorful writing. That's not enough. The writer needs to take a point of view, not simply to say, 'Look at this guy who was put into an institution for the retarded at the age of 6, and when he was 18 some worker in the place saw that the kid wasn't retarded at all but had a learning disability.'

"The writer of this kind of piece has to be indignant at the tragedy. How can you be objective about this kind of inhumanity? A reader should be moved to indignation—not by the reporter's sounding off. We don't want that. But this kind of piece has to have the kind of facts and a story tone that gives a strong sense of human waste and bureaucratic inefficiency."

• Make sure the story has a good plot and is unusual enough to hold our interest. This means the central idea should have possibilities for drama, conflict, excitement, emotion.

• Don't tell us when you can show us people doing things.

Caution   Only inexperienced writers think they can write humorous stories and features easily. See *NRW Plus*: **Humor: Approach with Caution** and **Land Mines on the Way to a Good Feature.**

Brights

The *bright* is to the feature what the short story is to the novel—a distillation, a tightly written gem that brightens the reader's day. The bright can be one paragraph or several. The following article is about as long as a bright should run:

POOLE, England—(AP)—"It was God who took out my tonsils," the little boy told his mother after his operation at Poole General Hospital.

"When I was taken into the big white room, there were two lady angels dressed in white. Then two men angels came in. Then God came in."

"How did you know it was God?" the mother asked.

"Well, one of the men angels looked down my throat and said, 'God, look at that child's tonsils.'

"Then God took a look and said, 'I'll take them out at once.'"

The conversation was reported by the hospital's staff newsletter.

Duck Talk

"You've got to tell those ducks what they want to hear," says Jimmy Goddard, a master duck caller Eric Lawlor interviewed for his piece about that fine art.

Lawlor let Goddard speak:

"Talk to them the way you'd talk to your lady. Say 'I love you honey, please come on back. . . .' You have to mean everything you say.

"Nothing alive spots a fraud faster than a duck. . . . You must be able to tell a duck's mood. I watch the bird. If he's happy, I'm happy. I tell him, 'If you'll just come on down here, the two of us can have a fine old time.' That's if he's happy. If he's lonesome, then you have to be lonesome. Ask him if he'd like to cry on your shoulder."

The last paragraph is an anti-climax. It belongs in the running story, probably at the end of the second paragraph. Then the reader would be left with that wonderfully innocent quotation from the child.

The Long Story

Despite the pressure on news writers to compress, to boil down the already distilled, long stories and broadcast documentaries are being written all the time. Some events and situations are so complicated, only a lengthy treatment suffices. Or the situation may be so interesting that length is an asset. Readers and viewers and listeners will stay with it all the way through, fascinated by every twist and turn.

Body Damage

The financial news was well known to those who follow business: The Body Shop franchises were in trouble, and the home office was undergoing a shakeup. Competition from similar merchandisers like Bath & Body Works had turned profits into losses.

To put a human face on the dollars-and-cents, profit-and-loss business story, Jeffrey A. Tannenbaum of *The Wall Street Journal* went to Mississippi to report the story of a couple who operate a Body Shop franchise and were not doing well. The full-page story, blending the experiences of Jim and Laura White with the company's woes, begins:

DOTTIE HITT, a trim 25-year-old real-estate agent, pops into the Body Shop outlet in Ridgeland, Miss. In less than a minute, she scoops up a pair of $5.95 nylon "scrubbing" gloves used for rubbing off flaky skin.

So far, so good for Body Shop franchisees Jim and Laura White, who run the store.

But hooked to Ms. Hitt's arm is a brown shopping bag from the Body Shop's arch-rival, Bath & Body Works. Minutes earlier, in the same shopping mall, Ms. Hitt had bought three bars of soap and four other products from the larger, cheerier Bath & Body Works store. She spent about $33 there—and would have bought the gloves at Bath & Body Works, too, if the store had them in stock. Bath & Body "is the chain people talk about," Ms. Hitt says.

Phrases like that crush Mr. White, the franchisee. "It turns my stomach to come in here every day," he says. "I have to take an anti-depressant"—Zoloft, a drug he says he didn't need until a year ago.

Body Shop's performance has indeed been depressing in the U.S., where its competitors are winning big. In the fiscal year ended Feb. 28, sales declined about 5% at Body Shop outlets open a year or more, on top of declines of 6% and 3% for the previous two years. More than 20 U.S. franchisees—some with multiple units—have quit the chain during the past two years, often citing financial and emotional distress.

The beginning of Tannenbaum's story provides the reader with a scene that shows the reason for the downward spiral of Body Shop. The business slide—really the theme of his piece—comes in the fifth paragraph. Tannenbaum has followed the two requirements of this type of the long story:

1. The anecdotal lead must be consistent with the theme of the story.

2. The theme must be no lower than the sixth paragraph.

Time and Labor

The long story travels on the legs of the reporter. "The first point about the long story," says Tannenbaum, "is that it usually requires a lot of work. For a profile of Rockefeller University, I conducted at least 20 interviews in person, and the typical interview lasted 90 minutes. I also did several more interviews by phone and read a great deal of background material."

Balance   The long story, he says, "is an interplay between the specific and the general." By "general" he means the key points or themes that the reporter has selected as the basis of the piece. A story about a breaking news event may have one or two points. The long story may have half a dozen. "Specific" refers to the details that illustrate and amplify the general points.

"For every generalization in the story," Tannenbaum continues, "there should be specific illustrations to buttress it. This means the reporter has to identify the themes and then must dig out the proof for them. The more specific and colorful the details that are used as proof or buttressing material, the more effectively the generalization or theme will be brought home to the reader."

Early Planning   Like all experienced journalists, Tannenbaum tries to sketch out his major ideas or key points as early as possible. This may come before any reporting is done, or soon after the reporting begins.

"For each key point, I want two things: Good quotes stating the point and colorful illustrations, anecdotes, examples," he says. "I know exactly what I am looking for from each interview subject."

In the reporting, additional points often will develop, and these, too, must be buttressed with specific quotes, illustrations, data and anecdotes.

Organizing the Story

No reader, viewer or listener will stay with a long story or a documentary unless the reporting develops interesting material and the writing is a cut above that acceptable for shorter pieces. The long article also must be well-organized to carry the reader or viewer through the long journey.

John McPhee, whom many consider one of the best reporters writing, had a formula when he wrote long pieces for *Time* magazine. "Each had to have a beginning, a middle and an end, some kind of structure so that it would go somewhere and sit down when it got there," McPhee says.

Saul Pett, for many years one of the AP's stellar writers, was called on often to write long pieces. He had a procedure he followed:

> There is my basic material. But it's all kind of in bunches. So then I sit down, and this is just dull donkey work, and I hate it, but I find it necessary, and I kind of outline my material. I don't outline my story because I don't know that yet. I'm outlining the material. I try to put it in piles.

Like Things Together He describes how he went about organizing a story about tempestuous New York Mayor Ed Koch:

> Here's stuff about Koch's wit. Here's stuff about his independence. Here's stuff about how he can be tough with minorities. Here's stuff about his background. All that exists in my notebooks scattered throughout. So the advantage of the outline is that I've got it on paper in logical segments. . . .
>
> I'm getting more familiar with the material so that when I'm ready to write I don't have to go fishing around in notebooks or in stacks of clips. By then I almost don't have to consult my notebooks

McPhee's Procedure McPhee admits that in organizing ideas for his long pieces he goes "nuts trying to put it all in focus." But his procedure gets him through the thicket of notes. First, he identifies the major themes of his piece, puts them on index cards and tacks the cards on a bulletin board. Then the cards are arranged in the order the themes will appear in the final version.

"Strange as it may seem to the beginner anxious to set words to paper, structuring the story challenges a reporter's creative talents as much as the writing. What's most absorbing is putting these stories together," says McPhee. "I know where I'm going from the start of the piece. It's my nature to want to know. Because I'm interested in structure, I must sound mechanistic," he told an interviewer. "But it's just the opposite. I want to get the structural problems out of the way first so I can get to what matters more. After they're solved, the only thing left for me to do is tell the story as well as possible."

Four Steps

1. Identify all themes. Summarize in a sentence or two.

2. Place each summarized theme on a separate index card. Put the cards in the order that the themes will follow in the story.

3. Cut up notes by theme and place them next to theme cards. Reread and again arrange cards and notes in the order in which they will be written.

4. Look through the cards for the major theme that will serve as the lead or the integrating idea for the article. Write it on another card.

As the notes are lined up (step 3), a reporter may discover a lack of adequate documentation or illustrative material to buttress some of the themes. More reporting will be necessary.

Reporters check their notes at this stage for the high-quality quotes and illustrations that can be placed high in the various sections of the story. A representative incident could begin the article if the piece lends itself to a delayed lead. Some reporters use a colored pencil or pen to mark these high-quality quotes, anecdotes and incidents to call them out for use.

Caution: Resist the temptation to use a dramatic quote or telling incident simply because it is attention getting. The material must illustrate the theme it accompanies. If the fit is loose, put the example with a more appropriate theme or toss it out—however much work went into digging it up, however exciting the material.

Remember: Keep clearly in mind or in view the major theme for the piece (step 4). Toss out any material that is irrelevant to this integrating idea.

Changing Directions

Once the story is organized, do not assume that the structure cannot be changed. If the piece does not seem to be flowing properly, shift some of the elements around.

Some of the other problems that come up are:

• A theme has too much material to organize: Divide it into subthemes that can be handled more easily. Consider dropping, or at least drastically subordinating, some themes.

• A theme is too minor to be worth the space being given it: Blend it into another theme or discard it.

• The transition from one theme to another is awkward: To go from one theme to another smoothly, reorder the themes so that the linkage is more natural.

• A long block of background material does not move; it impedes the flow of the article: Break up this background, history, explanatory material and blend sections into the narrative.

See **The Magazine-Story Formula** in *NRW Plus.*

A Television Documentary

Let us watch the producer of a television documentary as he tries to focus on a theme for his subject—the decline of many of the country's older cities.

If the city is the heart and brain of civilization, then the troubles afflicting the city cores of Denver, Detroit, Cleveland, Philadelphia, Boston, Baltimore, St. Louis, Los Angeles, New York and dozens of others threaten a way of life—cultural, commercial, educational, religious. For in the heart of the cities are the opera houses and philharmonic halls, the factories and the offices, the schools, and the temples and the cathedrals. The city gives a center to modern life.

The producer has a national audience and must make one or two cities illustrate the plight of the many. He must draw common elements from the tangled problems of many cities and then find a city that symbolizes most of these elements.

The Racial Factor

Howard Weinberg, the producer, wanted to show the forces, especially racism, at work in causing neighborhood deterioration.

"I went to Chicago," Weinberg says. "My associate and I spent a week there, interviewing real estate agents, mortgage bankers, open housing leaders, community leaders, journalists, government officials and others on the south, west, north sides of Chicago."

When he returned to New York he had no idea how he would tell such a complicated story in half an hour. Tentatively, he decided to use the neighborhood of Austin where black and white community groups had organized to preserve and improve their neighborhood. Also, one organizer, Gale Cincotta, lived in Austin, and Weinberg wanted to have a person as a focus for the program.

"In discussions with Bill Moyers, I was forced to rethink and refine my outline," he says. In looking back at his original outline, Weinberg found he had written, "It is beginning to be understood in communities of the inner cities that deterioration is not an accident, it is the inevitable result of a lack of faith. Expect deterioration—and you'll get it."

Redlining

This idea of a self-fulfilling prophecy kept coming back to Weinberg, and he continued to do more reporting. Gradually, a theme and a strong point of view emerged. "It became clearer that 'redlining' was the story I wanted to tell."

Redlining takes its name from the red circles that banks and other lending agencies reportedly draw on maps around certain neighborhoods. The banks decide that people in these neighborhoods will not be given mortgage money because the banks consider the neighborhoods to be deteriorating. The practice makes it difficult for residents to improve their homes or for buyers to move into the neighborhood. Further deterioration results.

Weinberg was struck by the material he turned up in his reporting. "A savings and loan association was licensed to serve a neighborhood—and clearly, it was not doing that when it openly admitted that it received 80 percent of its deposits from its neighborhood and reinvested 20 percent in its neighborhood," Weinberg says.

Weinberg visualized the booming suburbs—which the savings of inner-city residents were helping to build—and the deteriorating inner city. This would make for dramatic pictures.

He decided to shift the main focus from Austin to Rogers Park, which was beginning to go the way of Austin. Here is how the script of "This Neighborhood Is Obsolete" begins:

BILL MOYERS: The skyline of Chicago thrusts a handsome profile above the shores of Lake Michigan, suggesting the serene self-assurance of a city and its architecture, its wealth and its power and its tolerance for new ideas in urban living. But opulent skylines point up and away from the reality in their shadows. And in Chicago, as in every large American city, the grand vista is misleading.

Out beyond the soaring, secular temples of commerce, before you reach the shopping centers of suburbia, the future of Chicago is being decided every day in less spectacular surroundings: in neighborhoods where drugstores and delicatessens, taverns, laundromats, barbershops, and small churches on treelined corners express a lifestyle in danger of extinction.

For the way the economic game is played these days, these neighborhoods hardly have a chance. There's a profit in moving people out and hang the human cost.

In the next half hour, we'll look at two Chicago neighborhoods where the neighbors are fighting back.

I'm Bill Moyers.

This neighborhood is obsolete.

The people who live here don't think so, but some of the banks and savings and loan associations do. They stopped lending money because they believe the community's deteriorating and the risk is too great. But without money to improve people's homes or to give them a chance to buy another, the decay speeds up and the fear becomes a self-fulfilling prophecy.

In this and similar neighborhoods in Chicago, people accuse the savings and loan associations and the banks of redlining. Redlining means an entire geographic area can be declared unsuitable for conventional loans and mortgages. A redline is, in effect, drawn like a noose around a neighborhood until for want of good housing the working and middle classes are driven to the suburbs and the neighborhood is left to the very poor.

A side effect of redlining is something called disinvestment. You probably haven't heard of that term before. I hadn't until I came here. Disinvestment is a process of collecting deposits in one neighborhood and investing them somewhere else. The lending agents say it's necessary to spread the risk, but it leaves a neighborhood like this short of capital and hope. Gasping for its very life.

The people who could afford to, move on. And that's what the savings and loan associations would like to do. After they've helped to build up the suburbs and make them affluent and attractive, they want to move there, too, or at least to open a suburban branch. Only then does an old neighborhood like this discover where its money has gone, but by then it's too late.

The Results   The documentary had results. A month after the broadcast, the Illinois Savings and Loan Commissioner issued a regulation against redlining that prohibits savings and loan associations from refusing to lend money in a neighborhood because of its age or changing character. Then Congress passed legislation to end redlining by banks.

Notice that Weinberg had to reduce his ideas to the dimension of his program. Like the writer of a 300-word story or a 30-second news item, he had to focus on a single theme and toss out all extraneous material.

The Theme

A theme can always be expressed in a simple sentence or two. David Belasco, the American theatrical producer, once remarked, "If you can't write your idea on the back of my calling card, you don't have a clear idea."

Steve Lovelady, a veteran editor, uses the Belasco method. "I have yet to run across the story too complex or too nuanced or too important to be summed up in twenty-five words or less," Lovelady says. Once that is done, he says, "the heart of the story—the incisively stated, powerful paragraph—has been essentially written." This summary then is the blueprint for the long story or the series.

The Series

Some subjects are too broad, too deep, too complex for even the long story. Faced with such a problem, the reporter finds that the series of articles is the solution. When Sam Roe of *The Blade* decided to examine the decline in Great Lakes shipping, he knew that he could not handle the topic in a single article. Only a series would do.

Roe's task was to show how the collapse of the steel industry struck lake shipping with devastating effect. Most of the ships served U.S. steel firms, carrying iron ore to the giant plants. Toledo's port on Lake Erie handled 43.8 million tons of cargo in 1966. When the steel industry sputtered, the port handled 17.9 tons.

"To capture and hold a reader's attention throughout a series is no easy task," Roe says. "That's why it is important to have stories with action, particularly in the first installment." Roe's first part in his four-part series begins with a delayed lead:

ABOARD THE AMERICAN REPUBLIC—"Damn! She's swinging too wide."

Capt. Robert Tretter cuts the throttle, curses the current, and prays that the *American Republic,* a freighter longer than two football fields, can negotiate one final hairpin bend on the Cuyahoga River. A strong current is denying her a lefthand turn and is pushing her toward a concrete embankment.

"You got 12 feet over here," says wheelsman John Norton. "She'd better not get closer."

The men on the bridge are as tense as sailors aboard a battleship in combat. For the past two hours, the *Republic,* carrying 21,000 tons of iron ore from Lorain, has inched her way down the narrow river toward Cleveland's inner docks.

Tom O'Reilly, *The Blade*

A Port's Relentless Decline

As the steel industry collapsed, Great Lakes shipping went into decline. For the main story in his series on the slump in shipping, Sam Roe of *The Blade* went aboard a freighter and accompanied the crew on its voyage.

Just what does this have to do with his theme, the decline of Great Lakes shipping? In a deft maneuver, the journalistic equivalent of Capt. Tretter's handling of his freighter, Roe sets his story in the right direction:

Now, just when it appears the *Republic*'s port side will ram the embankment, the current lets her go. . . .

This time, the *American Republic* prevailed.

But ahead of her lies a far more formidable obstacle, one that her crew and all others in the shipping industry fear they can't beat: the relentless decline of Great Lakes shipping.

Numbers tell the story. This year there were only . . .

"This lead is more captivating, I thought, than diving into the statistics," Roe says.

Roe says he finds it useful to "walk the reader through" main stories. "For example, the main Great Lakes story was reported and written from the vantage point of a single ship on a single voyage.

"A cook in the mess talking about tough times allowed me to cite unemployment figures. Two decks below, in the cargo holds, an engineer pointing out new equipment allowed me to discuss technological changes in the industry. And so on. The story never really had to move off the ship."

Roe's series, "Struggling to Stay Afloat," won first place in an AP contest for enterprise reporting.

For more examples of Roe's enterprise journalism, see **Tecumseh Street** in *NRW Plus.*

The Crab Pickers

Anne Hull told her editor at the *St. Petersburg Times* that she thought the story would take a week or two. The story was to be a description of how Mexican women are recruited to work in North Carolina picking the meat out of hardshell blue crabs trapped off the coast. The recruitment was done under a federal program that permitted U.S. businesses to bring in foreign workers for jobs that U.S. workers will not do.

But as Hull dug into the story, her ideas shifted and she realized that there was a bigger, better story in following the young women from their small town in central Mexico to North Carolina.

She ended up becoming involved in a six-month journey that took her to Mexico, then with the women to the Outer Banks of North Carolina, and then home to Palomas.

Hull was with the young women when the call summoning them north came. Here is how she begins her series:

It was early afternoon when the girl stepped into the shade of Señor Herrera's small store. She unfolded her mother's shopping list and set it on the wooden counter. A hot wind blew outside.

Señor Herrera was cutting down a rope of chorizo for her when the telephone rang. "Ay," he said, wiping his knife.

Señor Herrera owned the only telephone in Palomas. When news came, he would step outside and shout the bulletin through cupped hands, knowing it would be passed from house to house. The priest is delayed. The medicine for the sick horse is coming.

But this time, he leaned on the counter and spoke to the young girl.

Ve dile a las señoras que ya es hora.
Go tell the ladies it is time.

The girl ran into the daylight, past the mesquite fences and the burro braying in the dusty street. She stopped at a blue iron gate, where a woman was pinning laundry to a clothesline.

The girl called out. *Señora, señora, teléfono.*

Juana Cedillo stood in her patio, blown with the powdery shale of the desert highlands. She'd been expecting the message. Now it had arrived. There would be no more waiting with the empty suitcase under the bed.

She went inside and gave her daughter the news.

Ya es hora de irnos.
The hour has come for us to go.

For more about the women leaving Palomas and Hull's comments about writing long pieces see **Una Vida Mejor—A Better Life** in *NRW Plus.*

Investigative Series

We begin with the series that Donald Barlett and James Steele planned for *The Philadelphia Inquirer* about a new federal tax law that exempted many rich people and large corporations. Then we'll go to Raleigh, N.C.

Leads The *Inquirer* reporters had a wealth of information documenting their theme of loopholes written specifically to help the well-to-do escape taxes. But how, they wondered, could they put the complexities of tax law into simple, everyday language for the leads to their planned seven pieces? How best to attract the readers to a complex topic?

Their editor, Steve Lovelady, was looking over the third in the series. "What does this mean to the average reader?" he asked himself. He answered his question, "That you'll never get a break." Unlike the well-connected types the reporters had uncovered, the average person would still be hit hard by taxes.

Lovelady showed Barlett what he had scribbled on an envelope, and Barlett said, "Forget part three, this is now part one."

Barlett and Steele worked it over, polished it. Here is the lead for the series they came up with:

Imagine, if you will, that you are a tall, bald father of three living in a Northeast Philadelphia row house and selling aluminum siding door-to-door for a living. Imagine that you go to your congressman and ask him to insert a provision in the federal tax code that exempts tall, bald fathers of three from paying taxes on income from door-to-door sales. Imagine further that your congressman cooperates, writes that exemption and inserts it into pending legislation. And that Congress then actually passes it into law. Lots of luck.

Long. Very long. But it works. The series had an enormous readership, and the newspaper was swamped with requests for copies. The series led to changes in the law.

Railroaded to Death Row Joseph Neff, a reporter for *The News & Observer* in Raleigh, N.C., had covered crime and the courts for years and then moved on to investigative reporting. But his old sources kept urging him to write about the death penalty. He told them the subject did not fit his new job. To one persistent source, he said, "If you ever have an innocent guy on death row, I'll do the story."

Months later, Neff received a call. "Joe, I've got one." Neff replied, "Got one what?" His caller said, "An innocent guy on death row."

This began Neff's investigation into the murder of a 56-year-old truck driver and the conviction of a small-time drug dealer sentenced to death for the slaying. The stories started with a description of the murder and the trial and continued for months as Neff described how the key prosecution witness gave conflicting testimony and key evidence was withheld from the jury by the prosecutor. A new trial was ordered, five years after Alan Gell went to death row, nine years after his conviction.

College Corruption

Brett Blackledge of *The Birmingham News* spent 14 months looking into Alabama's two-year colleges.

He found no-bid contracts going to favored businesses; legislators on college payrolls; nepotism and cronyism; the family of the head of one school was on the state's payroll for $560,000.

Blackledge was awarded the 2007 Pulitzer Prize for Investigative Reporting.

A year after his series began, Neff wrote this delayed lead:

WINDSOR—After waiting almost nine years, half of them on death row, Alan Gell sat between his lawyers Wednesday morning, his hands crossed in prayer, waiting for the jury to send him home or to prison for the rest of his life.

The seven men and five women didn't look at Gell as they took their seats facing Superior Court Judge William C. Griffin. The forewoman, Beverly Goodwin, stood.

"Is the verdict to first-degree murder not guilty?" Griffin asked.

"Yes sir," she said, clearly.

Neff's stories are available from www.newsobserver.com

American Heritage Center, University of Wyoming

Reaching into the Past for a Feature

Features based on historical material make for good reading, especially if there are interesting photographs to accompany the article. This photograph of a homestead in Wyoming reveals a lot about the roles of men and women on the frontier. The head of the household is seated comfortably at the center, and around him the women are shown with the tools of their work. One poses with her spinning wheel, and grandma is shown knitting. To the man's left a young woman poses with the butter churn, and to her left a mother fans a child in her lap.

Further Reading

Buchwald, Art. *You Can Fool All of the People All the Time.* New York: Putnam, 1985.

Halberstam, David. *The Powers That Be.* New York: Knopf, 1979.

McPhee, John. *Uncommon Carriers.* New York: Farrar, Straus & Giroux, 2006.

    The master reporter of our times, McPhee here tells the stories of Tom Armstrong, captain of a tugboat on the Illinois River; Don Ainsworth, with whom McPhee crosses the country in Ainsworth's chemical tanker truck; and Scott Davis, whose 10,000 ton coal train a mile and a half long makes the run, with McPhee aboard, from the Black Thunder mine in Wyoming to a generating plant in Tennessee. The portraits are of men who love their work and are masters of demanding professions.

Mitchell, Joseph. *McSorley's Wonderful Saloon.* New York: Grosset & Dunlap, 1943.

Nasaw, David. *The Chief: The Life of William Randolph Hearst.* New York: Houghton Mifflin Co., 2000.

Swanberg, W. A. *Pulitzer.* New York: Scribner, 1967.

Jeff Isaacs, AP Photo

On the air at the Associated Press Broadcast News Center.

Preview

Broadcast stories are written to be easily understood. Radio and television writers:

- Use everyday language.
- Write short sentences.
- Limit every sentence to one idea.
- Use the present tense whenever appropriate.
- Usually confine their stories to one major theme.

In addition to writing local stories, broadcast writers rewrite into broadcast form the stories they pick up from news wires. The material is compressed and sentences are shortened.

For television journalists what is written and how it is written often depend on the available video.

Rely on nouns and verbs. Avoid adjectives and adverbs.

We've been discussing writing for the eye. Now we turn to writing for the ear. Broadcast news is written to rules different from those that guide writers for print and online.

Watch the evening news, stopwatch in hand. You'll find that most stories are short. They usually run less than 30 seconds. These are called *tell* stories and are also known as *readers* because they are not accompanied by visuals.

Broadcast news serves a purpose different from that of the newspaper. Its intent is to provide the public with basic information quickly and succinctly. The broadcast writer's job is to get the story idea across without detail. To communicate events in such short bursts to an audience that cannot read or hear the material again, the broadcast journalist follows a special set of guidelines.

Like the jockey or the weight watcher who thinks twice about every slice of bread, the broadcast journalist examines every word and idea. Too many words and the story may squeeze out another item. Too many ideas and the listener or viewer may be confused.

Broadcast newswriters set their writing rhythm to a few guidelines: Keep it tight. Write simple sentences. One idea to a sentence. When attribution is necessary, begin the sentence with it.

An Early Guide

When the United Press hired reporters they were handed a green booklet about the size of a small greeting card. It was titled *United Press Radio News Style Book* and was written by Phil Newsom, the UP Radio News Manager.

Though more than 50 years old, and written before the days of television, Newsom's advice holds up today. Here are some of Newsom's guidelines:

> To write effectively for radio you must unlearn the prose writer's rules about sentence structure. Disregard such forms as dependent clauses and balanced sentences. You can even forget the first grammatical rule you ever learned—that a sentence must have a subject and a verb.

> Some of radio's most effective sentences are not complete sentences at all. They are descriptive phrases. They save a lot of words and go over very smoothly on the air.

> Ordinarily, short sentences are the best for radio. But the real test is whether they can be read aloud, whether the announcer finally can arrive at the end without gasping for breath.

> Don't try to tell too much in your opening sentence. The radio listener requires a little time to get adjusted after each story. We call it "warming up the listener."

> Never lead into a story with a question. The similarity between such leads and commercials is apt to be confusing.

> There has always been a rule in radio news reporting against hanging phrases, since they break up the flow of thought. For example, a newspaper lead might say:

> "Fourteen persons were killed today in an explosion at King's Powder Mill, state police announced."

> The radio news report would say:

> "State Police announce that 14 persons have been killed in an explosion at the King's Powder Mill."

These days we would not have the state police "announce" the 14 deaths. If it's an established fact, we would not even have to attribute the deaths. But his point that in broadcast writing attribution precedes assertion remains valid.

Newsom suggests that broadcast writers study their notes for the "most interest-compelling angle" and use it for the lead. He goes on to advise writers to emphasize the aspects of the event that affect people personally. Stories written with people in mind hold their attention, he says.

Rewriting the Wires

Most of television's nonlocal news is rewritten from the news wires. Let's see how this is done.

News Wire

SAN FRANCISCO (AP)—Leaders of the University of California on Thursday voted to drop race-based admissions following a tumultuous meeting in which Jesse Jackson and other demonstrators drove the panel from its meeting room.

The 14–10 decision by the UC Board of Regents was a major victory for those working to roll back affirmative action programs around the nation, including Republican Gov. Pete Wilson, who has made that fight the key plank of his presidential campaign.

"It means the beginning of the end of racial preferences," said Wilson, who grabbed the national spotlight from his vantage point as president of the regents. "We believe that students at the University of California should achieve distinction without the use of the kind of preferences that have been in place."

Jackson said after the vote, "California casts either a long shadow or a long sunbeam. This is a long shadow. July 20 will live a long time in California history."

(Ten more paragraphs follow.)

Radio Wire

[San Francisco]—The University of California Board of Regents voted tonight to end race-based preferences in school admissions.

The vote came soon after demonstrators interrupted the regents' meeting, singing "We Shall Overcome." The regents were forced to another room to vote on the admissions policy.

Earlier tonight, the regents voted to eliminate the school's affirmative action-based policies on the hiring of faculty and contractors.

Nixon Library Let's watch Mervin Block rewrite a wire story for a 20-second tell story for network television news. Here is the wire copy Block had before him:

News Wire

YORBA LINDA, CALIF [AP]—Construction of the long-delayed Richard M. Nixon presidential library and museum will require the demolition of the home of a 93-year-old widow who doesn't want to move, officials say.

"I love my house. I don't want them to take it from me," said Edith Eichler, who knew Nixon as a boy here and supported him for president.

"Why should I have to move into a more crowded, dinky retirement place away from my family and friends? Do you think Richard Nixon would want his mother to move?"

Yorba Linda, Nixon's birthplace 30 miles southeast of Los Angeles, was chosen for the $25 million library last month after a nine-year search. Years of delays by San Clemente city officials forced Nixon to give up building the library in that coastal community, where he kept the western White House during his presidency.

At a news conference Monday night, city officials said they would appraise Eichler's one-story, wood-frame cottage within a month and make her an offer.

Eichler, a former schoolteacher who has lived in the house for 65 years, will be the only person displaced by the museum.

Eichler said she knew the Nixon family well.

"Richard was a nice enough little boy, always running around like any other kid. Who would believe he would become a president?

"And who would ever imagine they'd want to build this big library for him right in my own back yard?" she asked.

That is the way AP wrote it for the eye. Here is the way Block wrote it for the ear:

Broadcast Version

They're putting up a library for former President Nixon near Los Angeles, but they say they first have to tear down the home of a 93-year-old widow. She says she loves her home and does not want to move. Officials of the city of Yorba Linda say they'll appraise her wood-frame cottage and make her an offer. The woman says she knew Nixon as a boy and supported him for president.

Here is how Block, now a broadcast writing coach, thought the story through:

I tell news writers, "Avoid premature pronouns." Yet I started my script with "they." Why? Although I refrain from starting a story with a pronoun, I know that in conversation we often start tidbits with "they." F'rinstance: "They say onions and garlic are good for you—but not for your companions."

I certainly don't want to start with a yawner: "Officials in Yorba Linda, California. . . ." In the first sentence, I want to mention *Nixon, library* and *L.A.*, but I don't see how I can sensibly start with any of

Learning from the Mistakes of the Pros

In his Television News-writing Workshop, (www.mervinblock.com), Block analyzes scripts of professional newscasters. Too often, the scripts are found wanting. Here are some of Block's comments about an ABC *World News* newscast:

Script: "Robert Alan Soloway did today plead not guilty to the charges lodged against him."

Block: ". . . did today plead"? Ungainly, unnatural, unconversational.

Script: "There is a major scandal rocking the world of NASCAR just days before the most prestigious race of the season, the Daytona 500."

Block: The main problem: starting with *there is,* a dead phrase. Better: "A scandal is rocking the world of NASCAR. . . ." *Major?* Do networks report minor scandals?

them. So I turn to our old friend "they." I make it clear that it's "they" who say the home must be torn down.

I don't use the widow's name because it doesn't mean anything outside Yorba Linda. I defer mentioning the name of the town, because it's not widely known. I save words wherever I can: I don't call it a *presidential* library; what other kind would they put up for a former president? And I'm just as stingy with facts: I don't mention San Clemente, the western White House, the widow's background and other details in the wire copy.

"Newsbreak"

"Newsbreak" ran on the CBS television network several times a day. In less than a minute, several major stories are read. One day, Block compressed seven wire stories into 50 seconds. Here are three items from the script and his explanation of how he wrote them:

Script	Explanation
A former employee of the Westchester Stauffer's Inn, near New York City, was arrested today and charged with setting the fire that killed 26 corporate executives last December.	Rather than start a story with a place name, "In White Plains, New York," I always try to fix the place up high but unobtrusively. In the third line, I wrote "outside," then realized that "near" is closer and shorter. I didn't use his name because he was an unknown, and his name wouldn't mean anything to anyone outside White Plains, which is largely unknown itself except as the site of a Revolutionary battle.
The government's index of leading economic indicators last month rose slightly, one-point-four percent. The increase reversed three straight months of declines.	To save words, I didn't say the U.S. Department of Commerce issued the statistics. It's sufficient to say "the government." I originally wrote, "rose slightly last month." Then I caught myself, remembering Strunk's rule to "place the emphatic words of a sentence at the end."
A British truck driver admitted today he was the "Yorkshire Ripper," pleading guilty to manslaughter in the deaths of 13 women. By not pleading guilty to <u>murder</u>, Peter Sutcliffe could be sent to a hospital for the criminally insane— and not prison.	This is a simple, straightforward, no-frills account of a dramatic development in a sensational story. But there's no need here for any supercharged language to "sell" the story. (As the architect Ludwig Mies van der Rohe used to say, "Less is more.") My second sentence gives the "why" for his plea. I underlined "murder" because I thought it was a word the anchor should stress. (Some anchors welcome this. In any case, in the pressure-cooker atmosphere of a network newsroom, the stress is usually on the writer.)

Voice-Over Videotape

Television writing is complicated by the need to write to visuals. Block was told to write a lead-in and 20 seconds of voice-over videotape for the "CBS Evening News" from this wire service story:

> CRESTVIEW, Fla. [AP]—Tank cars carrying acetone exploded and burned when a train loaded with hazardous chemicals derailed here today. Thousands were evacuated as the wind spread thick yellow sulfur fumes over rural northwest Florida.
>
> Only one injury was reported. A fisherman trekking through the woods near the wreck inhaled some of the fumes and was hospitalized for observation.
>
> Oskaloosa County Civil Defense director Tom Nichols estimated that 5,000 people had fled homes or campsites in the 30-square-mile evacuation area, which included several villages and about half of Blackwater River State Forest.
>
> "It's a rural area and houses are scattered all through it," said Ray Belcher, a supervisor for the Florida Highway Patrol. "It's about half woods, half farms."
>
> Civil Defense officials put the approximately 9,000 residents of nearby Crestview on alert for possible evacuation as approaching thunderstorms threatened a wind-shift that would push the fumes in that direction. . . .

Block was writing "blind" to the tape. That is, he did not have access to the videotape his copy would refer to. Here is Block's thinking:

> **First, I see the dateline, Crestview, Florida, and I know that in writing for broadcast I have to put the dateline up near the top as unobtrusively as possible. It has to be done deftly.**
>
> **When I started writing for broadcast, I was told by an editor that it's inadvisable to begin a story by saying, "In Crestview, Florida. . . ." The editor told me that was a lazy man's way of starting a story. In London today . . . in Paris today. . . . He didn't say never. But in 90 or 95 percent of the cases, it's best not to begin that way.**
>
> **We see in the first line of the AP story that one of the trains is carrying acetone. My reaction is that most people don't know what acetone is. That probably is a reflection of my ignorance. If we were to use it on the air, it could sound like acid-own. In any case, there's no need to identify the chemical, or any of the chemicals, perhaps. The most important element is the explosion and the evacuation.**
>
> **In the second paragraph of the story, it says that only one injury was reported. I didn't mention the injury. It seems slight. The third paragraph gives the name of the county. In writing news for broadcast, you have to eliminate details and focus on the big picture.**
>
> **In my script, beginning with the second paragraph, I had to write 20 seconds of voice-over. As so often happens, I had no chance to see the**

More from Block

Script: "If you or anyone you know are flying tonight, we have information on airport delays and arrivals."

Block: That sentence needs more than first aid; it needs reconstructive surgery. *Anyone* is singular, so *are* should be *is*. . . . opening with *if* is not promising; *if* is the weakest word in the dictionary. Better: For you or anyone else flying tonight, we have information. . . ." But I'd skip the *you* stuff; only one person in 200 might be flying that night. And all those already aloft—or sitting on a runway—wouldn't hear the newscast.

Here is the script as Block wrote it:

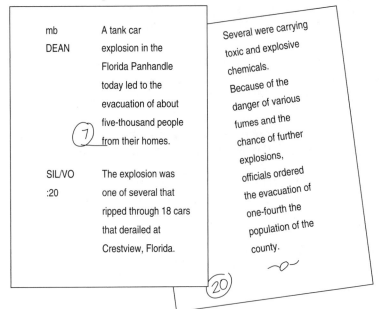

```
mb          A tank car
DEAN        explosion in the
            Florida Panhandle
            today led to the
            evacuation of about
            five-thousand people
   (7)      from their homes.

SIL/VO      The explosion was
:20         one of several that
            ripped through 18 cars
            that derailed at
            Crestview, Florida.
```

Several were carrying
toxic and explosive
chemicals.
Because of the
danger of various
fumes and the
chance of further
explosions,
officials ordered
the evacuation of
one-fourth the
population of the
county.
(20)

videotape in advance, so I had to write in a general way without getting specific. I made an assumption at this point, and although it's dangerous to assume, I have seen so many derailments on TV films or tape that I figured the opening shot would be of derailed cars. So I presumed my paragraph covering the tape of the accident would be appropriate.

I was looking for facts in the AP story that would be essential in my script. As you can see, my script consists of about a five-second lead-in and 20 seconds of voice-over for the tape. Within the tight space, I can use only the most important facts because a script cannot consist of a string of dense facts.

In his column in *RTNDA Communicator,* Block shows how to avoid using datelines to begin stories. See **Starting the Story** in *NRW Plus.*

Sentence Structure and Language

From our window into the thinking of a broadcast newswriter, we can generalize about writing for the ear.

Write short, simple sentences. Use everyday language. Make most sentences conform to the S-V-O structure (subject-verb-object). Keep one idea to a sentence. Write the way you talk. "Be conversational," says the editor. Here are some other guidelines and examples:

- **Begin sentences with a source, with the attribution, if needed:**
  WRONG: The city needs new traffic lights, the mayor said.
  RIGHT: The mayor says the city needs new traffic lights.

- **Do not start a story with a participial phrase:**
  WRONG: Hoping to keep the lid on spiraling prices, the president called today for wage-price guidelines for labor and industry.
  RIGHT: The president is calling for wage-price guidelines to keep prices down.

- **Use ordinary, one-syllable words whenever possible:**
  WRONG: The unprecedented increase in profits led the Congress to urge the plan's discontinuance.
  RIGHT: The record profits led Congress to urge an end to the plan.

- **Use vigorous verbs.** Avoid adjectives and adverbs:
  WEAK: He made the task easy for his listeners.
  BETTER: He simplified the task for his listeners.
  WEAK: She walked slowly through the field.
  BETTER: She trudged through the field.

- **Use the active, not the passive, voice:**
  WEAK: He was shown the document by the lawyer.
  BETTER: The lawyer showed him the document.

- **Use familiar words in familiar combinations.**

- **Write simply, directly.** Omit useless words.

- **Write in language that can be read easily.** The writer should test his or her writing by reading it aloud. Not only will the reading catch sounds that do not work, it will reveal whether a newscaster can read one idea in a single pulse. The newscaster must be able to breathe, and each breath closes out an idea. Also, reading aloud you may catch double meanings.

  Simple, direct writing can be elegant. This is the language of Mark Twain, Charles Dickens, and Edward R. Murrow. Here is a lead by Charles Kuralt, a correspondent for CBS television who was doing a piece about exploitation of the environment:

      Men look at hillsides and see board feet of lumber. Men
      look at valleys and see homesites.

- **Use a phrase to indicate someone is being quoted:** as he said, as he put it, and these are his words. Do not use "quote," "unquote," or "end quote." For routine quotes, paraphrase.
  WEAK: He said, "I am not a crook."
  BETTER: He said, and these are his words, "I am not a crook."

- **Place titles before names.** Spell out all numbers through 11. (Why 11? Because it resembles two l's.) Do not use initials for agencies and organizations unless they are widely known, such as FBI and CIA. In a script, hyphenate letters that are read aloud. Use contractions for informality. Keep sentences to fewer than 20 words.

Tenses

Where appropriate and accurate, use the present tense or the present perfect tense:

> The state highway department **says** it will spend six million dollars this year improving farm-to-market roads.
> The state highway department **has announced** it will spend six million dollars this year improving farm-to-market roads.

When the present tense is used in the lead, the story may continue or shift to the past tense. When the present perfect tense is used in the lead, the story shifts to the past tense to indicate when the event occurred:

> A federal judge **has issued** a temporary order stopping efforts to put a reservist on active army duty because he refused to shave off his beard.
> Yesterday, the judge **gave** the army ten days to answer a suit filed by the American Civil Liberties Union for the reservist.

Following the past tense, the story can shift back to the present perfect or even to the present tense if the writer believes the situation is still true or in effect. The AP radio story continues:

> The ACLU **filed** the suit on behalf of a high school teacher, John Jones of Bristol, Rhode Island.
> The suit **asks** the court to declare unconstitutional a regulation forbidding beards and **claims** the teacher was marked absent from several drills that the suit **says** he attended.

Caution: Don't strain to use the present or present perfect tense. When something has happened in the past, the past tense is appropriate.

Wrong: Two men are dead after a head-on collision on State Highway 68.

Correct: Two men died in a head-on collision on State Highway 68.

Wrong: Freeport is without a budget director today.

Correct: Freeport Budget Director Albert Heffner resigned last night.

Attribution

Where attribution is needed, broadcast copy places attribution at the beginning of sentences. This makes for clarity.

News Wire

ALBUQUERQUE [AP]—The death of a man whose body was found set in 500 pounds of concrete in a 55-gallon drum may be connected to a counterfeiting case, a federal agent says.

"I believe there is a connection. We won't be 100 percent certain until we know if the guy is who we think he is," said David Saleeba, special agent in charge of the U.S. Secret Service office in Albuquerque. . . .

Broadcast Wire

(Albuquerque)—A federal agent in Albuquerque says the death of a man whose body was found set in 500 pounds of concrete in a 55-gallon drum may be connected to a counterfeiting case. Police and federal agents say they believe the body recovered is that of 21-year-old Derek Suchy.

More on Writing

Block conducts broadcast newswriting workshops, scrutinizes news scripts and on his Television Newswriting Workshop (www.mervinblock.com), and in his columns in *RTNDA Communicator,* he examines bloopers, blunders and questionable writing. "Too many of us think we're not only the messengers but also part of the message," he writes. For example:

Carrollton police tell us one person was injured during a car chase overnight.

Sometimes, the broadcast writer will introduce the station into copy, or the media, as this Nebraska news writer did:

It was a full-fledged media event that brought every TV station in the state to northwest Nebraska today.

"The media are not the story," says Block. "The *story* is the story."

In one of his columns, Block culled these sentences from clips. Look at the words in italics:

- The attorney for defendant Henry Watson *dropped a bombshell* in his closing argument.

- City officials and union leaders have been *burning the midnight oil.*

Sentence Length: Always keep in mind that someone has to read the words you write for broadcast—and has to read them aloud. Very long sentences, especially those with lots of clauses, cause broadcasters to stumble.

If a sentence goes over two lines on your terminal screen, it may be too long. Take another look at it. Read it aloud, slowly. Can you get through it without gasping for air or stumbling?

If you can, then ask yourself if the listener will be able to comprehend all the facts you've presented in that one sentence. Would you convey the information more clearly in two sentences? If so, rewrite.

The Lead: The shorter the better. Don't summarize the day's major development in a long, complex sentence. Instead, provide a short and compelling reason for the listener to keep listening.

Helping the Broadcaster: Read copy one more time to root out typos and awkward phrasings and to provide pronunciation guides, called *pronouncers,* wherever the anchor is going to encounter a strange or difficult name or word.

- The workers were *visibly shaken* but not hurt.
- Lopez was sitting with friends on a courtyard bench at the Marlboro Houses in Coney Island when *shots rang out* Sunday.

Yes, you're right. They are clichés, the "language of newspeople churning out copy in a race against the clock," Block says. And he goes on to quote George Orwell's warning to writers: "Never use a metaphor, simile or other figure of speech you are used to seeing in print."

The Lead

Some events are too complex to plunge into immediately. Or there may be a confusing array of personalities or numbers. The script then has to be set up for the theme of the piece.

Newspaper Lead

As Gov. Alfred Caster neared the end of his seven-day working vacation aboard a riverboat today, his aides said that he was unconcerned about some editorial criticism that he had become an absentee governor whose administration was adrift.

Broadcast Lead

Some newspaper editorials have criticized Governor Caster as an absentee governor. But officials aboard a riverboat with the governor say the criticisms don't bother him. The governor is nearing the end of his seven-day working vacation on the boat.

Broadcast Reporting

Let's look at how broadcast reporters work. First, we go to an all-news radio station.

At the largest stations, the news director or assignment editor makes up an assignment sheet for reporters. The editor goes through the futures file, notes continuing stories and consults the wire services' schedules of stories. Breaking news stories also are assigned.

In the field, the reporters, who carry tape recorders, may each cover three or four stories—a feature, a running story from city hall, a talk by a congressman and a traffic accident that tied up a major artery. For each, the reporter phones the editor, who decides whether the reporter should go on live or be recorded.

If the reporter is to go on live, the editor places the reporter on a newscast. If recorded, the reporter talks to an aide, who makes sure the material is being recorded properly by an engineer. The recording, called a *cart* (for *cartridge*), is labeled by slug and time and given to the editor.

Radio reporters cannot rely on pictures, so they supply much of the descriptive material for their stories. Sound bites from their interviews are essential to give the listener a sense of immediacy and what reporters call "you-are-thereness." The radio reporter develops a keen ear for the high-quality quote, the quotation that sums up the situation. The rest is ruthlessly discarded.

One of the most important tasks of the broadcast journalist is to ask relevant questions. Good interviews are made by the right questions.

As tape can be edited, the reporter can ask a question again if the answer is too long or complicated.

Television journalism involves a more complex technology than print or radio. The TV reporter is always conscious of the need for a video, for action of some sort. If the reporter is to be on air, the prevailing wisdom has it, she or he should be speaking over action.

Reporting and Writing to Tape

The feature or timeless piece may include an interview, voice-over silent tape, or tape with sound of an event and the reporter's summarizing the event. The story may take days of planning and hours of shooting, editing and writing, and then when it is finally broadcast it may run for only a minute and a half.

For a story on a new reading program in the city schools, an interview with the superintendent of schools may set out the intent of the curriculum change. Additional interviews will allow viewers to hear the specific plans of teachers. School children will be interviewed. Locations might include classrooms, teachers discussing the program, the superintendent in his office.

The producer will want a variety of shots—medium, close-up and cutaway—to build a visual story to accompany the reporter's narration and interviews.

Newsreaders

"Most local television stations hire readers, not journalists or newspeople. Local anchors are hired for their personalities or their looks, good hair, for instance. . . . They should be called newsreaders, as they are in Europe."

—*Walter Cronkite*

Text to Video

"Text should enhance a video, not describe what the viewer already sees. If you see a woman crying, do not write, 'The woman is crying,' but say, 'The woman is mourning the death of her son.' Also, let the video 'breathe.' Let it play out; you do not have to write a word for every frame. Sometimes the pictures tell a story without any text; you can use natural sound and sound bites as your narrative."

—*Herb Brubaker, president, Television News Center*

Stories for newspapers usually follow a straight-line form—most important material at the beginning, least important at the end. But for longer broadcast pieces, the form is often a circle because the ending usually has a reminder of the theme.

The reporter's task is to marry natural sound, visuals and interviews. Sometimes the reporter muffs the opportunity. In a piece about a cloistered order of nuns who vow perpetual silence, the reporter wrote a narration with no pauses. He wrote about silence but never stopped talking. In effect, the viewer could not hear the silence. He might have captured the event had he stopped talking in some places, a few seconds at a time, to allow viewers to hear the clatter of knives and forks at a silent dinner, the footsteps of nuns in darkened hallways. The tone of the story should match the event.

Blunt Writing

The news all week had been grim. The World Trade Center ruins were still smoldering, and there was little hope of any one of the thousands missing being found alive. The intro for the weekend edition of ABC's *World News Tonight* reflected the state of affairs.

> the president prepares the country for a war, he says, unlike any we have fought. a sixth grueling day of digging and searching in the world trade center rubble, and at the pentagon, the victims of tuesday's terrorist attacks are remembered in services near and far.

For more of the script prepared for the program, see **Terror Folo**, *in NRW Plus*.

Packaging Short News Features

Let's watch a television news student, Cathy, as she puts together a news feature. The story is about a program designed to prevent children from committing crimes when they grow up. Cathy has an interview with the psychologist who developed the program. She also has videotaped the children in the program as they talk to the psychologist and play. Cathy has interviewed the children for their reactions to the program.

After her reporting, Cathy has 40 minutes of tape. On her way back to the station, Cathy starts blocking out her story:

I'll tell the editor to start with pictures of the children in a circle for 20 seconds while in my script I'll give some facts about the project.

Then a 20- to 30-second sound bite from the psychologist explaining the "substitute family" technique. As he talks about the substitute parents, the editor will show pictures of the children and parents greeting one another affectionately.

Then I'll write a short transition into the interviews. I think that to get into this section I'll pose the question, "But does the program work?" and have three or four short interviews with the answers.

She'll close with a quote from the psychologist and then her own wrap-up from the scene to answer questions she thinks have been left unanswered. She estimates the feature will run from 2:30 to 2:45, just what the producer wants.

Interviewing

Much of what Cathy did was the result of planning. For her interviews, she devised questions that sought to get to the heart of the story quickly. Interviews have to be kept short, to the point. This requires gentle but firm direction by the reporter. Here are some interviewing guidelines:

Before shooting the interview:

1. Make the subject comfortable.

   a. Describe the general area your questions will cover, but don't tell the subject what the questions will be. The first, spontaneous response to a question is often the truest.

   b. Explain the setting—which mike the subject should speak into and so on. Tell her or him to look at you or other questioners—not the camera—unless she or he is going to show the audience how to do something that requires direct communication between the speaker and the audience.

   c. Before the interview chat easily to dispel any nervousness. Show an interest in the subject's area so he or she will gain confidence.

   d. Don't act like you know it all. Prepare so you do know enough about the topic so that your subjects believe you understand what they are talking about.

   e. Know what your are looking for. Most short items must be carefully focused because of time limits.

   f. Don't waste the subject's time with questions whose answers could be found elsewhere—age, job, education, residence. Such questions make the subject wonder about your interest. Prepare background ahead of the interview.

During the interview:

1. Start with easy-to-answer questions. Leave the tough ones for the end. If the first questions are too demanding, the person can walk away. An early easy question puts the person at ease.

2. Don't ask questions that can be answered yes or no.

3. Don't ask long, involved questions.

> **Advice**
> Studs Terkel, for 45 years a major figure on National Public Radio whose interviews have won prizes and acclaim, advises: "Listening leads to truth. . . . You can't fake interest. . . . Let the little guy tell his tale. . . . Stay patient."

4. Don't suggest answers to interviewees.

5. Build on the subject's answers—don't ask questions just because you prepared them. Listen to his or her answers and ask questions about what he or she says.

6. Ask only one question at a time. Don't ask multiple questions.

7. Develop a sense of timing. Cut in if the subject starts to be repetitive or long-winded. Don't cut the subject off just when he or she is about to say something important.

8. Try to stick to one topic.

9. Adjust the tone of the questions to the interviewee's experience. A politician may need to be pushed and asked direct questions.

Variety for Newscasts

Most stations and networks blend the day's top news with features and theme stories. Some stations have staffs large enough to assign reporters to investigative projects.

Sexual Harassment

KTRH NewsRadio in Houston had cultivated sources in the Houston police department over the years of covering its activities. One of its sources told Stephen Dean of KTRH that women officers and other workers who complained of harassment suffered retaliation.

Dean investigated and verified the tip. Some women officers were transferred to desk jobs or to distant posts. Nothing was done to the officer against whom the complaint was filed.

Here's his lead-in to the first story:

> Charges of retaliation and unfair treatment are raised by cops who claim they are victims of sexual harassment on the job. NewsRadio's Stephen Dean has the results of an exclusive KTRH investigation.

Dean then picks up the story:

> Women who wear Houston police badges find themselves quickly transferred to desk jobs or cross-town assignments when they file sexual harassment complaints.
>
> Some say they're treated harshly by supervisors and coworkers as the complaints are being processed.

Internal Affairs Sergeant Patsy Chapman filed a complaint against an office supervisor, saying he made repeated advances and stuck his tongue in her ear. When she turned him away, overtime requests she turned in for his approval suddenly disappeared. She was out $800 of pay.

So her last resort was a written complaint, and she says it caused her life to get even worse. . . .

Disappearing Songbirds

As cities expand into the countryside and as industry replaces forest and grassland, the environment changes. Pavement replaces grass, duplexes and factories rise where pine and birch once grew. KOTV in Tulsa wondered whether in this changing environment the songbird would be silenced.

It embarked on a documentary, an "ecocampaign," the station called it, to alert viewers to the plight of grassland songbirds. One of the imperiled birds is the state bird, the scissortailed flycatcher. The reporting and filming took more than three months of arduous work.

"For those who've never noticed, once a songbird alights on a perch, it generally doesn't stay very long," says Scott Thompson, the reporter for the documentary. "We would spend hours in nearly inaccessible prairie draws and sloughs and desolate mesa plateaus, waiting for a chance encounter with a songbird or raptor."

The photographers shot vast amounts of videotape to be able to capture a few seconds of usable footage.

The labor paid off. KOTV distributed more than 12,000 viewer guides, and proceeds from the sale of the videotapes of the program went to a research center. The documentary won the Public Service Award from the Society of Professional Journalists, whose judges found the subject of "Songs of the Prairie" to be "just as important as it was when Rachel Carson published *Silent Spring*. The writing, photography were excellent, practically lyrical. The videography deserves special recognition."

Investigative and Public Service Reports

Phil Williams and Bryan Staples of WTVF-TV in Nashville examined invoices and e-mails in statehouse records and found that friends of the governor had received contracts without competitive bidding.

Reporters for WFAA-TV in Dallas looked into the local police department's pursuit of drug dealers. The station questioned the legitimacy of police work and the department's confidential informants. As a result of the reporting, drug charges against more than 50 defendants were dismissed.

Dedrick Russell and the staff of WBTV in Charlotte, N.C., assembled in-depth profiles of the 10 lowest performing high schools in the Charlotte-Mecklenburg school district. On 10 consecutive nights, Russell showed the schools' plans for improvement.

The Power of TV

In 1958, Edward Murrow said, "This instrument can teach, it can illuminate, yes, and it can even inspire. But, it can only do so to the extent that humans are determined to use it to those ends. Otherwise it is merely wires and lights in a box. There is a great and perhaps decisive battle to be fought against ignorance, intolerance and indifference. This weapon of television can be useful."

Unclaimed Bodies

Every month, the Cook County coroner sends the bodies of unclaimed dead to a distant cemetery where they are placed in an unmarked mass gravesite. WBBM Newsradio 780 wanted to tell their stories.

Reporters traced the body of Alphonso Knox, who died in his room on Chicago's West Side. Although his roommate told investigators Knox was a Korean War veteran, the government had no such record. Newsradio 780 located Knox's honorable discharge, and instead of being buried in an unmarked pauper's grave, his body now lies in the Abraham Lincoln National Cemetery.

Newsradio 780 won a public service award for the stories.

A Dozen Deadly Don'ts

Thou shalt not:

1. Scare listeners.

2. Give orders.

3. Start a story with

   - "as expected."
   - "in a surprise move."
   - "a new development today."
   - "our top story tonight is."
   - *there is* or *it is.*
   - a participial phrase.
   - a personal pronoun.
   - a question.
   - a quotation.
   - an unknown or unfamiliar name.
   - someone's "making news" or "making history."
   - *another, more* or *once again.*

4. Characterize news as "good" or "bad."

5. Use any form of *to be* as the main verb in your lead.

6. Bury the verb in a noun.

7. Use *yesterday* or *continues* in your first sentence.

8. Use *no, not* and negatives in your first sentence.

9. Use newspaper style, language or rituals.

10. Cram too much information into a story.

11. Lose or mislead a listener.

12. Make a factual error.

Adapted from Mervin Block's *Writing Broadcast News—Shorter, Sharper, Stronger,* 2nd ed. (Chicago: Bonus Books, 1998).

For more of Block's advice on writing for broadcast, see **Top Tips of the Trade** in *NRW Plus.*

Through the words and voice of a troubled teen-ager, WBEZ-FM in Chicago detailed the abuses at the city's juvenile detention center.

WKRC-TV in Cincinnati examined charter schools and found them offering poor-quality education. The reporting staff found taxpayers were supporting second-class education and wasting millions of dollars in public funds.

At WBBM in Chicago, Steve Miller went through the records of hundreds of people licensed to work in daycare centers and found many who had been convicted of drug dealing and possession, spousal and child abuse and other criminal offenses. Miller's work led the legislature to pass a bill tightening up the procedures for obtaining a license to work in daycare centers.

Telling the Whole Story

Little of what goes through the broadcast station's editing rooms reaches the public. Interviews are cut as editors search for the brief sound bite. Background material, if any, is compressed. Sometimes, the meaningful shades of gray that make the story complete don't make the broadcast, especially when they complicate the theme or story line.

Critics have accused broadcast journalists of allowing office holders and candidates to pass on to the public what one disparagingly described as "sound bites that were simply advertising."

A Conveyor Belt

People in public life have long considered broadcast news a more direct route to the citizen and a more congenial medium than print. Franklin D. Roosevelt was famous for his radio fireside chats in which he soothed a country mired in a deep depression. Dwight D. Eisenhower began the televised presidential news conference to reach the public directly, without the interpretations and possible criticism of the print press. Eisenhower used television, historian Stephen Ambrose wrote, to "set the national agenda" and also to "obfuscate an issue when he was not sure how he would deal with it."

Mario Cuomo of New York, when governor, told newspaper reporters, "Don't flatter yourselves into thinking you're the best way to reach the public.

"When I go to you, I don't reach the public directly; you do. When I go electronically, I reach the public. If I want to reach the public, I shouldn't be talking to you. I should be talking to a radio microphone."

Ethical Imperatives

Broadcast journalists are aware of attempts to use them as the conveyors of messages. Although broadcast journalists operate within tighter deadlines and are called on to be more concise than print journalists, they try to give fair, well-rounded and accurate accounts of events.

The TV camera has enormous power, and its users are conscious of this. When news crews were slow to arrive in Somalia, a CBS medical reporter said, hundreds of thousands of starving people died.

Local News: Mostly Crime

Studies of local news on TV stations show that they are the number one source of news for the public. But the studies also show that most of the news focuses on crime and little on social issues, education and other news of significance.

A study of local TV news by eight journalism schools found almost a third of news time went to crime and criminal justice stories, and a sixth to government and politics. Education averaged a minuscule 2 percent of news time. A study of 100 local TV newscasts by the Rocky Mountain Media Watch found crime took up 30 percent of newscast time.

An Exception In Austin, KVUE-TV instituted "community standards" guidelines for deciding whether to broadcast a story about a local crime. The station decided it would use a crime story if people in charge of news could answer yes to questions such as: Is there an immediate threat to public safety? Is there a significant community impact? Do viewers need to take some kind of action?

The Reason
Marty Haag, senior news vice president for the A.H. Belo stations, says that "covering crime is the easiest, fastest, cheapest, most efficient kind of news coverage for TV stations. News directors and station owners love crime because it has a one-to-one ratio between making the assignment and getting a story on-air."

Entertainment
"If people who listen to the news, and watch the news, become so conditioned by the frivolous treatment of news that they come to regard news primarily as entertainment, how can they really care about the news? Or really *think* about the news, think about what they see and hear in terms of meaning in their community, in their country, in their world?"
—*Edward Bliss, Jr.*

A TV Newsman's Critique

The power of television to inform and influence the public worried Charles Kuralt, a veteran network reporter and writer. He thought too many stations follow the advice of news consultants who "would cut the Iliad or King Lear to 90 seconds." He was disturbed by the inadequate news training of the "earnest young man or woman" who opens the six o'clock news: "'Good evening, here is the news.' This is said very urgently and with the appearance of sincerity—most often by an attractive person who would not know a news story if it jumped up and mussed his or her coiffure."

In a talk at the University of Nevada–Reno, he told journalism students and faculty members:

> The real rewards—both in the giving and the receiving—are in the patient, hard work of the careful writer who seizes a fact or an event out of the air as it flashes past and hammers it like a blacksmith on his anvil, and tempers it, and dissatisfied, discards it and rekindles the fire in the forge, and comes back to it until at length it becomes a useful and pretty thing—and a bit of truth. Television news is papier-mâché. Real writing is wrought iron.

Austin was recorded in the study as devoting 5.7 percent of airtime to crime, whereas Indianapolis devoted 36.7 percent of airtime to the subject. KVUE has been number one in ratings for news in the Austin area for several years.

The guidelines influenced many stations. At KGUN9, the result was a "Viewers' Bill of Rights." For this ethical code and the Code of Ethics of the Society of Professional Journalists, see **Appendix D** in *NRW Plus*.

Comments: Pluses and a Few Minuses

Joan Barrett, KVUE-TV, Austin, Tex.: One of the first questions we ask at our morning meeting is, "What are people talking about today?" And then it's, "What do people need to know? What should they know? What do they want to know?" You know, producers play a key role in our shop. Yet we don't get many students who say "I want to be a producer." But they're the ones shaping the decisions in the newscasts for the most part.

Andrew Lack, former president, NBC News: We are spawning a generation of reporters and news directors who no longer place any value on the written word, the turn of phrase, the uncut, long, hard question. All we care about are the almighty pictures, the video, the story count—and that it moves like a bat out of hell. We barely listen to what is said any more.

Kirk Winkler, KTVK-TV, Phoenix, Ariz.: The most important problem (among journalism students) is a simple lack of curiosity. One in ten students now graduating has enough of it to make it as a successful reporter. Also: They do not know how to report on deadline and some don't know what a city directory is and don't read a daily newspaper.

Walter Cronkite, "CBS Evening News" anchor and managing editor for 19 years: Some anchorpersons are inadequately educated and poorly trained. Their only qualifications seem to be pretty clothes and stylish hairdos—and this applies to both sexes. Too many are interested in becoming stars rather than journalists. They aren't interested in news except as it resembles show business. However, a talented genera-tion of young people is coming out of journalism schools with the hearts and guts—and educational background—to be called journalists.

Summing Up

Preparation: Examine your notes and all other material for the broadcast to determine the key material. Highlight it. Know the time allotted for the seg-ment you are writing. Decide on the lead.

Writing: Begin with the best. Make it short, to the point, interesting. Use S-V-O construction, present tense, familiar words and phrases.

Last-minute check: Read what you have written. If you sound too formal, stumble on a word or run out of breath, rewrite.

Further Reading

Bliss, Edward, Jr. *Now the News: The Story of Broadcasting.* New York: Columbia University Press, 1991.

Block, Mervin. *Writing Broadcast News—Shorter, Sharper, Stronger,* 2nd ed. Chicago: Bonus Books, 1998.

Block, Mervin. *Rewriting Network News: WorldWatching Tips from 345 TV and Radio Scripts.* Chicago: Bonus Books, 1990.

Block, Mervin. *Broadcast Newswriting: The RTNDA Reference Guide.* Chicago: Bonus Books, 1994.

Persico, Joseph E. *Edward R. Murrow: An American Original.* New York: McGraw-Hill, 1988.

Schieffer, Bob. *This Just In: I Couldn't Tell You on TV.* New York: Putnam Publishing Group, 2003.

Schieffer covered stories big and little over his 40-year career, mostly in broadcasting with CBS News. His recollections cover reporting the integration battles at the University of Mississippi, JFK's assassination and the Washington political scene where, he says, most news "becomes public because it is in someone's interest for it to come out."

Schonfeld, Reese. *Me and Ted Against the World: The Unauthorized Story of the Founding of CNN.* New York: HarperCollins, 2001.

A quick-paced account of how entrepreneur Turner, who had no real interest in news, and Schonfeld, a veteran TV newsman, made what in its early days was called Chicken Noodle News into a major cable news service.

Schorr, Daniel. *Staying Tuned: A Life in Journalism.* New York: Pocket Books, 2001.

From CBS, where he worked with Murrow, to CNN and PBS, Schorr has covered power in all its shades and voices.

Smith, Sally Bedell. *In All His Glory: The Life of William S. Paley, the Legendary Tycoon and His Brilliant Circle.* New York: Simon & Schuster, 1990.

Sperber, Ann M. *Murrow: His Life and Times.* New York: Freundlich Books, 1986.

Preview

Many of the news stories and features that journalists write are based on news releases. A release stands a good chance of being used if it:

- Is newsworthy.
- Has an attention-getting lead.
- Is accurate, interesting and contains sources for a follow-up.

Other factors:

- Impact on the public.
- Proximity to local people.
- Timeliness.

Burson-Marsteller Photo

Preparing a news release.

The men and women we have been watching at work describe themselves as providing news for the public interest. Now we turn our attention to those whose job it is to speak for clients, for General Motors and Ford, for the Rainforest Alliance and Save the Children, for the Los Angeles Lakers and the Seattle Mariners, for Northwestern University and Dutchess Community College and for the thousands of other organizations, companies, colleges and businesses that hire public relations practitioners.

"We are advocates," says Harold Burson of Burson-Marsteller, one of the largest public relations firms in the world. "We are being paid to tell our client's side of the story. We are in the business of changing and molding attitudes, and we aren't successful unless we move the needle, get people to do something."

One of the ways public relations practitioners move the needle is by reaching journalists through the news release. When United Way wants to announce its goal for the year's fund drive, it sends out a news release. When the North Point Press published a collection of the journalism of A.J. Liebling, it sent out a news release.

These releases were used because they were newsworthy and timely. News release writers know that unless there is a newsworthy element in their work, it will be discarded.

Misspell a word and the reader presumes you're stupid. You are.

News Tie-in   The Ladies Professional Golf Association sent out a news release in early October, which, the release said in an editor's note, is Breast Cancer Awareness Month.

> CHELTENHAM, Pa.—LPGA Tour star Cristie Kerr, as a three-time tournament winner already this season, knows a thing or two about making birdies. But when her mother, Linda, was diagnosed with breast cancer in July 2003, Kerr decided to turn her on-the-course successes into support for a life-altering disease. Through her Breast Cancer program, Kerr has been pledging $50 for each birdie she makes on Tour, which is matched by sponsors and other supporters. So far this season, Kerr has raised more than $40,000 for the fight against breast cancer.

The release goes on to give details of the breast cancer drive and concludes with a brief description of Kerr's career as a golfer, which "began in 1997 at the age of 18." She won more than $5 million in her career. The final sentence reads:

> Her mother, Linda, is currently in remission and doing well.

Sports pages carried the news release, mostly in rewritten form.

At an Agency

We're sitting alongside Molly Wright, a senior associate with Burson-Marsteller, watching her write a news release. Wright is one of the public relations agency's 2,000 employees spread over 97 offices in 57 countries. Wright is in Chicago where she has agreed to take a few minutes to chat about her work.

"The most important point about a news release is that it needs to include news," she tells her visitor.

The Key: Is It Newsworthy?

Since the release is distributed to editors and reporters it must have a compelling "news hook" to attract them, says Wright.

"For example, say you are writing a news release about a new food product. It's not newsworthy simply to announce the product. What are the most compelling attributes of the new product? Is it innovative? Does it help alleviate a common problem affecting consumers? Will it help consumers save time or money?

"If your analysis fails to uncover any special quality or qualities, you need to tie it to existing news. In this case, you might tie it to National Food Lovers Day. Or with research you might find a unique contribution to an existing trend or topic of national interest.

"Keep in mind that you have a small window of opportunity to convince your audience of the news value of the information.

"The best approach is to think and write as though you are a reporter or editor. If you believe that you'd find the information compelling and interesting, it's likely that a reporter or editor would also."

Purpose
"Public relations is about not paying for placement in print or on the air."
—*Michael Levine,*
A Branded World:
Adventures in Public Relations and the Creation of Superbrands

Code of Ethics
"Be honest and accurate in all communications. Act promptly to correct erroneous information for which the practitioner is responsible."
—*Public Relations Society of America*

Editing a Release

Molly Wright in the Chicago office of Burson-Marsteller edits her news release about pairing pasta and pasta sauce, which she has described in her lead as "one of the greatest culinary marriages."

"A news release is a written statement created by a company or an organization for distribution to the media," she informs a visitor. "It contains information that a reporter needs in order to write an article on a particular subject."

Nearly 60 percent of articles in leading newspapers were generated by news releases, she says that a study found. "News releases are a critical component of journalism because they provide reporters with information they can use to create, refine and enhance their stories."

John W. Hill, founder of Hill and Knowlton, advised his writers to "use facts that are understandable, believable and presented with imagination."

For the Food Editor

Here's how Wright wrote a release that was used by many newspapers around the country because of the information it contained.

"The release was designed to educate consumers on the best ways to pair pasta and pasta sauce for authentic Italian meals," Wright says. "It was not overly commercial. Rather it was written to engage the reader with solid, factual information of interest to a wide range of readers."

The lead provides a nugget of information—pasta's longtime pairing with sauce. "The quotes from a well-known chef boosted the credibility of the claims being made," she says.

Wright mentions the company in passing in the second paragraph but positions information about Barilla at the end of the release. "This strategy sets up the story, encourages sell-in of the facts and then provides the source of the information."

Did the release work? "The 20 million media impressions in papers throughout the country indicates an overwhelming success," says Wright. (Media impressions are the number of people estimated to have been reached by the message. Included in the calculation is the circulation of the newspapers that run the release multiplied by 2.5 for the "pass-around" effect.)

FOR IMMEDIATE RELEASE   CONTACT: Molly Wright for Barilla
                                                             312-596-3457
                                                             molly_wright@chi.bm.com

A MATCH MADE IN ... ITALY
Pasta and Sauce Pairing Is the Key to Delicious Italian Meals

Chicago (Oct. 14, 2003) – Chocolate and strawberries, champagne and caviar, fine wine and gourmet cheese – all celebrated food pairings of the century. Yet the longest and most enduring pairing took place in the 17th century and is still happily united today. Pasta and pasta sauce, one of the greatest culinary marriages, are the cornerstones of authentic Italian cooking and when paired appropriately, optimize Italian cuisine.

Widely known and used throughout the regions of Italy, the pairing process aims to harmonize the shape and surface of the pasta cut with the color, consistency and flavor of the sauce.
James Beard, award-winning Chef Roberto Donna and Barilla have joined together to bring years of Italian culinary knowledge to home chefs through tips, guidelines and recipes showcasing this pairing art form, enabling them to recreate endless perfect pairs in their own kitchens.

"The pairing concept is extremely helpful in bringing out the flavors and textures of a delicious, authentic Italian meal," said Chef Donna. "It all starts with considering the size and texture of both the pasta and the pasta sauce. For example, angel hair pasta, which has a light, delicate surface texture, doesn't have the strength to hold chunky sauce, so it's best paired with less dense sauces like pesto, tomato and basil, and béchamel (white) sauces."

Another important consideration is to feature ingredients that best complement the pasta cut and the pasta sauce pairing. For example, chunkier, heartier sauces can withstand large, more substantial vegetables and meats, while more delicate sauces and pasta cuts need smaller, more delicate ingredients.

- more-

Why It Worked

Wright says there are several reasons for the success of the release. "Although there was no timely news to communicate, the release creatively incorporated the client into a larger education story that would be of interest to food editors throughout the country," she says.

"The release had a creative lead that drew the reporter into the topic. Another positive feature of the release is the positioning of the Barilla name in the release. If a journalist decides to use any of the content he or she would need to list Barilla as the source, which positions the company as a credible leader in the education and dissemination of quality Italian food products, a key communications objective."

Headline and Lead   The headline "is engaging and attention-grabbing," says Wright. It meets the requirements of headline writing that the headline contain the key news element, that it "convey the crux of the story," she says. When possible, the headline should have a noun and a verb and, if possible, the client's name.

The lead also meets the requirements for a sound lead. "The lead needs to pique the reader's interest and to keep the reader interested enough to continue reading through the entire release," Wright says.

The Body   "The body of the news release completes the story that was introduced by the headline and the lead," Wright says. "The message must be written concisely. Delete any words that fail to convey the message." It's also important to have an "insightful quotation from a company or organization spokesperson or from a third-party expert," she says. "The quote should communicate a key message for the product or service."

Photos   Photographs that accompany news releases can help the releases find their way into print. See **Photos Help** in *NRW Plus*.

The Writing Process

Let's look more closely at how a release is written. We'll take it step-by-step beginning with a few questions the writer asks himself or herself.

To begin, says Diane F. Witmer of the news bureau at California State University–Fullerton, "You must have a clear focus on the PR goal. Why is this release being written? What are you trying to accomplish?" Is the release informative, telling the public about a personnel change, a new product, a grant to a university department, the year's earnings for the company?

Or is this a reactive release, telling the public your client's side in some controversy? Or is it a reinforcement release, telling people about the good job, the positive works, the stellar performance of the client?

Once that is settled, the writer has to think about where the release is to go, the intermediary who will—you hope—pass it on to the public or to a special audience.

That intermediary is the man or woman in a newsroom who is sitting there thumbing through a dozen news releases and deciding which, if any, to use.

The Audience

"Knowing and understanding the audience is a key requirement to creating strong press release content," says Wright. Is your release going to a trade publication or to the general news media? If it is to go to a publication about retail merchandising, the release can be more technical than the release that is sent to newspapers and broadcast stations.

You should direct the release to an individual whenever possible. The sports information office at the University of Washington will send a release about a widely recruited basketball player from Everett who decides to attend the University to the sports editor of *The Herald* in Everett and to sports editors of other newspapers in the state.

The release for a travel agency about trips to Costa Rica's bird sanctuaries will go to travel editors.

The *Year Book* published by Editor&Publisher lists the names of daily and weekly newspapers and their staffs.

Subject Matter

First, identify exactly what you want to say. Then obtain sufficient information to convey the idea that will be the theme of your release.

Tips and Alerts

Instead of sending out full news releases, some news bureaus and agencies distribute brief paragraphs about a situation or an upcoming event.

The University of Wisconsin–Eau Claire News Bureau's "Tip sheet" carried these Story Ideas one week:

- UW–Eau Claire football players are meeting weekly for study tables. Guests talk with players about study skills, time management, values and other topics that help student-athletes succeed in the classroom and in life. They also discuss support resources available to students. And the sessions provide time for players to focus on course work. Contact head football coach Todd Hoffner at (715) 836-3093 or hoffnert@uwec.edu; or Joel Hornby, assistant football coach and program coordinator, (715) 836-5779 or hornbyjo@uwec.edu.

- UW–Eau Claire's Preparatory Arts Program provides performing arts instruction to Chippewa Valley children and adults. The fall program provides lessons to community members—beginners through advanced—in piano, voice, flute, oboe, saxophone and strings. For details, contact La Vone Sneen at (715) 836-5179 or sneenl@uwec.edu.

At the University of Arkansas–Little Rock, Amy Oliver Barnes, director of the Office of Communications, uses Media Alerts. She says they are effective in "piquing the interest of reporters for an upcoming event. They work especially well with the electronic media. The alert gives reporters the Who, What, When and Where quickly, with two or three paragraphs of Why."

Wright asks herself the Five W's and an H—who, what, when, where, why and how—as aids in information gathering. She usually conducts additional research on the Internet and in the library. This material plus the input from the client adds up to considerable material, a pile of papers or a batch of stored information. The next task is to organize it. But before you do, will this be a feature or a straight news story?

Hard or Soft?

Writers distinguish between straight news stories and features, or hard news stories and soft news stories. The pieces that have a short shelf life because they demand immediate telling are called hard news stories, and they almost always take a direct news lead. The stories that can be used tomorrow or next week—in some newsrooms called evergreens because they stay fresh for a long time—usually take a delayed lead. (See Chapter 5, **The Lead.**)

When Hurricane Jeanne hit the eastern states, the Pennsylvania Department of Transportation issued a news release whose lead stated that "three state highways remain closed in the five-county Philadelphia region." That's a direct lead on a hard news story.

After the Phoenix Suns basketball team hired a new coach, the news office of the National Basketball Association distributed by e-mail a feature story about the hiring that began this way:

Although Mike D'Antoni is entering his first full season as the Phoenix Suns' head coach, he can hardly be classified as

Terse and to the Point

a rookie. The West Virginia native has spanned the basketball globe, both playing and coaching in the U.S., across Italy and throughout Europe.

That's a delayed lead.

Oops The NBA release ends this way:

Check out what Coach D'Antoni had to say about the teams youth, it's outlook and more.

Two grammatical errors in one sentence. Send in the subs.

For a rundown of common errors by news release writers, see **Check the Errors** in *NRW Plus*.

Outlining

Wright likes to prepare a written outline, though some professionals go directly to the writing. For her, "outlining is an essential approach to organizing information and thoughts."

Outlines come in all shapes and sizes. Some writers scribble a few words that reflect the order in which the information will appear in the release. Others prepare a more formal outline that will serve as their guide. Wright bases her outline on the inverted pyramid form the story will eventually take:

Lead

Buttressing, amplifying the lead

Background

Secondary material

Writing

Outline in hand, or in mind, the writing begins. The first effort should contain all essential information but may not be as smoothly written as you would like. Not to worry. Most professionals consider their first effort a first draft.

Reviewing the Copy   In going over the first version of the story, the writer checks:

- Is my theme in the lead?

- Have I amplified the theme at once or have I drifted off to another theme?

- Is all the key information included?

- Do I have a good quote from a reliable source, an interesting anecdote, a useful tip for the reader?

- Is the form correct—a punchy headline, all essential sources and how to reach them?

Wright often reads her releases aloud. "By doing this, you can find mistakes in wording that you might not have caught," she says.

The online wire service PRWeb advises its contributors to "pay attention to the content of your press release." See PRWeb's **Press Release Content Tips** in *NRW Plus*.

Next, let's look at how news releases played a part in a public relations campaign, the replacement of the old-fashioned Good Humor Man with a rappin', jivin' man.

The Good Humor Man

Planning Stage

Tamara Strentz goes over the draft of a news release with a colleague.

Everyone knew the Good Humor Man in his spotless white uniform as he cruised the streets or stood on a street corner next to his wagon. Well, maybe not. That's what the company that makes the ice cream decided. The image was too old-fashioned. It needed something consistent with the hip new generation.

What emerged was a public relations–advertising campaign: a search for a young man who would be the new image, the new Good Humor Man, and then when he was named, a series of news releases for news coverage.

Making It Newsworthy

Tamara Strentz helped handle the account. Her job, she says, was to turn the search and selection into "a newsworthy event." Strentz conducted research to find the history of Good Humor and obtained anecdotes "to add newsworthiness to the commercial story," she said. She and Laura Bokowy wrote several news releases.

Here is the beginning of one of them about the new Good Humor Man:

FOR IMMEDIATE RELEASE

NEW GOOD HUMOR MAN TAKES THE WHEEL

GREEN BAY, WI—After a coast to coast search, Good Humor–Breyers, America's number one ice cream company has found its man—make that the Good Humor Man. Seventy-six years after the first trucks rolled onto the streets, the company is introducing a new Good Humor Man.

From more than 500 hopefuls, the man selected to be the official Good Humor Man is Robert Gant, age 27, who left a promising legal career for a shot at being America's ice cream icon. With this new role, there are many shoes to fill. Gant represents the thousands of men and women who, since 1920, have delivered ice cream and happy memories to children of all ages.

"Robert embodies the characteristics that built the legend of the Good Humor Man: enthusiasm, dedication, an entertaining flair and a desire to bring a bit of laughter to everyone's life," said Dick Newman, vice president of marketing for Good Humor–Breyers.

"We share a rich tradition with Americans, and the new Good Humor Man brings back treasured memories for those who remember hearing the truck's famous bells jingling and buying the first Chocolate Eclair Bar of the summer. We want to get America into a Good Humor, and Robert's the man for the job," said Newman.

From child actor, singer and dancer to adult legal eagle, Gant has always been a performer. After receiving his law degree from Georgetown University in 1993, Gant headed to California and worked at a prominent L.A. law firm, but after four months he left the world of casebooks and courtrooms to pursue his lifelong dream of performing.

As the new Good Humor Man, Gant will be the ambassador of Good Humor from coast to coast, making appearances at select events. He will also be featured in the new Good Humor television advertising campaign.

Looking Back   As part of the Good Humor campaign, Strentz and Bokowy wrote a feature about the history of the Good Humor Man. Here is how it began:

Through the years, Good Humor Men have traveled 200 million miles and found a place in the hearts of Americans from coast to coast. These men delivered more than ice cream

The Scope of PR Practice

When environmentalists bombarded StarKist Seafood with calls and postcards protesting the slaughter of dolphins by tuna fishermen, the company called on Edelman Public Relations Worldwide for guidance. Edelman engages in **corporate** public relations, one of several PR fields that include:

In-House—Many businesses have their own PR specialists who write news releases, edit company publications and perform other tasks.

Sports Information—Attached to universities and colleges, the staff produces media guides, profiles of players, statistics.

Personal—Basketball players, movie stars, TV personalities hire PR firms that specialize in advising individual clients.

Public Affairs—Employed by governmental units, they publicize programs and policies through brochures, pamphlets and news releases.

Political—These consultants are considered indispensable to those seeking public office. Political PR practitioners write speeches, news releases and establish contacts.

The Old and the New

to American neighborhoods—they created memories that would grow through the decades with each new generation.

The first appearance of the distinctive white ice cream truck with the tinkling bells and the smiling driver took place in 1920 in Youngstown, Ohio. Candy maker Harry Burt came up with a unique way to market his new Good Humor Bars—by bringing them to the customer's door with a fleet of trucks driven by Good Humor Men: chauffeurs wearing crisp white uniforms, starched hats, bow ties and black belts.

Good Humor was an immediate success, and soon expanded into other Midwestern cities. . . .

There's nothing immediate about this release. It's an evergreen.

The news releases found their mark. Newspapers and stations picked up the news about the switch from the sedate Good Humor Man to a new image. As *USA Today* put it in the lead to its story about the new ice cream salesman:

The Good Humor Man is alive, swell—and rappin'.

Next to the newsroom, the destination of thousands of news releases each week.

In the Newsroom

The news release must make it past the newsroom gatekeeper in order to be used. These gatekeepers—editors and reporters—decide whether to:

1. Toss it in the wastebasket.

2. Use as is.

3. Rewrite it.

4. Use it as the basis of a story the reporter will develop.

Tossed

The fate of most releases is the trash can. Why? Ask a gatekeeper, Frank Herron of *The Post-Standard* in Syracuse, N.Y., what he looks for in a release. "Accuracy, timeliness and newsworthiness," he answers. He also looks to see whether there is an unusual aspect of the situation described in the release.

"We received a release about the plan of a local musical group to award scholarships to high school singers," Herron says. "What made it interesting is that the decision will be made by audience members—some 1,200 of them—during a show. That generated a couple of articles."

Newsworthy   As they scan news releases, gatekeepers look for a news angle. The elements of newsworthiness are described in Chapter 3. One of the most important of these elements is *impact*. The greater the impact on the public, the more likely the release will be used. When the drug company Merck announced that it would stop selling its arthritis and pain medicine Vioxx, it was front-page news across the country. Almost 2 million people take the drug, which a study found can cause heart attacks and strokes.

Proximity   "Like many journalists," says Herron, "I try and keep an eye peeled for a local connection. The good news release takes that into account.

"That can mean the person was born here, went to elementary school or college here, owns a summer home nearby, used to work here."

In the margin here is a photograph that was distributed by the news division of the U.S. Navy along with a news release. It shows a sailor aboard an aircraft carrier laying navigational tracks. He is from Falls Church, Va., the release says.

The release and photo stand a good chance of being used by the weekly newspaper in Falls Church, perhaps by the newspaper in Arlington, Va., and stations in the area. But no journalist in Richmond or Blacksburg will bother with the material.

Use As Is

Newspapers and stations with small staffs often use news releases with little or no editing. This may make the writer of the news release happy, but it can prove embarrassing for the newspaper or station and for the agency distributing the release if the release is short of the mark.

When *The Atlantic Journal-Constitution* ran word-for-word a news release from the University of Georgia about the hospitalization of two students, the *Columbia Journalism Review* took note. The *Review* described the newspaper as suffering from "journalistic malaise" for failing to use the release as the basis of reporting.

The *Review*'s criticism of the newspaper can be applied to the news release writer as well: Why didn't you do a Google search for background material about the transmission rates for the disease among students, for dorm residents? Why didn't you point out the fact that it can be transmitted by kissing? Why didn't you include the fatality rate?

Had the writer of the news release done the necessary research, even though the newspaper used the release unedited there would have been little cause for criticism—and a more interesting story.

Rewrite

When a release passes the first test—is this newsworthy?—its next hurdle is answering the reporter's questions: Is there enough material in here for me to make this into a news story? Is the newsworthy material sufficiently amplified, buttressed, supported? If not, does the release have the names and numbers of contacts and sources who can be reached to provide what's lacking?

You may spend a full day gathering material for a news release and half a day writing it only to find it's been rewritten. Frustrating? Perhaps. But that's the way it goes. Journalists rewrite releases as a matter of course.

U.S. Navy

Journalists List Their Complaints
Public relations practitioners and journalists have a "delicate and often contentious" relationship, Elizabeth A. Johnson of the University of Tennessee and Lynne M. Sallot of the University of Georgia say their studies have found.

"Journalists perceive practitioners to be deficient in journalistic standards, practices and traditions," they write in *Journalism & Mass Communication Educator.* "Seventy-two percent of the journalists interviewed complained that practitioners lack news sense, news values, accuracy, timeliness, news style such as inverted pyramids, and local angle; that practitioners are overtly and overly self-serving; and that practitioners are poor writers."

Look at the first two paragraphs of a release prepared by the sports information office of Northeastern University in Boston:

Season Outlook

The Huskies posted a 3–7 mark last season, but the record could have been 7–1 just as easily. The Huskies swallowed close losses against Delaware State (3–11), New Hampshire (28–31), Massachusetts (27–31) and Maine (26–29).

With experienced players returning, and an influx of promising young recruits, the Fall of the new decade looks like a good one for the Red & Black. But each Fall brings a new schedule, and this year's looks to be as difficult as ever.

Here is how John Connolly of *The Boston Herald* rewrote the release:

There is a strong belief that a dark cloud hovers over Parsons Field even on sunny afternoons.

For if there has been one New England team which has somehow managed to clutch defeat from the jaws of victory each Saturday in autumn, it is certainly the hard-luck Northeastern Huskies.

A year ago is a prime example. NU posted a 3–7 mark, but the record was slightly misleading. Three losses came by a total of 10 points (31–28 to New Hampshire, 31–27 to Massachusetts and 29–26 to Maine. . . .

Connolly's story went on to quote some of the players and the coach about the frustrating season for the Huskies' football team. He used the release for background, put a feature touch on it and added some reporting of his own. This is the classic practitioner-reporter relationship at work—or here we might say at play.

Compressed   When the name of the winner of the Miss Texas beauty pageant was announced, it sounded familiar to Kevin Tankersley, director of sports information at the University of Arkansas, Little Rock. *Sunni Cranfill.* Yes this was the young woman who had been a UALR track runner and cheerleader for the basketball team before transferring to West Texas A&M University.

Tankersley wrote a story about her for the university Web site and sent it to local media. "I would usually never send a release that's this long (three single-spaced pages) since I know it will probably never run, but I was hoping that my story would cause a reporter to do a similar story."

He had a bit of luck, The release did generate an eight-paragraph item in Michael Storey's "Paper Trails" column in the *Arkansas Democrat-Gazette.*

Tankersley has better luck with brief items, one- and one-and-a-half-page releases on such subjects as a UALR runner named to the Academic All-America team, a new member of the basketball team's coaching staff, the basketball coach honored by city leaders. Tankersley was at the ceremony honoring the coach,

University of Arkansas–Little Rock
Sunni Cranfill

with his camera. "We try to use as many photos on our Web site as possible. So I usually end up shooting pictures."

Most of UALR's sports information releases go out by e-mail, many by fax.

Release as News Tip

On a slow news day in Syracuse, Herron received a news release that piqued his interest. It began this way:

> **Oneida Nation Homelands**—The Oneida Indian Nation and the Milton J. Rubenstein Museum of Science and Technology today jointly announced September events to honor the iron-workers who helped construct the buildings and bridges that have become landmarks around the country.

Herron made a few calls and arranged to attend a news conference the museum sponsored before the opening of an exhibit about the ironworkers. At the conference, he met one of the Indian ironworkers, whom he interviewed. He blended this interview with material from the news release to write a story about the exhibit and the history of the ironworkers.

See **Mohawk Ironworkers** in *NRW Plus.*

Summing Up: Checklist

Form

- —Name of organization distributing the release and its phone, fax and e-mail numbers.

- —Contact's name, phone, fax and e-mail numbers.

- —Release date, time.

- —Headline, preferably in capital and lowercase letters.

- —Wide margins.

- —One or two pages.

- —Names, addresses of people willing to be interviewed.

Content

- —Straight news form; inverted pyramid.

- —Human interest.

- —Quotations.

—Written for specific or general audience.

—Sent to specific person at publication, station, online.

—Conforms to Associated Press Stylebook.

—Objective; does not contain the writer's opinions or judgments; avoids exaggerated claims.

—Double-checked for correct spelling of names; accuracy of dates, addresses, contact numbers, etc.

—Is newsworthy.

Part 4: Reporting Principles

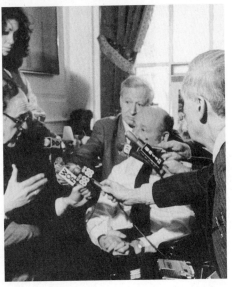

Leslie Jean-Bart

When? Where? How? Why?

Preview

The reporter's job is to gather information that helps people understand events that affect them. This digging takes the reporter through the three layers of reporting:

1. **Surface facts:** source-originated material—news releases, handouts, speeches, news conferences.

2. **Reportorial enterprise:** verification, investigative reporting, coverage of spontaneous events, background.

3. **Interpretation and analysis:** significance, causes, consequences.

Be a self-starter. Devise your story ideas.

The reporter is like the prospector digging and drilling the way to pay dirt. Neither is happy with the surface material, although sometimes impenetrable barriers or lack of time interfere with the search, and it is necessary to stop digging and to make do with what has been turned up. When possible, the reporter keeps digging until he or she gets to the bottom of things, until the journalistic equivalent of the mother lode—the truth of the event—is unearthed.

The reporter, like the prospector, has a feel for the terrain. This sensitivity— the reporter's street smarts or nose for news—helps unearth information for stories. Equally helpful is the reporter's general knowledge.

Let's watch a reporter for a Florida newspaper do some digging.

Finding the Lottery Winner

The word from Tallahassee was that the single winning ticket in the $5 million Florida lottery had been sold in Port St. Lucie. Sarah Jay, a reporter for *The Port St. Lucie News,* had heard rumors about the winner—that someone in a meat market knew the winner's name; that the winner could be found by talking to someone in the Roma Bakery. Jay tried the market. No luck. She fared better at the bakery, where a woman told Jay that her niece was the winner.

She gave Jay the woman's name—Pat Lino—but no phone number or address. Jay checked the telephone company—the number was unlisted. But she did find some Linos in the directory and called, thinking she might reach a relative.

"One guy was totally unrelated," Jay says. "Another was the winner's brother-in-law, and although he wouldn't give me her phone number he did mention that she lives in St. Lucie West, a new housing development."

Knowing that property tax records that list addresses are available, Jay checked the files for Pat Lino. She found the address and drove to the location, only to find no one there.

"It was all locked up. It looked as though I'd hit a dead end, but just to be sure I talked to a neighbor. He didn't know them, he said. Nor did another. But then I tried one more neighbor, and she knew Pat Lino. She had Pat Lino's daughter's phone number."

The neighbor called and Pat Lino was there. But she said she didn't want to be interviewed. "I told the neighbor that I only wanted to speak with her for a minute, that I'd been looking for her all day," Jay said. Lino gave in.

"In this small bedroom community, the naming of a $5 million lottery winner was the talk of the town. And we had it first."

The Reporting Process

As reporters go about their work of digging up information, they are guided by an understanding of the nature of reporting: Reporting is the process of gathering relevant material through a variety of means (direct observation, interviews, examination of reports and documents, use of databases and Internet resources) and subjecting the material to verification and analysis. When assembled in a news story or feature, the material gives the reader, listener or viewer a good idea of what happened.

Reporting
"It's the hardest job in the world that doesn't involve heavy lifting."
—*Pete Hamill*

The Layers

The state's senior senator is planning to give a talk tomorrow at a fund-raising dinner for the state Republican Party. The story that gives the time, place and purpose of the senator's talk is a Layer I story. That is, it simply relays information from a source.

If the reporter handling this story were to dig a bit deeper and ask the senator's press secretary whether the senator will support a particular gubernatorial candidate in the party primary, we can say that the reporter is now operating at a deeper layer, Layer II. We have seen how Sarah Jay worked Layer II by not waiting for the state to announce the name of the winner of the lottery.

As we move on in our examination of journalistic work we will meet reporters who are allowed to interpret their findings, to find causes and consequences of the events they examine. They work in Layer III.

The News Story and Its Layers of Truth

Layer I—Handouts, news conferences, speeches, statements.

Layer II—Reportorial enterprise, verifying material, background, reporter's observations, spontaneous events.

Layer III—Significance, impact, causes, consequences, analysis, interpretation.

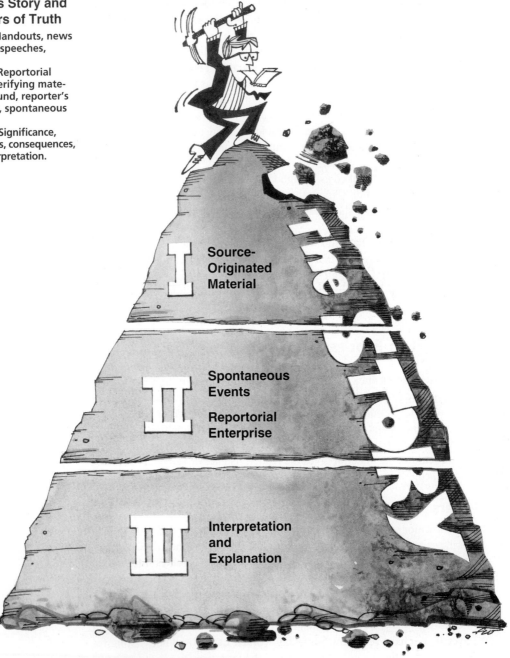

I Source-Originated Material

II Spontaneous Events

Reportorial Enterprise

III Interpretation and Explanation

Digging for the Story

Most journalists say that their most important task is to look beneath the surface. Lincoln Steffens, the great journalist of the muckraking period, said the reporter's task is "the letting in of light and air." Reporters base their work on the same conviction that guided Steffens. Their job is to seek out relevant information for people who cannot witness or comprehend the events that affect them.

Layer I Reporting

Layer I reporting is the careful and accurate transcription of source-originated material—the record, the speech, the news conference. Its strengths and its limitations are those of objective journalism.

Layer I is the source for the facts used in most news stories. Information is mined from material that originates with and is controlled by the source. Fact gathering at this level of journalism may involve going to the mayor's office to pick up a transcript of the speech he is to deliver this evening or it may involve calling the mortuary holding the body of the child who drowned last night. The stories based on these facts rely almost wholly on information a source has supplied.

Fact gathering at Layer I is the journalistic equivalent of surface mining. The reporter sinks no shafts into the event but is content to use top-layer material, some of which is presented by public relations and information specialists. Much of the reporter's task is confined to sorting out and rearranging the delivered facts, verifying addresses and dates and checking the spelling of names. Most stories appearing in newspapers and on radio and television are based on source-originated material.

Essential Information   Despite criticism of Layer I reporting, it serves an essential function. At its most basic level, it gives the people information about the happenings in their community. The local newspaper will publish photos of dogs awaiting adoption at the County Animal Shelter and tell parents that the school lunch on Monday will be hot dogs, junior salad bar, veggie dippers and fruit salad. Tuesday, meatball sandwich, salad, buttery corn and raisins. . . .

The newspaper also will provide an hour-by-hour police incident report:

> 1:03 a.m.: A loud party was reported on Lincoln Street. On request, the responsibles agreed to quiet down.
> 2:24 a.m.: William Young of 42 Broadway was arrested for driving under the influence of alcohol. He was booked in the county jail. . . .

In Layer I, journalists report city council meetings, legislative hearings, United Way fund raising, street closings, traffic accidents, basketball games, appointments of the new university president and human rights commissioner, the verdicts at trials—an enormous range of activities. Such coverage is essential, especially in the area of public affairs. The public must have access to the statements and activities of its officials, and these officials must have feedback so they know what's on the mind of the public. This give and take makes responsive, consensual government possible.

Pseudo-Events

As the mass media, particularly television, became the dominant dispensers of experience in American life, sources sought to manipulate reality to accommodate the media, especially television's need for pictures. The information sources realized that press releases and announcements unaccompanied by visual material of events would not merit more than 20 seconds on most newscasts, if that. As a result, sources learned to stage events for the press that resembled spontaneous events (Layer II) but were, in fact, as much under the control of the source as the news release and the prepared speech. These staged events are known as *media-events* or *pseudo-events.*

Following a presidential State of the Union speech, Russell Baker of *The New York Times* asked one of the president's advisers if the speech "was not mostly a media event, a nonhappening staged because reporters would pretend it was a happening."

"It's *all* media event," the adviser replied. "If the media weren't so ready to be used, it would be a very small splash."

Daniel J. Boorstin, the social historian, originated the term *pseudo-event* to describe these synthetic occurrences. He says that a "larger and larger proportion of our experience, of what we read and see and hear, has come to consist of pseudo-events." In the process, he says, "Vivid image came to overshadow pale reality." His book about image making opens with this short dialogue:

> ADMIRING FRIEND: "My, that's a beautiful baby you have there!"
>
> MOTHER: "Oh, that's nothing—you should see his photograph."

Boorstin says the pseudo-event has these characteristics: "It is not spontaneous, but comes about because someone has planned, planted or incited it. . . . It is planted primarily (but not always exclusively) for the immediate purpose of being reported or reproduced. Therefore, its occurrence is arranged for the convenience of the reporting or reproducing media. . . . Its relation to the underlying relativity of the situation is ambiguous. . . ."

Media Manipulation

The orchestration of events for public consumption is a frequent occurrence in government and politics. Needing public attention and approval, politicians often resort to media manipulation, and they often get away with their contrivances. In his memoirs, Richard Nixon wrote that modern presidents "must try to master the art of manipulating the media . . . at the same time they must avoid at all costs the charge of trying to manipulate the media."

Spinsters

People, wrote Walter Lippmann in his 1922 book *Public Opinion,* do not react rationally to information but respond to the "pictures inside their heads." This marked "the birthing moment of spin," says Stuart Ewen, Hunter College historian and author of *PR! A Social History of Spin.*

"We live in a world where everyone is always battling for the public mind and public approval," Ewen says. "I think the public believes there is no truth, only spin—in part because much of the educated middle class spins for a living."

Staged Confrontation   One of the most dramatic pictures of the civil rights movement in the South in the early 1960s showed a determined Gov. George C. Wallace blocking the entrance to a University of Alabama building, refusing to allow two black students to enroll. For Wallace, a symbol to southerners of resistance to federally imposed desegregation, this was a powerful and positive image. Even when confronted by federalized National Guard troops with a court order, Wallace stood firm.

Grudgingly, in the face of firepower, he stood aside.

The reality was far different: In secret meetings, the Justice Department and Wallace had worked out a scenario that would make President John F. Kennedy and Wallace look good. Wallace would be allowed to take a stand against desegregating the university but would permit the black students to enroll under the Guard's protection.

Wallace thus was able to make political capital in the South, and Kennedy appeared decisive to people who wanted the country to move faster toward desegregating its educational system.

The Kennedy-Wallace secret pact came to light years later. Another media event some 40 years after the Alabama agreement had a much shorter life.

Mission Exposed   Following the quick collapse of the Iraqi army, the media advisors to President George W. Bush arranged an event to celebrate the victory.

Photo Op Gone Sour
A classic photo opportunity that went awry was Richard Nixon's attempt to counter the image John F. Kennedy had established of being calm and thoughtful. Nixon's handlers had him walking on a beach, gazing out to sea. Reporters pointed out Nixon was wearing a coat, a tie and wingtip shoes for his stroll in the sand.

Stagecraft
The Associated Press caption for this photograph of President Bush aboard an aircraft carrier reads:
President Bush flashes a "thumbs-up" after declaring the end of major combat in Iraq as he speaks aboard the aircraft carrier USS Abraham Lincoln off the California coast, Thursday, May 1, 2003.
The carrier will arrive in San Diego May 2, 2003, following a record 10-month deployment including "Operation Iraqi Freedom."
Combat did not end in 2003 but intensified with increasing deaths to Iraqi civilians and U.S. troops.

AP Photo by Scott Applewhite

Before a battery of reporters and photographers, Bush landed in a fighter jet on the deck of an aircraft carrier. The president emerged in full flight gear to cheers and a huge banner, "Mission Accomplished."

The scene was dramatic, a made-for-TV moment. But reporters were quick to point out that the ship was close to shore. The captain had turned it about to make it appear to be at sea.

On page 1 of *The New York Times,* White House correspondent Elizabeth Bumiller wrote that the event "will be remembered as one of the most audacious moments of presidential theater in American history," and she went on to write that "it was only the latest example of how the Bush administration, going far beyond the foundations of stagecraft set by the Reagan White House, is using the powers of television and technology to promote a presidency like never before."

Bumiller wrote that President Bush's media handlers have made media events into "an art form." Her story is Layer III Reporting.

Trial Balloons

One of the ways government officials manage the media is through the floating of trial balloons. The technique involves letting reporters in on inside information, usually about an appointee or a possible new program. The material is to be used without attribution. The information is published or used on television, and public reaction is gauged. If the public rejects the floated material, no one can be blamed as there is no source named. If there is acceptance, then the official may be named, the program adopted.

Dangers of Layer I

When reporting is confined to Layer I, the distinction between journalism and public relations is hard to discern. The consequences for society can be serious, as Joseph Bensman and Robert Lilienfield, sociologists, explain:

> When "public relations" is conducted simultaneously for a vast number of institutions and organizations, the public life of a society becomes so congested with manufactured appearances that it is difficult to recognize any underlying realities.
>
> As a result, individuals begin to distrust all public facades and retreat into apathy, cynicism, disaffiliation, distrust of media and public institutions. . . . The journalist unwittingly often exposes the workings of the public relations man or information specialist, if he operates within a genuine journalistic attitude.

Worthwhile Information

Some staged events do produce news—the civil rights demonstrations in the 1960s, picketing by the local teachers union. Certainly, dozens of source-originated events are newsworthy—the text of the mayor's speech, the details the mortuary supplies about the child's death, the announcement that the university football program has been placed on probation for booster activities that included payment to athletes.

Conduit

"Increasingly, information is generated by those who wish to promote something or someone—a product, a cause, a political candidate or officeholder—without arguing their case on its merits or explicitly advertising it as self-interested material either. Much of the press, in its eagerness to inform the public, has become a conduit for the equivalent of junk mail."
—*Christopher Lasch*

Officials influence the news several ways:

Explanatory briefings: Complex events often require explanations by officials who use the opportunity to present the official point of view. These briefings may be off-the-record, which allows the sources to escape responsibility for the information should it prove unpopular.

Controlled timing: By holding news conferences close to deadline, sources make it difficult for reporters to verify material and to seek comments.

Feeding favorites: Information is offered on an exclusive basis to certain reporters, usually those at influential newspapers such as *The Washington Post, The New York Times* and *The Wall Street Journal.* The tendency for the newspaper with an exclusive is to play it up.

Security blanket: Embarrassing information can be covered by labeling it top security even if the material will not imperil security.

Heading off stories: Material with self-serving information is leaked when officials are worried about an unfavorable impending development or story.

Handling the Handout

"Don't be a handout reporter," Harry Romanoff, a night city editor on the *Chicago American,* would tell young reporters. One of Romanoff's charges was Mervin Block, who recalls an encounter with Romanoff:

> I remember his giving me a fistful of press releases trumpeting movie monarch Louis B. Mayer's expected arrival at the Dearborn Street Railroad Station. An hour later, Romy asked me what time Mayer's train would be pulling in. I told him, and when he challenged my answer, I cited the handouts: one from the Santa Fe, one from Mayer's studio (MGM), and one from his destination, the Ambassador East Hotel. All agreed on the time. But that wasn't good enough for Romy.
>
> "Call the stationmaster and *find out.*"

More Costly   When news releases from food chains in Chicago announced price cuts on thousands of items, the Chicago newspapers bannered the stories on their front pages. One such headline:

Inflation Breakthrough
Food Prices to Drop Here

Despite the rash of stories about how the shopper "may save 15% in price battle," as another paper said in a headline over one of its stories, consumers were actually paying more on a unit, or per-ounce, basis.

The Chicago commissioner of consumer affairs demonstrated that the city's consumers were being misled by the store announcements and consequently by the newspaper stories that took the handouts at face value. Many of the items that were reduced in price were also reduced in weight. Peanut clusters went from 72 cents a packet to 69 cents, an apparent saving of 3 cents. But the packet went from 6 ounces to 5¼ ounces. With a little arithmetic, a reporter could have figured out that this was actually an increase of 6 cents a packet. Some items were publicized because they stayed at the same price "despite inflation," according to the handouts and the

Which Says More?
Layer I
   Rudolph W. Giuliani has accepted the endorsement of publisher Steve Forbes for the Republican presidential nomination.
            —Radio news story

Layer II
   Rudolph W. Giuliani accepted the endorsement of Steve Forbes yesterday and embraced Mr. Forbes's signature issue, saying he liked the idea of a flat tax—something Mr. Giuliani denounced when Mr. Forbes was running for president.
      —*The New York Times*

stories. True enough. A 70-cent can of beef stew was still 70 cents. But the new can contained half an ounce less than the old can.

The moral of this little tale of the peanut clusters and beef stew is: Even when operating in Layer I, check and check again.

The Internet as Source

Journalists mine the Internet for background information, as a tip source for stories and as a communication channel with other reporters and with sources. A reporter with *The Knoxville News-Sentinel* says he refers to the World Wide Web "as much as to the city directory, telephone book and the newspaper morgue."

But there is a difference between the material obtained via the Internet and that from standard references. The references are checked and verified. When the journalist turns to the Web, often as not he or she is operating in Layer I with unverified, source-originated material—and sometimes the source may be spurious.

You can see what happened to a reporter who thought she had discovered on the Internet an idea for a fabulous feature. See **The Backyard Archaeologist** in *NRW Plus*.

Defamatory Entry   Wikipedia is billed as "the world's biggest encyclopedia." It is one of the 20-most-visited sites in the world; many students cite it in their work. But a false and scurrilous entry parted the curtain and like Dorothy confronting the Wizard of Oz, users learned this vast enterprise consisted of a single editor and a part-time helper who simply passed on the contributions of 17,000 volunteers, who are relied on to make corrections.

One of the contributions depicted John Siegenthaler, former editor of *The Tennessean,* as a suspect in the assassination of President Kennedy. A volunteer did make a correction in the Siegenthaler bio—he corrected the misspelling of the word *early.*

The libelous entry remained online four months before someone informed Siegenthaler about it.

Because of the unreliability of entries in Wikipedia, several colleges have told students they cannot cite it in their essays and research.

Layer II Reporting

When reporters initiate information-gathering and when they add to Layer I material, they are digging in Layer II. We could say that the ordinary beat reporting that journalists engage in has much of Layer II involved. When sports reporters cover a game, they are working in Layer II, for example.

Whenever the situation moves beyond the control of those trying to manage it, the reporter is working in Layer II.

The transition from Layer I to Layer II can be seen at a news conference. The reading of a statement provides the source-originated material (I). The give-and-take of the question and answer period is spontaneous (II). When the source declines to answer questions, the reporter should understand that he or she is back in Layer I, dealing with material controlled by the source.

The reporter who seeks verification from a second source that the governor will appear at the Lions Club ceremony is moving into Layer II. So is the reporter who, after she is told by the police that the hotel was burglarized at 5:46 a.m., looks up the time of sunrise that day. Her enterprise enables her to write, "The burglar left the hotel in early morning darkness."

The reporter who writes that the state purchasing agent has awarded to a local dealer a contract for a fleet of automobiles is engaged in Layer I journalism. The investigative reporter who digs into the records to learn that the contract was awarded without bids is working at the second level.

Standard Practice

If we look back at the reporters at work in Chapter 1, we can see how often journalists move from Layer I to II:

- Much of the work Dick did on his story about the Black Parents Association after receiving the handout from the group was on his initiative.

- The investigative stories by Cammy Wilson and Heidi Evans were carried out entirely in Layer II.

These reporters moved beyond merely relaying information originated and controlled by a source. Each checked the information, supplied missing materials, explained complicated details. None of these efforts is the activity of a reporter content with Layer I information.

Let's look at some other examples of Layer II reporting.

The Cost of the Gender Gap

After California passed a law prohibiting gender price discrimination, reporters for KRON-TV in San Francisco checked to see whether it was being complied with. The law had come about after a survey by a legislative office showed that women paid on average $1.79 more to launder an identical shirt than men, that they paid $5 more for a similar haircut and that clothing alterations were considerably more costly for women than for men.

KRON-TV reporters found "women were still being taken to the cleaners." Emerald Yeh and Christine McMurry found that of 30 hair salons in San Francisco, a third quoted higher prices for women than for men. When a woman took in a size 4 men's style shirt to be cleaned, she was charged $2.50. When a man took in the same shirt, he was charged $1.

Women for Sale

When Lena H. Sun, *The Washington Post*'s correspondent in China, heard of the practice of selling women to men seeking wives, she looked for a victim so

Mark Avery

Seeking Out Dissidents

Jan Wong of *The Globe and Mail* of Toronto maintained contacts with those working for a democratic China in the face of suppression and prison. To avoid wiretaps and inquisitive police, she would meet in public places like this park.

Lena H. Sun,
The Washington Post

Sold for $363

Although Ma Linmei is far from home and is married to a man she does not like, she is luckier than most bought wives. Many are brutalized, kept in virtual captivity.

she wouldn't have to rely on secondhand accounts. On the outskirts of Beijing, she found Ma Linmei who was, Sun wrote, "a virtual prisoner. The main road is more than an hour away by foot, down a steep, rocky path. She has no money, and she can barely speak the local dialect. No one will help her escape."

Her husband had been unable to find a bride locally and traveled thousands of miles to Yunan Province in southwestern China to buy a wife.

Sun interviewed Ma, who told her, "I miss my home. I miss my mother. I'm always sick. If I had money I would run away."

But in a way, Ma was luckier than many women, Sun found. Thousands of others "are abducted by traders in human flesh, who trick them with promises of good jobs and a better life far from home. The traffickers often rape and beat the women before selling them into virtual bondage, often with the full knowledge and cooperation of local Communist Party officials. . . ."

Some of the victims, she reported, are as young as 14. Some are locked up, others shackled to keep them from running away. "Some have had their leg tendons cut to prevent them from escaping," Sun reported.

Computer-Assisted Reporting Projects

Journalists who use the computer to analyze material work in Layer II. When he was database editor of the *Austin American-Statesman* Jeff South teamed up with reporters to write informative stories. Here's how one begins:

Some of the highest-paid employees of Austin city government aren't doctors, lawyers and department heads. They're electricians, water workers and mechanics who add thousands of dollars to their salaries through overtime.

Dozens of city employees regularly earn more than $15,000 a year in overtime. Ninety have received more than $50,000 in overtime pay over the past four and a half years, and two-thirds of those employees work for one department: the electric utility.

By examining city payroll records, South and Mike Todd found the city had paid out more than $8 million in overtime in a year.

In computer analyses of database and other material, South found 402 dams in Texas "could collapse" with heavy rains, that despite the law a sixth of Texas drivers do not have auto insurance, and a fourth of Texas public schools had no black or Hispanic teachers.

Peter Eisler of *USA Today* dug into old records—100,000 pages of declassified documents—for his series on government contracts that put workers at risk and led to the pollution of many areas in the country. The material was placed in an Excel spreadsheet. For Eisler's detailed explanation of how he handled the reporting, and excerpts from his stories, see **Poisoned Workers & Poisoned Places** in *NRW Plus.*

Investigative Reporting

Those who dig deepest in Layer II are called investigative reporters. Their work falls into two categories—checking on illegal activities and looking into systemic abuses. The city purchasing agent who awards contracts without calling for bids violates the law. The police department that regularly stops black motorists is engaging in a systemic abuse.

A Systemic Abuse

Judy Johnson of *The Anniston Star* heard that some people in an Alabama community were having trouble getting credit from banks and finance companies. She decided to investigate. She spent months examining records of mortgages and land transfers. "I compiled them into lists year by year, looking for patterns, building a history," she said.

She talked to people turned down by banks. Through the years of borrowing from a local businessman, one woman had accumulated $50,000 in high-interest loans. Among her loans was one for a four-year-old car she and her husband had bought from the businessman's used car lot. The model she bought cost her slightly less than a new car would have cost her.

Johnson showed how the poor, who cannot obtain credit from large lending institutions, are victimized by private lenders. Her series won national recognition.

Illegalities

Shortly after his graduation from journalism school, James Dwyer of *The Dispatch* in Hudson County, N.J., was checking the bids of merchants hoping to sell supplies to a vocational school. His instructor had told Dwyer that bids sometimes are manipulated and that examining them can be rewarding.

Strange Bids Dwyer noticed that some seemed to be typed on the same typewriter. He also noticed that the prices for ladders, dust cloths, shovels and other items were high. Even when the supplies were purchased in quantity, prices were higher than they would have been for goods sold as individual items in hardware stores. For example, the school paid $564 for ladders that local stores sold for $189. He visited the school and found enough dust cloths to keep the school's furniture glowing for a couple of centuries.

Dwyer tried to locate the firms that made the unsuccessful bids. He could not find them. He theorized that the agent through whom the goods were sold had invented bidders, and using these fake firms to enter high bids on faked stationery, the agent made his firm the low bidder. Dwyer's investigation confirmed his theory and a grand jury took over after his stories appeared.

Computer-Assisted Reporting Project A reporter had been told by an out-of-office politician that some city workers were political appointees who never

Shoe-Leather Columnists

Experienced columnists work in Layer III. They leave the comfort of their offices and "go out and interview people and reflect their views in the column," says *New York Times* columnist Clyde Haberman. "More often than not, I go out and eyeball an event, a person, a project.

"Obviously, observing something directly provides useful color, a helpful quote or a sense of time and place. But I like to see an event or talk with people even if the results are not necessarily reflected in the writing.

"Merely watching something somehow helps me organize my thoughts, helps me focus. Frankly, I don't understand how columnists who never leave their offices do it. It's so easy to get lost in yourself.

"To me, the best columns are rooted in real reporting."

Thomas L. Friedman, another *Times* columnist, says he was taught early in his career "that whether you're writing news, opinion or analysis, if it isn't based on shoe-leather reporting it isn't worth a bucket of beans."

showed up for work. An idea: Examine parking tickets in resort areas issued to vehicles with New York license plates. He compared the names on the tickets with names on the city payroll. Lo and behold, he found Florida traffic tickets for New York City employees on days they were supposed to be working.

Finding Sources

As you may already have gathered, there are two basic types of sources, physical and human. Physical sources range from databases of political campaign donations to the minutes of city council sessions. They include census data and crime statistics. We will be looking at sources in greater detail in Chapter 14, but we'll pause a moment here to look at how a veteran reporter handles human sources.

Jeffrey A. Tannenbaum of Bloomberg News puts the names of the most helpful sources in his files. "Someday, they may come in handy," he says. But what about finding sources for a subject entirely new to the reporter?

"First, look for institutional sources," Tannenbaum says. "If you're writing about pizzas, there's a national association of pizza chefs." For his story about the growing power of the states' attorney generals, he asked the New York attorney general if there was an association of all 50 officers. He was given the telephone number of the organization.

In gathering information from news sources, he says, "One source leads to another. Perhaps only the seventh one in the chain has what you need."

When do you know you have gathered all you need? "Only after the information the sources have provided is getting redundant, and the sources are failing to supply new sources," he says.

Layer III Reporting

Reporters face a public increasingly interested in knowing all the dimensions of the events that affect their lives. The result has been a journalism that has expanded beyond accounts of what happened. Reporters are encouraged to tell readers, viewers and listeners how and why it happened, to describe the causes and consequences of the event.

When the U.S. Senate passed a tax cut bill, Edmund L. Andrews of *The New York Times* wrote in his lead that the bill is "mostly for the nation's wealthiest taxpayers." He went on to point out that the Senate failed to act on tax breaks "including deductions for college tuition and a savings credit for low income people. . . ."

Layer III reporting tells people how things work, why they work that way, or why they don't work.

Bad Swap When *The Seattle Times* learned that the U.S. Forest Service had traded away a verdant area along the Green River for a logged-over, debris filled stubble, reporters dug into the program that permitted such disadvantageous exchanges. Then reporters went beyond their investigation to suggest ways to fix the program.

The *Times* suggested seven reforms, from selling unwanted government land to the highest bidder to allowing the public to have a voice in determining what land should be exchanged or sold and in negotiating the sale or exchange.

Quick Passage   In the early days of the presidency of George W. Bush, Congress enacted a law making it harder for people to erase their debts by filing for bankruptcy. Philip Shenon of *The New York Times* pointed out that President Clinton had vetoed a similar bill in his last weeks in office but that the current version had quick and easy sailing. Shenon showed why:

> The bill's quick resurrection after Mr. Bush's inauguration was seen as evidence of the generous campaign contributions made to each party by the credit industry. It also reflected the growing power of lobbyists in a government in which the White House and Congress are run by business-friendly Republicans.

Easy Credit   The AP story from Chicago began:

> William Rodriguez trudged home through rain and snow and wee-hour darkness.
>
> He was only 23, in good health and known as a happy-go-lucky fellow.
>
> Yet he would be dead before sunrise.

Rodriguez had purchased rat poison on his way home from work, and as he walked he ate the poison. Why? The AP assigned two reporters to find out. Their digging turned up the answer—easy credit. Rodriguez owed $700 to merchants for furniture, clothing, a television set. He couldn't meet the payments, and the creditors were threatening to tell his employer.

The story galvanized the city's enforcement agencies. Rodriguez had been sold low-grade merchandise and had been given credit at usurious rates. The legislature reacted by lowering interest rates. The law is known as the "Rodriguez Law."

Voter-Conscious   When the New Jersey state legislature passed a bill banning state Medicaid payments for abortions, it ignored nine federal district court decisions in eight states that ruled similar bills were unconstitutional. The reason for the legislators' action was described in this Layer III sentence from *The New York Times:* "Approval of the measure reflects the influence of the Catholic Church, which opposes abortion, in New Jersey: About 55 percent of the state's registered voters are Catholic."

Putting I, II and III to Work

Let us watch a reporter mine these three layers for his story.

City Planner Arthur calls the local stations and newspaper to read to reporters a statement about a new zoning proposal. The release contains facts 1, 2 and 3. At the newspaper, reporter Bernard looks over the handout, tells his city editor that 1 and 2 are of no news value but that 3—elimination of two-acre zoning north of town—is important and worth exploring in an interview with Arthur. The editor agrees and assigns Bernard to the story.

Before leaving for the interview, Bernard checks the newspaper library for a story about a court decision he recalls that may be related to the proposed regulation. He telephones another city official and a real estate developer to obtain additional information. With this background and Arthur's statement, Bernard begins to develop ideas for questions. He jots down a few, 4, 5 and 6.

During the interview, City Planner Arthur repeats 1, 2 and 3. Reporter Bernard asks for more information about 3, the elimination of the minimum two-acre requirement for home building. Bernard also brings up his own subjects by asking questions 4, 5 and 6. New themes develop during the interview: 7, 8 and 9.

Back in the newsroom, Bernard looks over his notes. He sees that his hunch about 3 was correct. It was important. Arthur's answer to question 5 is newsworthy, he decides, and fact 7—the possibility of low- and medium-cost housing in the area—which developed during the interview, may be the lead.

Bernard needs comments on the impact of 7 from developers. A couple of calls and the possible consequences, 10, emerge. The developers confirm their interest in building inexpensive housing. Looking over his notes, he spots background from the library, 11, that is now relevant and also will go into the story.

The story will contain facts 3, 5, 7, 10 and 11. Bernard decides he will fashion 7 and 10 into a lead, and he worries about how to blend 11 into the story at a fairly early stage without impeding the flow of Arthur's explanation. He has found that background is sometimes difficult to work smoothly into the story. He writes this lead:

A proposed change to eliminate the two-acre zoning requirement for home building north of town could open the area to people who can afford only low- and medium-cost housing.

Bernard's story will consist of the following:

Facts	Layer
3	I
5, 7, 11	II
10	III

Bernard has used almost all the techniques reporters have at their command to gather facts for stories. He was given information by a source. Then he used the newspaper library—a physical source—for background. He then interviewed his original source—a human source—and made independent checks by calling up additional sources.

Summing Up

Here is some down-to-earth advice about reporting from working reporters:

- Stay ready for any breaking news story by keeping up-to-date on developments in the community.

- There is a story behind almost any event. Remember, it was a third-rate break-in in a Washington building that began the Watergate revelations and ended in the resignation of a president.

- Always check all names in the telephone book, the city directory and the library to make absolutely sure they are spelled correctly.

- Follow the buck. Find out where money comes from, where it is going, how it gets there and who's handling it. Whether it is taxes, campaign contributions or donations, keep your eye on the dollar.

- Question all assumptions. The people who believed the emperor was clothed are legion and forgotten. We remember the child who pointed out his nudity.

- Question authority. Titles and degrees do not confer infallibility.

Further Reading

Boorstin, Daniel J. *The Image: A Guide to Pseudo-Events in America.* New York: Atheneum, 1961.

Crouse, Timothy. *The Boys on the Bus.* New York: Random House, 1973.

McGinniss, Joe. *The Selling of the President 1968.* New York: Pocket Books, 1973.

12 Making Sound Observations

Alejandro Videla

Capture the dreamy look, the weary posture.

Preview

To gather the reliable and relevant information essential to a story, the reporter should:

- Know what readers and listeners are interested in, what affects them and what they need to know.
- Find a theme for the story early in the reporting.
- Look for the different, the unusual, the unique aspect of the event that illustrates it and that sets it apart from other events like it.

Don't write writing.
Write reporting.

The Congo was torn by civil war and the United Nations sent Secretary-General Dag Hammarskjold to the African republic to try to arrange a cease-fire.

At dusk, reporters at the Ndola airport in Northern Rhodesia awaiting Hammarskjold's arrival saw a plane land and a fair-haired man emerge. The reporters, who had been held behind police lines a hundred yards away, ran to file bulletins on the secretary-general's arrival. Anticipating Hammarskjold's next move, the press associations soon had stories describing Hammarskjold's discussing peace terms. Many of these stories ran in early editions of the next day's newspapers.

But the man the reporters saw disembark was not Hammarskjold. He was a British foreign affairs official on a fact-gathering tour. At the time the reporters were filing their stories, Hammarskjold was aboard another plane that crashed in a forest 10 miles north of Ndola, killing the secretary-general and the others on board.

The UPI reporter told his boss later, "I saw a man I thought looked like Hammarskjold. Other reporters claimed they were sure it was. After comparing notes, we all agreed to file stories."

The incident reveals some of the problems reporters face in covering spot news stories. To make sound observations, the reporter has to see and hear the event clearly, but this is not always possible. In this case, rather than wait to be certain of their man's identity, the reporters did what reporters do when their observations are uncertain and they are under pressure—they made an inference.

Because the man had light hair and his build approximated that of the secretary-general, the reporters jumped to the conclusion that he was Hammarskjold. They had violated the reporter's maxim, "Beware of inferences. Do not jump from the known to the unknown."

To guard against individual error, they checked with each other and formed a consensus. The difficulty in covering events often causes journalists to consult each other for reassurance, which leads to what is known as *herd* or *pack journalism.* Reporters tend to chat about the lead, the credibility of the source, the reliability of the documentation they have been offered. They seek agreement in resolving the uncertainties.

Accurate observations are the basis of news stories and features. Learning how to report accurately begins with an understanding of the methods that are used in the search for relevant information for the task of truth telling.

> **Eye of the Beholder**
> "Some news happens; the rest is discerned."
> —*Thomas Griffith, former editor,* Time

The Art of Observation

In his short story, "The Murders in the Rue Morgue," Edgar Allan Poe has his character C. Auguste Dupin expound on the art of observation as Dupin goes about solving the grisly murders of Madame L'Espanaye and her daughter, which have stumped the Parisian police. He dismisses the way the police work:

> There is no method in their proceedings, beyond the method of the moment. . . . The results obtained by them are not unfrequently surprising, but, for the most part are brought about by simple diligence and activity. When these qualities are unavailing, their schemes fail.

> **Mistakes**
> "Accurate observation of complex situations is extremely difficult, and observers usually make many errors of which they are not conscious."
> —*W.I.B. Beveridge*

Although hard work is essential to good reporting, activity is not enough. A method is essential. Dupin says that the detective makes "a host of observations and inferences. So, perhaps, do his companions; and the difference in the extent of the information obtained lies not so much in the validity of the inference as in the quality of the observation. The necessary knowledge is of *what* to observe."

In other words, the vacuum-cleaner collector of information wastes time. Dupin says the proper method is to follow "deviations from the plane of the ordinary." This is how "reason feels its way, if at all, in its search for the truth. In investigations such as we are now pursuing, it should not be so much asked 'what has occurred,' as 'what has occurred that has never occurred before.'" This is an excellent definition of news.

France's Fiction = New York's Fact

Dupin may be Poe's invention, but his method of observation is as useful in New York City as in Paris. Robert T. Gallagher, a private detective who spent 18 years on the New York City police force, disarmed more than 1,200 gun-toting thugs before they could draw their weapons. He had, everyone on the force agreed, an uncanny ability to spot people carrying guns on the street. How did he do it?

"If you're not looking for the clues you don't notice them," Gallagher said. "But if you're looking for them, they're so obvious they begin to jump out at you."

The easy one, "the classic bulge," Gallagher dismisses. He knew that most street criminals stick their guns in their waistbands. As a consequence, when they walk the leg on the gun side takes a shorter stride and the arm a shorter swing.

Another clue: the "security feel." Those carrying guns unconsciously reach to touch the weapon. They also adjust it after getting out of a car, going up or down stairs and stepping off a curb.

He notices the way jackets hang in the front. Buttoned, one side clings more tightly to a thigh than the other.

Like Dupin, Gallagher looks for the different, the unusual, what Dupin calls the "deviations from the plane of the ordinary." Dupin talks of seeing the "matter as a whole," and Gallagher's procedure is to examine the clothing, the gait, the mannerisms of his suspect. Out of this picture may emerge the clue for Gallagher, the deviation for Dupin and the lead for the journalist.

The Reporter's Task   For the reporter, every assignment is a mystery to be unraveled. With a method of observation, the reporter can find the solution, the significant information that becomes the core of the story. What makes this basketball game decided in the last 30 seconds different from the dozens of others that are also won with a last-second basket? How does this school board meeting differ from the last one, and the one before that? What is the outstanding evidence in the prosecution's case, who among the many is the defense's key witness, the judge's most significant quote in his sentencing comments?

By knowing how to make the important, the pertinent, the relevant observation the reporter provides the public with insight.

"Make Me See"

When reporters see clearly and see as a whole, they are on their way to communicating not only truthfully, but graphically. Gene Roberts, former managing editor of *The New York Times,* learned this on his first job as the farm columnist for the 9,000-circulation *Goldsboro News-Argus* in Wayne County, N.C. Roberts' editor was Henry Belk, who was blind.

Roberts recalls that when he showed up for work in the morning, Belk would call him over and inform the young reporter that his writing was insufficiently descriptive.

"Make me see," he would order.

Thomas French, *St. Petersburg Times*

On Trial for Murder

"At times, he came across as harmless, anonymous, utterly forgettable; your eyes would sweep over him and barely register his presence. A minute later, he would shift in his chair or turn his head a certain way, and all at once he seemed intimidating, even menacing.

It was there in his size and obvious physical strength, in the enormous forearms that rested on the table before him, in the way he stepped so jauntily in and out of the courtroom under the bailiff's escort. For someone so big, he was surprisingly light on his feet."

Roberts says, "It took me years to appreciate it, but there is no better admonition to the writer than 'Make me see.' There is no truer blueprint for successful writing than making your readers see. It is the essence of great writing."

Murderer   In his series that traced the search for and the trial of the killer of a woman and her two daughters aboard a boat in Tampa Bay, Thomas French of the *St. Petersburg Times* lets us see the accused through the eyes of jurors:

The jurors could not stomach Oba Chandler.

Some of them, sick of the smile he had worn through so much of the trial, wanted to slap him. Others were terrified of him.

Especially the women.

Linda Jones, an office administrator seated in the back row of the jury box, could hardly make eye contact with Chandler. If he looked her way, she averted her gaze. Evelyn Calloway, a school bus driver who sat in the front row, next to the witness stand, had looked into Chandler's eyes as he testified and had seen such coldness in him, she did not think he was human. Calloway began to worry that he might actually lunge for her from the witness box.

Rose Welton, a grandmother at the other end of the front row, was also struck by the chill in Chandler's stare. When he looked into her eyes, Welton thought she could feel his spirit, crawling inside her body.

A single word went through her, over and over:

Devil, devil, devil.

French's exhaustive reporting and vivid writing—the seven-part series was three years in the making—earned him a Pulitzer Prize.

Relevant Observations

The reporter on assignment is confronted by a flood of facts. A meeting can last two hours, cover seven different topics and include four decisions. A speaker may deliver an address containing 4,500 words. To handle these stories, the reporter may have at most a column for each story, about 750 words, or 90 seconds on a newscast, less for an online report.

There are three guides to the selection of relevant facts:

1. **Know the community:** Develop a feeling and understanding of what people need and want to know.

2. **Find the theme:** Carefully identify the theme of the story as soon in the reporting as possible. This way facts that support, buttress and amplify the theme can be gathered, the rest ignored as irrelevant.

3. **Look for the different:** Seek out the unique, the dramatic, the unusual, the break from the normal and routine.

Know the Community

The way to know the people in a community is to talk to them, to watch them at work and play, to study their past and to listen to their aspirations for themselves and their families. Talk to people in the Home Depot, chat with the service station attendant at Exxon, ask the first-grade teacher what her most pressing problems are. Go to a Little League game, read the clips about past news events, talk to the 70-year-old barber and the new lawyer in town and to the men and women who clean offices in the early-morning hours.

A Texas Tale   Reporters who move from one area to another often have trouble adjusting to their new readers and listeners. The story is told about the veteran reporter for a Chicago newspaper who decided to forsake the big city for a more relaxed life in Texas. He accepted a job as the city editor of a west Texas daily newspaper. One day a fire broke out in town and the reporter's blood stirred in the city editor. He decided to go out on the story himself.

R.L. Chambers

Be Precise

Don't write that the university card catalog was sent to oblivion a "few years ago." Journalism is the art of the specific.

Write that the computer replaced the card catalog "in 2004."

On his return, he batted out a story, Chicago style—dramatic and well-written. The managing editor was pleased with his city editor's handiwork except for one hole in the story.

"How much water did they use to put out the fire?" he asked. In parched west Texas, that fact was as important to readers as the number of fire units answering the call would have been to Chicago readers.

Find the Theme

Our second guideline is based on the form of the news story, which places certain demands on the reporter that he or she must satisfy in fact gathering. We know that the story consists of the statement of a central theme or idea (the lead) and the elaboration of that theme or idea (the body). The reporter must find the theme quickly so he or she can ask the relevant questions and make the appropriate observations to flesh out the story.

The sociologist Irving Kristol observed, "A person doesn't know what he has seen unless the person knows what he is looking for." In his book, *The Art of Scientific Investigation,* the British scientist W.I.B. Beveridge writes that developing ideas or hypotheses helps a person "see the significance of an object or event that otherwise would mean nothing."

Let's watch two reporters at work.

On the Street   When the Salvation Army dispatched 4,000 of its soldiers to New York City to do battle against "sin and evil," a reporter for *The New York Times* accompanied some of the troops through the streets. Impressed by the work of the Army men and women, the reporter decided early in her reporting to emphasize their dedication and singled out this incident in her account to illustrate her theme:

"The Army believes in total abstinence," a young soldier was saying to a disheveled-looking man, whose breath reeked of alcohol. "You are the temple of the Lord and if you destroy yourself, you're destroying Him."

"Am I?" the older man asked, as they stood in front of the entranceway of the Commodore. "No, I'm not."

"Sure you are," the soldier replied, resting his hand on the man's shoulder. The man reached out his hand, too, and began to cry. So did the Salvation Army soldier.

At a Party   In another part of town, the veteran *New Yorker* reporter Lillian Ross is at a party for a Broadway opening. She notices many cast members of "The Sopranos" and a bunch of pre-teen-agers and their parents. Ross decides to stay close to "eleven-year-old Bianca Bethuna, a pretty girl with long dark hair" and Bianca's mother. Ross describes Bianca as wearing "a stiff, full-skirted, long white organdie dress, white stockings, white patent-leather slippers, a diamond necklace, a gold bracelet, a gold Mickey Mouse wristwatch, and a sparkling silver tiara, which she won in a 'Sunhurst Beauty Pageant' a few years ago."

Clearly, Bianca is being groomed for something, and this gives Ross her theme, and this theme guides Ross's observations and her questions. Ross learns that Bianca is driven from her home in New Jersey every day after school for dance lessons, and on weekends as well, "has a piano lesson once a week. She gets weekly private lessons with a voice teacher and an acting coach." Her mother tells Ross, "All this started when I took Bianca at eighteen months to Mommy and Me classes. As they say, you do what you got to do."

It is almost midnight at the party and Bianca is at last being photographed with the play's leading actress. Ross writes, "Someone asked Bianca's mother if she was ready to take the limo and go home with Bianca. 'No way,' Bianca's mother said. 'We've got to work the room.' " This is the concluding line in Ross's piece. It is not difficult to see what Ross has been getting at, what her theme is. Ross hasn't **told** us; she has **shown** us through her observations and the quotations she uses.

Caution   If the reporter discovers facts that contradict the theme, it is discarded and a new theme is adopted. In this way, the reporter is like the scientist whose conclusion can be no stronger than his or her evidence.

Devising Themes   Experienced reporters almost always have a theme or tentative idea as soon as they receive an assignment. If a reporter is sent to cover a fire in a college dormitory, the reporter immediately thinks of deaths and injuries and

Greg Lovett

Mourner

For the reporter who seeks out the unusual, the sting of defeat may make as good a theme as the joy of victory.

The unusual is not always at center court. It may be on the sidelines where the losers bury their heads in grief. It could be buried in the small print in a document, the last sentence in a press release that begins with optimism and self-congratulation but ends with the admission of an unprofitable business year.

Looking deeply, listening intently, the reporter discovers truths that fascinate and inform readers and viewers.

the cause as the theme or possible lead. If the assignment is about the rescue of a drowning man, the lead could be the courage or ingenuity of the rescuer. Six youths die in an automobile accident; the reporter cannot help but immediately think of alcohol and drugs or speeding.

As soon as the Bethesda Naval Center announced that Supreme Court Justice Thurgood Marshall had died, reporters knew the theme of their story and the direction it would take. The fact that a Supreme Court Justice had died was not the theme but that the first black to join the Court and a leading figure in the civil rights movement had died. And that is just how the AP story began:

> WASHINGTON—Retired Justice Thurgood Marshall, the first black to sit on the U.S. Supreme Court and a towering figure in the civil rights movement, died Sunday of heart failure. He was 84.

Reporters knew what to write because of their knowledge of Marshall and his career.

Such knowledge tells the reporter "what to observe," to use Poe's language. It guides the reporter in asking questions, in doing background checks. In short, it allows the reporter to structure the reporting by providing a tentative theme for his or her story.

The theme or idea originates in the reporter's experience, knowledge of the subject, understanding of the essentials or necessities for this kind of story and in a vague area we can only describe as the reporter's feel for the subject.

Science in the Newsroom

O.K. Bovard, the great editor of Pulitzer's *St. Louis Post-Dispatch*, was said to take a scientific approach to news. He would advance a theory or hypothesis on the basis of a bit of information and then prove or disprove it through reporting. He said he and his staff used the approach "all day long in this room. The imaginative reporter does it when he refuses to accept the perfunctory police view of the mystery and sets himself to reason out all the possible explanations of the case and then adopts a theory for investigating the most likely one."

Bob Thayer,
The Providence Journal

Turning Point?

Did the steal open up a big inning? Or did the second baseman's grab of a poor throw keep the runner at second and prevent a rally? This play could be the lead for the game story.

Look for the Different

Learning to distinguish the unique from the routine is difficult enough, let alone for the sports reporter covering her 33rd basketball game, the education reporter covering his fifth school board meeting. Events seem to settle into a familiar pattern. Spotting differences is difficult. We grow up seeing likenesses, similarities. How many can distinguish the Jonathan from the Delicious, the Jersey from the Guernsey? To most of us, all apples are alike, and cows are just cows.

But journalists see differently. They learn early on to look at the world through the eyes of the innocent child while applying the discerning eye of the wise elder who can distinguish between the significant and the unimportant, the dramatic and the routine.

Red Smith, a sportswriter who covered so many baseball games he lost count, explained the basis of the journalist's artistry: "Every ball game is different from every other ball game—if the reporter has the knowledge and wit to discern the difference."

When Gustave Flaubert, the French novelist, was teaching Guy de Maupassant to write, he told the young man to pick out one of the cab drivers in front of a railway station in Paris and to describe him in a way that would differentiate him from all the other drivers. To do so, Maupassant had to find the significant details that would single out that one man. The moustache? No, four others have one. That slouch? No, they all seem to be collapsing. Ah, one has a red beret. The others are wearing black hats. Also, he is the only one without a cigarette dangling from his mouth.

Little differences make for big stories.

Individuality

Experienced reporters usually agree on the themes of the stories they cover. Beyond that, each reporter puts his or her individual stamp on the story. Some of that individuality comes from writing style. Much is based on the particular observations the reporter makes. What is a relevant detail to one reporter may be irrelevant to another.

When Homer Bigart, the winner of two Pulitzer Prizes and one of the country's great reporters, was sent to cover the military trial of Lt. William Calley, who had been accused of murdering civilians in the My Lai massacre during the Vietnam War, Bigart observed how Calley was brought into court. He linked this observation to his observations at another army officer's trial he had covered, and he wrote:

> Although he had just been found guilty of twenty-two murders, Calley was treated far more gently than was Army doctor Captain Howard B. Levy four years ago after receiving a sentence for refusing to give medical training to Green Berets on the grounds that the training would be used unlawfully in Vietnam.

Unlike Levy, Calley was not handcuffed and left the court unfettered. An officer explained: "His conduct has been exemplary throughout and he'll continue to be treated as an officer."

Bigart's editors at *The New York Times* apparently considered his references to the Levy trial to be irrelevant, for the section read simply:

Lieutenant Calley was not handcuffed when driven to the stockade.

Whose judgment was better, Bigart's or his editors'? Bigart's reference to the Levy trial provides the reader with some idea of the intense feeling of the military against the peace movement—of which Levy was a symbol—and its consideration for the accused murderer of civilians, a career army man.

Looking, Listening

A journalist may be sharp of sight, acute of hearing and blessed with wide experience and the best of news sense. But unless that journalist is in a position to see and hear what is happening, all these qualities are meaningless. Good observation begins with good vantage points. This usually means being close to the action.

Close to Clinton David Remnick of *The New Yorker* accompanied former President Bill Clinton on an extended trip to Africa, Europe and to the Parkside Middle School in Manchester, N.H., where several hundred children were sitting on the floor of the gym for the "obesity event."

Clinton "stripped off his jacket and sat on a high stool," Remnick writes, and then listens as Clinton starts to talk.

"When I was a little boy," he said to the kids, "I was bigger than almost all of you. Now there are more kids like I was." He told them about learning to exercise more and suggested they watch a show on Nickelodeon called "Let's Just Go Play Healthy Challenge."

When the question period began, a chubby kid, no more than seven, nervously held the microphone and asked Clinton, "What if you don't have the channel?"

His quavering voice betrayed such a sense of terror and deprivation that a lot of the kids laughed. *What? No Nickelodeon? It's basic cable!*

Clinton had clearly heard the laughter and seen the terror in the kid's eyes and he sensed the embarrassment that would likely haunt his nights, and so he said, "A *lot* of people don't have the channel. So that's a good question. A *great* question."

The jaws of life! The boy smiled. His whole body seemed to relax. The laughter stopped. It was a *great* question! And while Clinton went on to talk about other ways kids could learn about eating more sensibly, it was easy to believe that this kid—still a little shaken, but relieved of his shame—would vote for a Clinton one day if he could.

A Tense Exchange At a news conference, Gov. Kirk Fordice of Mississippi told reporters, "The United States of America is a Christian nation. . . . The less

Carlos Antonio Rios,
Houston Chronicle

Different Reason

Thousands cross the Rio Grande in search of work, but this pregnant woman wants her child born in the United States.

we emphasize the Christian religion the further we fall into the abyss of poor character and chaos in the United States of America."

Gov. Carroll A. Campbell Jr. of South Carolina differed, he wanted reporters to know. "The value base of this country comes from the Judeo-Christian heritage that we have and that is something we need to realize." Richard L. Berke, who covered the conference for *The New York Times,* watched Campbell as he returned to his seat on the dais next to Fordice.

"I just wanted to add the 'Judeo' part," Campbell told Fordice. Berke then writes, "Mr. Fordice responded tartly, 'If I wanted to do that I would have done it.' "

The exchange, brief as it was, provided a shaft of light for the reader, an insight into the positions and the feelings of the conservative and center factions of the Republican Party.

Berke had positioned himself so that he could overhear the conversation of the governors.

Checking It

So, not only get up close, but when what you think you've heard sounds strange, check it out. Look into that seemingly wild statement, rumor or situation. Don't write it off. The reward could be a footnote in journalism history, or a Pulitzer Prize.

Editors attending a luncheon at a convention of the American Society of Newspaper Editors were astonished when they saw Fidel Castro, the guest of honor, reach across the table and swap plates with the president of the Society.

Had an editor acted on that astonishment at the 1961 banquet and done what reporters are supposed to do—ask why—that editor might have been informed that Castro feared assassination. And that editor might have had a major story. For in 1975, the Central Intelligence Agency admitted that during the administrations of presidents Eisenhower, Kennedy and Johnson the United States government had indeed tried to murder Castro.

Down the Drain   No one could believe the rumors: The Internal Revenue Service was botching a huge number of returns. Some weren't being examined, some were tossed away. Arthur Howe of *The Philadelphia Inquirer* decided to check the rumors and he learned that the IRS had mishandled one of three returns for the previous year. In Atlanta, a worker flushed returns down a toilet. In Memphis, complicated returns were destroyed.

The IRS denied it all. But Howe persisted, and he corroborated everything. He was awarded the Pulitzer Prize for National Reporting.

Unbelievable   Deborah E. Lipstadt maintains in her book *The American Press and the Covering of the Holocaust* that many newspapers refused to publish reports of the Nazi Final Solution because the reports of death squads and gas chambers were "beyond belief." If the newspapers and radio stations had been less skeptical of the reports of refugees, she writes, they might have had an accurate description of Hitler's rise to power and his policies.

Listening in

Rodger Mallison of the *Fort Worth Star-Telegram* took photos and conducted interviews for a series on local crime. Here's what he wrote about the arrest of the young driver he photographed taking a sobriety test:

"In two hours I'll be out," the man says.

"I don't think so, dude. I'm not taking you to the drunk tank. I'm taking you to jail for DWI," Johnson says.

"You can't do that. I'm a very intelligent man."

"I can see that. It takes a lot of intelligence to get behind the wheel drunk. You could've killed somebody."

"That's right, and I'll kill you," the man says. "Stupid———. You'll get killed; we've already got your name. Come to Stop Six. You'll be six feet under. Your——— is going. I hate a black man that takes another black man down. . . . I'll kill you. I will slit your whole throat."

It is a long nine-minute ride to the jail.

"I had to bite my tongue a few times," Johnson says at the jail. "You definitely have to have a thick skin. You can't take it personally."

The Holocaust and the Castro incident point to an unseen dimension of reporting. Although the reporter is guided by reason and logic, he or she must be open to the most implausible facts and observations. Time after time reporters find aberrant facts and extraordinary observations and put them aside as too unusual for further examination. No report should be dismissed—no matter how outlandish it seems—without at least a quick check.

Notice the word *check.* The journalist's term for this is verification. By verification journalists mean direct observation and when that is not possible they mean statistical data, documents, reports, some kind of physical evidence. An anecdote or an isolated incident is not verification but can serve to buttress the observation and the evidence, give it a human dimension.

When physical evidence is impossible to obtain and direct observation is blocked, then human sources are acceptable if there is confirmation from several such sources.

Limitations of the Story

Although we may agree that the reporter's task is to continue the search for relevant facts until the theme is adequately supported, we also must admit that the search can never be completed, that there are facts beyond the reporter's reach. Just as a map can never be the complete guide to a territory, so a news story is rarely the definitive statement of reality.

Here are some of the obstacles reporters face:

- The deadline.

- The source the reporter cannot locate.

- The missing record, document or newspaper clipping.

- The incident the reporter cannot see or hear properly.

- The facts the source will not divulge.

- The material the copy editor cuts out of the story.

- The book or magazine the reporter fails to read. Yesterday's newspaper left unread beyond page 1.

- The phone call not returned.

- The question not asked.

For those who like ideas expressed in formulas, we can represent the concept of the limitations of the story with the Reporter's Equation:

$$\text{Truth} = \text{Story} + X$$

Actually, the capital letter X represents a series of small x's—those that we have listed as the obstacles reporters face.

The Tyranny of Time

The clock is the journalist's major obstacle. Unlike the historian or the sociologist, who face few daily or weekly demands for their work, the journalist submits to the requirements of nagging daily, sometimes hourly, deadlines while still seeking to present a complete and accurate account.

Complex events require time to unravel. The reporter may find that the newspaper or station cannot provide time in an increasingly competitive media environment. Discouraged, the reporter sometimes settles for the recital of what sources declare (Layer I journalism), which is truth of a sort.

Style as a Barrier

The journalistic style also may obstruct truth. The journalist is instructed to tell a story in simple, dramatic, personalized prose. Some important events are complicated. The reporter who seeks to make these events—usually ideas, trends, concepts—come alive may distort them by using exciting details that are colorful but not representative. For years, the newsmagazines emphasized this kind of detail. Their correspondents named the wines the diplomat drank, counted the cigarettes he smoked during a tense hearing. The significance of the event often was lost in the human-interest trivia.

The Reporter as Intruder

The act of reporting can itself be an impediment to accurate observations. Walter Lippmann characterized the journalist as a "fly on the wall," a detached observer whose presence does not affect the event being observed. But if reporting requires close-at-hand observation, scrupulous note taking, photographs, video or tape, how unobtrusive can the reporter be? The fly descends and buzzes around the event.

We know what happens when a television crew arrives at an event. Drones become animated. Reserved people begin to gesticulate. Reality is altered.

At a political rally in Central America, a reporter noted the calm, almost serene atmosphere. Even when a speaker released a dove from the center of the plaza, the crowd was hushed. Then the television and still photographers arrived, and the event suddenly took another shape. Fists were shaken. A Cuban flag was unfurled for the photographers, and revolutionary slogans were shouted into the recording equipment. When the photographers departed, the rally returned to its placid state. In the next day's newspaper, accompanying the reporter's story of a quiet protest against United States Foreign policy, was a photo of what seemed to be a fist-shaking mob.

Even the reporter's pencil and paper can distort the event. Every reporter experiences the trying moment when, after chatting with a source to put him or her at ease, it is time to reach for a pencil and notepad. In an instant, the mood changes. The simple tools of the reporter's trade have spooked the source.

Unobtrusive Observation

This type of reaction can be avoided by nonreactive or unobtrusive observation, methods that have the merit of allowing the reporter to be a fly on the wall. Let us follow a reporter as he uses this reporting technique.

Among the dozens of reporters gathered in central California to attend a Republican state conference was a reporter who was unknown to the delegates. He was able to mix freely, smiling and shaking hands with delegates. He knew he was being mistaken for a young delegate, and when one of the central committee secretaries told him there was an important meeting, he went along with her. They walked into the meeting together, and he sat near her, apparently doodling absent-mindedly on a pad in front of him.

All day long he moved in and out of caucuses, meetings and powwows. He heard Orange County delegates denounce the president, a Republican, as a liberal, a spendthrift, an enemy of the party's conservative principles. He listened as deals were made to try to attract labor and minority votes.

The week before when another political group held a convention, the reporter had plumped down in a soft chair in the lobby of the hotel and listened. He had heard delegates talk about the threat of leftists, the radicalism of the labor movement and the dangers of sex education in the public schools.

Ethics Debated

Some journalists condemn this kind of reporting. They point out that journalists have exposed intrusions into privacy by credit investigators and some governmental agencies. Journalists cannot, they say, set themselves apart from the rules they would apply to others.

A reporting technique that avoids the dilemma about concealing the reporter's identity is described by Helen Benedict of Columbia as "watch-and-wait" journalism. Sources know a reporter is present, but the reporter eases into the background, rarely asking a question. Lillian Ross, whose piece about an aggressive mother and her 11-year-old daughter we examined a few pages back, practices this kind of journalism. It is as close to the fly-on-the-wall reporting as journalism can reach.

Journalistic ethics are discussed further in Chapter 27.

Participant Observation

Another research method—participant observation—links social science and journalism strategies. An Oregon reporter who managed to fold his six-foot frame into a third grader's seat at school was a participant observer. The reporter who worked as a telephone operator and then wrote a series of articles based on her experiences was doing participant observation.

In this kind of reporting, the reporter discards his or her role as the uninvolved, detached observer and joins the activity of the person or group he or she is covering. The reporter who became a third-grader for a story participated in the children's school work, ate lunch with them and played ball at recess. The school children took him for a friend, a bit older and awkward about some things, but a companion nevertheless. They talked to him as an equal. His relationship with the students enabled him to gather material that the usual interview and observation techniques would not have revealed.

New Directions

Social scientists who studied people in their settings influenced journalists. Traditionally, journalism focused on centers of authority with their formalities—ceremonies, meetings, announcements. This was insufficient, journalists came to realize. They understood that they were not describing the reality of human experience and they became anxious to develop techniques that enabled them

Charles Buchanan, *Winston-Salem Journal*

Going Along for the Morning Collection

For her story about sanitation men, Phoebe Zerwick of the *Winston-Salem Journal* rides along on the orange garbage truck as the men make their morning rounds. She absorbs the sights and the sounds—and the smells, too. "A mist lingers on an unusually cool August morning. A few dogs bark, lunging at fences. Once in a while someone starts a car engine and backs out of a driveway. . . . The smell, sometimes sweet, sometimes sour, is still faint at 8 a.m. before the heat of the day cooks up stronger odors." She observes the workers: "The men keep up a furious pace, with Casey, 28, taking long strides in knee-high rubber boots and McLaurin, 34, running."

to expand their reporting. Sara Grimes, a reporter in Philadelphia, said after she had been covering the juvenile court for a year, "I wonder why so many reporters insist on quoting people in positions of power rather than observing people who are affected by power."

Listening to Youngsters   She listened closely to the young defendants in court, and she sought to understand the effect of the system on youngsters by talking to them. One day she learned that an 11-year-old boy—who was brought into court in handcuffs—had been held in a detention center for nine months although he had not committed a crime. He was a runaway. Grimes asked to talk to the youngster, who had been sent to foster homes after his parents were judged neglectful. He had not liked the foster homes and had run away. Here is part of the story she wrote:

"Jones, Jones," the guard's voice could be heard as he walked up and down the cell-block. Amid a few undistinguishable low grumblings behind the rows of bars came a small, high voice. "Yes, that's me."

Johnny was brought out to an anteroom. No longer crying, he sat with downcast eyes in dungarees and a gray sweatshirt. Quietly and slowly he answered questions.

He wished he had somebody to bring him soap because the institutional soap gives him a rash. He would like to leave YSC (Youth Study Center) and would go "any place they send me."

How does it feel to be handcuffed? In a barely audible voice, he answered: "It makes me feel like a criminal."

The Epidemic   Barbara Ferry of *The New Mexican* in Santa Fe found worry and fear in the usually placid northern New Mexico villages and towns. Drugs. Everywhere. In the village of Chimayo, she wrote, there are more than 30 dealers. "Villagers don't seem to be getting noticeably richer," she wrote. "They are dying." Her series included portraits of some of the victims, most of them young men and women. Some of these are in *NRW Plus* **The Damage Done.**

With an Addict   Loretta Tofani of *The Philadelphia Inquirer* watched as the young woman dropped her maternity pants past her swollen stomach. The woman, eight months pregnant, picked up a syringe and injected heroin into her right calf.

"He won't stop moving, this baby," the woman told Tofani. "When he moves a lot it means he's sick. He needs a fix."

Tofani stayed with the 30-year-old addict for months, watched her wheedle money from relatives for her drugs, stayed in her kitchen when she entertained a visitor for the $20 she needed for a fix.

And she stayed through the birth of the baby and watched the woman fight to retain custody of her daughter, who was born addicted to heroin, methadone and a pill the woman was popping before the birth.

A Ghetto Family

Leon Dash, a reporter for *The Washington Post,* spent several years with a woman and her family in a relationship so close that he was able to gather the most intimate details of their lives. Although sympathetic to the family, Dash was unsparing in his presentation of a family wracked by poverty, drugs, prostitution, crime and illiteracy.

The book Dash wrote later is dedicated to "unfettered inquiry."

The head of the family, Rosa Lee, in her 50s on welfare and food stamps, supports herself through shoplifting and drug dealing. She has eight children by five different men. Dash shows her strengths as well as her weaknesses—her love for her children, aspiration to a decent life, resourcefulness. But he is no soft touch for the tales his sources tell him. Ducky, Rosa Lee's youngest son, informs Dash that he has had a religious conversion and will hereafter serve Christ.

Dash tells Ducky, "You cook powdered cocaine into crack for New York City dealers . . . and you have been addicted to crack for some time now."

Drugs emerge as the major destructive force in the life of the family Dash portrays. Two sons manage to escape from the dysfunctional home life, and Dash says three factors were involved: They attended school longer than their brothers and sisters; an adult became concerned about them (one a school teacher, the other a social worker), and each was able to obtain a full-time job.

The Live In

Dash's extended participant observation can also be described as a Live In, a reporting technique introduced 45 years ago at the Graduate School of Journalism at Columbia University. Based on the work of Margaret Mead, Oscar Lewis and Robert Coles, the Live In sends students into homes and workplaces. To move closer to their sources, students have tutored addicts in drug rehabilitation centers and children in schools. They have slept on the floors of mission houses in the Bowery, in sleeping bags at a residence of the Catholic Workers and on cots in shelters for the homeless.

Students have walked the beat with police officers, gone on home visits with social workers and accompanied ambulance drivers on their calls. These experiences were not one-shot affairs. Students met the policeman's family, talked to the welfare mother's children and went into wards to talk to patients.

Behind the Doors

These reporters and the others we'll look at understand what the great Russian writer Anton Chekhov wrote about in his short stories, the struggle of people to overcome forces sometimes too powerful or incomprehensible for them. For Chekhov's insight, see **Behind the Doors** in *NRW Plus*.

The Students

Charles Young, a white, middle-class student from Wisconsin, did his Live In at a junior high school in Harlem in New York City. Let's join Young while he waits for the assistant principal in his office. The room is filled with students. Young describes the scene at the beginning of his Live In:

> Gus Marinos, known simply as "Marinos" to everybody, a Greek immigrant in his twenties with dazed but kindly eyes beneath his Coke-bottle glasses, returns to his office on the fourth floor. The room erupts with a deafening chorus of his name.
>
> "MAH-*REE*-NOS! HER FINGERNAILS BE POISON!" a girl screams, holding up her scratched right hand.
>
> "So die," says Marinos, examining some smudged papers on his desk.
>
> "WHY 'ON'T CHEW DIE!"

"You wanna go home?"

"YEAH, BUT CHEW CAN'T TELL ME HER NAILS AIN'T POISON!"

"So go home."

"HER NAILS GOT DIRT AN' SHIT IN 'M!" The girl leaves with a pass home.

"MAH-*REE*-NOS!" another girl demands, "GIMME A PENCIL!" He hands her a pencil from his desk. "I 'ON'T WANT NO PENCIL LIKE THAT! I WANNA BLACK PENCIL!"

"This *is* a black pencil."

"I MEAN A YELLOW PENCIL THAT WRITES BLACK!"

"We don't sell those here."

"I 'ON'T WANT TO BUY NO PENCIL! I WANT CHEW TO GIMME IT!" She grabs the pencil from his hand and in the process drops a textbook. "NOW SEE YOU MADE ME DONE DIRTY MY BOOK!"

"I made you done what?"

"DIRTY MY BOOK!" She leaves for class.

These girls read an average of two years below the national norm for their grade level (slightly ahead of the boys), but the ghetto has already taught them how to get what they want from life: yell until somebody gives it to you. The lesson is apt, because when they are graduated in three years or so, they won't be equipped to do anything anyway.

That these girls (all sent to the office for disciplinary reasons) want something is obvious. What they want is less obvious and increasingly important as the market for unskilled labor dries up.

The first step in finding out what they want is learning a new vocabulary, some of which would be useful to define here. To "come out your mouth" is to communicate. "On time" is an adjective or adverb of approbation meaning you have done something according to socially accepted procedure. "On cap" is synonymous with "in your head," referring to intelligence. . . .

The Disciplinarian

Young interviewed the assistant principal in charge of discipline, who, he writes, "carries a cane in one hand and a leather whip in the other when she wades into a group of warring Dominican and Puerto Rican youths."

His description continues:

She resembles an army tank—solid, low-to-the-ground, unstoppable, paradoxically maternal.

She is in fact known as the mother of the school. Teachers speak with awe of the dedication that brings her to the otherwise deserted building on weekends and vacations. Students speak with equal awe of her omniscience. Because they trust her, she knows exactly who is pushing what drugs and who is fighting with whom.

Standing at the main entrance to the building at 3 o'clock one Friday afternoon in anticipation of a gang fight, Williams catalogues a gathering of a dozen or so Puerto Rican school alumni.

"That one is on parole now. . . . That one is pushing. Look at his station wagon. . . . That one has a sawed-off .38 in his pocket. We'd tell the police about it, but it will pass fifty hands by the time they can react. . . ."

On Thursday, one of their little brothers dropped a piece of chalk from the fourth floor that hit a Dominican on the head. In the ensuing melee, another Puerto Rican was badly cut on the arm with a broken bottle. The Puerto Ricans seek vengeance.

Having no stake in the matter, the blacks are blasé and leave the area immediately. They've seen it all before and even the prospect of serious violence is a bore. The Hispanics gather in groups along the sidewalk and buzz with rumors, with more energy than they have shown all day in class.

Williams crosses the street and puts her arm around one of her former students who has an Afro bigger than the rest of his body. She makes small talk for a couple of minutes, then kisses him on his pockmarked cheek as the gang scatters off down the street. A group of Dominicans, observing the enemy from a block away, disappears to its lair on 133rd Street.

The aborted fight is typical of junior highs anywhere in that the participants seem willing to do battle over nothing. What is frightening is that the involved alumni range in age from 16 to the mid-twenties. They never grew up, just became better armed. They are the fruit of the American system of education.

"Even five years ago they at least expressed an interest in college," says Williams back in the dormitory-room-sized office which she shares with three other school officials and usually seven or eight students who have been thrown out of class. . . .

The Basketball Player

Young befriended a bright young black student in the school. After Young graduated and went to work for *Rolling Stone,* he decided to look up the youngster for a story for the magazine about his dream of becoming a basketball star. He found the youth in high school, playing basketball, struggling with his classes and still filled with hope. Young's piece, "Above 125th Street: Curtis Haynes' New York," begins:

"I'm growin' plants all the time," says Curtis Haynes, pouring half a glass of water over a geranium. The floor and window ledge of his bedroom are covered with leafy pots. "Plants are everything. They give us oxygen and food. They also a home for insects." He brushes an aphid off a leaf. "Insects gonna inherit the earth."

He continues the tour of his room—recently painted electric blue by his mother—by pulling a picture off a shelf full of basketball trophies. Judging by his fleeting eyes and reticent tone of voice, he doesn't know what to make of me—a pale, white, 26-year-old, bearded magazine editor with thick glasses from a myopic childhood of too much TV watching and book reading in Madison, Wisconsin. Nor do I know what to make of him—a handsome, ebony-skinned, 16-year-old, short-haired high-school student with sharp vision from a childhood spent on the basketball courts of Harlem. "This is my brother, Footie," he says, holding a blurred photograph of a teenager bearing a strong resemblance to Curtis. "Remember, remember, remember . . ." is inscribed around the margins. "We named him that because he had such big feet," he says. Curtis' Pro Ked basketball shoes equal my own 11½ Adidas—and I am 6' 2" while he is just 5' 10". "He died in a fight two years ago. Puerto Rican friend got in an argument at a party and the other dude pulled a gun. My brother jumped between them. I never go to parties no more."

The Crab Pickers

In Chapter 8 we read about the departure of a group of young women from a village in Mexico to North Carolina where they were to work in a crab plant. The elderly black women who had worked at the task of picking out the slivers of crab from the hard shells had gradually retired and a new source of workers was found in Mexico.

Two days after the phone call came, Hull was aboard a bus with the women for the four-day trip to the Outer Banks. She stayed with the women on and off for the length of their stay and returned home with them. Her four months of reporting was a Live In.

For more of Hull's work, see **Una Vida Mejor—A Better Life**—(II) in *NRW Plus*.

Problems of Involvement

Participant observation can cause problems. In addition to the possibility that the reporter's presence may affect the event, the participant observer can become too deeply involved with his or her sources, risking the possibility that feelings may override responsibility to the facts.

Participant observation also has been criticized as exploitation of the source. After all, the journalist is using the lives of people as the basis of a story, which could lead to the reporter's acclaim, help him or her win a pay raise and possibly a promotion. But the alcoholic, the addict, the welfare mother and the police officer are not reimbursed for their contributions. Nor is much done about the problems that overwhelm some of these people.

Prying Indefensible   The journalist James Agee agonized over prying into the lives of Southern sharecroppers. He and the photographer Walker Evans were assigned to do an article on cotton tenantry, the system by which farmers worked the fields of landowners in return for a share of the crop less what was advanced to them for seed, living quarters and tools. The sharecroppers were poorer than dirt poor, for not even the earth they tilled was theirs. The magazine article was not published, but in 1940 the work became a book, *Let Us Now Praise Famous Men.* Agee knew the justifications for his intimate observations, but they did not console him. Early in the book, he describes his reservations:

> It seems to me curious, not to say obscene and thoroughly terrifying, that it could occur to an association of human beings drawn together through need and chance and for profit into a company, an organ of journalism, to pry intimately into the lives of an undefended and appallingly damaged group of human beings, an ignorant and helpless rural family, for the purpose of parading the nakedness, disadvantage and humiliation of these lives before another group of human beings, in the name of science, of "honest journalism" (whatever that paradox may mean), of humanity, of social fearlessness, for money, and for a reputation for crusading and for unbias which, when skillfully enough qualified, is exchangeable at any bank for money (and in politics, for votes, for job patronage, abelincolnism, etc.). . . .

In Defense of Prying

In rebuttal to these criticisms, reporters who use the technique say that public awareness is increased by stories about the lives of people. They say this awareness can lead to reform by involving the public emotionally in the situations described by the reporter.

Steven Almond, a reporter for the *Miami New Times,* spent weeks at the James E. Scott housing project to reveal "what life is really like for the women and children living in Miami's inner city." Almond said he was bothered by one aspect of his work:

By far, the most difficult aspect of the work was realizing that I was merely another male figure who would eventually abandon the kids that I had befriended. And facing that, in some deep sense, I was exploiting the kids by using their lives as journalistic fodder. It was betrayal.

Hopefully, The Canyon managed to convey a little bit about what it is like, day to day, for women and children who live in inner-city housing projects. That's not a story often told.

A Corrective for Detachment

Participant observation can help correct a detachment that can lead to callousness. A student who said he considered drug addicts weak and worthless conducted a Live In with a young female addict. The woman's daughter was being put up for adoption because the mother had been judged unfit to raise her. The woman's agony at the prospect of losing her daughter—which the student felt intensely—led him to do a series of revealing articles about the city's adoption laws.

The experience of participant observation allows the reporter to step outside routines and familiar environments to achieve new insights and to avoid another trap—the tendency to stereotype. Working under pressure, reporters fall back on stereotyping people, which permits them to simplify complicated events and to communicate complexities in easily understood terms. Forgetting that life is endless variety and change, some reporters look at the world through a kaleidoscope that is never turned. As a consequence, their observations reflect only a narrow, static vision. In Chapter 17, we will examine these stereotypes and the ways of thinking that determine how reporters look at events.

Summing Up

The key to first-rate observation is the quality of the theme the reporter has in mind. The reporter's theory or idea—call it the possible lead to the story—"suggests and coordinates observations," says the scientist and teacher-writer Stephen Jay Gould of Harvard. "Theory can prod, suggest, integrate and direct in fruitful ways."

But it "can also stifle, mislead and restrict," Gould adds. He calls the business of devising themes as a prelude to making observations the "double-edged sword . . . as both liberator and incarcerator. . . ." It is liberating when the theme is borne out by information gathered by detached observation. It is incarcerating when the reporter's observations are made with eyes and ears determined to see and hear on the basis of hope and belief that the theme or lead is on target.

In the next chapter, we will look at how reporters build the background on which they structure sound observations for their stories.

Further Reading

Agee, James. *Let Us Now Praise Famous Men.* Boston: Houghton Mifflin, 1960.

Beveridge, W.I.B. *The Art of Scientific Investigation.* New York: Vintage Books, 1962.

Dash, Leon. *Rosa Lee: A Mother and Her Family in Urban America.* New York: Basic Books, 1996.

Lipstadt, Deborah E. *The American Press and the Covering of the Holocaust, 1933–1945.* New York: Free Press, 1985.

Preview

Journalists work at building two kinds of background knowledge:

- **General:** The overall knowledge that the reporter takes to the job. This storehouse is based on wide reading and varied experience.
- **Specific:** The specialized information that helps the reporter handle his or her beat. It includes, for example, knowing about one judge's preference for jail sentences and another's for probation, or the mayor's determination to reassess property values to increase revenues.

The reporter's storehouse of general information serves two purposes:

1. Provides necessary explanatory detail for stories.
2. Leads to stories that anticipate events.

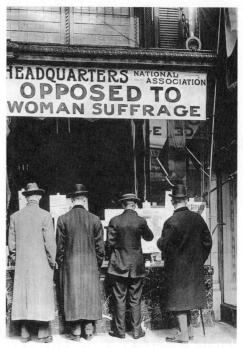

The Library of Congress
Non-voters then. Sought after now.

The journalist is expected to know it all. An error, a missing fact or a misinterpretation cannot be explained away.

Demanding as this may seem, it is the lot of the professional to be unfailingly certain in performance. The doctor is expected to identify the ailment that plagues the patient. The attorney is an authority on the law. The teacher is a wise, unfaltering guide who takes students through the complexities of phonics, irregular Spanish verbs and William Blake.

But we know professionals are fallible. Doctors misdiagnose, and sometimes their operations fail. Lawyers lose cases they should win. Teachers are human, too, like the grade school teacher who assigned her class the task of writing sentences containing words from a list she

You can't write if you can't think.

supplied. One youngster, who consulted his collection of baseball cards for inspiration, chose the word *cap,* and he wrote, "Catfish Hunter wears a cap." The teacher returned the boy's paper with the sentence corrected: "*A* catfish hunter wears a cap."

Should the teacher have known Catfish Hunter was a baseball player? Well, perhaps we do make excuses for teachers, as well as for doctors and lawyers. But we do not excuse the journalist who errs through ignorance.

Should the journalist really be expected to know everything? "Yes," said the reporter Murray Kempton. "When you're covering anything, and you're writing about it at length, you use everything you know. And in order to use everything you have to be interested in an extraordinary range of things."

Should you have known that the photograph that opens this chapter depicts a long period in American life: Women could not vote in national elections until 1920 when Tennessee ratified the 19th Amendment.

For more photographs with which you can test your background knowledge, see **Important Parts of the Past** in *NRW Plus.*

Da-Da Journalism

David Cay Johnston said he decided to cover tax policy because most of the reporting was bad. "Our whole system depends on taxes," *The New York Times* reporter says, "whether it's educating children, or enforcing your rights under a contract or military defense of the country.

"The first thing I learned was most of the reporters covering this, like most reporters covering most subjects, engaged in 'he said' journalism: 'da, da, da, he said.' So what they ended up doing was accurately quoting people, whether they knew what they were writing about or not."

Twain's and Mencken's Complaints

In Mark Twain's *Sketches,* he describes his experiences as a newspaperman in "How I Edited an Agricultural Paper." Twain is telling a friend that little intelligence is needed to be a journalist:

> I tell you I have been in the editorial business going on fourteen years, and it is the first time I ever heard of a man's having to know anything in order to edit a newspaper. You turnip! Who write the dramatic critiques for the second-rate papers? Why, a parcel of promoted shoemakers and apprentice apothecaries, who know just as much about good acting as I do about good farming and no more. Who review the books? People who never wrote one. Who do up the heavy leaders on finance? Parties who have had the largest opportunities for knowing nothing about it. Who criticise the Indian campaigns? Gentlemen who do not know a war whoop from a wigwam, and who never have had to run a foot race with a tomahawk, or pluck arrows out of the several members of their families to build the evening camp-fire with. Who write the temperance appeals, and clamor about the flowing bowl? Folks who will never draw another sober breath till they do it in the grave.

H. L. Mencken, a journalist whose prose skewered presidents, poets and bartenders with equal vigor, used some of his most choice execrations to denounce his fellow journalists. In an editorial in the *American Mercury,* October 1924, he wrote of journalists:

> The majority of them, in almost every American city, are ignoramuses, and not a few of them are also bounders. All the knowledge that they pack into their brains is, in every reasonable cultural sense, useless; it is the sort of knowledge that belongs, not to a professional man, but to a police captain, a railway mail-clerk or a board boy in a brokerage house. It is a mass of trivialities and puerilities; to recite it would be to make even a barber or a bartender beg for mercy. What is missing from it is everything worth knowing—everything that enters into the common knowledge of

educated men. There are managing editors in the United States, and scores of them, who have never heard of Kant or Johannes Müller and never read the Constitution of the United States; there are city editors who do not know what a symphony is, or a streptococcus, or the Statute of Frauds; there are reporters by the thousand who could not pass the entrance examination for Harvard or Tuskegee, or even Yale. It is this vast ignorance that makes American journalism so pathetically feeble and vulgar, and so generally disreputable no less. A man with so little intellectual enterprise that, dealing with news daily, he goes through life without taking in any news that is worth knowing—such a man, you may be sure, is as lacking in true self-respect as he is in curiosity. Honor does not go with stupidity. If it belongs to professional men, it belongs to them because they constitute a true aristocracy—because they have definitely separated themselves from the great masses of men. The journalists, in seeking to acquire it, put the cart before the horse.

GBS: Two Views

The practice of journalism arouses considerable passion among outsiders, sometimes leading them to excesses of inconsistency. George Bernard Shaw, the eminent playwright and critic, was of two minds regarding journalism. In a note to a journalist, he wrote:

Dear Sir,
Your profession has, as usual, destroyed your brain.

But he also wrote:

Journalism can claim to be the highest form of literature. For all the highest literature is journalism, including Plato and Aristophanes trying to knock some sense into the Athens of their days and Shakespeare peopling that same Athens with Elizabethans. Nothing that is not journalism will live as long as literature or be of any use while it does live. So let others cultivate what they may call literature. Journalism for me.

Improvements?

Twain's and Mencken's comments were made years ago. Journalists are now college trained, often in schools of journalism (a hopeful sign, Mencken said in the same editorial quoted above). And yet: What are we to make of the current generation, one of whose representatives wrote in a college newspaper about a presentation of *The Merchant of Venus,* instead of *The Merchant of Venice?*

And what can we say to the journalism student who wrote of the sculptor Michel Angelo? Or to the reporter who wrote when crimes in town doubled that they went up 200 percent?

Should the journalist be expected to know the plays of Shakespeare, the world of art and how to derive a percentage, calculate a ratio and find the median in a

A Deep Tradition

Government officials have been attacking journalists from the earliest days of the nation. John Quincy Adams, the sixth president, declared, "Journalists are a sort of assassins, who sit with loaded blunder-busses at the corner of streets and fire them off at any passenger they may select."

At the Maryland state-house 180 years later, Gov. Robert Ehrlich, Jr., ordered all government workers to deny "any and all" information to two *Baltimore Sun* reporters because they failed to "objectively report" his administration.

group of figures? Would it terrify would-be journalists to suggest that the answer has to be yes?

This storehouse of knowledge is the reporter's essential background, and it should be constantly replenished. Reporters need to have at their fingertips a wide assortment of information: They should know who tops the charts, what the Emancipation Proclamation accomplished, how local schools are financed and what agency compiles the list of the 10 most-wanted criminals.

Background Defined

The term *background* has three definitions:

- A reporter's store of information. This knowledge may be amassed over a long period or picked up quickly in order to handle a specific assignment. Without background knowledge, a reporter's fact gathering can be nondirected.

- Material placed in the story that explains the event, puts it into perspective. Without background, a story may be one-dimensional.

- Material a source does not want attributed to him or her. It may or may not be used, depending on the source's instructions.

Here, we are dealing with the first two meanings.

The Contents of the Storehouse

Journalists have a deep and wide-ranging fund of general information that they have developed through extensive reading, a variety of experience and their continuing education. Much of this stored information is about how things work, processes and procedures: the workings of the political system; the structure of local government; the arrest process; how governments pay for schools, streets and police and fire protection. The list is long.

Such knowledge is important because it is the bedrock on which news stories are built. The American philosopher John Dewey said, "We cannot lay hold of the new, we cannot even keep it before our minds, much less understand it, save by the use of ideas and knowledge we already possess." Irving Kristol, a writer on social and political affairs, said, "When one is dealing with complicated and continuous events, it is impossible to report 'what happened' unless one is previously equipped with a context of meaning and significance."

Specific knowledge is also required. When a candidate for the school board refers to "Brown versus Board of Education," the reporter knows the school desegregation court ruling she is referring to. When a luncheon speaker says that "the country took the wrong turn under the New Deal," the reporter knows the speaker is talking from a conservative perspective. And when a reporter does a profile of a country singer, he knows what the singer means when he says he is drifting from the "Nashville sound."

The Basis
"Unless you've had experience and lived, what could you have to say on your instrument?"

—*Milt Hinton, bass player*

Classic Photos That Symbolize Historic Events

The Library of Congress

Joe Rosenthal, AP

Lewis Hine, International Museum of Photography at George Eastman House

What They Don't Know

The National Assessment of Educational Progress tested 8,000 17-year-olds of different races, both sexes and in all regions of the United States.

Some of the findings:

- 20 percent or fewer could identify Joyce; Dostoyevsky, Ellison, Conrad or Ibsen.

- 36 percent knew Chaucer is the author of *The Canterbury Tales.*

- 37 percent could equate Job with patience during suffering.

- Fewer than 25 percent knew that Lincoln was president between 1860 and 1880.

- 32 percent could place the Civil War between 1850 and 1900.

- 57 percent could place World War II between 1900 and 1950.

- 30 percent could identify the Magna Carta.

Vacuums

". . . while they may be trained to write and while they may be trained to articulate what is written, the fact remains that many who call themselves journalists and are employed in local stations have no notion whatsoever about history, geography, political science, economics and other things about which an informed individual should have some grasp."
—Frank Magid, CEO, Frank N. Magid Associates, TV consultants to 140 local stations

Lost

"The unprepared mind cannot see the outstretched hand of opportunity."
—Alexander Fleming, discoverer of penicillin

Zoning Favoritism   The knowledge of how things work can turn a routine assignment into a significant story. When a reporter for a Long Island newspaper was sent to cover a fire in a plastics factory, she noticed that the plant was located in a residential zone. On her return to the office, she told her editor, "I've got the information on the fire, but I want to check out why that factory was built there in a residential zone. Was it zoned industrial when the factory was built, or did the company get a variance?" The reporter knew that variances—exceptions to general zoning patterns—are sometimes awarded to friends or political donors. Although the reporter was not a city hall reporter or a specialist in real estate, she knew about zoning through her overall understanding of city government. Her curiosity and knowledge led to a significant story.

The Clone   When Gina Kolata, science reporter for *The New York Times,* was thumbing through her copy of *Nature,* a magazine for scientists, she came across an article titled "Viable Offspring Derived from Fetal and Adult Mammalians." She leaped up.

"It didn't say the word clone and there was no clue in the article that there was anything interesting," she said. "People missed this story because they had to be able to understand the title and the abstract," which, she says, "was in the most abstruse scientific language in the whole world."

But she immediately called her editor and said, "Do you know what? I think they have actually done something amazing. I think they've cloned an adult."

Kolata's understanding of the abstruse technical article led to an exclusive page 1 story.

Covering the 500   When Joe Munson, a photographer for *The Kentucky Post* in Covington, Ky., was covering the Indianapolis 500, the daring tactics of a driver caught his eye. Munson knew that there is an imaginary line that race car drivers must follow around bends in order to keep their cars under control.

Joe Munson, *The Kentucky Post*

Cutting the Turn Too Closely: Crack-Up at the 500

"I noticed driver Danny Ongais straying six inches from that imaginary line and I suspected he was destined for a crash," Munson recalled.

"So I kept my camera focused on him."

Munson was ready when Ongais lost control and his car cracked into the wall. Munson was able to gun off 20 shots of the fiery crash that seriously injured Ongais. One of them took first place in the sports category of a National Press Photographers Association regional competition.

Set Point   Christopher Keating, chief of *The Courant*'s Hartford capital bureau, noticed an item on the state bond commission's agenda that struck a bell. The item called for raising $800,000 in bonds for construction and renovation of tennis courts and other park facilities. The "tennis courts" was the bell ringer. Keating knew that during his successful gubernatorial campaign John G. Rowland had criticized the incumbent governor for winning approval of more than 100 projects in the final meeting of the bond commission.

"We're not going to be bonding tennis courts in my administration," Rowland had said.

"Now, six months later," Keating wrote, "the Rowland-led bond commission is scheduled to vote today on a similar item: $800,000 for construction and renovation

Suspect in Slaying Once Got 30 Days
Instead of 15 Years

Calvin Jackson, who is said by the police to have "implicated himself" in the murder of at least nine women, was arrested in Manhattan 10 months ago on felonious robbery and burglary charges that could have sent him to prison for 15 years, an examination of court records disclosed yesterday.

Instead, the 26-year-old former convict was sent to jail for 30 days after the felony charges against him and two others were reduced to misdemeanors.

He had pleaded guilty in plea bargaining in Criminal Court to the lesser charges, which arose from the robbery last November of a young man, a resident of the Park Plaza Hotel, where Mr. Jackson lived and where six of his alleged victims were killed.

Mr. Jackson's experience is no different from that of thousands of others who yearly pass through the city's court system.

. . . the year of Mr. Jackson's last arrest, there were 31,098 felony arrests in Manhattan, according to the crime analysis unit of the Police Department. Of these, only 545 cases went to trial on the original felony charges, including possession or sale of narcotics. . . .

—Marcia Chambers
The New York Times

of tennis courts and other improvements at three parks—in Rowland's hometown of Waterbury."

The story hit home. Rowland withdrew the $800,000 request that day.

Knowing the Records Marcia Chambers, who covered the Criminal Courts Building for *The New York Times,* scored many exclusives because she had mastered the procedures of the criminal justice system. Chambers used files, records and background that led to an exclusive she wrote on the arrest of a mass-murder suspect. Here is her description of how she went about digging up the information for her story:

On the day Calvin Jackson was arrested, I covered the arraignment where the prosecutor announced that Jackson had been charged with the murder of one woman and had "implicated himself" in several others. At the time, we wanted to find out more about Jackson's prior criminal record, but given the hour—5:30 p.m.—we couldn't get the information. In a sidebar story that appeared the next day, Joe Treaster, the police reporter, said Jackson's previous arrest had occurred 10 months before. But the disposition of the case, the story said, was unknown.

From my experience, I knew that nearly all cases are disposed of through plea bargaining, the process whereby a defendant agrees to plead guilty in exchange for a lesser charge. Several weeks before I had obtained from the Office of Court Administration data that showed that last year only 545 out of 31,098 felony arrests went to trial, including drug cases. The rest were plea bargained.

On Monday, at 10 a.m., I went to the court clerk's office. My premise was that Jackson's last arrest, like the thousands of others that pass through the criminal court system, had probably involved plea bargaining, a reduction of charges and a minimal sentence.

From the docket book, I obtained the docket number of the mass-murder case, and since case records are public information, I asked the clerk for the case. I took it to the side of the room, and quickly copied the file that contained information about his previous arrests. (In addition to carrying change and a phone credit card for phone calls, reporters should carry at least two dollars in change at all times for the copying machine as well as a backup pen or pencil.)

Blunders

Reporters with ample background knowledge do not embarrass themselves or their editors by blundering in print or on the air. Witness these bloopers, the result of a lack of background:

• In one of her columns, Harriet Van Horne referred to Canada as having a "tough and happily homogeneous population. . . ." (The columnist ignored the large Indian and Inuit populations and the almost six million French-speaking Canadians. Not only is the country not homogeneous, the French- and English-speaking Canadians are hardly happily ensconced together. Many of the French-speaking people contend that they are second-class citizens, which has led to the separatist movement in the province of Quebec.)

• When the basketball coach at Boston College accepted the head coaching job at Stanford, a CBS sports announcer said that the coach had "followed Horace Mann's advice to go west." (The advice is attributed to Horace Greeley, founder and editor of *The Tribune:* "Go west young man." Horace Mann was an educator.)

• In a feature on food served during the Jewish holidays, a reporter for the *Press-Enterprise* in Riverside, Calif., described Yom Kippur as "marked by rich, indeed lavish meals." (Yom Kippur, known as the Day of Atonement, is the most solemn of all Jewish holy days and is observed by fasting.)

• A *New York Times* story of mourning for victims of a terrorist bombing in Jerusalem said the mourners' clothing was "rented." (In funerals, clothing is *rent*—torn—not rented.)

Botched
In the journal for journalism faculty, *Journalism & Mass Communication Educator,* an author referred to the American philosopher "Thomas Dewey." Wrong Dewey. Thomas Dewey was the Republican candidate for president in 1944 and 1948, losing once to Franklin D. Roosevelt and then to Harry S Truman. John Dewey is the philosopher, considered one of the most influential theorists in education as well as philosophy.

Anticipatory Journalism

A solid grasp of the past and the present is essential to a growing area of reporting—*anticipatory journalism.* It consists of spotting trends, identifying movements in their earliest stages, locating individuals with an important message.

Journalism has not been good at this kind of reporting. It ignored the feminist movement, was late to sense the civil rights surge, was hesitant about the lifestyle changes of teen-agers.

Anticipatory journalism can be as simple as making journalism out of the realization that the city's revenues are inadequate to meet new expenses and that payrolls and services will have to be cut or taxes increased. With this knowledge, the reporter can interview the mayor, city council members and community leaders about what solutions they recommend.

More Than Writing
"The vocabulary of a writer is his currency but it is a paper currency and its value depends on the reserves of mind and heart which back it."
—*Cyril Connolly*

The Past Illuminates the Present

To those who despair over today's racism and environmental damage, a knowledge of the past provides perspective. For years after gold was discovered in California, mining companies used hydraulic water cannons to wash down mountains for the gold ore they contained. Silt clogged once pristine rivers, causing floods downstream and irreparable damage was done to the terrain. After considerable public pressure, the practice was outlawed.

Now only a footnote in the history of racism, the Ku Klux Klan once elected governors and paraded its cause down the main avenues of cities and state capitals. Klanswomen even marched down Pennsylvania Avenue in Washington, D.C.

Plumas County Museum

National Archives in Washington, D.C.

This is public service journalism. It gives people time to discuss and decide issues rather than having to react quickly when last-minute problems arise.

An essential to the practice of anticipatory journalism along with a grasp of background is a good string of sources, a subject we shall next look into in the next chapter.

Don't Guess   Speculative reporting is not anticipatory journalism. The reporter who speculates about events or predicts outcomes is guessing. The reporter who anticipates uses evidence and makes no leaps to judgment or opinion.

When Vicente Fox challenged the candidate of the Institutional Revolutionary Party, which had governed Mexico for 71 years, his candidacy was written off by a speculative article in *The Christian Science Monitor.* The basis for the write-off?

". . . the so-called 'family' issue is taking on decisive importance," the reporter wrote. Fox is divorced and his four children are adopted, the newspaper reported, and it quoted several women voters as saying that Francisco Labistida, the candidate of the IRP, was their favorite because he stood for "strong families."

The result: Fox defeated Labistida.

Summing Up

The best journalists know a lot. They know the past as well as the present. They are exceptions to the charge leveled by *The New York Times* columnist Bob Herbert who describes the United States as "a nation of nitwits." As evidence, he cited a Gallup Poll that found:

- Sixty percent of Americans are unable to name the president who ordered the atomic bomb dropped on Japan. (Truman)

- One of four didn't know Japan was the target of the bomb.

- A fifth didn't know that such an attack had occurred.

"We are surrounded by a deep and abiding stupidity," he wrote.

Further Reading

Boylan, James. *Pulitzer's School: Columbia University's School of Journalism,* 1903–2003. Columbia University Press, 2003.
> Joseph Pulitzer tried Harvard and was rebuffed. But Columbia accepted his offer of $2 million (about $40 million today) to build a school of journalism and to underwrite the Pulitzer Prizes. The school opened in 1912 and has had a roller coaster ride since—critics calling it a trade school, deans clashing with faculty members, the curriculum ever changing, some graduates running major media enterprises.

Lewis, Anthony. *Gideon's Trumpet.* New York: Random House, 1964.

Steel, Ronald. *Walter Lippmann and the American Century.* Boston: Atlantic Monthly Press, 1980.

Teachout, Terry. *The Skeptic: A Life of H.L. Mencken.* New York: HarperCollins, 2002.

  Teachout contends that Mencken was the greatest of all American journalists. In his review of this biography in *The Atlantic Monthly,* Johnathan Yardley writes that, "the only other American journalists whose names can be mentioned without embarrassment in the same paragraph as his own—Ring Lardner, A.J. Liebling and Russell Baker. . . ." Yardley says of Mencken that "the most important thing about him is that he was a newspaperman," and he quotes Teachout's praise of Mencken's "firmly balanced prose rhythms and vigorous diction."

Classic Photos

Upper left: **President Franklin D. Roosevelt** tours farm country. During the 1930s the United States was mired in what was known as the Great Depression. Among its victims were the country's farmers. The president visited Midwestern farms to promise help under an agricultural program in the president's New Deal.

Upper right: **Iwo Jima** flag raising. During World War II, U.S. forces captured the island at great human cost. This photograph of the flag being planted on its highest peak, Mount Suribachi, became a symbol of the conflict in the Pacific.

Bottom: **Child worker** in a New England mill. Lewis Hine recorded child labor throughout the U.S. from 1908 to 1915. His photographs aided in the support for the passage of child labor laws. Hine went on to document the problems of refugees and other effects of the Great Depression.

Finding, Cultivating and Using Sources   **14**

Preview

The reporter relies on three types of sources:

- **Human sources,** which consist of authorities and people involved in news events. When using human sources, reporters find the person most qualified to speak—an authority on the subject, an eyewitness, an official, a participant.
- **Physical sources,** which consist of records, documents, reference works, newspaper articles.
- **Online sources,** which include a vast array of human and physical sources, from academicians to government data.

Chris Hardy, *San Francisco Examiner*
Sources come in all sizes.

Journalists have a saying that a reporter can be no better than his or her sources. These sources include officials, spokesmen and -women, participants in events, documents, records, tape recordings, libraries, films and books. The quality of the reporter's story depends on the quality of the sources.

Reporters spend a lot of time looking for and cultivating people who can become sources and contacts. A county courthouse reporter in California puts in a couple of hours a day passing time with his sources. He also chats with guards, secretaries, elevator operators, whom he describes as contacts, people who can provide tips for stories. An elevator operator tipped him off about a well-known businessman who had been summoned by a grand jury and was taken to the jury room by a back elevator.

Jere Downs, who covers transportation for *The Philadelphia Inquirer,* heard that the local transit agency, SEPTA, was considering a fare hike. "I called sources at the agency and requested that we have a cup of coffee

Question your assumptions . . . and theirs.

and talk about the new prices," she says. "That was how I learned that the agency was raising prices against the advice of $1 million in consultant studies that advised dropping fares was the best course of action."

Making Nice at the Courthouse

Jeff Klinkenberg of the *St. Petersburg Times* shows us Milt Sosin, the Associated Press courthouse reporter in Miami, at work:

He pokes his head into offices and makes small talk with secretaries. He chats with a lawyer in an elevator. He shares respectful words with a newspaper reporter outside a courtroom. With a charming smile, he even opens a hallway door for a sweaty man in a three-piece suit.

For Sosin, who is probably the best reporter you *never* heard of, charm is part of his giant bag of journalist's tricks. His job is getting information. Being chummy, though it may come unnaturally, could pay off one day: He may need these courthouse people to provide news that might lead to an Associated Press exclusive.

"It's no big deal," Sosin says later, sounding almost embarrassed. "They're just sources. You treat them right. You stop by and ask them if anything is going on, that's all. If they give you something you can use, you protect them. You never betray their confidences."

In Washington

"The key to this job is sources, sources, sources," says Amie Parnes, a reporter with the Washington bureau of the Scripps Howard News Service. "When I first arrived here, someone told me, 'Get to know the Hill contacts very well. Take them out to lunch, get to know their kids' names, know everything about them.'"

Cultivating sources paid off for Parnes when Rep. Mark Foley, R-Fla., was revealed to have sent inappropriate messages to male congressional pages. (Parnes' special area of coverage is the Florida delegation.) She broke the story of Foley's resignation.

"I had a great relationship with his office," she says. "I hung out there on a weekly basis, talking with the congressman, his chief of staff, his legislative assistants and his press secretary. I spent a lot of time building those relationships, and they knew and trusted me."

Massive Tire Recall

It was a "call from a source who does research for trial lawyers," says Sara Nathan, that led her to a major story. The source told her that Firestone tires on Ford Explorers were being recalled in six foreign countries but not in the United States. Nathan checked with several safety organizations, and they confirmed the tip and told her that they had urged a tire recall in the United States.

Tim King
Scripps News

Amie Parnes

After first denying that their tires were defective, Firestone recalled 6.5 million tires in the face of stories like this one by Nathan and fellow *USA Today* reporter James R. Healey that began a series of articles:

Millions of people in the USA are riding on tires that are the focus of a federal safety probe, and that have been recalled and replaced in six other countries, according to government files.

The National Highway Traffic Safety Administration (NHTSA) also said Tuesday that it has reports of 21 deaths—up from just four it knew of earlier this week—and 193 crashes involving Firestone ATX, ATX II and Wilderness tires. Reports of the incidents say the treads inexplicably peeled off the tire casings, causing skids.

For more from the original series in *USA Today,* see **Tire Recall** in *NRW Plus.*

Reliability of Sources

The distinction between human and physical sources, and their relative reliability, was nicely put by Sir Kenneth Clark, the British writer and critic: "If I had to say who was telling the truth about society, a speech by the Minister of Housing or the actual buildings put up in his time, I would believe the buildings."

The difference in the reliability of these sources became startlingly clear in the Iraq war. In the buildup to the invasion, the United States asserted Iraq had a stockpile of weapons of mass destruction. Much of its evidence came from the same source that a *New York Times* reporter was using for her stories, an Iraqi expatriate. The source supposedly had many contacts inside Iraq and was considered reliable.

Inspection teams had not turned up such weapons in the past, and they urged caution. The invasion went ahead, and despite intensive searches, no weapons were found.

Human Sources

A person with information the reporter needs for a story or for background is called a *source.* Arthur L. Gavshon, diplomatic reporter for the AP, says:

> To me anyone on the inside of any given news situation is a potential source. But they only turn into real sources when they come up with a bit, or a lot, of relevant information.

Gavshon says he finds sources anywhere and everywhere. He develops his sources "just as you would get to know a friend and nurture a relationship in everyday life (always assuming you can live a normal life as a journalist)—through the exercise of patience, understanding and a reasonable capacity to converse about shared interests."

Authoritative Sources   Sometimes an assignment is so complex or so unfamiliar that a reporter hardly knows where to begin. The clips on the subject prove to be too sketchy, and the reference material presumes some knowledge of the subject. The reporter needs a crash course in the topic, but the assignment is due and there is no time for in-depth research.

On her second day as the marine news reporter for *The Gazette* in Montreal, Jan Wong was given an assignment and told to handle it quickly because her editor had another story for her to cover.

Wong did what reporters do in such circumstances. She turned to people who know, authoritative sources:

"I must have called 20 people," she says. "I called everyone I could find in the marine directory. People were very helpful."

Sources need not be mayors or directors of companies. The city hall reporter knows that the town clerk who has served a succession of mayors has a comprehensive knowledge of the community and the inner workings of town government. The courthouse reporter befriends law clerks, court stenographers and security guards. Business reporters cultivate switchboard operators, secretaries, mailroom help.

Tactics   Reporters have gone out of their way to do favors for their sources. At one newspaper in California, the reporters who handle obituaries send birthday candy and flowers to the mortuary employees who call to report the deaths of important people. A death called in near deadline means the newspaper or station telephoned first will have that much more time to write the obituary. A difference of two minutes can be the difference between making or missing the last edition or the 6 p.m. newscast.

Some reporters cultivate sources by reversing the news-gathering process. One Midwestern newsman says that instead of always asking sources for news, he puts his sources on the receiving end. "I see to it personally that they hear any gossip or important news. When I want news, I get it," he says.

The source needed for information on a single story need not be cultivated with the care reporters lavish on sources essential to a beat. But courtesy and consideration are always important. In speaking to a source for the first—and perhaps the only—time, the reporter identifies himself or herself immediately and moves to the questions quickly. A different pace is necessary for the source essential to a beat. Gavshon cautions:

> Don't ever rush things. Don't make the ghastly mistake of thinking only in terms of tomorrow's headline. . . . One-night stands rarely satisfy anybody.

Be Careful

Sources may not be what they seem. When a federal agency called for a moratorium on silicon-gel breast implants, a woman made herself available to reporters, saying she was a breast cancer patient and had implants. She said she was satisfied with them. Three local television stations and *The Boston Globe* used her comments.

Terry Schraeder of WCVB-TV in Boston checked out the woman and found she was a paid spokeswoman for Dow Corning, manufacturer of the implant

Source?

"Only a fool expects the authorities to tell him what the news is."

—*Russell Baker*

Paying Sources

"We pay for information," says Steve Coz, editor of *The National Enquirer.* "We pay them to be sources." Among the recipients of handsome checks from the weekly supermarket tabloid are chauffeurs, maids, bartenders, caterers, the modestly paid people who work for the famous. Payment for information, known as checkbook journalism, is frowned upon by the mainline media, though sometimes tempted by the possibility of exclusive information, a newspaper or network will write a check.

material, which had provided her with training in handling the media and a list of reporters to contact.

Pseudo-Sources

When some members of Congress wanted to find out the plight of farmers hard hit by rising costs and falling income, they called Sissy Spacek and Jane Fonda to testify. The women had played the wives of farmers in films.

Who's Being Quoted?

Journalists have been criticized for calling upon a narrow band of sources for information for stories—business executives, bankers, government officials, college presidents, political leaders—usually white, middle-class men. This narrow demographic bandwidth skews stories, the critics say.

For stories about the economy, experts at the think tanks are called upon—the Cato Institute for the conservative point of view, the Urban Institute for the liberal and the Brookings Institution for the centrist positions. But the economy is about people—whether they keep their jobs, how inflation affects them. And the people make up a wide range of individuals.

To make up a representative sample of the community, as the polling people would say, it's important to have a mix of ages, races, ethnic groups and, of course, men and women. And if the story is about the economy sagging or soaring, we will want to hear how it affects families.

Mutual Dependency

The source is the reporter's life blood. Without access to information through the source, the reporter cannot function. The reporter is just as necessary to most sources, for without the journalist the source has no access to the public. Sources in the public sector need reaction to their proposals and policies.

Out of this mutual need a source–reporter relationship develops: The source will provide the reporter with information and will brief him or her on developments. In return, the reporter will write a fair account of the material.

As events become more complex, the reporter's dependence on sources increases. When a reporter learns of a probable future event, such as the presentation of the municipal budget to the city council, he or she may ask a source for background so that the difficult story can be written authoritatively. The courthouse reporter who learns through the grapevine that the grand jury is about to return an indictment against the city clerk will ask the district attorney for a briefing. Sources usually are happy to comply because they prefer an accurate story to a rush job.

Protecting Sources

Occasionally, a reporter is asked to protect a source's identity. An investigative reporter learns from a police officer that a convict serving a life term for murder was convicted on perjured police testimony. In return for the tip about the frame-up, the reporter must promise not to name the source.

Bias

". . . there is no such thing as an independent source, and the first thing a reporter should ask himself when he is talking to anyone whom he thinks may be a source is, 'Why is this source talking to me? What is in it for him?' First, I have to find out what is in it for him before I find out what is in it for me. . . . I would never assume that any source is telling me the whole truth, because I don't think the source knows the whole truth. . . ."

—*Murrey Marder*

Too Close

"A reporter who could call Henry Kissinger by his first name wasn't worth a damn on the Watergate story."

—*Benjamin Bradlee*

All states have some kind of protection, but in some states, a reporter who tries to protect a confidential source may face contempt charges and jail. State press associations usually distribute pamphlets about reporters' rights.

Sometimes reporters have to overcome their reluctance to embarrass a friendly source with a tough story. Walter Lippmann said there must be a "certain distance between the reporter and the source, not a wall or a fence, but an air space." Once a friend becomes an official, he said, "you can't call him by his first name anymore."

Protecting Michael   Early in Michael Jordan's career with the Chicago Bulls basketball team, he asked reporters not to reveal that he had a child since he wasn't married. They went along, says Robert Blau, associate managing editor for projects and investigations at the *Chicago Tribune.* "They liked him. They wanted to be liked by him. And they needed him," Blau says. "There's a healthy debate to be had over whether the out-of-wedlock child born to a basketball player, even a superstar, is newsworthy. It certainly has nothing to do with performance on the court. But given Jordan's carefully choreographed image, the information might have been useful in assessing the man," Blau says.

"Protecting sources and currying their favor so they will remain sources, whether in a sweaty locker room or a swank boardroom, too easily crosses the line from common sense to conspiracy, cheating the public and betraying the truth," he says.

The Expert

People tend to believe those in authority. The more impressive the title, the higher the social position, the more prestigious the alma mater, the more faith people have in the expert or authority. This trust in authority is known as the "hierarchy of credibility"—the higher on the scale the authority is, the more believable the source is thought to be. When the journalist surrenders to this tendency, he or she allows those in power to define events and situations.

Reporters must be careful to use sources only within their areas of expert knowledge. A banker can talk about banking, a general about the strategy and tactics of war. But it is unwise to rely on a banker for comments on the nation's economy or on a general as an authority on international affairs. They may be less useful than the labor department area representative or the assistant professor of international affairs at a local college.

"The real news," says James McCartney, who covered Washington for the Knight Ridder newspapers, "frequently does not come from the top, from authorized statements at the White House or State Department or other agencies. Normally those words are spin. Often important news comes from the deep bowels of the bureaucracy or from no-name staff members of congressional committees. It comes from those who know what is going on and who think it is important for the public to know."

A reporter's best sources are those who have demonstrated their knowledge and competence. Reporters should drop sources who are proved wrong in their observations

James Woodcock,
The Billings Gazette

She Knows Best

For a story on crowded classrooms, the best sources are the teachers and the students, not the president of the board of education.

The Care and Feeding of Sources

Lucy Morgan of the *St. Petersburg Times* capital bureau in Tallahassee has a list of suggestions for the treatment of sources. Here are her top four suggestions:

1. Be nice to everyone. This may sound like something you should have learned in kindergarten but you'd be surprised how many reporters ignore this advice. Get to know everyone's name, including the janitors. You can never tell when one of them will give you a good tip.

     Sources usually prefer nice reporters to nasty ones. At least, the nice sources do.

2. Ask people to help you. Tell people you are interested in what they are doing and ask them to call you later if something develops. You'll be surprised how many people will do just that.

3. Help the people you encounter each day understand what news is. You may have to teach them one story at a time, but when they realize what you are interested in, you'll hear from them.

4. Listen. Let people tell you their story, even if it's more than you want to know. Be patient. Get to know the whole person.

and assessments, whether they served in the president's cabinet, ran a multi-million-dollar import business or graduated *summa cum laude* from Harvard.

Reliability Tests

For sources on the beat, those the reporter is in touch with on a regular basis, reliability is usually determined by consistency. That is, the source is considered reliable if in the past the information he or she supplied proved accurate.

For transient sources, those interviewed for a particular story, the test is more complicated:

- Was the person an observer of the incident, or did he or she hear about it from someone else?

- Is the person a competent observer? An airline employee would be a better source for information about an airplane crash than would a student or a salesperson.

- Can the source supply precise details that have the ring of truth and seem consistent with the facts?

- Are several sources offering the same information? Generally, when several people provide the same version of an event, chances are good that the accounts are reliable.

Checking the Prospectors   Kevin Krajick's magazine story about diamond prospectors led him to think about making a book out of the prospectors—a strange and secretive group—and the forbidding far north country in Canada where they searched.

"When I started on the book, I discovered that my reporting work had just begun," Krajick says. "In digging deeper into the details, I found all sorts of

> **Blogs as Sources**
> Blogs and more blogs. A score of new blogs are born every few minutes. Some are froth, some sediment, some sludge. A few are useful. Thomas L. Friedman, columnist for *The New York Times,* says: "I like blogs, but the only bloggers who appeal to me are those who do reporting and aren't just sitting at home in their pajamas firing off digital mortars."

subsidiary characters who also had tales to tell—some in conflict with those of the main characters. Sometimes people who were in the same spot at the same time had differing versions.

"This led me to examine more deeply who had a stake in the story coming out a certain way—and who could be considered an impartial witness.

"Sometimes it even came down to a rough sort of vote. If four people saw the same event and three told the same story, it seemed likely the fourth guy was either misremembering or fudging it.

"Sometimes I would go back to the fourth person and run the other version of the story past him. Human memory is a funny thing. Even the smartest people forget things, remember things that never happened, are open to suggestions afterwards. They make their own myths, about themselves and others. Eyewitnesses are not always reliable.

"The best a writer can do is to get reasonable agreement among the parties, or else give the conflicting versions, point out no one agrees and move on fast . . . unless you *really* know what happened and can prove it."

Krajick's book is *Barren Lands: An Epic Search for Diamonds in the North American Arctic.*

Bill Clinton—182 IQ

Internet Reliability

Experienced journalists approach the Internet cautiously. They know that Web pages can remain for years without being updated and that little is available about events before 1995 because that was when material began to be placed on the Web.

Liars, hoaxsters, promoters and leakers thrive on the Internet. "You can't be sure of any of it," said Henry Stokes, managing editor of *The Commercial Appeal.*

Richard Nixon—155 IQ

Rating Presidents   The study by the Lovenstein Institute reported on the Internet detailed the findings of a four-month investigation into the intelligence quotient of presidents over the past 60 years. In its ratings of the 12 presidents from Franklin D. Roosevelt to George W. Bush it found IQs for Bill Clinton to be 182; Jimmy Carter 175; John F. Kennedy, 174; . . . Ronald Reagan, 105; George Bush, 98; George W. Bush, 91.

The material made its way to newspapers and stations and was reported on several academic listservs. It continued to make the rounds until someone checked the so-called Institute and learned it does not exist, that the study was a hoax.

Internet Checks   "Check and confirm before using Internet material," says Elizabeth Weise of *USA Today.* To confirm, Weise will talk to someone she knows to be reliable or make a telephone call to the source to verify the information. "Unless the person is already known to you, as a general rule never quote an individual without speaking to him or her on the telephone to confirm his or her identity."

George W. Bush—91 IQ

Jan Alexander and Marsha Ann Tate, librarians at Widener University, have five tests for Web page reliability:

Authority—Who put the page together? Can you reach the people who put it together? Can you tell who wrote the information on the page and what their qualifications are?

Accuracy—Is there a source for information that you can check with to verify the information?

Currency—Is the page updated? Can you tell when the information was written, when posted?

Coverage—Is the material thorough? Are issues neglected?

Objectivity—Is advertising clearly separated from information? If there is bias, is it made clear?

Reliability Ratings   Here is a reliability scale devised by Steve Miller of *The New York Times:*

1. **Government data**—Material from federal, state and local sources. The figures, not the comments about them, are almost always reliable.

2. **Studies by universities and colleges**—These materials, usually in the form of articles in scholarly journals, are peer-reviewed before publication.

3. **Special-interest groups**—Although these have agendas they pursue, some have reputations as reliable sources.

4. **Home pages**—The least reliable and most questionable.

Physical Sources

The range of physical information is enormous. The availability of physical sources is limited only by the reporter's knowledge of their existence.

Databases provide quick access to dozens of excellent sources, from census material to local arrest records. Donald Barlett and James Steele turned to *The Philadelphia Inquirer* databases for material for their prize-winning series about the federal Tax Reform Act. "Once you would come up with a name of somebody, you could go right to one of these databases and see what was known about him very quickly," Steele said. The database made it possible to pack large amounts of convincing detail into their stories, such as the description of the widow who inherited $4 million more from her late husband's estate under the giveaway terms of the act.

Not All Sources Are Equal

Not all physical sources are of equal reliability. Tables of vital statistics are more reliable than the city official's summary introducing the tables. The world almanac is more reliable than a newspaper clipping of the same event, for the

Specialized Publications
If you are doing a piece on the fast food industry, says a reporter, look at the *Nation's Restaurant News.* Want to know whether Americans drink more soda pop than water, consult *Beverage Industry.* These publications are part of the massive trade press, and they are a valuable source of specialized information.

almanac is usually the work of professional researchers, and the news story may have been written in a hurry before all the facts were in.

Paper Trail

Much can be learned by tracking a person through the many documents he or she leaves behind. Such searches are described as "following the paper trail." The trail is strewn with material: a birth certificate, hospital records, school records, real estate transfers, marriage and death certificates. Two examples of what can be learned:

Home: What it cost; what was paid and what was borrowed for the down payment; who holds the mortgage and how much it amounts to; liens on the property; the amount of property taxes paid and any delinquencies.

Automobile: Registration number; title information; name and model of vehicle; year of manufacture; license plate number. Automobile records also include data on the owner—name, age, height, weight, offenses.

Databases

Reporters mine the vast array of databases available:

Drunk Drivers   When the Paddock papers in the Chicago area wanted to know what happened to people arrested for drunk driving, reporters fed into the computer 1,500 drunk driving arrests and their dispositions. The finding: More than two-thirds of those arrested avoided conviction. Only 1 in 15 was jailed or fined heavily. The *Atlanta Constitution* used local bank records to show a pattern of racial discrimination in housing loans, and it won a Pulitzer Prize for its stories.

Led to Slaughter   Martha Mendoza of the AP used the computer to track the handling of a multi-million-dollar federal program designed to protect thousands of wild horses on public lands. Under the direction of the Bureau of Land Management, the program allows individuals to adopt up to four horses each and care for them. After a year, the adopters are given legal title to the animals. At that point, Mendoza found, many of the owners, some of them BLM employees, were selling the horses to slaughterhouses—at a profit of $700 a horse. After her revelation, the BLM admitted that about 90 percent of the horses in the program were sold for slaughter.

For a listing of sources on the Internet, see **Appendix E, Sources Online** in *NRW Plus.*

How Reporters Use Sources

Let us accompany some reporters as they work with various kinds of sources for their stories. The first story is the type that puts reporters on their mettle, the late-breaking event that must be handled quickly and accurately.

Check Think Tanks
Funding sources can bias seemingly independent organizations that offer background material. Reporters often quote officials of these organizations and cite their studies but fail to indicate who is funding the think tank. For funding information see The Foundation Center, http://fdncenter.org.

A Fatality

The story takes us to a New Jersey newsroom where a reporter is making late police checks, which consist of calling area police departments not personally covered by the police reporter. Here, the reporter must rely on human sources. There is little opportunity to examine police records.

The reporter is told that a car plowed into a motorcycle at a stoplight and the two young people on the motorcycle were killed. The driver was arrested three miles down the highway and charged with drunken driving. The reporter knows this is a good story, but little time remains before the last edition closes. The rule in the newsroom, she remembers her editor telling her, is simple: "In baseball, if you get your glove on the ball and don't handle it cleanly, it's an error, no matter how hard it's hit to you. If you get a story before deadline and don't have it written for the next edition, you're not a reporter."

She has seen baseball games in which fielders managed to touch a ball but were not given errors when they failed to throw the batter out. But she had not called that to her editor's attention. She knows better.

Basic Information   She quickly learns the names of the victims and the driver as well as the location and circumstances of the accident. Knowing that the investigating officers are still writing their report, she asks if they are available at the station. They will have details she needs, especially about the chase for the driver. She then calls the mortuary to obtain background about the victims. Mortuaries usually have the exact spelling of a victim's name, and his or her age, address and occupation.

She glances at the clock to see whether she has time to call the parents of the victims for more precise information. Also, relatives often are around after an emergency to help out, and they might be able to tell her something about the deceased. But she decides that first she will see whether the victims' names are in the newspaper files.

During her interviews with the investigating officers, one of them mentions that this was the third motorcycle accident in the last month. She notes that on her pad for a quick check in the files, too.

Background Check   The check discloses this was actually the fourth motorcycle accident in the county, one of the others having been fatal to a young man. She also finds a story about the young woman who was killed. She was the daughter of a prominent local family, and the story indicates she used a middle name, which was not in the reporter's notes.

The reporter then decides to locate the parents of the man who died in the accident. She realizes that she had decided not to make those calls because of her distaste for intruding on the family's tragedy. At some newspapers, reporters do not have to make such calls, she recalls a colleague telling her, but that is not the case at this one. The younger sister of the man answers the telephone and is able to supply some details about him.

The reporter used physical and human sources. One key to the story is her knowledge that the investigating police officers might be at the police station writing up the report of the accident. She knows that the best sources are those close to the scene. Although they had not seen the accident, they had arrived quickly and had conducted the investigation. The names of the officers will add authenticity to the story.

She begins to write, some 20 minutes before the last edition closes. She knows she has time because she had been organizing her notes as she was reporting.

An Enterpriser

We turn from this spot news story to a story that begins with a chat between friends.

Jeffrey A. Tannenbaum, a reporter with *The Wall Street Journal,* is in the newsroom when a call comes in from a former college classmate, Ralph Sanders.

Sanders, who is blind, tells Tannenbaum he is active in an organization called the National Federation of the Blind and that the group is planning a demonstration. Sanders says that the blind are tired of being denied rights granted to sighted people.

Sanders suggests the demonstration will make a good story. Sensing a broader story than the coverage of an event that is being staged for the media, Tannenbaum arranges to have lunch with Sanders.

"I was fascinated with the possibility of writing a story about the blind comparable to early stories on the civil rights movement," Tannenbaum says later. "In the course of a long interview, Sanders provided the theme for the story. I used it in the sixth paragraph of the finished story.

"What I needed to do after the interview was to document the central thesis. I needed to find examples of ways in which blind people are discriminated against. And I needed to find cases of discrimination in which blind people were militant."

At lunch, Sanders provides some sources and examples of militancy. Tannenbaum finds other examples by calling organizations of the blind. He learns about discrimination by checking with social agencies and human rights commissions. He is able to find more than a dozen examples of discrimination.

Examples "As a rule of thumb," Tannenbaum says, "I like to have half-a-dozen highly readable, colorful, to-the-point examples in a story. Each one should illustrate a different aspect of the general problem, buttressing the main theme but not duplicating one another."

He checks with people who might have another point of view on what the blind charge is discrimination. Tannenbaum says, "More than fairness is involved here. A good reporter knows that the best stories are multidimensional. Conflict and controversy do make a better story, but they also accurately reflect reality."

Tannenbaum now has sources with specific complaints and incidents. He has a feeling an incident at a Washington, D.C., airport described by Keith and Elizabeth Howard should be well up in his story, perhaps the lead.

He interviews the head of Sanders' organization and a blind professor of American history at Seton Hall College in New Jersey, who provides an excellent quote that gives an overview. He consults some references for data about the blind. He has now interviewed 40 people and is ready to write.

THE WALL STR

VOL. CLXXXVI NO. 7   ★ ★   EASTERN EDITION   THURSDAY, JU

New Crusaders

Angry Blind Militants, Seeking 'Equal Rights,' Try Tougher Tactics

Sightless Stage Walkouts, Sue Landlords, Bosses, Reject 'Excessive' Pity

The Fight With Sky Glider

By JEFFREY A. TANNENBAUM
Staff Reporter of THE WALL STREET JOURNAL

Keith and Elizabeth Howard were all set to board an Allegheny Airlines flight from Washington, D.C., to Philadelphia. The airplane wasn't fully booked. Yet an airline official suddenly insisted they must take separate flights.

The reason: The Howards are both blind.

The couple say they were told the pilot didn't want more than one blind passenger on the flight because he assumed that blind people might cause a safety problem or require extra service. While his wife went on ahead, the 43-year-old Mr. Howard waited for the next flight.

Far from being helpless nuisances, the Howards both successfully manage their own lunch counters in Washington. They angrily protested to Allegheny, which confirms their story. Allegheny apologized, and says that Ransome Airlines, which operated the flight under contract, has changed its policies to prevent a repeat of the incident. But the Howards figure their problems are far from over. They say the airline incident was typical of the "common discrimination—a normal thing" that society practices almost routinely against the blind.

But nowadays, blind people like the Howards are moving with increasing fervor to protest such discrimination. They are voicing complaints, turning to the courts and even staging strikes and demonstrations. As a result, employers, landlords and businesses generally are finding they must either change their policies or face protests and lawsuits.

"A Dash of Leprosy"

"Society will give charity to the blind, but it won't allow us to be first-class citizens," charges Ralph W. Sanders, president of the Arkansas unit of the National Federation of the Blind. "Like the blacks, we've come to the point where we're not going to stand for it anymore," he adds.

Ironically, this militancy occurs at a time when conditions for the blind are improving significantly, particularly in the realm of jobs. Several states in recent ~~ave gr~~ ~~mprov~~ ~~broad~~

What's News—

★ ★ ★
Business and Finance

OIL'S EXPORT PRICE was cut by Ecuador in what may be the first major crack in the oil cartel's pricing structure. Ecuador's cut was through a reduction in the income-tax rate charged oil companies.
(Story on Page 3)

● ● ●

A tax on most crude oil and refined petroleum products of up to three cents a barrel was proposed, as expected, by President Ford to help pay for damages caused by oil spills.
(Story on Page 3)

● ● ●

A Honduran commission urged steps to nationalize the concessions and property of units of United Brands and Castle & Cooke to increase that country's participation in the banana-export business.
(Story on Page 2)

● ● ●

Developing nations' efforts to negotiate new international agreements fixing commodities prices will be resisted by the U.S., a top Treasury official said.
(Story on Page 2)

● ● ●

General Motors is being countersued by a former dealer for $33 million in connection with a tangled series of criminal and civil cases involving alleged warranty fraud. Separately, GM said its supplemental benefit fund for laid-off employes could soon resume payouts for a brief period.
(Stories on Page 4)

● ● ●

Ford Motor confirmed that it quietly paid for repairing about 69,000 rust-damaged 1969-73 models even though normal warranties had expired.
(Story on Page 4)

● ● ●

Great Atlantic & Pacific Tea reported a $6.5 million loss, less than predicted, for its May 24 first quarter; a year earlier it earned $10.3 million.
(Story on Page 4)

● ● ●

International Paper's second quarter earnings slid 37% to $47.2

★ ★ ★
World-Wide

A MIDEAST AGREEMENT isn't "anywhere near," Kissinger said.

The Secretary of State, beginning a European trip during which he will meet with Israeli Prime Minister Rabin, said reports that an Egyptian-Israeli accord had been all but wrapped up are "totally wrong." Hearst Newspapers quoted Egyptian President Sadat as indicating that basic terms of a new interim Sinai agreement had been worked out. But Prime Minister Rabin said some key issues remain to be settled.

Sources suggested that an agreement would involve an electronic surveillance system, operated by the U.S., to warn of any attack through the Gidi and Mitla mountain passes in the Sinai.

Rabin conferred with West German Chancellor Schmidt in Bonn, who urged the Israeli premier to take advantage of the current chance for a settlement with Egypt. Kissinger arrived in Paris and will meet with Soviet Foreign Minister Gromyko in Geneva before seeing Rabin Saturday in Bonn.

The Palestine Liberation Organization said in Beirut that it had failed to win the release of an American Army colonel kidnapped last week. It said the colonel was being held by two radical Palestinian groups that don't belong to the PLO. The deadline the abductors set for the U.S. to meet their ransom demands passed.

● ● ●

A TURKISH-ARMS COMPROMISE was offered to the House by Ford.

After meeting with 140 House members, the President proposed legislation partially lifting the ban on military aid that was imposed after Turkey used U.S. weapons in invading Cyprus. Under the plan, undelivered arms already paid for by Turkey would be shipped and more weapons could be bought for cash, but Turkey wouldn't be eligible for grants. Ford would report to Congress every two months on arms sales and on the chances for a Cyprus settlement.

The three leading House opponents of arms for Turkey weren't invited to the meeting with Ford. One of them, Rep. John Brademas (D., Ind.), denounced the proposal as a fraud.

Speaker Carl Albert predicted the House would approve Ford's plan. The Senate last month voted 41-40 to end the arms embargo. Turkey has demanded that negotiations on the status of U.S. bases begin next Thursday if the embargo hasn't been lifted by then. It wasn't known whether Turkey would accept Ford's compromise.

● ● ●

PORTUGAL'S ARMED FORCES will form local units bypassing political parties.

An Enterpriser: A Reporter-Initiated Story

Tannenbaum finds the writing goes quickly. "A well-reported story—one reported logically with a central theme in mind—tends to write itself," he recalls an editor telling him. He begins with the Howards in a delayed lead and presents the theme in his words in the fifth paragraph and then in Sanders' words in the sixth paragraph. The next two paragraphs are background.

Tannenbaum's first version had the blind professor's quote lower in the story, but he remembered the guideline that good quotes should be put up high in a story.

Summing Up

Good reporters rely on human and physical sources. A study by Kathleen A. Hansen of the University of Minnesota journalism faculty found that Pulitzer Prize winners used a greater variety of physical sources in their stories than did nonwinners. The winners used more documents, reports, books and other printed matter and fewer interviews than did the nonwinners.

Yet many reporters rely on the interview for almost all their reporting. Stephen Hess found in his study of Washington reporters that journalists used no documents in almost three-fourths of their stories. When reporters are given more time to do stories, he says, "they simply do more interviews."

Interviews are, of course, essential to reporting. We will next examine how to conduct them and we will consider their place in the reporter's arsenal of methods for digging out useful and relevant material.

Further Reading

Abel, Elie. *Leaking: Who Does It? Who Benefits? At What Cost?* Winchester, Mass.: Unwin Hyman, 1987. (This is a 20th Century Fund study that examines leaks and their consequences to government and to journalism.)

Kovach, Bill, and Tom Rosenstiel. *Warp Speed.* New York: The Century Foundation Press, 1999.

Ritchie, Donald A. *Reporting from Washington: The History of the Washington Press Corps.* New York: Oxford University Press, 2005.

Ritchie describes a press corps, male and white until fairly recently, that has more often failed than succeeded in piercing the bureaucratic maze in Washington. He traces the origin of the shift in American politics when candidates began to be packaged "like bars of soap" to Richard Nixon's 1968 presidential campaign which was crafted "by a savvy team of media advisors."

Interviewing Principles 15
and Practices

Preview

Reporters conduct two types of interviews:

- **News interview:** The purpose is to gather information to explain an event or situation in the news.
- **Profile:** The focus is on the individual.

Sources respond to interviewers they consider competent and trustworthy. Questions are directed at a theme the reporter has in mind, but if a more important theme emerges, the reporter develops it.

Reporters listen for what they call high-quality quotations, the words that breathe life into their stories. Quotations are placed high in the story when they address its theme: "Good quotes up high," editors tell their reporters.

Curt Hudson
Relevant questions elicit newsworthy replies.

In the stadium locker room, the half-dressed hurdler was stuffing his warm-up suit and track shoes into a battered black bag. Seated on a bench nearby, a young man removed a pencil and a notepad from a jacket pocket.

"I'm from the paper in town," the young man said. "You looked sharp out there. Mind if I ask you some questions?"

The athlete nodded and continued his packing.

"First time you've been to this part of the West or this city?" the reporter asked. Another nod. This was not going to be easy, the reporter worried. The editor had told him to make sure he brought back a good story for tomorrow's paper, the day the National Association of Intercollegiate Athletics would begin its outdoor track meet at the local college. The tall, lithe young man standing in front of the bench was a world record holder in the hurdles, the editor had said, and worth a story for the sports section.

The secret to good stories is asking the right questions.

The reporter tried again. "What do you think of our town?" The athlete seemed to see the reporter for the first time.

"I don't know anything about this town," he replied. "I'm here to run. I go to the East coast, the West coast, here. They give me a ticket at school and I get on a bus or a plane and go. My business is to run." He fell silent.

Rebuffed, the reporter struggled to start the athlete talking again. In the 20-minute interview, the hurdler never really opened up.

Back in the newsroom, the reporter told the editor about his difficulties. They seemed to begin with his first question about whether the athlete had been to the town before. His boss was not sympathetic.

"First, you should have checked the clips and called his college for information about your man," the editor said. "That way you could have learned something about him, his record or his school. You might have used it to break the ice. Or you could have asked him about the condition of the track, something he knows about."

Then the editor softened. He knew that interviewing is not easy for young reporters, that it can be perfected only through practice.

"I think you have a good quote there about the business of running," he told the reporter. "Did you get anything else about the places he's been? That could make an interesting focus for the piece."

Yes, the reporter said, he had managed to draw the hurdler out about where he had been in the last few months. With the editor's guidance, the reporter managed to turn out an acceptable story.

Types of Interviews

The major story on page 1 of a September issue of *The Hawk Eye* in Burlington, Iowa, was about a three-alarm fire that destroyed a two-story building that housed an automobile sales agency and a body repair shop. The reporter interviewed several people for information to supplement his observations. Here are the people he interviewed and a summary of their comments:

- **The owner:** 15 cars destroyed; exact loss as yet unknown.

- **A fire department lieutenant:** The building could not have been saved when firefighters arrived. They concentrated on saving the adjoining buildings.

- **An eyewitness:** "I didn't know what it was. It just went all at once. I seen it a-burning and I was scared to death."

- **The fire chief:** The state fire marshal will investigate the cause of the fire.

News Interview

Although the reporter was not present when firefighters battled the fire during the early morning hours, the interviews with the lieutenant and the eyewitness give his story an on-the-scene flavor. Because these interviews help explain the news event, we describe them as *news interviews.*

Another local front-page story also relies on a news interview. A head-on automobile crash on Iowa Route 2 near Farmington took the life of a Van Buren County woman and caused injuries to four others. The story is based on a call to the Iowa Highway Patrol.

Personality Interview

The other type of interview story is the *profile* or *personality interview* in which the focus is a person rather than an event or situation.

Phoebe Zerwick of the *Winston-Salem Journal* writes profiles for a feature called "Tarheel Sketch." In one, she profiled a federal district judge with a reputation as a hero to the disadvantaged.

"Over the past 20 years," Zerwick writes, "advocates for black children sent to inferior schools, poor people awaiting public assistance, disabled people who have been kicked off the Social Security rolls, and mentally disturbed children locked away in state hospitals have climbed the stairs to that courtroom. And over the years, McMillan has provided them with relief." (See Zerwick's story on the next page.)

Before we examine the two types of interviews in detail, let's look at the principles that guide journalists when they interview sources.

Four Principles

From our examination of the interview of the hurdler, the coverage of the fire in Burlington and Phoebe Zerwick's profile of a federal judge, we can settle on a few basics for the interviewer. Our sportswriter went off on the wrong foot when he failed to obtain background about the athlete he was to interview. Lacking this information, he was unable to draw out his subject, much less to establish a relationship with him.

Zerwick's profile is successful because she was well prepared before she interviewed the judge, having examined his decisions in key cases and talked to people who had appeared in the judge's courtroom.

The reporter who covered the local fire asked the people involved in the incident questions whose answers developed the information essential to the story.

Here are the four basic guides to good interviewing:

1. **Prepare carefully,** familiarizing yourself with as much background as possible.

2. **Establish a relationship** with the source conducive to obtaining information.

3. **Ask questions that are relevant** to the story and that induce the source to talk.

4. **Listen and watch attentively.**

Tarheel Sketch

JAMES MCMILLAN

Big Mac's understanding of the Constitution
made him into a champion of the oppressed

By Phoebe Zerwick
JOURNAL REPORTER

CHARLOTTE — Something about the way the attorney was arguing his case didn't sit too well with Judge James B. McMillan.

The case before McMillan, a federal judge in the Western District, concerned a judge who had been opening court with prayer.

The judge, H. William Constangy, said that prayer helped him set a dignified tone for the day's proceedings and also expressed his reverence for the Lord.

But five public defenders in Charlotte were offended by the prayer. They thought that it came too close to government endorsement of religion and violated the First Amendment to the Constitution. Several weeks ago they brought their complaint to McMillan.

As McMillan said afterward, the case was riveting. The evidence was succinct, and the attorneys were well organized. But still, as Constangy's attorney delivered his closing argument, McMillan kept interrupting, fixing on a seemingly minor detail, the possessive pronoun his.

"I'm interested in the theory that it's his courtroom," McMillan asked, at least four or five times, each time raising more extreme examples. Does the judge have a right to pray even though he offends some and bores others? What if he wanted to turn toward Mecca and kneel upon a prayer rug? Does he have the right to do that?

Looking up from the bench, McMillan said, "It's not my courtroom. It's a place where I work."

McMillan's place of work is the federal courthouse in Charlotte, which faces Trade Street, a broad, tree-lined avenue that runs into the city's downtown. He works in a courtroom on the second floor.

Over the past 20 years, advocates for black children sent to inferior schools, poor people awaiting public assistance, disabled people who have been kicked off the Social Security

> **RESUMÉ**
>
> **FULL NAME:**
> James B. McMillan.
>
> **AGE:** 73.
>
> **PUBLIC POSITION:**
> U.S. District Court judge in the Western District.
>
> **BIRTHPLACE:**
> McDonald, Robeson County
>
> **EDUCATION:**
> B.A., University of North Carolina at Chapel Hill; Law degree, Harvard University.
>
> **FAMILY:**
> Married to Holly Neaves McMillan; one son, one daughter.

rolls, and mentally disturbed children locked away in state hospitals have climbed the stairs to that courtroom. And over the years, McMillan has provided them with relief.

In 1970, he ordered the Charlotte-Mecklenburg Board of Education to bus black children into schools in white neighborhoods and white children into schools in black neighborhoods. The case was the first busing case to be upheld by the U.S. Supreme Court and led to the desegregation of schools across the state and nation.

That was the first major case McMillan heard, and no case since then has triggered the kind of controversy that raged around him during those years. But since then, he has become a kind of hero among advocates for the poor by ruling in favor of the disadvantaged in numerous lesser-known cases.

Theodore O. Fillette, the deputy director of Legal Services of Southern Piedmont, said, "I can say without a doubt he has had the greatest impact on improving the rights of low-income people than anyone else in the state. I would include people without power, racial minorities, prisoners, and physically and mentally handicapped people."

In 1975, McMillan ordered the N.C. Department of Human Resources to process applications for welfare and Medicaid, the federal insurance program for the poor, within the required 45 days.

Some applicants were waiting as long as six months. During that time, some were evicted because they couldn't pay their rent. Others went hungry or cold.

The state is still under court order,

See McMILLAN, Page A20

Preparation

There's a saying in newsrooms that good interviews follow the two "P's"—persistence and preparation. Persistence is necessary to persuade people to be interviewed, and it is essential in following a line of questioning that the subject may find uncomfortable.

Preparation may consist of a few minutes spent glancing through a story in last week's newscast before dashing out to interview a congresswoman on a flying visit to look at the local Veterans Hospital where cutbacks have affected care. For a profile of the new university president, it may be a prolonged examination of clippings and material that databases have turned up.

Clyde Haberman, a *New York Times* columnist, says "exhaustive research is the basic building block of a successful interview."

Research   A. J. Liebling, a master reporter who moved from the newspaper newsroom to *The New Yorker* magazine, is quoted in *The Most of A. J. Liebling,* edited by William Cole: "The preparation is the same whether you are going to interview a diplomat, a jockey, or an ichthyologist. From the man's past you learn what questions are likely to stimulate a response."

When Liebling interviewed the jockey Eddie Arcaro, the first question Liebling asked was, "How many holes longer do you keep your left stirrup than your right?"

"That started him talking easily, and after an hour, during which I had put in about twelve words, he said, 'I can see you've been around riders a lot.'"

"I had," Liebling said later, "but only during the week before I was to meet him." In his preparations, Liebling had learned that most jockeys on counterclockwise U.S. tracks help balance their weight and hug the rail by riding with the left stirrup longer than the right. A rail-hugging journey is the shortest distance from start to finsh.

Research begins with the files about the subject. If the interviewee is well-known, *Who's Who in America* and other biographical dictionaries can be consulted. Most reference works are accessible online. People who know the interviewee can be asked for information.

Research serves four purposes: (1) It suggests tentative themes for the interview and specific questions. (2) It provides the reporter with a feel for the subject. (3) It provides useful background. (4) It enables the reporter to establish an open, friendly relationship with sources, who are pleased that the reporter took time to learn something about them.

Axel Schultz-Eppers, AP

Preparation Pays Off

Reporters interview a wide range of people, from six-year-olds and governors, even Mali tribesmen, as Sydney Rubin of the AP is doing here.

Establishing a Relationship

When Sheryl James of the *St. Petersburg Times* was interviewing sources for her prize-winning series on abandoned infants, she realized that many of those she was interviewing were unaccustomed to talking to a reporter. "I was dealing with good but somewhat unsophisticated people," she says, "who would have been easy to manipulate. It was a challenge to be sure they understood what I was doing and to keep promises made during the reporting process that I could have broken with impunity."

Interviewing Tips—Useful Guides

"Different people have to be approached different ways. You have to treat people differently based on the circumstances."

—David Cay Johnston, *The New York Times*

"'You want a good interrogator?' Jerry Giorgio, the New York Police Department's legendary third-degree man, asks. 'Give me somebody who people like, and who likes people. Give me somebody who knows how to put people at ease. Because the more comfortable they are, the more they talk, and the more they talk, the more trouble they're in—the harder it is to sustain a lie.'"

—Mark Bowden, *The Atlantic Monthly*

Memory is good within a day of the experience but dims with time. "With the passage of time, memory shifts from a reproduction of the past to a reconstruction that is heavily influenced by general knowledge and beliefs."

—Daniel L. Schacter, professor of psychology, Harvard

"List question topics in advance—as many as you can think of, even though you may not ask all of them and almost certainly will ask others that you do not list."

—Fred Zimmerman, *The Wall Street Journal*

"You ask a question that may be very meaningful. Then you move away from it. I do it sometimes even if the person doesn't get particularly fidgety, because I don't want him to think what he has told me is necessarily important to me. I'll move to another question and say, 'What's that on the wall?' Whatever. Anything that will divert him . . . and then come back and ask another very pointed question."

—Wendell Rawls Jr., veteran newsman

James focused on a woman who was charged with leaving her baby in a box near a Dumpster. She had to develop a relationship with the woman. "I simply tried to be straightforward about what I was doing," James said, "and get her to trust me, to know that I would keep my word to her.

"When I finally did interview her, I felt as I do with many people I interview— I try to establish a relaxed rapport, to be human myself so that they know I'm not a media monster."

Give-and-Take   The early stage of the interview is a feeling-out period. The interviewee balances his or her gains and losses from divulging information the reporter seeks, and the reporter tries to show the source the rewards the source will receive through disclosure of the information—publicity, respect and the feeling that goes with doing a good turn.

When the source concludes that the risks outweigh the possible gains and decides to provide little or no information or is misleading, the reporter has several alternatives. At one extreme, the reporter can try to cajole the source into a complete account through flattery—or by appearing surprised. At the other extreme, the reporter can demand information. If the source is a public official, such demands are legitimate because officials are responsible to the public. The reporter can tell the source that the story—and there will be some kind of story—will point out that the official refused to answer questions. Usually, the source will fall into line.

The Questions

Careful preparation leads the interviewer to a few themes for the interview, and these, in turn, suggest questions to be asked. But before the specific questions are put to the interviewee, a few housekeeping details usually are attended to, vital data questions. Questions of this sort are nonthreatening and help make for a relaxed interview atmosphere. Also, they are sometimes necessary because of conflicting material in the files, such as discrepancies in age or education.

Harold Ross, the brilliant and eccentric former newspaperman who founded and edited *The New Yorker,* slashed exasperatedly at the pages of profiles and interviews that lacked vital data. "Who he?" Ross would scrawl across the copy.

Direct Questions   Most questions flow from what the reporter perceives to be the theme of the assignment. A fatal accident: Automatically, the reporter knows that he or she must find out who died and how and where the death occurred.

A reporter is told to interview an actor who had been out of work for two years and is now in a hit musical. The reporter decides that the theme of the story will be the changes the actor has made in his life. He asks the actor if he has moved from his tenement walk-up, has made any large personal purchases and how his family feels about his being away most nights. These three questions induce the actor to talk at length.

Open- and Closed-Ended Questions   When the sportswriter asked the hurdler, "What do you think of our town?" he was using what is known as an *open-ended question,* which could have been answered in general terms. The sports editor's suggestion that the reporter ask the athlete about the condition of the track would have elicited a specific response—fast, slow, or slick—as it was a *closed-ended question.*

The open-ended question does not require a specific answer. The closed-ended question calls for a brief, pointed reply. Applied properly, both have their merits. Two months before the budget is submitted, a city hall reporter may ask the city manager what she thinks of the city's general financial situation—an open-ended question. The reply may cover the failure of anticipated revenues to meet expectations, unusually high increases in construction costs, higher interest rates and other factors that have caused trouble for the city. Then the reporter may ask a closed-ended question, "Will we need a tax increase?"

Reporters often begin their interviews with open-ended questions, which allow the source to relax. Then the closed-ended questions are asked, which may seem threatening if asked at the outset of the interview.

Television and radio interviews usually end with a closed-ended question because the interviewer wants to sum up the situation with a brief reply.

Tough Questions   Sometimes a young reporter finds that posing the right question is difficult because the question might embarrass or offend the interviewee. There is no recourse but to ask.

Oriana Fallaci, an Italian journalist famous for her interviews, says that her success may be the result of asking the world leaders she interviews questions that other reporters do not ask.

"Some reporters are courageous only when they write, not when they face the person in power. They never put a question like this, 'Sir, since you are a dictator, we all know you are corrupt. In what measure are you corrupt?'"

Beatle Talk

Interviewer: Sorry to interrupt you while you are eating, but what do you think you'll be doing in five years when this is over?

John Lennon: Still eating.

Interviewer: One of your hits is "Roll Over Beethoven." What do you think of Beethoven?

Ringo Starr: He's great, Especially his poems.

Interviewer: (after the Beatles were honored by the Queen): What do you think of the Queen?

Paul McCartney: She's lovely, great. She was just like a mum to us.

Interviewer: What do you call your haircut?

George Harrison: Arthur.

The Right Moment

When an interview begins, says Carol McCabe of *The Providence Journal,* people are wary, stiff. Gradually "they lean back, they are open. Then you can begin to move," she says. "The time to ask your most sensitive question is when the 'mirroring' starts. Mirroring is when they are doing the same thing you are doing. You begin the test: You push back in your chair and watch to see if they push back in theirs. You cross your right leg over the left one and see if they do it. You put one arm on the other arm, and see if they do it. That means they like you, you are together and that's the time to ask your tough questions."

Remarkably, heads of state, kings and guerrilla leaders open up to Fallaci. One reason for this is her presumption that the public is entitled to answers and her unwillingness to be treated with indifference. When the heavyweight champion boxer Muhammad Ali belched in answer to one of her questions, she threw the microphone of her tape recorder in his face.

Another reason for her effectiveness is "her talent for intimacy," as one journalist put it. "She easily establishes an atmosphere of confidence and closeness and creates the impression that she would tell you anything. Consequently, you feel safe, or almost safe, to do the same with her," writes Diana Loercher in *The Christian Science Monitor.*

In her interview with Henry Kissinger, the U.S. secretary of state at the time, Fallaci had him admit that his position of power made him feel like the "lone cowboy who leads the wagon train alone on his horse." His image of himself as the Lone Ranger caused an embarrassed Kissinger to say later that granting Fallaci the interview was the "stupidest" act in his life. It was, he said, "the single most disastrous conversation I have ever had with any member of the press."

Intrusive Questions   Some questions are necessary, some not. The guidelines for relevance and good taste are constantly shifting, and reporters may find they are increasingly being told to ask questions that they consider intrusive. This is the age of intimacy.

Reporters who dislike asking these questions, preferring to spare sources anguish, are sometimes surprised by the frank replies. A reporter for *Newsday* was assigned to follow up on an automobile accident in which a drunken youth without a driver's license ran a borrowed car into a tree. One of the passengers, a 15-year-old girl, was killed. In doing his follow-up story, the reporter discovered that most of the parents were willing to talk because, as one parent said, the lessons learned from the accident might save lives.

Listening, Watching

"Great reporters are great listeners," says Carl Bernstein of the Woodward-Bernstein reporting team that exposed the Watergate cover-up that led to President Nixon's resignation.

The good listener hears relevant quotes, revealing slips of the tongue, the dialect and diction of the source that sets him or her apart.

In an interview with Luis Manuel Delgado whom Diana Griego Erwin encounters at a motor vehicle office in Santa Ana, Calif., she finds Delgado unable to tell the English-speaking clerks what he needs. Does that bother him? Erwin asks. Here is an excerpt of their conversation from *The Orange County Register:*

"I should know how to speak English," he said with a quiet simplicity. "This is the United States."

"My kids are very good," he said. "They get good marks in school. They speak English. No accent. One wants to be a doctor. When they first came here I told them to study English and learn it well. Don't let them treat you like a donkey like they treat your papa."

I asked him if it didn't hurt, being treated "como un burro," as he said.

"No, I am not a donkey and my children know it. They know I do all this for them.

"They are proud of me. Nothing anyone else says or does can make me sad when they have pride in me.

"And they will never be donkeys."

Sometimes, a single quote can capture the person or illuminate the situation the interview is about. In an interview with a former governor of Arkansas, Sid McMath, one quotation told a great deal. First, the background.

School Desegregation   In 1957, Gov. Orval Faubus defied a federal court order to desegregate Little Rock's Central High School. Although President Eisenhower responded by ordering the 101st Airborne to enforce the court order, Faubus had legitimized resistance and there was violence when the few black students tried to enter the high school.

Faubus had been a small-time politico when McMath plucked him out of Madison County.

Years after the Little Rock spectacle, McMath was asked about Faubus and he replied: "The sorriest thing I ever did as governor was to build a paved road into Madison County so Orval Faubus could come down it."

School Cruelty   Listen to Wendy Williams, a bright 13-year-old, talk to a reporter. She lives in a trailer park in Dixon, Ill. Her teacher recommended her for an advanced math class, but she said no. "I get picked on for my clothes and for living in a trailer park," she said. "I don't want to get picked on for being a nerd."

Louisiana Politics   Earl K. Long, a member of the powerful Long political dynasty, was getting on and a reporter interviewed him for a profile. Long told his interviewer, "When I die—if I die—I want to be buried in Louisiana so I can stay active in politics."

The Interviewer's Ground Rules

Both parties in an interview have certain assumptions and expectations. Generally, the reporter expects the interviewee to tell the truth and to stand behind what he or she has told the interviewer. The interviewee presumes the reporter will write the story fairly and accurately.

Having said this, we must admit to the exceptions. Sources may conceal, evade, distort and lie when they believe it is to their advantage. The reporter must be alert to the signs of a departure from truth.

The rules that govern the reporter's behavior in the interview can be detailed with some certainty. Most journalists agree the reporter should:

1. Identify himself or herself at the outset of the interview.

2. State the purpose of the interview.

Listener

Lynn Hirschberg, whose profiles of Hollywood's stars appear in many magazines, skewers her subjects as often as she applauds them. Yet they rarely turn down her request for an interview, and they always open up to her. Why? "It comes down to how interested you are in what they have to say. It's just a matter of how much you want to listen."

3. Make clear to those unaccustomed to being interviewed that the material will be used.

4. Tell the source how much time the interview will take.

5. Keep the interview as short as possible.

6. Ask specific questions that the source is competent to answer.

7. Give the source ample time to reply.

8. Ask the source to clarify complex or vague answers.

9. Read back answers if requested or when in doubt about the phrasing of crucial material.

10. Insist on answers if the public has a right to know them.

11. Avoid lecturing the source, arguing or debating.

12. Abide by requests for nonattribution, background only or off-the-record should the source make this a condition of the interview or of a statement.

Who's in Control?

Reporters usually have specific information they seek in an interview, and sources who readily supply it need little coaxing or guidance. Some sources, usually experienced public officials and heads of corporations, try to take over the interview situation, to put it on their terms. If they supply the needed information, the reporter willingly plays the passive role. Increasingly, however, these sources attempt to use tactics to avoid direct answers.

In fact, many of these sources are coached to do just that. "For $4,000 to $10,000 a day trainers who are ethically and intellectually as diverse as journalists themselves teach the art of performing for the press," writes Trudy Lieberman in the *Columbia Journalism Review.* "Today it's a rare public soul who has not been media trained." She says that politicians, government bureaucrats and "as many as 70 percent of corporate CEOs are taught how to parry reporters' questions and deliver predetermined messages.

"Even flower sellers coached by the Society of American Florists know they should talk about the color of roses when reporters call about price gouging on Valentine's Day."

With these sources, a reporter has no choice but to wrest control.

The Profile

The profile is a minidrama, blending dialogue, action and description. Through the words and actions of the subject, along with those of his or her friends and associates, and with the reporter's insertion of background and explanatory matter, a life is illuminated.

Anticipate Questions Subjects May Have

Interviewers should anticipate these questions that a subject may be asking himself or herself at the outset of an interview:

- Why is this reporter talking to me?

- What is her purpose? Is she here to hurt, embarrass or help me?

- What sort of story does she intend to write?

- Is she competent, trustworthy or will she misunderstand, hurt me?

- Is she bright enough to grasp some of the complexities, or should I simplify everything?

- Will I have to begin at the beginning, or does she seem to have done her homework?

Momentum is the key requirement for the profile. One of the obstacles to movement is the necessary background of the person profiled. Inserted in clots, the background brakes the story, stills its movement. The writer's task is to blend background into the moving narrative.

> On most days, his commute from Burlingame to his downtown law office in San Francisco took about half an hour. But on that Tuesday, he left at 8 a.m. as usual, turned on the radio and did not. . . .

The writer is describing how her subject heard a news story that influenced a career change. She goes on to tell us that he pulled off the highway, parked his car in a Wendy's lot and began to think about becoming a teacher. Along the way, we learn that he lives in an affluent suburb and is a lawyer.

Reporting Is the Key

Reporting makes the profile. Joseph Mitchell, whose profiles for *The New Yorker* are considered the standard for the form, is described by Brendan Gill in *Here at The New Yorker,* a history of the magazine, as having had the ability to ask "just the right questions." The questions would open up his sources, and Mitchell would closely attend their recollections and reflections. He encouraged sources to a loquacity no one suspected they possessed. Mitchell knew that everyone has a good story and that good reporting will flush it out.

In the dedication of one of his books, Calvin Trillin, a *New Yorker* writer, wrote, "To the *New Yorker* reporter who set the standard, Joseph Mitchell." Note Trillin's description of Mitchell as a "reporter." Trillin, like all good writers, knows that reporting is at the heart of the journalist's work.

Quotes, Quotes

Look back, and chances are that you will recall that your interest perked up when you came across quotation marks. As the novelist Elmore Leonard says, "When people talk, readers listen." In interviews, the writer listens for the telling remark that illuminates the person or the situation. Leonard says he lets his characters do the work of advancing his story by talking. He gets out of the way.

"Readers want to hear them, not me."

Love Song   Listen to the singer Lorrie Morgan talk about her problems: After her husband, the singer Keith Whitley, died of alcohol poisoning, Morgan was only offered slow, mournful ballads by her songwriters, she said in an interview with *The Tennessean* of Nashville.

"I mean, it was all kinds of dying songs," she said. But then she fell in love with Clint Black's bus driver, and she decided to change her tunes.

"I said, 'I'm not going to do that. I'm not basing my career on a tragedy.' I live the tragedy every day without it being in my music." Her life, she said, has turned around, thanks to her new love. "He's a wonderful, wonderful guy. This

Track Talk

In her book *Seabiscuit,* Laura Hillenbrand describes a famous match race between Seabiscuit and War Admiral. Seabiscuit's regular rider, Red Pollard, was unable to ride because of an injury and George Woolf was substituted. Pollard advised Woolf to let Seabiscuit run eye-to-eye with War Admiral, that the Admiral was not game.

When Seabiscuit left War Admiral behind, Woolf said he saw "something pitiful" in the Admiral's eyes. "He looked all broken up. Horses, mister, can have crushed hearts just like humans."

Colorful Quotes—Poisoned Darts

"A $400 suit on him would look like socks on a rooster."

—Gov. Earl Long of Louisiana

"Nixon is the kind of politician who would cut down a redwood tree and then mount the stump to make a speech for conservation."

—Adlai Stevenson

"Bill Clinton's foreign policy experience stems mainly from having breakfast at the International House of Pancakes."

—Pat Buchanan

He is "lower than the regurgitated filth of vultures."

—FBI Director J. Edgar Hoover on Jack Anderson, muckraking columnist

guy is very special, and I'm into him real bad." However, not too long afterward Lorrie's love life took a detour—her affections switched to a politician.

Listening and Hearing

There is an old saying that most people hear but few listen. Noise surrounds us, and we survive the clatter by tuning out. But reporters must listen. Their livelihood depends on it. To become a good listener:

- Cut down your ego. You are conducting an interview to hear what others say, not to spout your opinions.

- Open your mind to new or different ideas, even those you dislike.

- Grant the interviewee time to develop his or her thoughts.

- Rarely interrupt.

- Concentrate on what the person is saying and make secondary the person's personality, demeanor or appearance.

- Limit questions to the theme or to relevant ideas that turn up in the interview.

- Don't ask long questions.

Swallowed   Good listeners will have in their notes the quotations that give the reader or listener an immediate sense of the person being interviewed—what are known as high-quality quotes. Oscar Lewis, the anthropologist who wrote about Spanish-speaking peoples, began his article, "In New York You Get Swallowed by a Horse," about Hector, a Puerto Rican, this way:

We had been talking of this and that when I asked him, "Have you ever been in New York, Hector?"

"Yes, yes, I've been to New York."

"And what did you think of life there?"

"New York! I want no part of it! Man, do you know what it's like? You get up in a rush, have breakfast in a rush, go to work in a rush, go home in a rush, even shit in a rush. That's life in New York! Not for me! Never again! Not unless I was crazy.

"Look I'll explain. The way things are in New York, you'll get nothing there. But nothing! It's different in Puerto Rico. Here, if you're hungry, you come to me and say, 'Man I'm broke, I've had nothing to eat,' and I'd say, 'Ay, Benedito! Poor thing!' And I'd give you some food. No matter what, you wouldn't have to go to bed hungry. Here in Puerto Rico you can make out. But in New York, if you don't have a nickel, or twenty cents, you're worthless, and that's for sure. You don't count. You get swallowed by a horse!"

Recollection   In her profile of the great jazz pianist Oscar Peterson in *Smithsonian* magazine, Marya Hornbacher lets Peterson recall one of his road trips 50 years ago with Dizzy Gillespie. The group was "traveling down South, in some of the bigoted areas," Peterson begins.

So it was two o'clock in the morning, or something like that, and we pulled up to one of those roadside diners. And I looked, and there was the famous sign: No Negroes. And the deal was, we all had duos or trios of friendship, so one of the Caucasian cats would say, What do you want me to get you? And they'd go in, and they wouldn't eat in there, they'd order and come back on the bus and eat with us. But Dizzy gets up and walks off the bus and goes in there. And we're all saying, "Oh my God, that's the last we'll see of him." And he sits down at the counter—we could see this whole thing through the window. And the waitress goes over to him. And she says to him, "I'm sorry, sir, but we don't serve Negroes in here." And Dizzy says, "I don't blame you, I don't eat 'em. I'll have a steak." That was Dizzy exactly. And do you know what? He got served.

A Champion   Ira Berkow, a sportswriter for *The New York Times,* lets Rulon Gardner talk. Gardner had defeated Aleksander Karelin in the Olympic super-heavyweight wrestling division for the gold medal. Gardner describes himself in the interview as a standard-bearer for wrestling and "maybe some kind of inspiration, a way of giving some people a little hope." Berkow continues quoting Gardner, "a school teacher who grew up on a farm in the metropolis of Afton, Wyo. (pop 1,394)":

"I had a learning disability," Gardner said. "People were always telling me that I wasn't good enough: 'You're not going to make it in junior college, then four-year college.' Then, 'You're not going to get a degree.' People were always putting restrictions on me, or trying to. I don't think they were being mean. They were just being honest, as they saw it.

"But I never listened to those people. I might have. Coming from a small town, the rest of the world looked very big. It was a big event if we were able to get to Salt Lake City once a year. But I was very competitive. I just kept giving myself opportunities in difficult situations."

With these few quotations, we are shown a good man, a man large in spirit and generosity as well as in girth.

A Tryout   Barry Singer of *The New York Times* lets Anne Wiggins Brown talk. Brown was the original Bess in George Gershwin's famous folk opera *Porgy and Bess* in 1935. The first African-American vocalist admitted to the prestigious Juilliard School of Music, she was a graduate student when at the age of 21 she heard that Gershwin was writing an opera "about Negroes in South Carolina." She applied and was called for an audition at which she sang Brahms, Schubert and Massenet for Gershwin, who then asked her, "Would you sing a Negro spiritual?" She flared at the request. She explains:

I was very much on the defensive at that age. I resented the fact that most white people thought that black people should or only could sing spirituals. "I am very sorry," I said, "but I haven't any of *that* music with me." And then I broke out, "Why is it that you people always expect black singers to sing spirituals?"

He just looked at me. He didn't say anything or do anything at all; he didn't appear angry or disturbed. But I saw that he understood my reaction. And as soon as I saw that, my whole attitude just melted away and I wanted more than anything else to sing a spiritual for this man. I said, "I can sing one spiritual without an accompaniment, if that's O.K." He told me it was. And I sang "City Called Heaven." It's a very plaintive, very melancholy spiritual. And I knew when I finished that I'd never sung it better in my life, because I was so emotionally involved at that moment.

He was very quiet for some time. Finally he spoke: "Wherever you go, you must sing that spiritual without accompaniment. It's the most beautiful spiritual I've ever heard." And we hugged one another.

Brown continues her reflections on her career, and then she thinks of what might have been:

"If I had been born 20 years later, I might have sung at the Metropolitan Opera," she mused.

"I might have marched for civil rights. I would have been here for that. I would certainly not have lived in Norway and my life would have been very different."

"Of course," she conceded, her eyes bright, "I would not have met Mr. Gershwin and that would have been a shame."

Interview Others   The reporter interviews friends, associates, relatives of the main subject. The profile of a popular psychology professor would be incomplete without comments from her students. After all, it's their reactions to her lectures and her personal interest in them that makes her liked.

A Guide for the Profile

Let the reader:

- See the person—physical characteristics.

- Hear the person—lots of quotations.

- Watch the person—lots of action.

- Know the person—education, job, age, family, income, likes-dislikes, hobbies, successes-failures.

When a young *New York Times* reporter turned in a piece about a nun who was an alcoholic and who counsels other similarly afflicted nuns, the story did not move past Charlotte Evans, an editor.

"As it stands," Evans told the reporter, "all you have is a moderately interesting interview with Sister Doody. You sat in a chair, and she sat in a chair and you had a chat. That's not very good, considering the story material."

"Did you talk to any nuns in treatment or just out of it?"

"Where is the anguish, the embarrassment, the guilt?"

"It doesn't sound as if you had done any real reporting, digging, pushing. Where are the people, the quotes, the color?"

The Miner Listen to Linda Raisovich-Parsons, one of the first women to go into the coal mines, talk to Bharati Sadasivam:

> I went into the mines when I was 18 years old and had just finished high school. There was not a whole lot of career opportunities for a girl back then in West Virginia. My father was a coal miner. He had multiple sclerosis and I didn't want to burden him with the expense of a college education. . . .
>
> Initially, he didn't like the idea because he didn't want his daughter working in that kind of environment. But when he saw that I was not just testing the waters and was determined to make a go of it, he taught me the ropes and looked out for his baby daughter. . . .
>
> There was a lot of heavy lifting and carrying to do and that was what I found the most difficult. Most of the men took the position that well, if you're here, you've got to pull your weight and I was determined that no one was going to prove that I wasn't able to do the job.

Advice
Samuel Johnson, the brilliant 18th century English writer, advised those plying his trade that "more knowledge may be gained of a man's real character by a short conversation with one of his servants than from a formal and studied narrative, begun with his pedigree and ended with his funeral."

All Quotes Sadasivam's magazine article consists entirely of direct quotes. She allows Raisovich-Parsons to tell her story. After several years in the mines, the United Mine Workers union offered her a job as a mine inspector. She would have been the first female inspector. At first, it was not easy.

> There were some safety committees that simply couldn't accept a woman and would bypass me and go to my male co-workers. And I often got the same reactions from the coal companies. But there were others that were more accepting of me. I found the older miners more helpful and respectful than the younger ones. Sexual harassment was a problem initially but we've grown with these men and I think we're just one of the crew now.

309

Gay Talese probably got closer to revealing the character of Frank Sinatra than any of Sinatra's biographers. Yet Talese never interviewed the singer. He watched him at a New York saloon and a California night club, and he spoke to many of Sinatra's friends. In his piece, "Frank Sinatra Has a Cold" in *Esquire,* Talese has scores of mini-profiles, all contributing to the Sinatra portrait. Here's one about Brad Dexter, "one of Sinatra's constant companions."

Whenever he is among strangers with Sinatra he worries because he knows that Sinatra brings out the best and worst in people—some men will become aggressive, some women will become seductive, others will stand around skeptically appraising him, the scene will be somehow intoxicated by his mere presence, and maybe Sinatra himself, if feeling as badly as he was tonight, might become intolerant or tense, and then: headlines. So Brad Dexter tries to anticipate danger and warn Sinatra in advance. He confesses to feeling very protective of Sinatra, admitting in a recent moment of self-revelation: "I'd kill for him."

I found women on the whole more safety-conscious than men. They took all precautions, made sure that all the equipment was working properly. You find a very low accident rate among women.

I'm comfortable here, but there are times when I've felt like a token woman. But the few women that are there are very outspoken, the type of people who get out and get involved because they've had to be fighters and scrappers to get the job. I have a button from a women miners' conference that says, "Just Another Mouthy Union Woman."

Sadasivam wrote the story just this way, a first-person account.

The Miniprofile

When Mark Patinkin and Christopher Scanlan were assigned to profile the black community in Rhode Island for *The Providence Journal-Bulletin,* they focused on individuals—the people who symbolize the facts and figures they were gathering.

For their report on crime in the Providence ghetto, the reporters interviewed a prostitute:

Voices: Debbie Spell on Hustling

"Being a hooker is all I know," said Debbie Spell. "It's how my mother supported me. That's all I seen when I was a kid, broads jumping into cars. Put me in a factory and I just couldn't hack it."

In poor neighborhoods, where unemployment and welfare rates are high, many blacks turn to hustling to survive. Debbie Spell turned to prostitution. Although she is 20, she looks 15. She is already the mother of three children. She normally works on Pine Street in Providence, where most of her customers are white.

"If it wasn't for them, then I wouldn't have food for my kids," she said, "or Pampers for my baby." Nor would she have her color television and living-room furniture.

"I'm not proud of it," she added, "but it's the way I make a living. Why should I work in a factory for $100 a week when I can make that much on a Thursday night?"

Andy Dickerman, *The Providence Journal-Bulletin*

Follow-Up to a Tragedy

After he had written a profile of Debbie, a young woman who spoke freely of her life as a street walker, Christopher Scanlan learned that she had hanged herself in jail two days after her arrest.

To find out something about Debbie's life, Scanlan returned to the streets Debbie frequented. He interviewed the women who engaged in the same trade as Debbie. They spoke freely but did not want their faces to appear in the newspaper.

Although blacks make up only 3.4 percent of the population in Rhode Island, they make up 24 percent of the population at the Adult Correctional Institutions and 7.5 percent of admissions to state drug abuse programs.

In Providence, blacks account for about 10 percent of the population, but a much higher percentage ends up in the city's arrest books. Last year, of the 243 juveniles Providence police arrested for major crimes, 37 percent, or 90, were black. As blacks get older, their arrest percentage grows. . . .

Getting Close "Tim Madigan can talk to anybody," says Madigan's editor at the *Fort Worth Star-Telegram.* Madigan interviewed 10 people for the newspaper's "Angels Among Us." Here is one of Madigan's miniprofiles:

Jeanette Martin: Inspired Teacher

Dominique entered Jeanette Martin's Forth Worth classroom still in diapers, a profoundly handicapped 3-year-old boy barely able to walk, speak or eat solid foods. When he left three years later, Dominique graduated to a regular kindergarten class.

"You'll have to excuse me," says Martin, the ex-banking executive, who for the last seven years has taught disabled children in Forth Worth public schools "I get kind of emotional when I talk about this. I'm doing something now I would do for free."

That sense of making a difference was absent in her 20-year banking career, she says now. So when her Arlington bank closed in 1989, Martin, then a senior vice president, began to volunteer at the Jo Kelly School for disabled students in Forth Worth.

"You're a natural," Jo Kelly Principal Leslie James told her then.

With that encouragement, and support from her husband, Don, she set off on a career path that would pay her roughly half of what she earned as a banker. In purely financial terms, that is.

"If I have influenced their lives even half as much as they've influenced mine, then I'll consider myself a success," Martin says now. "I see these kids every day who have to struggle for things you and I take for granted or the things that are so easy for us.

"But they are so willing to do that and they try so hard. To me that's an inspiration more than any football player or politician. They inspire me. Every day they inspire me to do the best that I can."

Appearance and Behavior

A carefree, casual attitude and dress can tell a subject that you, the reporter, do not take him or her seriously. Hair and dress, tone of voice, posture, gestures and facial expressions convey messages to a source. Anthropologists say that what people do is more important than what they say, and the first impressions the reporter conveys with his or her dress, appearance, posture and hand and facial movements may be more important than anything the reporter says.

A reporter can choose his or her garb, practice speaking in a steady, modulated voice and learn to control gestures. But age, race, sex and physical characteristics are beyond the reporter's control, and some sources are affected by these.

Where there is identification with the reporter, the source is much more likely to speak freely than he or she is with an interviewer of another sex, race, religion or age. People feel comfortable with those who are like them.

From Friend to Authority Figure

Reporters can adopt the role of friend, confidant and companion when sources appear to need encouragement before they will talk. When a source indicates he will cooperate only if he is sure that he will benefit from the story, the reporter is reassuring, promising that her story will be fair and balanced.

Some stories require pressing sources to the point of discomfort or implying a threat should they fail to respond. Journalism often becomes the business of making people say what they would prefer to keep to themselves. Much of this is properly the public's business, and the reporter who shifts roles from friend to authority figure or threatening power figure can justify his or her role as being in the public interest.

Compassionate Listener

The compassion and understanding that Diana Sugg of *The Sacramento Bee* took to the police beat resulted, she says, in "incredible stories about ordinary people."

Mike Roemer

Cover Up, Remove

The tattoo can be discreetly covered by a sleeve, but the pierced tongue may prove so fascinating to the interviewee that it becomes the subject of discussion rather than the topic the reporter came to ask about.

Disarming

"I am so physically small, so temperamentally unobtrusive and so neurotically inarticulate that people tend to forget that my presence runs counter to their best interests."

—Joan Didion

R.L. Chambers

Bharati Sadasivam

Working People

The diverse ways people make a living are worth chronicling: The Indian jewelry craftsman, the coal mine inspector, the railroad worker, the billboard installer. Each has a fascinating story to tell.

Joseph Noble, *The Stuart* (Fla.) *News*

Mike Roemer

Interviewing Klansmen

Peter Francis of *The Stockton* (Calif.) *Record* questions two leaders of the Ku Klux Klan about their plans to organize additional California chapters. The KKK national leader (on left) and the head of the California Klan said their program, which included racial segregation, was attracting new members "every day." Although the men were wary of the reporter's intentions, Francis was able to draw them out about their plans for enlarging their base in California.

Rich Turner, *The Stockton Record*

The suicide of a homeless man, Joseph King Jr., recorded in a brief note in the police reports, interested Sugg. "The detective who had worked the case knew me, and he told me how sad it was because before the suicide King and his homeless friend had been talking about trying to get jobs." Sugg tracked down King's friend. "He told me how shy and skinny King was, and that he always needed protection. 'I wasn't finished teaching him yet about how to live on the streets, about how to deal with the cold,' his friend said."

Sugg began her story of the death of an anonymous street man this way:

Joseph King Jr. was a tall guy, but he wasn't a fighter, and on the streets where he lived, his best friend had to watch out for him.

Even in the Sacramento parks where they sometimes slept, King was in the middle, with a friend on either side of him as protection through the night.

But the 49-year-old man was weary, friends said. Tired of moving from homeless shelter to homeless shelter. Tired of missing his former wife.

About 7 p.m. Thursday, after discussing with his best friend ways to get a job, the homeless man dove 20 feet over a ledge behind the Sacramento Memorial Auditorium.

With his buddy crying at his side in the dark loading area, King died.

"He was my best friend. That was the only friend I ever had that was something to me," said Michael Lockhart, 31, who had been living on the streets with King for the past four years.

A Child Dies   Sugg spent two hours interviewing the family of a youngster who had died. When Randy Ray Harlan was four weeks old, his father—strung out on drugs and alcohol—had beaten Randy mercilessly. Since that beating, the child had been blind and brain damaged. Randy's grandmother provided constant, loving care. Now, Randy could fight no longer. Five years after he was beaten so badly, he died.

She recalled her interview with Randy's grandmother:

"He was beautiful before all this happened," the grandmother told Sugg, "perfect in every way." When Randy's sister asked, "Where's Randy? Where's Randy?" Sugg noted the grandmother's reply: "I told you, he's in heaven." Then the grandmother turned to Sugg and said, "He was very special to Carrie. She would hold onto him and hug him and kiss him, but she knew he couldn't do it back. All we could do was tell her he was sick."

Again, the grandmother recalled Randy:

"That little boy was a real fighter. I can imagine what he would have been like if this had never happened. He would have gone places."

"But it happened."

Nonjudgmental

The spacious brick home is indistinguishable from those that surround it in the middle-class neighborhood of South Arlington. . . . But something is different about this place and the couple who live here. The man of the house, Dean Jones, a high-paid supervisor in the aerospace industry, is rarely seen. It is Mary Jones who comes to the front door, always Mary Jones lest the visitor be a child selling candy. Her husband does not engage in neighborly fraternization, and is especially careful to stay clear of the boys across the street or the teen-age girl living on the corner.

This is how Tim Madigan begins "The Man Next Door," his interview with a convicted child molester. His editor said Madigan "can talk to anybody." And those Madigan talks to speak openly to him:

"'The fact is,' concedes Jones, a heavyset man with brown hair and eyeglasses, 'I have a deviant attraction to young females.'"

"With great reluctance, Jones says he has come to terms with the truth. 'Pedophile' applies to him."

Jones tells Madigan about his attempts to control his deviant tendencies. "He has thrown out his collection of pornographic movies. . . . He does not visit a shopping mall unaccompanied by his wife."

Mrs. Jones is also open with Madigan, telling him that she has learned to stand between her husband and any children that may be nearby in a line at a restaurant.

"If my daughter comes and spends the night and I wake up and Dean's not in my bed and I find him coming from the front of the house, I should call his probation officer," she tells Madigan.

> **Balancing Act**
> "An interview is frequently the course you chart between what you came in knowing and what you're finding out as it's happening."
> —*Terry Gross, National Public Radio's "Fresh Air"*

Jones goes along with all this, he says. "I've had the therapy. I've seen it work. As long as I'm not around kids, I haven't molested any kids.

"I can't control what trips my triggers. Just like you can't control what trips your triggers. What I can do is control what I do with it next."

Alcoholics   Eric Newhouse took the same nonjudgmental approach to his series about alcohol abuse when he dealt with the alcoholics in his area. He was neutral in interviewing Tara Fatz, manager of the Lobby Bar, who tells him that people are lined up at the door when she opens for business at 8 a.m. And he was nonjudgmental when he talked to Tom Jerome, drunk at 9 a.m. from the stash he keeps in an alley.

For Newhouse's comments about how he gathered material for his Pulitzer Prize–winning series in the *Great Falls Tribune* and excerpts from some of his stories, see **Alcohol: Cradle to Grave** in *NRW Plus*.

Invasive Questions

Thousands died when terrorists struck the Pentagon in Washington, D.C., and the World Trade Center towers in New York City. One of the tasks reporters faced was to interview survivors.

"It was one of the most emotionally gruelling assignments I've had in years," one *USA Today* reporter said. "To have to talk to people who lost loved ones was shattering," says Haya El Nasser.

Some of those whom reporters reached were angry. "Many people wanted nothing to do with me," says Traci Watson, another member of the *USA Today* reporting team assigned to write obituaries. "One person even sent an e-mail saying that everything possible should be done to stop us from writing about a particular victim. My correspondent, who'd been a good friend of the victim, seemed to think it would be demeaning to have the victim reduced to 'a blurb in a national newspaper.'"

But some friends and family did want to talk and "seemed to draw some comfort from doing so," Watson says.

Mel Antonen says, "I started every conversation with, 'I don't want to be invasive or insensitive, but we are gathering stories about the victims, and if you'd like to answer some questions we'd appreciate it. If not, we certainly understand.'"

One reporter looked back on the assignment, which lasted several days, and remembered: "The most heart-wrenching experience was hearing victims' voices on answering machines. I'm known as a pretty tough cookie around here. But I'll admit it: I cried many evenings."

Tough Questions

Reporters who work on investigative stories use an interviewing technique that requires a straight face and a knowing tone of voice. Bruce Selcraig, a special contributor to *Sports Illustrated,* calls this the "assumed-truth question."

Analysis
A psychiatrist at the University of California at Berkeley medical school says that if the subject of an interview thinks longer than you believe the answer to your question requires, this indicates a coverup or lie. Also, he says, the length of an eyeblink is indicative—the longer the blink, the more likely the subject is making up a story for his or her response.

"You're trying to confirm whether the FBI has begun an investigation at Steroid University," he says. "You may get nowhere if you simply ask an agent, 'Can you confirm this or that?' Instead, try: 'What's the bureau's jurisdiction in this case?' 'Which agent will be supervising the investigation of the university?'"

Selcraig suggests reporters watch how their subjects handle questions:

> Notice stress indicators like frequent crossing and uncrossing of legs, constant handling of desk items (paper clips, pencils), picking at one's clothing, and obvious signs like sweating or stuttering. He may not be lying yet, but you may be getting uncomfortably close to the right question. Try asking: "Have I made you nervous?" or "You seem bothered by something today."

With difficult stories and closed-mouthed sources, Bob Greene of *Newsday* would take an approach he calls "building a circle." He would conduct many interviews for his investigative stories. The first one, he says, is general, "far off the goal. Then you move closer and closer until the person you are checking becomes tense. He or she is then primed for the final interview." Along the way, Greene says, a subject hears that you have been calling on people to check him. "He suggests that you might want to come over and talk to him."

The Careful Observer

You are entering the office of the chairman of the English department. You had telephoned to ask if you could interview him about the department's plans to cope with the increasing numbers of high school graduates who arrive on campus poorly trained in reading and writing. He had told you to drop in about 3 p.m.

As you enter, you notice two paintings of sea scenes on a wall and two novels, a dictionary and a world almanac on his desk. Books in a floor-to-ceiling bookcase line one wall. These impressions do not particularly interest you because this will be a news interview focused on the situation, not the individual.

The chairman is worried, he says, about the growing numbers of students unable to understand college-level material. The chairman pauses often in his answers and occasionally goes to a shelf to take down a book that he reads to amplify a point.

"A friend of mine calls this the cretinization of American youth, and I used to laugh at him," he says. He reads from a copy of *McGuffey's Readers.*

"This grade-school material is now at the high school level," he says. "I wonder if anyone cares." He then reads from a Wordsworth poem that he says used to be memorized in grade school. No more, he says.

Musings   "I wonder just what they are teaching students in high school," he says, "Not much, I fear, and that continues in college." He stops speaking to toy with a battered cigarette lighter. You wonder whether to ask about it.

"A member of our department told me the other day that he received a note from a publisher that his book proposal made too many demands on students. Said the vocabulary was beyond college students. And the publisher gave a

couple of examples—'incomprehensible' and 'pernicious.' I am afraid we are living in a period of lowered expectations, and students pick up on that. They know that they don't have to do much to get by."

He goes back to his cigarette lighter. "Am I asking too much of students? Am I damaging their self-esteem by suggesting that their reliance on the spell checker is foolish, that they should read more than the comics and the movie ads, spend less time on video games?"

The Human Element   Suddenly, you decide that the interview should include more than the plans of the department to offer more courses in remedial writing and grammar. The story will include the chairman's musings, worries and personality as well as his plans. That will help personalize it, make it more readable.

Quickly, you reexamine the office to make note of the artists of the paintings, the titles of the books on the desk, and you ask about the cigarette lighter. (You learn the chairman uses it to relieve tension; he is trying to stop smoking.)

As the chairman talks, you note his mannerisms, his slow speech, his frequent stares out the window. A student enters the office and asks for permission to drop a course, and you watch him persuade the freshman to give the course another week.

Noticing the family pictures on the chairman's desk, you ask for their identities. Smiling, the chairman complies and then says, "You must be a believer in Whitehead's remark that genius consists of the minute inspection of subjects that are taken for granted just because they are under our noses."

You make a note of that, too, more for yourself than for the story.

Back in the newsroom, the editor agrees that the story is worth two columns, and he sends a photographer to take a picture of the chairman—toying with his cigarette lighter.

Details, Details

The reporter was acting in the best reportorial manner by noting specific details of the setting and the interviewee's mannerisms as well as watching for any interaction with third parties. In looking for details, the reporter was seeking the material that gives verisimilitude to an interview.

It was not enough to say that the chairman toyed with a cigarette lighter. The reporter wrote of the "lighter that he fingered to remind him of his no-smoking pledge." The reporter did not write that the chairman had read from an elementary school reader used in U.S. grade schools generations ago. He gave the book's title. The reporter did not merely quote the chairman when he spoke about the low scores of entering freshmen on the English placement test. The reporter noted the dejected slope of the chairman's shoulders, and he checked with the college admissions office to obtain the scores.

Too much for you, these warnings to be alert to every little detail? Then ponder the bewilderment of the *Baltimore Sun* reporter who turned in a story about a murder and was asked, "Which hand held the gun?"

The question is asked in newsrooms when a reporter writes a story that lacks convincing detail.

To Tape or Not to Tape?

"I tape, therefore I am," says Studs Terkel, whose radio programs and books utilize the tape recorder. For his books, Terkel, an excellent interviewer, transcribes his taped material, then edits it carefully. "It's like prospecting," he says. "The transcripts are the ore. I've got to get to the gold dust. It's got to be the person's truth, highlighted. It's not just putting down what people say."

Jan Wong, who did personality interviews for *The Globe and Mail* in Toronto, is a believer in the tape recorder. "If things get so tense that you need to stop taking notes for a moment, the tape is still running," she says. "That happened with John Hurt, the British actor. I had asked him about his wives and girlfriends, some of whom cuckolded him. He got so mad he started shaking. I didn't dare write or he would explode.

"But the tape kept going, so I didn't lose a word."

Wong says she keeps her recorder running even after she has closed her notebook. "This is often when you'll get the best stuff," she says.

When Wong sits down to an interview she automatically turns on her tape recorder. "I don't ask," she says. "I just turn it on."

Lillian Ross of *The New Yorker* has no use for the tape recorder and says flatly, "Do not use a tape recorder. The machine, surprisingly, distorts the truth. The tape recorder is a fast and easy and lazy way of getting a lot of talk down. . . . A lot of talk does not in itself make an interview. . . . A writer must use his own ears to listen, must use his own eyes to look."

Another *New Yorker* writer, John McPhee, often described as the country's foremost journalist, says, "All writing is a process of selection, and a tape is unselective. When you are writing without a recorder you make your selection right then. The tape is intrusive. When do you turn it off and on?"

Retroactive Requests

Sometimes a person being interviewed will suddenly stop and realize that he has said something he does not want to see in print or hear on television or the radio.

"Please don't use that," he will say. "It's off-the-record."

Should the reporter honor that request? It depends: If the source is a good contact and the material is not crucial to the story, the reporter probably will go along, particularly if the source is not a public figure or official. However, if the source has said something important, or the information is of concern to the public, then the reporter will usually reply that because the source knew he was talking to a reporter, he cannot suddenly go off-the-record retroactively.

When Jessica Mitford was interviewing Bennett Cerf, one of the owners of the Famous Writers School, he chatted freely with the amiable but sharp-penned writer. In the middle of his discourse, Cerf realized he sounded contemptuous of the people who took the school's correspondence course.

Cautions

Studies of memory and the use of handwritten notes have found that those who rely on their memories may omit some material, but copious note takers sometimes irritate sources or influence their responses.

The author Truman Capote said that note taking makes people say "what they think you expect them to say." Annette Garrett, author of a book on interviewing, said that note taking can interfere with the interviewer's participation in the interview. Experienced reporters rely on notes to jog their memories, but few take verbatim notes.

Here is how Mitford describes what happened, in her *Atlantic Monthly* article "Let Us Now Appraise Famous Writers":

While Mr. Cerf is by no means uncritical of some aspects of mail-order selling, he philosophically accepts them as inevitable in the cold-blooded world of big business—so different, one gathers, from his own cultured world of letters. "I think mail-order selling has several built-in deficiencies," he said. "The crux of it is a very hard sales pitch, an appeal to the gullible. Of course, once somebody has signed a contract with the Famous Writers School he can't get out of it, but that's true with every business in the country." Noticing that I was writing this down, he said in alarm, "For God's sake, don't quote me on that 'gullible' business—you'll have all the mail-order houses in the country down on my neck!" "Then would you like to paraphrase it?" I asked, suddenly getting very firm. "Well—you could say in general I don't like the hard sell, yet it's the basis of all American business." "Sorry, I don't call that a paraphrase, I shall have to use both of them," I said in a positively governessy tone of voice. "Anyway, why do you lend your name to this hard-sell proposition?" Bennett Cerf (with his melting grin): "Frankly, if you must know, I'm an awful ham—I love to see my name in the papers!"

When the source states beforehand that something is off-the-record and the reporter agrees to hear it on that condition, the material may not be used. Never? Well, hardly ever. Witness how Clifford D. May handles his source in this article, "Whatever Happened to Sam Spade?" in the *Atlantic Monthly*. A private detective, Jeremiah P. McAward, has been describing his difficulties in shadowing people:

"It's harder than you'd think," McAward continues. "Don't print this, but I once lost a pregnant Indian who was wearing a red blanket and had a feather in her hair, in Macy's." I reply that he cannot tell me something like that and expect that I won't use it. "Really?" he asks. I nod. "All right, then." There is a pause and then he adds. "But she just evaporated. A two-hundred-pound Indian."

Using and Abusing Quotes

Many reporters cleanse the language of free-speaking sources before putting their quotes into stories. They also correct grammatical errors and ignore absurd and meaningless statements that are not central to the story.

When the Canadian track star Donovan Bailey defeated the American Michael Johnson, Bailey was quoted in *The New York Times,* "He's afraid to lose. We should run this race again so I can kick his rear one more time." A reader e-mailed the newspaper to say that he had heard Bailey on Canadian TV and that Bailey had actually said, ". . . so I can kick his ass one more time." In a note to the staff, an editor wrote, "We shouldn't have changed it to 'rear.' We don't change quotes. (Since we also wouldn't want to use the word 'ass,' the proper course would have been a paraphrase.)"

On the other hand, several newspapers quoted Rep. Patricia Schroeder's response when she was asked how her congressional colleagues treat women. She replied, "A lot of men still don't know that harass isn't two words."

Use It? Fix It? or Cut It?

When an exact quote is ungrammatical and may cause the source embarrassment, do we rephrase it? Another question: Can we eliminate three or four sentences between the two that are relevant? The answers: Yes, and Yes.

"You ain't did nothing wrong," the mother was quoted in the first edition as telling her son. In the next edition, it was paraphrased: Telling her son he had done nothing wrong. . . .

When the exact quotation captures the character of the speaker, most writers let it stand. Speaking of the blues, the musician John Lee Hooker said, "Since I was a kid it's been a healing force for me. Since I was 12 years old. The blues done followed me. And I'll never get out alive."

Carol McCabe of *The Providence Journal-Bulletin* says, "I feel very strongly that it is condescending to make everyone sound as if they're speaking Standard English when they're not."

As for splicing sentences, it's OK so long as it does not change meaning.

Legal Angle

Alice Neff, a media lawyer, has these suggestions about quotations in the light of court decisions:

- If you use a tape recorder, listen to it to verify quotes.

- Corrections of grammar, syntax, stuttering and filling in explanatory words are all acceptable changes to quotations.

- It is acceptable to edit out irrelevancies and wandering.

- It is acceptable to substitute words, without changing the meaning.

- If you do make changes, consider the whole. Have you conveyed accurately what you think the person meant to say?

The Tabloid Approach

Listen to Jack Alexander of the *Weekly World News* describe his interviewing technique:

> I always tell them I'm doing a series of articles, that I'm a religious editor or a travel editor. That puts them at ease. I say I'm with *The News* in Palm Beach and I try not to say more than that. I want to put questions in (the source's) mouth, so he just says "yes" or "no." Then we will quote him as saying that. (I ask the source,) "Could this happen?" He says, "Oh yeah." Then as far as we're concerned, it did happen.

Holy Writ or Amendable?

"We regard quotations as absolutely sacrosanct. If there is any reason at all to be tempted to change them, then you take the quotation marks off and paraphrase it."

—*The New York Times*

"Quotations should be exact. The words should not be rearranged for more felicitous phrasing."

—*The Washington Post*

The magazine engages in "what is commonly known as cleaning up the quotes."

—*The New Republic*

"(W)riters and reporters by necessity alter what people say, at the very least to eliminate grammatical and syntactical infelicities. If every alteration constituted the falsity required to prove actual malice, the practice of journalism, which the First Amendment standard is designed to protect, would require a radical change, one inconsistent with our precedents and First Amendment principles."

—Justice Anthony Kennedy, U.S. Supreme Court

Sal Ivone, managing editor of the *News,* describes his paper's news policy: "If someone calls me up and says her toaster is talking to her, I don't refer her to professional help. I say, 'Put the toaster on the phone.'"

Wendy Henry, editor of the *Globe,* explains the philosophy of these newspapers: "The great thing about working here is the simplemindedness that sales are everything, and a great honesty about what sort of paper we are and who we are aiming at."

Literal Quotes

To some sources, reporters apply the whip of exact quotations. They know the validity of the statement by Arnold Gingrich, former editor in chief of *Esquire* magazine, "The cruelest thing you can do to anybody is to quote him literally."

One of the delights for the reporters covering Chicago Mayor Richard Daley was quoting him exactly as he spoke. Angry at being attacked, Daley was quoted as saying, "They have vilified me; they have crucified me—yes, they have even criticized me." And, on another occasion when he sought to inspire the citizens of his city, he said, "We will reach greater and greater platitudes of achievement."

Daley had an uneasy relationship with reporters, who frequently pointed to corruption in his administration. Once, while lecturing reporters, he said that "the policeman isn't there to create disorder; the policeman is there to preserve disorder." Reporters delighted in quoting Daley's introduction of the poet Carl Sandburg as Chicago's "poet lariat."

Chicago journalists are equal-opportunity quoters—everyone is fair game. When a candidate for mayor attacked aides of an opponent for visiting a "house of prosecution," he was quoted as he spoke. And when another candidate remarked that he would be a "drum major for education" and would "get out in front and beat the banner," he, too, was quoted as he misspoke.

Generous Journalists

Lest you conclude from all this that reporters are always intent on humiliating their sources and that you are much too compassionate to join this cut-throat company, here's evidence to the contrary:

When a politician took the microphone at a meeting to defend a fellow political candidate and said, "He is not the orgy some people think he is," reporters substituted *ogre* for *orgy*. When Sen. Dennis DeConcini of Arizona endorsed a balanced budget amendment to the Constitution at a news conference by announcing, "It's going to be a great day because we're going to finally wrestle to the ground this gigantic orgasm that is just out of control, that absolutely can't put itself together."—well, what would you have done?

Instructive No generosity was shown by a *New Yorker* writer who attended a press conference for entrants in the Miss Universe contest. Miss U.S.A. is introduced and is telling reporters that the Miss Universe contest has helped her express her feelings and widen her knowledge:

"For instance, Miss India has a red spot on her forehead. And do you know what? She says it's an Indian custom. . . .

"One of the experiences I've had was just this morning," Miss U.S.A. says. "I'm rooming with Miss South Africa, and I just saw their money. You see people, but you never realize their money was different."

The reporters try to think of another question. Finally, one of them says, "What do you think of the feminist movement?"

"Oh, I think femininity is the best thing on this earth," she says.

"What about masculinity?"

"That's just as wonderful."

Nostalgia for Tough Reporters

"Senator Christopher Dodd of Connecticut complained to me recently about the degradation in the quality of news since he first came to Washington in 1975. He said he actually longed for many of the reporters who he said used to grill him about issues because they asked questions about matters of substance.

"'Now it's give me a quote,' he said, thrusting his wine glass at me like it was a microphone. 'You've got all these reporters who don't know anything . . . ,' he complained before waxing nostalgically about reporters who understood Pentagon procurement and other issues that informed their work."

—*David Cay Johnston,* The New York Times

E-Mail Interviews

A fierce debate emerged on the journalism instructor's listserv. On one side were those defending the use of the computer to conduct an interview. Just as adamant were the no-sayers.

Yes It's handy and fast. Unlike the telephone, it provides a printed record of the interview, which is useful in capturing the precise language of the subject. Younger subjects respond more readily on the computer keyboard than on the telephone. The computer produces more thoughtful responses than the telephone. In friendly interviews, especially with features, nothing is wrong with an online interview. With technical interviews, the printed record is helpful. Stopping e-mail questioning is similar to someone trying to stop the use of telephones in a 1940 newsroom. Students need to learn all the techniques of information gathering, and sometimes an e-mail is all you will get.

No Posing questions by e-mail isn't an interview at all—it's an exchange of correspondence. You can't write "he said" for an e-mail interview. How does this sound: "Gov. James Jones wrote in an e-mail message"? How do you know who's at the other end? It isn't safe. It's OK for setting up interviews, but it doesn't provide copy that's lively and real. There's no chance to ask follow-up questions or to read facial expressions, change in voice, body language. I tell my students it is a distant third to in-person and phone interviews, an absolute last resort. A hideous trend.

A Student Speaks   "I am a journalism student, and in my (very little) experience writing for a school newspaper (*The Elm* at Washington College) I found that e-mail interviews seemed more convenient at first, but ended up getting me in more trouble than they were worth. Besides, it was better experience for me to go out and interview face to face."

Anonymous and Confidential

Sources do not always want to be identified, for a variety of reasons. The low-level official whose boss demands all material from the office go out under his name requests anonymity for the information she provides. The whistle-blower does not want to endanger his job by being identified.

The most notable example of an unknown source is Deep Throat, the informant for a considerable amount of material about Richard Nixon during his presidency. The reporters who handled the Watergate revelations, Carl Bernstein and Bob Woodward, never disclosed the identity of this key source until he identified himself in 2005.

Clear at the Outset
"... the identification of a source now is one of the opening parts of the negotiation in a journalistic conversation. ... the first thing you say is we have to agree on how you are to be described. That's a negotiating point."
—*David Shribman,*
Washington bureau chief,
Boston Globe

Plus and Minus   The anonymous source is not accountable for the information he or she provides. Without being accountable, the source can be less than fully forthcoming, can even mislead or lie.

"No newspaper worth its name could fulfill its mission without using confidential sources," says Harry M. Rosenfeld, former editor of the *Times-Union* in Albany, N.Y. "Without them, much of the very best in journalism would not be possible. At the same time, nothing so much brings our blood to boil. We decry their use and we despair of their ubiquity."

"I don't think we ever named a source," Carl Bernstein says of his and Bob Woodward's coverage of Watergate. "Because it would have been impossible to pursue the story without the use of anonymous sources."

Joel Kramer, executive editor of the Minneapolis *Star Tribune,* says, "Anonymous sources are like fireworks. Used properly, they can produce a spectacular display. But they can also explode in one's pocket."

USA Today will not use such sources: "Unidentified sources are not acceptable at *USA Today*," a policy memo states. Michael Gartner, editor of the *Ames Daily Tribune* in Iowa and former president of NBC News in New York, worries that "the anonymous source is taking over journalism. It's a lousy trend that is eroding the credibility of newspapers and adding to the unresponsibility of newspapers."

Some Guides

- Use of anonymous and confidential sources should be avoided if at all possible.

- Sources should be told exactly what is being promised them in terms of anonymity or confidentiality.

- Anonymous sources should not be used to criticize a person's character or credibility. The exception is rare, and then only with the permission of the editor.

- An anonymous source should be told that although his or her name will not appear, the reporter is obligated to give the source's name to the editor.

Summing Up

A pleasant appearance, a neutral first question, a willingness to listen usually put an interviewee at ease. Jules Loh of the AP says the first question he asks is, "'When were you born?' He replies, '1945.' I say, 'What date?' He says, 'October 1.' Now you pull the notebook out.

"You're getting a matter of fact. Then a couple more questions like that. This impresses the subject that you are interested in accuracy. The first thing they've heard about reporters is that they get everything wrong."

Sometimes you deliberately avoid taking notes, says Dan Wakefield, journalist, novelist and screenwriter. "If people were saying something I thought really embarrassing I would try not to be writing because I didn't want them to see my hand moving and clam up," he says. "I would wait until they said something kind of innocuous and that's when I would write down the awful thing they said."

Studs Terkel, the master radio interviewer and author of books based on interviews, puts people at ease by saying, "'Oh yeah, that happened to me.' If I bring some of my own stuff in, maybe that person will feel more akin."

Further Reading

Capote, Truman. *In Cold Blood.* New York: New American Library, 1971.
Cole, William, ed. *The Most of A.J. Liebling.* New York: Simon & Schuster, 1963.
Fallaci, Oriana. *Interview with History.* Boston: Houghton Mifflin, 1976.
Garrett, Annette. *Interviewing: Its Principles and Methods.* New York: Family Association of America, 1982.

Kadushin, Alfred. *The Social Work Interview.* New York: Columbia University Press, 1983.

Liebling, A.J. *Just Enough Liebling: Classic Work by the Legendary New Yorker Writer.* New York: North Pointe Press, 2004.

Liebling's scope was wide. He wrote well and perceptively about food, boxing, politics in the south, World War II (he was embedded with the Army Air Corps) and was a press critic. He is credited, says *The New York Times* writer-at-large Charles McGrath, with discovering "how to turn the old-fashioned feature story into full-fledged narrative."

Mitchell, Joseph. *Up in the Old Hotel.* New York: Vintage Books, 1993.

Mitford, Jessica. *Poison Penmanship.* New York: Vintage Books, 1980.

Terkel, Studs. *Hope Dies Last: Keeping the Faith in Difficult Times.* New York: New Press, 2003.

Among the scores interviewed are residents of housing projects, civil rights workers, union activists, peace workers, teachers in tough neighborhoods. The writer Margaret Atwood says of Terkel that he is "the American interviewer par excellence: Terkel became a practiced listener. He learned how to take the measure of what he was hearing, and to assess who was saying it."

The books by Garrett and Kadushin, which are used in schools of social work, are excellent guides to interviewing. Capote's coverage of a pair of Kansas killers—their act and their trial—is a classic, as are Mitford's and Fallaci's acid-dipped writings. Liebling and Mitchell are considered among the reporters whose writing matched their interviewing skills.

Speeches, Meetings and News Conferences 16

Preview

- **Speech** stories include the name and identification of the speaker, the theme of the talk, the setting and ample quotations.
- **Meeting** stories usually begin with the major action taken. They include the purpose of the meeting, background to the major action and quotations from those who spoke.
- **News conference** stories begin with the speaker's major point unless a better lead turns up in the question-and-answer period.

Stories should include plenty of quotations. "The story always matches the nature of the event," editors tell their reporters.

Bob Thayer, *The Providence Journal*
Watch the gestures, the mannerisms.

Speeches

"Ours is not to wonder why but to cover the speech or die," the reporter muttered as he put on his overcoat and stepped into the cold for a three-block walk to a downtown hotel where a testimonial dinner for the mayor was to be held. "I'll bet it's creamed chicken again," he said to himself.

The reporter's exasperation was caused as much by the fare he thought the speaker would offer as by the menu. But this was a slow news day, his editor had told him.

Realizing that not every speech can be covered, speakers and organizations deliver a prepared text to the newspaper and station ahead of time so that the story can be written in the office. (The reporter inserts the phrase, "In a speech prepared for delivery tonight . . ." or something similar.)

Speeches by prominent people are usually covered, whatever the subject. Nothing could have been more mundane than the testimonial dinner set for Betty Ford, wife of President Ford, at the New York Hilton one warm June evening. She was

Good quotes up high.

to be honored at the dinner launching a $6 million fund drive for an American Bicentennial Park in Israel. Her remarks were expected to be routine. Indeed, as the evening wore on, reporters became restless. A few of them left, asking those who remained to cover for them should anything unusual turn up.

Naturally, the unusual did occur, and it was front-page news in newspapers and a major item on evening newscasts. As Mrs. Ford was being introduced, the president of the Jewish National Fund of America, who had just finished speaking, slumped in his chair at the head table. In the confusion, Mrs. Ford went to the microphone and spoke to the stunned guests: "Can we bow our heads for a moment and say a prayer for Rabbi Sage," she said. The New York *Daily News* began its story this way:

> First lady Betty Ford led a stunned benefit dinner audience in prayer at the New York Hilton last night for a Zionist leader who collapsed at the affair honoring Mrs. Ford, and died of an apparent heart attack at a hospital a short time later.

Checklist: The Speech Story

The speech story includes:

- What was said: speaker's main point.

- Who spoke: name and identification.

- The setting or circumstances of the speech.

- Any unusual occurrence.

Any of these can provide the lead and theme of the story, although most speech stories emphasize what was said. Itabari Njeri of *The Greenville* (S.C.) *News* began her story with a delayed lead and moved to the speaker's main point in the second paragraph:

The three greatest lies, according to Dr. Eula Bingham, assistant secretary of labor: "The check is in the mail; Darling, I haven't looked at another woman in 27 years; and, I'm from the government and I'm here to help you."

The punchline got the desired laugh. But Dr. Bingham, who also directs the Labor Department's Occupational Safety and Health Administration, said she really is trying to help business and labor by eliminating or streamlining unnecessary government health and safety regulations.

Addressing the annual spring meeting of the South Carolina Occupational Safety Council, the former college professor and zoologist said: "We are attempting to revamp regulations that are burdensome and not meaningful. Our mandate is to protect the health, life and limb of working men and women. We are not interested in harassing or catching anybody."

Locate the Theme   A tip-off to the theme may be the title of the speech. Some speakers use forensic devices to drive home their major points—pounding the podium, raising the voice, suddenly slowing down the delivery. The main point may be in the summary at the end.

When the reporter is unsure of the theme, it makes sense to interview the speaker after the talk. When combining material from a speech and an interview, the journalist should tell the reader or listener where the information came from. Otherwise, those who attended the speech or heard it on radio or television will find the story puzzling.

Occasionally, a reporter will find a lead in what the speaker considers a secondary theme. Then, the reporter should lead with what he or she considers the more important element but summarize high in the story what the speaker considers the major theme.

For example, the president of a large investment firm is speaking to a local civic club about the role of the small investor. The morning papers have a story from New York about a sudden selling wave on the stock exchange late yesterday that sent prices tumbling. The speaker sticks to his subject that noon but in a digression predicts that the bottom of the market has not been reached. Obviously, the lead is his prediction of a continued decline. The reporter will probably want to ask the speaker after his talk for his comments on the market decline to give still more information to readers about his newsworthy prediction.

A speech consists of spoken words. So must the story. Unless there is an incident during the talk that would make the circumstances and the setting the most newsworthy item, the story will emphasize what was said with ample quotations at the top of the story. Resist the quote lead unless there is a highly unusual statement.

Tough to Handle

Now and then a reporter sits through an incoherent speech in which illogic and vagueness prevail. What should he or she do—confuse the reader with an accurate account? The reader will only blame the reporter.

The reporter should seek out the speaker and attempt to clarify the confused points. If these tactics fail, the only recourse is to write a brief story.

John R. Hunt, who turned from prospecting in the wilds of northwestern Quebec to newspapering, has been covering the North country of Ontario for the *North Bay Nugget* for more than 40 years. "As a small-town newspaperman, I have covered hundreds of speeches," Hunt says. "It is an interesting fact that a dull and boring speech can often become an interesting story. But I don't know of anything more difficult to write about than a funny speech." The best tactic is to use plenty of quotations and hope the humor carries through.

Off-the-Record

Reporters have the right to be present at an official, public meeting and can use anything they see and hear there. They have no legal right to attend a meeting or talk by a private group, and they must leave if asked. But the reporter can report

Washington Post on Private Meetings
In a gathering of a private organization, where the reporter is present as a reporter and guest, he or she must protest any attempt by the speaker to go off-the-record. The reporter should point out that the meeting was open to the press and should declare that he or she will not be bound by the limitation.

what he or she learns from those who were there. Because some of those attending the session probably will talk to the reporter about the speech, the speaker may find the material garbled in the telling and should welcome an accurate report.

The reporter is not bound by requests for off-the-record status of any item if the request is made after the information has been disclosed.

Meetings

Meetings provide newspapers and broadcast stations with enormous amounts of news. Public bodies—school boards, city councils, legislatures, planning and zoning commissions—conduct much of their business at open meetings. Then there are the meetings of private groups—baseball club owners, the directors of corporations, protesting citizens.

On her first day as writing coach at the *Winston-Salem Journal,* Phoebe Zerwick encountered a reporter who confessed to her, "I think meetings are dull." Zerwick decided to find out the reason for this resistance and then to compile a tip sheet for "turning dull meeting stories into gems."

The Basics

At the outset of her investigation, Zerwick says she "found that reporters aren't doing some of the things that need to be done." She listed them:

Check the clips.

Obtain the agenda ahead of time.

Write out questions for interviews.

At the meeting, look for the offbeat and unusual.

Think about the people affected by a decision or policy.

In examining past stories on subjects the meeting will consider, reporters accumulate background that can put the issues in perspective. Also, the material may lead to additional sources and to people affected by an item on the meeting agenda.

A *Journal* reporter confessed to Zerwick that he missed a good story by ignoring an item on the agenda of the zoning board of adjustment. People in Boone complained about a sign advertising a flea market. The sign was in the shape of a lion, and people in Boone were angered by the size of the lion's penis.

"Not bad for a zoning story," Zerwick said.

Checklist: Meetings

The essentials of meeting stories are:

• Major business transacted: votes, decisions, adoption of policies.

• Purpose, time and location of meeting.

• Items on agenda.

- Discussion and debate. Length of session.

- Quotes from witnesses and experts.

- Comments and statements from onlookers, authorities and those affected by decision, vote or policy.

- Background.

- Unusual departures from agenda.

- Agenda for next session.

Delayed Lead   Not all meeting stories will contain every one of these items. Notice the items stressed in the first five paragraphs of this meeting story from *The Brattleboro Reformer* of Brattleboro, Vt. The reporter used a delayed lead to emphasize the unusually large number of people who turned out. The first paragraph sets the scene for the major business transacted by the town school board, which is described in the second paragraph:

Public Protests Budget Cuts in Elementary Programs

By Gretchen Becker

Nearly 300 people came to an emotional Brattleboro Town School Board meeting at Green Street School Tuesday night to protest proposed cuts in the elementary school art, music, and physical education programs.

Purpose
Day
Location

Caught between the strong public opinion at the meeting not to make these cuts and a strong Town Meeting mandate to cut 5 percent from their budget, the school directors reluctantly approved almost $35,000 in budget reductions.

Major business transacted

Approved were elimination of the elementary art instructor's position, the second physical education position, a part-time vocal instructor's position, the fifth and sixth grade basketball program, and rental of space at Centre Church.

The board took no action on the administration's proposals to eliminate the instrumental music position and the part-time principal's position at Canal Street School. Approval of these cuts would have brought the total cuts to $46,000.

Salary Controversy

At Town Meeting March 22, the representatives voted to cut 5 percent, or $74,200, from the elementary budget. Those urging the cuts requested that teachers' salaries be frozen. However, WSESU Superintendent James Cusick has noted several times that the proposed budget included only $25,000 for increases in salaries. . . .

Background

Direct Lead   Most often, the lead will focus on the major action taken at the meeting, as in this lead:

Seating Plan
Wayne Worcester of the University of Connecticut recommends making a seating plan for covering meetings when you are unfamiliar with the participants. "Key the people to numbers, and as you take quotes and notes assign your numbers to them. When you write, refer to your seating plan."

City Councilwoman Elizabeth T. Boskin successfully persuaded council members to approve additional funds for the city police department last night.

Major action

The council had been cutting requested funds for the 2008–2009 budget because of anticipated declines in tax revenues.

Purpose of meeting

But Boskin said violent crimes had increased 18 percent last year.

"The only way to handle this is with more police officers," she said.

Amplification of major theme that includes direct quote on theme

The department had asked for a 15 percent increase in funds over the current year's allocation for hiring an additional dozen officers.

Background

The council has been making cuts in the requests of city departments and agencies ranging from 10 to 20 percent.

Boskin's plea was persuasive, and the council voted unanimously to approve the request for an additional $287,000, an increase of 14 percent.

Amplification of theme

Then the council returned to wielding the hatchet. . . .

Transition to other actions

News Conferences

The Day Book, a listing of daily events used by New York City newspapers and broadcast stations as an aid in making local assignments, carried this item one Wednesday evening:

Manhattan District Attorney Robert Morgenthau holds news conference to produce evidence that confirms existence of ancient civilization in Israel between 2000–1500 B.C., 155 Leonard Street 10:30 a.m.

To local editors, it sounded like a good yarn. Moreover, many New Yorkers feel a kinship with Israel. So, when the district attorney began his conference, half a dozen reporters and two television crews were on hand. But the story took an interesting turn.

The reporters were told that a Manhattan school teacher visiting Israel had taken a clay tablet out of the country that was found to be an antiquity. Under Israeli law, no historical objects may leave the country, and the teacher was therefore in possession of stolen property, a criminal offense.

The DA's Compassion

The district attorney had decided not to prosecute. He had worked out an arrangement between the teacher and the Israeli government. Although all of this could have been announced in a press release, a news conference was called so that the district attorney could play midwife in the delivery of an important historical tablet to an Israeli representative. The district attorney, an elected official, would appear to the public as a man of compassion and wisdom. The media would benefit as well, for the story would interest readers and viewers.

The incident illustrates the mutuality of interests that the news conference serves. It permits an individual, group or organization to reach many reporters at one time with an announcement that will receive more attention than a news release because of the photo possibilities, and it is an efficient and economical way for the media to obtain newsworthy material.

Usually, the news conference has a prescribed form. A prepared statement is read or distributed to the reporters beforehand. Then reporters ask questions.

News Briefing

County Prosecutor Brent Davis informs the media that he will charge the two boys involved in the Jonesboro, Ark., school shooting with capital murder in Juvenile Court.

AP photo by Mike Wintroath

For Release: November 20
Contact: Gerda Handler
732-7300
Ext. 603/4

Robert M. Morgenthau, District Attorney, New York County, announced today the recovery of a priceless antiquity from ancient biblical times. The object is a sherd—a fragment of a clay tablet—bearing a cuneiform inscription of unique archaeological significance.

Mr. Morgenthau today returned this antiquity, dating from between 1500 and 2000 B.C., to Amos Ganor, Acting Consul General of the State of Israel.

The sherd was originally found at the site of the archaeological excavation of the ancient city of Hazor, located about ten miles north of the Sea of Galilee in Israel.

It was removed from Israel in violation of that country's Antiquities Ordinance, which requires the finder of any antiquity to notify the Government of the discovery and afford it an opportunity to acquire the object. A complaint was filed with the District Attorney by the Government of Israel through Dr. Avraham Biran, former Director of the Department of Antiquities in Israel. An investigation was undertaken by the District Attorney which resulted in the recovery of the sherd.

The sherd records a case of litigation, conducted in the presence of the king, concerning real estate in Hazor. It is of great historical value because it confirms that the excavation, begun in 1955 near the Sea of Galilee, is the ancient city of Hazor. According to Professor Yigal Yadin, who headed a four year archaeological expedition at Hazor, the sherd is a major link in the identification of the excavation as the ancient city of Hazor, that was mentioned in the Egyptian Execration Texts of the 19th century B.C., the Annals of the Pharaohs Thut-mose III, Amen hotep II and Seti I and in several chapters of the Bible.

At the district attorney's news conference, reporters wanted to know the size of the tablet, when it was discovered, how it was recovered and other details. The news stories that appeared differed substantially from the news release.

The Story Here is how Marcia Chambers began her account that appeared in *The New York Times*. Note that some material in the lead is not contained in the handout and was obtained through questioning. Also, the story places the district attorney in the third paragraph, whereas the press release begins with the district attorney's name:

News Release
District Attorney Robert Morgenthau's news release (above) on the recovery of an antiquity by his office. Compare this with the story a reporter wrote that was based on the release and additional information provided at the news conference.

A fragment of a clay tablet 3,500 to 4,000 years old that confirms the existence of the biblical city of Hazor in Israel was returned yesterday to the Israeli Government after a teacher who smuggled it out of Israel agreed to surrender it to avoid prosecution.

The odyssey of the 2-by-2-inch fragment, with a cuneiform inscription, began last year when the young teacher was on his honeymoon. The teacher, an amateur archaeologist, found the tablet at the site of an archaeological excavation some 10 miles north of the Sea of Galilee.

It ended yesterday, at a news conference, when Robert M. Morgenthau, the Manhattan District Attorney, turned over the priceless piece to Amos Ganor, Israel's acting consul general here. . . .

Checklist: News Conferences

The essentials of news conference stories are:

- Major point of speaker.

- Name and identification of speaker.

- Purpose, time, location and length of conference.

- Background of major point.

- Major point in statement; major points in question-and-answer period.

- Consequences of announcement.

Panel Discussions

In symposia and panel discussions, the presence of several speakers can pose a problem. But experienced reporters usually make their way through the tide of talk by emphasizing a thematic approach. They will find a basic theme—often an area of agreement—and write a summary based on that theme:

> Four members of the local bar agreed last night that probation is no longer a useful means of coping with criminal offenders.
>
> Although the speakers disagreed on most matters at the symposium on "How to Handle Crime," they did agree. . . .

Disagreement   Here are two leads based on disagreements:

Space exploration can be man's salvation, a physicist said today, but an astronomer worried that man might overreach himself and pollute the universe as well as his own planet.

The disagreement was voiced at a symposium last night, on "Space Travel," sponsored by the Science Club and held in the Civic Auditorium. More than 250 people turned out, obviously drawn by the promise of hearing one of the speakers discuss Unidentified Flying Objects.

But if they came expecting to hear a defense of UFO's they were disappointed, for Dr. Marcel Pannel said flatly, "They do not exist."

Bob Thayer,
The Providence Journal

"No Way"

Opposition can be made the theme of a panel discussion story as well as agreement. Opposition, in fact, is usually intense, whereas agreement is routine, tepid, neutral.

The above lead works because only two speakers are involved. The following summary lead was used because several speakers were involved:

There was no accord at the College Auditorium last night as four faculty members discussed "Discord in the Middle East."

The political scientists and historians disagreed on the causes of unrest in that troubled area, and they disagreed on solutions.

All they agreed upon was that the situation is thorny.

"We really don't know whether peace will break out tomorrow, or continued conflict is in the offing," said Professor Walter. . . .

After the theme is developed for a few paragraphs, each speaker is given his or her say. Obviously, the more newsworthy statements come first.

Singled Out   When one speaker says something clearly more interesting and significant than what the others are discussing, the newsworthy statement is the lead rather than a general theme. Here is how such a story runs:

A California research team may have found a potent opponent of the virus that causes the common cold sore.

The information was disclosed today at a discussion of bioscientists and physicians at the School of Public Health on the campus.

Dr. Douglas Deag, a naval biochemist, said that the enemy of the herpes simplex virus (types 1 and 2) may well be the popular seafood delicacy, seaweed. The red variety—known as Rhodophyta—contains a species that has an active agent that prevents the herpes virus from multiplying.

Herpes is responsible for keratitis—a severe eye infection—and a genital disease as well as the cold sore. But the research is in the early stages, Dr. Deag said.

He was one of five speakers who discussed "Frontiers of Medicine," which was concerned primarily with careers in the medical sciences. . . .

Summing Up

Here's a guide to establishing a procedure for covering speeches, news conferences and panel discussions:

1. Find the **subject.** The title is an indicator.

2. Determine the **purpose.** Generally, the speaker will be trying to report, explain or persuade, perhaps all three.

3. Locate the **main idea.** Here we get to the specific point that will constitute your lead.

4. Gather the **evidence** used to prove the point. This provides the body of the story.

Remember: These stories are based on spoken words. Your story should include plenty of quotations. The story always matches the nature of the event.

Also, show up early. That's the best way to talk to participants, to get a sense of what will follow.

Preview

Reporters rely on their hunches and feelings as well as rational, disciplined thinking:

- Hunches and intuition spring from the interaction of new information with the reporter's accumulated knowledge.
- Feelings and emotions can motivate the reporter to seek out systemic abuses and illegalities.

But hunches and feelings can distort reporting, as can a reporter's stereotypes. Reporters regularly check to see whether they have gender, racial, or religious stereotypes in their stories.

John Walker, *The Fresno Bee*
Compassion can lead to revealing stories.

Reporters go about their work in a rational, almost scientific manner. They cover events with detachment, weigh their observations against their general knowledge and the background of the event and then draw logical conclusions. Then they reconstruct these observations in objective stories.

Analysis and synthesis, the application of reason to experience—these are the processes that underlie the journalist's work.

Yet, this summary is misleading. It ignores hunches and intuition and emotional reactions that include feelings such as prejudice, hatred, friendship and love. "Our thought processes are only partially based on logic, and are inextricably mixed with emotions and desires and social interactions," says Freeman Dyson of the Institute for Advanced Study in Princeton.

Hunches and Intuition

Every reporter has had the experience on assignment of sensing the meaning of an event, of suddenly seeing through the thicket of details to the underlying concept

Follow your hunches and your hormones.

that shapes the event. Some reporters seem to possess an extrasensory perception that enables them to detect the real story, the actuality that lies beneath surface details. "I can smell something a mile away. It's just a fact of life," says Seymour Hersh, whose stories of the My Lai massacre by U.S. troops in Vietnam and brutalities inflicted on Iraqi prisoners by U. S. soldiers revealed the underside of these wars.

Hunches, guesswork and intuition come into play as soon as the reporter is given an assignment. Before leaving the newsroom, before gathering information, the reporter has feelings and insights about the story, and these suggest the reporter's coverage of the event.

There is nothing wrong with this. These intuitive concepts are sound starting points for reporting. "Feelings are not only reasonable but are also as discriminating and as consistent as thinking," said the psychiatrist Carl Jung. Even in that most rigorous of pursuits, science, bursts of insight open the pathways to discoveries. Karl Popper, a philosopher with enormous impact in science, said that scientific ideas are the products of human creativity and not, as commonly thought, the result of arduous experimentation. Albert Einstein wrote approvingly of "intuition, supported by being sympathetically in touch with experience."

The Cuban Missile Crisis   Murrey Marder of *The Washington Post* glanced at the check-in book at the State Department one Saturday evening. Strange, he thought, two people from the CIA (Central Intelligence Agency) had just checked in. On a Saturday night? Marder had a hunch: A crisis was at hand. But where?

He noticed the only lights on that late were in the Latin American Bureau and the Bureau of International Organization Affairs. As he raced around the building, Marder came upon Harlan Cleveland, who was attached to the International Bureau. Katherine Graham, publisher of the *Post,* recalls what happened:

> Marder had to think quickly of a question that might elicit a useful answer, which an open-ended one like, "What's going on?" clearly would not. So he asked, "How bad does it look to you, Harlan?" to which Cleveland replied, "Well, pretty bad."
>
> Marder felt he was on to something big. But what? He knew the United States was at sword's point with Cuba, then on intimate terms with the Soviet Union. Marder had his question. It was about "this Cuban thing," whether the administration was confronting Cuba. Cleveland responded, "I think we are."
>
> With a little more checking, Marder had an exclusive story—the onset of what was to become the Cuban Missile Crisis.

The Kennedy Assassination   In the turmoil minutes after President Kennedy was struck down in Dallas, reporters heard rumors they had little time to check. They had to make quick decisions. Tom Wicker of *The New York Times* said he had to set these reports against what he knew about the people supplying the information, what he knew about human behavior, what two isolated facts added up to—above all on what he felt in his "bones."

In looking back on his on-the-scene coverage, Wicker said, "I see that it was a hard story to put together, but at the time you really didn't have much time to think about what you were doing. You just had to do what you could do.

"In a crisis, if a reporter can't trust his instinct for truth, he can't trust anything."

The Process
Thomas Griffith, former editor of *Time,* describes the thinking process of reporters as "conjecture subject to verification."

The Agnew Payoffs   Jerry Landauer, a superb investigative reporter for *The Wall Street Journal,* had a gut feeling when he first saw Spiro Agnew, the governor of Maryland, then being nominated for vice president:

> There was something too tanned, too manicured, too tailored for the guy to have been living on a governor's salary, with no other known source of income. So I started going down to Towson, seat of Baltimore County, the bedroom community where Agnew got his political start; talked to lawyers who frequently appeared to be on the losing side of zoning cases, to engineers who didn't seem to be getting a fair share of state business. After a couple of visits some started talking.

Landauer found out Agnew was receiving payoffs.

Hunches Develop from Experience

We have watched four reporters develop big stories from feelings, hunches, intuition. But if we look closely at their reporting another pattern emerges. Marder and Landauer noticed a break in the normal, the expected, the routine. Wicker had experience with the people he was interviewing, and Hersh had learned that official versions cover up untidy and embarrassing truths.

In other words, experience and prior knowledge provided them with the mind set or memory to put the new material in perspective. They built the new on a foundation of the old, what they already had experienced, what they knew.

What seem to be intuition, hunches and luck is the crystallization of what is already known, a leap from the reporter's storehouse of knowledge to a higher plane of insight. A new situation, fact, observation or statement suddenly fuses with material from the storehouse.

In a review of R.A. Ochse's *Before the Gates of Excellence: The Determinants of Creative Genius,* Mary L. Tenopyr, testing director of AT&T, wrote of intuitive breakthroughs: "Nothing that was not already in the creator's mind comes forth, but what is produced is old information put to a new use or configured differently than it was before."

Reporters store thousands of facts about people, events, policies and the many incidents of their daily experience. This vast storehouse is organized subconsciously. When a new piece of information strikes the reporter as important, it triggers the subconscious into releasing related material.

Hunches and instinct usually work for the good reporters, rarely for the lazy or the talentless.

Gretzky's Genius   Ability plus practice and experience equals excellence in all fields. During the 1982 hockey season, a talented young center for the Edmonton Oilers set records no one thought possible. Wayne Gretzky had fans comparing his feats with those in other sports. His goals, 82, and his assists, 120, for the season were the equivalent of a .425 batting average in baseball, 55 points a game over a basketball season, 3,000 yards gained in a season of professional football.

Pure instinct, said those who watched him. Not so, says Gretzky.

Useful Memories
Marilla Svinicki, director of the Center for Teaching Effectiveness at the University of Texas, says, "When new information gets hooked up with a particularly rich and well-organized portion of memory, it inherits all the connections that already exist." The result is a jump to a higher plane of knowledge, she says.

Making Connections
"Human intelligence is not just knowing more, but reworking, recategorizing, and thus generalizing information in and new and surprising ways."
—*Israel Rosenfeld*

Still Better

Four years later, Gretzky did even better, breaking his 202-point total with 215 on 52 goals and 163 assists. Still later, he became the first National Hockey League player to record 2,500 points.

"Nine out of ten people think my talent is instinct," he said. "It isn't. It's all practice. I got it all from my dad."

When Gretzky was a 3-year-old in Brantford, Ontario, his father iced down the backyard and had the youngster practicing. At the age of 10 he was skating five hours a day.

Reporters make use of this same combination of talent, hard work and experience. The reporters who rarely develop good stories attribute the success of their colleagues to luck. It doesn't work that way. "Luck is what happens when preparation meets opportunity," says Raymond Berry, a former coach of the New England Patriots.

Awed by a technological society in which computers and data processing machinery seem to minimize human ability, reporters should retain their faith in their own reasoning. "The largest computer now in existence lacks the richness and flexibility in the brain of a single honeybee," writes Peter Sterling, a brain researcher at the University of Pennsylvania Medical School.

Einstein's Model for Thinking

This diagram is a way of looking at the kind of thinking we have been describing.

Albert Einstein drew this diagram for a friend who asked the famous physicist to explain the roles of experience, intuition and logic in making discoveries or in formulating a theory. Einstein did not limit his ideas about thinking to science. The "whole of science is nothing more than a refinement of everyday thinking," he said.

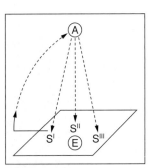

Everyday Thinking

Scientist or shopkeeper, mechanic or journalist . . . we all think this way, making the leap to some conclusion from our experiences. Einstein said the leap follows no logic, "only intuition." The more diverse the experience, the more insightful the theory or hunch for a story.

Einstein's diagram shows a cyclical process. The process begins and ends at **E,** of which Einstein says, "The **E** (experiences) are given to us." **E** represents the range of sense experiences and observations that Einstein referred to as a "labyrinth of sense impressions," a "chaotic diversity."

Intuitive Leap   Out of this plane of experiences a curved line rises toward **A** at the top of the model. This leap is the intuitive reach of the thinker, the reporter's hunch, the scientist's sudden breakthrough.

"**A** are the axioms from which we draw consequences," Einstein said. "Psychologically, the **A** are based upon the **E**. There is, however, no logical path from the **E** to the **A**, but only an intuitive (psychological) connection, which is always subject to revocation."

In his first paper on relativity, Einstein referred sketchily to some experiments and then wrote that they "lead to the conjecture," which he called the Theory of Relativity. "There is no logical path to these elementary laws; only intuition, supported by being sympathetically in touch with experience."

In the diagram, lines lead downward from **A** to **S′, S″, S‴**. These are deductions from the central idea, and they can be tested in the plane of experience.

This model and Einstein's concepts are useful to the journalist, for they illustrate the reportorial process. Reporters develop ideas, **A,** based on their experiences, observations and readings symbolized by **E.** From **A,** reporters draw consequences, **S′, S″, S‴**—which we can call tentative leads or story ideas. These leads or themes are the basis of reporting, which is the validating or disproving of the leads in the plane of experience, **E.**

This discussion of Einstein's theory about thinking may seem theoretical to you. The fact is that reporters apply it often. Look at how Marder developed his exclusive story about the sudden worsening in U.S.–Cuban relations.

He made the leap to **A** from his experiences, **E,** as a State Department reporter: the unusual Saturday night meeting; the fact that it was taking place in the Latin American Bureau; his knowledge that relations between the two countries were strained.

Once he concluded that the meetings might involve Cuba, he devised a story lead, **S′,** that the situation had become serious. He tested this idea or story theme by asking an official questions based on his theory. The replies confirmed Marder's hunch.

Feelings

Reporters welcome their hunches and intuitive guesses, but they are less cordial toward their feelings—that uncontrollable emotion that can hold us captive without warning, lift us to ecstasy at a glance or a touch and plunge us to bleakest despair from a word or a gesture.

This wilderness of feeling frightens most people, and it terrifies those who depend on their rationality, as reporters do. But reporters are human and must function within the limitations of the rationality of human behavior.

Feelings, in fact, can be an asset. "How can you write if you can't cry?" asked Ring Lardner. The poet Robert Frost commented, "No tears in the writer, no tears in the reader." Feelings help us develop value systems and keep them nourished. Moral indignation can direct a reporter to crowning achievements. The muckrakers, whose journalism was the supreme journalistic achievement in the last century, were propelled by a monumental moral indignation. Anyone who reads their work can sense the intensity of feeling behind it.

The Library of Congress

Ida Tarbell

One of the band of muckrakers who exposed the monopolistic practices of big business, Tarbell revealed the ruthless drive to power of John D. Rockefeller and his Standard Oil Company. She and Lincoln Steffens ran *American* magazine from 1906 to 1915 and attacked municipal and federal corruption and the robber barons of industry.

Exploited Women One muckraker wrote of a girl of 17 who had been working in department stores for three and a half years. Uneducated, from a poor family, the girl worked at a New York City department store "at a wage of $2.62 1/2 a week; that is to say, she was paid $5.25 twice a month. Her working day was nine and a half hours long through most of the year. But during two weeks before Christmas it was lengthened from twelve to thirteen and a half hours, without any extra payment in any form. . . ."

Rheta Childe Doar described maids' quarters that consisted of a den partitioned off from the coal bin; a maid's bed that consisted of an ironing board placed over a bathtub. Maids were rarely let out of the houses in which they worked.

Boys in the Coal Pits

Mary Alden Hopkins described unsafe factories in which women worked . . . and died. In Newark, N.J., 25 young women died when a fire broke out in a factory. Some leaped out of their top-floor workplace. Some stayed and died. "They lost their lives because they worked in a building that was not decently safe for human beings to work in," wrote Hopkins. She said there were at least 100 more unsafe factories in Newark, some without fire escapes.

Child Labor   The exploitation of child labor was another theme of the muckrakers. Edwin Markham wrote in *Cosmopolitan* of Helen Sisscak, who worked in the silk mills in Pennsylvania, "a girl of eleven who had for a year worked nights in the mill, beginning at half-past six in the evening and staying till half-past six in the morning. Haggard, hungry, and faint after the night's work shifting and cleaning the bobbins, this child had an hour's walk in the chill of the morning over the lonesome fields to her home." Her pay: three cents an hour.

Then there was Annie Dinke, a silk-twister, 13, who worked on her feet 13 hours, and Theresa McDermott, 11, whose wage was $2 a week.

John Spargo wrote in *Bitter Cry of the Children* of the 12- and 13-year-olds who worked for 50 and 60 cents a day in West Virginia coal mines:

> Crouched over the chutes, the boys sit hour after hour, picking out the pieces of slate and other refuse from the coal as it rushes past the washers. From the cramped position they have to assume most of them become more or less deformed and bent-backed like old men. . . . The coal is hard and accidents to the hands, such as cut, broken, or crushed fingers, are common among the boys. Sometimes there is a worse accident; a terrified shriek is heard, and a boy is mangled and torn in the machinery or disappears in the chute to be picked out later, smothered and dead.

This strong emotional reaction to the abuses of power by public officials and the titans of commerce and industry propels investigative reporters to their discoveries. The Teapot Dome scandal was exposed by a reporter for the *St. Louis Post-Dispatch* who spent years gathering evidence to prove that powerful oil interests had bribed the secretary of the interior in the Harding administration. The reporter, Paul Y. Anderson, was driven throughout his journalistic career by the need to expose wrongdoers.

Today's Crusaders

These feelings—compassion, indignation at injustice, the need to right wrongs—constitute a powerful, continuing force in journalism. Look at the photograph that opens this chapter and the one on the left. The photos are from a series in *The Fresno Bee* titled "Children: The Forgotten Farmworkers." The photograph that opens the chapter shows Melissa Hernandez collecting onions in the field for her parents who cut off the tops. Melissa is 4 years old. On this page, Aida Cruz Sanchez, hardly more than a child herself, is left at the migrant labor camp to care for her 10-month-old brother while her parents work in the fields.

Alex Pulaski, who wrote the articles, describes the children he has watched working in the fields as "part of a work force intentionally ignored by federal

**Baby Sitter—
A Child Herself**

lawmakers, who have carved out exemptions for agriculture. They allow children to labor in the fields at a younger age, in more hazardous jobs and for longer hours than their counterparts at fast-food outlets, retail stores and nearly every other business."

Pulaski estimates that 100,000 children "labor illegally in U.S. fields, forgotten because their sweat keeps down the price of the raisins, chilies and pickles we buy at the grocery store." These children work "in the cucumber fields of Ohio, the chili fields of New Mexico and the onion fields of Oregon and Idaho." Melissa was photographed in an onion field near Ontario, Ore.

Auditing Feelings

Despite the usefulness of strong feelings, the reporter is wise to check his or her emotions every so often, for they can distort observations and impede the processes of analysis and synthesis that are the foundation of reporting and writing.

A city hall reporter who finds the personal lifestyle and ideas of a councilwoman abhorrent may discover he is looking only for negative facts about her. A political reporter whose personal allegiance is to the Democratic Party may find she is overly critical of the Republican Party and its leaders. The idea of welfare payments to the able-bodied poor—or subsidies to farmers—might so violate a reporter's convictions that his coverage is distorted.

Cautions   Reporters cannot be neutral about life. Nor should they be. Enthusiasms, feelings, generalizations can be useful, as we have seen. But reactions that swing to an extreme should be examined carefully for their causes. Reporters must watch for uncritical enthusiasm and unreasonable hostility.

Some reactions may be based on what the semanticists call "short-circuited responses," ideas that burst forth without thought. A reporter may be positive about doctors or judges and negative about salespeople or stockbrokers without distinguishing among the individuals in these groups. This kind of thinking is known as *stereotyping,* a dangerous way to think, particularly for a reporter.

Stereotypes, Biases, Fears

We like to think that we are reasonable, modern folk. We make decisions on the basis of the evidence, physical proof. Yet, what are we to make of the fact that while viewing the same television programs, reading the same newspaper accounts of the O.J. Simpson civil trial, 74 percent of white Americans agreed with the civil court verdict that held Simpson liable for murdering his wife and her friend, whereas only 23 percent of black Americans agreed with the verdict?

The fact is that we carry with us attitudes, assumptions, biases, fears, desires, inclinations and stereotypes from an early age. We see the world the way our parents, friends, schools and racial and religious communities have defined it for us. We are creatures of the culture that surrounds us—our jobs, the reading we do, the television programs we watch and our government and economic system.

Racism
In 1902, President Theodore Roosevelt invited Booker T. Washington to the White House and people were scandalized that a black man was being entertained by the president. Not until 1930 was another black person invited to the White House.

All these influence the way we think and how we see and hear. And the way we think, see and hear affects the accuracy of our journalism. In a famous experiment, journalism students were shown to have made more errors when they wrote stories about a report that was contrary to their biases and predispositions than they did when the report supported their feelings.

The journalist sees much of the world through lenses tinted by others. The maker of images and stereotypes, the journalist is also their victim.

Victim of Images

Since Plato's time, philosophers have speculated about how and what people see. In the "Simile of the Cave" in *The Republic,* Plato describes a cave in which people are shackled so that they can only look straight ahead at one of the walls in the cave. They cannot see themselves or each other. Outside, a fire burns, and between the fire and the cave dwellers there runs a road in front of which a curtain has been placed. Along the road are men carrying figures of men and animals made of wood, stone and other materials. The shadows that these figures cast upon the wall are all the cave dwellers can see.

"And so in every way they would believe that the shadows of the objects we mentioned were the whole truth," Socrates says of what the prisoners can see.

The parable is striking, almost eerie in its perception of image making. It takes little imagination to replace the cave with the movie theater or to visualize the shadows on the wall as the images on a television or computer screen.

Plato goes still further with his insight into how images pass for reality. He examines what happens when the prisoners are "released from their bonds and cured of their delusions." Told that what they have seen was nonsense, they would not believe those who free them. They would regard "nothing else as true but the shadows," Socrates tells us. The realities would be too dazzling, too confusing.

Shadow Reality

A woman customer of a dating service that uses videotapes tells this story: She was reading the biographies of men in the service's reading room when she saw a young man who obviously was the man she was reading about. He seemed eminently suited for a young woman also in the room, and the older woman whispered to the young man that he ought to introduce himself to the young woman. He did, and he spoke to the young woman for some time. When he suggested a date, she replied, "Oh no. Not until I see your videotape."

The Seduction of Stereotypes

Now let us jump ahead some 2,250 years to the speculations of Walter Lippmann, whose classic description of how people see is contained in his book *Public Opinion.* Here is that description:

> For the most part we do not first see, and then define, we define first and then see. In the great blooming, buzzing confusion of the outer world we pick out what our culture has already defined for us, and we tend to perceive that which we have picked out in the form stereotyped for us by our culture.

Lippmann says that the "attempt to see all things freshly and in detail rather than as types and generalities is exhausting. . . ." Stereotypes allow us to fit individuals into categories defined for us, categories that are comfortable because they save time in a busy life and defend our position in society, Lippmann says. They also "preserve us from all the bewildering effects of trying to see the world steadily and see it whole," he writes.

But the reporter must try to see the world steadily and see it whole. When a student movie reviewer at Barnard College saw a film made by Luis Buñuel, she wrote in amazement, "How Buñuel at age 70 can still direct such marvelous, memorable, intelligent and worthwhile films is beyond me." Her comment illustrates one of the stereotypes common to youth, the belief that with age comes decrepitude. Stereotypes are held by every age group, by religious groups, nationalities and the sexes.

Racial, Religious Stereotyping

The most persistent stereotyping in the United States has been directed at women, at Jews, African Americans, Native Americans and Spanish-speaking people. Newspapers and broadcast stations have lent themselves to this stereotyping.

In the 1900s when mass migration brought many Jews to the United States, anti-Semitism spread rapidly, and newspapers were no deterrent. It was not unusual to see a criminal suspect described as a Jew or Jewish. "Jew banker" and "Jew peddler" were common descriptions, as was "Jew store." Bargaining was known as "Jewing down."

This persistent stereotyping had tangible consequences. In 1942, during World War II, a public opinion poll asked which groups menace the country most. Jews were third, just behind Germans and Japanese. Hotels and restricted neighborhoods carried signs, "No Jews or dogs allowed."

The media no longer set Jews apart in derogatory fashion, but other minorities contend they are stereotyped. Jesse Jackson accused the media of projecting black people in "five deadly ways every day. It projects us as less intelligent than we are, as less hard-working than we are, as less patriotic than we are, as less universal than we are, as more violent than we are."

Native Americans

"If Indians want to get the media's attention, they should focus on issues much more important than whether a team has an Indian for a mascot or over a beer named Crazy Horse." The advice stunned the audience of Native Americans. It was offered by the host of a major television network news show at a conference on the American Indian and the media.

The advice, well meaning though it may have been, revealed the insensitivity of whites to the feelings and frustrations of minority groups, in this case Native Americans.

"It has to do with self-esteem," said Tim Giago, then publisher of *Indian Country Today,* a national weekly published in Rapid City, S.D. "It has to do with children growing up believing they are better than mascots." Crazy Horse, Giago said, is a spiritual leader of the Lakota.

"What would happen if this company named a beer Martin Luther King Jr. malt liquor?" Giago asked. He went on, "Sure, there are more important issues facing us, but if we can't be treated as human beings in the small things, we will

---

Give the Relevance
The New York Times stylebook on mention of race, religion or ethnicity states:

> Race should be specified only if it is truly pertinent. The same stricture applies to ethnic and religious identifications.

Since that guideline was established, the newspaper has added another rule: The relevance of race, religion or ethnicity must be made explicit in the article itself.

never be heard when it comes to the big things." Giago concluded his newspaper column with this warning:

"Like the blacks who were forced to sit in the back of the bus, we will no longer serve as mascots for the sports fanatics of this nation. We refuse to move to the back of the bus anymore."

Success   Some protests have paid off. Colgate University, whose nickname was the Red Raiders, dropped "Red," which is considered offensive to Native Americans. In Minneapolis, the *Star Tribune* does not use nicknames for American Indians in its sports reporting, replacing Braves, Chiefs, Tribe, Skins and others with the city or another suitable identifier.

Sexism

One of the most persistent stereotypings has been that of women. They have been seen as emotional and dependent, whereas men are stoic and self-sufficient. They have been accused of being intellectually inferior.

Jeanette Rankin, the first woman elected to Congress, voted against the United States entering World War I, which led *The New York Times* to comment that her vote was the "final proof of feminine incapacity for straight reasoning."

That same year, 1917, the *Times* was upset when suffragettes picketed the White House for the right to vote. The *Times* described the women's picketing as "monstrous." The women were arrested and jailed for six months without trial.

Those days are past, but sexism persists in some ways, one of them in media writing that identifies women through their relationships with men. Our language itself often reflects male-centered thinking. The column on the left contains what is considered to be sexist language. The column on the right contains nonsexist forms:

Sexist	*Nonsexist*
man and wife	husband and wife
men and ladies	men and women
Jack Parsons and Ms. (Miss, Mrs.) Burgess	Jack Parsons and Joan Burgess
Parsons and Joan	Jack and Joan (or) Parsons and Burgess

Gay and Lesbian Stereotyping

Some of the most pervasive stereotyping has been directed at the gay and lesbian community. The Gay and Lesbian Alliance Against Defamation (GLAAD) made the media a "major target of gay activists because of the often derogatory images of gays and lesbians in mainstream media content," says Jack Banks of the University of Hartford. "These activists charge that such portrayals have nurtured homophobic attitudes in society at large and fostered self-loathing by gays and lesbians."

Historical Notes

In 1873, the Supreme Court ruled that a woman was not constitutionally entitled to practice law. The opinion of Justice Joseph B. Bradley stated, "The natural and proper timidity and delicacy which belongs to the female sex evidently unfits it for many of the occupations of civil life. The paramount destiny and mission of women are to fulfill the noble and benign office of wife and mother. This is the law of the Creator."

Despite the prejudice against hiring women as reporters and editors, the media had to bend because of the manpower shortage during World War II. One of those hired by the United Press was Priscilla Buckley, who recalls that when she was promoted to the sports desk, "I was never to mention it to anyone. My copy, even the nightly feature story, was unsigned. If anyone called for a clarification I was instructed to have a copy boy take the call."

GLAAD and other organizations conferred with TV producers and movie-makers, conducted letter-writing campaigns, sit-ins and boycotts. This activism has been fairly successful, but stereotyping surfaced during the discussion about legalizing gay marriage.

Substitutes for Observation

A news story grows out of the interaction between reporters and events. If reporters see the event in prefixed forms, they will prejudge the event, making it conform to the stereotyped pictures they carry. Robert L. Heilbroner describes an experiment performed with college students that shows how powerful these pictures can be. The students were shown "30 photographs of pretty but unidentified girls, and asked to rate each in terms of 'general liking, intelligence, beauty' and so on," Heilbroner says.

"Two months later," he continues, "the same group were shown the same photographs, this time with fictitious Irish, Italian, Jewish and 'American' names attached to the pictures. Right away the ratings changed. Faces which were now seen as representing a national and religious group went down in looks and still farther down in likability, while the 'American' girls suddenly looked decidedly prettier and nicer."

Stereotypes are, as the semanticist S.I. Hayakawa points out, "substitutes for observation."

Journalists who settle for stereotyped responses to events might heed the warning of F. Scott Fitzgerald: "Begin with an individual and before you know it you have created a type; begin with a type and you have created—nothing."

Patterns and Relationships

John Dewey said that "the striving to make stability of meaning prevail over the instability of events is the main task of intelligent human effort." These meanings are the patterns that establish relationships among facts and events. The great journalist of the muckraking period, Lincoln Steffens, said that his thinking about reporting was transformed by a prosecuting attorney during his investigation into municipal corruption in St. Louis.

"He was sweeping all his cases of bribery together to form a truth out of his facts," Steffens wrote later. "He was generalizing . . . he was thinking about them all together and seeing what they meant all together." Steffens said that this thinking led the prosecutor to conclude that the corruption was systemic.

Or, as the poet Robert Frost put it, thinking "is just putting this and that together."

Causal Relationships

The causal relationship is one of the most common patterns we form. The first state-by-state comparison of how public schoolchildren do on national tests

At the Movies
Scene from the 1939 movie *Torchy Blane* in which Glenda Farrell plays a newspaperwoman, Torchy Blane. She and a police detective are sitting in a car:

Detective—You Wait here. This rat hole is no place for a woman.
Torchy—But I'm a newspaperwoman.
Detective—You just sit quietly and maybe nobody will notice it.

Cause and Effect
In a traffic fatality roundup in a San Francisco newspaper, the reporter made clear the causal relationship:
Ten lives in 10 hours. Such was the appalling toll yesterday of two head-on crashes that chalked up the grimmest period in Bay Area traffic history.
Not one person in the four cars involved survived. An entire family of five was snuffed out. That family, and a sixth individual, were innocent victims.
Speed was the killer. And liquor a confederate.
Three died in an explosive, flaming smashup on the Bay Bridge at 11:40 p.m. yesterday. The killer car was going 90 miles an hour.
Just 10 hours earlier, at 1:40 p.m., seven met death in a jarring smackup. . . .

showed that only one in seven eighth graders is proficient in mathematics. Why? Authorities said the data showed:

> The states whose students had the best performances are also states with the lowest proportion of families headed by single parents.
>
> Students with the worst performances came from southeastern states where poverty is high and from states with large, disadvantaged urban areas.
>
> The top 10 states in student performance were also the 10 lowest-ranked states in the percentage of students who reported watching more than six hours of television a night.

Here we have to be careful. Just because a situation occurs before or in tandem with an event does not qualify the situation as the cause of the event. Scientists worry about ozone depletion in the atmosphere, but they don't think beer consumption is the cause although it has been shown that the decline in the ozone parallels the increase in beer drinking.

Make the Connection When a reporter has the necessary information, he or she should be willing to state the possibility of a causal relationship. When Gov. Mike Huckabee overruled a ban on smoking in restaurants voted by the Arkansas health board, reporters included in their stories that "Huckabee, a nonsmoker, has received tobacco industry campaign contributions." Reporters for the *Minneapolis Star Tribune* found that the milk producers lobby had channeled hundreds of thousands of dollars into the Republican Party treasury through dummy committees. Following these contributions, the reporters wrote, the White House decided to increase milk support prices.

There was no absolute proof that the contributions had caused the policy decisions. But the reporters decided that the suggestion of a causal relationship was legitimate.

In the obituaries of Joe Pyne, a television and radio talk show host, and Hal March, a master of ceremonies on television quiz shows, *The New York Times* reported the men died of lung cancer. Then the stories noted that Pyne had been a "heavy smoker" and that "Mr. March had smoked two packs of cigarettes a day for many years." There was no proof their cigarette smoking had caused their cancer, but the data collected by the surgeon general's office had indicated a high probability of such a relationship, and the newspaper was willing to suggest the cause-and-effect relationship for its readers.

Making causal relationships in print or on the air represents a certain risk to the reporter, but experienced reporters know when to take risks. In fact, risk taking may be one of the marks of a successful journalist. The British mathematician G.B. Hardy remarked that high intelligence is not important to the success of most people. No one, he said, can make the most of his or her talents without constant application and without taking frequent risks.

Polar Alternatives

Another potentially dangerous line of thinking common among harried reporters is the polar alternative. For instance, the reporter may think, "Either the Black Parents Association is right or it is wrong in its stand on schoolbooks." This either-or thinking can save the reporter time and energy, but it can lead to superficial journalism.

The reporter who looks only at the extremes of situations will be limiting observations to the most obvious elements of the event. The world is hardly bilateral and the reporter should resist what is called *bilateral consciousness* by being aware of the infinite colors and shades between black and white.

Linking Facts

Navigating a multitude of facets, faces and facts is half the task. The reporter's most difficult job is to put them into some meaningful pattern, to synthesize them in a story. But that is what journalism is about—linking facts to make stories.

As we have seen, these leaps to significant relationships are launched from solid ground. They are based on experience and the logical thinking of the kind described by the philosopher Isaiah Berlin: "To comprehend and contrast and classify and arrange, to see in patterns of lesser or greater complexity is not a peculiar kind of thinking, it is thinking itself."

The technique of patterning is described by T.S. Eliot, the poet, this way: "The poet's mind is a receptacle for seizing and storing up numberless feelings, phrases, images, which remain there until all the particles which can unite to form a new compound are present together." In describing the emotion in a poem, he says it "is a concentration and a new thing resulting from the concentration, of a very great number of experiences which to the practical and active person would not seem to be experiences at all; it is a concentration which does not happen consciously or of deliberation."

There is not much difference in the ways poets and journalists think, indeed in the ways all creative people think. The ability to pattern observations and feelings is the mark of the thinking person, whether we look at a reporter covering a story or a composer at her piano.

The good reporter has what the philosopher Alfred North Whitehead describes as an "eye for the whole chessboard, for the bearing of one set of ideas on another." In his book *The Powers That Be,* David Halberstam describes "the great reporter's gifts" as "limitless energy, a fine mind, total recall and an ability to synthesize material."

Finding the Links

Reporters are always looking for facts that relate to each other. The obituary writer wants to know the cause of death, especially if the death is sudden, unexpected.

A reporter covering such a death was given the explanation—accidental gunshot wound. But the reporter wonders. The death seems staged. Could it have been a suicide? That's playing games, he says to himself. Still, the death looks like that of a character in a novel. Thinking of this sort led the reporter to dig and then to write that Ernest Hemingway had killed himself, contrary to the explanation put out by the authorities, who had agreed to cover up the truth.

Military Protects Sex Offenders, Punishes Victims

First it was a hunch, say Miles Moffeit and Amy Herdy of *The Denver Post.* "A cluster of five spousal homicides at Fort Bragg last year suggested big problems with how the U.S. military handles domestic violence," they say. They decided to look deeper.

As they began their reporting, the story broke of dozens of female cadets at the U.S. Air Force Academy being sexually assaulted with no prosecution of their attackers. "We nailed a pattern," they say: Abusers were being treated lightly.

For nine months they interviewed victims and reviewed thousands of documents to support their conclusion. They found that "only a small fraction of batterers faced prosecution within the armed services." Their three-part series "Betrayal in the Ranks" found "sexual and domestic violence to be widespread in the armed services" and that the "military's unique justice system protects abusers while punishing the victims of domestic and sexual violence."

A Story Possibility   A reporter assigned to write a year-end summary of traffic fatalities begins with the data the police department has supplied. As she scans the figures of deaths and injuries, she notices that pedestrian deaths and injuries are up 16 percent, whereas the increase over the previous year is 8 percent. She decides to concentrate on pedestrian accidents.

Further examination indicates that most of those killed and injured were 14 years old and under. The reporter recalls that some months ago a parents' organization petitioned the city council to provide more play streets for the warm-weather months in areas where there is a heavy concentration of low-income families and few open spaces. She wonders whether the number of children who were killed and hurt in traffic accidents was high in the summer. She also checks the location of the accidents. A pattern is beginning to take shape. Now she must determine whether the facts support her ideas.

As she moves through the data, she notices the traffic department lists the times at which deaths and injuries occurred. She is surprised at the number of children who were killed or hurt in the evening. Well, she reasons, perhaps that is logical. Where else can kids play on hot summer evenings, especially youngsters from homes without air conditioning? She looks at her newspaper's clip file to check her recollections of the city council meeting. All this takes less than an hour. Next, she makes several telephone calls to gather additional information.

A reporter's approach to the story is as important as the fact gathering. She could have settled for Layer I reporting. Had she done so, her story might have begun this way:

> Pedestrian deaths and injuries in the city last year were 16 percent higher than the previous year, a year-end summary of traffic accidents disclosed today.

Dangerous Streets   Instead, after her first hour of checking the clips and another 45 minutes of calls, she is ready to write a story that she begins this way:

> For 10 of the city's children the streets they played on last summer became a death trap.

She then gives the total figures for all deaths and injuries to children under 14 and the total traffic deaths for the city. Then she works into her story the petition the parents had presented to the city council. Her finding that the evening hours were particularly dangerous for youngsters had not been discovered by the parents, who had asked for daytime restrictions on traffic.

Before writing, the reporter had called the head of the parents' group and told her about the evening accident rate. The reporter was told that the group probably will renew its petitioning, this time with the request that in the summer some streets be permanently blocked off to traffic. This new material—the concept of 24-hour play streets—went into the story also.

The reporter not only turned out a meaningful story by linking certain facts but performed a public service for her community as well.

Summing Up

Journalists use their intuition and feelings to provide insights into events and situations. Hunches and emotions are valuable but must be checked to see whether they are legitimate. Particularly sensitive are the sentiments we carry with us from childhood—some positive, some negative.

Further Reading

Hayakawa, S.I., and Alan R. Hayakawa. *Language in Thought and Action,* 5th ed. New York: Harcourt Brace Jovanovich, 1991.

Lippmann, Walter. *Public Opinion.* Mineola, N.Y.: Dover Publications, 1997.

Ochse, R.A. *Before the Gates of Excellence: The Determinants of Creative Genius.* New York: Cambridge University Press, 1990.

Part 5: Accidents to Education

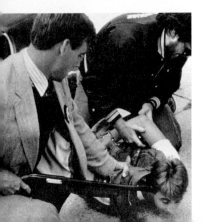

Part Five: Introduction

In the next seven chapters we will follow reporters on different beats as they report and write their stories. We'll look at a dozen of the most common stories that reporters handle. Also, each chapter contains a checklist. The checklist is a guide to the necessary elements that these stories should contain.

For example: An obituary requires the name, age and identification of the deceased; the cause, time and place of death; the survivors; funeral and burial plans and some background about the deceased. We can make similar lists of necessities for other story types.

Using the Checklist

When a reporter goes out on an assignment, the aim should be to gather information on the checklist, the essentials of the story. The checklist is a starter, a takeoff point. The elements on the checklist are not in the order they should appear in the story. Any one of the elements could be made into a lead, depending upon the circumstances. Reporters use their judgment to determine what constitutes the news angle or theme of the event. Also, not all of the elements will appear in every story, but most will.

Students should not regard the checklist as a cook approaches a recipe for flapjacks—a cup of pancake mix, one large egg, a cup of milk, a tablespoon of liquid shortening; stir until fairly smooth and then pour on a preheated, lightly greased griddle. That may make for a satisfying short stack, but this is a textbook, not a cookbook. Creative cooks always depart from recipes anyway. The reporter's task is to put his or her personal stamp on copy. The checklist is designed to point the reporter in the right direction.

Enterprise
"I was working as a sports writer when the city editor asked me to take a call about an automobile accident. I had no idea what I should say or ask. The police officer asked me, 'Whaddya need to know?' I froze. Then a light blipped and I said, 'Well, you know, the usual stuff.' Fortunately, he knew what the 'usual stuff' is and rattled it off."
— *Frank Herron*, The Post Standard, *Syracuse, N.Y.*

Types of Beats

There are two kinds of beats—topical and geographical. Some of the topical beats are education, politics, business—beats that take reporters over a wide area in pursuit of stories. Some of the geographical beats are the courthouse, city hall, police—beats that require the reporter to report from a specific location.

Beats come and go. When many Americans made their living on the farm, agriculture was a major beat. It remains so in only a few areas of the country. With the invention of the computer and the soaring developments in technology, new beats that required technical knowledge were installed in newsrooms. Long-established beats like business and education, once routinely covered, widened to include investigative reporting.

The beats and stories in the chapters in this section cover areas of reporting to which beginning reporters are most likely to be assigned.

Deskbound
"The biggest problem I have in the newsroom is getting the reporters off their asses and into the communities they are supposed to be covering."
—*Malcolm A. Borg, publisher,* The Record, *Hackensack, N.J.*

Covering a Beat

The reporter starting on a beat tries to meet everyone—clerks, secretaries, typists, assistants as well as those in charge of the offices and agencies on the beat. It's a good idea to give sources a business card or a note with your name, address and phone number.

"Shoot the breeze," says an experienced beat reporter. "That's the way to develop sources and how you find good stories. People usually are happy to chat with a reporter.

"You need to establish a relationship of trust with sources. But you make no promises you cannot fulfill or that interfere with your responsibilities as a reporter."

When he was the editor of *The Charlotte* (N.C.) *Observer,* Rich Oppel distributed to his staff eight tips for managing a beat. Here, in summarized form, are his suggestions:

1. **Get started fast** and get out of the office. Don't waste time. Not many stories are found in newsrooms.

2. **Set daily goals.**

3. **Build sources.** There is no substitute for regular, perhaps daily, contact.

4. **Do favors.** Where appropriate, do a favor for a source. The council member's daughter needs a copy of a month-old edition for a class project. Why not?

5. **Ask the sweeping questions;** ask the dumb questions. What's taking most of your time these days? What's the biggest problem you face in your job?

6. **Listen carefully, watch carefully.**

7. **Look at the record.** In managing a beat, go for original source material.

8. **Set up calls.** Make phone checks. Phone calls are a supplement, not a substitute, for direct contact.

Know the Beat

We can add a number 9 to this list: **Know the beat.** This means knowing the people in charge and those who work for them. It means knowing how the organization, commission, office works. A reporter said of a fellow reporter famous for his digging that resulted in many prize-winning stories, "He understands the process."

The following chapters will help you master the fundamentals of these beats.

Preview

Local stories about accidents and disasters must include:

- Names and addresses of dead and injured.
- Extent and cost of property damage.
- Time, location and cause of accident.
- Comments from eyewitnesses and authorities.

Interviews with those involved in the accident or disaster breathe life into these stories. Quotations, not paraphrases, are used as often as possible.

Reporters are careful about attributing the cause of accidents from the scene. They await official determination or the issuance of citation by authorities.

Dave Kline

On the scene at a stubborn fire.

Motor Vehicle Accidents

Every year more than 43,000 people die and 2.7 million others are injured in 7 million motor vehicle accidents. News of cars smashing into each other on fog-bound highways and buses tumbling off mountain passes are given good play in newspapers and on local broadcast stations. Only the routine "fender benders," as reporters describe minor accidents, are ignored or summarized. It's a rare reporter who has never written a *fatal,* a story about an accident in which at least one person died.

One accident story tends to read like another. But the enterprising reporter finds an aspect of the event that sets his or her story apart. In this story from

You never go out on an assignment as a blank slate.

The News-Gazette in Champaign-Urbana, Ill., the location of the fatality was newsworthy:

DANVILLE—A 55-year-old Martinsville, Ind., man was killed Wednesday night as he was walking across the highway in the 2500 block of Georgetown Road.

Harold Owens was killed when he was struck by a car and a pickup truck while walking across Illinois 1 in the Hegler area south of Danville at 9:40 p.m.

That dark stretch of the road has been the scene of numerous fatal pedestrian accidents, according to Vermilion County Coroner Lyle Irvin.

Mr. Owens was with a logging crew that is working in the county. He was staying at a motel in the area and was walking across the road to a tavern, Irvin said.

The "dark stretch of road" has an ominous sound to it. We all know dangerous places like that. The story would have been more effective had those words in the third paragraph been worked into the lead.

Checklist: Motor Vehicle Accidents

Expanding the Accident Story

When Mark Siebert of *The Des Moines Register* was assigned to write about the death of a teen-ager in an ATV accident, he decided to dig further into accidents involving all-terrain vehicles. He found the death was the second in 10 days of a youngster driving an ATV, the fourth in the state so far in the year.

Over the country, he reported, ATV-related deaths are increasing, a situation that worried Iowa officials. They worry, Siebert wrote, "because of recent law changes." One such change "eliminated the requirement that ATV's carry orange safety flags," he wrote. He quoted a state official who said that restrictions were also removed to allow ATV operators to drive in ditches.

___Victims: names, identification of dead and injured.

___Type of vehicles involved.

___Location.

___Time.

___Cause (from official source).

___Names and identification of other drivers and passengers.

___Cause of death, injuries.

___Where dead taken.

___Where injured taken and how.

___Extent of injuries.

___Heroism, rescues.

___Latest condition of critically injured.

___Funeral arrangements if available.

___Damage to vehicles.

___Arrests or citations by police.

___Unusual weather or highway conditions.

___Accounts by eyewitnesses and investigating officers.

___Speed, origin and destination of vehicles.

Sources

State highway patrol; local, suburban police; sheriff's office; hospital; ambulance service; mortuary; coroner.

Cautions

Art Carey of *The Philadelphia Inquirer* says that one of the first warnings he received about covering accidents was to be careful of inadvertently attributing blame when writing about the cause. Unless one of the drivers has been cited or arrested, it is best to avoid a detailed description of the cause. The reporter must be especially careful about saying which vehicle struck the other because such statements may imply responsibility. Also, be wary of eyewitness accounts, and verify addresses and the spelling of names in police reports.

Airplane Accidents

Airplane accidents make headlines. A motor vehicle collision in which two are killed will not receive the attention given the crash of an airplane with the same number of fatalities. Airline crashes are big news. Newspapers and stations will scan the casualty list carried on the wires for the names of local residents.

Checklist: Airplane Accidents

___ Number of dead and injured.

___Time, location and official cause of crash.

___Origin and destination of plane.

___Airline and flight number.

___Type of plane: manufacturer, number of engines.

___Victims: names and identification (including hometown).

___Survivors by name.

___Condition of injured.

___Where dead and injured taken.

___Cause of death: impact, fire, exposure.

___Altitude at time of trouble.

___Weather and flying conditions.

Careful

Resist the temptation to write that airplanes collided in midair, a word that has no meaning. Just write that they collided, says the AP. If they collide on the ground, say so in the lead.

Resist pressure to give the cause. The National Transportation Safety Board usually takes a year or more to find the reason. The Aviation/Space Writers Association advises, "Don't jump to conclusions. Avoid oversimplifications. Attribute statements and conclusions."

___Last words of crew from black box.

___Police, fire, rescue units at scene.

___Unusual incidents; heroism.

___Eyewitness accounts of survivors.

___Eyewitness accounts of people on ground.

___Comments by air controllers, officials, airline company.

___Cost of aircraft.

___Prominent people aboard.

___Fire and other destruction as result of crash.

___Direction aircraft heading before crash.

___Flight recorder recovered?

___If aircraft was missing, who found wreckage and how.

___Funeral arrangements, if available.

___Survivors of deceased, if available.

___Official inquiry.

___Previous crashes in area.

___Previous crashes of same type of plane or same airline.

Sources

Airline; police, fire, and other rescue units; Federal Aviation Administration (which in many large cities has a special telephone number for accident information); air traffic controllers; airport officials; National Transportation Safety Board; hospital; mortuary; coroner; morgue.

Cautions

Eyewitnesses on the ground are notoriously inaccurate about aircraft crashes. Early reports of casualties tend to be exaggerated. Passenger flight lists can be erroneous; verify if possible.

Quotes Useful

We listen for the quotes that set this particular accident we are reporting apart from other accident stories:

CADIZ, Ky., Dec. 16 (AP)—Seven teen-age boys who had squeezed into a compact car were killed in a head-on collision on Wednesday, plunging this small town into mourning.

None of the boys was wearing a seatbelt when their car crossed the center line and collided with a four-wheel-drive vehicle outside this town of 1,600 in southwest Kentucky.

"No community this size can take seven at one time," David Goodcase, administrator of Trigg County Hospital, said as the hospital filled with friends and relatives. Boys and girls sat in clusters and wept.

Katrina Folo   In the aftermath of Hurricane Katrina, tens of thousands of homeless people sought out friends and relatives to stay with. The AP moved a story from Lancaster, Pa., about 20 adults and 19 children showing up "at Patricia and Timothy Edwards' house a few hours before dawn Sunday, and now it's their home, even if some have to sleep four to a bed."

The story quotes Ms. Edwards response when her mother had called from New Orleans about the family's plight:

> "I said, 'Wait a minute, stop right now.'
> I didn't think twice: 'Bring them all, I don't
> care.'"

Lead Material   Sometimes the remarks of the coroner or an official can provide material for the lead, as in this story from the *Herald-Dispatch* in Huntington, W. Va.:

ELK CREEK, W. Va.—Two brothers died early yesterday when their car went off W. Va. 65 and struck a tree, a county official said.

The deaths were the second and third traffic fatalities in Mingo County in two days, said interim County Coroner Larry Wood.

He identified the victims as Jimmy Nichols, 16, of Varney, and Clyde R. Nichols, 18, of Columbus.

He said their car left the highway about 12:15 a.m., wrapped around a tree and "practically disintegrated."

Although wreckage was scattered over a wide area, evidence at the scene indicated that Jimmy Nichols was driving, the coroner said.

"From the appearance of the car and where it left the road, excessive speed probably caused the accident," said Deputy Bill Webb of the Mingo County Sheriff's Department.

There were no witnesses to the crash, he said. . . .

That partial quote in the fourth paragraph is too good to be buried. Try your hand at including it in the lead.

Here's a quote from someone who witnessed the path of a car after it hit an abutment on a bridge overpass:

> "I looked up and saw him flipping
> through the air and coming at me head-
> first," said John Pender of Havertown.

It, too, was far down in the story, as was the fact that the car traveled 250 feet in the air before striking cars when it landed. For the full story, see **Spectacular Crash** in *NRW Plus*.

Storms, Floods, Disasters

Floods, earthquakes, hurricanes, storms and drought—nature's excesses are the media's regular fare. Everyone is interested in the weather, and when it turns really bad it becomes front-page news and leads the evening newscast. Hurricane Floyd weakened when it struck eastern North Carolina, but it killed five, knocked out power to a million homes and caused massive flooding. It was news on page 1 of *The News & Observer* of Raleigh for two weeks, and stations sent out waves of teams to cover the damage.

The epic waves—called a tsunami—that struck Southern Asia at the end of 2004 took more than 300,000 lives and was the subject of massive coverage for weeks. Reporters described the onslaught of the waters as they engulfed fishing villages and resort hotels, children in school and sunbathers. They described the rescue at sea of a man who clung to an uprooted tree for eight days, the torment of a mother who watched her 8-year-old daughter being swept away and who could not hold on to her 4-year-old as the sea pulled the child from her grip. "I feel I should have died with the kids," she told a reporter.

"Unprecedented Storm Surge"

Here is a lead the Associated Press put on a story as Hurricane Katrina surged toward New Orleans:

NEW ORLEANS— Pounding wind and rain squalls strengthened each passing hour this morning as Hurricane Katrina charged toward the Gulf Coast and threatened to strike low-lying New Orleans with an unprecedented storm surge.

Hurricane Katrina A year later, a powerful hurricane struck New Orleans and nearby areas. Unlike the villagers in Indonesia and the tourists there, who had no idea of the incoming tidal wave, New Orleans residents had ample warning. Much of the early coverage concerned people driving away. It was not until TV showed pictures of those left behind that the public became aware that it was the poor and the black who were the major victims.

Herded into the Superdome, they had to contend with lack of water and inadequate medical care for the elderly and the sick.

The coverage following the storm concerned decisions about whether to rebuild, whether New Orleans could, or should, be returned to its former life. The hurricane, the costliest in U.S. history, is estimated to have been responsible for $81 billion in damages.

Accident or Disaster? The line separating accidents and storms from disasters is difficult to draw. If the difference is the number of lives lost, the amount of property damaged or destroyed, then who would set down the numbers that separate them? Katrina took 1,800 lives, a handful compared to the hundreds of thousands lost in the tidal wave that engulfed Indonesian islands a year before. To the Texas A&M community, the death of several students and a former student when a pile of logs collapsed was a disaster.

So was the loss of three volunteer firemen in the fire in a church in the small town of Lake Worth, Texas. When the Precious Faith Temple in Lake Worth, Texas, caught fire, several companies of volunteer firefighters answered the alarm. As the blaze spread, the roof collapsed, trapping three of the men inside. They were pronounced dead at the scene. To the small community, this was a disaster. The weekly *Times/Record* ran a banner headline across its front page: **Firefighters perish,** and below the headline a photo of the fire ran across the width of the page.

Some define a disaster as massive, widespread destruction of the kind usually associated with the vagaries of nature—floods, earthquakes, hurricanes, storms and drought. It might be a famine in Ethiopia, an earthquake in Mexico, a volcanic eruption in Colombia that takes 22,000 lives in one hellish night. Generally, journalists use the word *disaster* to cover large loss of life or massive property damage and the relocation of many residents.

Handling a Disaster

Dave Saltonstall was the rewriteman at the *Daily News* who wrote the major story following the attack on the World Trade Center in New York. He describes the day in the newsroom:

> I learned about noon that I'd be writing the "main bar," a story that was in fact an enormous group effort. *The News* had over 120 reporters and photographers on the street that day, some of whom were nearly killed by the collapsing towers. My job was to sort through the dozens of feeds that came in and weave them into something that was hopefully accurate, concise and clear-headed. In that, the story was not unlike any other major disaster take-out. But of course this wasn't like any other story.
>
> I think we all knew that Sept. 11th was one of those rare moments when the national psyche is transformed instantaneously and forever. And in a way, I think the weight of the day almost made the writing easier—the events were so powerful, so cataclysmic, that little flourish was needed.
>
> What was required was a clear recounting of an extraordinarily confusing and frightening day. We tried to do that, without losing sight of the deep emotional scars that the attacks would surely leave. Capturing the sheer scope of the damage and loss became the biggest rhetorical challenge, and at first the lead called it "the deadliest assault on the U.S. since the Japanese bombed Pearl Harbor." But by nightfall, it was slowly becoming clear that the loss of life would be much greater than Pearl Harbor or any other American conflict. That is well established now but seemed like much more of a reach in those first uncertain hours, when the death toll was still largely a guessing game.
>
> So we changed the lead at the last minute to "the deadliest assault on the U.S. in its history," which I think aptly and correctly conveyed the gravity of the day. The first edition left my desk at about 9 p.m., but we were able to update most stories until about 1 a.m.
>
> The challenge then became delivering the newspaper, which was a serious issue at the time since all bridges and tunnels into the city were closed and *The News* has

"Deadliest Assault"
Here is how Saltonstall began his story:

> On a day of unspeakable horror for New York and the nation, terrorists crashed planes into the World Trade Center and the Pentagon yesterday in the deadliest assault on the United States in its history.
>
> "Thousands of lives were suddenly ended by evil, despicable acts of terror," President Bush said in an address to the nation last night.
>
> The attacks involved four synchronized plane hijackings, two from Boston, one from Newark and one from Dulles International outside Washington. Each was bound for the West Coast, loaded with fuel for the cross-country flight, and they crashed within 90 minutes of one another.

been printed in New Jersey for years. But my understanding is that calls were made to Gov. Pataki's office and, given the obvious public service that all print media provided that day, our trucks were brought into the city under police escort. They hit the stands a little late but, like every other daily, were gone from most neighborhoods by 10 a.m. or so.

Rescues   Storm and disaster coverage includes stories of the work of rescuers:

Hurricane Floyd's drenching rain turned parts of Interstates 95 and 40 into treacherous passages Thursday, leading to at least two deaths and a pair of dramatic rescues in Nash and Pender counties.

The two victims couldn't be identified.

But there were plenty of witnesses to rescues by Marine Corps helicopters in Nash and a mix of Highway Patrol troopers and volunteers in Pender, both daring acts that kept the death toll from climbing.

—*The News & Observer*

OKLAHOMA CITY (AP)—Choking through dusty smoke and the overpowering stench of the decaying dead buried around them, they push on. At times forced to inch along on their backs through foot-high crawl spaces, they push on.

Haunted by creaks, groans and cracks, they eye small chunks of rubble that shower them sporadically and stay alert for the scream of "Get out!," the signal that the collapse of tons of debris may be imminent.

At Ground Zero

The firefighters refused to leave.

Sweaty and soot-covered, they were beaten down with exhaustion, pain and anger.

At ground zero, amid the twisted and ash-coated rubble that had rained down on Battery Park City, they sat stunned, resting their aching bodies against buildings like the homeless.

"If any of you have already completed your 24-hour shift, please go home and report back here at 0900 hours," a deputy chief barked through a bullhorn.

Two dozen shell-shocked firefighters stood up, as if to leave—only to sit down again once the supervisor left.

"Some guys have been here since 9 a.m., and they won't go home," explained one Bronx firefighter.

"Our brothers, our friends, our relatives are buried there. I'm not going anywhere," he said.

"My uncle is a firefighter assigned to a house near here, and we haven't heard from him."

The dozens of smashed-up and ash-covered emergency vehicles nearby graphically illustrated the disaster facing their buried comrades.

—*New York Post*

Folo Stories

The coverage also includes what is known as a folo, a follow-up story that assesses damages, physical and emotional. The folo may also tell stories of courage and endurance.

After Katrina struck along the southern coast of the United States, reporters spread out to cities where the displaced residents had fled. They described overwhelmed classrooms in Houston, overcrowded relatives in Baton Rouge.

The debate over whether to rebuild New Orleans to its former stature continued for many months, as did the racial aspect of the disaster: Much of the most devastated parts of the city were black sections several feet under sea level and the most likely to be flooded again should another Katrina-type hurricane strike.

Katrina's Legacy   A year after the disaster, residents were still living amid debris and garbage. But the reporters turned to cover the decline of personal and civic life. Suicides, post-traumatic stress and depression markedly increased. "The crime rate has soared," one reporter wrote, "and there are persistent feelings of sadness and hopelessness."

Hurricane Floyd   Peter St. Onge wrote folos for *The Charlotte Observer* when Hurricane Floyd receded, leaving in its wake the homeless and the penniless and some with stories of their rescue. For two stories St. Onge wrote, see **The Storm That Shocked N.C.** in *NRW Plus*. St. Onge also describes how he reported and wrote these stories.

Forecasting Failures   In the years that 45 hurricanes struck the United States since 1992, how well did the federal government's multi-billion-dollar weather-tracking system work? *The Miami Herald*'s Debbie Cenziper decided to try to find out. She spent eight months investigating. Her conclusion: The forecasting system had failed nearly half the time.

"Buoys, weather balloons, radars, ground sensors and hurricane hunter planes" often did not work. Staff shortages were chronic. She quotes a science officer at the Miami office of the National Weather Service, "It's almost like we're forecasting blind." Lack of equipment and obsolete equipment hampered the forecasters, she reported.

Service workers knew of the problems but were told not to go public with their concerns. But Cenziper's stories were effective. Less than a month after the final story in her series appeared, she wrote:

> WASHINGTON—A group of influential U.S. senators convinced Congress this week to help shore up the nation's storm-warning system, with new equipment and four more forecasters for the National Hurricane Center—the most significant increase in years.

Jack Andresen, *Daily News Tribune*

Checklist: Storms, Floods and Disasters

As in the accident story, the human toll is more important than the loss of property.

___Dead.

___Injured.

___Total affected or in danger.

___Cause of death.

___Estimated death and injury toll.

___Eyewitness accounts.

___Property loss:

___Homes.

___Land.

___Public utilities.

___Permanent damage.

___Rescue and relief operations:

___Evacuations.

___Heroism.

___Unusual equipment used or unique rescue techniques.

___Number of official personnel and volunteers.

___Warnings: health department, public utility commission, police and highway department statements.

___Looting.

___Number of spectators.

___Insurance.

___Suits.

___Arrests.

___Investigations.

___Cleanup activities.

Lloyd B. Cunningham, *Argus Leader*

Tornado Cleanup

Sources

In storm and disaster coverage, statements may be issued by presidents and prime ministers, local police and priests. The destruction may be so vast no single source is adequate for coverage. Usually, the first place the reporter turns is to the experts—meteorologists for the weather picture, the Federal Aviation Administration for plane crashes, the Red Cross for disaster assistance.

Experts sometimes speak in technical language and the reporter should know some of these terms. In a flood situation, for example:

Flood stage—The height of the river above which damage begins to occur, usually because the river overflows its banks.

Crest—The highest level that a river reaches.

Human Interest

When a cold wave swept through the East over Christmas, it left seven dead in New Jersey. For his story of the disaster, Jim Dwyer chose five of the dead and began his story with vignettes: One man had in his pocket a 16-year-old newspaper clipping about his son's death; another was found dead in the front seat of a truck in which he had sought shelter.

A homeless man had dozed off under the Atlantic City boardwalk. "The temperature was basically warm when John went to sleep," said a friend, "but then it dropped rather drastically. In that drastic drop was when he died."

Caution: Eyewitness accounts should be treated with care, especially if they are of events that unfold rapidly and particularly if the witness to the event is emotionally involved.

Writing the Disaster Story: Caution

With stories of the dimension of a disaster, the reporter is tempted to pull out every writing device he or she knows. Resist. If resisting is difficult, pause and reflect on the story—part fact, part fiction—told of the reporter from a Philadelphia newspaper sent to cover a mine disaster in Donora, Pa., where hundreds of miners were entombed dead or facing imminent death from mine gas. The mine was surrounded by weeping relatives, and when it was opened 200 bodies were taken out.

The reporter looked at this scene of death and grief and wired his newspaper the lead: "God sits tonight on a little hill overlooking the scene of disaster. . . ."

As these words came over the telegraph machine in the newsroom in Philadelphia, an editor shouted out, "Stop," and he handed the telegraph editor a message to send back to the reporter in Donora: "Never mind disaster—interview God."

19 Obituaries

R.L. Chambers

Grave markers tell stories:
   A renowned ornithologist and an anonymous miner—Paradise, Ariz., cemetary.

Preview

   Obituaries are among the most frequently read stories in the newspaper. The obituary sums up the activities and outstanding qualities of the individual.
   The obituary usually centers on the person's most
noteworthy accomplishment or activity.
   Interviews with survivors and friends often turn up
interesting material.
   Incidents in the person's life that are well-known to
the public are included in the obituary.
   Verification of the death from mortuaries or authorities is essential.

Tuck them into their
graves.

Here are two views of the obituary:

1. "The obituary is a routine story that no reporter enjoys writing."

2. "On the obituary page may be found the summing up of the glories, the
   achievements, the mediocrities, and the failures of a life which the rest of
   the paper chronicled day by day."

The first description is taken from a journalism textbook, the second from
a veteran journalist's article about writing obituaries. Both summaries are
accurate. Most obituaries are indeed routine, written by writers who rigor-
ously follow a formula so that only names, addresses, ages and the other
vital statistics differentiate one obituary from another. However, the writers
who use their reportorial and writing skills on obituaries develop interesting
stories. Obituaries are among the best-read parts of the newspaper.

   No reporter should approach any story with the intention of writing
routinely. Of course, some stories are difficult to make interesting, but the

obituary hardly falls into this category, for the reporter has a wide panorama from which to select material—a person's entire life. No life lacks drama, if the reporter has the intelligence and the time and the desire to look for it.

Guideline   William Buchanan of *The Boston Globe* was guided in writing obituaries by the thought "that what I wrote would probably be the last words ever printed about the person. That's why I always worked hard to include something in that person's life of which he or she would have been most proud."

> I recall one woman who worked for years in the office of a candy factory. The part of her life she loved most was playing the violin at special Masses at St. Peter's and St. Paul's Churches in Dorchester. Or, for another example, there was a man who started as a busboy in a restaurant and later became the owner; after he became the owner, no job was too menial for him to handle. That clearly showed his character.

Even when the life is brief, the obituary can be interesting, even moving. Here is the beginning of an obituary of a 12-year-old boy written by a young reporter, James Eggensperger, for the *Sanders County Ledger* in Thompson Falls, Mont.

> Ronald Laws, a rising star in Thompson Falls athletic competition, died Friday night doing one of the things he liked best, playing baseball. He was 12 years old.
>
> Ron, as his friends and teachers and coaches called him, was batting in a Little League baseball game when he was hit in the chest by a pitched ball.
>
> Then, according to one witness, he started running. After about 20 feet, he turned to the call of his coach, fell to the ground and never rose.

Eggensperger recalls the day he took the call about the accident:

> I remember feeling sick that such a thing should happen to such a good kid. But even more, that he had not had a chance to bloom into his potential and to enjoy all the things in life there are to enjoy. I put myself in his shoes and thought of all the memories, good and bad times, people and places I would have missed if I had not lived past 12, and the impact was overwhelming.
>
> And in the back of my head was something I had been taught, which ran something like this: "An obit may be the only time a guy gets into the paper, and it's his last chance."
>
> So I talked to some people and wrote what I felt.

Obituaries Can Enlighten Us

The obituary can tell us something about our past along with details of the life of the deceased. In the obituary of S.I. Hayakawa, a noted scholar on language usage who also served as a U.S. senator from California, it was reported that in 1937, while teaching at the University of Wisconsin, he married one of his students. "At the time, marriages between whites and Asians were not recognized in

Able and Willing
She had applied for a job with *The Miami Herald* after working for a small Florida newspaper but had heard nothing. Finally, she sent a one-word note: "Obits?" The city editor called Edna Buchanan the next day and put her to work.

The News Trinity
Who was born? Who got married? Who died?

some states, including California, and the couple lived for nearly two decades in Chicago," the obituary reported.

Emma Bugbee was a pioneer woman reporter in New York. When she died, her obituary stressed the unique niche she had filled in the days when women were a rarity on newspaper reporting staffs.

Bugbee worked for *The New York Herald Tribune* for 56 years. For many of those years, she was one of only two women reporters at the newspaper. They were not allowed to sit in the city room, the obituary recalled, "but had to work down the hall."

In the obituary of Louis Loss, a professor of law at Harvard, the writer noted that after Loss's graduation from Yale Law School "he was attracted to Washington by the excitement of the New Deal, and because he knew he could not go to the big Wall Street law firms because he was Jewish." And then the writer, no doubt with a smile on his face, wrote: "He would eventually become the William Nelson Cromwell Professor of Law at Harvard, a chair financed by one of those firms, Sullivan & Cromwell, in the name of one of its founders."

Causes Informative   The causes of death inform us of some of our personal and social problems:

- The obituary of Eddie Kendricks, the former lead singer of the Temptations, who died of lung cancer at the age of 52, stated, "He said the disease was caused by 30 years of smoking."

- The deadly combination of cold weather and alcohol—a too-frequent cause of death among Native Americans—was Jerry Reynolds' theme for this obituary in the newspaper *Indian Country Today:*

MARTIN, S.D.—The icy claw of winter claimed another young life in Indian Country last week.

Twenty-year-old Sidney Brown Bear of Allen was found dead in the back seat of a car in Martin the morning of March 5. Companions said he had been drinking at a bar in nearby Swett, S.D., the night before and fell down twice before leaving.

A preliminary autopsy report placed his blood alcohol content at almost four times the legal limit. . . .

The preliminary report indicated that exposure appeared to be the cause of death. . . .

Checklist: Obituaries

The following items are required in all obituaries:

___Name, age, occupation and address of deceased.

___Time, place and cause of death.

___Birthdate, birthplace.

___Survivors (only immediate family).

__Memberships, military service.

__Funeral and burial arrangements.

Many obituaries also will include:

__Outstanding or interesting activities and achievements.

__Memberships in fraternal, religious or civic organizations.

__Anecdotes and recollections of friends and relatives.

Sources

First news of deaths can come from different sources. Many newspapers rely on the death notices mortuaries send newspapers to be placed in the classified advertising section. The news department is given a copy. Some mortuaries will call in the death of a prominent person, and on some newspapers and stations reporters regularly make the rounds of mortuaries by telephone.

The police and the coroner's office will have news of deaths caused by accidents. Reporters scan wire service stories for the names of local people who may have been involved in disasters or accidents out of town.

Background material for the obituary is gathered from many sources. The starting point is the newspaper or station library. Friends and relatives can provide information, some of it human interest material that makes an obituary interesting, and they can clarify questionable or vague information.

Digging Pays Off

By checking the files and by talking to different people—his boss, her college classmates, a co-worker, the teacher's students, the merchant's customers—the writer can turn up the nuggets that make an obituary glitter. In the obituary of Saul Pett, the AP's gifted feature writer, *Los Angeles Times* writer Mathis Chazanov wrote that Pett wrote scores of profiles, including one of the writer Dorothy Parker that began with Parker asking Pett for assistance:

> "Are you married, my dear?"
> "Yes, I am."
> "Then you won't mind zipping me up."

The following incident was recalled by Robert D. McFadden in his obituary of *New York Times* reporter Peter Kihss:

> On the night of Nov. 9, 1965, moments after a huge power failure plunged the Northeast into darkness, an assistant metropolitan editor of *The New York Times*—candle in hand—groped his way through the newspaper's darkened newsroom.
>
> "Peter," he called. "Peter."

Homage to a Reporter

Here are excerpts from an obituary of the journalist-writer David Halberstam by Tim Rutten of the *Los Angeles Times*:

Halberstam was the exemplar of a courageous intellectual approach to journalism that found its first clear public expression in a young combat correspondent's refusal to buy the government line on Vietnam. They were there; they trusted the evidence of their eyes and refused to look away, no matter how much pressure successive American administrations and military commanders brought to bear. . . .

As he said . . . about his war coverage, ". . . we would have liked nothing better than to believe the war was going well and that it would eventually be won. But it was impossible for us to believe those things without denying the evidence of our own senses. . . . And so we had no alternative but to report the truth. . . ."

. . . not long ago, he spoke to students about what he took from those early years in Mississippi (when he covered the civil rights movement). "I learned how to work a story, how to talk to ordinary people, and what a joy doing legwork was. I learned that the best question of all for any interview: 'Who else should I see?' "

> In the face of crisis, it seemed only right
> for the editor to call on Peter Kihss, his best
> reporter, to do the story.

In an obituary of James B. Reston of *The New York Times,* a colleague, Tom Wicker, said of Reston, "He had far and away the best sense of where to look for a story and whom to question. Scotty was lucky, too, and nobody who isn't lucky will ever be a good reporter."

Check The Files Much is available about well-known people. In the AP's obituary of Frank Sinatra, material was included that had appeared in a magazine 18 years before the singer's death. Sinatra, Pete Hamill had written, "was the original working class hero. Mick Jagger's fans bought records with their allowances; Sinatra's people bought them out of wages."

In checking the files for an obituary of A. Leon Higginbotham Jr., one of the country's most prominent black judges, the writer came across a talk Higginbotham had given to the graduating seniors at Wesleyan University in 1966. He ended the obituary with Higginbotham's words:

> "I will make two requests of you. They are that you always attempt to see those human beings who become invisible to most people, and that you always try to hear the pleas of those persons who, despite their pain and suffering, have become voiceless and forgotten."

Writing the Obit

Richard G. West, whose comments on the obituary are quoted as No. 2 at the start of this chapter, says of the obituary, "Preparing an obituary is a delicate and exacting task, demanding the utmost diligence, insight and imagination. His obituary should be, as far as human judgment and ability may create it in the limits of a newspaper's space, a man's monument."

Monuments take time to carve, and the newspapers that attempt to carry obituaries for most of those who die within their circulation area cannot possibly devote much time or space to each. Still, some should be thoroughly reported and carefully written.

Beginning reporters often are broken in by a stint of obituary writing because it tests the journalist's accuracy in reporting names and dates and his or her ability to work under pressure—people are always dying on deadline. Some beginners— possibly those who used the textbook by No. 1 who is quoted beginning of this chapter—consider obituary writing a dull assignment of little importance. "What nonsense. What an opportunity," says Joseph L. Galloway, senior writer for *U.S. News & World Report,* who wrote his share of obituaries when he broke into newspaper work on a small Texas daily:

> The obits are probably read by more people with greater attention to detail than any other section of a newspaper. Nowhere else is error or omission more likely to be noticed.
>
> A good reporter gives each obit careful and accurate handling. He or she searches in the stack for the one or two that can be brought to life.
>
> Veteran of World War II, the funeral home sheet says. Did he make the D-Day landing on the beaches of Normandy? Taught junior high school English for 43 years? Find some former pupils who can still quote entire pages of Longfellow because somehow she made it live and sing for them.

Two Types   The circumstances of the death determine how the obituary is written. When the death is sudden, unexpected—as in a traffic accident, a disaster, an airplane crash—the lead highlights the circumstances of the death. When the death is anticipated, as it is for the elderly and those who are seriously ill, the obituary concentrates on the individual's background and accomplishments.

Here are some examples of the two types:

Unexpected

CHICAGO (AP)—Chris Farley, the blubbery "Saturday Night Live" comic whose specialty was sweaty, tightly wound characters who erupted in vein-popping frenzies, was found dead Thursday in his apartment. He was 33.

The cause of death was not immediately known.

Farley died young like his comic idol, John Belushi. Both had a hearty appetite for food, drink and drugs.

Police said Farley's brother John called 911 after finding his brother in his 60th floor apartment in the 100-story John Hancock Building on a stretch of Michigan Avenue known as the Magnificent Mile. There was no sign of foul play.

The Cook County Medical Examiner's Office said Farley's body, clad in pajama bottoms, was found on the floor. . . .

Anticipated

Ronald Wilson Reagan, a former film star who became America's 40th president, the oldest to enter the White House but imbued with a youthful optimism rooted in the traditional virtues of a bygone era, died yesterday at his home in Los Angeles. He was 93.

—The New York Times

The Story Behind the Babe Ruth Photo

On June 13, 1948, the assignment editor of *The New York Herald Tribune* sent Fein to Yankee Stadium for Ruth's farewell appearance. Fein showed up early and went to the Yankee locker room. He watched as two men helped put on his old uniform. With the assistance of a male nurse, Ruth went on the field to the cheers of more than 49,000 fans.

Most of the photographers lined up along the baseline facing Ruth. Fein held back. He said he had two thoughts about the photo. First, Ruth's face—haggard and drawn—was not the apple-cheeked image fans were familiar with. Second, Ruth's uniform number, 3, was being retired that day, and the number could only be seen on the back of the uniform Ruth was wearing.

Using available light rather than flash, Fein took what some consider the most famous sports photo. It showed Ruth, baseball cap in his left hand at his side, bat in his right hand, planted solidly on the ground, the Yankee team lined up at his right and in the background the fan-filled grandstand.

Three months later the 53-year-old Sultan of Swat, as sportswriters affectionately described Ruth, was dead of cancer. Fein received the Pulitzer Prize for his photo.

Find the Theme

As with any story, the obituary should emphasize a major theme. The writer usually finds the theme in the person's occupation or main accomplishment. When Richard Harwood, a journalist for *The Washington Post,* died, his newspaper based his obituary on Harwood's work:

> He was an exhaustive reporter, with a keen eye for distinctive detail. He understood and was able to communicate the structure of things—not just the politics of government programs but the underlying substance, how they worked, whom they did and didn't help, their histories.

Accomplishments   When Charles M. Schulz died, every obituary began with the fact that he had created the comic strip "Peanuts" that starred Charlie Brown and Snoopy, and that 355 million people around the world read it.

When Tom Landry died, the obituaries emphasized that as coach of the Dallas Cowboys for 29 years he had led the team to five Super Bowls.

Frank Wills died at 52 in Augusta, S.C., of what friends said was a brain tumor. Frank Wills? He was the night watchman, as all his obituaries noted, who discovered the 1972 Watergate burglary that ultimately led to the resignation of President Richard Nixon.

Nat Fein took thousands of pictures in his work as a newspaper photographer. His obituary singled out one in the lead: a rear-view photograph of a mortally ill Babe Ruth as he received applause in Yankee Stadium, known to baseball fans as the House That Ruth Built.

Just a Singer   Unlike Sinatra's obituaries, which emphasized his trigger-temper, notorious Mafia friendships and many tangled romances along with his fabulous voice, the obituaries of Perry Como were quiet, restrained—much like the man himself and his voice. Como's marriage lasted six decades, they noted. One obituary reported, "Mrs. Como always did the cooking and Mr. Como frequently dried the dishes."

It was his career—sales of 100 million records, a Grammy and several Emmys—that the obituary writers emphasized, not his personal life. The obituary in *The New York Times* ended this way:

> "I don't have a lot to tell the average interviewer," Perry Como once told a reporter. "I've done nothing that I can call exciting. I was a barber. Since then I've been a singer. That's it."

Yet this unexciting life merited five columns in the *Times* at its end.

Courthouse Man   In Chapter 14 we met Milt Sosin, Miami federal courthouse reporter for the AP. When Sosin died, *The New York Times* gave his obituary by Rick Bragg 20 inches plus a four-inch photo. The obituary consists of one anecdote after another:

Mr. Sosin, who often referred to editors as "amateurs," reacted with his usual contempt when an editor at *The News* once ordered the staff to write shorter, punchier paragraphs.

He sat down at his old typewriter, banged out his answer and stuck it on the bulletin board.

"Quit," it said. . . .

He regularly beat his competitors, scooping them even when he was old. In a time before cellular phones, when reporters raced to the courthouse pay phones to call in news of a verdict, Mr. Sosin carried a pad of yellow "out of order" stickers, which he would slap onto a phone before going into the courtroom.

One day a young reporter, Martin Merzer, now with *The Miami Herald,* sat beside Mr. Sosin in the courtroom.

"Hey, kid," Mr. Sosin asked him, "have you filed yet?"

Mr. Merzer told him the phone was out of order.

Mr. Sosin reached into his pocket and showed him the pad of stickers.

"He had this wonderful, evil smile on his face," Mr. Merzer remembered.

A Crusader   When William H. Jones, managing editor of the *Chicago Tribune,* died at the age of 43 of leukemia, his professional accomplishments as an investigative reporter and an editor were emphasized. The obituary noted his "tireless work, creative thinking and total integrity."

The obituary writer found in the newspaper files a story about a talk Jones gave to a graduating class at the Medill School of Journalism at Northwestern University. Jones had spoken about journalism as a career:

> It's a commitment to use your skills to improve your community, to speak loudly for the victims of injustice and to speak out against those who perpetuate it. Some of the best reporting begins with a single, voiceless citizen who seeks help from a newspaper that is willing to listen, and to dig out the facts.

The obituary quoted an investigator with the city's Better Government Association who worked with Jones on a series of stories that exposed widespread corruption in Chicago's private ambulance companies, which won Jones a Pulitzer Prize when he was 31. The investigator said, "Bill hated to see people abused, especially the helpless."

A Humorist   Henry Morgan was a radio and television performer years before the days of talk shows. Admired for his quick wit—he usually worked without a script—he was derisive about the media and his sponsors. It was natural, then, for his obituary to dwell on some of Morgan's caustic comments and their consequences.

Richard Severo's obituary in *The New York Times* recalled that one of Morgan's sponsors was the candy bar Oh! Henry. The sponsors thought that the similarity of names would incline Morgan to sheathe his rapier wit. Hardly.

"Yes, Oh! Henry is a meal in itself," the obituary quoted a Morgan monologue, "but you eat three meals of Oh! Henrys and your teeth will fall out."

"On another broadcast," the obituary continued, "Mr. Morgan said that if children were fed enough of such candy bars they would 'get sick and die.' The makers of Oh! Henry withdrew."

Use Human Interest

Too many obituaries read like the label on a bottle. The major ingredients are listed, but the reader has no idea of the actual flavor. Details, human details, help the obituary writer move readers close to the person being written about. Few lives lack interest, even drama, if the reporter digs deeply enough to find it.

In an obituary of Helen Childs Boyden, who taught science and mathematics at Deerfield Academy, the reporter used several incidents from her life. When Mrs. Boyden had applied for work, the obituary reported, the principal was "not at all enthusiastic about the young applicant. But the school was too poor to insist on someone more experienced. He hired her on a temporary basis." She taught there for 63 years. The obituary continues:

> . . . In a highly personal style she cajoled thousands of students through the intricacies of mathematics and chemistry.
>
> Even in a large class she taught the individual, not the group. Her tongue was quick but never cutting. One boy, later a college president, recalls her telling him:
>
> "Victor! When will you stop trying to remember and start trying to think?"

The Boy Is a Man
Some alert students at Syracuse University point out that the writer of the Boyden obituary has a "boy" doing the recalling in the second paragraph when obviously it is a man recalling something Boyden told him when he was a boy.

Use Quotations and Incidents

Baseball Player Willie Stargell, his obituary noted, "was an inspiration in a clubhouse where he forged unity across racial and ethnic lines." Playing for the Pittsburgh Pirates, he was known as Pops, the team as the Family, the obituary stated. But when he broke in with Pirates farm teams in Roswell, N.M., and San Angelo, Texas, racism was rampant.

In the obituary, the writer recalled the day Stargell was going into a ballpark in Plainview, Texas:

> Two men wearing trench coats approached him. One of them pulled out a revolver, uttered a racial epithet and said that if he played that day, "I'm gonna blow your brains out."

Stargell remembered: "I was real scared. But by the time the rest of the team got there, I decided that if I was gonna die, I was gonna die doing exactly what I wanted to do. I had to play ball."

Teacher, Principal   In the obituary of Abraham H. Lass, author and educator, Robert D. McFadden, master of many story styles at *The New York Times,* takes us back to Lass's childhood. Lass was "the son of Russian Jewish immigrants who settled in America early in the century. . . ." Young Lass "spoke only Yiddish when he entered elementary school in 1913. But he learned English in the streets and in schools where the teachers, he recalled, were women in pince-nez and high lace collars." Then he quotes Lass:

"They didn't seem to like us or love us. . . . But they taught us—firmly, thoroughly, relentlessly. They did not ask, nor did they seem to care, who we were, where we came from, what we wanted or what language we spoke. They knew what they were in school for: to civilize us, Americanize us, give us a common tongue and a common set of traditions."

Stargell's and Lass's quotations give us a sense of the men as well as an insight into the times in which they lived.

Who Is Chosen

Most small newspapers run at least a short item on every death in town. In large cities, where 50 or more people die daily, newspapers will run an obituary of a handful. Alden Whitman, for years the chief obituary writer for *The New York Times,* said for someone to rate an obituary in a metropolitan newspaper, a person has to be "either unassailably famous or utterly infamous."

Mostly Men   The majority of those selected are men. A study of 1,803 obituaries in *The New York Times* over a three-year period showed that 84 percent were of men. Traditionally, women have been housewives, teachers, clerks, typists and secretaries, not the activities that lead to careers in business, politics and law. The *Times* study also examined the obituaries of those who died at 45 and younger, those less affected by gender roles. The same ratio—five to one male—held up.

The perceptive reporter knows there is more to a person's life than his or her occupation. There is as much drama—perhaps more—in the life of a woman who reared three children or struggled to educate herself as there is in a man whose obituary is justified by his having run a local business for 35 years.

Quotes That Weren't Quoted

At the funeral of Louis B. Mayer, a tyrannical Hollywood studio head, Red Skelton observed the huge crowd and remarked, "It only goes to show that when you give the public what it wants, it will turn out."

In Paris for the funeral of French President Georges Pompidou in 1974, Richard Nixon said, "This is a great day for France."

Paid Obits

Many newspapers publish paid-for obituaries that friends or relatives submit. These allow a record for those of the deceased who do not make the news columns of the obit page.

The Rockford, Ill., *Register Star* runs free a "six- to nine-line obituary that lists the basic information," says Linda Grist Cunningham, executive editor. "Families who desire longer, more detailed obituaries pay for them."

Here is the beginning of an obituary in a Maine newspaper:

> Mrs. Verena C. Hornberger, 92, died
> Tuesday at a Waldoboro nursing home. She
> was the widow of Hiester Hornberger.
>   She was born at Bremen, daughter of
> Franklin and Emma (Hilton) Chaney. . . .

No Reporting   Not only is the obituary routinely written, it finds Mrs. Hornberger's prominence to be in her relationship to her husband, which might be newsworthy if he is shown to be prominent. He is not. But the obituary does contain some clues that, if followed up, might have made a fascinating story:

> . . . She graduated in 1910 from Colby
> College where she was a member of Chi
> Omega sorority.
>   She was a teacher, first working in local
> schools. She also taught in Essex, Conn.,
> and Verona, N.J., following graduate work
> in Germany at the University of Jena and
> Columbia's Teachers College.

Was she the last surviving member of the class of 1910? Does the college have any information about her? Do some of her students recall her? It was unusual for women in those days to finish high school, much less to graduate from college, and graduate work abroad was rare. Can someone cast light on this? Obviously, the writer simply took the mortuary form and rewrote the data. No one was interviewed. Contrast this obituary with the work of Nicolaas Van Rijn of *The Toronto Star:*

> Ann Shilton didn't become the first woman principal of an academic secondary school by being a pussycat.
>   The principal of Jarvis Collegiate Institute from 1975 to 1983, Miss Shilton "was a very strong single woman, with strong opinions and the will to make them known," her brother Paul said yesterday.
>   Miss Shilton, 69, died Thursday of abdominal cancer in Princess Margaret Hospital. . . .

Ordinary Folk   Deborah Howell, managing editor of the *St. Paul Pioneer Press,* says that "too many big-city dailies report just the deaths of important people—captains of industry and political leaders. That's a mistake. These newspapers ignore the woman who always feeds the ducks in the late afternoon at the city lake, the tireless youth worker at the neighborhood park, the druggist dispensing sage advice along with medicine for 50 years."

Howell recalled the obituary of a woman who died of cancer and who had asked for a party after her funeral. She was memorialized this way in the *Pioneer Press:*

> The ladies sat in a circle of lawn chairs in the neatly clipped backyard, between the pea patch on the right and the tomatoes and cucumbers on the left, sipping their gentle scotches and bourbons and beers, while the mosquitoes buzzed around their ears, and the evening slowly faded without pain into the night.

Of Tom Flaherty, Howell said, "To most folks, Tom might have seemed quite ordinary. He worked his whole life as a laborer on the Great Northern Railroad, as did many of the Irish immigrants in St. Paul. At first, I worried how I was going to make an obit on Tom interesting. Then I decided that his life represented so much that is so Irish, so Catholic, so railroad, so St. Paul. When any Irish railroadman died, Tom was at the wake. At the St. Patrick's Day parade, Tom led the Flaherty section.

"I explained the kind of obit I wanted to one of our better writers. His obit began:

> Tom Flaherty was an Irishman's Irishman, a John Henry of a man who for 50 years matched his mighty muscle against the hardest work the railroad had to offer.

"The trick is to make the dead person come alive again in an obituary, to remind family and friends and co-workers why someone was important," Howell said.

"Too often reporters come away with just the basic facts about birth, education, marriage, vocation and perhaps a few war medals. Obituaries can be examples of the paper's best writing, meaning reporters must search for the kind of detail—the unusual facts—that makes any news story interesting to read."

Accuracy Essential In the obituary of a physicist who worked in the development of the atomic bomb, the reporter wrote that he carried out his work "in the research center in the sands of Los Alamos." Los Alamos is high in the mountains of northern New Mexico.

In describing the physicist's background as a student, the reporter wrote that on the way to an eastern university "he stopped at the University of Wisconsin at Ann Arbor. . . ."

For a glimpse at some well-written sections of obituaries, see **Writing with a Flair** in *NRW Plus,* Chapter 19.

Double-Check

"The worst mistake I ever made in an obit was identifying the deceased as the same person who was shot and paralyzed in a holdup a few years earlier. I made that mistake because I didn't double-check information that had been volunteered by a colleague with a reputation for accuracy."

—Edna Buchanan

Frequently Asked Questions

Here are answers to some questions about writing obituaries.

Advance Obits

Q.   Does it make sense to prepare obituaries in advance?

   A.   Yes, even before a prominent person is ill. The AP keeps 1,000 "biographical sketches" on hand, frequently brought up-to-date. *The New York Times* has 1,200 on file. A newspaper, depending on its size, may have a score or a handful. When a well-known person dies, the background, or *B Matter,* is ready so that all the reporter need write is a lead and the funeral arrangements.

Late Reports

Q.   If we are days late with our obituary, do we try to bury the old time element?

   A.   This is an old wire service practice:

   NAJA, Mexico, Jan. 1 (AP)—Chan K'in Viejo, the spiritual leader of the Lacadone Indians in southeastern Mexico, has died. A son said he was 104.
   The son, Kayum Garcia, said his father died at his home on Dec. 23 and was buried the following day. . . .

This practice deserves interment. Be straightforward with the reader and state the date of death in the lead.

Verification

Q.   Do I verify reports of deaths?

   A.   Always. Do so by telephoning relatives, the funeral home or mortuary, the police or hospital.

KING D. ROME

AGE: 1½ • HIGHLAND PARK

King Demarest Rome died yesterday. He was 1½ years old.

He was born in New Brunswick and lived with his family in Highland Park.

Surviving are his mother, Debra; four brothers, Billy, Thorndyke, Kate, and Alex Demarest, and a sister, Sarah Meredith.

Cremation will be private.

Interviews

Obituaries in *The New York Times* were "bland factual digests of their lives," writes Arthur Gelb in his book *City Room.* To make them reflect the deceased's life, Gelb decided to send Alden Whitman, chief obituary writer for the paper, to interview prominent people for anecdotes and incidents that would go into a prepared obit in the files. "An uncanny number of his subjects died shortly after he interviewed them," Gelb writes, and Whitman "became known as the angel of death."

A few days later, the following appeared in the New Jersey newspaper:

Correction

Due to a reporter's error, *The Home News & Tribune* mistakenly published an obituary for a family pet in Sunday's editions. The obituary was published under the name King D. Rome. The error occurred because the newspaper's procedure of verifying all obituaries was not followed.

Embarrassing Material

Q. Should I omit material from a person's life that might offend some readers or embarrass survivors or friends?

A. Follow the policy of the newspaper or station. Generally, newspapers have become more frank since the 1930s when a new reporter for *The New York Herald Tribune* would be told by City Editor Stanley Walker that there were two rules for writing obits: "First, make sure he's dead. Second, if he's a rich drunk, call him a clubman and philanthropist."

We follow Walker's first rule by verifying reports of deaths, and we smile at his second rule.

In its obituary of D. Tennant Bryan, founder of the communications giant Media General Inc., *The New York Times* made a point of Bryan's opposition to the desegregation of public schools despite a Supreme Court ruling. In the second paragraph of the *Times* obituary that Edward Wyatt wrote, Bryan was described as "a leading voice against school desegregation in Virginia in the mid-1950's," and later in the story Wyatt said Bryan's newspapers "were leading supporters of the campaign of 'massive resistance' to racial integration in public schools. . . ."

Jerry Garcia, the guitarist for the Grateful Dead, died in a residential drug treatment center after years of LSD and heroin use. *The New York Times* said in the third paragraph of its page 1 obituary, "In the 1960s, he was known as Captain Trips, referring to his frequent use of LSD, and he struggled through the years with a heroin addiction."

Incidents well known to the public cannot be disregarded. On the other hand, when a man or woman had led a useful life after making a mistake years past, no harm to truth is done by passing over the incident. The obituary of the former city treasurer who was sentenced to the penitentiary for graft 30 years before his death will be handled differently by different newspapers. Some will include his crime; others will not, on the ground that he paid for his mistakes and thereafter led a blameless life.

Don't Ignore The Obvious

Here is how *The New York Times* began its obituary of a well-known but much-disliked owner of a hotel chain:

Leona Helmsley, the self-styled hotel queen whose prison term for income tax evasion and fraud was greeted by a public who regarded her as a 1980's symbol of arrogance and greed, died yesterday at her home in Greenwich, Conn. She was 87.

R.L. Chambers

Memorials

Posters were put up in New York City's Times Square subway station of those missing in the World Trade Center terror bombings. Soon they became memorials when the few survivors were accounted for.

Please Omit Flowers

Q.   When people request no flowers, what do I write?

    A.   Ask the caller if the family prefers that donations be made to an organization, scholarship or charity and name it: The family requests that remembrances be sent to the Douglas County Heart Association. Do not write that the family requests no flowers be sent.

Interviewing Survivors

Q.   Do I press grieving survivors to speak to me even though they may not want to?

    A.   Editors usually want background about the deceased that only people close to the person can provide. An obituary celebrates the person's life, and an interview with relatives can help capture that life. Few subjects have ample material in the clip file.

        Still, reporters must be sensitive to grief. If the source is unwilling to talk, do not press. But give reasons for needing the information, and try to conduct a personal interview if there is no deadline problem.

Cause of Death

Q.   Do I always use the cause of death?

    A.   The cause is given, unless policy is otherwise. For years, cancer—the country's second leading cause of death—was replaced in many obituaries by the euphemisms "long illness" or "lingering illness." The cause of death should be reported whenever possible.

Suicide

Careful

    Certain ways of describing suicide lead to "suicide contagion" or "copycat" suicides, reports the American Foundation for Suicide Prevention. It suggests:

• Do not romanticize or idealize a suicide.

• Avoid details of the suicide method.

Q.   How do I handle suicides?

    A.   Follow the newspaper's policy. Most are frank; some avoid the word. *The Record-Journal* in Meriden, Conn., describes the cause of death in the final paragraph of the obituary, which allows the family to cut off the paragraph before preserving the story or sending it to others. Be careful to attribute suicide to an authority, the medical examiner or the coroner. Without such attribution, do not state suicide was the cause of death.

First Person

Q.   If I knew the deceased well, can I write a first-person obituary?

    A.   Rarely. Obituaries are almost always in the straight news form. Now and then, a reporter may be permitted a personal reminiscence, but this is usually done in a column.

Localizing Obituaries

Q. Should I try to localize obituaries?

A. Yes, if the person is a resident of your community and died elsewhere or was a former well-known resident. For example:

> John A. Nylic, 68, a retired mainte-
> nance worker at General Electric Co., died
> Friday night after suffering an apparent
> heart attack while visiting in Lebanon
> Springs, N.Y.
>   Mr. Nylic, who lived at 78 W. Housa-
> tonic St. . . .
>   —*The Berkshire Eagle* (Pittsfield, Mass.)

Humorous Obituaries

Q. Must the obituary always be solemn?

A. Most are and should be. Now and then the subject lends himself or herself to lighter treatment. When the screenwriter Al Boasberg died, the lead to his obituary shocked some readers. Others found it appropriate. Boasberg had written many of the gags that were used in the Marx Brothers' movies. Some of his most famous sequences involved death, such as the one of Groucho Marx posing as a doctor taking a patient's pulse and intoning: "Either this man is dead or my watch has stopped." For the lead on Boasberg's obituary, Douglas Gilbert wrote:

> The joke's on Al Boasberg. He's dead.

The Specialist

A few newspapers assign specialists to write obituaries. Alden Whitman, for years the master obituary writer for *The New York Times,* was allowed to comment on the personal habits and the accomplishments of his subjects. When he wrote the obituary of Mies van der Rohe, the prophet of an austere modern architectural style, Whitman noted that the architect chose to live on the third floor of an old-fashioned apartment house on Chicago's north side.

In his obituary of André Malraux, the French writer, Whitman wrote that he was "a chain smoker of cheap cigarettes." In his lengthy obituary of the American socialist, Norman Thomas, Whitman said Thomas' socialism "was to Marxism what Musak is to Mozart."

Summing Up

The obituary is no different from any news story. In this case, the reporter finds the most newsworthy aspect of the person's life—she was the author of a best selling novel; he lived to be 105 and worked until he was struck down by a bus. Every life has something newsworthy, and it is the task of the reporter to find out what that was.

Further Reading

Baranick, Alana, Jim Sheeler and Stephen Miller. *Life on the Death Beat: A Handbook for Obituary Writers,* 2nd ed. Oak Park, Ill.: Marion Street Press, 2005.

 The authors, experienced journalists, outline the basic approach to obit writing and suggest answers to such questions as whether to write about past crimes and the use of old photos.

Johnson, Marilyn. *The Dead Beat: Lost Souls, Lucky Stiffs and the Perverse Pleasures of Obituaries.* New York: HarperCollins, 2006.

 Johnson describes the obituary as a "tight little coil of biography" that "reminds us of a poem" and "contains the most creative writing in journalism." She profiles some of the best obituary writers and provides examples of what she considers to be their best work.

Mitford, Jessica. *The American Way of Death.* New York: Fawcett Crest, 1978.

Whitman, Alden. *The Obituary Book.* New York: Stein and Day, 1971.

Whitman, Alden. *Come to Judgment.* New York: Viking Press, 1980.

Preview

Police reporters cover a vast array of news. Their beat calls upon them to handle:

- **Breaking stories:** Accidents, crimes, arrests, fires.
- **Features:** Profiles of police personnel, criminals; stories about police investigations.
- **Interpretative articles:** Law enforcement policies, changes in personnel and procedures.
- **Investigative reporting:** Examination of false arrests, corruption, lax enforcement.

Police reporters depend on sources in the department and on their knowledge of police procedure for their stories.

The Bureau of Justice makes crime data available online. The data enable reporters to compare crime figures of their cities with that of other cities.

The U.S. Department of Education and the FBI maintain Web sites with crime data for colleges and universities

Wayne Miller

Details from the crime scene.

Few beats produce as much news as the police beat, and few reporters are called upon to do as much as quickly as the police reporter. The police reporter covers:

- **Crime:** reports of crime, investigation, arrest, booking, arraignment.
- **Accidents:** traffic, airplane, drowning, rescue.
- **Fires:** reports and on-the-scene coverage.
- **Departmental activity:** personnel, policies, efficiency and accountability.
- **Departmental integrity:** standards, policies and procedures for dealing with internal and external allegations.
- **Other law enforcement agencies:** sheriff's office, state highway patrol, suburban police departments, federal marshals.

The Range and Cost of Crime

Which hand held the gun?

One of four households is hit by crime every year, mostly by burglary and theft. One in 35 households is struck by a violent crime—murder, rape, robbery, assault. A rape is committed every 6 minutes, a murder every 34 minutes.

The Beat With Everything
   "The police beat is about people and what makes them tick, what turns them into homicidal maniacs, what brings out the best in them, what drives them berserk. It has it all: greed, sex, violence, comedy and tragedy. You learn more about people than you would on any other newspaper job."
   —Edna Buchanan,
   The Miami Herald *police reporter*

The number of crime victims approaches 26 million. Of these, a fourth are the victims of violent crimes. The U.S. Department of Justice reports that almost 7 million people were the victims of murder, rape, robbery or assault last year.

The prison and jail population grew from 300,000 in the mid-1970s to 2.2 million today. More than 4.8 million are on probation or parole. The 7 million involved with the penal system amounts to 1 in every 40 adults. The U.S. incarceration rate is the highest in the world, seven times that of Italy and Germany, more than ten times that of Japan and Norway.

The crowded jails and prisons are the result of several converging forces—the public demand for longer sentences, the elimination of parole in some states, the belief that taking criminals off the streets will lower violent crime rates and the imprisonment of increasing numbers of men and women convicted of crimes involving drugs. In 25 years, the number of inmates in prisons for drug offenses went from 1 in 16 inmates to 1 in 5.

Although the number of violent crimes has been declining for a decade, the prison population has been increasing, up by 170 percent over the past decade to 2.2 million. One in 143 adults is in prison.

Fewer Crimes

No one is sure why the crime rate is dropping. One theory is that tougher law enforcement and longer prison sentences are keeping criminals off the streets. Another is that there are fewer men in their 20s, the high-crime age group.

Another suggested cause is the increase in what is known as "community-oriented policing." Police respond to a call about a crime no matter how petty. By moving quickly when windows in a housing project are broken, when loitering youths insult passersby, when graffiti mars stop signs, when playgrounds are vandalized—when the police react to these low-level activities that disrupt public order, more serious crimes decline. The police presence frightens away the drug dealers. The gangs stop loitering.

When the police began making disorder arrests, they found the people they arrested were carrying guns and many were wanted on felony warrants. The "Disorder Theory," as the low tolerance for minor crimes is known, has become common police practice.

Suburban Crime   Traditionally, crime rates are highest in the big cities. But the growth of the suburbs and increased police efficiency in the city have led criminals to the suburbs. Chicago street gangs, for example, have moved out of the city. The 70 gangs in the Chicago area have more than 70,000 members and are engaging in white-collar crime along with extortion and drug dealing.

Costs

More than $150 billion is spent each year on the police, and on courts, prisons and jails and the parole and probation systems by cities, states and the federal government.

The War on Crime—Costs and Consequences

The National Criminal Justice Foundation issued a report that found:

Many American cities spend more money on law enforcement than on education.

More prisons have been built in rural areas since 1980 than during the previous two centuries.

Corrections officer is the fastest-growing job category in government service.

Fifty percent of inner-city children have at least one parent in jail or prison, on parole or probation, or on the run from the law.

One of every four males has an arrest record.

Some prison guards earn more than college presidents.

The cost of confining an inmate can run to $60,000 a year in large cities. And when the public demands, as it has, less probation, more confinement and longer sentences, the costs skyrocket. Handling criminals costs more than $300 a person in taxes.

Interest in Crime News

You might think that over the years of intense crime coverage the public's appetite would reach the saturation point. Not so. Crime news remains high on the media agenda.

Perhaps it is the increasingly bizarre nature of crimes:

- The perfect neighbor who stabbed his next-door neighbor 13 times after she resisted his sexual advances.

- The Mormon church leader who had an entire family executed to protect his standing in the church.

- The teen-ager who persuaded his college classmates to kill his stepfather.

- The lawyer who had his buddies on the police force shoot his wife and dump her and her car into a Chicago canal.

- The widow who rid herself of a series of husbands by feeding them arsenic.

The Police

To cope with crime there are almost 600,000 state and local police officers, and efforts are constantly being made to add more. They are outnumbered by the 1.5 million private police, who guard office buildings, apartment complexes, shopping malls, gated communities and even the streets of some residential communities. Most universities use their own police to monitor campuses.

Rodolfo Gonzales,
San Antonio Light

Juvenile Crime

Law enforcement agencies devote considerable resources to juvenile crime. Gang membership totals about 650,000; 60 percent of the gang members are concentrated in California, Illinois and Texas.

Police Department Organization

The police department is organized around the three police functions—(1) enforcement of laws, (2) prevention of crime and (3) finding and arresting criminals.

The department is headed by a chief or commissioner who is responsible to the mayor, director of public safety or city manager. The chief or commissioner is appointed and although he or she makes departmental policy, broad policy decisions affecting law enforcement come from a superior and are often made in a political context. The chief's second in command may be an assistant chief or inspector. Commissioners have deputy commissioners under them.

The rest of the organizational chart depends upon the size of the city. In large cities, deputy inspectors are put in charge of various divisions or bureaus—homicide, detective, robbery, juvenile, rape, arson, traffic. The larger the city, the more bureaus. As the patterns of criminal activity change, organizational changes are made. After the World Trade Center terror bombings, some cities formed counterterrorism bureaus. These changes make good stories.

The next in command in large cities are captains, who are assigned to run precincts and are assisted by lieutenants. Sergeants are placed in charge of shifts or squads at the precinct house. The private in the organization is the police officer.

The beat reporter's day-to-day contacts are for the most part with sergeants and lieutenants. Reporters, trained to be suspicious of authority, are sometimes irritated by the paramilitary structure, secretiveness and implicit authoritarianism of the police department.

Diana K. Sugg, a police reporter for *The Sacramento Bee,* is blunt: "In most cities around the country, big or small, the cops don't like reporters." Often the reporter and the police work at cross purposes. "We want the information they can't or won't release." Let's accompany Sugg as she works her beat.

Making Her Rounds

It's 9 a.m. and Sugg is in the police station with her portable police scanner, pager, map and notepad. Some days she visits the sheriff 's office first and then the police station.

She flips through the watch summaries of the significant events of the previous day and night. With her scanner buzzing in the background, she goes over every page, every notation. "I'm looking for anything strange, anything particularly cruel.

"Once a woman managed to catch a rapist by running into her bathroom with a portable telephone and calling 911. Another time a man tied up three children and then raped their mother in front of them. Or you may find material for a short feature story—like the man named the 'inept robber' by the police because he made four robbery attempts at markets—and made off with only one beer."

She also reads the arrest reports, sometimes as many as 200 a day. For the detailed reports and the watch summaries, her eyes go automatically to the name, age and, "particularly the occupation. A 45-year-old unemployed man arrested for theft isn't much of a story. But a 45-year-old teacher? Why would he need to steal? When you contact him, will he tell you the arrest was a mistake?"

She looks at the section marked "Comments" at the bottom of the arrest sheets for unusual circumstances the officers may note. "Once a man threw a rock through a window and waited for the police to come because he wanted to be arrested—he was homeless and he had AIDS. He figured the jail officers would at least take care of him."

Consulting the Penal Code   Sugg occasionally consults a small handbook, the penal code, as crimes sometimes are listed only by the code number. "That's done to keep reporters from noticing certain arrests," she says.

Diana K. Sugg

She makes a point of looking in on the sergeant in charge that day. "Even if things are slow and I don't have anything to ask the sergeant, I always make a point to talk with him, sometimes sharing the hard parts of my job so he could understand why some stories were shorter, or why we weren't interested in covering some.

"During all this checking, the scanner is babbling and my pager is ringing as I am talking with a secretary. It can get nerve-wracking, because I am afraid I might miss something." Her ear is tuned to the code numbers for kidnappings, shootings, homicides, and she knows the police codes, too, those they use when they report they are going to eat, taking a bathroom break or going off duty.

To the Newsroom   Her morning checks completed, Sugg drives to the newsroom with a couple of items to run by her editor to see whether they are worth pursuing. She has to return a phone call to someone who read one of her stories and wants to add to it.

It's noon and she takes a break, her second Mounds bar, a diet Coke, maybe a giant chocolate chip cookie. The *Bee* is a morning paper, and Sugg has the afternoon to continue to gather information, to look deeper into some items, to call people on continuing stories.

Then she's off with her pager, scanner, portable radio, map and notebook. On the way to the scene, she's listening to officers talk to their supervisors. She moves fast. One day while working the night police shift—the newspaper covers the beat 'round the clock—she heard on her scanner a report of a shooting. She was off. On the way to the crime scene she heard officers report that one shooting was fatal, and then a second … and then a third. "Within half an hour I was dictating the story of a triple shooting over the portable radio," Sugg says. She made the deadline.

On the Scene   "Neighbors are incredible sources," Sugg says. "Especially if you find the one busybody who watches the street like a hawk and knows everything about the neighbors. People like this know where someone works, the hours he or she keeps, the age of his children, when he was divorced. All this information has to be checked out, but it's a starting point."

Many crimes do not have eyewitnesses, but Sugg looks for the neighbor who heard a shot, a scream. "Once I interviewed a 7-year-old boy who watched a shooting through his apartment window."

She always tries to interview the victims. "Often, when they discover your sincerity they open up and give you unbelievable details." She makes sure to absorb the scene—the ambulance door slamming shut, the smell of the burned house, the cold fog over the scene of the triple shooting.

Smaller-City Coverage

Crime receives considerable coverage, even in smaller cities. Although a newspaper or station may not have a regular reporter covering the environment or business, education or county government, most assign a reporter to cover the police on a daily basis.

The stories may include "juveniles throwing snowballs in front of the City Center, hindering pedestrians" and "moose on the highway" (*The Times Argus* in Barre-Montpelier, Vt.) and the kidnapping of a scarecrow "value $15" (*The Quincy Herald-Whig* in western Illinois). These brief items will run in a column like this one in the *Argus Leader* in Sioux Falls, S.D.:

Police Log

VANDALISM: Vandals spray-painted a pentagon, a pitchfork and assorted other graffiti on the Knights of Columbus hall at 315 N. Summit Ave. on Monday, police said. The graffiti, which was found on the back wall of the hall, caused $50 damage.

VANDALISM: Vandals uprooted a fence post and threw display items such as wooden geese into the Laurel Oaks Pool at 3401 E. 49the St. on Saturday or Sunday, police said. The damage amounted to $100.

VANDALISM: Someone broke the left headlight, removed the hood ornament and scratched and dented the driver's side of a 1984 Cadillac El Dorado, causing $725 damage, on Friday or Saturday, police said. The car's owner, Alvin R. Clausen, 69, 816 W. 15th St., said he wasn't sure where the vandalism occurred.

AGGRAVATED ASSAULT: A 15-year-old boy and his 14-year-old friend told police three boys pulled what resembled a black automatic handgun on them as they rode their bikes on Westview Road from their homes to a convenience store and back Friday, police said. The "handgun" turned out to be a squirt gun.

AGGRAVATED ASSAULT: A 16-year-old Sioux Falls girl told police that her ex-boyfriend slapped and punched her on the back of her head and then struck her with a green garden hose May 31, police said. The girl said the assault occurred at her ex-boyfriend's residence in the 3300 block of South Holly Avenue and was not the first time he had struck her, police said. No arrest was made.

New on the Beat

Editors like to assign their younger reporters to the police beat in the belief there is no faster way to test a reporter's competence and to immerse the new staffer into the life of the city.

On the job, the new police reporter immediately becomes acquainted with the organization of the police department and sets about making contacts

With the Police: Drugs, Teens, Death

Randy Piland, *The Macon* (Ga.) *Telegraph*

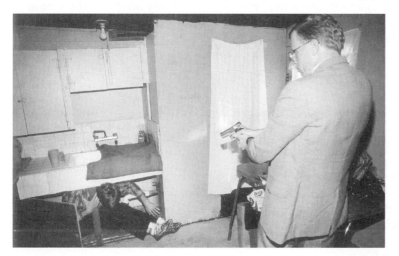

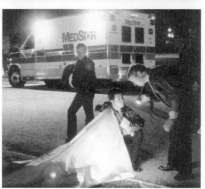

Other photos: Rodger Mallison, *Fort Worth Star-Telegram*

with key officers. Survival depends on establishing a routine and developing good sources.

The new police reporter quickly learns the difference between a minor crime, which can be a violation or misdemeanor, and a major crime, a felony. Stealing a scarecrow may violate a city regulation, but stealing $10,000 from the local A&P is a felony as defined in state law. Misdemeanors are punishable by less than a year in jail and/or a fine, whereas felonies send the convicted perpetrator to the state prison, or a federal prison, for more than a year.

Types of Felonies

There are seven types of felonies, which fall into two general categories, not including the so-called possessory felonies involving weapons and drugs.

- **Violent crime:** murder, rape, robbery, aggravated assault.

- **Property crime:** burglary, larceny-theft, motor-vehicle theft.

The FBI keeps crime data in these categories, as do local and campus police. Ten percent of all felonies are violent and 90 percent are crimes against property.

Sources Are Essential

Dangerous Cities
The Morgan Quitno Press of Lawrence, Kan., examined crime data to rank the most dangerous cities. Here are the top three by population group:

500,000 or More
Detroit
Baltimore
Washington, D.C.

100,000–499,999
St. Louis
Flint, Mich.
Richmond

75,000–99,999
Camden, N.J.
West Palm Beach, Fla.
Compton, Calif.

Police reporters depend on inside sources. Without them—given the guarded nature of the police—the reporter has a hard time covering the beat. This is why big-city media keep at least one reporter on the police beat for years. It takes time to cultivate sources.

Edna Buchanan of *The Miami Herald* is a veteran of the beat. "I talk to cops a lot," she says. "Talking to cops is the only way to get a lot of the stories I do. Of course, a lot of policemen don't recognize a good story, so you just have to keep talking to them so it'll come up in conversation." She recalls learning about a robbery where "a guy got robbed and knocked down. No big deal." But she learned from a contact that the victim had artificial legs and was pushed off his legs "for something like a dollar and forty cents."

The Arrest Process

The police reporter knows arrest procedures, and because on some smaller newspapers and on many radio and television stations the same reporter who covers an arrest might stay with the case through the trial, a knowledge of the criminal court process is necessary, too. Here, we will discuss the arrest process. In the next chapter, criminal court procedures are outlined.

A person may be arrested on sight or upon issuance of a warrant. Let us follow a case in which a merchant spots in his store a man he believes robbed him the previous week.

The store owner calls a police officer who arrests the man. The suspect is searched on the scene and taken to the station house. The suspect is then searched again in front of the booking desk. His property is recorded and placed in a "property" envelope. The suspect's name and other identification and the alleged crime are recorded in a book known to old-time reporters as a *blotter*. (The blotter supposedly takes its name from the work of turn-of-the-century police sergeants who spilled considerable ink in their laborious efforts to transcribe information and then had to sop up the splotches with a blotter.)

Miranda Warning   The police are required to tell a suspect at the time of arrest that he has the right to remain silent and to refuse to answer questions. (This is called the Miranda warning.) He also has the right to consult an attorney at any time and is told that if he cannot afford a lawyer one will be provided. Unless the suspect waives these rights, his statements cannot be used against him at his trial.

The signed waiver permits the police immediately to interrogate the suspect about his actions, background and whereabouts in connection with the crime. If it is a homicide case, the practice is to call in an assistant prosecutor to ensure the admissibility of any admission or confession.

The officer then prepares an arrest report, which is written in the presence of the suspect who also supplies "pedigree information"—age, height, weight, date and place of birth and other details.

The Complaint   The suspect may then be photographed and fingerprinted and will be permitted to make a telephone call. A record is made of the number and person called and the suspect is returned to a detention cell to await arraignment. The arresting officer goes to the complaint room to confer with the complainant and an assistant district attorney so that a complaint can be drawn up. The police officer may ask the complainant to identify the suspect again in a lineup.

The assistant district attorney has to decide whether the case is strong enough, the witness reliable, the offense worth prosecuting before a complaint is drawn. The prosecutor must also decide whether to reduce a felony charge to a lesser felony or to a misdemeanor. She may reduce the charge if she feels the reduction would lead to a guilty plea and thus avoid the expense of a trial.

The police officer may have to file additional reports. If he fired his weapon, he must file an "unusual incident report," as it is described in some jurisdictions, and if he shot someone, he files an "inspector's report."

The fingerprints are checked in a central state agency to determine whether the suspect has a record, and the suspect's file is sent to the courts, which require the information before arraignment. The presiding judge at arraignment decides whether bail should be set and the amount. A suspect with no record who is arrested for a minor crime may be released on his own recognizance—that is, without putting up bail.

Most large cities have overcrowded detention facilities and a backlog of untried cases. To cope, they may release suspects on low bail or none at all. Later, plea bargaining may be arranged in which the defendant agrees to plead guilty to a lesser charge so that the case can be disposed of at arraignment (see Chapter 21).

Safest Big Cities
The Morgan Quitno Press lists the following crime rankings for cities of more than 500,000:
   San Jose
   El Paso
   Honolulu
   New York
   Austin

Jails, Prisons
Jails are locally administered and hold persons who are awaiting trial or sentence or are serving sentences of a year or less. Prisons, state and federal, hold inmates with sentences of more than a year.

The Wichita Eagle

Arrested

A suspect in the murder of 10 people is arrested. He was later to plead guilty.

Arrest Stories

Most crimes are committed by young men, and a growing number involve teen-agers. Juveniles who are arrested are turned over to the juvenile court and their names are not released. In some states, in response to the rise in violent crime by youngsters, serious offenses by youths, particularly murder, are handled by the regular court system and their names can be used, as an upstate New York newspaper did in the following crime.

Murder   The battered body of a 77-year-old man was discovered in his home at 11 p.m. by a neighbor who called the police. The neighbor said she saw two youths running from the scene. Police conducted an investigation and within five hours arrested a 16-year-old and a 14-year-old. The two were charged with second-degree murder and at their arraignment entered pleas of not guilty.

The reporter for the local afternoon newspaper learns all this on his 7 a.m. check. He calls the coroner to obtain information about the cause of death,

The Arrest Process

The police reporter covers all aspects of the arrest process, from the report of the arrest through the arraignment of the suspect. Most arrests receive bare mention, but serious crimes are covered fully.

Reporters rely for information on the police, the district attorney and the suspect's lawyer. The reporter is aware that the original charge often is reduced by the prosecutor because either the original charge cannot be sustained or the prosecutor believes the suspect is more likely to plead guilty to a lessened charge than he or she would to the original charge.

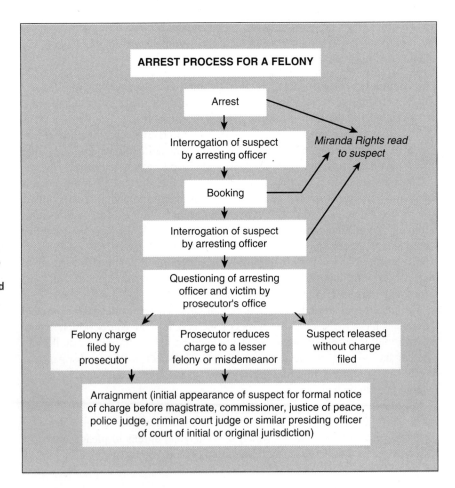

and he questions the police about the murder weapon and the motivation. He also asks where the youths are being held and the time they were arrested. With the information on hand, he calls his desk to report what he has and the city editor tells him to give the story 200 words. The dead man was not prominent.

The editor asks about the neighbor: Did she identify the youngsters, and if not, how did the police learn their identities? The reporter says the police will not comment about the neighbor. Nor will the neighbor talk. The story will have to be a straight murder-and-arrest piece. Here is how the reporter wrote it:

Two Saratoga youths were arrested early today and charged with the murder of 77-year-old Anthony Hay, a local fuel oil and coal dealer, whose battered body was found last night in his home.

Police identified the youths as Arthur Traynor, 16, of 61 Joshua Ave., and John Martinez, 14, of 15 Doten Ave. Police said a neighbor saw two youths fleeing from Hay's residence at 342 Nelson Ave. The arrests were made within five hours of the slaying.

The youths entered pleas of not guilty at their arraignment this morning on charges of second-degree murder and were being held in the county jail pending a preliminary hearing.

Hay's body was found at 11 p.m. in the business office of his home. He was "badly beaten about the head and face and had a fractured skull," Coroner Clark Donaldson reported. Police said they recovered the death weapon, a three-foot wooden club. They declined to give any motive for the slaying.

Caution: Be careful about identifying the arrested. A libel suit resulted when a newspaper identified a crime suspect who had stolen a wallet from which police took the name. "Use special care in reporting the arrest of a public figure," advises the AP. "It is not uncommon for crime suspects to give police false names, and frequently those they provide are from sports figures, politicians, etc." Press authorities for authentication of the identification.

Be especially careful about identifying anyone as a suspect before the person has been formally charged. Identifying a suspect had been common practice until a suspect in a bombing at the 1996 summer Olympics in Atlanta filed suit against the media that used his name in their accounts. *The Atlanta Journal-Constitution* reported the man had become a suspect and NBC and CNN picked up the story. Three months later, he was cleared. Rather than have to fight a libel suit, the networks settled out of court for large sums, but the newspaper claimed it accurately quoted authorities. The newspaper would not settle out-of-court and won when the court ruled that the suspect was a public figure and that the newspaper had not been malicious in naming him.

In Dallas, a woman who named two football players on the Dallas Cowboys team as having raped her was later charged with perjury. But the police department had released the names of the players to the media. The police later announced a policy of not identifying suspects until they are arrested or charged.

What Color Is the Blouse?

In his book *City Room,* Arthur Gelb describes the first breaking news story he covered on the police beat for *The New York Times*. A woman had been bound with neckties, strangled and stabbed repeatedly. A blouse had been spread over her face.

I phoned in the notes I had taken to Mike Berger.

"What color were the ties?" he asked.

"I'm not sure. I think one of them was brown."

"You think one of them was brown? I need to know the actual colors."

I said I'd go back and check. One tie was bluish-brown, another was brown and yellow, a third was gray. I called Mike and apologized for the oversight.

"Okay," he said. "What color was the blouse?"

I didn't know, so I went back again. "It was pink," I told Mike.

"Great. What kind of furniture was in the room?". . .

Gelb went back again, and then for the fourth revisit when Berger wanted to know the kind of fur coat that was draped over a chair near the body.

"Mink," Gelb Replied.

Not Me, Officer

Photographer O. Gordon Williamson Jr. of *The Orlando Sentinel* chanced to see a bearded man make a getaway from a bank he had just robbed. Williamson followed the man to a barber shop, and while the identifying beard was being removed, Williamson called the police . . . and then took this picture.

Crime Classification

Crimes are classified as violations, misdemeanors or felonies. The classifications are made by the states and differ slightly from state to state. Generally, the length of the sentence and the fine determine the classification. Violations are low-level crimes, punishable by small fines or short jail terms—loitering, committing a public nuisance. Misdemeanors are more serious and can lead to a jail sentence of less than a year—petty larceny, minor burglaries, traffic offenses.

Felonies are serious crimes punishable by a sentence of more than a year in a state prison. Felonies are the subject of most police reporting.

Hate Crimes

In 1990, in response to growing concern over bias crimes, Congress passed a law requiring the U.S. attorney general to collect data "about crimes that manifest evidence of prejudice based on race, religion, sexual orientation or ethnicity."

A recent year showed 8,152 incidents, with California leading the nation, reporting 1,942 incidents. Most were anti-black and anti-Jewish incidents.

For a breakdown of these offenses, see **Hate Crimes** in *NRW Plus.*

Murder

In some states, murder is rare—Vermont may have two homicides a year. When a murder is reported, coverage is intense. In metropolitan areas, where one or two murders are reported each day, only the prominence of the victim or the suspect merits full-scale coverage. Prominence clearly was the news value that motivated the minute coverage of the death of O.J. Simpson's ex-wife—not hers, of course, but his. Look at how the AP wrote the first lead on the discovery of the bodies:

> LOS ANGELES, (AP)—Hall of Fame football player O.J. Simpson's ex-wife and a man were found dead early Monday outside the woman's condominium, and Simpson was being interviewed by police.

This began what some critics described as a "media circus" or a "media feeding frenzy." Journalists countered by pointing to the near-insatiable public appetite for the story.

Story leads about the progress of the investigation and then the arrest of Simpson are in **O.J. Simpson** in *NRW Plus.*

NRW➕

Checklist: Homicide

Crime

___Victim, identification.

___Time, date, place of death.

___Weapon used.

___Official cause of death or authoritative comment.

___Who discovered body.

___Clues; any identification of slayer.

___Police comments; motivation for crime.

___Comments from neighbors, friends.

___Any police record for victim; any connection with criminal activity.

___Consequences to victim's family, others.

Arrest

___Name, identification of person arrested.

___Victim's name; time, date, place of crime.

___Exact charge.

___Circumstances of arrest.

___Motive.

___Results of tip, investigation.

Murder Rates

The national rate for murders was 5.5. Here are the cities and states with the highest rates:

Cities

1. New Orleans	25.5
2. Detroit	20.3
3. Jackson, Miss.	14.0
4. Pine Bluff, Ark.	13.1
5. Richmond, Va.	12.6

States

1. Wisconsin	11.8
2. Mississippi	10.5
3. Louisiana	9.6
4. North Carolina	8.8
5. Georgia	7.9

(Rate per 100,000 population.)

WANTED 187 PC WARRANT

Date: 6/12/2001
Case #:   01-4546
Name: JOSE FLORES
Address: 187 ATKINSON LANE
               WATSONVILLE, CA
Height: 5 Feet 8 Inches
Weight: 190
Age: 58
Sex: M
Eyes: BRN
Hair: BLK
Complexion: FAIR
Race: HISPANIC
Birth Date: 4/15/1943

OTHER INFORMATION BELOW

On 05-18-01, Jose Aguefe Flores shot and killed his employee during a work related dispute and in front of numerous witnesses. Flores fled the scene with his cellular phone and the murder weapon in hand. Although his current whereabouts are unknown, he has extended family in Mexico and may have fled there. A warrant of arrest is in the system for 187 PC.

If located use extreme caution. Flores should be considered ARMED and DANGEROUS.

Santa Cruz County Sheriff
(831) 454-2311

Homicide

Jose Flores, a foreman on a California strawberry farm, was furious when Mauricio Cruz picked some green berries. They argued. Flores went home and returned with a gun. Witnesses say he then shot Cruz in the back and while the worker was lying on the ground, he shot Cruz in the head. Flores fled and the sheriff's department in Santa Cruz County issued this poster.

___Officers involved in investigation, arrest.

___Booking.

___Arraignment; bail, if any.

___Suspect's police record (in states where it is not illegal to publish such information).

Burglary, Robbery

Burglary (B) is a crime against property, usually involving a home, office, or store break-in. Robbery (R) is a crime against a person, involving the removal of the person's goods or money with force or threat of force and is categorized as a violent crime.

Checklist: Burglary, Robbery

Crime

___Victim, identification.

___Goods or money taken; value of goods.

___Date, time, location of crime.

___(R) Weapon used.

___(B) How entry made.

___(R) Injuries and how caused.

___Clues.

Mug Shot

After a suspect is arrested, booked and interrogated, he or she is photographed. The pictures, called *mug shots,* go into the suspect's file, which also contains his or her criminal record, known as a *rap sheet.* This is a photo of Joseph (Crazy Joe) Gallo, a mobster whose rap sheet showed an extensive record. Gallo was gunned down by rival mob hit men as he celebrated his 43rd birthday in Umberto's Clam House a block away from New York City police headquarters.

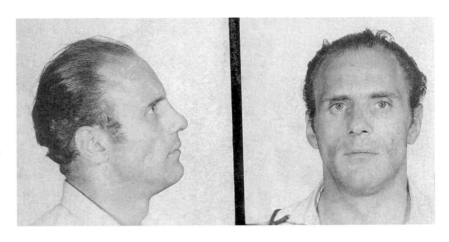

____Unusual circumstances (overlooked valuables, frequency of crime in area or to victim, etc.).

____Statements from victim, witness.

Arrest

____Name, identification of person arrested.

____Details of crime.

____Circumstances of arrest.

> **Robbery Rates**
> The cities with the highest robbery rates are:
>
> 1. Memphis   339.1
> 2. Miami   324.8
> 3. Detroit   322.1
> 4. Vineland, N.J.   268.7
> 5. Los Angeles   266.0
>
> The national rate is 136.7 per 100,000 population.

Additional Elements Some newspapers and stations have added these essentials to their stories about violent crime:

____Where was the weapon obtained?

____Were alcohol or drugs involved?

____Did the victim and the perpetrator know each other?

Note: Half or more of those arrested are not formally charged with the crime for which they were arrested. Some newspapers and stations will use the names of those arrested only after they have been formally charged with a crime.

Crime Coverage and Race

High crime rates in the inner cities have led to considerable coverage of the perpetrators and the victims, who are disproportionately members of minority groups. And this, in turn, has been the cause of criticism of the media.

One area of controversy has been racial profiling, the police practice of using race as a significant factor in stop-and-search activities. For an analysis of this practice see **Racial Profiling** in *NRW Plus.*

For a case study of how a reporter went about exposing racism practiced by a police department see **Targeting Blacks** in *NRW Plus.*

Database Reporting

Police departments keep good records, and most are available to reporters online. It is not difficult, for example, to take the list that the state provides of all school bus drivers and correlate that list with the names of those arrested in a given period. Reporters regularly do this to check whether child molesters, drunk drivers or felons are driving children to and from school.

Drunk Drivers You know drunk drivers are involved in traffic accidents. But how many of them are responsible for highway fatalities in your state? Easy.

Ask the U.S. Department of Transportation, www.dot.gov, for the percentage of fatalities in the state in accidents involving alcohol. The DOT's National Highway Traffic Safety Administration keeps the data.

You'll find Texas, Louisiana, Alaska, North Dakota, Nevada, New Mexico and Washington are high in the rankings, usually with more than half the fatal accidents involving drunk drivers.

Police Efficiency

How well the local police force does its work can be checked by using a few figures: What percentage of reported crimes led to arrests? Another comparison: What percentage of arrests led to complaints filed by the district attorney? Prosecutors will not take a case unless the police provide them with sufficient evidence and solid witness support.

Can a force be too forceful? Using databases with police figures, *The Washington Post* found that District of Columbia police killed more people per capita than any other police force. Its series on quick-trigger cops won a Pulitzer Prize for public service.

Another check of departmental efficiency can be made by examining the response to calls made to the police. A study of 2,000 calls to the St. Louis Police Department found that 25 percent of the calls were ignored. Of the 75 percent to which the police responded, arrests were made 50 percent of the time. Ten percent of those arrested went to trial, and 4 percent of those arrested were convicted.

Data Available

The Bureau of Justice Statistics makes available free copies of its reports that cover a wide range: national crime surveys, domestic violence, parole and probation, ages of rape victims, sentencing patterns, juvenile crime.

To be placed on the Bureau's mailing list, call toll-free 1-800-732-3277 or write: Justice Statistics Clearinghouse, P.O. Box 179, Dept. BJS-236, Annapolis Junction, MD 20701-0179. The Web site is www.ojp.usdoj.gov/bjs/.

Single copies are free. Public-use tapes of Bureau data sets are available from the Criminal Justice Archive and Information Network, P.O. Box 1248, Ann Arbor, MI 48106, telephone (313) 763-5010.

The Federal Bureau of Investigation makes annual crime figures available at www.fbi.gov/vcr/ucr.htm.

The Victims

Crime falls heaviest on the poor, the young and members of minority groups. Half the victims of violent crimes are aged 12 to 24 although they represent only a fourth of the population. Blacks and Hispanics across all age groups are more at risk from violence than whites of comparable age: 1 in 30 blacks, 1 in 35 Hispanics, 1 in 58 whites.

Murder rates of blacks are 8 times higher than that for whites—1 in every 894 blacks, 1 in every 7,334 whites. The lifetime chance of being a murder victim is 1 in 131 for white males, 1 in 21 for black males.

Violence Against Women

About 2.5 million women are the victims of violent crime each year. The most frequent crime committed against them is assault, often domestic assault. Studies by the Bureau of Justice found that the women "most vulnerable as the victims of violence are black, Hispanic, in younger age groups, never married, with lower family income and lower education levels and in central cities."

More than two-thirds of the women victims knew their attackers. Almost one-third of the attackers were husbands, boyfriends, or relatives; a third were acquaintances. Women victimized by strangers were six times more likely to report their attack to police as were those women attacked by relatives or friends. These women said they feared reprisals from their attackers.

Although the violent crime victimization rate for males has declined, the rate for females has not.

Rape

More than 350,000 rapes and sexual assaults are reported a year. Only about half the women report their victimizations to the police. The Bureau of Justice found about half of all rapes were perpetrated by someone known to the victim and that in one-fifth of the cases the offender was armed.

"Of female rape victims who took some self-protective action such as fighting back and yelling and screaming, most reported that it helped the situation rather than made it worse," the Bureau reported.

See *NRW Plus* **"Cracking an Unsolved Rape Case Makes History"** for an article on how DNA was used in California.

Domestic Violence

The home, figures tell us, is more dangerous for women than the streets. Domestic violence is the single greatest cause of injury to American women. The American Medical Association considers family violence a public health menace and estimates it affects one-fourth of all families in the United States. The AMA reports domestic violence is responsible for a third of all murders of women.

Yet, coverage of the subject is minimal, lost in the reporting of murders, gang wars and drug busts. Also, the actual dimension of the crime is not reflected in the police reports. Close to half of all incidents of domestic violence against women are not reported to police. Of married women not reporting their husbands, 41 percent were subsequently assaulted by them within six months. Of those who did report their husbands, 15 percent were reassaulted.

State Rape Rates
The national state rate for rapes is 32 per 100,000 population. The five states with the highest rates are:

Alaska	85
New Mexico	55
Michigan	54
Washington	46
Oklahoma	42

Child Abuse
The Justice Department reported child abuse and neglect reports tripled over the past decade, rising from one million to three million.
Idaho, Alaska and Washington have the highest rates of physical and sexual child abuse.

Donna Ferrato, *Domestic Abuse Awareness Project*

Behind Closed Doors

Domestic abuse is the silent plague of American households. Half the occurrences are not reported to police, and journalists rarely cover the crime. Yet it affects about a quarter of households and is the single greatest cause of injury to women.

A Reporter's Perspective

Edna Buchanan, the prizewinning police reporter for *The Miami Herald,* says:

> Sometimes, we are all the victim has got.
>
> Sometimes you feel like Wonder Woman, or Superman, going to the rescue. Reporters can find missing kids, lost grandmothers, and misplaced corpses. We fish out people who fall through the cracks. Publicity rescues people tangled in the hopeless mazes of government and bureaucracy. We recover stolen cars and priceless family heirlooms. A story in the newspaper can secure donations of blood, money, and public support—and occasionally that rarest gift of all: justice.

Skepticism   Police reporters say skepticism comes with the job. Things are seldom what they seem. A heartbroken father tells police a hitchhiker he picked up forced him out of his car at gunpoint and drove off with his 2-year-old daughter in the back seat. A distraught mother reports her 4-year-old daughter and 2-year-old son disappeared in a department store on Christmas Eve. Newspapers and television carry the woman's prayer for the safe return of her children.

Two days after the hitchhiker story is played up by newspapers and television, the child's body is found in a garbage bin. The father is charged with second-degree murder; authorities say he left the child in the car on a hot day and she was asphyxiated.

Two days after a mother's tearful prayer on TV, this lead appears on a story in a New York newspaper:

> Two small Queens children whose mother had reported losing them in a crowded Flushing department store on Christmas Eve were found dead in a rubble-strewn lot in East Harlem last night, and the mother and a man with whom she lives were charged with the murders.

Cautions

Garish details of rapes, homicides, suicides and assaults are considered unnecessary. Details essential to an investigation are not used, although there is no legal prohibition against using information obtained legally. Usually, police will not give reporters confessions, statements, admissions, or alibis by suspects; names of suspects or witnesses; details of sex crimes. (Publication of a confession or statement can jeopardize a defendant's rights.)

Double Checks   All names, addresses, occupations should be double-checked against the city directory, telephone book and any other available source.

Beware of sudden cleanup drives for vice, gambling. Usually, they are designed for public consumption.

When the police arrest a suspect, reporters ask for his or her arrest record or rap sheet. In many cities and states, the record may be denied or only a portion of it released. Sometimes the refusal is the result of state law. There has been a growing sensitivity among officials concerning the need to guarantee the accused a fair trial. Revelations about past crimes might compromise the defendant's rights.

Using Prior Convictions   Conviction data—information about a guilty plea, a conviction, or a plea of *nolo contendere*—usually can be used. Half the states make it illegal to use nonconviction data.

State laws that seal arrest records take precedence over sunshine laws. Where there are no explicit prohibitions against the use of such records, it is permissible to use them, whatever the disposition of the arrests. Reporters can use nonconviction information that they find in public documents that are traditionally open to the press: court records of judicial proceedings, police blotters, published court opinions, wanted announcements, traffic records.

Juvenile Records   Juvenile records usually are sealed, and family court rules almost always prohibit press coverage. But there are few state laws that make it illegal to identify a juvenile as a suspect or that prohibit stories about

---

Meaningless

". . . the media have done an increasingly poor job of developing a balance between what is interesting and what is important. This is the difference between a crime story and crime coverage, between a story about yet another anecdotal crime and one that identifies the anecdote as either representative of a trend or representative of absolutely nothing."

—*David J. Krajicek ("Scooped! Media Miss Real Story on Crime While Chasing Sex, Sleaze, and Celebrities," Columbia University Press, 1998.)*

a juvenile's conviction. Generally, the press has gone along with the contention that such publicity could make rehabilitation of the young offender more difficult.

When a 9-year-old boy turned himself in to the FBI as a bank robbery suspect, newspapers and television stations gave the story huge play. The youngster, who took $118 from a teller, held what looked like a pistol.

The newspapers and stations were unhappy about using the story but said they had no recourse. It was "pointless" not to publish a picture of the youngster, said the metropolitan editor of *The New York Times,* that was already "on television all over town."

Remember: An arrest is just that. It does not mean that the person has been charged with a crime. Charges are brought by the district attorney and indictments are made by a grand jury. When a person is arrested, the reporter can write that Jones was "arrested in connection with the robbery of a drugstore at 165 Massachusetts Ave." Or: "Jones was arrested in an investigation of the embezzlement of $45,000 from the First National Bank of Freeport."

The U.S. Department of Justice has found that half the arrests are disposed of prior to indictment.

Covering Campus Crime

Federal law requires colleges and universities to release data on crimes on the campus by Oct. 1 each year. The figures are available to the public.

Figures collected over recent years show an increase in burglaries and motor vehicle thefts on many campuses. Sexual assaults show a slight increase.

Source

The Student Press Law Center has booklets on campus crime for guidance of student journalists and offers advice to students needing information. It can be reached at Student Press Law Center, 1101 Wilson Blvd., Suite 1910, Arlington, VA 22209; www.splc.org.

Fire Coverage

The police reporter monitors the police radio for reports of fires. If a fire is serious or involves a well-known building or downtown area, the reporter will go to the scene. Importance can be determined by the number of units dispatched, usually expressed in terms of the number of alarms.

Ask for Information   At fires, as with any emergency situation, reporters seem to be in the way, and some hesitate to grab a police officer or firefighter to ask for details. Ask.

Causes
Studies show that 75 percent of violent juvenile offenders have suffered abuse by a family member and more than 60 percent of juveniles in custody have parents who abused alcohol or drugs. Says John J. Dilulio, Jr., of Princeton, "Very bad boys come disproportionately from very bad homes in very bad neighborhoods."

Data Available
The U.S. Department of Education maintains a Web site that includes reported criminal offenses for more than 6,300 public and private colleges and universities. The institutions provide criminal offenses that have been reported to campus security authorities and to local police agencies. The Department of Education Web site is www.ope. ed.gov/security for campus crime data.

The FBI site www.fbi. gov/ucr/ucr.htm contains crime data for colleges and universities. Recent figures:

Motor vehicle thefts—U. Arizona, 105; Arizona State, 82; Cal. U. at Long Beach, 82.

Burglaries—Harvard, 387; Ohio State, 349; UCLA, 297.

Entire block endangered by disabled

butane truck too near flaming building

Heroes

By PAM NEWELL SOHN
Star Staff Writer

They talked like it was all in a day's work.
. . . like anyone would work on a disabled, half-filled butane truck a few feet from a building burning out of control.
. . . like the expectation the truck might explode and level the entire block was of no more consequence than answering a ringing phone.

Their apparent attitude: It had to be done. And the handful of men did it.

WHILE POLICE were evacuating about 100 spectators from the scene of a savage fire Thursday at Virgil Coker Tire Service on Noble Street, and while firemen were trying to tame the flames, four men ignored warnings and made fast, makeshift repairs on the tank truck. Then they half-drove, half-dragged it out of immediate danger.

The four men were Anniston Police Sgt. Mike Fincher, wrecker driver Kenneth Garrett and brothers Lamar Crosson and Buford Crosson, both employees of Virgil Coker Tire Service.

The Southern Butane Co. truck, carrying about 400 gallons of highly flammable gas, was parked for repairs near the rear of the building when a fire broke out there at about 11:20 a.m.

The front-end of the truck was near a telephone pole and could not be moved forward. Two rear wheels and the drive axle

had been removed from the truck. The empty wheel space was on the side of the burning building. Coker employees said work on the truck had reached a standstill waiting for the delivery of a new wheel hub.

WHEN IT BECAME apparent that the fire could not be extinguished quickly, some firemen and the four men began contemplating how to move the disabled truck.

Lamar Crosson said he heard mention of pulling the truck away from the blaze just as it stood. "But the (gas) valve was right there on the bottom and it could have broke and burned," said Crosson.

Crosson said that at about that time, the new hub was delivered and he and his brother began to reassemble the wheel hub and mount the tire, working between the truck and the burning building. They were assisted by fireman Jimmy Crossley, fincher and Garrett.

The men said they had to work "on and off" because of the intense smoke from the fire. And at times, according to Garrett, flames were as close as 10 feet away. When the smoke wasn't blinding and choking them, they were being doused with water from a fire pumper truck spraying cooling water on the butane tank, they said.

FINALLY, the men were able to secure one

(See Truck, Page 12A)

Here are the beginnings of two fire stories that appeared in *The Tennessean* of Nashville:

A resident of an East Nashville rooming house suffered massive burns early today before fellow residents braved flames and yanked him to safety through a second-floor window.

The house at 256 Strouse Ave. was gutted by the blaze, which Metro fire officials have labeled "suspicious."

A 3-month-old Nashville girl asleep on a sofa-bed perished last night as her house went up in flames and relatives clawed in vain at an outside wall to rescue her.

The victim is the daughter of Janice Holt, who shares her 1925 16th Ave. N. home with several relatives, police said.

Firefighters arrived at the one-story dwelling off Clay Street shortly after the 6:45 p.m. call, and found the house consumed by flames, said Metro District Fire Chief Jordan Beasley.

Checklist: Fires

___Deaths, injuries.

___Location.

___Cause.

___When, where started.

___How spread.

___When brought under control.

___Property loss: how much of structure damaged.

___Estimated cost of damage.

___Type of structure.

___Measures taken to protect public safety.

___If rescue involved, how carried out.

___Who discovered fire.

___Number of fire companies, firefighters assigned. (How much water used.)

___Exact cause of deaths, injuries.

___Where dead, injured taken.

___Quotes from those burned out; effect on their lives.

___Comments of neighbors, eyewitnesses.

___Insurance coverage.

___Arson suspected?

___Any arrests.

___Unusual aspects.

Sources

* Fire chief, marshal, inspector.
* Police department.
* Hospital.
* Morgue, mortuary.
* Welfare agencies, rescue groups (Red Cross).
* City building, fire inspection reports.

If a fire is serious enough to merit a follow-up story, possible themes are the progress of the investigation into the cause of the fire and the conditions of the injured. Another may be the cost of replacing the destroyed structure.

Further Reading

Buchanan, Edna. *Never Let Them See You Cry: More from Miami, America's Heart Beat.* New York: Random House, 1992.

Coté, William, and Roger Simpson. *Covering Violence—A Guide to Ethical Reporting about Victims & Trauma.* New York: Columbia University Press, 2000.

Krajicek, David J. *Scooped! Media Miss Real Story on Crime While Chasing Sex, Sleaze, and Celebrities.* New York: Columbia University Press, 1998.

21 The Courts

Preview

Coverage of state and federal courts involves:

- **Civil law**—actions initiated by an individual, usually a person suing another individual or an organization for damages. Many actions are settled out of court.
- **Criminal law**—actions initiated by the government for violation of criminal statutes. The process begins with the arraignment of the accused and concludes with dismissal or a not-guilty verdict or sentencing after a conviction.

Most criminal cases are settled before they go to trial by plea bargaining in which the accused agrees to plead guilty in return for a lesser sentence.

The cases that go to trial are covered from jury selection through verdict and sentencing.

Rosemary Lincoln, *The Patriot Ledger*
Courtroom drama—forcible removal of defendant.

Be counter-phobic. Do what you fear or dislike doing.

For every one of the 2 million men and women behind the bars of jails and prisons, five others are being processed in the criminal justice system. At the same time, increasing numbers of lawsuits flood the civil courts.

The courts over the land have become overwhelmed. They are at the confluence of a swollen tide of lawmaking, arrests and litigation. Watching over all this, pencil poised, is the reporter.

The only way the reporter maintains stability in this swelling tide of words—most of which are dense and arcane—is through knowledge of the judicial system, good sources and the ability to pick out the significant and interesting cases.

The Basics

There are two judicial systems, state and federal. State systems differ in detail but are similar in essentials. There are two kinds of law, criminal and civil. In criminal law, the government is the accuser. In civil law, an individual or group usually initiates the action; the government also can bring an action in the civil courts. Because crime stories make dramatic reading, the criminal courts receive the most media attention. Reporters cover the civil courts for damage suits, restraining orders and court decisions on such issues as taxes, business operations and labor conflicts.

These criminal and civil proceedings take place in state courts with a variety of titles—district, circuit, superior, supreme. The lower-level courts of original jurisdiction at the city and county levels—criminal, police, county, magistrate and the justice of the peace courts—handle misdemeanors, traffic violations and arraignments. The federal court system includes the federal district courts, the circuit courts of appeals and the Supreme Court.

The county courthouse or court reporter covers state and local courts and the office of the district attorney. The federal courthouse reporter covers the U.S. attorney, the federal magistrate and the federal courts. The magistrate arraigns those arrested and sets bail.

There are special state and local courts, such as the domestic relations or family court, sometimes called juvenile or children's court; small claims; surrogate's court (where wills are probated) and landlord–tenant court.

The court reporter's attention is directed to the civil and criminal proceedings in the state courts of superior jurisdiction—district, superior, circuit or supreme courts—and in the federal system.

Before we go into our examination of court coverage, a note of caution: Reporting the courts has been the subject of considerable legal action. Some areas are off-limits—jury deliberations, certain activities of jurors—and some have been hemmed in by judicial decree. Chapter 25 surveys the continuing push-and-pull between journalists, who seek freedom to cover all aspects of

Terminology
A list of the officers of the court and court terms is included in *NRW Plus,* **Court Language.**

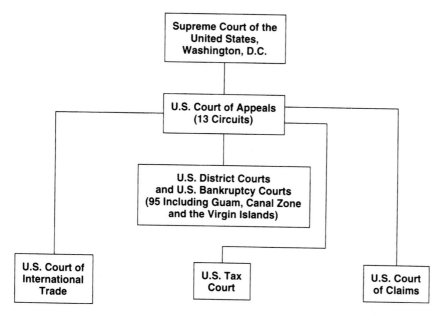

The Federal Court System

The federal judicial system has three tiers:
District courts: Trial courts located throughout the nation.
Circuit courts: Intermediate regional appeals courts that review appeals from the district courts.
Supreme Court: Takes appeals on a discretionary basis from circuit courts.
The federal courts have power only over those matters the Constitution establishes: "controversies to which the United States shall be a party; controversies between two or more states; between a State and a citizen of another State; between citizens of different states. . . ."

the judicial system, and the courts, which have sought to limit coverage on the ground that it can compromise the defendant's right to a fair trial. Many states have press-bar guidelines.

Civil Law

Civil law consists of two major divisions: actions at law and equity proceedings.

Actions at Law

These suits are brought—mostly in state courts—for recovery of property, damages for personal injury and breach of contract. The reporter who thumbs through the daily flow of suits filed in the county courthouse singles out those that have unusual, timely or important elements. They also are on the lookout for well-known people who may bring suit or against whom a suit is filed.

The Unusual   Here is a brief story about a freak accident in a baseball game. The circumstances made the suit worth writing about:

OREGON CITY—A 13-year-old who broke both arms during a Little League baseball game has filed a $500,000 suit in Clackamas County Circuit Court through his guardian. It charges the Lake Oswego School District and Nordin-Schmitz, Inc., a private corporation, with negligence.

According to the suit, plaintiff Martin K. McCurdy was injured when he fell into a ditch on the boundary between the school district and Nordin-Schmitz property as he was chasing a ball during a Little League game May 16.

Explanation Essential   Some cases involve complexities that the reporter has to explain so the reader or listener can make sense of the courtroom processes. Here is an example of how a radio reporter handled a court case that would have mystified listeners without an explanation:

The wife of a Dallas minister was found near death from what appeared to be an attempt to strangle her. Her husband was suspected, but police said they had no evidence to charge him. The woman is in a coma.

The woman's mother sued her son-in-law in civil court and has won a $16 million judgment, the money to be used for the lifetime care of the minister's wife.

> **Social History**
> "We as reporters are the witnesses to history, the eyes and ears of a public seeking information on some of the most important issues of our time. We are also the documentarians of a justice system that is evolving anew with every case that passes through it."
> —Linda Deutsch, AP court reporter

Whoa, the listener says. How can a man be ordered to pay for a crime the police say they cannot charge him with? The reporter answered the question with this sentence:

> Unlike the criminal system, which requires proof beyond a reasonable doubt to convict a defendant, a civil suit requires only a preponderance of credible evidence.

The Key Differences In a criminal trial, the issue is the guilt *beyond a reasonable doubt* of the accused. In a civil trial, in which damages, contracts and the like are involved, the issue is the *likelihood of the defendant's liability.*

In a criminal trial, the verdict must be unanimous. In a civil trial, 9 of the 12 jurors constitutes a verdict.

This difference between a criminal and a civil trial was a factor in one of the most heavily covered civil trials of the decade—the damage suit against O.J. Simpson that followed his acquittal of murder in a criminal trial.

O.J.'s Civil Trial In Simpson's criminal trial for the murder of his ex-wife and her friend, a jury returned a unanimous verdict of not guilty. The families of the two victims then filed a civil action, asking for monetary damages for their loss.

The fact that the former football star had been acquitted in a criminal trial did not count for much with the civil jury. It found Simpson "liable" for the deaths and awarded a total of $35.5 million in damages to one of the families.

Although there is a constitutional prohibition against double jeopardy, private civil suits have not been considered a violation of the prohibition.

Caution: Lawyers often file damage suits seeking large sums. A $1 million lawsuit is commonplace. Most damage suits are settled for far less or tossed out of court. Relatively few go to trial. The reporter examines the suit to see whether it has newsworthy elements in addition to the amount sought.

Equity Proceedings

The courts can compel individuals, organizations and government bodies to take an action or to refrain from an action. When such an order is requested, the complainant is said to seek equitable relief. Reporters come across these legal actions in the form of injunctions and restraining orders. Here is a story about a restraining order from the radio news wire of the UPI:

> PROVIDENCE, R.I.—A federal judge has issued a temporary order stopping efforts to put a reservist on active army duty because he refused to shave off his beard.

Criminal and Civil Actions

I

Jay-Z, the Grammy Award–winning rapper, was placed on probation for three years after pleading guilty yesterday in State Supreme Court to stabbing a record producer in a Times Square nightclub two years ago.

Jay-Z, 31 years old, whose real name is Shawn Carter, admitted stabbing Lance Rivera, 35, at the Kit Kat Club. Rivera dropped a civil suit against Jay-Z after they made an out-of-court settlement for an undisclosed amount.

II

DENVER (AP)—Kobe Bryant and the 20-year-old woman who accused him of rape nearly two years ago settled her civil lawsuit against him yesterday, ending a case that tarnished one of the NBA's brightest young stars.

Terms weren't released. A statement by Bryant's attorneys said the matter had been resolved "to the satisfaction of both parties." . . .

The lawsuit, filed three weeks before the criminal case against the basketball star collapsed last summer, sought unspecified damages. . . .

District Judge Edward Day in Providence, R.I., yesterday gave the army 10 days to answer a suit filed Friday by the American Civil Liberties Union. . . .

Temporary injunctions, also known as preliminary injunctions, are issued to freeze the status quo until a court hearing can be scheduled. Thus, it makes no sense to write that the petitioner has "won" an injunction in such a preliminary proceeding (which is also called an "*ex parte* proceeding") because a permanent injunction cannot be issued until an adversary hearing is held in which both sides are heard. The respondent is ordered to show cause at the hearing—usually set for a week or two later—for why the temporary injunction should not be made final or permanent.

In this equity proceeding, a party asked the court to compel another party to take an action:

> The developers of a proposed shopping center and office complex at the intersection of Route 13 and West Trenton Avenue have asked Bucks County Court to order Falls Township to issue a building permit.
> —*Bucks County Courier Times*

Pretrial and Trial

A complaint lists the cause of action, the parties to the action, and the relief sought. The defendant has several alternatives. He or she may file a motion seeking to delay, alter or halt the action. He or she can ask for a change of venue or a bill of particulars or can file other motions. When the defendant is ready to contest the action, or if motions to stop the action have not been granted, the defendant files an answer.

The case may then move to trial. Although there are more civil trials than criminal trials, few civil trials are covered. Reporters rely on records, lawyers and court personnel for information. Civil court stories are written on filing of the action and at the completion of the trial or at settlement.

Checklist: Civil Actions

___Identification of person or organization filing action.

___Background of plaintiff or petitioner.

___Defendant; respondent.

___Type of damage alleged.

___Remedy sought.

___Date of filing; court of jurisdiction.

___Special motivation behind action, if any.

___History of the conflict, disagreement.

___Similar cases decided by courts.

___Could suit lead to landmark decision? Is it a precedent?

___Possibility of an out-of-court settlement.

___Significance of action; effect on others.

___Lawyers for both sides; types of firms they are associated with.

___Date and presiding judge for trial, hearing.

___Judge's reputation with similar cases.

Should the reporter cover the trial, key points for reporting are selection of the jury; relevant evidence; identification and expertise of witnesses; demeanor of witnesses on the stand; judge's rulings; pertinent material from opening and closing statements of attorneys; the damages, if any are assessed; whether the losing party intends to appeal.

Checklist: Verdict Stories

Here are the essentials of verdict stories for civil actions:

___Verdict; damages, if awarded (same, less, greater than those sought).

___Parties involved.

___Judge's statement, if any; deviations by judge from jury's findings.

___Summary of allegations by plaintiff.

___Key testimony and attorneys' points.

___Length of jury deliberations.

___Comment by jurors on deliberations, verdict.

___Any appeals or motions.

Sources

Private attorneys representing plaintiff and defendant; judges and their law clerks and clerks of the court; court stenographers; county courthouse clerk or assistant who is in charge of filing such actions. The clerk is usually the best source for tips on important cases.

Court Documents Privileged   Documents filed in the clerk's office usually are privileged as soon as the clerk stamps the material as received. The reporter is

Don't Be Awed

The testimony of expert witnesses sometimes overwhelms reporters. Relax. Even the experts have troubles. Here is the Question-Answer exchange during one trial:

Q. Doctor, before you performed the autopsy did you check for a pulse?

A. No.

Q. Did you check for blood pressure?

A. No.

Q. Did you check for breathing?

A. No.

Q. So, then it is possible that the patient was alive when you began the autopsy?

A. No.

Q. How can you be so sure, doctor?

A. Because his brain was sitting on my desk in a jar.

Q. But could the patient have still been alive, nevertheless?

A. Yes, it is possible that he could have been alive, practicing law somewhere.

free to use privileged material without fear of libel because it has been given official status. Statements in court also are privileged.

Cautions

Negotiations between the sides often will continue even after a trial begins, and the reporter should be aware of the possibility of a sudden settlement. In many damage suits, the plaintiff threatens to go to court to support his or her demand for a certain sum or other remedy. In turn, the defendant appears to be unconcerned about the possibility of a court battle. In reality, neither side welcomes the inconvenience, cost and unpredictability of a trial. The judge, too, wants a settlement. The civil courts are overwhelmed.

Attorneys for the losing side usually indicate an appeal will be filed. Do not overplay these assertions, but when an appeal is filed it can be a good story.

In civil cases, the defendant may ask the judge to dismiss the plaintiff's complaint or cause of action. Make sure to use the word *dismiss,* not *acquit,* which is a criminal term and refers to a verdict after a full trial by either a judge or a jury. In either a civil or criminal case, after the matter is finally decided, the judge usually orders a *judgment* to be entered in favor of the party prevailing in the action.

Criminal Law

Whether it is night court where the sweepings of the city streets are gathered for misdemeanor charges, or a high-paneled district courtroom where a woman is on trial for the murder-for-hire of her wealthy husband, the criminal courts offer endless opportunities for coverage.

The assumption that underlies the criminal justice system is that an injury to the individual affects the general public. Crimes are therefore prosecuted in the name of the state as the representative of the people.

The public prosecutor, an elected official, is usually known as the district attorney, state's attorney, county attorney or people's attorney. In the federal system, the prosecutor, a presidential appointee, is called the United States attorney.

Criminal Court Process

The criminal court system goes into operation shortly after the arrest and consists of pretrial and trial periods.

The pretrial period has four phases: arraignment, preliminary hearing, grand jury action and jury selection. Usually, these are accomplished in line with the constitutional provision: "In all criminal prosecutions, the accused shall enjoy the right to a speedy and public trial. . . ."

Arraignment

At arraignment, the defendant is told of the charges and of his or her right to an attorney and can enter a plea to the charge. If the defendant cannot afford a lawyer, the court assigns one. Arraignments are held in courts of original or least

O.J. Arraigned

LOS ANGELES—O.J. Simpson, looking dazed and haggard, pleaded not guilty at his arraignment Monday to charges that he murdered his ex-wife and a friend of hers.

For most of the brief session, Simpson—who was dressed in a dark suit but without tie, belt or shoe-laces—stood with his head cocked to one side. He sighed deeply several times as he looked around the courtroom.

City and State Courts

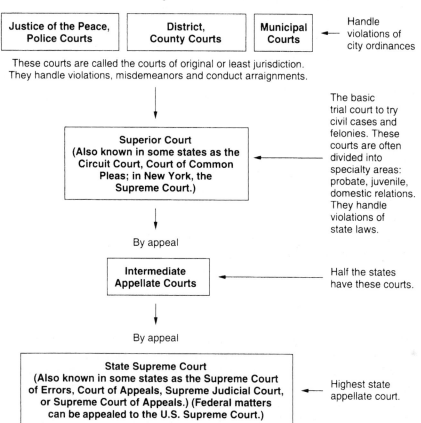

| Justice of the Peace, Police Courts | District, County Courts | Municipal Courts |

Handle violations of city ordinances

These courts are called the courts of original or least jurisdiction. They handle violations, misdemeanors and conduct arraignments.

Superior Court
(Also known in some states as the Circuit Court, Court of Common Pleas; in New York, the Supreme Court.)

The basic trial court to try civil cases and felonies. These courts are often divided into specialty areas: probate, juvenile, domestic relations. They handle violations of state laws.

By appeal

Intermediate Appellate Courts

Half the states have these courts.

By appeal

State Supreme Court
(Also known in some states as the Supreme Court of Errors, Court of Appeals, Supreme Judicial Court, or Supreme Court of Appeals.) (Federal matters can be appealed to the U.S. Supreme Court.)

Highest state appellate court.

jurisdiction. These courts are empowered to try only misdemeanors and violations, such as gambling, prostitution, loitering and minor traffic offenses. In a felony case, this lower court will determine bail. The prosecutor is present at arraignment, and she may decide to dismiss or lower the charge. If a felony charge is lowered to a misdemeanor, the case can be disposed of then and there.

The arraignment court, often called the criminal or city police court, acts like a fine-necked funnel, allowing only those felonies to pass through that the prosecutor considers serious. Others are reduced to violations and misdemeanors and handled forthwith.

If the defendant pleads guilty to a misdemeanor, the court can sentence immediately. If the defendant pleads guilty to a felony charge, the case is referred to a higher court.

If a plea of not guilty is entered to a misdemeanor, the judge can then conduct a trial or preliminary hearing. For felony not-guilty pleas, the case is referred to the appropriate court for a preliminary hearing. If the preliminary hearing is waived, the defendant is then bound over to the grand jury for action. Felonies are handled by courts which are variously called district, superior or circuit courts, depending on the state.

Checklist: Arraignments

___Formal charge.

___Plea.

___Bail (higher, lower than requested; conditional release).

___Behavior, statements of defendant.

___Presentation, remarks of prosecutor, defense lawyer, judge.

___Summary of crime.

Ordered to Trial

LOS ANGELES—Judge Kathleen Kennedy-Powell ruled today that O.J. Simpson must stand trial on murder charges.

The six-day preliminary hearing featured the presentation of blood samples from the crime scene by the district attorney's office. Simpson's lawyers, who did little to tip their defense at the hearing, are expected to file a motion asking for dismissal of the charges because of lack of evidence.

Preliminary Hearing

At a preliminary hearing, determination is made whether there are reasonable grounds, or probable cause, to believe the accused committed the offense and whether there is sufficient evidence for the case to be bound over to the grand jury. If the presiding judge considers the evidence insufficient, he or she can dismiss the charge. Also, bail can be increased, eliminated or reduced at the hearing.

The defendant has another opportunity to seek to have the charge lowered through plea bargaining at this point in the process. Some attorneys handling criminal cases prefer to have their clients plead guilty and receive probation or a light sentence rather than risk a trial and a lengthy sentence.

The prosecutor usually goes along with plea bargaining, but if the crime is serious, the defendant has a long record or the presiding judge is convinced there is reason to believe a serious crime was committed, the case will be sent to a grand jury to decide whether the defendant should be indicted.

Here is the beginning of a story of a preliminary hearing in the federal system:

BOSTON, Dec. 24—A Harvard Law School student, who allegedly enrolled under separate identities twice in the last seven years, was ordered yesterday bound over to a United States grand jury on charges that he had falsified a federal student loan application. . . .

United States Magistrate Peter Princi found probable cause yesterday that the student falsified applications for $6,000 in federally insured loans, which helped to see him through 2½ years of law school. . . .

Grand Jury Action

Criminal defendants can be brought to trial in three ways, depending on the state. In half the states, a grand jury indicts. A jury of citizens, usually 23 (of which 16 make a quorum), decides whether the evidence is sufficient for a trial on the charges brought. If 12 jurors so decide, an indictment, known as a *true bill,* is voted. If not, dismissal, known as a *no bill,* is voted. Only the state's evidence is presented to the jury.

In 20 states, the prosecutor files a charge called an *information* and a judge decides at a preliminary hearing at which witnesses testify whether there is cause for a trial. (See the marginal note **Ordered to Trial.**) In a few states, the prosecutor files affidavits to support the charge and the judge decides whether to move to trial.

Here are leads to grand jury indictments, the first by an Indiana state grand jury, the other by a federal grand jury:

INDIANAPOLIS—Former heavyweight champion Mike Tyson was indicted here today on a charge of raping an 18-year-old Miss Black America beauty pageant contestant and on three other criminal counts.

OKLAHOMA CITY—Timothy J. McVeigh and Terry L. Nichols, former army buddies who shared a hatred for the government, were indicted by a federal grand jury today on charges of blowing up a federal building here in April with a rented truck packed with 4,800 pounds of homemade explosives.

Rearraignment

After the indictment, the defendant is again arraigned, this time before a judge empowered to try felony cases. If the defendant pleads not guilty, a date for trial is set and bail is set. For example:

INDIANAPOLIS—Mike Tyson pleaded not guilty to charges he raped a beauty pageant contestant and was released on $30,000 bail.

In a 10-minute court appearance, Marion Superior Court Judge Patricia Gifford read Tyson the rape, criminal deviate conduct and confinement charges against him. If found guilty on all those charges, Tyson could face up to 63 years in prison. A trial date of Jan. 27 was set.

What Happens to the Defendant After Indictment

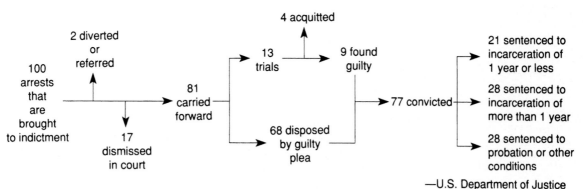

—U.S. Department of Justice

Plea bargaining continues at the rearraignment following grand jury indictment. Felonies, which usually are classified by degree—Class A, B, C, D and E—can be adjusted downward, a Class A felony moving down to a C or D, a Class C or D being negotiated down to a Class E felony or a misdemeanor.

Plea Bargaining

If every arrest were to be followed by a plea of not guilty and the accused granted the speedy trial promised by the Bill of Rights, the court system in every large city would collapse. The only way the courts can cope with the crush is to permit or to encourage arrangements whereby the defendant and the prosecutor agree that, in return for a lowered charge, the defendant will plead guilty. The nature of the sentence is often explicitly promised by the judge as a condition to the defendant's agreement to plead guilty.

Even serious crimes such as murder and rape are the subject of plea bargaining. In New York City, three-fourths of all murder arrests are plea bargained, and in Philadelphia three-fifths are plea bargained. In many major cities, nine of 10 criminal cases result in plea bargains.

Interrupted Trial Plea bargaining continues even as the criminal trial is under way. Here is the beginning of a court story that involves plea bargaining. It was written by Joseph P. Fried of *The New York Times:*

The last defendant in the St. John's University sexual-assault case interrupted his trial yesterday to plead guilty to sharply reduced charges, then admitted he had done virtually everything he had originally been accused of.

The wrenching case came to an end in an emotional scene in a Queens courtroom in which a female spectator yelled out that the 22-year-old defendant was a "rapist" and his mother responded with screaming vituperation.

The plea bargain allowed the defendant, a student at the largest Roman Catholic university in the country who was accused with five others of what is known as acquaintance rape, to be given three years' probation. They were accused of sodomizing the victim and sexually abusing her in other ways.

Offer Spurned Sometimes the bargaining is unsuccessful. Here is the beginning of a story from *The Humboldt Beacon* by Nancy Brands Ward:

EUREKA—The case of three Headwaters activists arrested in Rep. Frank Riggs' Eureka office on Oct. 16 moved one step closer to trial this week as attorneys failed to reach a deal on a plea bargain.

After Judge Marilyn Miles asked during a pretrial hearing Monday if the case could be settled short of going to court, Deputy District Attorney Andrew Isaac offered to let the three women plead guilty to trespass and resisting arrest. In exchange, vandalism charges would be dropped, though the prosecution would reserve the right to bring them to the court's attention during sentencing.

"It was no offer," said Mark Harris, who represents Terri Slanetz, Jennifer Schneider and Lisa Sanderson-Fox, who'd locked themselves in Riggs' office in an October protest.

Pretrial Motions

After the defendant has been formally accused, several kinds of motions can be filed:

• **Motion to quash the indictment:** The defendant can challenge the legality of the indictment. If the motion to dismiss is granted, the indictment is quashed. The prosecutor can appeal the quashing. He or she also can draw up another

Motions Prepared

LOS ANGELES—Attorneys for O.J. Simpson are laying out a battery of motions to try to undermine the case against the former football star, Simpson's lead attorney said in an interview today.

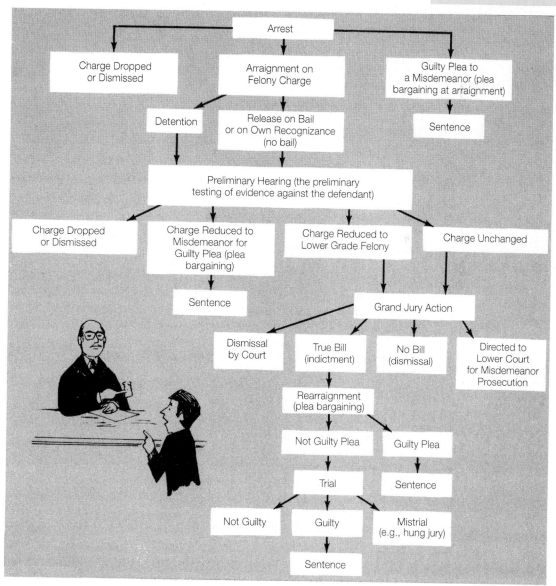

Court Process for a Felony

indictment if the grand jury again hands up a true bill, even if the first has been quashed, because the constitutional protection against double jeopardy does not apply.

• **Motion for a bill of particulars:** When the defense attorney wants more details about the allegations against the accused, such a motion is filed.

• **Motion to suppress the evidence:** Evidence shown to be seized or obtained illegally may not be used in the trial if the court grants such a motion.

• **Motion for a change of venue:** A defendant who believes he or she cannot receive a fair trial in the city or judicial area where the crime took place may ask that it be transferred elsewhere. Such motions also are filed to avoid trials presided over by particular judges.

Jury Selection

When a case emerges from the pretrial process and has been set for trial, a jury is usually empaneled. (The accused may waive the right to jury trial, in which case the judge hears the evidence in what is called a *bench trial.*)

Jurors' names are drawn from a wheel or jury box in which the names on a jury list were placed. The list is made up of names drawn from the tax rolls, voting lists, driver's license files and so on.

Twelve jurors and several alternates are selected in a procedure during which the defense attorney and prosecutor are permitted to challenge the selection of jurors. There are two types of challenges: *peremptory,* when no reason need be given for wanting a person off the jury, and *for cause,* when a specific disqualification must be demonstrated. The number of peremptory challenges allotted each side is set by statute, usually 10 per side. A judge can allow any number of challenges for cause.

Klansman's Jury   In the case of a former Klansman accused of a 1963 church bombing in which four black girls died, federal prosecutors used their peremptory challenges to remove 10 white men and 6 white women. The defense used 12 of its 16 challenges to strike blacks. The prosecutors relied on the advice of a jury consultant who organized two focus groups and polled nearly 500 Birmingham area residents to find out about attitudes toward racial issues and the church bombing 38 years before.

The jury took two hours to convict Thomas E. Blanton. It then sentenced him to life in prison. (The U.S. Supreme Court has ruled that peremptory challenges cannot be used to exclude people from juries on the basis of sex or race.)

Selection a Key   "Most trials are won or lost in jury selection," says Larry Scalise, a trial lawyer. In the trial of a woman accused of murdering her abusive husband, her lawyer said he concentrated on selecting a jury that was well-educated and sensitive to the victims of domestic violence. His client was acquitted.

Jury selection was a key factor in O.J. Simpson's acquittal at his criminal trial, court observers say. Through the use of surveys and focus groups, Simpson's lawyers learned that black men were three times more likely than black women to believe Simpson was guilty and that the more educated black men and women also considered him guilty.

In focus groups, Simpson's lawyers found, "Virtually every middle-aged African-American woman supported Simpson and resented the murder victim (Nicole Simpson)," says Jeffrey Toobin, the author of *The Run of His Life: The People v. O.J. Simpson.*

The criminal trial jury in the Simpson case included eight black women. The only whites were two women. In the civil trial that found Simpson liable for the deaths, there was not a single black juror.

"No one wanted to tell what I regard as the truth about the Simpson case—that race was always at the heart of it," says Toobin.

Jury Consultants   Jury selection is so important that it has spawned an industry—jury consultancy. Behavioral consultants advise attorneys how to select sympathetic jurors and how to use psychological techniques to persuade jurors.

Sometimes the advice works, as it did in the murder trial of O.J. Simpson. Sometimes not, as in the defense of Kenneth Lay, a major figure in the billion dollar collapse of the energy firm Enron. Lay's consultant sent prospective jurors a questionnaire that included queries about their TV-viewing and radio-listening. Did they watch Bill O'Reilly, listen to Rush Limbaugh? Watch "Market Watch" and "Boston Legal"?

Lay was found guilty on 10 counts that included wire fraud, securities fraud, bank fraud and false statements.

Reporter's Fare

A careful eye to jury selection will indicate the strategy of prosecutor and defense attorney. Does the defense attorney want women on the jury because he believes they will be sympathetic to the abused wife who shot her husband? Is the prosecutor asking questions about the television shows and movies the jury panelists watch? Does she prefer those who like westerns and police dramas? If so, what does that tell you?

We are ready to examine the procedure for trials, which the court reporter must master to do his or her job properly. But first a suggestion from the dean of court reporters, Theo Wilson of the New York *Daily News:* "Take the reader into the courtroom with you."

The Trial

A reporter cannot attend all the trials conducted in the courthouse that he or she covers. A reporter may sit through opening and closing statements and key testimony, but only the most celebrated cases are covered from opening statement

---

Jury Selection In Murder Trial

Here's how Jeff Eckhoff of *The Des Moines Register* began his story about the start of jury selection in a murder trial:

To his family and friends, Tam Minh Vu was a hard-working Des Moines newlywed who wanted to build a life for a new family.

But he was just "some Chinese dude" to the young women who approached him outside a University Avenue convenience store in August.

Court papers say Josette Williams and Portia Allen, desperate for a car on Aug. 23, cajoled Vu, a native of Vietnam, into giving them a ride to the 1400 block of Laurel Street, where they ordered him out of his green Honda Accord, shot him in the abdomen and left him to stagger down the street.

Now it's left for 12 Polk County jurors to decide what happened.

Jury selection begins today in Williams' first-degree murder trial. The Des Moines woman faces life in prison if convicted of firing the fatal bullet. . . .

**Spin Doctors
and Hired Hands**

Big trials attract public attention, and lawyers and others associated with the trials are sought after for comments. Sharon Waxman described one such trial for *NYTimes.com*

REDWOOD CITY, Calif.—There are two trials under way here over the killings of Laci Peterson and her unborn son.

One is the quiet proceeding inside the four walls of the town courthouse run by Judge Alfred A. Delucchi. That trial is all but bereft of drama and hard to follow. . . .

The other trial takes place in the hallways and on the esplanade in front of the courthouse, where a spin zone relentlessly churns before television cameras, which are barred from the courthouse itself. This one has drama and humor and pathos, played out breathlessly almost every day on Court TV and Fox News, on "Today" and "Larry King Live."

The spin masters Waxman is describing are mostly paid by television networks and programs for their commentaries. Another class of spin doctors is connected with the trial itself. Unless forbidden by the judge, lawyers freely comment on the trial, obviously with speculation favorable to their side.

The veteran court reporter for the AP, Linda Deutsch, says of those offering such insights: "It takes a careful eye to separate the spin from the substance."

to verdict and sentence. Reporters cover most trials by checking with the court clerk, the prosecutor and the defense attorney.

Court transcripts are used in important trials if they can be obtained in time for broadcast or publication. A friendly court stenographer can quickly run off key testimony in an emergency.

Trial Process

The trial procedure follows this pattern:

Opening Statements

1. Opening statements by prosecuting attorney and the defense attorney outline the state's case and the defense or alibi of the defendant and give a general preview of the evidence.

"The opening statement is the single most important part of the trial," says Joseph W. Cotchett, a Burlingame, Calif., lawyer. "This is the time you win your case. It's the rule of primacy; the jurors hear the details of the case for the first time. You give them the critical facts you're going to prove."

Direct Examination

2. The prosecution presents its case through testimony of witnesses and evidence. At the end of the presentation, a judge can direct a verdict of acquittal if he or she finds that the state has not established what is called a *prima facie* case, failing to present sufficient proof of the crime that is charged. The questioning by the prosecutor of his or her witness is called *direct examination.*

In direct examination of the woman who accused Tyson of raping her, the prosecutor led her to describe the event after her introductory statement: "If I was a quitter I wouldn't be here. I start what I finish," she told the jury. Then she described in three and a half hours of testimony what had happened. She said, "I was terrified. I was begging him, trying anything that would work. It just felt like someone was ripping me apart."

The story in the *Daily News* began:

INDIANAPOLIS—Mike Tyson's 18-year-old accuser testified yesterday that the former champ laughed while she wept in agony as he raped her in his hotel suite here last July.

"Don't fight me," Tyson growled menacingly during the attack as he grabbed her, pulled her clothing off and pinned her while she feebly pushed his heavyweight arms and back, she testified.

"I was telling him, 'Get off me, please stop.' I didn't know what to do," the woman said, her almost childlike voice captivating the hushed courtroom as she recounted the incident.

The prosecution calls other witnesses to support the contention of its major witnesses. In the Tyson case, the prosecutor drew from Tyson's chauffeur the statement that, when the woman left the hotel and returned to the limousine, "she looked like she may have been in a state of shock. Dazed. Disoriented. She seemed scared."

Cross-Examination by Defense

3. The defense attorney may cross-examine the state's witnesses.

In a criminal defense trial, says Cornelius Pitts, a defense lawyer in Detroit, "relentless cross-examination is necessary. The objective is to prevent the prosecution from winning and to do what you have to do to attack the complainant and the complainant's witnesses to the extent their testimony is no longer credible to the jury."

Nancy Stone, *The Plain Dealer*

Witness to His Mother's Murder

Here is the beginning of the story by Katherine L. Siemon and Eric Stringfellow of *The Plain Dealer* that accompanied this dramatic photograph by Nancy Stone:

Five-year-old DeVon Stapleton vividly remembers the night last spring when a stranger bludgeoned his mother to death while he watched from the back of a van.

Yesterday he spent about an hour trying to recount for a three-judge panel in Common Pleas Court what happened that night in April, how he and his mother tried to escape, and how he was left standing alone on a dark street corner after his mother was killed.

Barely tall enough to see over the witness stand and with a voice barely loud enough to be heard without a microphone, DeVon pointed to the man who is on trial for the death of Ruby Stapleton.

"There, he's right there," DeVon said, shaking his finger at Reginald Jells when Assistant County Prosecutor Carmen Marino asked the boy if he saw the stranger in the courtroom.

Jells, 21, faces the death penalty for Stapleton's killing last April 18. He also is charged with kidnapping and aggravated robbery. During opening arguments yesterday, Marino said Stapleton's blood was found inside Jells' van and a footprint matching Jells' was found near the body.

Jells has denied the killing.

(Jells was convicted and sentenced to death.)

In Martha Stewart's trial for lying to federal investigators to conceal her selling stock in violation of insider trading laws, the key witness against her was subjected to searching cross-examination. Under questioning, he admitted he smoked marijuana, and the jury was told he had pleaded guilty to a misdemeanor for initially lying in the case. But the jurors believed the witness's testimony against Stewart and a former Merrill Lynch broker who handled her account. Both were found guilty.

Redirect Examination

4. Redirect examination is permitted the prosecutor should he or she want to re-establish the credibility of evidence or testimony that the defense's cross-examination has threatened.

Motions

5. The defense may make a motion for a directed verdict of acquittal or of dismissal based on its contention the state did not prove its case.

Rebuttal

6. The defense may call witnesses to rebut the state's case. The defendant may or may not be called, depending on the defense attorney's strategy. The prosecutor is not permitted to comment on the defendant's failure to take the stand.

Tyson's attorneys called beauty pageant contestants to testify that his accuser had flirted with him and repeatedly talked about his money. Tyson did take the stand and under questioning by his attorney said he and his accuser had engaged in consensual sex. "No, she never told me to stop. She never said I was hurting her. She never said no. Nothing."

Cross-Examination by Prosecutor

7. The prosecutor may cross-examine the defense witnesses.

In cross-examination of the contestants, the prosecution elicited testimony that the plaintiff was naive and "not streetwise" about a date with Tyson. Tyson also was cross-examined:

> INDIANAPOLIS—A visibly rattled and slightly peevish Mike Tyson, after an hour of intense cross-examination, left the stand yesterday having had some inconsistencies in his testimony high-lighted but with his basic story intact.
>
> Attacking less with a sledgehammer than with a chisel, special prosecutor J. Gregory Garrison chipped away at Tyson's testimony but refrained from grilling Tyson about precisely what went on in Room 606 of the Canterbury Hotel on the morning of July 19, when an 18-year-old beauty pageant contestant says she was raped.
>
> —*New York Post*

Redirect Examination by Defense

8. Should the state seem to weaken the defense's case through its cross-examination, the defense may engage in redirect examination of its witnesses.

Strategies for Cross-Examination

"Great advocates intuit what will bother the witness and gnaw at it in their questions. They get the witness to speak without thinking, to contradict himself on small points. They move around the room, alter the rhythm of the questioning, change their volume and tone. They may be sarcastic one minute, then angry, then friendly. They switch topics often. The goal is always the same: To convince jurors that this is not the person they would trust with their car keys, much less rely on for a verdict."

—*Stephen Gillers,*
New York University
School of Law

Rebuttals

9. Rebuttals are offered on both sides. Witnesses may be recalled. New rebuttal witnesses may be called, but new witnesses ordinarily cannot be presented without the judge's permission after a side has rested its case.

Note: At any time during the trial, the defense may move for a *mistrial,* usually on the basis that some irregularity has made a fair verdict by the jury impossible. If the judge grants the motion, the jury is discharged and the trial is stopped. Because double jeopardy does not apply in such situations, the defendant can be tried again.

Summations

10. The defense and the state offer closing arguments in which they summarize the case for the jurors. These presentations, known as *summations,* provide reporters with considerable news. Attorneys sometimes make dramatic summations before the jury.

Maurice Rivenbark, *St. Petersburg Times*

Murder Jury

Jurors in the trial of a man accused of murdering a woman and her two daughters listen as the prosecutor makes his summation. The jury was sequestered for the trial that was widely covered because of the heinous nature of the crime and the dogged police work that resulted in the arrest of the accused murderer. The jury convicted him.

"Telecom Cowboy" Guilty on All Counts

NEW YORK (AP)— Bernard Ebbers, the once-swaggering CEO of WorldCom, was convicted Tuesday of engineering the largest corporate fraud in U.S. history—an $11 billion accounting scandal that capsized the big telecom company three years ago.

The verdict marked a colossal fall for Ebbers, who had turned a humble Mississippi long-distance provider into a global telecommunications power, swallowing up companies along the way and earning the nickname "Telecom Cowboy."

A federal jury in Manhattan returned guilty verdicts on all nine counts, including securities fraud, conspiracy and lying to regulators—a decision that could send Ebbers, 63, to prison for the rest of his life. Sentencing was set for June 13.

Ebbers reddened deeply when the jury returned its verdict after eight days of deliberation. . . .

Charge to Jury

11. The judge charges or instructs jurors before they retire for deliberations. The judge may review the evidence, explain the law that should be applied to the facts of the case and explain the verdicts that can be reached. The jury must accept the judge's explanation of the law but is the sole judge of the facts in the case.

Jury Deliberation

12. Jury deliberations may be short or extended. In important trials, the reporter may want to stay with the jury until deadline because verdicts make headlines. A jury may ask for further instructions on the law, or it may wish to review certain material from the trial. Stories can be written speculating on the meaning of lengthy deliberations or the questions the jury asks the judge.

Verdict

13. The verdict in a criminal trial must be unanimous—guilty or not guilty. If the jury reports it is deadlocked and has little chance of reaching a verdict, the judge declares a *mistrial* because of the *hung jury*. After a verdict of guilty, the defense may move to set aside the verdict or file a motion for a new trial. Such motions usually are denied, but the decision may be appealed.

After the jurors are discharged they are free to discuss their deliberations unless the judge gags the jury. In most states, the judge does not have that right. Following major trials, the reporter will interview jurors about their deliberations.

Verdict Essentials   The specific charges on which the jury convicted, the length of the possible sentence(s), the time the jury deliberated and a summary of the trial must be included in the story. Here is how Jeff Eckhoff of the *Des Moines Register* began his story of the jury verdict in a murder trial:

> Jossette Williams sat quietly Tuesday, roughly 20 feet from the Vietnamese woman she made a widow as 12 Polk County jurors sent her to prison for the rest of her life.
>
> Williams, 23, blinked slowly as she was declared guilty of first-degree murder for the Aug. 23, 2001, shooting of Tam Minh Vu.
>
> Under Iowa law, the crime carries a mandatory penalty of life in prison without parole. . . .

In the case of an acquittal, the time of deliberation, the charge and the length of the trial usually go into the lead. In some cases, the makeup of the jury is considered relevant:

> LOS ANGELES—O.J. Simpson was found not guilty of the murders of his ex-wife and her friend after a year-long trial that attracted worldwide attention.
>
> The jury of eight blacks, two whites and one Hispanic reached their verdict yesterday after less than four hours of deliberation. The verdict was announced today in Superior Court by Judge Lance Ito.

Juror Says Ebbers' Testimony Hurt Him

NEW YORK—"I didn't care for him. Everything he said was too laid out for me, too scripted."

Zina Gregory, 40, who was juror No. 8 at the fraud trial of Bernard Ebbers, said Ebbers' testimony that he was unaware of the massive accounting coverup did not impress the jury. "I find it hard to believe that someone who started a company and built it up like he did would suddenly pull away and let other people run it," she said.

Jurors were very emotional during deliberations, Gregory said. "Some actually broke down and cried." . . .

Sentence

14. The sentence may be pronounced immediately after the verdict or later, pending a probation report. State laws usually set ranges—minimum and maximum sentences—that may be imposed. Always include the probable time the defendant will serve.

INDIANAPOLIS, March 26—Mike Tyson, the former heavyweight champion who was convicted of rape last month, was sentenced to 10 years in prison today. But the judge suspended the last four years, meaning he will spend no more than six years behind bars.

In a rape case that has attracted worldwide attention and prompted debate about sexual roles and racial attitudes in the criminal justice system, Mr. Tyson is likely to be freed in three years with time off for good behavior.

—*The New York Times*

Convictions on more than one count can lead to concurrent or consecutive sentences. A judge also may issue a suspended sentence, place the defendant on probation or levy a fine.

A majority of offenders in all states are placed under community supervision of some kind rather than incarcerated.

In some states, in trials involving the possibility of a death sentence, the jury decides the sentence following conviction, or a new jury is empaneled to decide.

Checklist: Criminal Trials

A story written at any one of the 14 stages outlined here should include the current developments and the following basic information:

____Formal charge.

____Full identification of defendant.

____Circumstances surrounding criminal act.

____Summary of preceding developments.

____Likely next stage.

Sources

Private attorneys; prosecutor's office, which includes assistant prosecutors, investigators and bureau heads; legal aid attorneys; law clerks of the judges; clerks of the court; court stenographers; bailiffs and security guards; police officers; probation department; state parole office; trial judges, many of whom like to chat with reporters. Clerks also can tip off reporters to important motions, hearings and trial dates.

Theater

"I have always compared big courtroom trials to great theater filled as those trials are with revelations of human weakness and folly, with violence and sorrow and humor and pity and passion, all the more fascinating because these are real people, real life."

—*Theo Wilson*

Incarceration Rates

The United States has the highest incarceration rate in the world, 715 per 100,000 population. Russia is second with 584; Italy, third with 100.

Incarceration rates by ethnicity: white, 378; Hispanic, 922; black, 2,489 per 100,000 population of the group.

The five states with the **highest** incarceration rates are:

Louisiana	816
Texas	694
Mississippi	669
Oklahoma	649
Georgia	574

The five states with the **lowest** incarceration rates are:

Maine	148
Minnesota	171
Rhode Island	175
New Hampshire	187
North Dakota	195

The national rate is 432 state prisoners per 100,000 state population.

The Full Story

It's not enough to give the sentence in the story. Tell the reader when the convicted person could be paroled. Except for sentences that specify no parole is possible, most criminals are let out of jail long before their full sentences, even for murder. For example:

He will be sentenced Feb. 6 to a mandatory life term with a possibility of parole after 9½ years.

Also, some trials have broad consequences. When a former Bush White House aide was convicted of lying about his ties to a lobbyist, the reporter wrote that the verdict "created alarm on Capitol Hill" among "several Republican lawmakers. . . ."

Look for Color, Strategy, Tactics

Material that gives the trial individuality may include the behavior of the defendant or unusual testimony. Drama is enhanced by describing the setting, the reactions of spectators and the reactions of jurors.

Stories about testimony can be dramatized by using the question-and-answer technique for crucial testimony:

Q. Can you identify the man you say attacked you?

A. Yes, I can. He is sitting there, to your right at the other table where I'm pointing.

Material for the Q and A usually is taken from the court transcript to ensure accuracy.

Reporters understand the necessity of finding patterns of strategy and tactics during a trial. Every prosecutor has a plan, and every defense attorney keys his or her presentation to a theme. Each witness, every bit of evidence is presented with a purpose. The reporter's job is to discover the design of each side in this adversary proceeding. Strategy and tactics shift, requiring the reporter to be alert during each day's testimony. The reporter asks himself or herself: What is the purpose of this line of questioning, this witness, this piece of evidence?

This kind of coverage gives the reader, listener or viewer a sense of the movement and direction of the trial. All other coverage is episodic.

Appeals

Convictions may be appealed to a higher court. In criminal cases, the appeal usually concerns errors or improper actions by the presiding judge. Sometimes, jury selection is appealed.

Stories About the System

Courthouse reporters are increasingly being asked to take an overview of their beats. Editors want stories about trends in the handling of criminal cases, how Supreme Court decisions affect the local judicial system, plea bargaining, new investigative techniques by the prosecutor's office, politics and the courts. Some editors want their reporters to do accountability pieces: Does the system work; are judges efficient in clearing caseloads; are white-collar criminals being treated leniently; are sentences for drug possession too severe?

One of the most sensitive issues in setting crime control policy is pretrial detention. Denial of bail resulting in detention deprives the defendant, presumed not guilty, of freedom, limits his or her participation in preparing a defense and deprives the person of earnings. Pretrial release, however, makes it possible for the defendant to commit crimes or to flee.

Innocents Convicted

Journalists have been looking deeply into murder and rape cases. In some of them, reporters have found flawed lab tests that led to convictions of innocent men and women. With the increased use of DNA testing, men and women convicted by eyewitness testimony have been freed.

Phoebe Zerwick of the *Winston-Salem Journal* spent months examining the case of Darryl Hunt, who had spent 18 years in prison for a rape-murder. In her research, she found "138 convicted murderers and rapists nationwide have been exonerated by DNA." In the Hunt case, Zerwick's intensive coverage uncovered documents Hunt's defense lawyers were never given, judicial errors and a stubborn refusal to consider another suspect, a man whose DNA, as it turned out, matched the semen sample taken from the victim. Finally, Hunt was freed:

Darryl Hunt walked out of the Forsyth County Jail before noon yesterday.

It was a defining moment in a complex murder case—the 1984 rape and stabbing death of Deborah Sykes—that for nearly 20 years has divided Winston-Salem along racial lines and cast doubt on the local justice system.

"It feels great. . . . to finally be free and vindicated," Hunt said on the jail steps as television cameras crowded to get a good shot of him. "I don't think there's words to express how I feel." . . .

Deadbeat Dads

Bonnie Britt of the *Asbury* (N.J.) *Park Press* found that some parents—most of them fathers—were avoiding child support ordered by the courts. More than $650 million was owed in the state, but law enforcement officers did nothing. Some mothers who were owed child support, she wrote, were evicted from their homes when they could not pay rent.

Politics and the Courts

Elected or appointed, the judiciary has a deep involvement in politics. Mayors, governors, senators and the president reward party members and campaign supporters, despite their campaign promises of appointments to the bench on the basis of merit. Nominations to the federal judiciary are made by the president—often on the basis of ideology—and approved by the Senate.

In many areas, the path to the bench begins with a political apprenticeship, either in a campaign or in a party post. Or it may be paved with contributions to a campaign.

During the Clinton presidency, the Republican-controlled Senate refused to confirm two-thirds of the president's nominees to federal appeals courts, and during the administration of George W. Bush, Democrats stalled the nominees of President Bush. Political ideology was involved: Clinton wanting moderate judges; Bush nominating strict constructionists, those adhering to the theory of

Reality Check

"We are a government of laws, but we are also a government of men and women. It makes all the difference which judge is deciding a case or issue. Our judges reflect their personal backgrounds, idiosyncrasies and biases. A Supreme Court justice with daughters active in the pro-choice movement is more likely to strike down antiabortion laws than a justice with a fundamentalist religious upbringing. A judge who has been a private attorney for insurance companies may be less sympathetic to an injured worker than a judge with a labor union background. A judge who has lived all his life in an homogeneous small town is likely to be less understanding of those who oppose the establishment of religion."

—Alan M. Dershowitz

Danger: Reporter in the Courtroom

When I sat on the bench I always wondered about any reporter I saw in my courtroom. Often I knew that the reporter had no idea what I was doing, what the judicial system was about, what the language being used in the courtroom meant, and what rights were being protected and advanced through the legal system. Rarely do reporters have any expertise in the law; the vast majority come from journalism or liberal arts schools, not law schools. Covering "cops and courts" is usually an entry-level position at newspapers and is subject to general-assignment reporting at television stations. Trained court reporters are a dying breed. Turnover is high.

As a result of this ignorance of the system, the public usually gets superficial and inaccurate reporting on the judicial process. Reporters often portray the judiciary merely as an extension of the prosecutors and police, and commonly overemphasize the day-to-day proceedings of the court without looking at the entirety of the judicial system. Court reporting is therefore often inaccurate, sensational, over-simplified, distorted, and routine.

—Thomas S. Hodson

original intent, the idea that the law must be found, not made. It is also described as the theory of strict interpretation of the Constitution.

Elected Judges   In 39 states, judicial candidates must run for office or run to retain their posts. Many of these races have become costly and have descended to mud-slinging. In Ohio, the race for two Supreme Court seats cost $9 million, and elections in Michigan for three Supreme Court seats cost the candidates $16 million.

Good judges have come out of the political system. Some of the great justices on the Supreme Court of the United States owed their appointments to political considerations. The reporter who examines the system of election and appointment to the bench must be careful not to predict performance.

The Grand Jury

The grand jury may initiate investigations as well as act on charges brought by a prosecutor. It can look into the administration of public institutions and the conduct of local and state officials and investigate crime. In some states, grand juries must be empaneled to make periodic examinations of specific state institutions and official bodies.

Special grand juries can be appointed to look into matters such as mistreatment of patients in a state hospital or a tie-in between the police vice squad and organized crime. The district attorney or the attorney general's office directs the inquiry, although the governor may appoint a special prosecutor to direct the investigation.

When a grand jury initiates action on its own and hands up a report on offenses, the report is known as a *presentment.* A presentment may be a statement of the jury's findings or it can charge a person with a crime.

Grand jury deliberations are secret and any publication of the discussions is treated severely by the courts. However, reporters are free to write about the area of investigation, and witnesses can talk to the press about their testimony in most states. Reporters often will try to learn who is testifying by stationing themselves near the jury room. Knowing the identity of witnesses, reporters are free to speculate. But the morality of publishing the names of witnesses is questionable because the grand jury may question witnesses not directly involved in wrongdoing, and even those under suspicion are not to be considered guilty.

One way reporters have learned about witnesses is by watching for motions to dismiss subpoenas issued to require witnesses to appear before the grand jury. Such motions are usually part of the public record and thereby provide the reporter with a document that can be reported.

In covering grand jury matters, as any pretrial proceeding, the danger is that publicity may harm innocent people or impair a defendant's right to a fair trial. Several verdicts have been reversed because of newspaper and broadcast coverage. The reporter must balance the right of the individual with the public's need to know what its official bodies are doing. Once the grand jury takes formal action, its work can be reported and jurors interviewed.

Time Out for a Good Laugh

Court coverage is usually serious, often high tension. But courtrooms sometimes ring with laughter. Attorneys do crack jokes, judges deign to comment sarcastically on cases and witnesses unwittingly provide laughs:

- A reporter heard this aside in a South Dakota federal district court from a man charged with theft of livestock when the jury returned a not-guilty verdict: "Does this mean I get to keep the cows?"

- In his summation before a state district court in the Midwest, the lawyer for a man charged with armed robbery pleaded, "I ask you, ladies and gentlemen of the jury, to give the defendant your best shot."

- When a Minnesota county court judge was asked to perform a marriage for two men, the judge turned to one of them and asked, "Which one of you has the menstrual cycle?"
  "Not me," said one of the men. "I got a Harley-Davidson."

- The judge in a New York case looked at the divorcing couple and announced, "I am going to give Mrs. Sheldon $3,000 a month."
  "Great," her husband said. "And I'll toss in a few bucks myself."

These exchanges occurred in courtrooms:

Q. Doctor, isn't it true that when a person dies in his sleep, he doesn't know about it until the next morning?

A. Did you actually pass the bar exam?

Q. What gear were you in at the moment of impact?

A. Gucci sweats and Reeboks.

Q. What was the first thing your husband said to you when he woke up that morning?

A. He said, "Where am I, Cathy?"

Q. And why did that upset you?

A. My name is Susan.

Further Reading

Alexander, S.L. *Covering the Courts: A Handbook for Journalists.* Lanham, Md.: University Press of America, 1998.

Chiason, Lloyd Jr., ed. *The Press on Trial: Crimes and Trials as Media Events.* Westport, Conn.: Greenwood Press, 1997.

    A study of 16 major criminal trials from the 1735 trial of colonial printer Peter Zenger through the trials of John Brown, Lizzie Borden and Bruno Hauptmann to the O.J. Simpson murder trial and how they reflected the concept of justice at the time of the trials.

Toobin, Jeffrey. *The Run of His Life: The People v. O.J. Simpson.* New York: Random House, 1996.

    Two issues of the *Media Studies Journal* published by The Freedom Forum Media Studies Center are useful:

"Crime Story," a selection of articles about the police and courts by a variety of authors that include judges and reporters: Winter 1992 issue.

"Covering the Courts," articles about cameras in the courtroom, the Simpson and McVeigh trials and legal aspects of court coverage: Winter 1998 issue.

Preview

The most heavily read section of the newspaper after local and entertainment news is sports news. Television coverage draws millions of viewers. The nation is made up of fans, many of them experts on the sports they follow. The sports reporter handles:

- **Game stories:** Coverage requires the score, key plays and players, effect of the game on standings, turning point of the game and post-game interviews.
- **Profiles:** Personality stories on new players, athletes having outstanding seasons, game stars.
- **Illegal and improper activities:** Payoffs to college players, drug use, racism, academic violations by coaches and schools, penalties to colleges.

Dave Kline

Rallying the troops.

When Susan V. Hands went to her first job to cover sports for *The Charlotte Observer,* she was anxious to investigate the growth of participant sports and to promote the development of women's athletics. Hands quickly shifted gears.

"I learned that people buy the morning paper to find out what happened in last night's football or basketball game. And our readers would be angry if, instead of finding the highlights and statistics of yesterday's North Carolina State basketball game, there was an investigative piece on the lack of athletic training available to girls in Charlotte high schools," she says.

Readers want to read about the game. They want to savor the important plays again, despite having seen some of them twice—once as they unfolded on TV and once again, courtesy of instant replay. Fans also want to know what goes on off the court and the field. "We take you behind the scenes," says Mark Mulvoy, the publisher of *Sports Illustrated,* whose circulation of 3 million is said to reach 16 million men and 5 million women for each issue.

Don't root. Report.

The appetite for sports is voracious. The Super Bowl draws more than 150 million viewers, and advertisers line up to spend millions of dollars for a commercial. The Associated Press assigns 100 writers to cover sports, and they send out more than 150,000 words a day plus statistics—enough to fill 20 pages of an eight-column newspaper. The local sports staffs of most newspapers are larger than business, education and municipal government staffs combined.

Sports is so pervasive that the language and personalities of sports have become part of our common vocabulary and metaphor. We say of someone who has failed in an enterprise that he "struck out." When someone does a great job, we say he "hit a home run."

Public interest in games goes back a long way, and just about every culture and country has a history of sports. In modern times, Hearst and Pulitzer recognized the interest in sports when they waged their circulation battles a hundred years ago. But the plunge into sports mania, historians say, began with a boxing match in 1926.

The Fight That Did It

When the Manassa Mauler, Jack Dempsey, met the erudite Gene Tunney for the heavyweight championship, the nation—and parts of the world—stood still. Publishers who had paid sports scant attention now found that "it is impossible to print too much," reported Will Owen Jones, the editor of the *Nebraska State Journal.* Jones had been asked by the American Society of Newspaper Editors to look into the "national obsession for sporting intelligence" because serious editors were alarmed by the interest in what they considered entertainment.

Seven hundred reporters covered the fight. They dispatched two million words to an enthralled public, says Bruce J. Evensen of DePaul University in his article in the *Journalism Quarterly,* "'Cave Man' Meets 'Student Champion': Sports Page Storytelling for a Nervous Generation During America's Jazz Age." Evensen writes, "Press coverage of the Dempsey–Tunney 1926 title fight signaled the arrival of the modern sports page as a major player in the struggle for circulation."

The Long Count   Tunney won that match, dethroning the mighty Dempsey who had reigned as champion for seven years. The rematch the following year generated even more print, and it is still discussed on the sports pages. In the seventh round, Dempsey knocked Tunney down. But the referee did not begin to count over the downed new champ, because Dempsey failed to go to a neutral corner. Sportswriter Roger Kahn says that Tunney was on the canvas for a full 18 seconds. Later, when Tunney floored Dempsey with a sharp right hand to the jaw, the referee began the 10-count immediately, not pressing Tunney to go to a corner of the ring. Dempsey was counted out in what Kahn says was eight seconds. Kahn says there was much talk at the time of the interest of the mob in finding a referee.

Andrew D. Bernstein, NBA photo

Who Is He?

Considered by sportswriters to be the greatest basketball player of all time, the Chicago Bulls player was described by a writer: "The ease of his game makes the rest of the players, all of them stars in college, look rough, somehow-clumsy, a step slow."

Questions aspiring sportswriters also might be asked:

• What was the "shot heard round the world"?

• What quarterback achieved fame for his Hail Mary Pass?

• Who said.
— Slump? I ain't in no slump. I just ain't hitting.
— I am the greatest.

To test prospective hires, some sports editors ask the applicants: "What's the 'long count'?" Those who answer, "Dempsey–Tunney, 1927" get the job.

Game Coverage

All aspects of sports interest fans, but the most pressing question they want answered is, "Who won?" Radio and television answer that question quickly enough for most games. Still, fans want to know more—how the key play came about, why the star failed in the clutch, what the coach thinks of the team's performance. Fans will read about the game, already knowing the score, and they will watch replays on TV and listen to recaps on radio.

For most major sports, the news story is featurized in newspaper and sports magazine accounts.

Most game stories focus on one of the following: a key player, a pivotal play, a change in the standings or a record set in the game.

Featurizing the Game Story

The Auburn Tigers were ranked No. 2 in the nation when they took the field against Arkansas in a nationally televised football game. Arkansas had been humiliated by Southern California 50–14 and ranked at the bottom of Division 1-A teams in several categories. But Arkansas thoroughly outplayed Auburn to win 27–10, an upset well-known to fans when sportswriters sat down to write the game story.

Here's how one writer began his account of the game:

> The Auburn football team, ranked No. 2 in the nation, was considered a well-oiled scoring machine. But in its game against underdog Arkansas, the gears failed to engage. Auburn stumbled, faltered and failed to function.
>
> Arkansas looked nothing like the team that had been trounced by Southern California 50–14 and that ranked last among 119 Division 1-A teams in time of possession. This time, the Razorbacks held the ball almost 32 minutes and outplayed the Tigers in a 23–10 rout.

The unexpected also occurred when the New York Yankees, with the highest payroll in the major leagues, met the Detroit Tigers in an American League playoff series. The heavily favored Yankees fell to the Tigers without much of a fight. Here is one sportswriter's lead for her newspaper:

> Money doesn't talk. The New York Yankees, whose $200 million payroll supported a lineup considered the most formidable since the days of Babe Ruth, wilted before Detroit Tigers pitching in the American League division playoff series.
>
> After a first-game loss to the Yankees, Tigers pitchers checked the Yankee hitters for three successive games.

Oblivious

Red Grange, one of football's greatest players, was taken to the White House by a senator from Illinois to meet President Calvin Coolidge. "Mr. President," the senator began, "may I present Red Grange of the Chicago Bears." The president replied, "How do you do, Mr. Grange. I am indeed delighted to meet you. I've always liked animal acts."

Joel Sartore,
The Wichita Eagle-Beacon

Turning Point

The end-zone catch, the successful goal-line stand, the last-second missed three-point attempt, the ninth-inning double play—these turning points in the game usually are the ingredients of the game story lead.

Yankee batters went 2 for 21 with runners in scoring position over the three losses. The Yankees were scoreless for 20 straight innings in these games.

The fourth game in the series was no contest quickly, and ended 8–3, the Yankees' runs coming in the seventh and ninth innings, before a home crowd whose cheers were a mixture of delirium and disbelief. Their Tigers had humiliated the mighty Yankees.

See **Serena Wins** in *NRW Plus* for how a reporter handled a tennis match that most fans had seen on TV.

Checklist: Games

___Result: final score, names of teams, type of sport (if necessary, explain that it is high school, college, professional); league (NFL, AFC, Ivy League, Western Conference).

___Where and when game took place.

___Turning point of game; winning play; key strategy.

___Outstanding players.

___Effect on standings, rankings, individual records.

___Scoring; details of important baskets, goals, runs, etc.; summaries of others.

___Streaks, records involved, by team or player.

___Postgame comments.

___External factors: weather, spectators.

___Size of crowd.

___Injuries and subsequent condition of athletes.

___Statistics.

___Duration of game when relevant.

Game Details

Unless a game is exciting or important, sportswriter Ron Rapoport says he tends not to include much detail.

"Usually a couple of paragraphs are enough to sum up the key plays. I prefer to use the space to concentrate on one or two or three of the most interesting things that happened and to tell what the players involved or the manager thought about them.

"Often, a game story will be built around somebody who had a large effect—positive or negative—on the outcome," Rapoport says. "It is almost mandatory that we hear from this key player and, though there are some spontaneous talkers

From the Players' Perspective

To see the game the right way, look at it the way the players do. The advice is given by Thomas Boswell, a sportswriter for *The Washington Post,* in his book *Why Time Begins on Opening Day* (New York: Doubleday). Boswell writes about baseball, but his suggestions apply to most sports.

Judge slowly. "Never judge a player over a unit of time shorter than a month . . . you must see a player hot, cold, and in between before you can put the whole package together."

Assume everybody is trying reasonably hard. ". . . giving 110 percent . . . would be counterproductive for most players. . . . Usually something on the order of 80 percent effort is about right."

Forgive even the most grotesque physical errors. "It's assumed that every player is physically capable of performing every task asked of him. If he doesn't it's never his fault. His mistake is simply regarded as part of a professional's natural margin of error."

Judge mental errors harshly. "The distinction as to whether a mistake has been made 'from the neck up or the neck down' is always drawn."

Pay more attention to the mundane than to the spectacular. "The necessity for consistency usually outweighs the need for the inspired."

Pay more attention to the theory of the game than to the outcome of the game. Don't let your evaluations be swayed too greatly by the final score. "If a team loses a game but has used its resources properly . . . then that team is often able to ignore defeat utterly. Players say, 'We did everything right but win.'"

Keep in mind that players always know best how they're playing. "At the technical level, they seldom fool themselves—the stakes are too high."

Stay ahead of the action, not behind it or even neck and neck with it. "Remember that the immediate past is almost always prelude."

---

who begin at the sight of a notebook, it is almost always better to have a question in mind. This sounds simple enough, but often takes some thought. The right question will often do wonders.

"I also like to listen to what's being said by the players—not to reporters—but to each other. They often have funny conversations when they've won, sympathetic ones when they've lost. Good dialogue can dress up a story."

Actions sometimes are as revealing as words. The slight shift in the linebacker's position, a change in the way a guard plays his man—these details that the observant reporter picks up often mean the difference between victory and defeat. Watch a center fielder play each batter differently. Keep an eye on the way a forward moves to the basket in the second period after he missed all his shots in the first period.

For more advice on how to prepare for game coverage and how to keep statistics see **Coverage Preparation** and **Keeping Statistics** in *NRW Plus*.

Expanded Coverage

Sports reporters do more than cover games. They handle labor negotiations, the commercialization and sometimes corruption of intercollegiate athletics, the off-field and off-court activities of athletes and their personal lives. Sports editors want enterprise, investigative stories: Is fan support strong or waning? What's the role of player agents? Who goes out for lacrosse, wrestling, fencing?

Are sports-conscious parents pressing their children too hard? (A TV documentary reported that 70 percent of youngsters who are pushed into sports burn

Quiz
   Which sports events require the largest sports-writing team the AP sends out? The Olympics. But for annual events, it is the Indianapolis 500. The wire service stations men and women in the infield hospital, garages, the crow's nest, the pits and in the stands.

out by age 13 and that fewer than 1 percent of high school athletes qualify for any sort of college scholarship.)

Parents Spend   Despite the discouraging data, parents are spending money—some as much as $5,000 a year—on their children's athletic activities. Starting at age 4, children are being sent to private sports schools, given personal trainers and placed with teams that travel for games.

Parents can order for $135 a test called Smart which determines their youngsters' potential in 38 sports. They can also hire National Scouting Report for a promising young athlete. The company will market the youngster's skills to colleges. Also in the marketing package, a highlight video of the athlete on the field and a personal Web site with photos, sports page clippings and a bio. Cost: $2,300.

The camps for these youngsters, the experiences they have, their parents' concerns . . . all these make for stories that break up the endless game reporting. They can also tell us something about parental priorities.

Personal Lives

At one time, what athletes did off the field was their business, even if it affected their play. No one tried to find out why Hank Thompson played third base so strangely for the New York Giants. "I had always supposed it was simply Thompson's way to scoop up a grounder along with the bag and whatever bits of grass and gravel were in the area and hurl the entire package across the diamond, leaving the first baseman to sort it out as best he could," said Peter Andrews of the days he covered the team.

Today, he would find out and probably report that Thompson often played third base drunk.

Alan Robinson, an AP sportswriter, says, "We're people writing about people instead of people writing about heroes. That's healthy."

Athletes as Models

Covering Ali
   The veteran sportswriter Robert Lipsyte says many sports reporters would not write about some of Muhammad Ali's antics. "They figured it would deny them access if they did," he says.
   Lipsyte adds, "A lot of athletes tend to be ordinary people with extraordinary skills. He was an extraordinary person. He was beautiful. He was a genius at what he was."
   But he says. "He's not really being covered. He's being beatified. Access is carefully given."

Michael Jordan is considered by many sportswriters to be the greatest of all basketball players. With that came close scrutiny of his successes and failures off the court as well as on. Asked about his refusal to endorse an African-American candidate for the U.S. Senate from his home state of North Carolina who was running against a candidate with a deeply conservative stance on race relations, Jordan replied, "Republicans buy shoes, too." As the major sports figure for Nike, Jordan also never spoke out when it was disclosed that Nike exploited its workers in foreign countries.

A sports columnist wrote of athletes in general, though he obviously had Jordan in mind, "The times have produced a remarkable chemical reaction in some players; it has fattened their wallets and bankrupted their wits."

A Different Score   *Sports Illustrated* checked on the extracurricular activities of players in the National Basketball Association and came up with the report that many NBA players have fathered illegitimate children, one with seven by six different women. Another player has five illegitimate children to add to the two by his wife.

The detailed disclosure named several players on its "NBA All-Paternity Team." They include Patrick Ewing, Juwan Howard, Shawn Kemp, Jason Kidd, Stephon Marbury, Hakeem Olajuwon, Gary Payton and Scottie Pippen. Kemp pays an average of $6,000 a month for each of his seven children. Not to worry. He has a seven-year contract for $107 million.

One of the major basketball agents told the magazine, "I'd say there might be more kids out of wedlock than there are players in the NBA." He said he spends more time "dealing with paternity claims than negotiating contracts," *Sports Illustrated* reported.

Fans do not take kindly to negative stories about their favorite players. For their reactions, see **Outraged Fans,** *NRW Plus.*

Fans prefer the brighter side of sports, and there are plenty of stories about athletes' overcoming adversity.

A Tragic Childhood   When Terry Glenn of the New England Patriots set an NFL record of 90 catches as a rookie, Thomas George of *The New York Times* interviewed him and told of Glenn's childhood:

> Glenn's mother was murdered in his hometown, Columbus, Ohio, when he was 13. His father lives somewhere in Columbus and Glenn has never met or seen him. Glenn grew up in his earliest years on welfare and wearing goodwill clothes. There were days when there was no electricity in his home.

A Dream Realized   Jerry Tipton of the *Herald-Leader* in Lexington, Ky., wrote a moving profile of George Adams, a University of Kentucky tailback, from interviews with the football player and his friends and family. Tipton begins:

> When Ruth Adams, mother of nine, sits in the living room of her Lexington home, she can look at nine photographs of her children. Five of them are of her younger son, George.
>
> "The others get on me for having so much about George," she said. "I love them all, the grandchildren, too. But George has a special place."

Tipton develops his story slowly, and the picture that emerges is of a family with many difficulties. Adams' father drank. A brother and a sister have served time in jail. Another son, the mother said, is "in trouble."

"George never gave me no kind of trouble," she said, breaking a long pause. "He always brought good things home from school. He made me happy."

When others caused so much trouble, why didn't George?

"He saw so much pain in his mother's eyes," said Donnie Harville, who coached Adams in basketball at Lafayette High. "And he decided he wouldn't make his mother suffer more."

Tipton delves into the family's problems:

> Adams can remember seeing his father walking unsteadily down a street. The son would cross to the other side to avoid a face-to-face meeting. . . .
>
> "When I was young, it hurt a lot," Adams said. "I mean a whole lot. I told myself I'm not going to be like that."

Adams had a dream. "If I can play pro football, the first thing I want to do with my first contract is buy my mother a house," he told Tipton.

Adams was selected in the first round of the professional football draft. He signed a four-year contract for $1.5 million, and he did buy a house for his mother.

R. L. Chambers

Tomorrow's Major Leaguers

Little Leaguers   A stroll over to the local baseball fields some weekend to watch the youngsters playing Little League baseball can pay off with interesting features. So can recollections of Little League graduates in the major leagues.

"I still remember it like it was yesterday," Paul O'Neill, a New York Yankee outfielder, told a reporter about his Little League days in Columbus, Ohio. "I pitched the championship game and struck out a kid named Darren Waugh to end it. I remember every detail. The games then meant as much to you as these games do now. And you got to go to Dairy Queen afterward."

Looking back on a career with more strikeouts than any pitcher and more no-hit games, Nolan Ryan told Alan Schwarz of *The New York Times* his happiest memories of baseball were playing Little League in Alvin, Texas. "We played for the love of the game and the camaraderie. Little League was the first opportunity for children in Alvin to get involved in any organized activity. It was one of the biggest events in our lives," Ryan said.

The Beat

In addition to covering games, the sports reporter attends sports banquets, drops by the pro shops at the golf and tennis courts, chats with the unsung athletes on the high school swimming, wrestling and track teams. The high school and college athletes who may go through a season never playing before more than a handful of spectators make for good stories. Not many readers understand why a youngster will run 10 to 20 miles a day to prepare for a cross-country meet, what it is like to engage in a noncontact sport in which the only adversary is the athlete's own mind and body. The runners, the javelin throwers, the swimmers, the gymnasts, the fencers and the wrestlers should not be overwhelmed by the glut of basketball and football coverage.

Sports Writing

Some of the best as well as some of the worst writing appears on the sports pages and is heard on sports broadcasts and telecasts. Perhaps it is the excitement of conflict that encourages these extremes. A team wins; a team loses. An athlete overcomes adversity; an athlete fails miserably when he or she is called on.

Consider this gem by John Updike about the last at-bat of the Boston Red Sox outfielder, Ted Williams. Williams, one of the greatest hitters in baseball, had done the unbelievable: He hit a home run:

> Though we thumped, wept, and chanted "We want Ted" for minutes after he hid in the dugout, he did not come back. Our noise for some seconds passed beyond excitement into a kind of immense open anguish, a wailing, a cry to be saved. But immortality is not transferable. The papers said that other players, and even the umpires on the field, begged him to come out and acknowledge us in some way, but he never had and did not now. God does not answer letters.

When the New York Yankees were winning pennant after pennant and Mickey Mantle was the home run king, Jim Murray of the *Los Angeles Times* wrote, "Rooting for the New York Yankees is like rooting for U.S. Steel."

Now look at this not-so lustrous lead:

> Coach Paul Bergen tried his hardest, but neither starters nor subs could stem the avalanche of baskets tossed through the hoops by a tide of Mustang players last night as the Cougars took a 86–42 drubbing from their crosstown rivals.

The sportswriter is trying too hard: We have an *avalanche* caused by a *tide,* and we have basketball jargon, *hoops.* Sportswriters are particularly susceptible to words that have been used so often they were tossed in the wastebasket of the better writers years ago. When Stanley Woodward was a sports editor he came across a baseball game story in which a batter had *belted* a game-winning home run. Woodward tore off his belt and swung it around the sportswriter's desk. "You ever see a guy hit a ball out of the park with one of these?" he shouted.

Tough Beat

Professional basketball writers say theirs is the most grueling of all sports beats. Covering games in so many cities requires frequent travel, sometimes coast-to-coast twice in a week. "I take care of my body as if I were a player," says David DuPree of *USA Today.* "I don't drink or smoke." Jackie MacMullan of *The Boston Globe* says she works out daily on road trips.

Who Won?

When keen observation and a knowledge of the sport join writing ability the result can be memorable, as is this lead by boxing writer Jack Cuddy who sent this bulletin from ringside to the United Press:

> NEW YORK (UP)— Jersey Joe Walcott, the ancient dancing master from Camden, N.J., gave Joe Louis a 15-round boxing lesson tonight but the officials gave the fight and the title to Joe Louis.

Bonds or Bacsik?

After Barry Bonds of the San Francisco Giants hit his 756th home run, breaking Hank Aaron's long-standing record, reporters naturally interviewed him.

But the words that struck them and were played prominently in their stories came from the Washington Nationals pitcher Mike Bacsik, whose fast ball Bonds sent soaring into the night air.

Bacsik, a 29-year-old with mediocre record, said:

I put my head down for a second. But I'm still alive. I always dreamed about this as a kid, but when I dreamed of it, I thought I would be the one hitting the home run. But if I didn't give up this home run, nobody would remember me. I'm part of history.

Let 'em Talk

The experts on sports are the athletes themselves, and listening to them talk about their trade leads to good stories. The material can come in a locker room chat or a more formal interview.

In a piece about Billy Williams, a Chicago Cubs outfielder for many years and later its batting coach, Frederick C. Klein of *The Wall Street Journal* quotes him on hitting:

> "You hear fans saying that this star or that one was a 'natural,' but 99 percent of the time they're wrong. Sure, you gotta have ability, but you also gotta work, and every good hitter I knew worked hard to get that way. You have to practice your swing all the time, just like a golf pro. And if you think golf's hard, try it sometime with a guy throwing the ball at you."

One of the best places to listen to athletes, and to ask talk-inducing questions, is the locker room.

"Right after a game when you're talking with athletes . . . that's when they're at their most vulnerable, and that's when you get the most out of a player," says Suzyn Waldman, whose beat includes the New York Yankees and the Knicks. She says, "Sports is flesh and blood, people and stories, and so much humanity."

Enduring Quotes Some of the best lines of sportswriters are not of their making. All they have done is to quote their sources:

A North Carolina State basketball player explaining why he was nervous at practice: "My sister's expecting a baby and I don't know whether I'm going to be an aunt or an uncle."

Shaquille O'Neal, after returning from Greece, was asked whether he had seen the Parthenon. His answer: "I really can't remember the names of the clubs we went to."

A Florida State football coach to his players: "You guys line up alphabetically by height."

Joe Theismann, former football player, then sports announcer: "Nobody in football should be called a genius. A genius is a guy like Norman Einstein."

Steve Spurrier, when University of Florida football coach, after hearing that a fire at Auburn's football dormitory had destroyed 20 books: "The real tragedy is that 15 of them hadn't been colored yet."

A Texas A&M basketball coach to one of his players who had received a D and four F's: "Son, looks to me like you're spending too much time on one subject."

George Rogers, New Orleans Saints running back on the coming season: "I want to rush for 1,000 or 1,500 yards, whichever comes first."

University of Houston receiver on his coach: "He treats us like men. He lets us wear earrings."

Chicago Blackhawks forward explaining why he has a color photo of himself on his locker: "That's so when I forget how to spell my name, I can still find my clothes."

University of Pittsburgh basketball player: I'm going to graduate on time, no matter how long it takes."

The Losers

Pete Hamill, a veteran journalist, wrote these lines to introduce his comments on a book about a baseball pitcher in the twilight of his career:

All good sports reporters know that the best stories are in the loser's locker room. Winners are bores—assuming a false modesty or performing a winner's strut while thanking their mothers, their agents or God. Losers are more like the rest of us. They make mistakes that they can't take back. They are imperfect when perfection is demanded, and thus suffer the sometimes permanent stain of humiliation. If organized sports teach any lessons about life, the most important is about accepting defeat with grace.

Straight Talk Best

Good writing means retaining the colorful language of sports, not falling into the homogeneous prose that infects too much of newspaper and television writing. Russell Baker, a columnist on *The New York Times* editorial page and a die-hard sports fan, bemoaned the decline of baseball talk that, he wrote, once "crackled with terseness, vibrancy and metaphor."

Baker had heard a television sportscaster say, "Ryan has good velocity and excellent location." He meant, Baker wrote, that "Ryan is throwing very fast and putting the ball where he wants to."

Great Lines   Sportswriters have written some memorable lines, such as this one about a midwestern quarterback who was a wizard on the field, a dunce in the classroom: "He could do anything with a football but autograph it." (The line came back to some sportswriters when they wrote about a football player at UCLA who was arrested for killing his drug dealer. The player, it turned out, could not read—the product of the win-at-any-price philosophy of big-time sports.)

Red Smith was a master writer. Of a notorious spitball pitcher, he wrote that "papers needed three columns for his pitching record: won, lost and relative humidity." Look at this lead he wrote about Buck Leonard, a black first baseman whose career ended before baseball was integrated:

Wearing a store suit, horn-rimmed glasses, and a smile that could light up Yankee Stadium, a sunny gentleman of 64 revisited his past yesterday and recalled what it was like to be the black Lou Gehrig on a food allowance of 60 cents a day.

Goodbye

Dick Young of the *Daily News* in New York took a strong personal approach to his coverage. When the Brooklyn Dodgers owner Walter O'Malley decided to move the team to Los Angeles in 1957, Young wrote in his column the following farewell:

This is called an obit, which is short for obituary. An obit tells of a person who has died, how he lived, and of those who live after him. This is the obit on the Brooklyn Dodgers.

Preliminary diagnosis indicates that the cause of death was an acute case of greed, followed by severe political implications. . . . and, now, Walter O'Malley leaves Brooklyn a rich man and a despised man.

Nonarguable

In 1931 when Babe Ruth was negotiating for a salary significantly greater than what President Herbert Hoover was earning, the Yankees balked. Ruth responded, "I had a better year than he did."

Defeated Warrior

This is one of the most famous of all sports photographs. It shows not a winner but a loser, a quarterback tackled behind his goal line, and in his daze comes the realization that his career is about over. This photograph by Morris Berman of New York Giants quarterback Y.A. Tittle was almost tossed out by Berman's editors at the *Pittsburgh Post-Gazette* because it depicted a player on the losing team instead of a winning play or players.

Lasting

The lead that Grantland Rice wrote to the 1924 Notre Dame–Army football game is considered the most famous in sportswriting history:

Outlined against a blue-gray October sky, the Four Horsemen rode again. In dramatic lore they are known as Famine, Pestilence, Destruction, and Death. These are only aliases. Their real names are Stuhldreher, Miller, Crowley and Layden.

Rice thus gave lasting fame to the Notre Dame backfield that won the game that day.

The last few words chill an otherwise warm recollection. They sum up a period of American life in a phrase.

Dizzy and Yogi   The stilted writing of some reporters makes a sports fan long for Dizzy Dean, the St. Louis Cardinals pitcher and later a sports announcer who was known for his picturesque language. Once he was struck on the toe while pitching and a doctor examined him on the mound. "This toe is fractured," the doctor said. To which Dean replied, "Fractured hell. The damn thing's broken."

Sportswriters carry stories such as the Dizzy Dean incident in their hip pockets. They also have a collection of Yogi Berra's comments handy for use when appropriate:

- It's not over 'til it's over.

- It gets late early at Yankee Stadium.

- That place is too crowded; nobody goes there anymore.

- Ninety percent of baseball is half-mental.

- It's déjà vu all over again.

- When you come to a fork in the road, take it.

- If people don't want to come out to the ballpark, nobody's going to stop them.

- Slump? I ain't in no slump. I just ain't hitting.

Did Berra, former catcher for the New York Yankees and manager of a couple of major league teams, really say that, or are they creations of baseball writers who needed to brighten their copy? No one is talking.

Anecdotes

Sportswriters are insatiable collectors of anecdotes they tuck away for use at the appropriate moment.

When an imaginative boxing promoter was trying to schedule a match between Muhammad Ali, who had made a friendly visit to Arab countries, and Mike Rossman, who carried the nicknames the Jewish Bomber and the Kosher Butcher, James Tuite of *The New York Times* recalled in his story a similar ethnic promotion. Years before, Irish Eddy Kelly and Benny Leonard, a Jewish fighter, were in the ring. Leonard was battering Kelly. Finally, in a clinch, Kelly whispered to Leonard, "Hub rachmones. [Yiddish for "take pity."] I'm really Bernie Schwartz."

Rossman, Tuite pointed out, was born Mike DePuano and took to wearing the Star of David on his trunks along with his new name to help sell tickets. The Ali-Rossman match was laughed out of the ring by pieces such as Tuite's.

When Reggie Jackson was elected to the Baseball Hall of Fame, sportswriters trundled out a battery of anecdotes about Jackson, who once referred to "the magnitude of me," and told a sportswriter, "The only reason I don't like playing in the World Series is I can't watch myself play."

He bragged to fellow players that he had an IQ of 160, to which Mickey Rivers, a Yankee teammate, replied, "You don't even know how to spell IQ."

Rivers was a man of plain talk and said to Jackson one day as Jackson—whose full name is Reginald Martinez Jackson—was rattling on about his greatness: "You got a white man's first name, a Puerto Rican's middle name and a black man's last name. No wonder you're so screwed up."

Myth Exploded The story is one of baseball's most often told—of how the New York Giants came from way behind to snatch the National League pennant from the Brooklyn Dodgers in 1951 with a game-winning, pennant-winning home run by Bobby Thomson. It was, legend says, "the shot heard round the world." Some say it was the greatest baseball game ever played.

The story lasted decades, its undoing the result of digging reporting by Joshua Harris Prager of *The Wall Street Journal*.

"I was talking to a friend," Prager says, "and he mentioned hearing a rumor that the Giants were stealing the Dodgers signs." (These are the hand signals a catcher sends out to the pitcher's mound telling the pitcher what kind of delivery to make.) His friend said he didn't believe it. But Prager decided to check the story and interviewed all 21 living members of the 1951 Giants.

**Don't Guess:
Check It Out**

Sports fans have bottomless memories, and woe to the reporter who makes a mistake. Case in point:

In a review of cheating in sports, a *New York Times* reporter wrote, "Bobby Johnson's 'shot heard 'round the world. . . .'"

The telephone calls began minutes after the newspaper hit newsstands, and the letters continued for days.

Vocabulary

Sportswriters toss the word *hero* around indiscriminately. A last-second basket, a ninth-inning home run, a 75-yard pass and the athlete is called a hero or performed a heroic act. Hardly. As a letter writer to a local newspaper pointed out when the word appeared once too often for her, "Sportswriters should keep in mind the power of words and use them appropriately. The word *hero* should be used for those who truly are—those who help others in time of need, who make sacrifices for others. This is not to diminish athletes. Some are really great. But heroes are another matter entirely."

"I was surprised so many didn't want to talk about it," Prager said. "Many of them were not happy I was doing it." Thomson broke down and cried. Some were furious. But some, Prager said, "wanted to talk about it."

Prager even located the telescope that was used in center field to spy on the catcher's signals. And he tracked down the family of the electrician who set up the buzzer system to relay the stolen signals to the Giants dugout, where they were sent out to Thomson at the plate.

Reporting Is the Key

As Yogi Berra put it, "You can see a lot just by observing." And that's the basis of good sportswriting, of all journalism, for that matter.

The game trophy may seem to go to the writers of the trade. But that's a superficial assessment. Roger Angell, who covers baseball for *The New Yorker* and is called the laureate of the sport because of the high quality of his writing, calls himself a journalist, a working reporter.

He says that his reporting, his insistence on using carefully observed details in his writing, gives his work authenticity. He also knows his trade. He knows, for example, whom to interview.

Pick the wrong player, Angell says, and you get clichés.

The reporters who spend time on their beats know who the right players are, and they realize that, no matter how much they think they know about the sports they cover, there is always an insightful athlete who can add to their understanding. They seek out these players.

Sportscasters Bob Costas, considered one of the best sports broadcasters in the business, sees a decline in his trade, the result of bad journalism. Most sports broadcasting, he says, is "bland shilling and repetition of clichés—not just cliché expressions but clichéd takes on situations—broadcasting without any element of journalism or a fresh eye."

The essence of sports broadcasting, he says, is solid reporting of the sport and the event.

Be Prepared Sportswriters develop many of their best stories by chatting with athletes. These may seem to an outsider to be spontaneous, but behind the reporter's chit-chat is sports savvy. Listen to Ira Berkow, a *New York Times* reporter who has covered every major sport and sports figure:

> Try to say something positive without being overly flattering. But it helps to he prepared. I wanted to ask a veteran pitcher something. "Congratulations on a good season," I said. "I'm having a horseshit season," he replied. I had to gather myself for a second. I said, "Hey, look, you're in the major leagues. Any season is a good one."

Starting Out

Many sports reporters learn the basics covering high school sports. Cathy Henkel, sports editor of *The Seattle Times,* began her career covering high school football games for *The Register-Guard* in Eugene, Ore.

"It was the best start I could have gotten," she says.

Some aspiring sportswriters begin in high school as stringers for local and regional newspapers and stations. Then they go on to cover college sports. Sam Smith, who covers the Chicago Bulls for the *Chicago Tribune,* was an accounting major at Pace College in New York. He liked sports and decided to cover it for the college weekly newspaper, the *Pace Press.*

The newspaper adviser spotted Smith's talent and suggested he add journalism to his studies. He did, found it a close fit with his interests and abilities and sold his accounting textbooks.

To the young reporter who can quote the pass completion records of the quarterbacks in the National Football League, being assigned to cover a high school football game may seem a letdown, if not a putdown. Not so.

High School Sports

A veteran sports reporter remarked that despite the attraction of professional football, major league baseball and skilled professional basketball players, local high school sports remains a dominant factor in many cities. "An American may not be too familiar with the workings of his city hall, but he knows his high school football team lineup."

A journalism instructor with years of reporting experience was astonished one Friday night early in his job at a midwestern state university to hear roars in the distance. They were persistent and advanced on him like a tidal wave. Concerned, he asked a neighbor what was going on.

"That's the Tigers game," he was told. The local high school football team was playing a team from the western part of the state. The instructor learned that some of the high school games outdrew the university's games.

Don't Push

Young sportswriters sometimes try too hard. They push the language, reach too hard for words and phrases. When this happens, the result is sawdust and shavings.

Direct, slender, purposive prose flows naturally from the event. Sports has the built-in essentials of drama—conflict, leading characters, dramatic resolution. There are enough incidents and examples to highlight the event, anecdotes that illustrate the situation; high-quality quotations that reveal the nature of the individual and the event.

Good sportswriting is not confined to the big newspapers covering major teams. Jack Schlottman of *The Globe-Times* of Bethlehem, Pa., learned just before game time that the coach of a high school football team had benched 22 of his players

Breaking In

Although sports is proliferating on radio, cable and the Internet, there are more budding sportscasters than positions. The director of a talent agency that represents sports broadcasters says, "There's a lot of backstabbing because there are only so many jobs for so many people. All the radio guys want to be in TV. The TV guys want to go to the networks. And the network guys don't want to give up their jobs." The best way up, he says, is to start with an unpaid internship at a TV station or as a production assistant for on-air talent.

Football Powerhouse

"Evangel Christian (of Shreveport, La.) has won eight state titles and one 'mythical national championship' since opening in 1989. It represents the future: a 300-student high school that seems to have been created for its football program, rather than the other way around. Criticized for its recruiting practices, roiled when its coach took a year's leave after he was accused of sexual abuse; eager to play out-of-state powerhouses, Evangel comes across as a prototype of a gladiatorial marketing machine."
—*Don Wallace, author of* Two Teams, Two Dreams in the First-Ever National Championship High School Football Game

for the season-ending traditional game with an intracity rival. The players had been told to go directly to their homeroom, not to stop for breakfast the morning of the game. Instead, they stopped off at a restaurant and started a food fight that led to a disturbance.

After the game that night, which the team with the benched players lost 43–0, Schlottman interviewed the coach, whose comment ended the piece:

"I'm still in the boy business and I hurt some boys tonight," the coach said. "Hopefully, I made some men."

Imitate, Then Innovate

Red Smith said that his goal as he developed his craft was to purify and clarify his writing. "I have sought to become simpler, straighter and purer in my handling of the language," he said. "When I was very young I knowingly and unashamedly imitated others.

"But slowly, by what process I have no idea, your own writing tends to crystallize, to take shape. Yet you have learned from all these guys and they are somehow incorporated into your own style. Pretty soon you're not imitating any longer."

In talking about his writing, Smith would recall the words of his teacher at Notre Dame, John Michael Cooney, who taught journalism in a basement room of the library. Cooney told his students he wanted clear sentences, "so definite they would cast a shadow."

The secret of Smith's writing is twofold—simplicity and good reporting. "The essential thing," Smith said, "is to report the facts."

Learn and Keep Learning

Because many fans are experts in the sports they follow, sports reporters have to know as much as and probably more than their viewers or readers. Preparation is the key, and this includes mastering the elements of the sport being covered and its details. It means knowing the sports' history as well as the strengths and weaknesses of current athletes.

Baseball reporters know the names Willie Mays and Lou Gehrig, Jackie Robinson and Larry Doby. Basketball reporters know about Bob Cousy and Kareem Abdul-Jabbar. Football reporters know Bart Starr, Vince Lombardi and Joe Montana. They can place Sandy Koufax, Hank Aaron, Joe Louis, Dale Earnhardt, Billie Jean King, Bobby Jones, Jesse Owens, Wilma Rudolph, Whirlaway and Eddie Arcaro without having to resort to reference books.

Breaking the Barriers Some of these athletes established records. Gehrig, known as the Iron Man of baseball, held the record for playing in consecutive games until it was broken by Cal Ripken. Vince Lombardi was the greatest professional football coach of his time, leading the Green Bay Packers to spectacular successes. Whirlaway was one of the few horses to win the Kentucky Derby, the Preakness and the Belmont Stakes, horse racing's greatest triumph, the Triple Crown.

Advice from a Pro: Try Again, and Again

Red Smith was always helpful to young writers. When a college student sent Smith columns he had written for his school newspaper, Smith replied:

> When I was a cub in Milwaukee I had a city editor who'd stroll over and read across a guy's shoulder when he was writing a lead. Sometimes he would approve and sometimes say gently, "Try again," and walk away.
>
> My best advice is, try again. And then again. If you're for this racket, and not many really are, then you've got an eternity of sweat and tears ahead. I don't mean just you; I mean anybody.

Charles McCabe of the San Francisco *Chronicle* wrote a column shortly after Smith's death in which he said:

> Red was nearly always the last man to leave the press room. Like Westbrook Pegler, he was a bleeder. I well remember him at the Olympic Games in Squaw Valley. When everyone else left and was up at the bar, Red sat sweating, piles of rejected leads surrounding him. He hadn't really even started his story yet. But when the lead came he wrote fluently and always met his deadline.

Smith once remarked, "The English language, if handled with respect, scarcely ever poisoned the user."

Jackie Robinson and Larry Doby set records of a different kind. They broke the race barriers in baseball, Robinson in the National League, Doby in the American League. See **Breaking the Barriers** in *NRW Plus* for their stories and how women established themselves as sports reporters despite opposition.

Dark Past   Sports reporters know the history of their sports. One of the "defining events in the history of athletics," as sportswriter Gerald Eskenazi describes the victory in 1966 of the all-black Texas Western College in the NCAA basketball championship tourney, is recounted in *Glory Road* by the team's coach, Don Haskins. Texas Western's opponent—the all-white University of Kentucky team—was coached by Adolph Rupp. The Texas victory, Eskenazi says, is "reminiscent of the moment Jackie Robinson first wore his Brooklyn Dodgers uniform, or the day Joe Louis knocked out Max Schmeling."

Golf Barrier   When Annika Sorenstam, a star in golf's LPGA Tour, decided to challenge the men at a PGA Tour event, some male golfers welcomed her. But many told her to stay away. David Feherty, the CBS golf announcer, was unhappy with Sorenstam's cool reception. "There are so few willing to be gentlemen about this," he said. "She doesn't have to prove anything to me. She's the best woman ever to have played. To have the guts to play the men and to endure this mean-spirited stuff, God Almighty, it's petty stuff."

A Day at the Races   When they aren't sure of a new field they are assigned to, journalists do their homework. Andrea Sachs, a journalism student, learned how to learn when she was assigned to interview a jockey at a racetrack. Sachs had never seen a horse race. A city girl, she said, "I didn't know the difference between a horse and a goat."

But she learned fast. To follow Sachs as she went about doing homework and then doing her interview, see **Quick Learner**, *NRW Plus*.

Two Developments

As sports attracted more and more fans, two aspects emerged that concern the sportswriter. One is the tug of partisanship, the pressure by fans on the journalist to become a rooter as well as a reporter. The other is the role of money in sports and its pervasive and sometimes corrupting influence.

Partisanship

Sports reporters by and large are closer to the teams and the players that they cover than other beat reporters are to their sources. Out of this relationship there are positive and negative consequences, says Rapoport.

"If you are around a group of people a lot you are going to learn a great deal about them and this can only help your reporting," he says. "The flip side of this, of course, is that familiarity breeds both admiration and contempt. Some sports personalities are delightful human beings; others are selfish creeps. Yet you cannot—must not—play favorites in your coverage even while you are expressing your opinion. Likewise, the team must not become 'we.' You must guard against letting your prejudices show."

Distance Best   The sportswriter Jimmy Cannon wrote, "Sportswriting has survived because of the guys who don't cheer." He was friendly with some of the players whose teams he covered but never a cheerleader.

Stanley Woodward, the legendary city editor of *The New York Herald Tribune,* remarked when he was its sports editor and read stories in which his reporters idolized athletes, "Will you please stop godding up these ball players."

Red Barber, radio's great baseball announcer, described the Brooklyn Dodgers in his warm southern drawl with affection, but it was no greater than his feeling for the Giants or Cubs. His love was for the game, not the team.

His calling the game impartially probably cost Barber his job when baseball coverage on television came under the control of team owners.

Team Control   "Every radio and television broadcaster for the major league baseball teams is either paid by the club he or she covers or is hired with that club's approval," wrote Ted Rose in the media review *Brill's Content.*

"As a practical matter, these broadcasters are not independent journalists but conduits to the public for the team that directly or indirectly employs them."

Costs of Independence   Many athletes are accustomed to being idolized, but when "the media want to show some perspective about sports or get behind something more important than who won or lost, the athletes generally dislike them," says former pitcher Jim Bouton. "Generally speaking, athletes dislike the media in direct proportion to the extent that reporters exercise their journalistic responsibilities."

Some sportswriters have been such "homers"—rooters for the home teams—that they have ignored or downplayed NCAA violations, criminal acts by athletes and the mockery of sportsmanship.

The Dumb Athlete Stereotype

"Contrary to popular impressions, intelligence and athletic ability may be slightly correlated in the population as a whole," says Robert H. Frank, a Cornell University economist.

But the stereotype of the "dumb athlete" may have some grounding in reality, he writes in *The New York Times.*

". . . varsity athletes at any given university are actually less intelligent than their classmates since many were admitted primarily on the strength of their athletic skills, not because of their academic achievements," Frank says. The stereotype, then, results from the "choices others make about them than from any innate differences in mental ability."

Bob Thayer,
The Journal Bulletin

Fans Cheer, Reporters Observe

A former basketball coach at Clemson says sports reporters must have known of the corruption and sleaziness in collegiate sports. "When I say, 'What's going on?' and you reply, 'I don't know. I didn't see anything,' that's a lie. You see what kind of clothes he wears, you see his car, you've been to his room. And he comes from the Pulpwood city limits—you gotta be kidding."

Money

Sports is big business. The 100 major sports universities have revenues of more than $1 billion. The professional leagues continue to expand to tap new markets. Teams that were bought for a few million dollars 30 years ago sell for more than $100 million today.

Multi-million-dollar signings are no longer news unless they approach $100 million. The top basketball and baseball players make $5 to $10 million a year in salaries, and endorsements can double that.

Fans like a winner, and so the bidding for top athletes goes higher and higher, and the star player who at one time spent his career playing with one team—a Ted Williams, Joe DiMaggio, Bob Cousy—now is available to the highest bidder. Teams, too, shift locations, moving from market to market.

Cash Conscious

The historian Henry Steele Commager commented about the consequence of player and team mobility, "We have nothing to be loyal to."

Hank Aaron, the Hall of Fame baseball player and baseball executive, says money has corroded sports. "Today's players have lost all concept of history. Their collective mission is greed. Nothing means much of anything to them. As a group, there's no discernible social conscience among them; certainly no sense of self-sacrifice, which is what Jackie Robinson's legacy is based on. Where there is no conscience, there are no heroes."

Money is the name of the game in collegiate sports as well. Despite the crowded college stadiums and field houses, few universities make money from their teams. Only 10 to 20 schools take in more than they spend. Deficits can hit a million dollars a year, the losses made up by donations and tax revenues. Even college bowl games need money, and get it from states or cities. *USA Today* revealed that 11 of the 25 postseason games one year drew on various public funds, and officials of eight other bowls said they expected to ask state legislators to provide money.

The Goal: Win at Any Cost

The drive to build winning teams has led to lying, cheating and hypocrisy, some of which sports reporters have documented. They have shown that teams have recruited semiliterate athletes and that some schools have gone out of their way to keep the players eligible by having school work done for them, allowing them to take courses from professors who are known to pass athletes despite failing performance, and covering up infractions they commit.

New Style: Shout, Scream

Ralph Kiner, who has announced New York Mets baseball games for more than 40 years, says announcers like him and Vin Scully, the Dodgers announcer, would "never be hired today."

"Our style of broadcasting is different from that of the new commentators. Now they think the louder you talk and the more you scream, the better it is. I prefer the old style of broadcasting, in which you talk to the guy sitting next to you as if you were sitting together in the stands. But that isn't what they want. They want noise."

—*From* Baseball Forever: Reflections on 60 Years in the Game *by Ralph Kiner with Danny Peary*

Poor No More

Joe DiMaggio once remarked, "A ball player has to be kept hungry to become a big leaguer." In his day, the average salary of a major league baseball player was $35,000. Today, it is 100 times greater.

More than 70 players are paid in excess of $5 million a year, and every time Yankee third baseman Alex Rodriguez steps to the plate he earns almost $40,000. Several pitchers make $60,000 for every inning they go to the mound.

On a per-game basis, hockey players do best, several making $200,000 to $250,000 a game for the regular season.

High school and community college students with considerable athletic ability but little academic competence have been eagerly recruited. At small St. Bonaventure University in western New York, the president personally decided that a junior college student with only a welding certificate was eligible to play in Division I basketball. In the fallout from the revelation, the basketball coach was fired, the athletic director resigned, the president was pressured to resign, the chairman of the board of trustees committed suicide. The chairman left a note saying he had let down his alma mater by failing to prevent the scandal.

For a record of infractions and illegal practices see **A Miscellany of Misdeeds** in *NRW Plus*.

The annual study of graduation rates by the NCAA shows low graduation rates for black basketball players at many schools and high rates at a few. Some recent rates: University of Arizona, 13 percent; University of Georgia, 20; Georgia Tech, 22; University of Kentucky, 17; University of Minnesota, 25.

Among the institutions that graduate most of their black basketball players—all with 100 percent—are the University of Michigan, University of North Carolina, Stanford and Villanova.

For further material on graduation rates, see **Graduation Rates, Academic Records** *NRW Plus*.

Varied Recruits

The demand for winning teams by boosters, fans and television is intense, so much so that many colleges accept high school athletes with grade-school-level academic scores. They even take criminals.

Seton Hall University in New Jersey grabbed one of the country's leading high school basketball players although he did not earn more than a combined score of 700 on his SAT test. The university kept its offer open to the youth even after he pleaded guilty to sexual abuse in a plea bargain. He had sodomized a young woman on the high school stairway.

When journalists wrote about the incident, the university grudgingly rescinded its scholarship offer. Two weeks later, a major basketball power in Utah made the student an offer but he accepted a full basketball scholarship to a Long Island university.

A leading schoolboy basketball player in Hampton, Va., was convicted on three felony counts of malicious wounding by a mob. Would that affect his chances to play college ball? "Every school in the country wants him," Bob Gibbons, a top scout of high school basketball players, told *USA Today.* "If he was John Dillinger, they'd take him."

Why stop with recruiting high school players for college? High school sports is, as we've seen, a major attraction in hundreds of cities. High schools are recruiting. "Now the college fan is wanting to follow the kids," says Mike Lardner of Sports Channel. "Teen-agers are part of a $10 billion market."

Pampered Parkers

The Diamondback, the University of Maryland student newspaper, won a court order to open access to parking tickets issued to members of the men's basketball team and to the coach. The newspaper wanted to check reports that the coach and players were given preferential treatment in the payment of fines, but the university denied access on the ground that the material fell in the category of educational or personnel records. Not so, the court ruled. One athlete had $8,000 in parking tickets.

Sports Isn't the Way Out of the Ghetto

And the question arises: Can sports in fact help change the despair, and rebuild the community?

It hasn't. Once, many more of us believed that sports and sports figures as models could lead us to the promised land. . . .

But today's life in the inner cities demonstrates that sports as a vehicle for change is not nearly as vital as it once was, or as we had once hoped, or expected.

It was Arthur Ashe who said, rightly, that minority kids spend too much time on the playing fields and not enough time in the libraries. There has simply been too much exploitation and offerings of false or minuscule hope in regard to minority youths in athletics. . . .

—Ira Berkow, *The New York Times* columnist

The lengths to which coaches will go to lure promising athletes to their campuses can provide the makings of good stories. To see how one sportswriter handled the recruiting of a high school basketball player see **Recruiting a High School Player** in *NRW Plus*.

A Case Study

In a two-part series, Sam Roe of *The Blade* described how some Toledo high schools were violating state high school athletic association rules by recruiting athletes from other high schools and from junior high schools. More than half the players on one nationally ranked basketball team were transfers. Roe quoted the mother of one transfer as saying that the coach had pressured her to lie about her residence. At another basketball powerhouse, a player's mother said the coach and his aides found an apartment for her family within the school district and paid the security deposit and two months' rent.

Some parents transferred "legal custody of their children to relatives in other school districts so the students can be eligible to play for the best teams," Roe wrote.

The reaction to the series was immediate. The state high school athletic association announced an inquiry, and a coalition of ministers held a rally at which Roe was denounced. More than 500 people at the rally condemned Roe, chanting, "In the South, they had Jim Crow. In Toledo, we have Sam Roe."

The group demanded a front-page retraction of the series and Roe's dismissal.

Six months later, the high school athletic association completed its investigation and placed the two high schools Roe wrote about on probation for two years and fined them $1,000 each for recruiting violations for their basketball teams.

Basketball Factories   A series of articles in *The New York Times* sports section exposed the manufacturing of basketball players by pseudo high schools. These schools consisted of a gym and a faculty of a couple of basketball coaches. The students told the *Times* reporter that their studies consisted of basketball tutelage. Yet the so-called graduates were heavily recruited by colleges.

An Overview

Roger Kahn—who wrote a fine book about baseball, *The Boys of Summer*—has a basic approach to his reporting. Most good sportswriters do. Here, from one of Kahn's columns in *Esquire,* is how he describes his approach to his beat:

Sports tells anyone who watches intelligently about the times in which we live: about managed news and corporate policies, about race and terror and what the process of aging does to strong men. If that sounds grim, there is courage and high humor, too. . . .

. . . I find sport a better area than most to look for truth. A great hockey goalie, describing his life on ice, once said, "That puck comes so hard, it could take an eye.

I've had 250 stitches and I don't like pain. I get so nervous before every game, I lose my lunch."

"Some football players," I said to the goalie, whose name is Glenn Hall, "say that when they're badly scared, they pray."

Hall looked disgusted, "If there is a God," he said, "let's hope he's doing something more important than watching hockey games." Offhand I can't recall a better sermon.

Red Smith, who was writing his sports column for *The New York Times* until a few days before he died, said of sports:

Sports is not really a play world. I think it's the real world. The people we're writing about in professional sports, they're suffering and living and dying and loving and trying to make their way through life just as the bricklayers and politicians are.

This may sound defensive—I don't think it is—but I'm aware that games are a part of every culture we know anything about. And often taken seriously. It's no accident that of all the monuments left of the Greco-Roman culture, the biggest is the ball park, the Colosseum, the Yankee Stadium of ancient times. The man who reports on these games contributes his small bit to the history of his times.

Rapoport takes what he calls a practical view of sports coverage. "If you can't find something light or something that will make the reader smile or laugh, at least remember and try to show, in style or substance, that these are games these people are involved in, not foreign policy discussions," he says.

However, says Rapoport, "intensely dramatic and emotional things do happen, and when they do the reporter should not be afraid to haul out the heavy artillery.

"Just remember that in such cases the facts are usually enough."

For additional suggestions on covering sports, see **Post Scripts** in *NRW Plus*.

NRWPLUS

Further Reading

Anderson, David, ed. *The Red Smith Reader*. New York: Random House, 1983.

Angell, Roger. *A Pitcher's Story: Innings with David Cone*. New York: Warner Books, 2001.

————. *Game Time: A Baseball Companion.* Orlando, Fla.: Harcourt, 2003.

This anthology, edited by Steve Kettman, takes the reader from spring training through the season to the playoffs and World Series. Angell, a *New Yorker* writer, is a writer's writer. Samples: Babe Ruth's "debutante ankles," Yogi Berra's "gentle, seamed smile, like a Gladstone bag opening."

Berkow, Ira. *A Biography of Red Smith.* New York: Times Books, 1986.

Berri, David J., Martin B. Schmidt and Stacey L. Brook. *The Wages of Win.* Stanford, Calif.: Stanford, 2006.

These sports scholars challenge conventional wisdom about professional athletes. The high-priced baseball players and MVP basketball stars do not contribute as much to winning games as their less-publicized teammates. In basketball, it's not the scoring average but a combination of assists, steals, blocked shots, personal fouls, rebounds and turnovers that count.

Bouton, Jim. *Ball Four: The Final Pitch.* Champaign, Ill.: Sports Publications Inc., 2000.

The American Library Association selected this book by a former pitcher for the New York Yankees as the best sports book of the 20th century.

Cavanaugh, Jack. *Tunney: Boxing's Brainiest Champ and His Upset of the Great Jack Dempsey.* New York: Random House, 2006.

Applicants for sportswriting jobs are asked, "What was 'the long count?'" The answer is here, among other details of the life of a fighter who was troubled by the violence of boxing. Although the spectators wanted brawls, Tunney favored fast footwork and intelligent defense.

Cramer, Richard Ben. *Joe DiMaggio: The Hero's Life.* New York: Simon & Schuster, 2000.

Some reviewers said Cramer drew too dark a picture of DiMaggio. One reviewer said the biography "of one of the greatest of American heroes will tarnish more than just an idol. It will tarnish the American myth, make it appear a manufactured product of wishful thinking and commercialism." In his review, Russell Baker remarked, "Heroes age best by dying young."

Eskenazi, Gerald. *A Sportwriter's Life: From the Desk of a New York Times Reporter.* Columbia, Mo.: University of Missouri, 2004.

Glimpses of Joe DiMaggio, Willie Mays, Muhammad Ali, Joe Namath. Eskenazi describes the changes in sports reporting, some of which make him unhappy. He yearns for the days when reporters asked "deeper questions."

Kahn, Roger. *The Boys of Summer.* New York: New American Library, 1973.

Unbreakable Records

Records are made to be broken.

This is an old sports saying. But sports writers say the following records will never be broken:

Basketball: Career points in NBA, Kareem Abdul-Jabbar, 33,387, 1969–89. Points scored in a single game, Wilt Chamberlain, 100, 1962.

Baseball: Hitting streak, Joe DiMaggio, 56 consecutive games, 1941.

Football: Receiving yards, Jerry Rice 22,895, 1985-2004.

Golf: Consecutive tournament victories on PGA Tour, Byron Nelson, 11, 1945.

Hockey: Number of goals and assists in an NHL season, Wayne Gretzky, 215, 1985–6

Boxing: Longest reigning heavyweight champion, Joe Louis, 11 years, 8 months, 1937–49.

Kahn's profiles of Brooklyn Dodgers players is considered a baseball classic along with Bouton's book.

———. *The Head Game: Baseball Seen from the Pitcher's Mound.* New York: Harcourt, Inc., 2000.

Lewis, Michael. *The Art of Winning an Unfair Game.* New York: W.W. Norton & Company. 2003.

With the third smallest payroll in the major leagues, the Oakland Athletics manage to finish high in the standings. The reason: General manager Billy Beane discarded baseball wisdom for statistics. A walk is as good as a hit, so players who walk a lot are as valuable as the million-dollar .300 hitters, and a lot cheaper.

Montville, Leigh. *At the Altar of Speed: The Fast Life and Tragic Death of Dale Earnhardt.* New York: Doubleday, 2001.

———. *Ted Williams: The Biography of an American Hero.* New York: Doubleday, 2004.

The best hitter of his time—perhaps of all time—Williams lost key playing years as a pilot in the Korean War.

Prager, Joshua. *The Echoing Green: The Untold Story of Bobby Thomson, Ralph Branca, and the Shot Heard Round the World.* New York: Pantheon, 2006.

Behind the first-place Brooklyn Dodgers by 13½ games, the New York Giants went on a tear, winning 37 of their last 44 games and ended the season tied with the Dodgers. But darkness was descending on the Giants in the National League pennant playoff. Bottom of the ninth inning and behind 4–2, the Giants had two men on base with Bobby Thomson at bat. Branca later said Thomson went after a high fastball "like a tiger pouncing on some wounded antelope." Prager tells the story of the strange aftermath.

Shulman, James I., and William G. Bowen. *The Game of Life: College Sports and Educational Values.* Princeton, N.J.: Princeton University Press, 2001.

Snyder, Brad. *A Well-Paid Slave: Curt Flood's Fight for Free Agency in Professional Sports.* New York: Viking, 2006.

Flood, who played from 1958–71, mostly for the St. Louis Cardinals, upended professional sports by eliminating the reserve clause, which bound a player for life to his team. Flood took on his owners, despite court rulings that exempted baseball from the Sherman Antitrust Act. The Players Association told Flood his lawsuit had a million-to-one chance of succeeding. Flood's court case failed, but the public mood soon doomed the clause. Flood dropped out of baseball. Broke and ignored by fellow players who profited handsomely by the suit, Flood died at 59 of throat cancer.

Vaccaro, Mike. *Emperors and Idiots: The Hundred-Year Rivalry Between the Yankees and the Red Sox, From the Very Beginning to the End of the Curse.* New York: Doubleday, 2005.

In the review in *The New York Times,* Michiko Kakutani describes the 2004 American League playoff between the Yankees and the Red Sox as "the greatest choke job in baseball history, a monumental, mind-boggling collapse: being up three games to none against the long-jinxed Red Sox and a mere three outs away from the World Series" the Yankees blew the playoff. Vaccaro describes the long rivalry that included players along with their teams—Joe DiMaggio vs. Ted Williams; Thurman Munson vs. Carlton Fisk.

Kakutani also praises another book about the headline-making 2004 baseball playoffs and World Series: Shaughnessy, Dan. *Reversing the Curse: Inside the 2004 Boston Red Sox.* Boston: Houghton Mifflin. 2005.

Both books "capture the intensity of this rivalry—the hostility; no, make that hate—many fans and team members feel toward one another," Kakutani writes.

23 Business Reporting

R.L. Chambers

Businesses come in all sizes, in all places.

Preview

Business and economic activity affects the cost and quality of the goods we buy; job opportunities; whether people buy or rent a home; the kind of car a person buys; even the college a high school graduate attends. The business reporter handles:

- **Local spot news stories:** Store openings and closings, company personnel changes, new construction, changes in the business climate, annual reports of local companies, disputes between and within businesses.
- **Features:** New products developed by local enterprises, profiles of company officials and workers and business and consumer trends.
- **Interpretative stories:** Effects of national and international economic activity on local business, the influence of local business leaders on municipal policies and the budget, the impact of regulatory actions.

Experts aren't always right.

News about business and economics has become everybody's personal business. People want to know about the cost of living, how the economy affects job possibilities, how high or low interest rates may go, whether layoffs are imminent in local industries and the value of a bond or stock that they own.

Our food, clothing and shelter are produced by business enterprises, and their quality and the prices we pay for them are largely a result of business decisions. Even the quality of the air we breathe and the water we drink is affected by decisions made by the business community. We have a large stake in those decisions, and we want to be informed of them and to know how they are made.

Business and economic reporting has exploded. Newspapers publish business sections and have large reporting and editing staffs devoted to the subject. Television has grown from the nightly reading of the Dow Jones closing averages to full-scale coverage with several reporters assigned to the half-hour programs that cover business and the economy. Cable offers 24-hour business news. More than 12,000 men and women cover business. Specialized business publications from *NursingLife* magazine and *Computer Design* to *Food Management* and *Construction Equipment* examine their fields in depth. There are more than 4,000 magazines, newsletters and newspapers of the business press.

The Scope of Business News

On Friday night, Tom and Ann Ryan sit down after dinner to make a decision. The birth of their second child means they will need another bedroom. They must decide whether to rent a larger apartment or buy a house.

Tom Ryan spreads out a page of the local newspaper on the dining room table. He points to an article with a headline, "Mortgage Shopping." It begins:

> New York (AP)—Attention mortgage shoppers: Today's specials are 30-year conventional loans—just a 7.5 percent rate and no points if you buy your home now.

The story says that "at no time have there been so many loan options available for those looking to buy or refinance a home. Not since nearly 20 years ago have rates been so low and home prices so stable."

That clinches it for the Ryans. They decide to buy a new home.

Interest rates also are a concern of the Goldensohn family. Robert, a high school senior, wants to attend a private college. The tuition is high and he must have a student loan. The family income meets the necessities and little more. Robert may have to borrow at least $10,000 a year.

If they cannot handle the loan, Robert will have to attend a community college. Their newspaper carries a story on the latest information about student loans and interest rates. The Goldensohns decide they can afford a loan. Robert will go to a private college.

From Cattle Prices to French Fries and Snow Cones

In homes in every part of the city, people look to business stories for information. Workers whose contracts are tied to the cost of living watch the papers and television to see how their paychecks will be affected by the latest figures from Washington. Farmers follow the livestock and commodity markets. Vacationers search through the list of foreign exchange rates to see what the dollar is worth abroad before deciding where to spend their vacations. Residents north of the city hear that a new shopping center will be built there; they look through the business pages to find out more about it.

When the interest rates on savings accounts and certificates of deposit sank below 3 percent, people began to look for higher-interest investments and were lured by advertisements: "Good News for C.D. Holders." What the ads did not point out is

Straight Talk
"The business of America is business."
—*Calvin Coolidge*

Good Writing
Business stories need not be dull:

BURBANK, Calif.—After a year and a half of courtship, Mickey Mouse left Miss Piggy at the altar.

This *Wall Street Journal* lead began a story of the breakdown in plans by Walt Disney Co. to acquire the Muppet characters.

Economics 1A
"Prices determine who gets what goods and services. Prices are determined by supply and demand. In a market economy, profit is the incentive for entrepreneurs, and competition is the regulator."
—*Ralph James Charkins, California State University, San Bernardino*

Mike Roemer

Entrepreneurs

The enterprising reporter will pull up alongside the two girls and will stop on a lunchtime stroll when the street vendor is spotted. The perennial question: "How's business?"

that unlike the certificates of deposit, whose principal is guaranteed by the Federal Deposit Insurance Corporation, the touted new investments had high risk.

Business reporters warned their readers of the risk, as they did when investment firms pushed closed-end government bond funds. Investing in such funds, wrote a *Wall Street Journal* reporter, was like paying $1.10 for a roll of 100 pennies.

Richard Read of *The Oregonian* followed a load of frozen French fries from the state of Washington to fast-food stores in the Far East to document how the Asian economic crisis affected potato growers. His reporting led to a Pulitzer Prize.

The Des Moines Register reports that a "ribbon-cutting ceremony for a snow-cone business in Pleasant Hill will begin at 12:30 p.m. Wednesday." Also: "A Mexican restaurant made popular by former University of Iowa football coach Hayden Fry will close. Owners of La Casa said Iowa City's new alcohol and smoking ordinances have hurt the family business."

And More   Business reporters go beyond Layer I reporting. They dig. "Tucked into the Coast Guard budget bill," writes David Cay Johnston of *The New York Times,* is language that "seems innocuous enough." The bill merely states that a section of existing law "is amended by striking the second sentence.

"But what that language would do is allow one company, Nabors Industries, to gain permanent access to business open only to American companies. The language is needed because Nabors, a big oil drilling company, moved its tax headquarters to Barbados in 2001 to avoid American taxes."

Two of *Commercial Carrier Journal*'s editors posed as businessmen and traveled thousands of miles from Chinatowns in the United States to Hong Kong, Singapore and Taiwan to expose "the flood of counterfeit merchandise pouring into the United States from the Far East."

The Human Element

Because business stories can be complicated, writers try to introduce human interest whenever possible in their copy. Vivian Marino—the AP business writer whose story on mortgage rates influenced the Ryans to buy a home rather than rent—says, "I try to keep my stories as interesting and memorable as possible, often by using anecdotal examples to which readers can relate."

In a story about the financial problems of some retirees, she began with a retired worker trying to get by on his pension:

NEW YORK (AP)—After three decades laboring in the grimy steel mills around Pittsburgh, Richard L. Walters thought he earned a clean retirement.

But since taking early leave from LTV Corp., Walters, 60, and his wife Audrey, 54, have been barely getting by. His $922 monthly pension check isn't enough for the loan payments on the couple's New Brighton, Pa., Victorian, along with food bills and other escalating expenses.

So he's trying to go back to work. "Right now, it's pretty hard to get a job around here. I've been tinkering around on people's cars, making a couple of dollars here and there. I would like to just stay retired, but the way things are now I can't."

Business Writer

When Vivian Marino joined the Miami bureau of the AP, she was assigned to do a series on the labor problems of Eastern Airlines. When she had done that, she was given more business assignments.

"I decided to carve out my own niche by concentrating on business and finance." Soon she was appointed regional business writer.

Then she was transferred to New York. "I had to learn about the markets and more complicated business and financial issues. I learned from my colleagues and from many of my sources. I also read a lot."

Marino writes a column on consumer affairs and personal finance for the AP.

Personal Finance

The Ryan and Goldensohn examples and Marino's story about Walters' retirement are called personal finance stories. A survey of readers found that personal finance is the most sought-after material on the business page. Readers—and listeners, too, stations have learned—seek information about solving credit problems, making decisions on investments, deciding whether to buy or lease.

The Atlanta Journal-Constitution carries a page weekly on personal finance. For the page, individuals open their checkbooks and bank books to reporters. The *Journal*'s business page feature "Money Makeover" deals with subjects such as planning for retirement and recovering from bankruptcy.

For a personal finance story about saving for college despite the downturn in the economy see **College Savings** in *NRW Plus*.

The Beat

The business reporter ranges widely: retail and consumer products, investing and the financial markets, the airline and automotive industries, management, corporate finance/investment banking/securities industries, the media and entertainment industries, advertising and marketing, labor and employment.

In the morning of one busy day for Susanne, a business reporter for a medium-sized midwestern daily newspaper, she interviewed local service station dealers about the escalating cost of gasoline, and that afternoon she localized a story about the effects of the failure of the coffee crop in Brazil.

Local stories she has covered include:

- Store openings, expansions and closings.

- Real estate transactions. New products from local enterprises. Construction projects planned.

- Plants opened, expanded, closed. Personnel changes, awards, retirements. Layoffs, bankruptcies.

- Annual and quarterly business reports. Annual meetings.

- Bond offerings by local government units.

In addition to spot news stories, the business reporter is aware of trends and developments in the community and area. The business reporter knows the relationship between the prime rate and the local housing market and understands how the city's parking policies affect downtown merchants.

Local Stories

Here is how Bob Freund of *The Times-News* in Twin Falls, Idaho, began a roundup that blended local and national business and economic activity with area trends:

TWIN FALLS—As spring turned into summer, the brightest news for the Magic Valley economy was coming from consumers.

They climbed into new cars at an accelerated pace, and sought credit both to pay for the new wheels and for improvements at home.

They benefited from a vicious war of price cutting and couponing among area grocery stores.

Indicators compiled by *The Times-News* for the second quarter ending June 30 show some momentum in the Magic Valley economy, but also some significant drags.

Despite lower mortgage rates and a national surge in homebuying, the biggest consumer of all, the home buyer, still is not pounding down the doors at Magic Valley real estate agencies.

A Drugstore Opening

In small communities the line between news and free advertising is so narrow it approaches invisibility. A large department store opening will be reported by the biggest newspapers. But a drugstore opening will not. The smaller newspaper or station will carry the drugstore opening and might cover the enlargement of a hardware store.

Here is the beginning of an 11-paragraph story that appeared in a newspaper in Massachusetts:

For 10 years, tailor Frank Saporito plied his trade with Davis & Norton Inc. on North Street here, where he was in charge of all alterations. When that business closed last month, Saporito was out of work—but not for long.

Saporito landed on his feet and decided to go into business for himself at 251 Fenn St., just across the street from the post office. He's been open there a little more than a week.

"I wanted to try it by myself," Saporito said. "I think it's a good move. I sure hope so."

Chain Store Alert

Business reporters keep an eye open for any moves into town by the major chain stores. Such moves can have a major impact on local business.

When Wal-Mart started building a store two miles outside Hudson, N.Y., local store owners took notice. The massive chain, the nation's largest retailer, has in other areas driven out local businesses because of its pricing policies. In Hudson, local businesses spruced up their stores and decided that they will profit from the new shoppers who will be attracted to the area.

In other areas, the mood has been pessimistic. In Greenfield, Mass., local residents voted to bar Wal-Mart from moving into town.

Local story possibilities: Sale of land for a new mega-store or new housing; new employment figures; new tax revenues.

Coffee Beans and Burritos

The photo on the right accompanied an article by Sherri Buri in the Sunday business section of *The Register-Guard* in Eugene, Ore., that begins:

Before Sony opened its compact disc factory in Springfield, it held a coffee tasting to decide which brand would flow through the company cafeteria's espresso machine.

One morning about two years ago, several local vendors set up shop at Sony's temporary offices in the Delta Oaks shopping center in Eugene. Nearly two hours and three gallons of coffee later, Eugene-based Full City Coffee walked away the winner.

"Money was never a question," recalled Michael Phinney, who owns Full City with his wife, Terril. "In fact, they never asked me how much we charge."

The 6-year-old coffee roasting company is just one of a huge network of local businesses that supply everything from coffee to custom steel work to the 375-employee high-tech company. These local suppliers demonstrate how high-tech giants, such as Sony and Hyundai, send out economic ripples far beyond the factory's payroll when they enter Lane County. . . .

Josh Estey,
The Register-Guard

Ready to Go

In another article in the section, Jim Boyd profiles a local woman who decided to expand her weekend business:

It wasn't getting the financing. It wasn't finding a location. It wasn't recruiting good workers. The biggest obstacle that Ritta Dreier had to overcome when she recently expanded her business was simply deciding to do it.

For 19 years, Dreier has operated the 10-by-10-foot Ritta's Burritos booth at Saturday Market and other regional events. Despite its nomadic nature, the booth has been a money-maker.

"I can say there's some booths down at Saturday Market—food booths—that are probably happy to make $400 on a Saturday, and I would say there's several Saturday Market vendors that can—on a really, really busy day—reach probably $1,800 dollars on a Saturday," she said. "And I'm one of the top-grossing vendors at Saturday Market and always have been."

Josh Estey,
The Register-Guard

New Business

Earnings, M&A and Executive News Stories

When the publisher and the editor of the *Los Angeles Times* made news by balking at cutting the newsroom staff, the story was basically a business story. Executives of the Tribune Company, owners of the *Times,* had felt the pressure of stockholders who were dissatisfied with the paper's earnings. Reporters quickly looked at the company's earnings and put the figures and those of other media companies into their stories.

Earnings figures are available for all public companies as they are required to file them regularly with the government.

M&A

Merger and acquisition stories frequent the news pages as companies are increasingly devouring one another or merging to form a single entity. Usually, the news is broken by a press release or a news conference.

These stories have serious consequences in the communities of the affected companies. A deal may lead to layoffs, or it could mean that a community would lose company headquarters to another city, says Chris Roush, who teaches business journalism at the University of North Carolina. He says M&A stories should answer these questions:

1. What is the total price and the per share price of the deal?

2. Is the acquisition paid for with cash, stock, debt or a combination?

3. If a stock transaction, what is the exchange ratio?

4. How does this price compare with similar transactions in the industry?

5. Who must approve the deal, and when will it be completed?

6. What's the reason for the deal? Does it make the company the largest in the industry or business line?

7. How did investors react to the acquisition announcement?

8. Will specific competitors be affected?

9. Did the stock trading activity of the companies involved in the deal increase shortly before the deal was announced?

10. Will the deal be accretive or dilutive to the acquiring company?

Executives

The top executives of a business are its public face and are often in the news. Business reporters maintain contact with CEOs and others high in the company's hierarchy, often interviewing the CEOs of local companies on a regular basis.

Roush says reporters should be aware of any tensions among company management, of a strain between the board and the CEO and between management and the employees. The turnover at the executive level is high.

When stockholders in the Tribune Company complained that the *Los Angeles Times* was not returning 25 or 26 percent profits, management of the company asked the publisher of the *Times* to cut back the news staff. He refused. He said the cuts would imperil the quality of the newspaper. He was fired.

Puff Pieces

The wall that separates the advertising and editorial departments at stations and newspapers is more than physical. It is a moral separation that says the news columns and news personnel are not for sale.

Advertising salespeople sometimes promise an advertiser a story about a store expansion or about the cashier who has spent 25 years behind the Hamburger Heaven checkout counter. When the publisher orders a story, the piece is known as a BOM (business office must).

These stories are considered free advertising. Still, it could be argued that some of these events can make good stories. The perceptive business reporter sent to interview the hardware merchant who is enlarging his store might find that the store owner is staking his last dime on this gamble to keep from losing business to the Wal-Mart outside town. And the Hamburger Heaven cashier could become a human interest story.

Writing About the Economy

A few pages back we listened in on the Ryan and Goldensohn families as they discussed how new interest rates would affect whether the Ryans bought a house or rented and whether young Robert Goldensohn would go to an expensive private college or enroll in a community college. The news stories they read were about the economy, which increasingly is part of the business reporter's coverage.

Economics reporting helps readers understand issues that affect their finances, says Roush. It takes many forms, he says, ranging from an explanation of how the inflation rate affects the wallet and pocketbook to why the unemployment rate is growing or declining.

Data as Story Source

Economic newswriting is based mostly on data compiled by the federal government. Reporters take these figures and put them in human terms, as we have seen in the Ryan and Goldensohn stories. Roush lists these economics stories that are regularly reported:

1. The unemployment rate for the state or metropolitan statistical area.

2. The consumer price index, which measures inflation.

3. Consumer confidence, which details how likely consumers will spend their money in the future.

Sources, Rewrites and Buried Leads

James McNair spent 15 years on the business beat for *The Miami Herald*. Here are some of his observations about coverage:

I have a problem with the motives of sources. I have to say that reporters' independence is under attack constantly by corporations that aim to have news slanted in a certain way. . . .

Business reporters give away their independence most often without accepting any forms of gratis or goodwill that shows in their stories. These are often nothing more than rewrites of a corporate press release, which is a carefully crafted, heavily lawyered statement, notorious for its omissions and distractions.

When corporations speak of "rationalizations of operations," reporters don't always know to ask, "How many workers are going to be laid off?" When corporations hire investment bankers who examine options to enhance shareholder value, that item might be buried or omitted in the story when it's probably the lead: The company is for sale.

4. Interest rate changes, which affect how much interest consumers pay when they borrow money to buy homes, cars or make other large purchases.

5. Trade, which documents how the economy imports and exports goods.

6. The gross domestic product, which measures the growth or decline of the nation's economy on a monthly basis.

Dig into the Data   Numbers sometimes do not speak for themselves. They must be interpreted by the knowledgeable reporter. For example, the unemployment rate is often cited as a key to the health of the economy. But it should be handled with care. The rate does not include the number of jobless who are not looking for work. When they do join the job hunt the unemployment rate goes up. Roush cautions that this may be a sign of a stronger economy because it could indicate that some of the previously discouraged jobless may find hope in a resurgent economy.

As is the case with most business and economy stories, the reality might be uncovered by talking to the individuals involved, in this case jobless men and women.

The Reporter's Requirements

The business reporter is a specialist who feels at home with numbers and is not frightened by lengthy reports and press releases, many of which contain rates, percentages, business and consumer indexes and the jargon of the business world.

Among the skills and attitudes the business reporter takes to the job is the recognition of the power business exerts and the willingness to ask tough questions when the numbers do not add up or the answers do not make sense. Along with this, the reporter has a healthy skepticism that keeps him or her from being awed by the muscle and money that business power generates.

Corporate Raider   The business reporter approaches the money managers and manipulators with the same objectivity and distance that any reporter takes on an assignment. In his profile of a corporate raider, Michael A. Hiltzik of the *Los Angeles Times* was able to find sources and anecdotes to get to the heart of his subject, Irwin L. Jacobs of Minneapolis. Jacobs acquires and merges companies, usually at great profit.

Jacobs usually would pledge to operate rather than to dismantle the firms "on the insight that Americans lionize industrialists and not liquidators," Hiltzik says. For his piece, Hiltzik was able to show that Jacobs dismantled one firm in 17 days, despite his promise to operate Mid American Bancorporation of Minnesota "for his children and his children's children," the story said. Jacobs' profit: an estimated $4 million.

Sour Investment   Specialist though he or she may be, the business reporter must know much more than the world of finance. When Hiltzik was assigned to cover the tribulations of a precious metals investment firm, he had to look through court documents with the same scrupulous and knowledgeable attention a courthouse reporter gives the records. Hiltzik found in one of the documents a human interest lead to his story about the complicated activities of the firm.

He began his lengthy account of Monex International Ltd. with the story of Kathleen Ann Mahoney, a professional singer who was living in Newport Beach, Calif., when she bought $10,000 worth of silver through Monex. The price of silver went up, and Hiltzik reports, she "invested another $12,000, then another $10,000, and then her last $13,000, relying on what she says was a Monex salesman's pitch that silver prices were rising so fast they might earn $100,000 for her over a year's time." The price of silver reached $50 an ounce.

"Four days later, Mahoney was wiped out. Silver had plunged to $28, and the crash had taken most of her investment with it," Hiltzik wrote.

Sources of Information

Most reporters deal with public officials. Laws and a long tradition have made the public sector public.

The business world, however, is generally private, secretive and authoritarian. The head of a company can order his or her employees not to talk to reporters. Because businesspeople usually are in competition, secrecy is a natural part of business life. True, businesses are required to file many kinds of reports with various governmental agencies, and these are excellent sources of information. But in the day-to-day coverage of the beat, the business reporter must cultivate human sources.

Human Sources

Good contacts and sources can be made among the following:

- Bank officers, tellers.
- Savings and loan officials.
- Chamber of Commerce secretaries.
- Union leaders.
- Securities dealers.
- Financial analysts.
- Real estate brokers.
- Trade organization officials.
- Teachers of business, economics.
- Transportation company officials.
- Federal and state officials in agencies such as the Small Business Administration, Commerce Department, various regulatory agencies.
- Employees and former employees.

Close-Mouthed
The owners of small businesses are the most reluctant to reveal profits and losses to reporters. Small business is the riskiest commercial enterprise, says Karen Hallows of George Mason University, and shows the largest numbers of bankruptcies as well as the highest returns. Few owners want to reveal that they are going down the drain or making a pot of money.

Two Types of Companies

Publicly held: Company owned by investors who bought its stock. Stock is traded on exchange or market where its price or market value is determined by what investors pay to own it. Must file documents with SEC and publish annual reports, which are sources of information for reporter.

Privately or closely held: Company is usually controlled by a small group or a family. Stock is not publicly traded on an exchange. Value is set by owners. Information is difficult to obtain. Company may be regulated by state or federal agency, which will have some information about it.

Cultivating Sources

On first contact with a reporter, the business source is likely to be wary, says James L. Rowe Jr., of *The Washington Post.* "As a result, it is often difficult to gain the source's trust.

"But if the reporter does his or her homework, learns what motivates business-people, is not afraid to ask the intelligent questions but doesn't have to ask the dumb one, more than enough sources will break down."

Doing the Homework   Geanne Rosenberg, who teaches business journalism at the City University of New York, advises those who report larger companies: "Read up on the business; look at recent news about the company; take a look at the company's Web site and review recent press releases. Try to understand the elements of the business—how many employees the company has, the location of its divisions, and how the divisions or parts are organized and fit together, the management team, how long senior managers have been in their positions.

"If it is a public company, look at its stock performance and its filings with the Securities and Exchange Commission. These reveal a great deal about the company's financial health, its management team and any lawsuits it faces.

"Read up about any competitors, where the business fits into the general industry, whether the company is an industry leader or laggard and whether the industry is expanding or facing serious challenges."

The reporter who does this homework will have no trouble impressing sources, who are reluctant to open up to reporters with scant knowledge.

The Right Sources   In developing sources for background material, the reporter will want to find people who can put events into perspective and who can clarify some of the complexities the reporter cannot. Caution is important. Not only must the sources be dependable, they must be independent of compromising connections and affiliations. Obviously, such sources are hard to find. The traditional independent source was the academician, the cloistered professor who had no financial stake in the matters he would comment about. But no more. Academicians now serve on the boards of banks, chemical companies and pesticide manufacturers. The alert reporter makes certain that background information from such sources is neither biased nor self-serving.

When quoting a source, note all of the person's business affiliations relevant to the story. In a banking story, it's not enough to say that Professor Thomas Graham teaches economics at the state university. His membership on the board of directors of the First National Bank should also be included.

Background Source   The source who provides background material is infrequently quoted, and so readers and viewers cannot assess the information in terms of the source's affiliations. Because background sources influence reporters by providing perspective, the independence of these sources is essential.

The business office of the station or newspaper has access to the local credit bureau and the facilities of Dun and Bradstreet, which can provide confidential information. These are helpful in running a check on a local business.

Chris Welles, a veteran business writer, says, "By far the most important sources on company stories are former executives. Unconstrained by the fear of being fired if word gets out that they talked to you, they can be extremely forthcoming about their former employer." Competitors are another good source, as are suppliers, the managers of investment portfolios, bankers and others who are likely to know the company's financial situation, such as the financial analysts who prepare reports on public corporations.

In interviews, Welles will share his problems in obtaining material. "Most people are predisposed to respond favorably to someone who, in a non-threatening way, asks for a little help." Welles says he listens "with great interest and sympathy." He says that "sources have a great deal of trouble terminating a conversation with someone who seems to be hanging on their every word."

> **Exceptions**
> "My general practice when examining a financial document is to look for the exceptions, the deviations. Few journalists are trained accountants or can know much about every single industry they cover, so the trick is to look for numbers that stand out: If the debt a company is carrying goes each year—$80 million, $75 million, $85 million, $300 million; if companies A, B, and C in the cosmetics industry record profit margins of about 8 percent and company D is 4 percent, or 15 percent, there's a story."
> —*Michael Hiltzik,*
> Los Angeles Times

Physical Sources

At the local level, reporters know how to use tax records. The city and county keep excellent records of real estate transfers, and the assessor's office has the valuation of real property and of the physical plant and equipment—whatever is taxed. The sales tax shows how much business a firm is doing. Many local governments issue business licenses on which the principals involved are named and other information is given.

State governments also issue business licenses. State boards license barbers, engineers, cosmetologists, doctors, morticians, lawyers, accountants and others. These agencies usually keep basic information about the businesses they oversee.

The state corporation commission or the secretary of state will have the names, addresses and sometimes the stock held by directors of corporations incorporated in the state and of firms that do a large amount of business in the state. The company's articles of incorporation and bylaws are also on file. Insurance companies are regulated by states and companies file their annual reports with the state insurance department.

For a list of Web sites for federal agencies that are useful to the reporter covering business and the economy see **Useful Sites** in *NRW Plus.*

The Effects of Business Closures

In towns across the country, merchants are shuttering their stores, some because of the competition from big box retailers like Wal-Mart. In other towns, the business base—farming, mining, livestock raising—eroded, leaving behind unemployment and tension.

Joel Sartore, *The Wichita Eagle*

Bankruptcies

The commercial on the all-news radio station is friendly, helpful. "Deep in debt? Let us help you with your bankruptcy filing." The commercial goes on to tell the listener that bankruptcy is benign, no headaches afterward. The soothing voice of the announcer indicates everyone is doing it. Well, not exactly. But a lot of people in debt are: In 20 years, bankruptcy filings went from 200,000 to more than 1.3 million a year.

It's true that people seemingly with plenty of money are filing. Toni Braxton filed for bankruptcy under federal law, and news reports said she owned a Porsche, Lexus and baby grand piano. "I'm gonna go out and enjoy myself," she told a reporter as she left the federal building. Also filing: M.C. Hammer, Burt Reynolds and Kim Basinger.

But most people who file are really in trouble, and this is where there are stories. A local merchant opens a jewelry store with high hopes, and within a year he files. Why? Was it a poor location? Did he fail to have sufficient funds for a varied stock? Did a chain store open and undercut his prices?

Credit Card Debts   There are personal bankruptcies as well as company filings, many of them the result of credit card debt that finally overwhelms the cardholders. It's estimated that almost 60 million households carry a credit card debt of more than $7,000 from month to month. Interest on credit cards can average 18 percent.

Covering the Business Beat Better

Here are some suggestions from Henry Dubroff, a veteran business editor:

- Become a financial news junkie. Pay attention to developments on your beats even if there is no obvious local angle.

- Look for hidden hooks in releases and routine earnings announcements. Hint: Read the last line first.

- Use your sources for insight, not necessarily quotes.

- Be comfortable with basic financial terms.

- Never be afraid to go back to a company or a source two or three times to get the whole story.

- The best stories often are the ones that break late on your beat.

- Learn from reading and rereading major publications like *The Wall Street Journal, Forbes* and *Barron's*. Not just for content but for how they approach a big research project or for how they tell a story.

- It's always better to get off the phone and get on the streets to actually see what a company looks like up close and personal.

College students are big on credit cards, and there are stories there, too. Many students carry three, four, five cards so that when they reach the maximum credit allowance on one they use another, and then another.

Many credit card issuers make no check of applicants' ability to pay. A fourth of households with less than $10,000 annual income have credit card debt as do more than 40 percent of those with income from $10,000 to $25,000.

For more about covering bankruptcy proceedings, see **Bankruptcy** in *NRW PLUS.*

Reading

Daily reading of *The Wall Street Journal* is necessary for the business reporter. Written for businesspeople and those with some involvement in financial matters, the stories nevertheless are written in everyday language. The newspaper is both record keeper for the business community and its watchdog. Its investigative reporting is among the best in the country.

BusinessWeek, a weekly business newsmagazine, is staffed by journalists with a good command of business, finance and economics. The magazine concentrates on the major industries and companies. Its long articles are aimed at the men and women who are in executive posts in business. *Fortune* magazine and *The Economist* are also avidly read by business journalists.

Forbes is addressed to investors, people who own stock in companies. The *Journal, BusinessWeek,* and *Forbes* are pro-business. Although they do go after the bad apples in the barrel, they never question the barrel, the system itself, as former *Journal* staffer Kent MacDougall puts it. The most pro-business publication is *Nation's*

Business, which is published by the U.S. Chamber of Commerce and the National Association of Manufacturers.

Many publications have online versions of their newspapers and magazines.

References

A good local library or any business school library at a college or university will have the following references that business reporters find useful:

- **Dun and Bradstreet directories:** One covers companies with capital under $1 million; another is for those whose capital exceeds $1 million. (Provides address, corporate officers, sales, number of employees.)

- **Who Owns Whom:** To find the parent company of a firm you are checking.

- **Standard & Poor's Register of Corporations, Directors and Executives.**

- **Moody's Manuals.**

- **Standard & Poor's Corporation Record:** Seven volumes of basic information on almost every publicly traded stock.

Most of these references are available online.

Enterprise

Don Moffitt, a *Wall Street Journal* editor, says that business reporters "should consider that they have a license to inquire into the nuts and bolts of how people make a living and secure their well-being.

"For a local paper, the fortunes of the community's barbers, auto mechanics, bankers and public servants are business stories. Business is how people survive.

"If people are falling behind in their mortgage payments, show how and why they are falling behind, how they feel about it and what they're trying to do about it," he says.

"Local government financing and spending is, in part, a business story. Who's making money off the local bond issues, and why? Is the bank keeping the county's low-interest deposits and using the cash to buy the county's high-yielding paper? Who suffers when the township cuts the budget, or can't increase it? Show how they suffer."

Always go beyond the press release, business reporters say. When a $69 million reconstruction job at a shopping center was announced, the developers sent out stacks of press releases. By asking why so much money was being spent on releases, a reporter learned that sales at the center had sharply declined recently—a fact not mentioned in any of the releases.

Steve Lipson, business news writer for *The Times-News,* develops ideas for stories by a simple technique—keeping his eyes open. "I read ads, I notice changes in the businesses where I shop. I count the number of cars in a car dealer's lot, and I look at what people wear, eat and drink," Lipson says.

"I look for unique stories," he says. He did one on the growing popularity of potato-skin appetizers. "This big boost to potato consumption would land

Five F's

Bloomberg News, a worldwide business and financial news service, tells its reporters:

Be *first* to report the news. Be *fastest* to report the details. Be the most *factual.* Have the *final* word; be the definitive source. What does an event indicate for the *future?* Explain today's news in the context of tomorrow's.

someone in the Idaho Hall of Fame if anyone knew who was responsible. Alas, my story found no one really knows."

Ideas can turn up anywhere, even in the small print in the back of the business section under "Foreign Exchange." The figures show how much the U.S. dollar is worth abroad. The exchange rates affect business. To see how, consult **The Dollar's Value Abroad** in *NRW Plus*.

Municipal Bonds

The school system and the city, county and state often decide on major construction projects. To finance them, large amounts of money have to be raised by selling bonds.

The bond story involves interest rates, the financial standing or rating of the local government and related matters that may seem complex for readers but that can be simplified with good reporting. First, check the rating of the governmental unit.

If the local government is not rated financially healthy, the bonds would not be seen as a good investment. To attract buyers of the bonds, the interest rate then would have to be set high. Just half of 1 percent more in interest could mean millions of dollars more that the taxpayers will have to pay in interest over the life of the bonds.

Reporters can learn about the health of the local government by examining two kinds of documents, the bond prospectus and the analysis by the rating agencies:

Prospectus: This document is required by law for the information of potential investors. It contains considerable information about the government entity offering the bonds.

Rating: The government entity's debt (which is what a bond is) is rated by organizations such as Moody's and Standard & Poor's. The lower the rating, the higher the interest rate on the bonds and the greater the cost to taxpayers. Reporters can obtain these ratings.

University Bonds

Almost all governments issue bonds and so do many private entities. Your university probably has issued bonds for a dormitory or classroom construction, possibly for building a stadium or field house. Just as governments that issue bonds are rated, so are colleges and universities. Some are given high ratings, others less than the best. Here is a story about a rating one university was given:

Standard & Poor's today announced it has upgraded Columbia University's debt rating from AA+ to AAA.

Only eight other universities are in the rating agency's top bracket: California Institute of Technology, Grinnell, Harvard, MIT, Princeton, Rockefeller University, Stanford and Yale.

Standard & Poor's upgraded Columbia's rating on the basis of a successful fund-raising campaign, effective financial strategies and the selectivity of the undergraduate and graduate programs.

Hospitals, Too

"Standard & Poor's today announced it has lowered from BBB to BBB– Englewood Hospital and Pascack Valley Hospital bond ratings because the market has become so competitive that hospitals are trying to gain market share by providing a wider range of costly services and specialty care."

In good times, these bonds can be easily repaid, says Thomas E. Calibeo, a senior vice president in the higher-education ratings group of Moody's Investors Service. But when the stock market declines, revenue sources for universities—earnings from endowments, gifts and tuition—are pinched and it is more difficult to meet interest payments

Skepticism and Doubt

"The business page is singularly marked by credulity," says Bernard Nossiter, a veteran business reporter. "Corporate and even Treasury pronouncements are treated as holy writ. Corporate officials are likely to be regarded with awe, at least until they are indicted."

One reason, he says, is that "reporters are literate rather than numerate," more at home with words than with figures.

One of the stories business interests find reporters eager to write is the new business or development piece. Anything that promises new jobs or an expanding economy in town is snapped up, even when the venture is speculative. In Alexandria, Va., a developer put up a huge sign announcing an 800,000-square-foot office building, and *The Washington Post* ran a picture and story. No tenant was ever signed up. Reporters need to dig deeper:

- **Questions for new ventures:** What evidence is there of secure financing? Who are the lenders?

- **Questions for developers:** What tenants have signed leases? Are they being given free rent? Have building permits been issued?

Morton Mintz, for many years a digging reporter at *The Washington Post* who exposed corporate greed that resulted in danger and death to the public, says that the press has failed to audit "impersonal crime committed by the large corporation." He recalls the response of Alfred P. Sloan Jr., head of General Motors, when GM was urged to use safety glass for windshields, as Ford had been doing for years.

GM was using ordinary flat glass, which, Mintz says, "breaks into shards, disfiguring, slashing, killing." Sloan's response:

> Accidents or no accidents, my concern on this matter is a matter of profit and loss. . . . I am trying to protect the stockholders of General Motors and the Corporation's operating position—it is not my responsibility to sell safety glass. . . . You can say, perhaps, that I am selfish, but business is selfish. We are not a charitable institution—we are trying to make a profit for our stockholders.

Stockholders' Pressure Publicly-held companies are owned by investors who have bought companies' stock. Their interest is in the growth of the company and its dividends. If they feel the company they have invested in is not

Handout Watchout

Here are the beginnings of three news releases. What do they have in common?

- Unites States Steel Corp. today announced a series of moves designed to ensure that its steel sector will continue as a major force in world steel markets for the balance of the century and beyond. . . .

- Greenbelt Cooperative Inc.'s Board of Directors unanimously approved a plan to strengthen the organization's financial position and continue expansion. . . .

- W & J Sloane, the retail furniture company long noted for its reputation for quality, style and trend-setting furniture, is once again taking the lead in the furniture industry. . . .

If you found the companies are about to report high earnings or an expansion, go to the rear of the class. The firms were all announcing bad news. U.S. Steel cut 15,600 jobs and closed plants in several cities. Greenbelt closed its cooperative supermarkets and gas stations. And W & J Sloane closed a store and sharply reduced its range of furniture in other stores. All this was in the releases—buried.

returning adequate dividends, the stockholders can call for executive changes, demand the sale of the firm or even liquidation. It was this pressure that led to the breakup of the Knight Ridder chain of 30 newspapers and the sale of the papers.

To learn how to read stock tables, see **Stock Tables** in *NRW Plus*.

Numbers Count

Pauline Tai, former director of the Knight-Bagehot Fellowship Program in business journalism at Columbia University, says business reporters must be able to "analyze numbers. You can't just accept what a CEO tells you. You should be able to calculate. You have to know how the CEO came to a figure and what it means. You just don't take what you are being told as the truth. You have to look into it, and sometimes you have to stick your neck out and make judgments."

Note: More than a third of business executives polled by the Freedom Forum First Amendment Center said they regularly lie to the media. See *The Headline vs. The Bottom Line* by Mike Haggerty and Wallace Rasmussen, available from the Center at Vanderbilt University, 1207 18th Avenue, Nashville, TN 37212, (615) 321-9588.

The ability to blend the qualitative and the quantitative is essential to the business journalist. Numbers alone do say a lot, but when these barometers are matched with human beings, they take on dramatic significance. When home loan applications increase (quantitative), the reporter finds a family like the Ryans we met a while back and shows why this family decided to buy rather than to rent (qualitative).

Better Stories
Paul Hemp of *The Boston Globe* makes these suggestions for improving business and economic stories:

- Avoid economic jargon.
- Define economic terms.
- Use statistics sparingly.
- Humanize business news.
- Go beyond the press release.
- Get both sides.
- Show the significance of statistics.

This material was prepared by Jim O'Shea for *The Des Moines Register*.

Business Terms

assets These are anything of value the company owns or has an interest in. Assets usually are expressed in dollar value.

balance sheet A financial statement that lists the company's assets, liabilities and stockholders' equity. It usually includes an *Earnings* or *Income Statement* that details the company's source of income and its expenses.

calendar or **fiscal year** Some companies report their income or do business on the regular calendar year. Others do it on a fiscal year that could run from any one month to the same month a year later. Always ask if the companies do business on a fiscal or calendar year. If the answer is fiscal, ask the dates and why. You might find out something unusual about the company.

capital expenditures This is the amount of money a company spends on major projects, such as plant expansions or capacity additions. It is important to the company and the community as well. If the company is expanding, include it in the story. Frequently, such plans are disclosed in stock prospectuses and other SEC reports long before the local paper gets its press release.

earnings Used synonymously with *profit.* Earnings can be expressed in dollar terms (XYZ earned $40) or on a per-share basis (XYZ earned $1 per share for each of its 40 shares of stock). When used as an earnings figure, always compare it to the earnings for the same period in the prior year. For example, if you want to say XYZ earned $1 a share during the first quarter, half or nine months of 2005, compare that with the 50 cents per share the company earned in the first quarter, half or nine months of 2004. That would be a 100 percent increase in profit.

liabilities These are any debts of any kind. There are two types of liabilities: short term and long term. Companies consider anything that has to be paid off within a year a short-term liability and anything over a year a long-term liability.

sales or **revenues** These terms are used synonymously in many companies. A bank, for example, doesn't have sales. It has revenues. A manufacturer's sales and revenues frequently are the same thing, unless the company has some income from investments it made. Always include the company's sales in a story with its earnings. If you say a company earned $40 in 2005 compared to $30 in 2004, you also should tell the reader that the profit was the result of a 100 percent increase in the company's sales, from $100 in 2004 to $200 in 2005. Use both sales and earnings figures. Don't use one and not the other.

stockholders' equity This is the financial interest the stockholders have in the company once all of its debts are paid. For example, say XYZ company has assets of $1,000 and total debts of $600. The company's stockholders' equity is $400. If that figure is expressed on a per-share basis, it is called *book value.* (If XYZ had issued 40 shares of stock, each share would have a book value of $10.)

Deficit:
The difference between expenditures and revenues.

Debt:
The total of all deficits. It is covered by debt obligations such as Treasury bonds and bills.

To examine business stories that are concerned with numbers, see **Annual Report** and **Stories About Earnings** in *NRW Plus*.

Depth Reporting

The Founding Fathers were concerned about the dangers of a strong central government. They could not have imagined the power that business would acquire. International banks and the conglomerates exercise enormous influence over the lives of people everywhere, and this power is worthy of scrutiny by the press in its role as watchdog.

Such examination starts at the local level. How much power do local real estate dealers and contractors have over planning and zoning decisions? What role does money play in elections? Does local government really have to give businesses and developers tax write-offs and abatements as an incentive? Is the tax structure equitable or does it fall too heavily on families, working people, home owners? In states with natural resources, is the severance tax properly balanced with other taxes, or are the extractive industries penalized or given preferential treatment?

Business reporters who dig deeply can come up with answers to some of these questions. Their articles are called public service journalism, journalism that gives people insights into the deep currents that swirl about us and are, to most of us, impenetrable.

Regulatory Agencies

All levels of government regulate business. Local laws prescribe health, fire and safety regulations to which businesses must adhere. The state regulates some banks, savings and loan institutions, insurance companies and public utilities. State licensing boards also regulate the trades and professions.

At the federal level, businesses are regulated by several agencies, among them the Securities and Exchange Commission. For the key documents large businesses must file with the SEC that are useful to reporters see **SEC Filings** in *NRW Plus*.

Further Reading

Eichenwald, Kurt. *Conspiracy of Fools: A True Story.* New York: Broadway, 2005.

In 1999, Enron, the Houston-based energy company, pledged $100 million to name the new Houston Astros baseball park "Enron Field." Thirty-two months later, Enron declared bankruptcy. This is the story of the company's implosion by a *New York Times* business reporter. Eichenwald made exhaustive use of documents and conducted scores of interviews for this story of greed and arrogance that cost employees their jobs and pensions and stockholders their investments.

Fink, Conrad. *Bottom Line Writing: Reporting the Sense of Dollars.* Ames, Iowa: Iowa State University Press, 2000.

Galbraith, J. Kenneth. *The Affluent Society.* Boston: Houghton Mifflin, 1958.

Leckey, Andrew, and Allan Sloan. *The Best Business Stories of the Year: 2003 Edition.* New York: Vintage Books, 2003.

Martin, Paul R. *The Wall Street Journal Guide to Business Style and Usage.* New York: Wall Street Journal Books, 2003.

Mintz, Morton. *At Any Cost.* New York: Pantheon Books, 1985.

Roush, Chris. *Show Me the Money: Writing Business and Economic Stories for Mass Communication.* Mahwah, N.J.: Lawrence Erlbaum Associates, 2004.

Silk, Leonard. *Economics in the Real World.* New York: Simon & Schuster, 1985.

Smith, Adam. *The Money Game.* New York: Random House, 1976.

Thompson, Terri, ed. *Writing about Business: The New Columbia Knight-Bagehot Guide to Economics and Business Journalism.* New York: Columbia University Press, 2001.

Toffler, Alvin and Heidi. *Revolutionary Wealth.* New York: Knopf, 2006.

The authors, known as futurists, describe the impact of the techno-revolution: massive wealth and worldwide changes.

Local Government 24
and Education

Preview

Local government reporters cover the actions of municipal agencies and departments and the interplay of citizens, interest groups and local government in making policy. Some areas of coverage are:

- Budgets, taxes, bond issues.
- Politics.
- Zoning and planning.
- Education.

Reporters check on whether city agencies and departments are carrying out their responsibilities efficiently, effectively and economically.

Mike Roemer

Give voice to citizen participation in local government.

People are more interested in local events than in any other kind of news. They want to know what the city council did about the proposal for free downtown parking, why the principal of the Walt Whitman High School was dismissed and how the new city manager feels about lowering the property tax.

Newspapers and stations respond to this interest by assigning their best reporters to key local beats, and usually the best of the best is assigned to city hall, the nerve center of local government. From city hall, elected and appointed officials direct the affairs of the community. They supervise street maintenance and construction, issue birth and death certificates, conduct restaurant inspections, collect and dispose of waste and collect parking meter coins.

The city hall reporter is expected to cover all these activities. To do this, the reporter applies his or her understanding of how local government works—the processes and procedures of agencies and departments, the relationship of the mayor's office to the city council, how the city auditor or comptroller checks on the financial activities of city offices.

Follow the buck.

City Government Activities

The city government engages in many essential activities that the reporter covers:

1. Authorization of public improvements such as streets, new buildings, bridges, viaducts.

2. Submission to the public of bond issues to finance these improvements.

3. Adoption of various codes, such as building, sanitation, zoning.

4. Issuance of regulations affecting public health, welfare and safety. Traffic regulations come under this category.

5. Consideration of appeals from planning and zoning bodies.

6. Appointment and removal of city officials.

7. Authorization of land purchases and sales.

8. Awarding of franchises.

9. Adoption of the expense and capital budgets.

The city is a major buyer of goods and services and is usually one of the city's largest employers. Its decisions can enrich some businesses, as indicated in the beginning of this story by Josh Getlin of the *Los Angeles Times:*

During the last year, Los Angeles Councilman Howard Finn and his wife enjoyed a free weekend in Newport Beach and Councilwoman Peggy Stevenson was wined and dined at some of New York's finer restaurants.

In both cases, Group W Cable TV officials were wooing council members to round up votes for the East San Fernando Valley franchise that could be worth $75 million.

Lavish entertaining is just part of a multi-million dollar campaign by six firms to win the city's last major cable franchise. . . .

Three Branches   The city is the creature of the state. The state assigns certain of its powers to the city, enabling the city to govern itself. The city has the three traditional branches of government—a judicial system and executive and legislative arms. In some cities, the executive is a powerful mayor who has control over much of the municipal machinery. In others, the mayor's job is largely ceremonial.

Legislative branches differ, too. But for the most part, the city council or commission has the power to act in the nine areas outlined above. The council or commission takes action in the form of ordinances and resolutions. An *ordinance* is a law. A *resolution* is a declaration or an advisory that indicates the intention or opinion of the legislative branch.

An ordinance is *enacted:* "The city council last night enacted an ordinance requiring dog owners to have their pets inoculated against rabies." A resolution is *adopted:*

"City commission members last night adopted a resolution to make June 18 Frances Osmond Day in honor of the longtime city clerk who died last Tuesday."

Forms of Local Government

The city council–mayor system is the most common form of local government. In large cities, the mayor is usually a powerful figure in city government, the centerpiece of what is called the strong mayor system. In this system, the mayor appoints the heads of departments and all other officials not directly elected. This system enables the mayor to select the people he or she wants to carry out executive policies.

One way to classify local government is by the strength of the office of the mayor, the power the chief executive has to initiate programs and policies. The two systems have variations:

Weak Mayor	**Strong Mayor**
Commission	Council-mayor
Commission-manager	Mayor-manager
Council-manager	

Strong to Weak, Back to Strong

The weak mayor systems and the creation of the post of city manager were reactions to the misuse of power by strong mayors. To be elected and to hold office, the mayor had to be an astute politician, not necessarily an able administrator. The wheelings and dealings of the strong mayors—exposed by such muckrakers as Lincoln Steffens—led people to reject a system that its critics said encouraged corruption. A movement toward less-politicized and more efficient local government developed early in the 20th century. It took the form of the council-manager system.

The manager, who is hired by the council, is a professionally trained public administrator who attends to the technical tasks of running the city government—preparing the budget, hiring, administering departments and agencies. Although the manager does increase the managerial efficiency of local government, the system has been criticized as insulating government from the electorate by dispersing responsibility and accountability. Several cities have returned to the strong mayor system in an effort to place responsibility in the hands of an identifiable, elected official.

An offshoot of the council-manager system is the mayor-manager plan, the most prevalent system today. This combines the strong mayor, politically responsive to the electorate, with the trained technician who carries out executive policies and handles day-to-day governmental activities.

Governing the City

Mayor-Manager Form

Strong Mayor System
The mayor appoints most department and agency heads and the city manager, who is responsible for day-to-day operations.

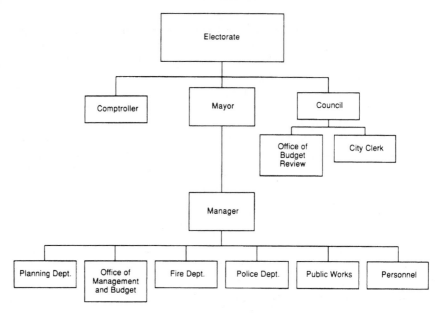

Council-Manager Form

Weak Mayor System
The mayor serves as a member of the city council, which makes most of the major appointments of agency and department heads. The mayor's powers are mostly ceremonial.

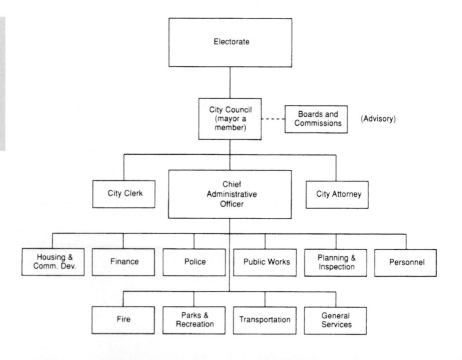

In weak mayor systems, elected commissioners serve as the legislative branch and the executive branch. The commissioners are legislators and also head various municipal departments—finance, public works, public safety, planning, personnel.

Often, the commissioner of public safety also serves as mayor, a largely ceremonial post in this system. The commission form has been criticized for blurring the separation of powers between the legislative and executive branches. In the commission system, there is no single official that the electorate can hold responsible for the conduct of local affairs.

The Public Interest

As we saw, the city manager plan was initiated during a period of reform as a means of taking politics out of local government. Other means have been advanced: the nonpartisan ballot, extension of the merit system and career services to protect city jobs from being used for patronage, the payment of low salaries to mayors and council or commission members to take the profit out of public service. Many cities have been the battlegrounds between the good government groups and their opponents, who contend that the result of taking power from party leaders and elected officials is its transfer to nongovernmental groups and bureaucracies that are not answerable to the public.

There are few identifiable public interests that most people agree upon. There can be a consensus on such matters as public safety and good roads. But the majority of issues resolve into a contest among differing special interests. The political process involves much more than the nomination and election of candidates. We can define the political process as the daily interaction of government, interest groups and the citizenry.

Participants in the Political Process

Professors Wallace S. Sayre of Columbia University and Herbert Kaufman of Yale put the political process in terms useful to the government reporter. They describe the participants as actors in a contest for a variety of goals, stakes, rewards and prizes. The police officer on the beat whose union is seeking to fend off reductions in the police force is an actor in the contest, as is the mother of three who is urging her school's Parents Association to speak out for more crossing guards at an elementary school. They are as much a part of the political process as the mayor who journeys to the state capital to seek a larger slice of state funds for welfare and health or who decides to seek re-election and lines up backing from unions and ethnic groups.

We can group the participants in the city's political process as follows:

• **The political party leaders:** The leaders and their organizations have a strong hand in the nominating process, but the other participants have increased their power and influence as the political party has declined in importance in local elections. Insurgents sometimes capture nominations, and the leaders must compromise their choices for the highest offices in the interest of finding candidates who can win.

Covering the Candidates

The Nieman Watchdog Project asked journalists how to improve the coverage of political campaigns. Here are some of their suggestions:

- Cover issues rather than events.
- Set agendas based on issues that are important to the public and aggressively pursue responses from candidates.
- Avoid he-said, she-said coverage.
- Pay attention to how the votes are counted.
- Don't let candidates get away with platitudes and sound bites. Press them on issues.
- Develop sufficient background so that you can define the relevant issues the candidates should address.
- Get away from polls and focus groups. Walk the neighborhoods, talk to people of different race, class, gender.

(The Nieman Foundation awards fellowships to experienced journalists to study at Harvard.)

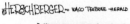

WHAT ARE THEY BIDDING FOR?

SCHOOL TEACHERS, COPS AND PRISON GUARDS...

• **Elected and appointed officials:** The mayor, members of the city council or commission and their administrators occupy key roles in governing the city. As the party's power has waned, the mayor and the visible elected and appointed officials have become independent decision makers.

• **Interest (pressure) groups:** Every aspect of city policy making is monitored by one or more political interest groups. Business groups are especially interested in the school system and the tax structure. When a school district reported that 66 percent of third-graders were reading at grade level compared to 88 percent in other districts, parents were concerned. So were real estate agents. Their reason: Poor schools would make it harder to sell homes in the district.

As for the city's tax structure, real estate interests want a low property tax to attract home buyers. They will also want large and efficient police and fire departments because these keep insurance premiums low.

The banks are interested in policies about the city's indebtedness because they are the buyers of the bonds and notes the city issues to pay for large-scale construction projects such as roads and schools. Contractors push for public improvements. The bar association checks on law enforcement and the judiciary.

Religious groups and educational organizations keep track of school policies. Medical and health professions examine the activities of the health department. The nominating process and the election campaigns attract ethnic and labor groups as well as the good government groups.

Interest groups compete with each other to influence the city leadership and its bureaucracy, and this balances their influence. An interest group may control the decision making of a department or agency, as when, for example, the real estate interests take over the planning and zoning department or the banks and bond market control decisions about the sale of bonds.

• **Organized and professional bureaucracies:** City employees became independent of the party organization with the development of the merit system, unionization and the professionalization of city services. Police, firefighters and teachers have been among the most active in influencing the political process.

• **Other governments:** The city government is in daily contact with a variety of other governmental units: the county, the state, the federal government, public authorities and special assessment districts. These governments are linked by a complex web of legal and financial involvements. State approval is often necessary for certain actions by the city. State and federal governments appropriate funds for such city services as education, health and welfare. City officials are almost always bargaining with other governmental units.

• **The press:** "The communication media provide the larger stage upon which the other participants in the city's political contest play their parts with the general public as an audience," says Kaufman. But, he continues, the media "do more than merely provide the public stage." They also take a direct part in the process. Having its own values, emphasis, stereotypes and preoccupations, the press is not an exact mirror or reporter, he says. The media highlight personalities, are fond of exposés, are too zealous in looking for stories about patronage crumbs—and are too skeptical of officials and party leaders, he says.

Auditing the Community

Along with covering the nine governmental activities listed at the beginning of this chapter, reporters keep tabs on the city's economic and social conditions.

The Economy

Much of the community's health depends on its economy—the availability of jobs, the ability of the city to meet its bonded indebtedness and to support first-rate schools and services. Reporters use several measuring sticks to gauge the local economy:

- Employment and unemployment rates.

- Housing construction and sales.

- Telephone and utility connections.

- Automobile sales.

- Hotel and motel occupancy rates.

- Sales tax revenues.

These factors also are considered by the agencies that rate the city's credit. A high rating means the city will be able to sell bonds at a low interest rate. A low rating means the city is in poor financial condition and will have to offer high interest rates as an inducement to buy its bonds, which furthers the city's tight financial condition. The local reporter regularly checks the city's credit rating.

Job Search   The Bureau of Labor Statistics makes monthly checks on employment in every state and for large metropolitan areas. It calls people at their homes and asks if they are working; if not, whether they are looking for work. The BLS also questions employers about their payrolls. Are they growing, shrinking? It asks about wages. The results of these surveys provide reporters with what *Baltimore Sun* business reporter Jay Hancock says is "the single best piece of current, state-based economic information you can get."

The data for states and large cities are available from the BLS home page: www.stats.bls.gov. Click *Data* on the main menu. Then click *Most Requested Series,* which gives you another menu. Go down to the *Employment and Unemployment* heading and click *State and Area Employment, Hours and Earnings* under the category *Nonfarm Payroll Statistics from the Current Employment Statistics.*

Click in your state and zero in on *Total Nonfarm Employment.* Hancock says not to base stories on a single month but to look for trends. Or take several months and strike an average. Then compare this current average with the same months from a year and five years ago.

Choices

"What I try to do is to show people that they have to choose, and my job is to make that choosing informed. I heard a saying once, 'Choice is fate.' You want more police? What do you have to give up to pay for them? You want smaller class size? Where's the money to come from? From higher school taxes? Smaller pay raises for teachers? Cutbacks in administrative costs? Our job is to see, understand and explain the consequences."

—*City hall reporter*

The Schools

Good schools help make the city financially secure because industry and business are attracted to communities with an educated work force. Telemarketing has created new business centers around the country to handle catalog orders, to make hotel reservations, to plan vacations, even to help computer owners get back on track. These businesses look for pockets of hard-working, well-educated people to do their work.

The "toll-free capital of the U.S." is located in Omaha where tens of thousands of people work in telemarketing. South Dakota's major industry is processing credit card transactions. North Dakota workers handle half the reservations of a large travel company in Philadelphia. These areas are marked by above-average national test scores and high graduation rates for their high school students.

But the overall picture of educational attainment is bleak, according to a study by the Rand Corporation. The authors of the study, Sloan McCombs and Stephen J. Carroll, write that educational reforms have helped raise reading achievement among children in the primary grades. "But many children are not moving beyond basic decoding skills—deciphering words and sounding them out—to fluency and comprehension. . . . This trend is especially troubling because today's adolescents (defined as students in the 4th through 12th grades) are facing a job market that demands high literacy and critical-thinking skills."

Education reporters are following such studies as the one by Rand to see whether their local schools are offering children a first-rate education.

Additional Checkpoints

Journalists also keep track of other facets of community life: how the city is meeting its obligations to all its residents, how people get along with each other, whether problems are being solved.

The larger the city, the more pressing the problems of race. But race is entwined with class—that is, minority groups are poor: 46 percent of black and 40 percent of Hispanic children live in poverty.

Another indicator of social conditions is teen-age motherhood. The United States has the highest rate of unwed teen-age childbearing. More than 1 million adolescent girls become pregnant every year, and half give birth.

In most communities, these indicators point to pockets marked by drugs, crime, poverty, poor health, high infant mortality rates, low educational attainment and unemployment.

NRW *PLUS*

For a closer look at these problems, see **Inner-City Problems,** *NRW Plus.*

The Demographics

Who lives in the city? What's the average age of the population, the male–female ratio, the income brackets, the educational attainment, the racial and ethnic makeup? What's the birthrate, the deathrate? Is the infant mortality rate higher than the state

From Idyllic Village to Urban Nightmare

". . . Not only are the streets dominated by the criminal element, but the schools and the housing projects as well. One's life is up for grabs, one's children will either be victimized by the criminal element or recruited into criminal enterprise. Almost nothing can be done to help the law-abiding majority of the ghetto unless and until crime and the drug trade are brought under control. . . ."

—Irving Kristol, *The Wall Street Journal.*
Right, Mel Finkelstein,
© *New York Daily News,* Inc.
Above right, Larry C. Price,
The Philadelphia Inquirer Magazine.
Above left, The Plumas County Museum.

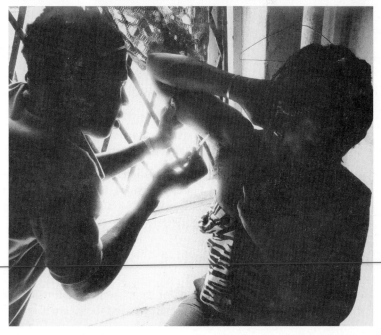

or national average? What is killing people in the community, heart attacks, cancer, AIDS, accidents?

Reporters who seek the answers to these and related questions give the public an insight into the changing nature of their communities and the consequences of these changes. As the Hispanic population grew in many states, political tensions developed, among these a battle for power between African-American and Hispanic blocs. Though both are minority groups, each has a distinct political agenda.

The Hispanic population is larger and growing faster than the black population. It makes up 14.4 percent of the U.S. population; the black population is 12.8 percent of the total population. This growth has been seen throughout the country. See **Demographics** in *NRW Plus* for the way a midwestern newspaper handled the influx in its area.

Guidelines

In addition to covering the breaking news in the community—city council meetings, school board decisions, zoning actions—what should the local reporter look for so that citizens can tell whether the community is meeting their needs? What guidelines can we establish?

An African proverb states, "It takes a whole village to raise a child." This can be our starting point: How well is the community protecting, nurturing, educating and caring for its children? Here are some indexes that help us establish quality of life guidelines for children:

Health: infant mortality rate, percentage of low-birth-weight infants, percentage of births to teens, number of physicians per 10,000 population.

Economics: unemployment rate, percentage of children in poverty, median family income.

Crime: violent crimes per 1,000 population, property crimes per 1,000, juvenile arrests.

Education: student–teacher ratio, dropout rate, scores on national tests (ACT, SAT, NAEP).

Physical environment: number of bad air days, pounds of toxic releases per 1,000 population, hazard ranking (toxic wastes).

All of these figures are available to the journalist from online sources.

For city rankings, see **The Good and the Not So Good,** *NRW Plus.* Also, see **State Rankings** for a list of the most and least livable states based on data in 44 categories.

Politics

Many of the most important issues that face communities are settled in elections. Candidates and their parties differ in the solutions they offer, and it is the task of the reporter covering politics to make clear the positions that define and differentiate the candidates so that an informed choice can be made.

Politics has been given a bad name over the years, and some reporters approach coverage with a disdain for the whole affair. Given the incessant attack on government, this distaste is understandable. But it's no way to approach the job. Not only that, but the assumption that government is the enemy is simple-minded.

When President Clinton remarked, "Government is not the solution," the historian Stephen Ambrose responded, "The government surely was the solution to the Depression and in World War II and on the civil-rights front and on providing a decent life for old folks in this country."

Penetrating the Package   Jena Heath of the *Austin American-Statesman* describes political reporting as the "push and pull between the candidate's need to control the message and our need to tell the real story." She found candidates aim their messages to "the TV folks, the real power in a business where beaming a neatly packaged candidate into voters' living rooms is the bottom line."

It is, of course, the reporter's job to shave away the fluff and get behind the camouflage.

Self Study   It is also the reporter's job to look within to see whether his or her attitudes and biases obstruct coverage. Everyone carries preferences, sympathies, likes and dislikes through life. For the reporter covering politics, personal feelings cannot be allowed to influence coverage.

For guidelines to covering politics and political campaigns, see **Some Tips on Campaign Coverage** *NRW Plus*.

Money Talk

The city school system needs teachers for the new high school west of town—money has to be budgeted by the school board. The health department needs special equipment to test for biological agents—it is asking the city council to increase its appropriation. Whether these expenditures are necessary, and if so whether the amount sought should be allocated—these determinations are made in a political context.

We next turn to how budgets are made.

Vern Herschberger,
Waco Tribune-Herald

The Budget

Covering local government—indeed, covering all levels of government—requires a knowledge of how money is raised and how it is spent. Money fuels the system.

"I've had to learn how to cover five governmental units, and I find the single best way to learn what they are doing is to attend budget hearings," says David Yepsen, political reporter for *The Des Moines Register*. "They let you know the current situation, what the problems are, the proposed solutions and where government is headed."

"Follow the buck," says the experienced reporter. The city hall reporter follows the path of the parking meter dime and the property tax dollar as they make their way through government. The path of these dimes and dollars is set by the budget.

The budget is a forecast or estimate of expenditures that a government will make during the coming year and the revenues needed to meet those expenses. It is, in short, a balance sheet. Budgets are made for the fiscal year, which may be the calendar year or may run from July 1 through June 30 or other dates. The budget is made by the executive branch (mayor, governor, president, school superintendent) and then submitted to the legislative body (city council, state legislature, Congress, board of education) for adoption.

A Compromise   The budget is the final resolution of the conflicting claims of individuals and groups to public monies. Aaron Wildavsky of the University of California at Berkeley describes the budget as "a series of goals with price tags attached." If it is followed, he says, things happen, certain policy objectives are accomplished.

The budget is a sociological and political document. As Prime Minister William Ewart Gladstone of Britain remarked more than 100 years ago, the budget "in a thousand ways goes to the root of the prosperity of the individuals and relation of classes and the strength of kingdoms."

The budget can determine how long a pregnant woman waits to see a doctor in a well-baby clinic, how many children are in a grade school class, whether city workers will seek to defeat the mayor in the next election.

Here is the beginning of a budget story by Paul Rilling of *The Anniston* (Ala.) *Star:*

A city budget may look like a gray mass of dull and incomprehensible statistics, but it is the best guide there is to the plans and priorities of city government.

Rhetoric and promises aside, the budget says what the city council really sees as the city's top priorities.

Tuesday, the Anniston City Council will consider for formal adoption the proposed city budget for fiscal . . .

Cover the Whole Process

City hall, education, county and state legislative reporters handle budget stories on a regular basis. Reporters on these beats begin to write stories several months before the budget is adopted so that the public can be informed of the give-and-take of the process and participate early in the decision making. In a six-week span, Bill Mertens, city hall reporter for *The Hawk Eye,* wrote more than a dozen stories. Here are the beginning paragraphs of two of them:

School crossing guards may be one of the programs lost if Burlington city councilmen intend to hold the new budget close to the existing one.

The city council has asked Burlington fire department heads to cut $30,000 from their budget request.

Income

General Revenues

Property Tax
  & Spec. Asses.
Returned State Funds
License & Privilege
Fines & Fees
Sales & Charges
Federal Aid
Transfer from Utilities
Other

Utility Revenue

Revenue
from
Water & Electric & Gas
Utilities
(Where City-Owned)

New Borrowing

New Bond Issues
&
Temporary Notes

City's Money Flow

This chart shows the major sources of revenues and the major outlets for expenditures of a city.

By following the lines, you can see that general revenues are used for general purposes, except for utility expenses in cities in which the utilities are municipally owned. Utility revenue is used for all types of expenditures, but new borrowing is used for capital outlays for the most part.

Occasionally, temporary notes are issued in the form of anticipation notes sold to banks to pay for bills due immediately. These are short-term loans.

The anticipation notes take the following forms:

RANS—Revenue Anticipation Notes. Paid off when anticipated revenues develop.

TANS—Tax Anticipation Notes. Paid back when taxes are collected.

BANS—Bond Anticipation Notes. Paid off when bonds are sold.

City
Treasurer

Expenses

Current Operations

General Admin.
Police & Fire
Parks & Recreation
Garbage & Trash
Band & Music
Cemetery
Trust Funds
Airport
Library
Public Health
Streets, Alleys,
  & Sewers
Other

Debt Service

Retirement of
  Bonds, Temporary
  Notes & No
  Fund Warrants
Principal &
  Interest Pay-
  ments

Utility Expenses

The Cost of
  Operating Electric,
  Water & Gas
  Utilities

Capital Outlay

New City Bldgs.
Street Paving
New Sewers
Utility Expansion
Flood Control
Airports
Hospitals
Sewage Disposal
  & Sanitation
  Plants
Parking Meters
Other

Most of the dozen-plus stories were enterprised by Mertens. In his stories, he was conscious of the consequences of the belt tightening. By writing about possible cuts in such areas as school crossing guards and the fire department, Mertens alerted the public. Residents could, if they wished, inform their council members of their support for or their opposition to the cuts.

Types of Budgets

Two types of governmental expenditures are budgeted—funds for daily expenses and funds for long-range projects. At the local governmental level, these spending decisions are included in two kinds of budgets: expense budgets and capital budgets.

Expense Budgets   The expense or executive budget covers costs of daily expenses, which include salaries, debt service and the purchase of goods and services. Expense budget revenues are gathered from three major sources:

- Taxes on real estate—the property tax—usually the single largest source of income.

- General fund receipts, which include revenues from fines, permits, licenses, and taxes such as income, corporation, sales and luxury taxes. (States must give cities permission to levy taxes.)

- Grants-in-aid from the federal and state governments.

Capital Budgets   The capital or construction budget lists the costs of capital projects to be built, such as roads and schools, and major equipment and products to be purchased. Capital budget funds are raised by borrowing, usually through the sale of bonds pledged against the assessed valuation of real estate in the governmental unit. Bonds are approved by the voters and then sold to security firms through bidding. The firms then offer the bonds for public sale. The loan is paid back, much like a home owner's payments on a mortgage, over an extended period, 10, 20 or 30 years. Principal and interest are paid out of current revenues and are listed in the expenditures column of the expense budget as "debt service," which should run under 10 percent of the total budget for the city to be on safe economic footing.

Making the Budget

Most budgets are adopted in this series of steps:

1. Budget request forms go out to all department heads, who must decide on priorities for the coming year and submit them to the budget officer, mayor or school superintendent.

2. Meetings are held between the budget officer and department heads to adjust requests and formulate a single balanced program.

3. The budget is submitted to the city council or commission, the board of education or other legislative arm of the governmental unit. The budget is sometimes accompanied by a narrative explaining the requests.

4. The legislative body examines budget items for each department and agrees on allocations for each.

5. Public hearings are held.

6. The budget is adopted.

The reporter covers each stage of this process, the behind-the-scenes bickering, dickering and politicking as well as the formal activities of the various department heads, executives and legislators. All sorts of pressures are brought to bear on the budget makers. Property owners and real estate interests want the budget held down, for increased expenditures usually mean higher property taxes. The businessmen and -women who rely on selling goods and services to the city seek hefty budgets for the departments and agencies they serve. Employees want salary increases, generous fringe benefits and more lines in the budget for promotions. Politicians seek to reward constituencies and to fulfill campaign promises.

The Aftermath   After the budget is adopted, the reporter watches the consequences. Few, if any, agencies and departments are given what they request, which usually does no harm as most units purposely hike up their requests. Sometimes damage is done. In Ohio, the *Akron Beacon Journal* investigated school finances and found that "legislators and governors have siphoned hundreds of millions of dollars from education for other purposes." The result: "High school seniors in tears when their football season and marching band are canceled . . . elementary school children have to wait after school because there are not enough buses in working condition to take them home."

Checklist: Budgets

Adoption

___Amount to be spent.

___New or increased taxes, higher license and permit fees and other income that will be necessary to meet expenditures.

___Cuts, if any, to be made in such taxes, fees or fines.

___Comparison with preceding year(s) in dollars and in percentage increase or decrease. How much will an increase cost the typical home owner?

___Justification for increases sought, cuts made.

___Rate of current spending, under or over budget of previous year.

You Haul
  Here is the beginning of a budget story that appeared in *The Anniston Star* at step 3 in the budget-making process:

  Anniston residents may have to start carrying their garbage cans to and from curbsides and commercial customers may be charged for garbage service to help the city of Anniston live within its budget.

___Patterns behind submission and subsequent adjustments, such as political motives, pressure groups, history.

___Consequences of budget for agencies, departments, businesses, public. Which had significant cuts, increases.

Follow-Up

___Per-person comparison of costs for specific services with other cities or school districts of same size.

___Check of one or more departments to see how funds are used, whether all funds were necessary, whether cuts created problems.

Sources

There are five major interest groups that seek to influence budget making and constitute the reporter's sources:

1. **Government:** chief executive, who submits the budget; mayor, governor, school superintendent, president; city manager; head of budget bureau or budget director; department heads; finance and taxation committees of the city council or commission; council members. (Party leaders outside government are sometimes helpful.)

2. **Money-providing constituencies:** local real estate association; property owners' association; chamber of commerce; taxpayer organizations; merchant and business groups; banks; savings and loan associations.

3. **Service-demanding groups:** lobbyists for education, health, welfare and other services.

4. **Organized bureaucracies:** public employees; municipal unions; civil service associations; the public employees' retirement fund manager.

5. **Independent groups:** League of Women Voters; National Municipal League; National League of Cities; U.S. Conference of Mayors; Advisory Commission on Intergovernmental Relations.

Compulsory Costs

Promises to cut spending and therefore lower taxes make for political rhetoric that entices voters, but the truth is that many items in the budget are mandated costs that cannot be shifted or eliminated without massive political changes. The mandated funds include salaries, debt service, pensions and matching funds that localities must produce to meet state and federal grants, particularly for such services as health, welfare and education. When the city accepts grants from the state or federal government, it must abide by rules and regulations that often require local expenditures.

This means that the actual maneuvering room in most budgets is not great, especially because salaries, which represent the largest single expense item, are

---

Trickle Down

When New York State slashed taxes—a popular political move—the cities in the state suffered as costs for pensions and Medicaid shifted to the cities. The cities had to cut back on services in order to meet these mandated costs.

Affected were the people "who never vote in large numbers," says Andrew White, the director of the Center for New York City Affairs at New School University. They are "low-income mothers, teens in foster care, parents in Family Court and others who rely on social programs" and who have little influence on state lawmakers, White said.

set by contract in many cities. Because of mandated costs, less than 10 percent of the budgets for most large cities is discretionary.

Costs can be reduced if commitments to the poor, the elderly and the ill are cut back. This, however, would antagonize the service-demanding constituencies. Maneuvering room could be created by changing earmarked funds, such as those for education, to general funds. Teachers and parents would object.

Trade-Offs and Rewards The competition for the limited free-floating general funds is always intense, and the perceptive reporter will examine this contest during the budgetary process. In this competition, the administrator finds it necessary to trade off the demands of various groups. The trade-offs make good stories.

Some aspects of the process are hidden from view. The reporter must dig them out and learn which constituencies are involved, the motives of the participants. Are political debts being paid by building a school in one section of the city or by increasing salaries in a particular agency? Have cuts been made in the department of a critical or independent administrator?

Budget Politics

During a legislative session, the Republican governor of New York proposed a new formula for the distribution of state aid to local school districts that reflected the demands of big-city school officials. A few days later, a group of Republican state senators and assembly members from Long Island met with the governor, who was facing re-election. Following the meeting, the governor's aid formula was changed to give more aid to suburban school districts.

"What happened at the gathering," reported *The New York Times*, "was summed up later by Joseph M. Margiotta of Uniondale, the powerful Nassau County Republican leader, who related that the Long Island delegation had simply delivered to the governor the stern message that without more state education aid, Long Island property taxes would skyrocket in September and the governor's campaign would sink in October."

When Mayor John Lindsay of New York "dropped the broom and picked up the nightstick"—the graphic phrase the *Daily News* used to describe the shift in budget priorities from clean streets to public safety—it was widely interpreted as Lindsay's recognition that law and order would make a more attractive national issue than sanitation. Lindsay had presidential ambitions.

Property Tax

The property tax is the largest single source of income for most municipalities, counties, special districts and school systems. It affects more people than any other local tax but the sales tax. Considerable local, county and school coverage centers on the action of the council, commission or board in setting the property tax.

The tax is formally known as the *mill levy.* A mill is .1 cent (1/10¢), and the property tax technically is expressed in terms of mills levied for each dollar of

Federal–State–County Trickledown

As the federal government faced deficits, it cut funds to states. The states, also facing declining revenues, cut funds to counties and cities, which then had to tighten spending and ask for more money from its residents.

The Des Moines Register reported:

Homeowners in most Iowa counties will pay a few dollars more in property taxes because of the state's budget crisis.

State officials decided this spring against reimbursing counties for the full amount of homestead, military, and elderly and disabled exemptions on residential property taxes.

In response, most Iowa counties have decided to reduce the amount of homestead credit residents are entitled to, said John Easter of the Iowa State Association of Counties.

"The majority have chosen to pass along the shortfalls from the homestead credit to the property taxpayers. . . ."

assessed valuation of property. One-tenth of a mill per dollar works out to 10 cents per $100 in assessed valuation, or $1 per $1,000 in valuation.

Here is the formula for figuring the property tax or mill levy:

$$\textbf{Mill levy = taxes to be collected} \div \textbf{assessed valuation}$$

Let us assume budget officials estimate that $1 million will have to be collected from the property tax and that the assessed valuation of real estate in the city or school district is $80 million. Here is how the tax is figured:

Mill levy = $1 million ÷ $80 million

Mill levy = $1 ÷ $80 = $.0125

Mill levy = 1.25 cents on each $1 of assessed valuation

Because mill levies are usually expressed against $100 or $1,000 in assessed valuation, the levy in this community would be $1.25 for each $100 in valuation, or $12.50 for each $1,000 in valuation.

Note that the mill levy is applied to assessed valuations, not to actual value as determined in the marketplace. Assessed value is usually a percentage of market value.

Budget Adoption   Here is the beginning of a story about the adoption of the city budget:

The Mt. Pleasant City Council adopted a $217 million budget last night and set a tax rate of $108.50 for each $1,000 in assessed valuation.

The rate represents a $6 increase in the tax rate for property owners for next year.

Those owning homes assessed at $50,000, which is the average Mt. Pleasant assessment, will pay $5,425 a year in city property taxes. The current bill for a $50,000 home is $5,125.

Many Other Taxes   Remember that the property tax is a major source of revenue for several governmental units—city, county, school, special assessment districts, each of which sets its own tax levy on property. When covering the action of one unit in setting a tax rate, it is necessary to inform the reader that this particular property tax is not the only one the property owner will pay.

Property taxes levied by special assessment districts can add a large chunk to the tax bill. These special districts construct and maintain services such as power and water lines, hospitals, sewage systems and community development projects. Each district has the power to levy taxes on property within the district.

Property valuations are made by the tax assessor and are public record. The tax rate is set each year, but valuations on individual pieces of property are not changed often. Total assessed valuation does change each year because of new construction and shutdowns that add to or subtract from the tax rolls. The taxing district must establish the total assessed valuation each year before a new tax rate can be set.

See **Assessment Districts** in *NRW Plus*.

Reassessments

When the assessor does make new valuations, the intensity of feeling is considerable, as revealed in this story:

SPRING VALLEY, N.Y., Dec. 12—Listening to people here, a visitor would almost think that someone was stalking the streets, sowing horror and destruction.

But it is only the tax assessor, equipped with a collapsible 10-foot measuring stick, a set of appraisal cards, a practiced eye that can tell the difference between a toilet and a water closet and experience that tells him which adds more value to a house.

This village of 22,450 persons, 2,219 dwellings and 109 commercial properties is nearing the end of a year-long reappraisal. . . .

The purpose of a reassessment is to bring valuations up to date and to attempt to distribute the tax burden fairly. Generally, reassessments result in increased revenues from the property tax since assessors will often use the current market value of property as the guideline, not the original cost of the property.

When a community decides it must raise more revenue through the property tax, it has two alternatives: It can raise the property tax or it can raise property valuations. A reassessment is considered more equitable as the heaviest burden falls on those with the greater ability to carry the increase.

Borrowing

Most cities need seasonal funds to tide them over while waiting for income from taxes or grants to arrive. They also need money to finance major construction projects.

Anticipation Notes

For seasonal borrowing or for emergencies when small amounts are needed, the city may issue and sell anticipation notes to banks. Future tax collections and anticipated grants-in-aid are pledged as security. Usually, the state must approve.

Short-term low-interest borrowing consists of three types of anticipation notes—revenue, tax and bond. All notes must be repaid in a year.

Bonds

The idea behind the sale of bonds is that the costs of such long-range projects as schools, hospitals, streets, sewage plants and mass transit should be borne by those who use them over the anticipated lives of the projects.

There are three major types of bonds. They differ as to the type of security pledged to repay them:

• **General obligation:** Most frequently issued. Security is the general taxing power of the city. Bonds are retired by taxes on all property in the city.

District Check

Tom Philp of *The Sacramento Bee* looked into the Sacramento Suburban Water District—one of more than 1,000 special districts in the area—and found abuses that led to a federal grand jury and indictments of three employees for collecting $1 million in undocumented expenses.

Philp went on to examine these districts around the state and found many abuses. The state decided to tighten the requirements for these independent special districts.

Ratings

Bond rating agencies assess the financial standing of cities and states that issue bonds. The higher the rating, the lower the interest rate. Here is Standard & Poor's rating schedule.

AAA: Highest.

AA: High-grade, slightly riskier than AAA.

A: Upper-medium-grade. Secure finances, but if problems arise, paybacks could suffer.

BBB: Medium-grade. Finances precarious. Lowest level of investment-quality bonds.

BB, C, CCC: Speculative. Uncertain whether long-term bonds can be repaid.

- **Special improvement:** For construction of sidewalks, sewers and similar public works. Taxes are levied on the property owners who will benefit from the construction. Charges levied on the property are called *special assessments.* Special assessment districts are set up to levy and collect the taxes.

- **Revenue bonds:** To pay for the acquisition, construction and improvement of such properties as college dormitories and public utilities. The pledge is a lien on earnings, which are used to redeem the bonds. These earnings come from room charges in dormitories; water, gas and electric collections from utility customers; toll charges on bridges and highways.

Bonds are paid off in two ways:

- **Term bonds:** The securities are retired at the end of the specified term, 10, 15, 20 years. Meanwhile, money is set aside regularly in a sinking fund and invested to be used to retire the bonds at the end of the term.

- **Serial bonds:** Most common. A portion is retired each year.

Give Total Cost   In writing bond stories, the reporter should make sure to include the cost of the bonds to taxpayers. Some readers will be astonished to learn how much a seemingly small rate of interest can add to the principal.

When Nassau County in New York sold $103 million in bonds for roads, land purchases and new sewers, officials estimated that interest would cost about $50 million over the life of the bonds. One reason for the high cost of debt was the downgrading of the county by bond-rating agencies as a result of the county's financial problems. The downgrading resulted in the county having to offer higher interest rates to attract investors worried about the lowered rating of the bonds.

Here is the beginning of a story about a credit downgrading:

> TROY, N.Y. (AP)—The City of Troy, which continues to struggle with a four-year-old financial crisis, had its credit rating reduced below investment grade Friday by Moody's Investors Service.
>
> Moody's said it had cut Troy's credit rating from B-aa to B-a, one step below investment grade. . . .

Exposé

A lengthy series in the *Asbury Park Sunday Press* exposed the way New Jersey legislators used the state treasury to enrich themselves.

Coverage of government—on the local, county, state and federal levels—requires frequent checks through investigative reporting.

Checking Up

Wherever public money is involved, audits are made to see that the money is spent properly. Most governmental units undergo internal checks made by their own auditors, and these make good stories. Here is the beginning of a story by Jayne Garrison of the *San Francisco Examiner:*

> OAKLAND—A Social Services Department audit says mismanagement and internal squabbling are so severe that clients would be better off if the agency were dismantled.

In addition, checks are made by an independent government agency or office. Cities, states and the federal government have a department or office independent of the executive that checks the financial activities of all agencies within government. At the federal level, the Government Accountability Office does this work. At the state level, the state auditor or comptroller is the watchdog, and at the city level an elected official, also known as the auditor or comptroller, examines the financial records of city offices.

A regular or preaudit examination determines whether there is money to pay for the goods, whether there are certified receipts for the delivered goods, whether there has been competitive bidding when required by law and whether the prices are reasonable.

Increasingly, auditors and comptrollers are conducting performance audits, which check the efficiency of the services, the quality of the goods and the necessity for purchasing them.

Preaudit example: A state official claims travel reimbursement for an official trip between Boulder and Denver. The auditor will determine whether the 39 miles claimed on the official's expense account attached to a pay order is the actual distance and will see whether the 29 cents a mile claimed is the standard state payment.

Performance audit example: The comptroller has decided to make a check of welfare rolls to see whether money is going out to ineligible people. The office makes a computer check of the welfare rolls against (a) death lists; (b) marriage certificates (if a person receiving aid to dependent children has married, the working spouse is obligated to support the children); (c) children in foster care homes still listed as at the residence; (d) city and state payrolls to determine if any employed people are receiving welfare.

Looking at the Files

Journalists make their own checks. They regularly look through vouchers and pay orders in the auditor's office, and they look at the canceled checks in the treasurer's office.

When a governmental unit wants to buy something, it sends a purchase order to the comptroller's or auditor's office, which makes a preaudit. Records are kept

Covering Religion

Religion is now a major beat for much of the media, and even reporters assigned to other beats often find themselves involved in covering religious issues. Politics: The religious right is a powerful political force. Education: The battle over the role of religion in public schools is incessant. Courts: Religious issues frequently make their way into the legal system.

The Religion Newswriters Association (www.RNA.org) provides up-to-date information on these issues and also offers background information. The RNA publishes *Reporting on Religion: A Primer on Journalism's Best Beat* by Diane Connolly, former religion editor of *The Dallas Morning News.* It is available online and in book form from the RNA.

The RNA booklet offers journalists guidance on such issues as:

Do I reveal my personal faith to sources?

What do I do when visiting places of worship?

Where can I find resources on covering religion?

The *Primer* states, "Religion shapes people's actions and reactions in very private and very public ways across the range of news and features. Without it, you're often not getting the whole story."

by the number of the purchase order, by the agency involved and often by the name of the vendor.

On delivery of the goods or services, a voucher is made up with the accompanying bill, and this starts the payment to the vendor. The payment is made in the form of a check, a warrant.

High-Level Thievery   An examination of vouchers and warrants enabled George Thiem, a reporter for *The Chicago Daily News,* to expose a multi-million-dollar corruption scheme by the Illinois state treasurer. Thiem could see that a number of checks were endorsed by typewriter. Interviewing some of those who supposedly were paid by these checks for work done for the state, he learned that the people listed on the checks had never done state work; nor had they received the checks. The treasurer went to prison as a result of Thiem's investigation.

For more information on how to check government, see **Investigating Government** *NRW Plus.*

Zoning and Planning

For centuries, the mentally ill were locked up. The reasons seemed logical: Isolated, the mentally ill could be overseen easily; free in society, their conditions worsened; they were a danger to others and to themselves. Gradually, the truth seeped out. Journalists showed that institutions for the mentally ill were snake pits where the patients were treated inhumanely. Few were cured, and many were made worse. With the development of tranquilizing drugs and other treatment, it became possible to offer outpatient care. But there had to be a transition, a halfway house to help the patient adjust after institutionalization.

In New Jersey, the Catholic Diocese of Trenton decided to administer several such houses. The state intended to deinstitutionalize its mental patients, and the diocese sought to help. The diocese found a structure in Willingboro that fit its needs. But permission was required from the zoning board because the building was in a residential area.

The Willingboro zoning board, like thousands of other such boards, carries out the community's planning goals, which are usually set by the planning commission. The zoning boards divide an area into zones or districts and designate them residential, commercial or industrial. The boards then grant building and construction permits consistent with these designations.

The boards also regulate the height of buildings, lot size, yard dimensions and other aspects of construction. City councils enact the ordinances that the zoning boards enforce.

Zoning can be restrictive, a way of keeping certain people out of an area. By requiring that new construction be of single-residence homes on one-acre lots, a zoning regulation will effectively keep out of the area all but the well-to-do. When Laura King, who covered Willingboro on her suburban beat, attended the zoning board meeting at which the diocese requested a variance for its halfway house, she was struck by the hostility of the spectators. King decided that the opposition to the house was the story.

Neighborhood Stories

City hall reporters spend too much of their time in city hall, says a veteran municipal government reporter. He recommends that they make regular trips out of the protected environs of the municipal building and into the neighborhoods of the community to see what is on the minds of people, to check how city programs and policies have been carried out. Here is the beginning of a neighborhood story by Jayne Garrison of the *San Francisco Examiner:*

OAKLAND—In the heart of the Oakland flatlands, the moms and pops of small business are plotting to sweep out the rubble: dope, litter and boarded buildings.

About 35 merchants meeting in churches and stores the last few weeks have organized a voice they hope will boom across town to City Hall—the Central East Oakland Merchants Association.

This is the first time in more than a decade that merchants along central East 14th Street have tried to wield clout together. The odds against them are steep.

They have little political pull and even less money. They face absentee landlords who own some boarded storefronts, and youths who have no work outside the drug trade.

But they do have determination.

"You see that red church down there?" said Al Parham, nodding toward a tall brick steeple half a block past Seminary Avenue on East 14th Street. "They just built that. So people are coming back into the community. And they're going to church. They care."

CAR   A lot of local reporting is based on records and files that are kept online. For an examination of how these records are put to use by reporters see **Computer-Assisted Reporting,** in *NRW Plus.*

Covering the Schools

Communities spend more money on public education than on any other single tax-supported activity. Public education has a long history, going back to colonial times. In 1642, the Massachusetts Bay Colony made education compulsory in the primary grades and required towns to establish public schools. The cost is borne by all in the community, whether the individual has children in the public school or not. The reason was given succinctly by Thaddeus Stevens to the Pennsylvania state legislature in 1835 when some legislators objected to the general financing of the schools.

"Many complain of the school tax," Stevens said, "not so much on account of its amount, as because it is for the benefit of others and not themselves. This is a mistake. It is for their own benefit, inasmuch as it perpetuates the government and ensures the due administration of the laws under which they live, and by which their lives and property are protected."

James Woodcock,
The Billings Gazette

Crowded

Bonnie Olson tries to cope with the 26 children in her Billings, Mont., classroom. The state sets 20 as the classroom limit, but the school district did not have money to hire enough teachers.

Graduation Rates

The ninth grade is the last schooling a third of U.S. students receive. A report by *Education Week* says that 69.6 percent of students who enter the ninth grade graduate in four years with a diploma. New Jersey has the highest graduation rate in the country, 84.5 percent. The federal Education Department puts the high school graduation rate nationally at 73.9 percent.

Education Week posts graduation rates for every school district in the country at edweek.org/dc06.

The faith in education as the underpinning of democracy is a constant theme in American life, along with the belief that a good education can pave the way to a good job, if not to the good life. Education pervades the life of most families because they have children in school.

The interest in schools—which really means a concern for the community's children—led *The Fincastle Herald* in Virginia to run a banner across page 1 when the Scholastic Aptitude Test (SAT) scores for the county were made public. "Low SAT scores surprise school officials," read the headline. The story was accompanied by a large box comparing county scores with others in Virginia, southern states and the nation. The story by Edwin McCoy begins:

> Botetourt County students scored at least 20 points below the state and national averages on both parts of the Scholastic Aptitude Test (SAT), according to figures provided by the county school system this week.

McCoy described education as the "focal point in the community" in an editorial accompanying the news story. "The quality of education is important to industrial or commercial development because developers are interested in the quality of life in any area they choose to expand in or move to."

Structure of the System

The school system is based in school districts. The schools are independent of municipal government and are subject to state regulations through a state board of education. School boards, usually with five to seven members, are elected in nonpartisan elections, although in some cities board members are appointed by the mayor. The board hires a superintendent of schools who is responsible to the board.

Stories from the board and the superintendent's office involve such subjects as changes in the curriculum and personnel, teacher contracts, the purchase of new equipment, aid to education, teacher certification, school dates for opening, closing and holidays and the vast area of school financing that includes budgeting and the issuance of bonds.

The school administration can provide material for assessing the performance of the system and its schools. Dropout and truancy records are kept, as are the results of standardized tests. Reporters can compare the scores in their communities with those of other cities. Comparisons also can be made of schools within the system. Do the students in the low-scoring schools come from economically depressed areas with serious social and economic problems? Is there a correlation between income and academic achievement?

A check of high school graduates would indicate what percentage is going to college from each school. Interviews with the students may uncover information just as revealing as the students' test scores.

Financing Schools

Schools receive funding from several sources. The averages work out to 48 percent from the state, 45 percent from local taxes and 7 percent from the federal government. In some states, the local property tax makes up more than half the school district's income. The result is that children in low-income districts, who usually need small classes, personal tutoring and experienced teachers, are short-changed. A survey by the U.S. Department of Education reports that fourth-grade children in low-income areas are three grade levels behind students in high-income areas.

Education Week reports: "Most fourth graders who live in U.S. cities can't read or understand a simple children's book, and most eighth graders can't use arithmetic to solve a practical problem."

The imbalance in school financing is the subject of stories by education writers. One result of these stories has been the enactment of school equalization laws. Several states have altered their school-financing formulas to make the state the major provider. In New Mexico, for example, 90 percent of school operating funds are provided by the state.

In the Classroom

The education reporter's responsibility is to hold the school system accountable to parents and to the community. The United States has committed itself to an educational system that will turn out large numbers of educated people. How well is it doing this?

The best way to begin to find out is to visit the classroom, to look at what is happening day after day and to check your observations against test scores and the assessments of parents and educators. When Bob Frazier of the *Register-Guard* in Eugene, Ore., covered education, he would scrunch all 6'4" into a grade-schooler's chair and sit in class. The stories he wrote were more significant than any release from the superintendent's office.

School visits are essential for the education reporter. Are elementary classrooms filled with books? Are the teachers working with a few students, not lecturing the whole class? William G. Ouchi in his book *Making Schools Work: A Revolutionary Plan to Get Your Children the Education They Need* says principals should take you into classrooms. If they prefer to walk down the hall that's "one of the most telltale signs" that something's wrong at the school.

A classroom visit will reveal the professional level of teachers, whether they are given respect and whether they, in turn, give students respect and attention. The school environment is checked: Is the school safe? Is there a strong code of behavior, and are violators punished? Is truancy increasing or declining? Records can be examined for the frequency, number and type of discipline problems and vandalism.

Does the high school have various tracks for its students, such as academic, vocational and general, and, if so, what percentage of students is in each? In the early 1960s, one of 10 students nationally was in the general track; today, almost

More Reading, Less Homework

There is little correlation between homework and achievement for elementary and middle school students, Sara Bennett and Nancy Kalish contend in their book *The Case Against Homework: How Homework Is Hurting Our Children and What We Can Do About It*. High school students do profit from homework to some extent, they say.

". . . most experts believe reading is the most important educational activity," the authors say. Yet reading "declines sharply after age 8. The No. 1 reason given by parents: too much homework."

half are. (The general track usually gives credit for physical and health education, work experience outside school, remedial English and mathematics and developmental courses such as training for adulthood and marriage.)

How much homework is given? A national survey of eighth-graders found youngsters spent 5½ hours a week on homework, 21 hours a week watching television. *The Raleigh Times* put at the top of page 1 its education reporter's story that half the state's students in the sixth and ninth grades do less than three hours of homework a week.

The School Budget

The allocation of federal, state and school district funds is made in the following process:

A budget for the following year is drafted by the schools superintendent and then submitted to the school board. The board holds hearings at which the superintendent defends the budget. Parents groups are heard, and if the teachers are organized into a union, the union speaks for raises for teachers.

Usually, the schools seek as much as possible and the board attempts to cut back to keep the mill levy (property tax) as low as possible. The board members have mixed motives. Although sensitive to the needs of the school system, they also reflect the larger community, which includes real estate interests that push to keep property taxes down.

The board then adopts a budget. In some states, the voters must approve this budget.

Hanging Out

Student life outside the classroom is worth covering, too. Thomas French of the *St. Petersburg Times* spent a year at Largo High School, listening to students talk about music, their sexual activity, their studies. He watched them sport chunks of gold jewelry, beepers and speed by the school in their late-model cars, "monster stereos with up to 1,000 watts" blaring.

The student culture is, some educators say, more important than the influence of the schools and of parents. Reporters have found a culture that pressures students to do the minimum work or be called "nerds." Students say they purposely do not do well because they want to avoid being ostracized. Many don't bother to do the homework, with no punishment by their instructors.

Asked what their parents think of their schoolwork, the little time they spend on homework, their C or worse grades, students say their parents are indifferent. French pointed out that student performance cannot be separated from the problems students take to the classroom.

"It was startling to learn from students how many of their families are disintegrating, no matter what their background," French said. "No one is immune any more. The sense of loss and emptiness and deep-seated anger is palpable in virtually every classroom I visit, from kindergarten through high school."

For French's description of how he went about reporting life inside and outside Largo High School see **A Year at School** in *NRW Plus.*

Maurice Rivenbark,
St. Petersburg Times

Inside Largo High

"I wore my Nikes and stayed away from ties," says Thomas French. Students talked openly with him.

Widening Scope

Some education reporters consider themselves consumer reporters whose job it is to check on the quality of the teachers, the textbooks and the product. They also understand that the schools have become the focus of an intense political battle that ranges from what students should be allowed to read to how the schools should be financed. Every week seems to see battle lines forming in the community over a school issue. Let's start with one of the most contentious—textbooks.

Dumbed Down Textbooks   A study of textbooks by the U.S. Department of Education found that many have decreased in difficulty by two grade levels since the mid-1970s. Few, if any, publishers aim their books at above-average students, the federal study found.

In one Massachusetts school district, the board dropped books by Mark Twain, John Steinbeck, Charles Dickens and others because they feared the authors' books might bore students. Among the books tossed out: *Tom Sawyer* and *A Tale of Two Cities.*

In *The New York Review of Books,* Alexander Stille writes, "The most recent textbooks appear to be designed on the debatable premise that they must compete with Nintendo games and MTV." Such books, he continues, "appeal to the lazier teachers who want both to keep the class busy and to avoid working with longer and more detailed texts."

Dumb Textbooks   Not only have textbooks become less rigorous, but they seem to be seriously flawed. "It is common nowadays to see schoolbooks that are packed, from cover to cover, with blatant factual and conceptual errors," says William F. Benetta who heads a textbook watchdog organization and is editor of its *Textbook Letter.*

The Sun of Baltimore examined textbooks in a lengthy article and found U.S. publishers wanting. It pointed out that a middle school physical science textbook mixed up velocity and acceleration, made two elements liquids that are solids and had grammatical as well as many factual blunders.

It quoted an education official that she was told "by the best mathematicians in the country that the U.S. does not produce a textbook of the caliber we were looking for."

The editor of a major publisher's English composition textbook told prospective authors that they had to anchor their works "in the pop culture" in order to appeal to students, and a journalism textbook writer says her publisher wanted a book revised with "less text."

Library Books   Periodic attempts are made to purge books from school libraries, especially the books that deal with sex, race and sensitive contemporary subjects. Sometimes even the librarian is purged. The West Valley School Board of Kalispell, Mont., fired its grade school librarian after she had helped two seventh-grade students with their research for a class report on witchcraft in the middle ages.

R. L. Chambers

Hopeful Sign

Some educators see the computer literacy of increasingly younger children as an indicator of improvement in educational attainment.

Most Often Banned

Of Mice and Men, John Steinbeck; *The Catcher in the Rye,* J.D. Salinger; *The Adventures of Huckleberry Finn,* Mark Twain; *I Know Why the Caged Bird Sings,* Maya Angelou; *The Color Purple,* Alice Walker.

In Ouachita Parish, La., more than 200 books were removed from a high school library after the principal ordered the librarians to get rid of anything having to do with sex.

In Georgia, a minister asked for the removal of art books from an elementary school library because they contained nudity. He was especially offended by reproductions of Michelangelo's Sistine Chapel and his statue of David.

For additional areas that education reporters look into see **Subjects for Coverage,** in *NRW Plus.*

Politics and Education

The conventional wisdom is that education is "above politics." The proof: The administration of the schools is separated from city government and placed in an independent board whose members are chosen without regard to party affiliation, usually in elections set apart from the partisan campaigning of the regular local election.

The truth is that education is inextricably bound up with politics. Politics enters the scene because, to put it simply, people differ in their notions of how youth should be trained, who should pay for it, who should control it. These differences are resolved in a political context. The conflict and its resolution should be at the heart of much of the reporter's coverage. The political debate runs from the White House to the local school board that meets in the little red schoolhouse.

Prime Example California is the glaring example educators use to prove that education is hip-deep in politics. Once considered to have one of the nation's best public school systems, California's schools have been in "precipitous decline," according to a Rand Corporation education study. The state has 13 percent of the nation's students and is looked to as "an immense laboratory for nearly everything that can go right or wrong with education in America," the Rand study states.

The wrong started with the passage of Proposition 13 in 1978, which limited property tax rates to 1 percent and capped annual increases in property taxes. It was, says the Rand study, "a dramatic turning point in funding for K–12 public education in California." California schools spend far less than the national average, from $600 above the national average in 1978 to $600 below in 22 years.

Property owners want lower taxes, and the political campaign to pass Proposition 13 gave them what they wanted. But they also want good schools, which they have not had: The state's students sit in classes of 21 children. The U.S. average is 16.

Pleased Parents, Disturbing Data

Surveys have shown that a majority of parents are pleased with their children's education. Yet every measure of school achievement contains alarming material about student achievement in many states.

The education reporter who consults the National Assessment of Educational Progress conducted by the U.S. Department of Education has available an unbiased insight into his or her state's schools. A recent NAEP survey found that fourth-graders in 13 states could not read at the "basic" level, defined as "partial mastery" of the knowledge and skills in reading that are expected of a fourth-grader.

These states are Alabama, Arizona, Arkansas, California, Delaware, Florida, Georgia, Hawaii, Louisiana, Maryland, Mississippi, New Mexico and South Carolina.

Nationally, 42 percent of fourth-graders score below the basic level. If we divide this overall figure into ethnic and racial groups, we find these percentages of low-scoring students:

White	32 percent
Black	72
Hispanic	67
Asian	23

The 10 states with the highest scoring fourth-graders in the NAEP test were Connecticut, Indiana, Iowa, Maine, Massachusetts, Montana, Nebraska, New Hampshire, North Dakota and Wisconsin.

For up-to-date NAEP test scores, see http://nces.ed.gov/nationsreportcard/.

Behind the Numbers   Data alone do not tell the full story.

The enterprising reporter will try to find causes for these figures. Among the factors that educators consider to affect academic performance are class size and pupil–teacher ratio. The better performing states showed a much higher overall percentage of classes with fewer than 25 students. Also, the highest pupil–teacher ratio in the better states was 15.8 whereas the lowest ratio in the poor-performing states was 16.6. The median class size for the high-scoring states was 15.3; the median class size for the low-scoring states was 17.3.

Maine's class size averaged 14, California's 21.

Approach With Care   Under the reporting provisions of the No Child Left Behind Act (NCLB), states are given discretion about reporting data on their schools' performance. Some states reported that 80 to 90 percent of their students were reading at the proficient level. But under the more stringent requirements of the National Assessment of Educational Progress (NAEP), the figures were considerably lower for many of these states.

Under NCLB, Mississippi reported that 89 percent of its fourth graders were reading at the proficient level, the highest score in the nation. But the NAEP score for proficiency of the state's fourth graders is 18 percent, next to last in the country. High school graduation rates reflect the same disparities.

Some states, Maryland and Massachusetts among them, are said to give truthful NCLB reports. But in all cases, journalists need to approach NCLB figures with caution. The differences are accounted for by how high or low the state sets its academic standards, which is the area reporters should check.

Covering a School Board Election

Increasingly, school board elections have become the focus of community tensions. As special-interest groups with a conservative agenda put candidates on the ballot, the lines dividing residents grow sharper.

Parents Matter
"If every parent in America made it their patriotic duty to find an extra 30 minutes to help their children learn more each and every day it would literally revolutionize American education."

—*Richard Riley,*
Former Secretary
of Education

Media Generation
The Henry J. Kaiser Family Foundation found children 8 to 18 years old are ravenous electronic consumers. On an average day, their media time is:

Watching TV	3:16
Listening to CDs or tapes	1:05
Listening to the radio	:48
Reading	:44
Using the computer	:31
Playing video games	:27
Using the Internet	:13

In Sioux Falls, S.D., in a school board election, two conservative candidates challenged two incumbents seeking re-election. The incumbents were part of a 3–2 liberal majority, and the local newspaper made it clear that much was at stake in the election: What values shall the community's children be taught, and how would the school board respond to property tax concerns?

Early in the campaign, the *Argus Leader* asked the candidates about these two issues, and it ran their replies along with biographical information about the four candidates. The newspaper was stating what it believed were key issues the candidates should speak about so that voters would have relevant material on which to base their votes.

One of the candidates said that to save money he would eliminate sex education and "social agenda items not academic." As for teaching values, this candidate stated, "We need Bible reading back in the school, not interpretation, but reading."

In her coverage of the election campaign, Corrine Olson explored the candidates' approaches to the teaching of "values." The challengers were quoted as emphasizing "values in the instruction and discipline of children." The incumbents contended that the schools in Sioux Falls have been teaching values and stressed the importance of "tolerance" as "one of the values that should be embraced." One challenger said that Christian teachers should be able to practice their faith in their instruction in the schools.

Paralleling the news coverage, the editorial page set the issues out early. Rob Swenson, the editorial page editor, wrote a month before the election, "Voters will determine whether the board stays the present course or turns further to the right." In a final editorial before the vote, Swenson wrote that voters faced a choice between "ideologues of the radical, religious-tinged right" and the incumbents, described as "moderates" who would join with a liberal member to form a majority of three on the five-member board. The other two incumbents were described as having "reactionary views on issues such as patriotism and sex."

Olson's story of the election results begins:

> Sioux Falls voters decided Tuesday to stick with incumbents just one year after they supported a new direction for the school board.
>
> The incumbents won by a vote of almost two to one.

Board of Education Meetings

School board meetings are often political battlegrounds on which important issues are fought out. The well-prepared reporter is able to provide depth coverage of these issues. The reporter is aware of the positions of the key players on some of the important matters that have come before the board and has kept track of developing issues. Here is a guide to covering board meetings.

Meetings Checklist

___Actions taken.

___How each member voted. If no formal vote but an informal consensus, get nods of heads or any other signs of approval or disapproval. Ask if uncertain.

___Size and makeup of audience.

___Reaction of audience to proposal(s).

___Position of groups or organizations with a position on issue. (Obtain beforehand, if possible.)

___Arguments on all sides.

___Statements from those for and against proposal on what decision of board means.

Mike Roemer, *Argus Leader*

"Control Spending, Emphasize Values"

A candidate in a school board election in Sioux Falls, S.D., outlines her program for the local schools. She wants administrative cutbacks to protect teaching positions and calls for a return to "basics" in instruction, along with an emphasis on "values."

Education Rankings

The Morgan Quitno Press in Lawrence Kan., issues annual state rankings in various fields. In its education report, it considered 21 factors to establish a state's rank, among them: financial support for teachers and students; high school graduation rates; reading, mathematics and writing scores of fourth and eighth graders; pupil–teacher ratios; class size; teacher safety. Here are the top and the bottom five:

Top
Vermont
Connecticut
Massachusetts
New Jersey
Maine

Bottom
California
Nevada
New Mexico
Mississippi
Arizona

New Educational Programs

Many meetings of school boards are concerned with new programs. Here is a checklist of items for the reporter:

Checklist

___Source of idea.

___Superiority to present program as claimed by sponsors.

___Cost and source of funding program.

___Basic philosophy or idea of program.

___Other places it has been tried and results there. (Make independent check of this, if possible. How well is it working there? What is cost?)

___Whether it has been tried before and discarded.

___How does it fit in with what system is doing now? How it fits with trends in area, state, nation.

___If someone is suggested to head it, who?

___Arguments pro and con, naming those involved.

Knowing the Community

In this chapter, we have looked at how local government works, the role of money in the community, politics and education. There's much more to covering a community, of course, and the following 20 questions touch on some of these areas of community life the reporter should know about. The list was compiled by Gloria Brown Anderson, executive editor of *The New York Times* news service:

1. How is your community different from others in your state? How did it come to be established where it is?

2. Who are the major employers? What's the unemployment rate?

3. What are the most popular entertainment activities? What single event in the past year drew the biggest crowd?

4. What are the major institutional assets (museums, colleges, tourist attractions, sports teams, etc.)?

5. Who are the town characters? Who's the most powerful person in town (politics, business, sports, education, etc.)?

6. Who are your experts and what are their fields of expertise?

7. What's the dominant religion/philosophy? How are people treated who are not part of it?

8. What's driving the economy? (May not be the same as dominant employers.)

9. What are the major social problems?

10. Who are the most creative people in town (business, the arts, education, social scene, etc.)?

11. How many people move into your community every week? How many people leave? Why are they coming and going?

12. What's been the biggest change in the nature of the community in the past 10 years?

13. What's the high school dropout rate? Do most high school students go to college?

14. What legends or true stories do old-timers tell and retell?

15. How old is the oldest business and what is it?

16. What famous/accomplished people have roots in the community?

17. What kinds of books have been your community's best-sellers over the past five years?

18. What are the most popular TV shows? How many people have cable?

19. What happens in your community that has a significant impact on people elsewhere?

20. What's the demographic profile of your town? How does it compare with nearby communities?

Further Reading

Cremin, Lawrence A. *Transformation of the School: Progressivism in American Education.* New York: Random House, 1964.

French, Thomas. *South of Heaven: Welcome to High School at the End of the Twentieth Century.* New York: Doubleday, 1993.

Kozol, Jonathan. *The Shame of the Nation: The Restoration of Apartheid Schooling.* New York: Crown, 2005.

> Kozol says schools throughout the country are as racially imbalanced as they were before *Brown v. Board of Education,* and that in many of the minority classrooms there is little meaningful instruction. Kozol devotes much of his research to interviews with school children rather than school administrators.

Nathan, Rebekah. *My Freshman Year: What a Professor Learned by Becoming a Student.* Ithaca, New York: Cornell University Press, 2005.

> Nathan, an anthropology professor, disguised herself as a first-year college student at an unidentified state university. (Nathan is a pseudonym.) She found few students involve themselves in the intellectual life of the university and few are involved in extracurricular activities. Student–teacher relationships are few, and classroom discussions steer clear of controversy. (The ethics of disguises is discussed in Chapter 27.)

Rathbone, Cristina. *On the Outside Looking In.* Boston: Atlantic Monthly Press, 1998. (The author spent a year in a high school for rejects.)

Ravitch, Diane. *The Language Police.* New York; Knopf, 2003.

Ravitch documents the self-censorship of publishers as they surrender to pressure groups, and the timidity of schools in giving in to such political correctness as:

- The elimination of "Founding Father" because it is "sexist."
- Men may not be shown as strong and brave but as nurturing helpmates.
- Older people cannot age into feebleness and dependency but must fix the roof and jog.
- No disobedient children may be depicted.
- "Men may not appear as plumbers and lawyers; women can."

Sayre, Wallace S., and Herbert Kaufman. *Governing New York City.* New York: Norton, 1965.

Wildavsky, Aaron. *The Politics of the Budgetary Process,* 2nd ed. Boston: Little, Brown, 1974.

Part 6: Laws, Taste and Taboos, Codes and Ethics

Part Six: Introduction

The final three chapters contain general guidelines for the journalist. As in most of journalism, there are few absolutes in these areas, and even those we tend to think of as unchanging do shift in time. Take libel law: Before 1964, libel was state law and journalists had to exercise special care, for what was acceptable in one state could be the basis of a lawsuit in another. But with the Supreme Court decision in *The New York Times v. Sullivan* everything changed. In Chapter 25, we will examine the wide latitude this decision has given journalists.

Considerable changes have occurred in the area of taste as well. When once journalists were hemmed in by a long list of taboos and agreed-upon prohibitions, in this Age of Candor, little seems off-limits, as we shall see in Chapter 26.

The last chapter, 27, takes us to the area of ethics, and here, too, journalism has changed. Once-acceptable practices are now considered unethical, such as racial and religious identifications.

The areas overlap, as the photo of a family's grief on page 546 illustrates. It was legal for the photographer to snap this public scene at a California beach. But is it so wrenching that it approaches bad taste to spread the photo across the page of a newspaper? Another question: Is it an invasion of this family's privacy to show them grieving moments after the child's body was recovered? This is a matter of ethics, the morality of journalism. The newspaper apologized later, but the photographer said use of the photo was a public service in that it illustrates what can happen when water safety rules are not observed.

Preview

The laws of libel and privacy limit what reporters may write.

- **Libel:** Most libelous stories are the result of careless reporting. The courts have made it more difficult for public figures or public officials to prove libel.
- **Privacy:** The right to privacy is protected by law. The personal activities of an individual can be reported if the material is about a newsworthy person and is not highly offensive.

Journalists can use material without worrying about libel if the report is full, fair, accurate and free of malice. Also, statements in legislative hearings and courts can be reported.

Hidden electronic devices used in newsgathering intrude on a person's privacy.

Dave McDermand,
The Bryan-College Station Eagle
Mourning students' deaths—an intrusion of privacy?

One of the thorniest areas for the journalist is libel. To the beginner, libel inhabits a land of mystery in which all the guideposts read, "Don't." To the experienced reporter, libel is a cautionary presence in the newsroom.

Libel is published false and malicious information that defames a person. It is writing or pictures that:

- Expose a person to hatred, shame, disgrace, contempt or ridicule.
- Injure a person's reputation or cause the person to be shunned or avoided.
- Injure the person in his or her occupation.

Of course, many articles and pictures do libel individuals. In most cases, the defamatory material may be safe for publication or broadcast if it is *privileged.* By privileged, we mean that the article is a fair and accurate report of a judicial, legislative or other public official proceeding and of anything said in the course of such sessions, trials or proceedings. The contents

When in doubt, check it out.

of most public records are privileged. Those who made our laws recognized that open debate of serious issues would be impeded unless the public had full access to official actions.

Another defense against libel is *truth.* No matter how serious the defamation may be, if the statement can be proved to be true and to have been made without malice, the defamed individual cannot successfully bring legal action.

A third defense, *fair comment and criticism,* usually involves editorial writers and reviewers. As long as the comment or criticism is directed at the work and not at the individual, the writing is safe.

In summary, the libel laws hold that a reporter is not in danger if the material is from a privileged proceeding (public *and* official) or if the material is substantially accurate or constitutes fair comment.

For broadcast journalists, defamatory statements made from a prepared script fall under libel, whereas extemporaneous defamatory remarks are treated as *slander,* which is defined as oral or uttered defamation.

Grounds for Libel Suits

Matter that might be held libelous by a court would have to:

1. Imply commission of a crime.

2. Tend to injure a person in his or her profession or job.

3. Imply a person has a disease, usually a loathsome disease that might lead to the individual's ostracism.

4. Damage a person's credit.

5. Imply unchaste behavior.

6. Indicate a lack of mental capacity.

7. Incite public ridicule or contempt.

For years, libel was a great weight on the shoulders of the press, particularly for newspapers that handled controversy and emphasized investigative reporting. The press associations and national publications had special concerns, for libel law was state law and was beyond the protection of the Constitution. What was legal in one state might have been libelous in another.

In effect, libel laws restrained the press, as the Supreme Court recognized in an epochal decision in 1964 that was to lighten the burden on the press. The court ruled that defamatory statements could have First Amendment protection. Our seven danger points are still to be watched, but the press now has much stronger defenses, thanks to the Supreme Court. To understand that decision—and to understand the organic nature of the law—we must travel back in time to Montgomery, Ala.

An Incident on a Bus

When Rosa Parks boarded the Cleveland Avenue bus in December 1955, she spotted an empty seat just behind the section reserved for whites. Tired from a day's work in a downtown department store, she eased into the space, only to be ordered to move as more white passengers boarded. Seats were for white passengers only.

Mrs. Parks, a quiet, reserved woman, refused to give up her seat. She was taken off the bus and arrested. That weekend, plans were made by the black community to boycott Montgomery's buses.

Martin Luther King Jr., a black minister who helped plan the boycott, recalled how he awoke early Monday morning to see whether Montgomery's black residents would heed the word that it was better to walk in dignity than to ride in shame. The bus line that passed by the King home carried more blacks than any other line in the city. The first bus went by at 6 a.m. It was empty. Another, 15 minutes later, was empty, too.

That was the beginning of the boycott. Some 42,000 Montgomery blacks said they would walk to and from work or use volunteer vehicles and black-owned taxis until the bus system altered its seating arrangements and hired black drivers for buses along the predominantly black routes.

For 381 days, they stayed off the buses rather than be told to move to the back. Many people went to jail for violating the state's anti-boycott laws, including Mrs. Parks and Dr. King. Finally, the Supreme Court ruled bus segregation illegal.

Tension Mounts

The struggle against segregation intensified. The response was lethal. In 1963, Medgar Evers, a black civil rights worker, was murdered in the doorway of his home in Jackson, Miss. The following year, three young civil rights workers were murdered in Philadelphia, Miss.

Newspapers and television stations sent waves of reporters to the South to report the conflict. Viewers saw fire hoses, police dogs and cattle prods used on blacks in Birmingham, and they saw the clubs of state troopers in Selma. The press reported the cry of blacks for an end to humiliation, economic exploitation, segregation in schools and discrimination at the polls.

It was also obvious the South was hardly budging. The border areas, portions of Tennessee and Kentucky and metropolitan communities such as Atlanta and Richmond accommodated. But not the towns and parishes of the Black Belt—Selma, Plaquemines, Yazoo City. Here, nonviolence met intractable resistance. Blacks might wait patiently outside the courthouse in Selma to register to vote. But the doors would stay closed to them, unless they were broken down by the federal government and the courts.

Press Coverage Increases

Because of the intensive coverage in the press, a consensus was developing outside the Black Belt. Most of the nation saw the anguish of the blacks who were

Press Role

Some newspapers, notably *The Arkansas Gazette,* called for an end to segregation. Others, notably the Media General chain, supported the status quo. Those calling for an end to discriminatory practices suffered financially. (See Chapter 27.)

hurling themselves against the wall of segregation. Some believed the nation was heading toward a race war.

In 1963, President Kennedy, aware of the developing conflict, declared that the struggle of blacks for civil rights was a "moral issue." Then four girls attending Sunday school in the black Sixteenth Street Baptist Church in Birmingham died in a bomb blast at the church.

The press stepped up its coverage. In some northern newspapers and on network television, the South was presented as a forbidding region of racism, its law officers openly defiant of the law, its white citizens unwilling to adjust to the changing times. Some southerners were so angered by the coverage they assaulted reporters covering civil rights demonstrations. The retaliation also took the form of suits against the press and television.

A Legal Club

Millions of dollars in damages were claimed by officials, who asserted they had been defamed by press and television. By 1964, libel suits seeking $300 million were pending against news organizations covering the racial story. One of the largest suits was brought against *The New York Times* by five officials in Alabama who contended that they had been inferentially damaged in an advertisement in the *Times* in 1960 that sought to raise funds for the civil rights movement. The advertisement, headlined "Heed Their Rising Voices," described the treatment of black schoolchildren by the Alabama police. The five officials brought suit for a total of $3 million.

Sullivan Case   The first case to be tried involved L.B. Sullivan, a Montgomery city commissioner responsible for the police department. The judge in the case ordered segregated seating in the courtroom, and after he praised the "white man's justice" that had been brought to the country by the "Anglo-Saxon race," the all-white jury heard testimony. The jurors, whose names and photographs were printed in the local press, were told that although Sullivan's name had not been mentioned in the advertisement, his reputation had been damaged by the erroneous statements about the police.

During the trial, it was evident that the advertisement contained errors. It stated that Montgomery students had been expelled from school after singing "My Country 'Tis of Thee" on the steps of the state capitol. Actually, they were expelled for a sit-in in the courthouse grill. The advertisement also said students had been locked out of their lunchroom to "starve them into submission," which was false.

The jury agreed that Sullivan had been libeled and awarded him $500,000 in compensatory and punitive damages from the *Times.*

In a headline over the story about the suits against the *Times,* a Montgomery newspaper seemed to reveal the motives behind the libel suits: "State Finds Formidable Legal Club to Swing at Out-of-State Press."

The Court Acts

It was in this atmosphere that the Supreme Court considered the appeal of the *Times* from the state court decision. The case of *The New York Times v. Sullivan* (376 US 254) in 1964 was to mark a major change in the libel laws. But more important, by granting the press wider latitude in covering and commenting on the actions of public officials, the decision gave the press greater freedom to present issues of public concern, like the racial conflict that was tearing the country apart.

The Supreme Court understood the unique nature of the appeal. The Court commented, "We are required for the first time in this case to determine the extent to which the Constitutional protections for speech and press limit a state's power to award damages in a libel action brought by a public official against the critics of his official conduct."

In its decision, the Supreme Court took from the states their power to award damages for libel "in actions brought by public officials against critics of their official conduct." The Constitutional protections for free speech and free press would be seriously limited by state actions of the kind the Alabama court took, the Court said.

Brennan's Opinion

Justice William J. Brennan wrote, "The Constitutional guarantees require, we think, a federal rule that prohibits a public official from recovering damages for a defamatory falsehood relating to his official conduct unless he proves that the statement was made with 'actual malice'—that is, with knowledge that it was false or with reckless disregard to whether it was false or not."

The Court apparently agreed with the argument of Herbert F. Wechsler, who wrote in a brief for the *Times*, "This is not a time—there never was a time—when it would serve the values enshrined in the Constitution to force the press to curtail its attention to the tensest issues that confront the country or to forgo the dissemination of its publications in the areas where tension is extreme."

Justice Brennan noted in his opinion that the Supreme Court had seen in the use of such legal concepts as "insurrection," "contempt," "breach of the peace," "obscenity" and "solicitation of legal business" attempts to suppress the open discussion of public issues. Now it was libel.

First Amendment Extended   In the Sullivan libel case, the Court extended the First Amendment in order to accomplish a social-political purpose—the protection of dissident voices in a repressive atmosphere. The right to criticize government, Brennan wrote, is "the central meaning of the First Amendment."

The decision, establishing what became known as the Times Doctrine, noted that the "Constitutional safeguard was fashioned to assure unfettered interchange of ideas for the bringing about of political and social changes desired by the people." To accomplish this, there must be "maintenance of the opportunity for free political discussion to the end that government may be responsive to the will of the people and that changes may be obtained by lawful means, an opportunity essential to the security of the Republic. . . ."

"Erroneous statement is inevitable in free debate," Brennan said. Running through the decision is the belief that free discussion will lead to a peaceful settlement of issues. Free expression, he was saying, has social utility. The Court seemed to be addressing itself to the millions of Americans in trauma because of the racial conflict.

Politic Action

The Sullivan case, like the school desegregation case 10 years before and the Nixon tapes decision 10 years later, reflected the need for a unanimous court decision in order to show the nation that certain issues were beyond debate.

The Sullivan decision supported a searching, vigorous and free press. *Brown v. Board of Education, Topeka,* said the 14th Amendment guaranteeing equal protection under the laws made school segregation unconstitutional.

The Watergate tape decision came at a time the president was under grave suspicion and a crisis of leadership threatened the nation.

"Throughout history," said an editorial writer for *The New York Times,* "the Court has been a vital factor on the political scene, even when trying to float majestically above it."

Robert T. Willett,
The News & Observer

No Question

Politicians and those in elective and appointive offices are public figures and must prove actual malice to prevail in any libel suit they may bring.

Coaches, Too

A Kentucky court ruled that an assistant basketball coach at the University of Kentucky was a public figure and thus had to prove actual malice. The coach had sued the *Lexington Herald-Leader* for its series on recruiting violations. The coach said the series had defamed him and ruined his career. A circuit court judge issued a directed verdict that the coach had failed to prove actual malice and dismissed the libel suit. The judge said there had been "no reckless disregard" for the truth.

"Actual Malice" In summary, the decision in the case makes it clear that, under the Constitution, no public official can recover damages for defamation in a newspaper article or "editorial advertisement" concerning his or her official conduct unless he or she can prove the article is defamatory and false and also show that:

1. The publication was made with the knowledge that it was false; or

2. The statement was made with reckless disregard of whether or not it was false.

Items 1 and 2 constitute the Court's concept of "actual malice."

The decision is the law in every state and takes precedence over federal and state laws, state constitutions and all previous state and federal court decisions. The decision applies to public figures as well as to public officials.

Courts Differ

Just where is the line that divides a public figure from a private figure? The Supreme Court has not clarified the point. Lower courts have differed.

The Washington Post escaped a libel judgment when a federal district court ruled a police informant was a public figure and had to prove actual malice. The *Post* had incorrectly stated the informant was a drug user. But three months later, a federal judge in Maryland ruled that a police informant was a private individual and thus need only prove that a Baltimore newspaper was careless in mistakenly stating he had broken into a lawyer's office to steal documents for the police.

In state courts, a Kansas judge ruled that a lawyer appointed to defend a penniless criminal defendant was a public official. Two months later, a Michigan judge said that an attorney appointed to represent an impoverished defendant was neither public figure nor public official.

In Virginia, a circuit court ruled that a high school English teacher was a public figure. The teacher had sued the *Richmond Times-Dispatch* for a story that criticized her teaching. She appealed and the state Supreme Court concluded she was not a public figure because she was in no position to influence or control "any public affairs or school policy." The newspaper appealed to the U.S. Supreme Court and lost. The teacher was awarded $100,000.

Police Officers The Supreme Court may have clarified the status of police officers. In 1989, it ruled that an officer that *The Danville* (Ill.) *Commercial News* had linked to a suspected burglary ring was a public official and would have to prove actual malice. A student newspaper at Cleveland State University profited from this decision when a suit in which a campus police officer sought $300,000 in damages was dismissed. The newspaper had stated in an editorial that the officer had a reputation for "excessive force, brutality and discrimination."

Caution: Events that are the subject of gossip or public curiosity and have no significant relation to public affairs usually do not confer on the persons involved in them the status of public figures. This means that no matter how public a person's marriage rift may be, that person is not necessarily a public figure.

Public Officials and Public Figures

Public officials: Government employees who have responsibility for governmental activities—elected officials, candidates for political office, appointed officials such as judges, police officers and some others engaged in the criminal justice system. The Supreme Court has said that not all public employees are public officials.

Public figures: People who have considerable power and influence and those who "voluntarily thrust" themselves into public controversy. Newspaper columnists, television personalities and some celebrities who seek to influence the public are included. But not all prominent people are covered.

If the reporter can prove that an event relates to public affairs or an important social issue, then the persons involved may be classified as public figures. For example, if a physician or a lawyer injects himself or herself into a controversy over a local bond issue, then the person has become a public figure for news about the bonds but not about his or her personal life.

Attributing a Libel Is No Defense

In a story about a development scheme in an area adjacent to the university, a student newspaper said that a member of the local planning board had received a "kickback" from the developer. (A kickback is an under-the-table payment for special treatment.) Asked whether he knew that such a charge is clearly libelous, the student replied, "But I attributed it."

His instructor could only shrug in exasperation. A reporter can be held liable if he or she repeats a libelous statement or quotes someone making such a statement unless the original material is privileged.

If the assertion had been made in court or at an official meeting, the statement—even if untrue—would be privileged and the privilege would be a defense against claims for damages, provided the report was fair and accurate.

Costly Attribution   When the FBI zeroed in on a suspect in a deadly bombing at the Summer Olympics in Atlanta, the media identified the supposed bomber. Tom Brokaw on NBC said the investigators were close to "making the case" and that they "probably have enough to arrest him right now, probably enough to prosecute him, but you always want to have enough to convict him as well. There are still holes in the case."

Yes, there were holes in the case, holes so wide the FBI finally admitted it had spent two months investigating the wrong man, a security guard who had seen a suspicious backpack just before the explosion.

The *Atlanta Journal-Constitution* also used the FBI's identification: "Richard Jewell . . . fits the profile of the lone bomber."

When the media hunt was over, Jewell clearly had grounds for a libel suit. Rather than contest it, NBC settled for what was reported to be $500,000. The

New York *Daily News* headlined the settlement story: BROKAW GOOFED AND NBC PAID. CNN also settled with Jewell.

Court Battles　The Atlanta newspaper refused to settle and a lengthy and costly court process ensued. One court ruled that Jewell had become a public figure, which required him to prove that the newspaper report was made with "actual malice." Jewell's suit collapsed when the newspaper showed that it had acted in good faith by quoting official sources about Jewell as a suspect.

But Jewell appealed and his lawyer showed the court videotaped depositions by several of the newspaper's copy editors who said they were concerned the paper's coverage could be libelous. The depositions would support Jewell's contention that involving him in the bombing was in "reckless disregard" of whether the material was false. Jewell died while his appeal was pending.

A similar case arose in Wichita, Kan., when a television station named a suspect in the BTK serial killings. The police had raided the man's home but he was never charged in connection with the killings. A jury ordered KSNW-TV and its news director to pay the man $1 million in damages. The man died before he could collect. (Kansas law holds that a libel award does not survive the plaintiff's death.)

The Lesson　The point is clear: Reporters must make sure that charges have been filed before naming suspects in criminal matters. What the police or other officials **say** they are doing or **plan** to do are not official actions and thus are not privileged.

Conditional and Absolute Privilege

The privilege to those participating in court cases and legislative sessions is an "absolute privilege," meaning the participants—the judge, lawyers, witnesses—cannot be held legally accountable even for malicious and deliberately false statements that are made within the scope of their participation in the proceedings. A newspaper or station, however, cannot use absolute privilege as a defense in libel suits. Their protection is known as "conditional" or "qualified privilege." The newspaper must present full, fair and accurate reports that are free of actual malice in order to be granted privilege.

A candidate for re-election to Congress who says of his opponent, "That man is a swindler" on the floor of the House of Representatives can make the statement with impunity, and a reporter can publish the accusation. (Obviously, the reporter would also carry the accused's reply.) But should the congressman make the charge in a political rally and the reporter's newspaper print the allegation, both are in trouble, unless the reporter can prove the man is indeed a swindler, and this would require proof of the man's conviction on that charge.

Warning: These protections do not cover proceedings, meetings, or activities that are private in nature. They also do not cover records that are sealed by law or court order.

Hot News and Time Copy

The Supreme Court has been generous to reporters who make mistakes under pressure of deadline. But reporters who have time to check material may not fare so well under the Court's distinction between "hot news" and "time copy." The differences were spelled out in two companion cases decided in 1967, *Curtis Publishing Co. v. Butts* and *Associated Press v. Walker* (both 388 US 130), involving public figures.

Edwin Walker was a former Army general who had become involved in the civil rights disputes in the South and had taken a position against desegregation. He was on the campus of the University of Mississippi in September 1962 when it erupted over the enrollment of James Meredith, a black student.

The AP moved a story that Walker had taken command of a violent crowd and had personally led a charge against federal marshals on the campus. The AP said Walker had encouraged rioters to use violence and had instructed white students how to combat the effects of tear gas. He sued for $800,000 in damages. Walker testified that he had counseled restraint and peaceful protest and had not charged the marshals. The jury believed his account and awarded him the sum he sought. The trial judge cut out the $300,000 in punitive damages because he found no actual malice in the AP account.

Game Fix   Wally Butts was the athletic director of the University of Georgia in 1962. He was employed by the Georgia Athletic Association, a private corporation, and so, like Walker, he was a private citizen when, according to *The Saturday Evening Post,* he conspired to fix a football game between Georgia and Alabama in 1962. An article in the magazine said an Atlanta insurance salesman had overheard a conversation between Butts and Bear Bryant, coach of the Alabama football team, in which Butts outlined Georgia's offensive strategy in the coming game and advised Bryant about defending against the plays.

Butts sued for $5 million in compensatory damages and $5 million in punitive damages. The jury awarded him $60,000 on the first charge and $3 million on the second, which was subsequently reduced to $460,000.

Winner, Loser   The Curtis Publishing Co., publishers of *The Saturday Evening Post,* and the AP appealed to the Supreme Court. Butts won his appeal, but Walker lost. The Court ruled that the evidence showed that the Butts story was not "hot news," but that the Walker story was. The *Post*'s editors, the Court stated, "recognized the need for a thorough investigation of the serious charges" but failed to make the investigation.

In the Walker case, the Court noted, "In contrast to the Butts article, the dispatch which concerns us in *Walker* was news which required immediate dissemination. . . . Considering the necessity for rapid dissemination, nothing in this series of events gives the slightest hint of a severe departure from publishing standards. We therefore conclude that Walker should not be entitled to damages from the Associated Press."

Punitive Damages
"Money a court awards to an individual who has been harmed in a malicious or willful way. The amount is not related to the actual cost of the injury or harm suffered. Its purpose is to keep that sort of act from happening again. Punitive damages serve as a deterrent."

—*Daniel Oran,
Law Dictionary
for Non-Lawyers*

Accuracy the Best Route

Most libel cases originate in a reporter's error. The lesson is clear: Follow Joseph Pulitzer's three rules for journalism, "Accuracy, accuracy, accuracy," or risk trouble.

Well, you might say, look at how many cases the media won despite the mis-takes. True, but in most of these cases the legal costs were ferocious. It can cost up to a million dollars for the average case, and *Time* estimated that had it not won its case quickly when the Scientology organization sued, its legal fees might have amounted to $10 million to $15 million in a drawn-out case.

Accuracy means checking everything yourself, not accepting someone's word or work as fact. This lesson was hard-learned by the authors of an ethics handbook published by the Society of Professional Journalists and the Poynter Institute for Media Studies. An anchor at KXAS-TV in Dallas filed a libel suit alleging he was unfairly portrayed as having a conflict of interest in acting as a "master of ceremonies during rallies for [George W.] Bush at several campaign stops." The publishers apologized and paid the anchor's $18,000 legal fees. In its statement of apology, the publishers said a researcher had incorrectly summarized information that had been published in a Fort Worth newspaper.

Libel Online

The U.S. Supreme Court has given the Internet the same First Amendment protection as the print media, but the laws are being written about where respon-sibility lies for libel.

Matt Drudge, the Internet tipster-gossip who puts out The Drudge Report, car-ried an item that the communications adviser to President Clinton, Sidney Blu-menthal, had beaten his wife. His sources were identified as "top GOP operatives" who told Drudge "there are court records" to prove their charge. Drudge did not produce the records, and Blumenthal sued.

Drudge retracted, saying he had been used "to broadcast dirty laundry. I think I've been had."

Who is liable? Not the carrier, AOL. Online service providers were immu-nized from libel suits in the Internet Decency statute. But Drudge is not exempt.

Next, to another cautionary area, that of privacy, an area that is increasingly troublesome to journalists because of the public's anger at the media for what it considers media intrusiveness.

Privacy

Whereas truth is the strongest defense against libel, it is the basis of inva-sion of privacy suits. Invasion of privacy is said to occur when an individual is exposed to public view and suffers mental distress as a consequence of the pub-licity. Unlike defamation, which has deep roots in the common law, the right to privacy is a fairly new legal development and one in which there is less certainty for the reporter than in the area of libel.

A balance must be struck by the courts between the public's right to know—a right commonly accepted though not in the Constitution—and the individual's right to privacy.

Three categories of privacy concern the reporter:

1. Publicity that places a person in a false light in the public eye. The Times Doctrine applies, provided the matter is of public interest.

2. Public disclosure of embarrassing private facts about an individual. If the facts are in an official document, they can be published, but not if they are private acts of no legitimate concern to the public.

3. Intrusion by the journalist into a private area for a story or a picture without permission—eavesdropping or trespassing. The use of electronic devices to invade a home or office is illegal. Newsworthiness is not a defense.

The Test: Newsworthiness

Except for intrusion, the newsworthiness of the event is a defense against invasion of privacy suits. A public event cannot have privacy grafted on it at the behest of the participants. However, the reporter cannot invade a person's home or office to seek out news and make public what is private. Nor can he or she misrepresent the purpose of reporting to gain access to home or office. There is no prohibition against following and watching a person in a public place, but the reporter cannot harass an individual.

Although the law of libel and the right of privacy are closely related, they involve distinctive legal principles and are fundamentally different. Libel law is designed to protect a person's character and reputation. The right of privacy protects a person's peace of mind, feelings, spirits and sensibilities. Generally, privacy guarantees an individual freedom from the unwarranted and unauthorized public exposure of the person or his or her affairs in which the public has no legitimate interest.

The right of privacy is the right of a person to be let alone unless he or she waives or relinquishes that right. Certain people, defined by the federal courts as "newsworthy," lose their right to privacy, but the material published about them cannot be "highly offensive."

In making rulings on the claim of invasion of privacy, the Supreme Court has applied the Times Doctrine. That is, even if the claimant could prove that the report was false, if it were a matter of public interest, the person bringing the action would have to show the error was made "with knowledge of its falsity or in reckless disregard of the truth."

"Calculated Falsehoods"

In one case, decided in 1974 by the Supreme Court, such disregard of the truth was proved by a claimant. The Court in *Cantrell v. Forest City Publishing Co.* (419 US 245) upheld an award against *The Plain Dealer* in Cleveland

---

Ride-Alongs

The U.S. Supreme Court ruled that police officers who take along a reporter into a private home during a search or seizure operation violate the Fourth Amendment. The police are liable, and the reporter risks being sued for trespass or invasion of private property.

Pictures

The picture was stark and it led to a suit for invasion of privacy. The photo in *Today* of Cocoa, Fla., showed a woman covered only by a towel as she fled from a house where her estranged husband had kept her hostage. A lower court jury awarded her $10,000 in damages, but the state Supreme Court upheld an appeals court decision that overturned the verdict.

The appeals court said the law is clear "that when one becomes an actor in an occurrence of public interest, it is not an invasion of privacy to publish her photograph with an account of such occurrence. . . . The published photograph is more a depiction of grief, fright, emotional tension and flight than it is an appeal to other sensual appetites."

on the ground that a reporter's story about a visit to the home of the claimant "contained significant misrepresentations." Although the woman was not at home when the reporter visited, the article said she "will talk neither about what happened nor about how they were doing. . . ." He wrote that the widow "wears the same mask of nonexpression she wore at the funeral." A lower court jury awarded her $60,000 to compensate for the mental distress and shame the article caused. An appeals court reversed the verdict, and the woman appealed to the Supreme Court, which found the reporter's statements implying that the woman had been interviewed were "calculated falsehoods."

Rape Victims   Some months later, the Supreme Court ruled on the second category involving privacy—the rights of private individuals to keep their personal affairs from public disclosure. In this case, the Court nullified a Georgia law that made it a misdemeanor to print or broadcast the name of a rape victim. The case involved the father of a young woman who had been raped and killed by a gang of teen-age boys. An Atlanta television station had used the victim's name, and the state court had ruled in favor of the father under the state law. The station appealed.

In setting aside the Georgia law, the Supreme Court stated that "once true information is disclosed in public court documents open to public inspection, the press cannot be sanctioned for publishing it." The Court stated (in *Cox Broadcasting Corp. v. Martin Cohn,* 420 US 469):

> The commission of crimes, prosecutions resulting therefrom, and judicial proceedings arising from the prosecutions are events of legitimate concern to the public and consequently fall within the press' responsibility to report the operations of government.

In both cases, the Supreme Court cautioned against broad interpretations of its rulings. Nevertheless, the first case clearly indicates that the press must take care in publishing material about individuals that is false, and the second indicates the Court will not extend the right of privacy to private persons involved in actions described in official documents.

Privacy Guideline   Here is a useful guide from a federal appeals court ruling:

> A reporter or publication that gives publicity to the private life of a person is not subject to liability for unreasonable invasion of privacy if the material (1) is about a newsworthy person—who need not be an elected official or a celebrity—and (2) is not "highly offensive to a reasonable person, one of ordinary sensibilities and is of legitimate public concern."

Secret Taping

The courts are not sympathetic to the use of hidden electronic devices for newsgathering. When used, the courts have ruled, they can intrude on a person's right to privacy. In a 1998 decision, the California Supreme Court ruled that newspapers and television stations can be sued for intrusion if reporters or photographers are "unlawfully spying on them in the name of news gathering." And the following year, the Court ruled against an ABC News reporter who had secretly recorded an employee of a psychic hot line.

Telephone Taping   Reporters routinely tape their telephone conversations with sources who are sensitive about being quoted accurately. In most states, one-party consent (the reporter's) is all that is necessary. But in 10 states all parties involved must agree to the taping—California, Connecticut, Illinois, Maryland, Massachusetts, Montana, New Hampshire, Pennsylvania, South Dakota and Washington.

Avoiding the Dangers

The guide in libel and invasion of privacy suits seems fairly clear. Caution is necessary when the following are *not* involved—public officials, public figures, public events. When a private individual is drawn into the news, the news report must be full, fair and accurate. Of course, no journalist relies on the law for loopholes. He or she is always fair and accurate in coverage.

Libel suits usually result from:

- Carelessness.

- Exaggerated or enthusiastic writing.

- Opinions not based on facts.

- Statements of officials or informants made outside a privileged situation.

- Inadequate verification.

- Failure to check with the subject of the defamation.

When a libel has been committed, a retraction should be published. Although a retraction is not a defense, it serves to lessen damages and may deprive the plaintiff of punitive damages.

Rush + Inference = Libel Troubles

Most libel suits result from a reporter's rush to publish or broadcast the story. The usual care is not exercised in the speed-up. When the *New York Post* reported that Whitney Houston had been hospitalized in Miami after overdosing on diet pills, a $60 million libel suit was filed. The reporters handling the story would have learned it was a hoax had they called the hospital, which had no record of the singer's admission or treatment. The newspaper retracted the story the next day.

Libel suits also result from one of our old enemies—the inference, or jumping from the known to the unknown. A copy editor for an Indiana newspaper wrote this headline over the story of the closing of a restaurant: "Health board shuts doors at Bandido's; Investigators find rats, bugs at north-side eatery." The restaurant owner sued, contending the investigators did not find rats in his eatery.

The copy editor testified in the trial: "When I saw the word 'rodent' or 'rodent droppings,' that said rats to me."

The jury awarded the restaurant owner $985,000, and the newspaper appealed. See **A Rodent Is Not a Rat** in *NRW Plus.*

The Reporter's Rights

The press carries a heavy burden. It has taken on the task of gathering and publishing the news, interpreting and commenting on the news and acting as watchdog in the public interest over wide areas of public concern. The burden of the press has been lightened by the foresight of the Founding Fathers through the guarantee in the First Amendment of the Constitution that Congress shall make no law abridging freedom of speech or of the press. This means that the press has the right to publish what it finds without prior restraint.

To journalists, it also means that they have the freedom to gather and prepare news and that the processes involved in these activities are shielded from a prying government and others. Also, journalists understood that their sources, their notes, their thoughts and their discussions with sources and their editors were protected.

Wide Protection

They had good reason to believe all this. State legislatures and the courts interpreted the concept of press freedom to cover wide areas of news gathering and publication. In 1896, for example, the state of Maryland passed a law allowing reporters to conceal their sources from the courts and from other officials. The concern of the public traditionally has been that the press be free and strong enough to counterpose a powerful executive. This sensitivity to central government began with the revolution against the British Crown. It was reinforced by the generations of immigrants who fled czars, kings, dictators and tyrants.

But Not Absolute

There is, however, no clear-cut constitutional statement giving the press the privileges it came to consider immutable. Absolute freedom of the press has never been endorsed by a majority of the Supreme Court. In the 1970s following Watergate, as the press started to dig and check with growing tenacity, a former ally in its battles with governmental power—the judiciary—began to render decisions the press found to be increasingly restricting. Many of these decisions—particularly those of the Supreme Court—convinced the press that its assumptions about its privileges were false. The press, the courts ruled, has no greater rights than any citizen of the land.

In its balancing of the public right to know against individual rights to privacy and the accused's rights to a fair trial, the courts denied the confidentiality of sources, the protection of unpublished material and the privacy of the editorial process. The courts gradually limited the press' access to information, and some newsgathering was specifically prohibited.

News Gathering

There are, of course, still wide areas of news gathering open to the press. Generally, the actions of official bodies are accessible to journalists. Judicial, legislative and executive activities can be freely covered—with some exceptions. A reporter has the right to cover a city council meeting, except for executive sessions. But the reporter has no legal right to sit in on a meeting of the board of the American Telephone & Telegraph Co., a private company.

Journalists have rights—along with all citizens—to vast areas of official activities. The Supreme Court ruled in 1972 (*Branzburg v. Hayes*) that the press has protection in some of its newsgathering activities. The Court stated that "without some protection for seeking out the news, freedom of the press would be eviscerated."

But the Court also ruled in *Branzburg* that a reporter cannot protect information a grand jury seeks, and that grand jury proceedings are closed to the press. When *The Fresno Bee* published material from a grand jury inquiry and its staff members refused to tell the court how they had obtained the information, they were sent to jail for contempt of court.

Executive sessions of public bodies may be closed to the press, but the reason for holding closed-door sessions must not be trivial. Usually, state laws define what constitutes an executive session. Reporters are free to dig up material discussed at these closed meetings.

Material of a confidential and personal nature held by such agencies as health and welfare departments is not available to the press. A reporter has no legal right to learn whether a certain high school student was treated for gonorrhea by a public health clinic. But the reporter is entitled to data on how many people were treated last month or last year and at what cost, how many people the clinic has on its staff and so on. Nor are there prohibitions against a reporter interviewing a clinic user who is willing to talk about his or her treatment, just as a person who appears before a grand jury may tell reporters about the testimony he or she gave to the jury.

News Gathering Process Not Protected

The courts have allowed plaintiffs to examine how a story was obtained and written. When a copy editor at *The Washington Post* wrote a memo saying she found the thrust of an article "impossible to believe," the memo was admitted in the suit. The existence of e-mail records has complicated matters for the media as it has been difficult to remove e-mails from computers and servers, and these can be used in suits. This has given pause to some journalists who use the computer for e-mail interviews. The unedited, unused portions are available to plaintiffs.

Free Press—Fair Trial

Judges contend that some news can prejudice jurors and thus compromise a defendant's Sixth Amendment "right to an impartial jury," making a fair trial impossible. Criminal convictions have been set aside because of such publicity.

End of the Line

Ten of the 19 witnesses who testified in the perjury and obstruction of justice trial of Lewis Libby Jr., the chief of staff of Vice President Dick Cheney, were journalists. Three of them, reported *The New York Times,* "played a central role in the conviction of Mr. Libby, their former source, by testifying about conversations they had once fought to keep secret by invoking the majesty of the First Amendment and the crucial role that confidential informers play in informing citizens in a free society."

Legal advisers to the media say that the prosecutorial grace period since *Branzburg* that kept reporters out of grand jury rooms ended with the Libby trial.

Brennan on Stuart

"Free and robust reporting, criticism, and debate can contribute to public understanding of the rule of law and to comprehension of the functioning of the entire criminal justice system, as well as improve the quality of that system by subjecting it to the cleansing effects of exposure and public accountability."

Judges do have ways to protect the defendant from damaging publicity that would compromise the defendant's right to a fair trial. In *Nebraska Press Association v. Stuart* (427 US 539), the Supreme Court discussed changing the location of the trial, adjourning the trial until pretrial publicity that may be prejudicial has dissipated, careful questioning of jurors during the voir dire (jury impaneling), sequestering the jury and other strategies.

Confidentiality Requires Protection

Constitutional Guarantees

First Amendment:
Congress shall make no law . . . abridging the freedom of speech or the press.

Sixth Amendment:
In all criminal prosecutions, the accused shall enjoy the right to a speedy and public trial, by an impartial jury of the State and District wherein the crime shall have been committed . . . and to have the assistance of counsel for his defense.

Fourteenth Amendment:
. . . nor shall any State deprive a person of life, liberty, or property without due process of law, nor deny to any person within its jurisdiction the equal protection of the laws.

The courts have been determined to seek out the sources of information to assist law enforcement officers and defendants. The press has been equally determined to honor its promise of confidentiality to sources.

A Boston television reporter was sentenced to three months in jail for contempt of court for refusing to identify a source who told her he saw police officers loot a pharmacy. A grand jury was looking into the matter and a prosecutor told the judge his office was stymied without the testimony of the witness.

Journalists traditionally have honored the request for confidentiality, sometimes at a heavy price. In 17th-century England, a printer, John Twyn, refused to give the Star Chamber the name of the author of a pamphlet about justice that Twyn had published. The Chamber called the pamphlet treasonous, and when Twyn would not speak, it passed the following sentence:

> (You will be) . . . drawn upon an hurdle to the place of execution; and there you shall be hanged by the neck, and being alive, shall be cut down, and your privy members shall be cut off, your entrails shall be taken out of your body, the same to be burnt before your eyes; your head to be cut off, your body to be divided into four quarters, and your head and quarters to be disposed of at the pleasure of the King's Majesty.

No Privilege   Today's journalists do not face Twyn's fate, but they can be sent to jail for refusing to reveal their sources. Judith Miller, a *New York Times* reporter, spent 85 days in jail when she did not divulge her source for stories about weapons in Iraq prior to the U.S. invasion.

Despite one reading of *Branzburg* that sees in it the absolute protection of sources, and another reading that sees it as permitting a qualified privilege, a recent comment by an influential federal judge seems to have settled the matter. Circuit Court Judge Richard Posner wrote that *Branzburg* cannot be read to provide a privilege for reporters against compelled testimony. Posner's opinion that *Branzburg* does not provide First Amendment privilege to journalists is widely cited by judges in their decisions denying privilege to reporters.

Shield Laws

One effect of the attack on confidentiality was the enactment of state shield laws, in effect in 31 states and the District of Columbia. These laws provide some protection to reporters in state courts. There is no federal shield law. In federal prosecutions, state shield laws do not help the reporter.

Reporters contend that their notes—which may include the names of confidential sources as well as the reporters' own investigative work—should be treated as confidential. State shield laws grant the reporter this protection unless in a criminal case the defense can prove that the notes are relevant and that alternative sources of information have been exhausted.

Shield laws are important. When the highest state court rules on matters covered by the state constitution, the issue cannot be reviewed by the U.S. Supreme Court because the state court is the final authority on the meaning of the state's constitutional guarantees. Some state constitutions have even broader protections than the U.S. Constitution.

The shield law is a helpful successor to the sunshine law, which requires public bodies to meet in public unless there is a compelling reason for privacy.

Confidentiality Necessary   Newspapers and broadcast stations contend that confidentiality is essential to freedom of the press. The press points out that the power of the government to punish people involved in unpopular causes led the courts to safeguard anonymity in many areas. The courts recognize the doctor–patient and lawyer–client relationship as generally beyond legal inquiry. Journalists have sought the same protection for their sources.

If the press is to be the watchdog of government, as the press believes the framers of the Constitution intended, then the press must be free to discover what public officials are doing, not limited to publishing what officials say they are doing. In order to ferret out the activities of public officials, insiders and informants are necessary. These informants usually must be promised anonymity. The courts, however, have not been sympathetic to reporters who seek to honor confidentiality in the face of court demands for disclosure.

Keep the Promise   Once a reporter promises confidentiality, he or she must honor that pledge, the Supreme Court ruled in *Cohen v. Cowles Media* in a 1991 decision. St. Paul and Minneapolis newspapers promised a source that damaging information he gave them about a candidate would not carry his name.

After the newspapers decided to use the source's name, he was fired from his job. The source sued, and the court ruled that First Amendment protections do not prevent a newspaper from being held liable for violating a promise of confidentiality. The state law on an implied contract was violated, the court ruled.

Tips and Tidbits

Here is some useful advice taken from court decisions, laws and the experience of journalists:

Interviewing Jurors   Jurors are free to talk about their experiences once a trial ends. But contact with jurors while they are deliberating can lead to contempt-of-court charges.

The same general rule applies to those serving on grand juries. The laws affecting witnesses appearing before grand juries vary from state to state. Some allow witnesses to talk about their testimony, but others forbid it until the grand jury inquiry is over.

Taping   The courts have ruled that it is illegal to use a tape recorder secretly while posing as someone else. This is invasion of privacy through *intrusion.*

Don R. Pember of the University of Washington, author of a mass media law textbook, advises his students to turn on the tape recorder and to ask permission. Then the consent is recorded. Generally, he says, be "up-front with recorders."

Wire Service Defense   Newspapers that publish wire service stories with libelous material have been protected by the "wire service defense." This legal concept holds that if the newspaper was not aware of the defamatory material in the story, could not reasonably have been expected to detect such material and reprinted the material without substantial changes, then the publication will not be held liable, whether private or public figures are defamed by the article.

Altering Quotes   The U.S. Supreme Court has ruled that changing a quote does not necessarily constitute libel unless the change gives a different meaning than the source intended. The Court stated:

> If every alteration constituted the falsity required to prove actual malice, the practice of journalism, which the First Amendment standard is designed to protect, would require a radical change, one inconsistent with our precedents and First Amendment principles.

Illegal-Legal   The Supreme Court ruled that the First Amendment protects journalists who use material that was improperly obtained and passed along to them. This covers such material as telephone conversations, corporate documents and government memos. The Court stated: "A stranger's illegal conduct does not suffice to remove the First Amendment shield from speech about a matter of public concern."

Press Disclosures Affect Freedoms

The press considers itself a critic not only of public officials and public figures, but also of sacred institutions. This disturbs those who want and need ideals and heroes, men and women to look up to, institutions to be loyal to. Few individuals or institutions can stand up under the scrutiny to which the press subjects them.

The public reaction has been to resort to the ancient technique of blaming the messenger.

Tyrone Brown, a law clerk to Chief Justice Earl Warren in the 1960s, then general counsel for Post-Newsweek Broadcasting and later a member of the Federal Communications Commission, said the Court's rulings reflect attitudes toward the press.

"All those so-called absolute principles like the First Amendment are functions of the time when they're decided," Brown says. "The Justices' role is a process role—making accommodations between various power groups in the country at various times."

In several decisions affecting the press, some justices have suggested that the Times Doctrine be re-examined. They have asserted that subsequent rulings favorable to the press have permitted the press to abuse privacy and to be held exempt from responsibility for its coverage.

The courts have been more willing to close judicial proceedings and to gag those involved in civil and criminal trials. And countless officials are more reluctant to allow reporters access to public records and entrance to meetings.

"There is an attitude of too many public officials that the material they are caretakers for belongs to them and not to the public," said Paul K. McMasters, the deputy editorial director of *USA Today*.

Although every state and the District of Columbia have open records and open meetings laws, "many newspapers ranging in size from the smallest to the largest national dailies find themselves almost continually snarled in disputes over one of our most basic democratic rights: To find out what branches of the government and its agencies are doing," reported the American Society of Newspaper Editors.

Summing Up

- The police cannot arbitrarily deny a press pass to a reporter.

- Except for placing reasonable restrictions on access to events behind police lines, the police cannot interfere with a reporter engaged in newsgathering activities in public places.

- Reporters cannot be denied access to open meetings of legislative or executive bodies.

- The reporter can try to use state law to open certain hearings of public bodies that have been closed as "executive sessions." But there is no constitutional right to attend. Several states have adopted "sunshine laws" that require public agencies to have open meetings and open records.

- Reporters do not have a constitutional right to documents and reports not available to the general public. (The Supreme Court has equated the press' right to access with the right of access of the public.)

- Reporters cannot guarantee a source confidentiality, should be careful about what they print about the criminal past of defendants, may be required to surrender documents to a grand jury or testify before it, should be careful about assuring sources they are protected by a state shield law.

A Free Press and Its Limits

"The press was protected by the First Amendment so that it could bare the secrets of government and inform the people. Only a free and unrestrained press can effectively expose deception in government."
—*Justice Hugo Black, Pentagon Papers case*

"This may involve a certain loss of innocence, a certain recognition that the press, like other institutions, must accommodate a variety of important social interests."
—*Justice William J. Brennan Jr. in response to a Supreme Court decision that went against the press*

". . . the ultimate good desired is better reached by free trade in ideas. . . . That, at any rate, is the theory of our Constitution. It is an experiment, as all life is an experiment. . . . While that experiment is part of our system I think that we should be eternally vigilant against attempts to check the expression of opinions that we loathe and believe to be fraught with death. . . ."
—*Justice Oliver Wendell Holmes Jr.*

"Of course not every claim of First Amendment protection has succeeded. But freedom of expression gets more protection today in this country than in any other. No other country, in particular, protects defamatory publications or hate speech in the expansive way that American law now does."
—*Anthony Lewis*

Further Reading

Abrams, Floyd. *Speaking Freely: Trials of the First Amendment.* New York: Viking, 2005.

Abrams, "the country's leading practitioner of First Amendment law," according to Anthony Lewis, writes that journalists should have a legal right not to disclose their sources. But he and co-counsel Alexander M. Bickel took a pragmatic approach in the Pentagon Papers case that resulted from President Nixon's attempt to stop *The New York Times* from publishing material from a secret history of the Vietnam War. Aware of the Supreme Court's rejection of an absolute view of the First Amendment, Abrams writes that the task of the lawyer in constitutional cases is to win them. The strategy resulted in a 6–3 decision against Nixon. Abrams discusses the Wayne Newton libel case and derides Rudolph Giuliani's attempt when mayor of New York City to shut the Brooklyn Museum because he objected to a painting in an exhibit. "I found myself confronted with an authoritarian Giuliani, a bullying Giuliani, a Giuliani deeply contemptuous of the First Amendment," Abrams writes.

Chaffee, Zechariah Jr. *Free Speech in the United States.* Cambridge, Mass.: Harvard, 1948.

Hand, Learned. *Liberty.* Stamford, Conn.: Overbrook Press, 1941.

Lewis, Anthony. *Make No Law: The Sullivan Case and the First Amendment.* New York: Random House, 1992.

Pember, Don R., and Clay Calvert. *Mass Media Law,* 15th ed. New York: McGraw–Hill Companies, 2007.

Sanford, Bruce W. *Synopsis of the Law of Libel and the Right of Privacy.* New York: World Almanac Publications, 1991.

Taste—Defining the Appropriate 26

Preview

Material that is obscene, vulgar or profane can offend readers and listeners.

Decisions to use such material depend on:

- **Context:** If the event is significant and the material is essential to describing the event, offensive material may be used.
- **Nature of the audience:** A publication for adults or a special-interest group will contain material that a mass medium might not.

Newspaper, online and magazine reporters have wider latitude than broadcast journalists in language and subject matter.

Editors say that pictures are the source of most reader complaints.

Khalid Mohammed, Associated Press
A grisly celebration in Iraq—four burned bodies strung on a bridge.

When an Iraqi mob murdered four American contractors and mutilated and burned their bodies, newspapers and magazines published photos of the bodies dangling from bridge girders, people celebrating in the foreground.

Some readers were angry. They called and they wrote letters. An outraged mother told *The New York Times,* which ran a large page 1 photo, that hereafter she would "hide the front page from my 7- and 9-year old children." A woman wrote *U.S. News & World Report* she was "appalled and disgusted by the photos of the horrendous act."

Other readers saw the grisly photographs as a realistic and stark portrayal of "Iraqis opposed to the occupation," as one letter writer put it.

Trade Center Photos The anger and the acceptance were similar to the responses to the photographs of bodies falling from the World Trade Center three years before

Keep your opinions to yourself.

Richard Drew,
Associated Press

Death Plunge
   Photographer Drew described this photo he took moments after the World Trade Center was attacked as "the most famous picture nobody's ever seen." Tom Junod wrote in *Esquire* magazine that "the images of people jumping were the only images that became, by consensus, taboo."
   Editors who did not use Drew's photo said it was too horrific for their readers and viewers. Bill Keller, executive editor of *The New York Times,* which published the photo, conceded the difficulty in deciding whether to run the photo. "Photos are trickier than words," he said, "because their content is in large measure emotional, visceral, and because you can't edit their contents."
   For other comments on the use of this photo see **Falling Bodies** in *NRW Plus.*

when terrorists struck the Twin Towers. Then, editors like Naomi Halperin, photography editor of *The Morning Call* in Allentown, Pa., responded to complaints. "It was the truth. The most horrific part of this tragedy is the loss of life," she said.

To those complaining of the photos of the Iraqi murders, Bill Keller, executive editor of *The New York Times,* replied, "You can't shy away from the news, and the news in this case is the indignities visited upon the victims and the jubilation of the crowd."

Apologetic   But Brian Duffy of *U.S. News & World Report* apologized. "Our intention was not to offend," he said, "but to present a faithful record of a transformative moment. In doing so, however, we did offend, and for that I apologize. We erred."

The major television networks edited the images to eliminate the most graphic scenes. Steve Capus, executive editor of NBC Nightly News, said, "Quite honestly, it doesn't need to be seen in full order to convey the horrors of this despicable act."

"Gruesome"   The video shows the body of Daniel Pearl, a TV journalist, lying on the floor. A hooded Palestinian approaches and hacks off his head with a large knife. The video was distributed by Pearl's killers and in the United States it was shown on the Web site of the *Boston Phoenix,* which a week later published two black-and-white photos from the video on its editorial page—one of Pearl talking about his Jewish heritage, the other of his severed head.

To outraged viewers and readers, the publisher of the *Phoenix,* Stephen Mindich replied, "This is the single most gruesome, horrible, despicable, and horrifying thing I've ever seen." But allowing the act to be seen made the public witness to evil, he said.

Bob Steele of the Poynter Institute's ethics faculty took issue with the *Phoenix.* "Any journalistic purpose in publishing the photos of his death is considerably outweighed by the emotional harm to Pearl's widow and family. At the least, publishing these photos is insensitive and disrespectful. It may be cruel."

Hardly New   Questions of taste have bedeviled the media ever since Benjamin Franklin set type as a colonial printer. He responded to complaints, "If all printers were determined not to print anything till they were sure it would offend nobody, there would be very little printed."

During the Civil War battle of Antietam, photographers took pictures of the dead, and when they were published there were objections. To which Oliver Wendell Holmes replied, "Let him who wishes to know what war is look at this series of illustrations." However, he suggested they be viewed only once because of their power.

Standards Vary   As we can see, the guidelines used to determine what is acceptable and what is in bad taste vary from editor to editor, medium to medium. What one editor decides is essential to the story, another finds offensive.

No one wants to offend readers or viewers. Nor—in the case of broadcast journalists—is there sense in offending the Federal Communications Commission, which has rules about obscenity, indecency and profanity. But how does a reporter or an editor decide when to risk giving offense in order to provide essential information? Just what is the "good taste" that journalists are supposed to exercise? Let's try to establish some guidelines.

Taste Is Relative

Taste is usually defined as a set of value judgments in behavior, manners, or the arts held in common by a group or class of people. Generally, these values help keep society stable and insulate it from sudden and possibly destructive change. Those who advocate strict controls on pornography, for example, argue that such material stimulates anti-social behavior.

These values are not absolute. Several factors are involved in setting standards. First, to a history lesson that shows us that what was once deemed offensive is now yawned at. We go back 35 years to a space shoot.

Time

Two Cornell University astronomers had an idea for the Pioneer 10 spacecraft flight. For its journey beyond our solar system it would carry a drawing of a man and a woman as well as information about the planet Earth. Should the space-craft then nuzzle down on some distant civilization the inhabitants could visualize what Earth man and woman look like.

The National Aeronautics and Space Administration accepted the sugges-tion, and when Pioneer 10 was launched in 1973, a gold-plated aluminum plaque engraved with a sketch of the Earth and its solar system and a drawing of a naked man and woman standing next to each other was aboard. NASA released the sketch to newspapers, thereupon confronting many editors with a dilemma. The picture was newsworthy, but would its publication be in bad taste?

"When I found my daughter's birth control pills, I hit the ceiling."

Planned Parenthood®
Federation of America, Inc.

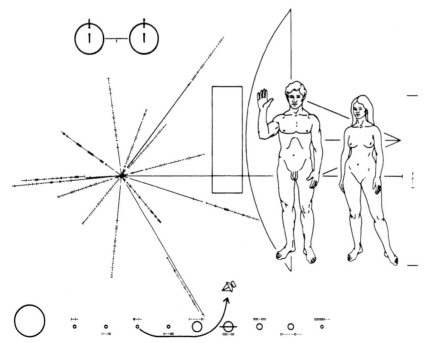

Changing Times

When this drawing, which was carried on the first human-made object to leave the solar system, was reproduced in the *Los Angeles Times*, a reader complained that it was "filth," and many news-papers removed various parts of the bodies of the man and woman before running it. Twenty years later, newspapers were carrying stories about AIDS and condoms and running advertisements about birth control by the Planned Parenthood Federation of America.

Castrated   The *Chicago Sun-Times* published the drawing in an early edition after an artist had removed the man's testicles. In a later edition, the rest of the genitals were erased. *The Philadelphia Inquirer* did even more brushwork: The male had no genitals and the nipples had been removed from the woman's breasts. The *Los Angeles Times* ran the drawing untouched. "Filth," a reader wrote in protest.

Shocked   In 1939, people were scandalized when in the movie *Gone With the Wind,* Rhett Butler turned to Scarlett O'Hara and said, "Frankly, my dear, I don't give a damn." The word *rape* was taboo in many newspapers until the 1950s.

Today, movies, theater, books and magazines leave little to the imagination. For those with exotic tastes, a $7 billion a year pornography industry caters to every conceivable fantasy, with not much legal interference. In time, journalism dropped many of its taboos, too.

Let's track some of these changes. First, we'll look at language, to the use of words that have been taboo but with the years have become acceptable for publication.

Offensive Words

The story that appeared in the April 18, 1966, issue of *The New York Times* about the Masters-Johnson study of the physiology of sex used words such as *vagina, vaginal lubrication, intravaginal diaphragms* and *orgasm.* As the story was being edited, a problem came up on the copy desk.

As the event is recounted by a *Times* copy editor, the desk noticed the frequent and explicit references to the female sex organ (six) and only euphemistic references (two) to the penis—"genital organ" and "the organ." The question was referred to an assistant managing editor who served as the arbiter of language and taste at the *Times.* He decreed *vagina* for the woman and *genital organ* for the man as proper.

Two years later, the *Times* was more forthcoming in its use of explicit language. Reporting the changes *The Washington Post* and *Chicago Tribune* had made in a review appearing in their Sunday book review supplement, "Book World," the *Times* reported that the newspapers had stopped a press run of the supplement to delete a section that "consisted of a paragraph containing reference to the penis in a discussion of the sexual behavior of primates."

Here is the paragraph that so offended the sensibilities of decision makers at the *Post* and *Tribune* that they called back a million copies of the press run at a cost of $100,000:

> Many a cocktail party this winter will
> be kept in motion by this provocative chit
> chat; man is the sexiest primate alive; the
> human male and not the gorilla possesses
> the largest penis of all primates. . . .

The *Post* and *Tribune* were clinging to the concept of the newspaper as family reading, although *Life* and *Newsweek* had used the word in their stories about the book, *The Naked Ape* by Desmond Morris, and although it was commonplace among millions of nursery school children who had been instructed to call a penis a penis.

Integration Battles   In 1960, during a school integration demonstration in New Orleans, the AP quoted some of the women who were shouting at the leader of the school sit-ins: "Jew bastard, nigger lover." In response to protests that the use of such words was in bad taste, the AP said it "judged them essential to establishing the temper and the mood of the demonstrators."

Gradually, pertinence or significance was becoming the guideline in determining whether an obscenity or profanity should be included in news accounts.

Watergate Tapes   A major turning point was reached during Watergate when the tapes of the White House conversations revealed a profusion of vulgarities and profanities. As the West Coast journalism review *feed/back* put it, the "Nixon administration made inoperative the detente that existed in the daily press against words once excised by editors."

The words *shit* and *fuck,* used in the White House, appeared in such papers as *The Washington Post,* the *St. Paul Pioneer Press,* the *Atlanta Journal,* the *Kansas City Star* and *The Seattle Times.*

It would have been impossible, many editors felt, to have changed the emphatic language of a statement by President Nixon from the key tape of March 22, 1973:

> I don't give a shit what happens. I want you all to stonewall it, let them plead the Fifth Amendment, cover up or anything else if it'll save the plan. That's the whole point.

The AP made a survey of newspapers using the Watergate material and found nearly a third of them printed all or nearly all of the obscenities without alteration. Slightly more than half sanitized the word *shit* or other words, and 15 percent of the papers completely edited out the vulgarities and profanities by paraphrase or deletion.

One of the newspapers that did not use Nixon's language was the Huntington (W. Va.) *Herald-Dispatch* and *Advertiser,* whose executive editor said, "In this very Fundamentalist market, we came to the conclusion that there was no reason to offend unnecessarily."

Clearly, the importance of the issue and the prominence of the people involved motivated some editors to use the words as spoken. Several said the issue was of such importance that sanitizing the language would have altered the public record. On the other hand, some editors considered the vulgarities too strong for their readers.

AIDS   At first reluctant to use direct language and graphic descriptions, television, radio and newspapers finally faced the reality of AIDS reporting. They dropped the euphemism *safe sex* and spoke and wrote about *condoms.* They replaced vague allusions to *sexual practices* and used *anal intercourse* in describing how the disease can be transmitted.

Freud on Language

"Anyone who considers sex as something mortifying and humiliating to human nature is at liberty to make use of the more genteel expressions 'Eros' and 'erotic.' I might have done so myself from the first and spared myself much opposition. But I did not want to, for I like to avoid concessions to faintheartedness. One can never tell where that road may lead; one gives way first in words, and then little by little in substance too. I cannot see any merit in being ashamed of sex. . . ."

—*Sigmund Freud,*
Group Psychology
and the Analysis
of the Ego *(1921)*

**Public Outrage,
Private Delight**

When it was discovered that Miss America was being displayed in the nude in *Penthouse* magazine (the photos had been taken before she won the title), the public was outraged and the pageant took away her crown. The issue with the photos sold 6 million copies, twice the magazine's normal circulation.

Cleansing a Quotation

After a campaign rally in Naperville, Ill., featuring the Republican candidates for president and vice president, the microphone was inadvertently left open and the following was heard:

> George W. Bush: "There's Adam Clymer, major-league asshole from *The New York Times.*"
> Richard Cheney: "Oh, yeah. He is, big time."

Most newspapers, including the *Times,* stepped back from direct quotation, using "expletive deleted" or "a——." *The Washington Post* and the *Los Angeles Times* used the vulgarity as uttered. *Post* Managing Editor Steve Coll said the paper's policy is not to publish vulgar language offensive to family readers. But this seemed a case where a word was essential to the meaning of a news event.

The New York Times, hardly an innovator among newspapers, ran a story headlined, "Among Women, the Talk Is of Condoms." Here is an excerpt from the piece:

> "I keep them with me," said Rebecca Pailes, a 25-year-old fashion designer. "I have them in my house. I won't have sex without them."
>
> She uses a diaphragm also for birth control. "I use condoms," she said, "just to prevent disease."
>
> "I don't trust anybody," said Judith, the 37-year-old owner of a small employment agency, who asked that her last name not be used. "I'm cynical about men. Nobody's worth the risk. Who knows who the people they've been with have been with? But I'm not going to give up sex."
>
> Judith, who described herself as alternating between celibacy and promiscuity, keeps a drawerful of condoms in her kitchen.
>
> "I give them to my friends who are celibate and say 'Here, now you can have sex,'" she said.

This was quite a change from the guarded coverage of the death from AIDS of the movie star Rock Hudson in 1985. Although many publications used the death to illustrate the danger of unsafe sex, only *Time* used the word *condom.*

Offensive Subjects

Disease and Disability   For reasons now difficult to understand, mentioning certain diseases and disabilities was considered poor taste in days past. It was considered improper to call attention to the fact that President Franklin D. Roosevelt used a wheelchair and that he could not stand unaided. No one wrote about his physical condition—the result of polio—and no one photographed FDR in ways that would reveal his disability.

When President Eisenhower had a heart attack in 1955, the press did follow that closely. But two years later when his wife underwent a hysterectomy reporters were satisfied with the explanation that she had undergone a "two-hour operation . . . similar to those many women undergo in middle age."

Gradually, good sense took over. When Betty Ford, wife of President Ford, underwent a mastectomy in 1977, the press reports were explicit.

But some frank language remained taboo longer.

Sexuality The taboos against explicit reference to intercourse and other sexual activities were broken by news events that made it impossible to avoid the specifics. We've seen how the AIDS epidemic was one of these events. President Clinton's sexual liaisons were another. If journalism is the mirror held to life, then a journalism prohibited from chronicling important events in our lives offers a distorted image.

The prominence of the individuals involved plays a major role in deciding whether to use graphic details of sexuality. When the Los Angeles Lakers basketball star Kobe Bryant was accused of rape, many newspapers carried this description of Bryant's preliminary hearing:

EAGLE, Colo. Oct. 9—The woman who has accused Kobe Bryant of rape told police he invited her into his hotel room, gripped her neck with both hands, forced her to lean face first over a chair and assaulted her.

The detailed account of events in Bryant's room was presented by Doug Winters, a detective with the Eagle County sheriff's department during a preliminary hearing to determine whether the Los Angeles Lakers All-Star guard should stand trial on a charge of sexual assault.

Rape The subject of rape has seen several changes from the days when a *Chicago Tribune* reporter, frustrated by the newspaper's taboo against using the word *rape* in print, wrote, "She ran down the street shouting, 'Help! Help! I've been sexually assaulted.' "

Generally, newspapers and stations do not use the names of rape victims, even when they testify at trials. The reasons:

• The victim risks being blamed. Some people believe the victims want to be raped.

• Publication would stigmatize the woman.

When she was editor of *The Des Moines Register,* Geneva Overholser said that although her newspaper did not run the names of rape victims she favored their publication because it would help erase the stigma and focus attention on the crime which is one of "brutal violence" rather than a "crime of sex."

In the Bryant case, some stations and newspapers used the name of Bryant's accuser. Their reason: A rape case is no different from any other criminal case where those involved are named.

Gay Activities Another area in which the taboos were almost total was the single-sex relationship. Slowly, and despite complaints from some religious groups, newspapers acknowledge gay and lesbian activities, public and personal.

In 1993, *The Salina Journal* published the first gay wedding announcement ever carried in a Kansas newspaper. A handful wrote to support the newspaper, but most wrote in shock and dismay and 116 readers canceled subscriptions. Today, many newspapers carry such items as the following:

Catherine Overby and Kristen McCarthy celebrated their partnership yesterday at the Chapel of the Seaman's Church Institute. The Rev. Bertram Aiken, an elder of the Disciples of Christ, led the ceremony.

No one calls to protest or cancels the newspaper in anger. Not to say that homosexuality is an acceptable lifestyle to many. Witness the furious debate about legalizing homosexual marriage. Nevertheless, the subject is out of the closet.

Place and Context

We know that communities differ. Some are more easy-going, cosmopolitan, more accepting of the different, the unique, the unusual. Language inoffensive in a newspaper or on a station in San Francisco would be tasteless to many residents of Salt Lake City.

Taste also is a function of the context in which the material is used. A story in *Rolling Stone* would contain language and references abhorrent to a reader of *The Christian Science Monitor.* Here is a sidebar to an article by Karen Rothmyer in the *Columbia Journalism Review* about her attempt to interview Richard Scaife, a major contributor to conservative causes:

Meeting Mr. Scaife

Richard Scaife rarely speaks to the press. After several unsuccessful efforts to obtain an interview, this reporter decided to make one last attempt in Boston, where Scaife was scheduled to attend the annual meeting of the First Boston Corporation.

Scaife, a company director, did not show up while the meeting was in progress. Reached eventually by telephone as he dined with the other directors at the exclusive Union Club, he hung up the moment he heard the caller's name. A few minutes later he appeared at the top of the Club steps. At the bottom of the stairs, the following exchange occurred:

"Mr. Scaife, could you explain why you give so much money to the New Right?"

"You fucking Communist cunt, get out of here."

Well. The rest of the five-minute interview was conducted at a rapid trot down Park Street, during which Scaife tried to hail a taxi. Scaife volunteered two statements of opinion regarding his questioner's personal appearance—he said she was ugly and that her teeth were "terrible"—and also the comment that she was engaged in "hatchet journalism." His questioner thanked Scaife for his time.

"Don't look behind you." Scaife offered by way of a goodbye.

Not quite sure what this remark meant, the reporter suggested that if someone were approaching it was probably her mother, whom she had arranged to meet nearby. "She's ugly, too," Scaife said, and strode off.

The *Review*'s editors wanted to show its readers the full dimension of Scaife's personality. Because most of the readers are journalists, the editors knew this brief exchange would enlighten rather than offend them.

Commercial Pressures

The media seek those who will buy the products its advertisers want to sell to, the young and the affluent. These readers and viewers have grown up with MTV, nudity in the movies, a multitude of cable channels that offer programming that leaves little to the most far-out imagination.

The NY Times On Obscenity

The *Times* stylebook states that the newspaper "virtually never prints obscene words, and it maintains a steep threshold for vulgar ones. The *Times* differentiates itself by taking a stand for civility in public discourse, sometimes at the acknowledged cost in the vividness of an article or two, and sometimes at the price of submitting to gibes."

The stylebook cites three exceptions to its "steep threshold":

*The 1974 White House conversations that figured in the Watergate hearings.

*The 1991 Senate hearing on the nomination of Clarence Thomas to the U.S. Supreme Court.

*Wording from the Starr Report concerning the impeachment of President Bill Clinton.

Lifestyles have changed for this generation of 21- to 45-year olds from that of their parents, when a premarital relationship was hushed by the family, and a premarital pregnancy brought family shame. Today, the once austere *New York Times* regularly points out in its wedding announcements that a couple had lived together before deciding to marry, and the newspaper publishes photos of obviously pregnant brides.

Reality   Feature stories reflect the dating and mating scene of the audience the media seek to reach. Here is the beginning of a feature in *The New York Times:*

> Chris London remembers the first time an impotence drug came to his emotional rescue. A 31-year-old lawyer and executive recruiter in Manhattan, Mr. London had been on a few dates with a lawyer who told him she couldn't judge a man without first having sex with him. The two made plans to meet after work. . . .

The story goes on to report that London had "a tablet of Viagra on hand" . . . and "later that evening he overheard his date giving his performance a rave in a phone call to a friend."

Inconsistency (1)   Too much for the breakfast table in Peoria and the classroom newspaper reading in Farmington? Probably. Yet, what are we to make of the silence when Bono, the U2 lead singer, barked out the infamous four-letter word when he was awarded the Golden Globe for the best song? No one complained to the FCC. But when Janet Jackson's blouse opened for a brief glimpse of her nipple, the wrath of a nation descended on TV and the FCC listened and responded: It fined CBS $550,000.

Suddenly, the shock jocks whose sexually explicit shows had been airing for several years were heavily fined, and Congress passed an indecency bill 391–22.

Inconsistency (2)   It did not take long for his sponsors and the network to descend on Don Imus, whose morning radio and TV talk show attracted several million listeners and viewers. In discussing the loss by the Rutgers women's basketball team in the NCAA playoffs, he described the mostly black players as "nappy-headed hos." American Express, General Motors, Staples and others pulled their advertising and MSNBC and his radio network pulled the plug.

Imus had defenders. Some said he used the phrase affectionately and that it was often used by rappers. A senior fellow at the New America Foundation complained that he was singled out, whereas the conservative commentator Ann Coulter's description of an Iranian as a "raghead" and her reference to a Democratic presidential candidate as a "faggot" did not result in editors pulling her newspaper column.

Silence
When Congress overwhelmingly voted to enforce a "decency code" on the media, *Broadcasting & Cable* magazine was angered by the failure of the media to respond. In an editorial, the magazine said the silence deserved a "hard-hitting exposé on how cowed the media have become."

Obscenity and the Law

On matters of obscenity, indecency and profanity, *Miller v. California* in 1973 (413 US 15) is the standard for determining whether a printed work is obscene. The Court set state rather than national standards. It asserted, "Diversity is not to be strangled by the absolutism of imposed uniformity."

The test is whether the work, taken as a whole, (a) appeals to the prurient interest as decided by "an average person applying contemporary community standards," (b) depicts or describes in a patently offensive way sexual conduct specifically defined by the applicable state law, and (c) lacks to a reasonable person any serious literary, artistic, political or scientific value.

For the work to be ruled obscene, all three elements must be present.

Although the courts have ruled that obscenity is not constitutionally protected, they have been reluctant to rule against printed material, even the pornographic publications that are sold at newsstands.

Limits on Broadcasting

The Federal Communications Commission is empowered to enforce federal statutes and the decisions of the courts in the areas of obscenity, indecency and profanity. The FCC can fine a station or revoke its license if it finds that it violated section 1464 of the federal Criminal Code, which provides for penalties for uttering "any obscene, indecent or profane language by means of radio communication." ("Radio" includes television.)

But even broadcasters and the FCC have changed with the times. In 1960, NBC censored the use of the initials *W.C.* on a nightly televised network talk program. *W.C.* stands for *water closet,* which in Britain means *toilet.* A dozen years later, the Public Broadcasting Service showed an "education entertainment" called the "V.D. Blues." There were no protests about the initials, and there were surprisingly few objections to some of the language in such songs as "Don't Give a Dose to the One You Love Most" and "Even Dr. Pepper Won't Help You," which was about the futility of douching as a contraceptive practice.

Although some stations made cuts, and stations in Arkansas and Mississippi did not carry the program, the majority of public broadcast stations decided that the program was a public service. When "V.D. Blues" was followed by a 2½ hour hotline on a New York City station, 15,000 people called with questions about venereal disease. One of the city's V.D. clinics reported the next day that the number of persons seeking blood tests went up by a third.

The Case of the "Filthy Words"

In 1973, in a broadcast in the early afternoon over station WBAI (FM) in New York City, George Carlin gave a comedy monologue entitled "The Seven Words You Can't Say on Radio and Television." Carlin said his intent was to show that the language of ordinary people is not threatening or obscene. The station later said in its defense that the broadcast was in the tradition of satire. In the broadcasts Carlin had said:

> I was thinking one night about the words you couldn't say on the public airwaves . . . and it came down to seven but the list is open to amendment and in fact has been changed. . . . The original seven words were shit, piss, fuck, cunt, cocksucker, motherfucker and tits. . . .

He repeated the tabooed words several times in what he said later was a purposeful "verbal shock treatment."

There was one complaint, and the FCC investigated. In 1975, it issued a declaratory order finding that the words were "patently offensive by contemporary community standards for the broadcast medium and are accordingly 'indecent' when broadcast by radio or television. These words were broadcast at a time when children were undoubtedly in the audience."

The station was not prosecuted. The finding, however, was made part of the station's file. In effect, the station was put on probation.

Limited Protection   The station appealed to the federal courts, and many stations and civil rights advocates joined the appeal against what was seen as a threat to freedom of expression. The case—which became known as the "Filthy Words Case"—reached the United States Supreme Court, and in 1978 in *FCC v. Pacifica,* the Court ruled five to four that radio and television stations do not have the constitutional right to broadcast indecent words. It said that the government has the right to forbid such words because of the broadcast medium's "uniquely pervasive presence in the lives of all Americans." The Court stated that "of all forms of communication, it is broadcasting that has received the most limited First Amendment protection."

The Supreme Court emphasized the limits of its ruling:

> It is appropriate, in conclusion, to emphasize the narrowness of our ruling. . . . The Commission's (FCC) decision rested entirely on a nuisance rationale under which context is all important. . . . The time of day was emphasized by the Commission. . . .

Political Pressure

Fines and other pressures on broadcasters do not arise spontaneously. Like much else involving the government, FCC actions are touched by politics. Pressures from the American Family Association, the Religious Roundtable and other religious and so-called family-values organizations led Congress to confirm FCC nominees who took a hard line in enforcing the rules against indecency.

Pictures

The front-page color photograph of the dying racing bicyclist infuriated many readers of *The Sacramento Bee* as did the equally graphic photo on page 1 in *The Press-Enterprise* of Riverside, Calif., of a woman who had hanged herself in Bosnia. (See p. 545.)

Over the Line

"I think we've gone too damned far."

—Chris Marrou, anchor for KENS-TV in San Antonio after the station's local newscast showed footage taken by a hidden camera of two men having oral sex in a park restroom. The segment from "Perverts in the Park" aired during the ratings sweep when viewership is measured.

The *Bee*'s ombudsman, Art Nauman, said, "Only a few times in my 15-year tenure as an ombudsman have I had as an intense outpouring of negative reader comments as I had on this picture."

Readers, says the Reader Representative of *The Hartford Courant,* may be appalled at a news story, but they are shocked and outraged at a news photo."

The Defense

In response, editors are equally vehement. Managing Editor Mel Optowsky of *The Press-Enterprise,* responded: "The story that picture tells is a horror. What is going on in Bosnia is a horror. It is a holocaust, the destruction of a people's body, mind, spirit and their worldly goods.

"The picture tells the story of the holocaust in a way that tens of thousands of words cannot."

Optowsky said the staff had a long discussion about using the photo.

"We discussed, for instance, the failure of much of the American press 60 years ago to adequately describe another holocaust and the consequent failure of a good people, the American people, to do something about it."

The Flint (Mich.) *Journal* published a photo of a Somali mother mourning the death of her young son whose emaciated body is clearly visible in the photo. Readers complained and in an editorial, the newspaper responded:

Good. It should.

It should offend all of us.

We should be outraged and incensed—not that newspapers would publish such a graphic and tragic image, but that the world would allow such suffering, such violence to continue.

Yes, the picture was horrifying. It made people uncomfortable. That was the point in publishing it. It was to open people's eyes to the catastrophe that continues to unfold there.

When the *Daily News* in New York ran a photo of a severed hand found near the World Trade Center terror bombings, readers complained. The photo was described by some critics as the most horrific picture ever published by an American newspaper. To those who complained, Editor in Chief Ed Kosner replied, "It's no time to be squeamish." However, the grim photo ran in only one edition.

See *NRW Plus,* **Severed Hand.**

Photo Guidelines

Claude Cookman, who worked as a picture editor for newspapers, says that these questions must be resolved:

1. What do the pictures really show?

2. What are the readers likely to add to or read into their interpretation of the photos' content?

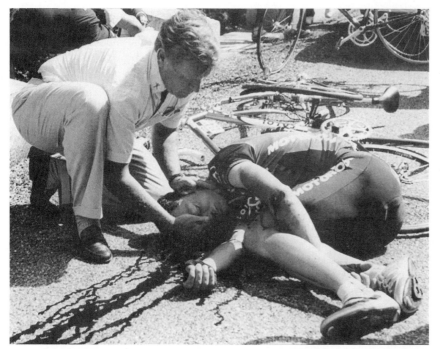

Anger and Acceptance

The photographs of the dying cyclist and the hanged woman provoked angry responses from the readers of the newspapers that published them. But no one protested the photograph in *The News & Observer* of Sgt. Joey Bozik and his wife Jayme taken at Walter Reed Army Medical Center shortly after their wedding.

Bozik lost both legs and his right arm when the Humvee in which he was riding was bombed near Baghdad.

Melanie Sill, executive editor of *The News & Observer,* said, "The photograph provides an enduring statement about the human cost of war and the spirit of those who make sacrifices that few can comprehend."

AP photo by Pascal Pavani

Ethan Hyman, *The News & Observer*

AP photo by Darko Bandic

Part 6 Photos

From page 511

Upper left: Reporters often interview victims, in this. case a mother and daughter who fled a home fire. Intrusive? Yes, hut not illegal. Discretion advised.

Upper right: The lifeless body of a child pulled from a pond was published in a local newspaper. Many newspapers would not use this photo. Intrusive.

Lower left: Local dentist surprised as he plays outfield by Strip-O-Gram birthday card arranged by softball teammates. Not used.

Lower right: Lynching victim used in historical features.

3. What are the circumstances under which the photographs were obtained?

4. How compelling is the news situation out of which the photos arose?

5. How compelling or significant are the photos in terms of what they teach us about the human experience?

6. Do the positive reasons for publishing the photos outweigh the almost certain negative reaction they will elicit from a sizable portion of the readership?

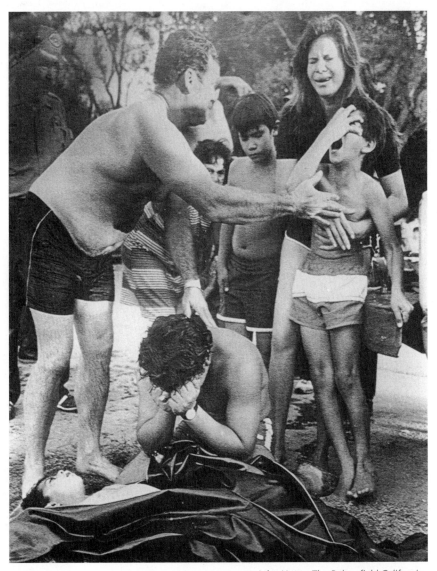

John Harte, *The Bakersfield Californian*

Application

The photo of a family crying over the body of the drowned child below remains one of the most disputed photographs published. Many readers protested its use in *The Bakersfield Californian* as an invasion of the family's privacy. The managing editor apologized: "We make mistakes—and this clearly was a big one."

The photographer, John Harte, did not apologize for taking it or for his newspaper's using it:

> Our area is plagued by an unusually high number of drownings annually. During the week this photo was taken, there were four drownings, two that day, in our area's public waters. . . . We hoped that by running this one our readers would have gotten the message that we felt it was important they witness the horror that can result when water safety is taken lightly.

Harte was applying No. 6 in Cookman's list. Is this sufficient to defend the use of the photograph?

Christopher Meyers, a member of the philosophy department at the California State University at Bakersfield, wrote that the basic defense for use of the photograph was its journalistic merit: "It was timely; the 'story' was relevant to *Californian* readers; the photograph is both artistically compelling and emotionally gripping. . . ."

But he finds its use morally indefensible. It was an invasion of the family's privacy and it reduced the family to objects of our interest, denying them their status as "part of the human family." As for the argument the photographer presents, Meyers says that it would be impossible to determine that the photograph did indeed save any lives. This use of utilitarian ethics as a defense might "justify some use of the photo," he said, but not the way it was used.

There was in this case, he says, "too much emphasis on journalistic values and not enough on moral values."

Death

Nora Ephron, a media critic, says of pictures of death: "I recognize that printing pictures of corpses raises all sorts of problems about taste and titillation and sensationalism; the fact is, however, that people die. Death happens to be one of life's main events. And it is irresponsible—and more than that, inaccurate—for newspapers to fail to show it."

A sensitivity to personal feelings is essential to the journalist, not because invasions of privacy are illegal but because compassion is a compelling moral demand on the journalist. The photograph can be as callously intrusive as the television crew at the scene of a disaster poking camera and microphone in the faces of the bereaved. Yet death is part of reality, and it is possible to be overly sensitive to it.

Death has provided the press with almost as many problems as has sexual material. We cringe at confrontation with our mortality. Morticians try to make death resemble life. Wakes are no longer fashionable. Black for the bereaved is a

Response

Richard Drew, the Associated Press photographer whose photo of the man falling to his death from the World Trade Center is shown early in this chapter, also took photos of a bloody Bobby Kennedy moments after he was assassinated in 1968. Unlike the falling-man photo, the Kennedy death photos were widely used.

Drew says the difference is that Kennedy was well-known, "an American prince," whereas the falling man was anonymous, the fellow who turns up each day to work in some tall office building, one of a throng. In defending his Trade Center photograph, Drew says, "He is you and me."

Murrow's Memorable Buchenwald Report
"Murrow follows the Third Army into Buchenwald and was profoundly moved, depressed, angered. His anger was his greatest weapon, but he knew how to control it. He described people being piled up like cords of wood. No adjectives. I don't think I ever heard him use an adjective. People piled up like cords of wood, ten deep, and the smell. Without saying that he vomited, you knew he did."
—*Fred Friendly on Murrow's broadcast from the Buchenwald concentration camp at the end of World War II.*

past practice. Children are kept from funerals by solicitous relatives. Death is said to be our last taboo.

Young reporters sometimes go to the other extreme. Carried away by the drama of violence, they may chronicle the details of death—the conditions of bodies strewn alongside the airliner, the mutilated homicide victim, the precise plans of the youngster who committed suicide in the family's garage.

This enthusiasm is as tasteless as prurient sexual interest, for it uses the tabooed subject as the means to shock readers, to call attention to the reporting rather than to the subject. Death can be terrible and horrifying. But its terror and horror are best made known through understatement. In sensitive areas, the whisper speaks louder than the shout.

Summing Up

Standards of taste traditionally were set by the upper class and the elders and religious leaders of the community. This held on, more or less, until the Depression of the 1930s, World War II and the postwar social upheavals.

With the economic collapse of the Depression came a questioning of the old ways, an unwillingness to accept edicts from authorities and a willingness to experiment with new, daring and different ideas. The old ways had given the country malnourished children, had uprooted families and had forced poor but proud men and women to seek welfare.

Social Ferment   World War II thrust an isolationist nation into a maelstrom. Not only did the shrinking of the protective oceans force the country to change its geopolitical assumptions, the war caused massive social disruption: Millions of young men were uprooted, hundreds of thousands of women were enlisted in the work force, blacks migrated from the agrarian south to the industrialized Midwest and Northeast. Classes, sexes and races mixed and mingled.

At the same time, unspeakable atrocities occurred over Europe and Asia. The Nazi brutalities, at first disbelieved as too vile, too incomprehensible to be true, were verified. Murder of the children, the disabled and the different had become German state policy. A nation that had given the world Beethoven and Goethe had acquiesced in the state's policy of slaughter.

The pictures of stacks of dead, Edward R. Murrow's broadcast from Buchenwald, the testimony of the killers at their trials could not be overlooked.

Nor could the changes at home.

Old Balances Upset   The civil rights struggles of the 1950s and the liberation movements of the 1960s involved actions and language the old rules of taste would have deemed improper. But journalists knew that they had to be reported. The profanities and obscene acts that accompanied the country's crises were symbols of the collapse of the old order. The battles and the new balances—the young, for example, were exerting greater social and political power—had to be reported.

Although some of the more conservative members of the community considered the young to be the modern counterparts of the barbarians at the gates, the young unquestionably were causing significant changes in society. But to report the full dimensions of these activities—the language and slogans—the press would risk censure by the upholders of order in the community. Radio and television station managers had less leeway. The FCC, they said, required them to conform to contemporary community standards.

But new technology widened the gap between those who tried to uphold the old rules and those who were offering words and pictures. Cable TV moved a wide variety of experiences, including explicit sexual material, into the home.

But taste is not a free-for-all for journalists. Those who work for the standard media need guidelines.

General Guidelines

First, some personal rules of the road. Although journalists are told that decisions on matters of taste are made by their editors, individual criteria are helpful.

Obviously, what and how a reporter sees are influenced by his or her attitudes and values. A censurious reporter may block out relevant material. A prurient reporter may overindulge his or her fantasies. An open attitude toward these issues is a corrective to the natural propensity to be guided, and consequently victimized, by impulse and sentiment.

By their nature, editors are conservative. Like libel lawyers, when they are in doubt they tend to throw out questionable material. Reporters learn early in their careers to fight for stories. The reporter who has a set of standards from which to argue his or her story past the desk will be better able to do a good job of presenting to readers and listeners the world of reality.

The self-appointed guardians of good taste no longer have the power to enforce dicta. Now, it's the journalist who decides what is essential and what is offensive and unnecessary. Guidelines are essential for responsible use of this power. Here are some:

1. Is the questionable material essential to a story of significance? If so, there is compelling reason to use it.

2. Use depends on the nature of the publication's readers and the station's listeners. But care should be taken to see to it that all are considered, not just those who are most vociferous.

3. The tradition of the publication or station is a consideration.

4. The private as well as the public actions of public officials and public figures are the subject of journalism if they bear on matters of public concern.

27 The Morality of Journalism

Joseph Pulitzer's Credo

Above knowledge, and above news, above intelligence, the heart and soul of a newspaper lie in its moral sense, in its courage, its integrity, its humanity, its sympathy for the oppressed, its independence, its devotion to the public welfare, its anxiety to render public service.

Preview

Journalism ethics has developed in two directions:

1. News organizations have adopted codes of ethics and guidelines that prohibit taking material from other newspapers or magazines, books, the Internet without full credit; prohibit accepting anything of value from a source; limit activities that pose a conflict of interest.

2. Reporters subscribe to a personal code that stresses willingness to look into abuses of power and to place responsibility for the failure of policies on those who made them; compassion for the poor, the disabled, the different; commitment to the improvement of their skills.

Power prevails when you are morally neutral.

"I don't mean to seem unfriendly," the fragile old man said, "but I just don't want people to see any stories about me." He looked down for a moment and then back to his young visitor, Kevin Krajick, a reporter for *Corrections* magazine. Krajick was on assignment to interview elderly prisoners, and during his stop at the Fishkill, N.Y., state penitentiary, he had been told about one of the oldest, Paul Geidel, 84 years old and in his 68th year behind bars for murder.

Geidel offered to make toast and tea for Krajick, and he accepted. Geidel had turned away many reporters before, but a guard had suggested Krajick try anyway, and he had led the young reporter to Geidel's 10 × 10 room in the prison infirmary.

With the gentleness of his age, Geidel said he understood that Krajick's job was "to get a story." He respected that calling, he said, but he really didn't want to talk about himself.

"I began slipping in questions about his past, his feelings about his life," Krajick recalled. "He answered several of them, but he said several times, he did not want 'any story.'"

The Dilemma

"He had tried to live in solitude and repentance, he said, and any notoriety upset him. He wanted to die in obscurity," Krajick said. A reporter had visited Geidel a few years before and had promised that no story would come out of their conversation, Geidel told Krajick.

"I thought they would leave me alone, but then one day I pick up the paper, and oh, there's my name and my picture splattered all over the front page."

Geidel, the son of an alcoholic saloon keeper, was put in an orphanage at seven. At 14, he quit school and worked at menial jobs. When he was 17, he broke into a hotel room in New York, stuffed a chloroformed gag in a guest's mouth, grabbed a few dollars and fled in a panic. The victim suffocated. Geidel was sentenced to life in prison for second-degree murder.

It was all in the newspaper, again, 60 years later.

"It was terrible, just terrible," Geidel said.

No Story . . .

"I had decided at that point that I would not put him through the pain of printing a story about him," Krajick said. "I told him that I would not. I figured there were plenty of interesting elderly prisoners who wouldn't mind being written about."

The two drank their tea, chatted about an hour and parted good friends.

"Then I learned that Mr. Geidel had served the longest prison term in U.S. history. I started to waver. I checked the files and found that several magazines and television stations had run stories on him when he refused parole at the age of 81. I then called the state corrections and parole authorities to find out how Geidel had been held for such an incredible term—a point that had not been made clear in the previous articles.

"It turned out that he had been classified as criminally insane on what turned out to be a pretty flimsy basis and then totally forgotten about. He had not stood up for himself during all those years and had no one on the outside to do it for him."

. . . or a Story of Significance?

"This obviously was a story of more significance than I had first thought. It was the most dramatic demonstration possible of the abuse of power under the boundless mental commitment statutes that most states have. What could be more moving than the story of the man who had spent the longest term ever, whom everyone acknowledged as meek and repentant and who, under other circumstances, would have been released before he reached the age of 40?

"The public clearly had reason to know about this man's life. It would be difficult to justify leaving him out since I was writing what was supposed to be a definitive article on elderly prisoners for the definitive publication on prisons."

Krajick faced a moral dilemma. Were the reasons for publishing his story sufficiently compelling to outweigh his promise to Geidel and the pain that the article would certainly inflict on the old man?

"I was anxious not to hurt a man who had, as prison records and he himself said, spent his life in mental anguish. I was sympathetic with his wish to remain obscure."

In his work, Krajick had faced situations in which people had been imprudently frank with him and had asked to be spared publicity. Those decisions had not been hard to make. He had reasoned that those who are hurt or embarrassed by the truth usually deserve to be. But Geidel deserved neither society's curiosity nor its condemnation. He had paid his debt to society.

Balancing Values

In the balance Krajick was striking—a balance of conflicting values—were two other factors: Articles had already been written about Geidel and he had become a statistic in the *Guinness Book of World Records,* which would soon draw other reporters whose articles, Krajick felt, would be more flamboyant and less accurate than his.

"On this basis, I decided to print the article, though not without misgivings," Krajick said. "I realized that if Mr. Geidel were to see the article he would be distressed, and he would feel betrayed by the young man who was nice to him but ended up lying. I only hope those around him have the sense not to show him the article. That would be the only escape for my conscience."

The piece appeared in the magazine under the title, "The Longest Term Ever Served: 'Forget Me.'" The concluding paragraph of the article reads:

> As his visitor left, he offered to write to Geidel. "Oh, no, please," he said. "Please. I don't mean to seem unfriendly. But please don't write. Forget me. Forget all about me." A distressed look crossed his face and he turned and hobbled down the hall to clean the teapot.

For a description of another ethical dilemma and its resolution by a photographer of domestic abuse see **Privacy Invasion or Public Service?** in *NRW Plus.*

Guiding Values

As we have just seen, reporters and their editors are constantly making decisions about what to cover, what to include in the story and what to leave out. Selection is at the heart of journalism, and it is guided by values established by journalistic practice and society.

These values are especially helpful to journalists when the choice is between alternative actions, each of which has some claim to principle. This is no different from the decision making most of us face almost daily. "We are doomed to choose," says the philosopher Isaiah Berlin, "and every choice may entail an irreparable loss. The world we encounter in ordinary experience is one in which we are faced with choices between ends equally ultimate and claims equally absolute, the realization of some of which must inevitably involve the sacrifice of others. . . . If, as I believe, the ends of men are many, and not all of them are in principle compatible with each other, then the possibility of conflict—and of tragedy—can never be wholly eliminated from human life, either personal or social. The necessity of choosing between absolute claims is then an inescapable characteristic of the human condition."

Journalists, then, must choose, just as we watched Kevin Krajick choose between keeping his word to an aged convict or exposing a system that had unjustly confined him for too many years. Was he wrong? Berlin would say, no, and he would add that yes, Krajick did harm the elderly prisoner.

Life as Referent

Can the journalist refer to some universal values as guides to choice, or is decision subject to particular circumstances—what the philosophers call a *situational ethic?* Traditionally—perhaps instinctively—people have sought absolutes as guides. And as often as the priest or the guru has supplied them, they have been found to be impractical. Or they have been discovered to be a way of keeping a religious, political, economic or social system in power.

Even so, we may find in these searches for an ethic to live by some suggestions for a useful journalistic morality. The concern for the good life, the properly led life, is almost as powerful as the need for sustenance. We may find some guides from religion and philosophy, from the Prophets and Plato, from the guru who traces his ethic to the Bhagavad-Gita and from contemporary philosophers.

"Life is the referent of value," says Allen Wheelis, a psychiatrist, who writes about ethics. "What enlarges and enriches life is good; what diminishes and endangers life is evil." If we start our search for an ethic by first defining life as physical survival and apply Wheelis' referent to one of the immediate problems of industrial societies, we see that what poisons the air, water and earth is bad. Industries that endanger the lives of their workers or nearby residents are bad. Safety procedures—or plant closures if this cannot be accomplished—are good.

But some factory owners and some automobile manufacturers have opposed strict environmental protection standards. To clean up a plant, to make a car that does not emit pollutants, to make a process safe in the factory would increase the price of the car or make operating the plant so expensive it might have to be shut down, owners have said. This means unemployment, a loss of taxes to the local community, a decline in business where the plant or factory is located. No wonder that workers and politicians often join industrialists to oppose proposals for safety, clean air and clean water.

Is it the responsibility of the journalist to continue to point out that the factory is poisoning the air? Or does the reporter turn away? If he or she does, jobs may be saved, the profits of the company assured and taxes kept low, surely good ends.

Agenda
" . . . those of us who have been granted the great gift to be journalists, the great gift to perform a public service, must seize the moment. If we don't, we will have failed. . . . We can never stop dealing with the issues that surround us and threaten to overwhelm us: Hunger and housing, health care and elderly care, education for our children and their children, jobs and taxes, our air and land and water and the kind of repressive social environment that doesn't allow every man and woman to live in dignity."
—Gregory Favre,
former Executive Editor,
The Sacramento Bee

The Journalist
"A journalist, in any effort to render truth, has three responsibilities: to his reader, to his conscience and to his human subjects."
—*John Hersey,*
New Yorker *writer*

The reporter's obligation is to "serve the public—not the profession of journalism, not a particular newspaper, not the government, but the public. . . ."
—*Clifton Daniel,*
former managing editor of
The New York Times

Timeless Dilemma   The dilemma is not new. The playwright Henrik Ibsen describes it in his play *An Enemy of the People.* Dr. Thomas Stockman, medical officer of the municipal baths, a considerable tourist attraction, discovers that the baths—the source of the town's economic resurgence—are being poisoned by the nearby tanneries. He wants to close them as a menace to public health.

But any revelation about the pollution will lead people to shun the baths, and this will cause economic problems, among them unemployment and higher tax rates for property owners. Dr. Stockman is reviled as an enemy of the people.

The practical concerns of a money-based society have occupied many writers. Dickens' novels cry out against the "cash-nexus" as the "only bond between man and man," as one literary critic put it.

"Breathe the polluted air," Dickens says in *Dombey and Son.* "And then, calling up some ghastly child, with stunted form and wicked face, hold forth on its unnatural sinfulness, and lament its being, so early, far away from Heaven—but think a little of its being conceived, and born, and bred, in Hell!"

No Choice   If "life is the referent of value," what other choice has the professional, whose reason for being is service to the public, than to see and to speak out so that others may see and understand? In the calculus of values, life means more than the bottom line on a ledger sheet. Joseph Conrad said, "My task which I am trying to achieve is, by the power of the written word, to make you hear, make you feel—it is, before all, to make you see. That—and no more, and it is everything."

Harold Fruchtbaum, a Columbia University social scientist, describes as "one of the intellectual's primary functions" the task of placing "responsibility for the failures of our society on the people and the institutions that control the society." Translated into a moral concern for the journalist, this is the task of holding power accountable, whether the power be held by a nation's president or a school superintendent.

See **A Journalist's Moral Framework** in *NRW Plus.*

Decency
Mary McGrory, for many decades a Washington correspondent much admired by her colleagues, said journalists could profitably keep in mind the author Jane Austen's "informing principle that politeness serves a purpose, that civility and kindness are moral imperatives."

Communal Life

In holding the powerful accountable to the people, the journalist takes to his or her job a sense of communal life. That is, the reporter has a set of values that reveal when power is being abused to the point that the quality of life in the community suffers. Philosophers through the ages have talked about the "good life," which has its starting point in a communal life whose underpinnings are freedom, tolerance and fairness. In such a society, individuals have basic rights that neither the state nor other individuals may violate, and the individual has, in turn, obligations to the community.

In writing about the American philosopher John Dewey, Sidney Hook said that Dewey believed

> . . . the logic of democracy requires the elimination of economic, ethnic, religious and educational injustices if the freedom of choice presupposed by the ethos of democracy is to be realized.
>
> One man, one vote is not enough—if one man can arbitrarily determine the livelihood of many others, determine where and under what conditions they can live, determine what they can read in the press or hear on the air.

A Religious Perspective

Dewey believed that the community has the responsibility for eliminating hunger and poverty, that political power must be harnessed to solve the problems of group and individual welfare. Economic conditions must be such, he wrote, that the equal right of all to free choice and free action is achieved.

Communal life is an unfolding process in which the experienced past and the desired and anticipated future are considered in making the present. The journalist plays a key role in this process. Every day, the reporter describes the immediate and the past while showing the possible future in his or her work.

The Good Life as Guide

When moral philosophers speak of the good life they mean a life in which people can read, speak and choose freely; that they need not live in fear of want; that they can count on shared values such as the desirability of equal opportunity and the undesirability of crime.

Journalists enrich and promote these activities through the values that they take to the job. For example, a journalist is told that at the local university the political science department is promoting a liberal point of view, that instructors are doing more than describing the ideology; they are endorsing it. To check on the charge, the reporter disguises herself as a student and sits in on lectures. In her story, she describes her experiences, quoting class lectures and discussions, using the names of students and instructors. The charge is found to be groundless.

We do know that posing and using disguises are generally not acceptable in society. Let us strike a balance in deciding whether the use of a disguise by the reporter was ethical:

- **The benefits:** An irresponsible allegation was proved false. The reporter was able to do firsthand reporting, which is more persuasive and closer to truth than transcribing the instructors' denials.

- **The costs:** Deception was used as a journalistic method. Privacy was violated.

Worthwhile

In addressing the graduating class at Rice University, the novelist Kurt Vonnegut said most of the graduates "will find themselves building or strengthening their communities. Please love such a destiny, if it turns out to be yours, for communities are all that is substantial about what we create or defend or maintain in this world.

"All the rest is hoopla."

Behavior

"The art of acting morally is behaving as if everything we do matters."

—*Gloria Steinem*

We can say that the costs of some of these actions—no matter how well intended—outweigh the benefits if we keep in mind that the good life is the healthy communal life. What kind of campus community will we have if we cannot speak freely and openly to one another in class because we fear our words may be broadcast or published? What kind of community will we have when we fear peering eyes so much that we must shred our garbage or fear our telephone conversation is being taped?

Actions that hurt people or disrupt the community are immoral, unless justified by powerful moral considerations, we all agree. A story about a convicted rapist will hurt the rapist; but we justify the story because punishment of those who commit crimes shows the community that society does not tolerate and will punish crimes. Crime unpunished can lead to the breakdown of the community.

Survival and the good communal life—are there additional guidelines, more specific guidelines that we can find that are of use to the journalist in helping him or her to make choices? Let's look at some ethical problems journalists have encountered in their reporting. We may be able to establish some guidelines from their experiences.

Some Case Studies

First Incident   Seymour Hersh, who won the Pulitzer Prize for his disclosures about the My Lai massacre in Vietnam and more than a dozen other major journalism awards, told a gathering of journalists at the Nieman Foundation at Harvard that he found out "some pretty horrible stuff" about a former president. "There was a serious empirical basis for believing he was a wife beater, and had done so—at least hospitalized her a number of times. I had access to some records. Okay? I'm talking about trauma, and three different cases," Hersh said. Should Hersh write the story?

Second Incident   A prominent businessman died and in preparing the obituary it was learned that 30 years before when he was a county official he was sentenced to prison for embezzling funds from his office. Since then, he had led an exemplary life. Does the conviction go into the obituary?

Third Incident   Shortly after a rape charge was filed against a young member of the Kennedy family, a London newspaper and then a U.S. tabloid, NBC and *The New York Times* identified the woman. Was it right to use her name?

Fourth Incident   The news shocked the people of Missoula. The 21-year-old daughter of a well-known couple had been stabbed to death outside her Washington, D.C., apartment house. She had been a high school honor student and an accomplished musician and had won a scholarship to Radcliffe.

Less than a week later, Rod Deckert, the managing editor of *The Missoulian,* a 32,500 circulation daily in the city, had an even more shocking story on his desk: The young woman had been a streetwalker in Washington, "a $50-a-trick prostitute" who "used to talk freely about her work and bragged about being 'a pro,'" according to a story *The Washington Post* planned to run the next day under the headline, "A Life of Promise That Took a Strange and Fatal Turn." The *Post* had learned she had returned to Missoula after dropping out of Radcliffe and one night in a bar she had been approached by a man who asked her to return with him to the East. He was a pimp who recruited young women around the country.

Deckert was confronted with a difficult decision. If he ran the story, the family would suffer new anguish. If he did not, he would be suppressing news that was bound to be known because papers distributed in Missoula and nearby might carry the dramatic story of a small-town girl who came to a sordid end in the East. It was, Deckert said, "the most painful day in my 11 years of life in the newsroom." What should he do?

Fifth Incident   Two months after terrorists used box cutters to commandeer commercial airliners that were flown into the World Trade Center and the Pentagon, Jan Wong of *The Globe and Mail* in Toronto suggested to her editor that she test Canada's airline security by trying to take a box cutter and other devices aboard Air Canada planes. Would this be seen as a newspaper stunt or a public service if her editor went along?

The Decisions

1. **Wife Beater** No, Hersh said, he did not write the story. He decided not to because he said he could not "find any connection between what he did in his private life" with his public life as president.

2. **Obituary** The newspaper did include the embezzlement conviction, and after readers complained the newspaper apologized in an editor's note.

3. **Rape** NBC and the *Times* defended their breaking the practice of not naming rape victims by pointing out that her name was already in circulation. However, at the *Times,* dozens of staff members protested the decision.

4. **Murder** Deckert reasoned that the young woman's experience could be a warning to other young women in the university community. However, he had to weigh this against the pain it would cause the family and friends.

Deckert decided to run an edited version of *The Washington Post* story with some locally gathered inserts. Deckert played the story on page 12 with no art under an eight-column headline.

5. **Airline Safety** The editor gave Wong the go-ahead and she was allowed to board four domestic flights "variously equipped with a box cutter, an X-acto knife and an assortment of penknives," she wrote. The lead to one of her stories:

> Aboard Air Canada Flight 109 from
> Toronto to Vancouver, nobody recoils
> when I take out the tweezers. Nobody

Public or Private?

A city councilwoman has AIDS. A candidate for governor is known as a womanizer. Newsworthy?

Some guidelines provided by Carl Sessions Stepp of the University of Maryland:

- Does it affect the person's public performance?

- If the fact is well-known, no good is served by keeping it out of print.

- If a competing station or paper uses it, the fact is now public. Use it.

Ratings

Asked to rate "the honesty and ethical standards" of people in various occupations, respondents rated high or very high (in percentages):

Druggists	61
Clergy	54
Dentists	51
College teachers	50
Medical doctors	47

Television reporters and commentators had a 22 percent rating, newspaper reporters 17 percent.

flinches when I produce nail clippers. Then I take out my **box cutter.**

Nobody seems to notice. Wong writes:

> "Hot towel?" asks a flight attendant as she sweeps by.

Right or Wrong?

We cannot say with absolute certainty that the decisions made in each of these incidents was right or wrong. We can, however, examine them with some guidelines in mind and reach some reasonable conclusions.

1. Hersh was acting responsibly in not using the material if, as he said, he could see no connection between the president's behavior in his personal life and his behavior in his public office. Today, though, he says he would use it on the assumption that the story would get out anyway. What he is saying is that he would use it so that he would be the first with the revelation. Presumably, his sources leaked the information to him so that he would use it, and when he did not, they would give it to someone else. Somewhere along the line, the material would be used, Hersh reasoned.

A reporter's instincts are to score exclusives, not to be beaten by a competitor. This, of course, leads to a kind of journalism that short-circuits verification and emphasizes revelation. This kind of journalism is clearly immoral. But in this situation, Hersh had what he considers proof of the president's wife beating.

Making the decision on the basis of scoring a beat is questionable. There is, however, a rationale for using such material, and it was made by the reporters who delved deeply into President Clinton's personal life to reveal his sexual escapades. Their contention was that his infidelities showed a duplicity that could affect his performance in office.

Journalists were, and remain, deeply divided over the relevance of personal behavior to public office. In Clinton's case, the extensive revelations made by the investigation in his impeachment made news of much of Clinton's personal life, and that material had to be reported.

Clearly, a person whose behavior in office is so erratic that he cannot perform his duties surrenders his or her right to privacy. But no one accused the president Hersh knew about or Clinton of being unable to perform their presidential duties because of personal misbehavior.

2. Disclosure of a white-collar crime committed 30 years before by a person who is dead seems to serve no end but the purpose—often sound enough—of full disclosure. If truth is served by presenting all the facts, then certainly we are on sound moral ground if we include unsavory but factual detail in an obituary. But the journalist knows that he or she is forced to select for use from a stockpile of information the few facts that can be fitted into the restricted time

and space allocations. In this selection process, the journalist applies to the material the tests of utility, relevance and significance within a value system.

Had the crime been well-known at the time of the man's death, the journalist could not ignore it. What the public knows the press cannot skip over without risking charges of covering up information.

3. The defense is based on an old journalistic maxim: If my competition has it, I will use it. In the rough-and-tumble of competition in the media market, the use of the name passes the reality test. But it doesn't pass the ethical test. Without having their permission, we generally avoid using the names of victims of sex crimes.

But suppose she were well-known, someone whose name is in the media often. Can we justify holding back and risking the accusation that we are protecting the person in order to curry favor? Reality again intrudes: People who live in the public eye pay a price for their fame.

4. The Missoula situation resembles Incident 3 in that the identification of the victim was known. There was no way the community would remain ignorant of the death of the young woman. Had the newspaper failed to run some story, accusations could have been made that the newspaper showed partiality to a middle-class family, whereas day after day it chronicles the troubles of others less affluent and influential. The newspaper could have handled the story with an editor's note admitting its dilemma, which might have alleviated the violent reaction to publication—the newspaper's editorial writer condemned the story and scores of people protested with calls and cancellations. (Krajick's dilemma might have been less intense had he considered an editor's note. Although readers usually need not be told the reporter's problems, situations such as these can be less troublesome with full disclosure.)

Suppose the Missoula newspaper alone had learned that the young woman died a prostitute. Should it have included the fact in its story? If her work had been an inextricable part of the crime, there would have been no way to avoid it. But she had been found dead near her apartment house, the victim of an unknown assailant. No newspaper dredges up every aspect of an individual's past, whether for an obituary or a straight news story.

However, as it turned out later, her work was part of her death, for the man charged with her murder was her pimp. The sordid affair would then have to be told when her murderer was arrested and charged.

Postscript: Eight months after the *Missoulian* published the story of the young woman's murder, a late model Chrysler New Yorker rolled into Missoula and the four occupants went to work. Two cruised bars, and two went to the high schools. Within hours, the police were informed by an alerted public. The four men were arrested and convicted of criminal trespass and soliciting for prostitution.

5. The government launched an investigation of airline safety, but readers were less than enthusiastic about Wong's work. One wrote the newspaper, "I hope she is investigated and, if evidence is found that she broke the law, that she is charged."

A Calling

"At its best, journalism is a calling for people, just like it is for academics. People often sacrifice much larger incomes to pursue this vocation. Journalism is also imbued with this sense of autonomy and independence, along with a spirit of public responsibility. That is the sense of journalism I picked up while working on my father's paper."

—*Lee C. Bollinger, president, Columbia University*

Poses, disguises and similar attempts to mislead in pursuit of a story go back a long way in journalism, and the ethics of the undercover work are still debated. Nellie Bly posed as a mental patient to expose the horrors of the mental care system, and she is honored by a U.S. postage stamp. Pulitzer Prize jurors refused to consider an exposé of payoffs to officials because the stories were based on reporters posing as owners of a neighborhood bar that was violating liquor laws.

Something New

The concern for the people involved in news events is fairly new to journalism. For many years, outsiders had urged on the media a sense of responsibility, that the First Amendment was not a license for sensation mongering in pursuit of unconscionable money making.

As the criticism grew and as journalism aspired to status as a profession, journalists paused and examined their practices. A study showed that four of five newspapers accepted free travel. Gifts were seen to flow into the newsroom from those who sought special treatment. Some reporters had side jobs as publicists for the people and organizations they covered.

The situation cried out for change, and one route seemed the adoption of rules, codes of conduct. But these were slow to catch on. In 1974, one of ten newspapers had such a code. Within a decade, most papers and many stations had codes that called for accuracy, impartiality, the avoidance of conflicts of interest. They proscribed activities such as the acceptance of gifts from sources.

Codes of Conduct

The codes not only prohibited specific practices, they sought to establish ethical norms. Journalists were reacting to practices that had tainted journalism with a grubbiness inconsistent with the standards of professional conduct.

The renewed interest in establishing journalism as a profession found a base on which to build in the report of the Commission on Freedom of the Press. The study, issued in 1947, was a response to criticism of the U.S. press as insular, often sensational and sometimes irresponsible. The members of the Commission—most of them prestigious faculty members at leading universities—concluded that the press had not been "adequate to the needs of society."

One finding was particularly pertinent—that the press had failed to give "a representative picture of the constituent groups in the society." Vast segments of society had been ignored by the press, particularly the young and the aged, racial minorities, the poor and women.

Gradually, the press became more responsive to external criticism. Journalists themselves became outspoken about practices they considered compromising, and their criticisms began to appear in the various press reviews that sprang up around the country. Journalists began to take their trade more seriously—possibly because of the steady infusion of college-trained reporters who were questioning

---

Theory of Responsibility

In its report, the Hutchins Commission included five requirements for the media:

1. The press must give a truthful, comprehensive and intelligent account of the day's events in a context that gives them some meaning.

2. The press must provide a forum for the exchange of comment and criticism.

3. The press must project a representative picture of the constituent groups in the society.

4. The press must present and clarify the goals and values of the society.

5. The press must provide full access to the day's intelligence.

Ethics Code

The Code of Ethics of the Society of Professional Journalists is in Appendix D in *NRW Plus*.

some of the assumptions of the craft. The climate was established for journalists to codify good practices, to set lines between the acceptable and the morally indefensible.

For an examination of some of the practices the codes discuss see **Sins of Commission** *in NRW Plus.*

Limitations of the Codes

Although the codes clearly describe what constitutes unethical behavior, they have not deterred journalists who are determined to steal the work of others (plagiarism) and to invent characters and events (fabrication). *The New York Times* has a lengthy (52 pages) code, but Jayson Blair made massive fabrications, and *USA Today* has a strong code of ethics, but Jack Kelley plagiarized and invented events and people.

Difficult Choices   Nor can the codes resolve some of the most difficult problems journalists face. These involve dilemmas in which the choice is between conflicting moral or ethical actions similar to those Kevin Krajick faced after interviewing the elderly prisoner.

Looking to codes for guidance, we find in one of them, that of the Society of Professional Journalists, that the journalist should "serve the general welfare." Krajick would serve the general welfare with publication. The same code stresses "respect for the dignity, privacy, rights and well-being of people encountered in the course of gathering and presenting the news." Clearly, respect for Geidel would mean heeding his plea not to write about him. The codes are no help here beyond identifying the clear moral choices.

No code can make a journalist a person of good conscience. Only a personal commitment to a journalistic morality can do so. Also, most codes emphasize prohibitions, actions not to take, practices not to undertake.

But the great failure of the press, as the Commission on Freedom of the Press stressed, is not its sins of commission, but rather its sins of omission, its failure to look into the significant actions of the powerful and the travails and the longings of the powerless.

> **Inventive Media**
> "One of the most disturbing revelations of the Blair scandal was that few subjects of his bogus stories. . . . called *The Times* to complain about his fictions. They just assumed that reporters make stuff up."
> —*Frank Rich,* New York Times *columnist*

Sins of Omission

Sins of omission occur when the journalist fails to act in situations in which revelation is required. The philosopher Jeremy Bentham described this immoral act as "Keeping at rest; that is, forbearing."

We will be looking at other examples of journalists who refused to forbear. Before we do that, first a fact of life about journalism and next some reassurance.

Money   The fact of life is that journalism is a business. Most of the media operate to make a profit, and the trend is to maximize profit, sometimes at the expense of good journalism. One of the ways the media are working at keeping their profit margins acceptable to stockholders is by cutting back on the newsroom staff.

For a more reassuring insight into the currents that have grown into a strong stream of activist journalism, let's step back and survey what is known as public service journalism.

Morality Underlies Journalism

Morality is basic to the theory and practice of journalism. The press justifies its freedom in terms of moral imperatives; it rationalizes much of its behavior with moral declarations.

If public consent freely given is essential to the proper functioning of a democracy, then for the consent to be meaningful the public must be adequately informed by a press free of government or any other control. Thomas Jefferson expressed this simply: "Where the press is free and every man able to read, all is safe." The First Amendment makes this consensual system possible. Although neither the Constitution nor any laws require that the press carry out its essential role in the system, the press takes on the responsibility for setting before the public the issues it considers important so that they can be openly discussed. The cultural historian Christopher Lasch says, "The job of the press is to encourage debate."

See **The Democratic Commitment** in *NRW Plus.*

Recorders and Activists

Journalists differ in their interpretation of their role as suppliers of information. Some contend that it is sufficient for journalism to create a record, to report the deeds and declarations of those in power. Others go further. They would initiate coverage, make searching examinations of power, practice what some of them describe as an activist or watchdog journalism.

The first group believes that journalists are called upon to present matters that the public is interested in, and some of these editors conduct focus groups and have reader-advisory panels to inform them of their readers' concerns.

The second group goes further. It leads from its own conception of community needs, its own insight into what constitutes community deeds and misdeeds that require attention and correction. These are activist journalists like David Willman of *The Washington Post* who took it upon himself to expose laxity in the Food and Drug Administration in allowing a drug to be sold that was killing people. Thomas Winship, former editor of *The Boston Globe,* was labeled an "activist editor" by colleagues, a label he bore proudly, he said. He learned about this kind of journalism when he was breaking in as a reporter at *The Washington Post.* The publisher, Philip L. Graham, "burned into my young, impressionistic head the idea that the license to print carried with it the obligation to give something back to the community," Winship says.

Activist and watchdog journalism go back to the work of the colonial printers in a tradition that has taken journalism to its most notable achievements in rendering public service.

This tradition embraces tempered skepticism (see **A College Education,** *NRW Plus*) and the practice of **Adversary Journalism,** *NRW Plus*.

Past and Present

During the American colonial period, journalists in the 13 colonies vigorously opposed what they termed "onerous taxes" and the lack of representation in decision making. These journalists became a major force in the struggle for independence. The colonial journalist had a point of view and expressed it.

Before the Civil War, an outspoken and active abolitionist press called for the emancipation of the slaves. And after the abolition of slavery, as Jim Crow laws and practices became commonplace in some parts of the country, journalists spoke out. Ida B. Wells exposed lynch law and mob rule at great personal risk.

As people moved to the cities and the country grew from an agrarian economy to become an industrial behemoth, exploitation and abuses proliferated. Industrialists—some described as "robber barons" because of their ruthless practices—took control of major industries. Workers were exploited and prevented from forming unions, sometimes at the point of a gun. Crooked politicians ran many large cities. In response, a group of journalists began to tell the story as the 20th century opened.

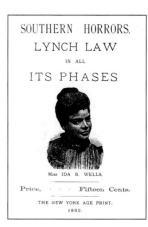

SOUTHERN HORRORS.
LYNCH LAW
IN ALL
ITS PHASES

Miss IDA B. WELLS.

Price, · · · Fifteen Cents.

THE NEW YORK AGE PRINT.
1892.

The Muckrakers

Four-fifths of the people in the United States were living in poverty. People were commodities. The mines and mills exploited child labor. Blacks were treated as chattel.

At first derisively described as *muckrakers,* this group of brilliant men and women took on the robber barons, the labor exploiters and the political hacks. They became known as the nation's voices of conscience. Some wrote books and others magazine articles, several took photographs and some worked for the daily press.

Racism

Ray Stannard Baker in 1908 described racism in Southern courts.

> One thing impressed me especially, not only in this court but in all others I have visited: a Negro brought in for drunkenness, for example, was punished much more severely than a white man arrested for the same offense. . . . The white man sometimes escaped with a reprimand, he was sometimes fined three dollars and costs, but the Negro, especially if he had no white man to intercede for him, was usually punished with a ten or fifteen dollar fine, which often meant he had to go to the chain-gang.

Chain Gangs Baker points out that one reason for the large number of arrests is the profit to the counties and state in hiring out convicts to private contractors. "Last year the net profit to Georgia from chain-gangs, to which the commission refers with pride, reached the great sum of $354,853.55. . . . The natural tendency

The Journalist as Watchdog

Bill Kovach, former curator of the Nieman Foundation at Harvard, said, ". . . watchdog journalism should be an integral part of the daily work of the news department."

The Nieman Watchdog Project maintains a Web site that discusses investigative projects: www.niemanwatchdog.org.

The Library of Congress

Child Labor

The muckrakers took their note pads and cameras into factories and out to the cotton fields to expose the exploitation of children. This six-year-old labored all day in a Texas field.

is to convict as many men as possible—it furnishes steady, cheap labour to the contractors and profit to the state. . . ."

These journalists did not condemn some vague system. They named names and held individuals responsible for their actions. Baker wrote that "some of the large fortunes in Atlanta have come chiefly from the labour of chain-gangs of convicts leased from the state." He described a banker who was also a member of the city police board and the owner of brickyards where many convicts were used on lease from the state at cheap rates.

Like the other muckrakers, Baker was adept at using files and records:

> From the records I find that in 1906, one boy 6-years-old, seven of 7 years, 33 of 8 years, 69 of 9 years, 107 of 10 years, 142 of 11 years, and 219 of 12 years were arrested and brought into court, 578 boys and girls, mostly Negroes, under 12 years of age.

Pulitzer's Journalism

One of the major practitioners of muckraking journalism was Joseph Pulitzer, the owner of the *St. Louis Post-Dispatch* and the New York *World.* Pulitzer's editors conducted crusades, newspaper campaigns to expose and remedy practices they considered illegal, unfair, unjust. They took their cue from Pulitzer's edict that the newspapers should never be content with "merely printing the news."

Instead, he said, his newspapers should be concerned "with the things that ought to happen tomorrow, or the next month, or the next year," and that they "will seek to make what ought to be come to pass." The "highest mission of the press," he said, "is to render public service."

His legacy continued under editors who were committed to using the press as an instrument of justice, reform and change. One Pulitzer reporter, Paul Y. Anderson, doggedly followed a paper trail that led to the exposure of the collusion of two of President Harding's cabinet members who conspired to lease federal oil field reserves to oil companies.

Making Journalism of Injustice

Pulitzer's edict to his editors to seek out issues, to make news of injustice and wrongdoing could be described as instruction to journalists to establish agendas for their communities. This is an approach to journalism that has no borders.

Deformed Children Harold Evans, editor of London's *Sunday Times,* said the "real power" of the press consists of its ability "to create an agenda for society."

Fair play was on Evans' mind when he heard that the manufacturers of the drug thalidomide had pressured parents of children deformed by the drug to accept a pittance in damages. Through its coverage of the issue, Evans said, the *Times* forced the crippled children "into the conscience of the country." The stories led to settlements 50 times greater than the original stipend.

Terror in Argentina When Argentina was in the grip of a murderous dictatorship in the 1970s and 1980s, few protested the arrests, torture and killing of schoolchildren, pregnant women, college students . . . anyone who spoke out against the tyranny. People were snatched from their homes, grabbed on the streets. Tortured, never given a trial, many were drugged, their stomachs slit and then were tossed out of navy planes over the ocean.

Some risked death to speak out. Robert Cox, an American who was editor of the English-language *Buenos Aires Herald,* published lists of the missing on the front page. Death threats flooded his office. He was arrested, taken to a cell past a huge Nazi flag on the wall, briefly imprisoned and then forced to leave the country.

The journalist Rodolfo Walsh could not remain silent. He wrote a public indictment of "the most savage reign of terror Argentina has ever known"; that its rulers had created "virtual concentration camps in all the principal military bases"; that the torturers felt a "need to utterly destroy their victims, depriving them of all human dignity. . . ."

Walsh knew he was signing his own death warrant through his reporting. He closed his indictment by saying that he had to speak out to be "faithful to the commitment I made a long time ago to be a witness in difficult times." The day after his statement was released, he was abducted. His body has never been found.

> **Democracy's Base**
> "Representative democracy is inconceivable without forms of mass communication—to create awareness of public issues that face a society whose members are not personally in touch with each other, who lack common geographic reference points, and whose central institutions are remote from the people they serve or exploit."
> —*Leo Bogart*

Two Courageous Women

In the United States, racial justice has been a pursuit of activist journalists. Courageous editors and publishers have bucked community traditions—and advertisers—to expose racism.

In Florida "Perhaps I'd have had the time to enjoy my growing daughter, my home and community life if I had concentrated on the till, and not worried about the word 'justice.' I am certain, now, that my concern over justice interfered with the cash register.

"I was advised time and again by wiser heads than mine to watch out for the pitfalls of 'taking a stand'—that to mount a high platform of principle was taking a downward plunge economically. I refused to listen, and so I am badly bruised by all the plunges I have taken.

"But I could not have done it any other way."

This is Mabel Norris Reese looking back on her turbulent years as publisher of the Mount Dora, Fla., *Topic.*

When the county sheriff shot and killed one Negro prisoner and wounded another while returning them from the state prison for retrial, Reese said she "opened both barrels."

Costly Coverage "I covered the inquest in which the sheriff contended that the Negroes had tried to escape, and I used all the language at my command to describe the wounded Negro and relate his account of the shooting."

The result: "Our printing plant began to suffer from lost revenue."

When the Supreme Court ordered the desegregation of public schools, Reese defended the ruling. "I pleaded for tolerance, for cool heads to guide the transition."

The result: "There was an explosion of fire in my yard soon after this—flames licked at a great, gasoline soaked wooden cross that had been planted there. Two nights later, the *Topic*'s office windows were smeared with big red crosses and beneath them were the initials 'KKK.'"

Next, the sheriff ordered five children out of the public school because, he said, they looked like Negroes. Reese condemned the sheriff. Advertising declined, and the business community financed the installation in town of a competing newspaper. More seriously, an attempt was made to burn down the home of the children and bombs were tossed into Reese's yard.

Communal Silence By 1960, a new sheriff was in office. But things had not changed. "Here the sheriff is regarded as the one man who can 'protect' the white people from integration. And he's considered the one man who can keep the labor unions from doing anything about the low wages in the citrus industry. So he is backed blindly by the powers that be." The churches, she said, "were silent," and "the average merchant feels it is a matter of life and death to mind his own business. His mind works to the tune of the cash register, not to the beat of his heart."

Despite the attacks and the coolness of the business class, Reese's paper survived. Not so lucky was another courageous woman editor.

In Mississippi Hazel Brannon Smith, the editor of two weekly newspapers in the Mississippi Delta country, would not forbear. She refused to be silent in the face of injustice. In 1946, she was found guilty of contempt of court for interviewing the widow of a black man who was whipped to death.

In an editorial she wrote in 1954, she accused the sheriff who had shot a young black man in the back of "violating every concept of justice, decency and right." The sheriff sued for libel and was awarded $10,000. The state supreme court overturned the ruling.

That year, Smith was invited to join "something called a 'Citizens' Council,'" she said, by "a local prominent man." The idea was to maintain segregation in the schools. Legal, nonviolent tactics would be used, she was told. "If a Nigra won't go along with our thinking on what's best for the community as a whole," Smith said the man told her, "he'll simply have his credit cut off." The idea was to use fear, he told her. Smith refused to go along. Her refusal cost her dearly.

Communal Silence She said the community became a battleground with intimidation the weapon, not only against blacks but against those who opposed the Council. "It finally got to the point where bank presidents and leading physicians were afraid to speak their honest opinions because of the monster among us," she said. "The idea was that 'we' would present a solid, united stand.

"I dissented by presuming to say that the truth had to be printed."

She was one of the few who dissented, and the pressure grew.

"My newspapers were boycotted, bombed and burned, a new newspaper was organized in Lexington to put me out of business, my life was threatened, and my husband lost his job as county hospital administrator—all because of pressure brought by this professional hate-peddling organization," she said.

Still a Problem
"Let me now be very specific about the one area where America's newspapers remain far too timid. An area that needs bold coverage and aggressive editorial leadership across the board—not just at a few newspapers. It's in the topic of race and inclusion. Quite simply, this is the biggest story of the first decade of our new century."
—*Frank A. Blethen,*
publisher
The Seattle Times

Truth-Telling

She and her husband managed to keep going, but the income was never enough and she had to mortgage her home to pay her bills. Finally, in 1985, she gave up. The bank took her home. Soon thereafter she died, penniless.

For more about journalists who stood up to protest racial injustice, see **Standing Strong . . . and Alone,** *NRW Plus.*

Next, let's look at some more recent examples of activist journalism, which is another way of describing public service journalism. This kind of journalism has long been considered the moral justification for journalism's privileges.

Activist Journalism

- ***The Toledo Blade:*** The Army spent almost five years investigating an elite Army platoon, Tiger Force, that tortured, murdered and then mutilated the bodies of civilian men, women and children in South Vietnam. The Army concluded 18 men had committed war crimes, but then hid the material. Thirty-seven years after the event, three *Blade* reporters dug out the material. "We undertook the project because the public has a right to know that American soldiers committed atrocities, and that our government knew about it and kept it from the public," said Ron Royhab, the executive editor. The revelations won the Pulitzer Prize for investigative reporting.

- ***The Courier-Journal:*** A yearlong investigation found that coal mine operators routinely ignored safety rules and faked air-quality tests.

- **ABC News' 20/20:** "Made in America" showed oppressed Chinese workers housed in crowded, rat-infested barracks were making clothing in U.S. territory Saipan for Ralph Lauren, Gap and other firms.

Abuse, Neglect

Alison Young went through stacks of nursing home inspection reports and found needless suffering, poor care, bad hygiene, physical abuse, affronts to human dignity. Her five-part series for the *Detroit Free Press* was based on public records. "I got into this business to give voice to the voiceless and to effect change," she says.

Weaponry
"If your aim is to change the world, journalism is a more immediate short-term weapon."
—*Tom Stoppard, British playwright*

• **Pacifica Radio:** Revealed the complicity of Chevron in the death of two Nigerian environmental activists.

• *The Orange County Register:* Warned of widespread poisoning of children by lead-tainted Mexican candy.

• *South Florida Sun-Sentinel:* Exposed the federal government's widespread mismanagement of Hurricane Katrina aid, which led to indictments and remedial action.

• *The Record:* An eight-month investigation of the area Ford left behind when it closed its assembly plant found that huge quantities of poisonous paint sludge had been dumped by Ford into streams and near mountains and farms. Ford had made deals with so-called waste management firms run by criminals. The New Jersey newspaper learned that rare and fatal illnesses were common.

• *The Ledger,* **Lakeland, Fla.:** Revealed that a fungicide caused crop and nursery damage and that the manufacturer, DuPont Co., knew that the fungicide had the potential to cause harm but was silent.

• *Star Tribune,* **Minneapolis:** Revealed that the state's foster care system allowed known criminals and sex offenders to become foster parents.

• *The Muskegon* **(Mich.)** *Chronicle:* Showed that the founder of a chemical plant made huge profits while knowingly exposing his workers to a cancer-causing chemical.

An activist journalism calls on the community to act: To see that city officials rid the local water supply of carcinogens (*The Washington* (N.C.) *Daily News*); to make the government regulate the American blood industry (*The Philadelphia Inquirer*); to force the Federal Aviation Administration to do a better job of the medical screening of airline pilots (*The Pittsburgh Press*); to require the county child-welfare agency to protect neglected and abused children *(The Blade).*

Results Activist journalism does achieve results. After the *Winston-Salem Journal* series that showed that the county's high infant mortality rate had not changed in 10 years although the state's rate steadily declined during the decade, the county hired an infant-mortality coordinator and community leaders pledged to undertake a forceful program.

Sam Roe of *The Blade* in Toledo, Ohio, went beyond "merely printing the news" to expose problems with tragic consequences in a county children's service. See "**Abused by the System**", in *NRW Plus.*

A Personal Guide

Some of the practices that have made journalism a powerful force in communities have changed through the years. One is the taboo against reading copy back to a source before publishing or airing it. No longer. For a rationale for the change, see **Checking Back** in *NRW Plus.*

Still, some practices and guidelines have persisted. Young journalists might consider these as guidelines for the practice of their journalism. From a variety of sources—from the Greek philosophers to today's police and White House reporters—the following emerge as suggestions for your consideration:

- A belief in and a commitment to a political culture in which the cornerstone is restraint in the use of power.

- Moderation in life and behavior.

- A secular, scientific attitude toward the work at hand. Knowledge is allowed to speak for itself. The professional does not believe on the basis of hope but of evidence.

- An open-mindedness that seeks out and tries to comprehend various points of view, including those in conflict with those the reporter holds.

- Responsibility to one's abilities and talent. To leave them fallow, to fail to labor to develop them through indolence or want of seriousness of purpose demeans the self and punishes the society whose betterment depends on new ideas vigorously pursued. For Homer, the good was the fulfillment of function. For Aristotle, the good was living up to one's potential, and for Kant the development of one's talents was a duty, and adherence to "duties" constituted the moral life. The reporter who fails to report and write to his or her potential is immoral.

- An understanding of and a tolerance for the ambiguities involved in most important issues and the ability to act despite these uncertainties and doubts. The willingness to take responsibility for these actions.

- The willingness to admit errors.

- A capacity to endure solitude and criticism, the price of independence.

- A reluctance to create heroes and villains to the rhythm of the deadline.

- A knowledge of the pathfinders in fields of knowledge, including journalism.

- A commitment to work.

- A sense of the past. W.H. Auden said, "Let us remember that though great artists of the past could not change the course of history, it is only through their work that we are able to break bread with the dead, and without communion with the dead, a fully human life is impossible."

- Resistance to praise. Humility. "You have to fight against the praise of people who like you," said I.F. Stone, the crusading journalist. "Because you know darn well it wasn't good enough." He tells the story of the great conductor Arturo Toscanini who was engulfed by admirers after a concert. "Maestro, you were wonderful," one said. Toscanini knew the oboe had not come in at the right time and that the violins were off. And Toscanini burst into tears because he knew it had not been good enough.

Eye of Conscience

During the Depression, a group of photographers set out to show the dire results of poverty. The most noted was Dorothea Lange, who said of herself, "All my life I tried very hard to make a place where what I did would count." Her photos of migrant workers and their children were reproduced in newspapers, magazines and books.

Pare Lorentz, the great producer of film documentaries, said of Lange that she did "more for these tragic nomads than all the politicians of the country." *The New York Times* said, "She functioned as our national eye of conscience. Her constant concerns—the survival of human dignity under impossible conditions, the confrontation of the system by the individual, and the helpless ignorance of children—were perfectly suited to the subject."

• Duty. John Dewey said, "If a man is burdened with an idea, he not only desires to express it; he ought to express it. He owes it to his conscience and the common good. The indispensable function of expressing ideas is one of obligation—to the community and also to something beyond the community, let us say to truth."

• Avoidance of the desire to please. Self-censorship is a greater enemy than outside censorship. Pleasing an editor, the publisher or the source is commonplace. Setting one's values to the "pragmatic level of the newsroom group," as Warren Breed puts it, can lead to timid, status-quo journalism.

• A wariness about making words an end in themselves. André Maurois, the French writer and political activist, writes:

> Power, Glory and Money are only secondary objects for the writer. No man can be a great writer without having a great philosophy, though it may often be unexpressed. A great writer has respect for *values*. His essential function is to raise life to the dignity of thought, and he does this by giving it a shape. If he refuses to perform this function he can be a clever juggler and play tricks with words such as his fellow writers may admire, but his books will be of little interest to anybody else. If, on the contrary, he fulfills it, he will be happy in his writing. Borne aloft by the world as reflected in himself, and producing a sound echo in his times, he helps to shape it by showing to men an image of themselves which is at once true and disciplined.

Summing Up

Reporters should seek to give voice to all groups in society, not to report solely those who hold power.

The public's need to know is an immanent value.

In determining what shall be reported and what shall be included in a news story, the reporter should consider the relevance of the material to the real needs of the audience.

If the reporter cannot disclose in the story the tactics and techniques used to gather information for the story, such tactics should not be used.

The reporter should:

• Be wary of treating people as a means.

• Believe on the basis of facts, not hope.

• Be committed to a value system but be free from ideologies and commitments that limit thought.

• Be wary of promising to help a source in return for material.

In balancing moral alternatives, the choice can be made on the basis of:

• The importance of the possible actions to life. (Life is the referent of value.)

- The public interest as against the private interest.

- The extent of knowledge of the event. If it is public knowledge or is likely to become so and the material is significant and relevant, the information should be used.

- Serving the needs of society. If the material assists people in participating justly, equally and freely in a meaningful community life, then it should be used.

Further Reading

Alterman, Eric. *What Liberal Media? The Truth About Bias and the News.* New York: Basic Books, 2003.

> This is the answer to conservative criticism of the media as having a liberal leaning. Among the targets of conservatives—CBS News, *The New York Times, The Washington Post* and others. Alterman, media columnist for the liberal *Nation* magazine, says the right is better organized, more powerful and hides its power behind its fusillades against the left, "a near-hopeless battle in which they (liberals) are enormously outmatched." Alterman says the rightward drift is the result of right-wing talk-show hosts and new media ownership. Of TV news, he writes, "unabashed conservatives dominate. . . ."

Black, Max, ed. *The Morality of Scholarship.* Ithaca, N.Y.: Cornell University Press, 1967.

Commission on Freedom of the Press. *A Free and Responsible Press.* Chicago: University of Chicago Press, 1947.

Downie, Leonard Jr., and Robert G. Kaiser. *The News About the News: American Journalism in Peril.* New York: Alfred A. Knopf, 2002.

Erlick, June Carolyn. *Disappeared: A Journalist Silenced.* Emeryville, Calif.: Seal Press, 2004.

> Journalist Irma Flaquer disappeared from the streets of Guatemala in October 1980 and was never seen again. Her disappearance took place during a frenzy of killings and disappearances of journalists, academics, religious figures and peasants. As a result of Erlick's investigation for the Inter American Press Association, which developed into this biography of Flaquer, the case was reopened by the Guatemalan government, which assigned a Special Prosecutor for Crimes Against Journalists.
>
> The government paid reparations of thousands of dollars to Flaquer's family, a street was named in her honor, the Irma Flaquer Peace Salon was established at San Carlos University documenting the country's peace process and displaying the journalist's writings. No one has been charged in the case. Flaquer's body was never recovered.

Gardner, Howard, and Wendy Fischman, Becca Solomon and Deborah Greenspan. *Making Good: How Young People Cope with Moral Dilemmas at Work.* Cambridge, Mass.: Harvard University Press, 2004.

This is a companion to an earlier work, *Good Work: When Excellence and Ethics Meet* (2001), in which Gardner examined how experienced workers in genetics and journalism maintain their ethics despite pressures. In this new book, Gardner and his young researchers explore the ways a young worker (again in journalism and genetic research) can produce work that is good—in the technical sense (being performed with skill) and in the moral sense (responding to the needs of society). The authors devote much attention to examining how young workers respond to "the potentially corrupting influence of money."

Ibsen, Henrik. *An Enemy of the People.* 1882. (Available in many anthologies and collections.)

Kovach, Bill, and Tom Rosenstiel. *The Elements of Journalism: What Newspeople Should Know and the Public Should Expect.* New York: Three Rivers Press. 2007.

The authors say that the elements of journalism are:
- Journalism's first obligation is to the truth.
- Its first loyalty is to its citizens.
- Its essence is a discipline of verification.
- Its practitioners must maintain an independence from those they cover.
- It must serve as an independent monitor of power.
- It must provide a forum for public criticism and compromise.
- It must strive to make the significant interesting and relevant.
- It must keep the news comprehensive and proportional.
- The practitioners must be allowed to exercise their personal conscience.

MacPherson, Myra. *"All Governments Lie": The Life and Times of Rebel Journalist I.F. Stone.* New York: Scribner, 2006.

I.F. Stone's Weekly had a small circulation, but its penetrating reporting had considerable impact. This biography of advocacy journalist Stone shows how a determined reporter can mine documents and reports for revealing stories. "Establishment reporters undoubtedly know a lot of things I don't," Stone said. "But a lot of what they know isn't true." He described the job of the journalist as "providing greater understanding of the complexities in which your country and your people and your time find themselves enmeshed." Pamphleteer, forerunner of the bloggers, Stone practiced an investigative journalism for readers who wanted more revealing information than journalism's stringent objectivity of the time provided.

McChesney, Robert. *Rich Media, Poor Democracy: Communication Politics in Dubious Times.* Champaign, Ill.:New Press, 1999.

Okrent, Daniel. *Public Editor #1: The Collected Columns (With Reflections, Reconsiderations, and Even a Few Retractions) of the First Ombudsman of* The New York Times. New York: Public Affairs. 2006.

In December 2003, in the aftermath of the fabrications of Jayson Blair and the heated-up reporting of supposed weapons of mass destruction in Iraq, the *Times* hired Okrent as its first ombudsman, also known as public editor and readers' representative. This collection based on his 18 months' work demonstrates Okrent's independence: he criticizes the paper, for example, for taking "so long" to examine its pre-war Iraq reporting. He also questions the use of anonymous sources for all but whistle-blowers.

Pierce, Robert N. *A Sacred Trust. Nelson Poynter and the St. Petersburg Times.* Gainesville, Fla.: University Press of Florida, 1994.

Roberts, Gene, and Hank Klibanoff. *The Race Beat: The Press, the Civil Rights Struggle and the Awakening of a Nation.* New York: Alfred A. Knopf, 2006.

Swados, Harvey. *Years of Conscience: The Muckrakers.* New York: World Publishing, 1962.

Waldron, Ann. *Hodding Carter: The Reconstruction of a Racist.* Chapel Hill, N.C.: Algonquin Books of Chapel Hill, 1993.

Glossary

These definitions were provided by the press associations and working reporters and editors. Many of the brief entries are from the *New England Daily Newspaper Study,* an examination of 105 daily newspapers, edited by Loren Ghiglione.

Print Terms

A

add   An addition to a story already written or being written.

assignment   An order to a reporter to cover an event. An editor keeps an assignment book that contains notations for reporters such as the following:

Jacobs—10 a.m.: Health officials tour new sewage treatment plant.

Klaren—11 a.m.: Interview Ben Wastersen, possible Democratic congressional candidate.

Mannen—Noon: Rotary Club luncheon speaker, Paul Robinson, the district attorney.

attribution   Identification of the person being quoted. Also, the source of information in a story. Sometimes, information is given on a not-for-attribution basis.

B

background   Material in a story that gives the circumstances surrounding or preceding the event.

banger   An exclamation point. Sometimes called a bang. Avoid. Let the reader do the exclaiming.

banner   Headline across or near the top of all or most of a newspaper page. Also called a *line, ribbon, streamer, screamer.*

B copy   Bottom section of a story written ahead of an event that will occur too close to deadline for the entire

story to be processed. The B copy usually consists of background material.

beat   Location assigned to a reporter for regular coverage—for example, police or city hall. Also, an exclusive story.

body type   Type in which most of a newspaper is set, usually 8- or 9-point type.

boldface   Heavy, black typeface; type that is blacker than the text with which it is used. Abbreviated *bf.*

Joel Sartore,
Wichita Eagle-Beacon

break   When a news development becomes known and available. Also, the point of interruption in a story continued from one page to another.

bright   Short, amusing story.

bulldog   Early edition, usually the first of a newspaper.

byline   Name of the reporter who wrote the story, placed atop the published article. An old-timer comments on the current use of bylines: "In the old days, a reporter was given a byline if he or she personally covered an important or unusual story, or the story was an exclusive. Sometimes if the writing was superior, a byline was given. Nowadays, everyone gets a byline, even if the story is a rewrite and the reporter never saw the event described in the story."

C

caps   Capital letters; same as *uppercase.*

caps and lowercase   Initial capital in a word followed by small letters. See **lowercase.**

caption See **cutline.**

column The vertical division of the news page. A standard-size newspaper is divided into five or more columns. Also, a signed article of opinion or strong personal expression, frequently by an authority or expert—a sports column, a medical column, political or social commentary.

computer-assisted reporting The use of online research or data analysis for a news story. Also called database reporting, analytic reporting and precision journalism.

copy Written form in which a news story or other material is prepared.

copy flow After a reporter finishes a story, it moves to the city desk, where the city editor reads it for major errors or problems. If it does not need further work, the story is moved to the copy desk for final editing and a headline. It then moves to the mechanical department.

correction Errors that reach publication are retracted or corrected if they are serious or someone demands a correction. Libelous matter is always corrected immediately, often in a separate news story rather than in the standard box assigned to corrections.

correspondent Reporter who sends news from outside a newspaper office. On smaller papers, often not a regular full-time staff member.

crony journalism Reporting that ignores or treats lightly negative news about friends. Beat reporters sometimes have a tendency to protect their informants to retain them as sources.

crop To cut or mask the unwanted portions, usually of a photograph.

cut Printed picture or illustration. Also, to eliminate material from a story. See **trim.**

cutline Any descriptive or explanatory material under a picture.

D

database A collection of information organized in a uniform way, usually as columns and rows. A database can consist of one list (called a table) or multiple tables that can be linked. Information compiled as a database can be searched and manipulated with computer software.

Reporters obtain databases from government agencies and analyze them for stories. Modern newsrooms have database systems for organizing and linking stories, photos, page layouts and other editorial content.

dateline Name of the city or town and sometimes the date at the start of a story that is not of local origin.

deadline Time at which the copy for an edition must be ready.

E

edition One version of a newspaper. Some papers have one edition a day, some several. Not to be confused with *issue,* which usually refers to all editions under a single date.

editorial Article of comment or opinion, usually on the editorial page.

editorial material All material in the newspaper that is not advertising.

enterprise copy Story, often initiated by a reporter, that digs deeper than the usual news story.

exclusive Story a reporter has obtained to the exclusion of the competition. Popularly known as a *scoop,* a term rarely used in the newsroom.

F

feature Story emphasizing the human or entertaining aspects of a situation. A news story or other material differentiated from straight news. As a verb, it means to give prominence to a story.

file To send a story to the office.

filler Material used to fill space. Small items used to fill out columns where needed. Also called *column closers* and *shorts.*

flag Printed title of a newspaper on page 1. Also known as *logotype* or *nameplate.*

folo Story that follows up on a theme in a news story. When a fire destroyed a parochial school in Chicago, newspapers followed up the fire coverage with stories about fire safety precautions in the Chicago schools.

free advertising   Use of the names of businesses and products not essential to the story. Instead of the brand name, use the broad term *camera* for Leica or Kodak.

futures calendar   Date book in which story ideas, meetings and activities scheduled for a later occurrence are listed. Also known as a *futures book.* Kept by city and assignment editors and by careful reporters.

G

good night   An expression meaning there is nothing further for the reporter from the desk for the day. Reporters call in when they take a break. Desks need to know where their reporters are in case of breaking stories.

graf   Abbreviation for *paragraph.*

Guild   Newspaper Guild, an international union to which reporters and other newspaper workers belong. Newspapers that have contracts with the Guild are said to be "organized."

H

handout   Term for written publicity or special-interest news sent to a newspaper for publication.

hard news   Spot news; live and current news in contrast to **features.**

head or headline   The display type over a printed news story.

head shot   Picture featuring little more than the head and shoulders of the person shown.

HFR   Abbreviation for "hold for release." Material that cannot be used until it is released by the source or at a designated time. Also known as *embargoed material.*

I

insert   Material placed inside a story. Usually, a paragraph or more to be placed in material already sent to the desk.

investigative reporting   Technique used to unearth information that sources often want hidden. This type of reporting involves examination of documents and records, the cultivation of informants, painstaking and extended research. Investigative reporting usually seeks to expose wrongdoing and has concentrated on public officials and their activities.

In recent years, industry and business have been scrutinized. Some journalists contend that the term is redundant, that all good reporting is investigative, that behind every surface fact is the real story that a resourceful, curious and persistent reporter can dig up.

italics   Type in which letters and characters slant to the right.

J

jump   Continuation of a story from one page to another. As a verb, to continue material. Also called *runover.*

K

kill   To delete a section from copy or to discard the entire story; also, to *spike* a story.

L

lead (pronounced *leed*)   First paragraph in a news story. In a direct or straight news lead, it summarizes the main facts. In a delayed lead, usually used on feature stories, it evokes a scene or sets a mood.

Also used to refer to the main idea of a story: An editor will ask a reporter, "What's the lead on the piece?" expecting a quick summary of the main facts.

Also, a tip on a story; an idea for a story. A source will tell a reporter, "I have a lead on a story for you."

localize   To emphasize the names of persons from the local community who are involved in events outside the city or region: A local couple rescued in a Paris hotel fire; the city police chief who speaks at a national conference.

lowercase   Small letters, as contrasted with capitals.

LTK   Designation on copy for "lead to come." Usually placed after the **slug.** Indicates the written material will be given a lead later.

M

makeup   Layout or design. The arrangement of body type, headlines and illustrations into pages.

masthead   Formal statement of a newspaper's name, officers, place of publication and other descriptive information, usually on the editorial page. Sometimes confused with *flag* or *nameplate.*

mug shot   See **head shot.**

N

new lead   See **running story.**

news hole   Space in a newspaper allotted to news, illustrations and other nonadvertising material.

O

obituary   Account of a person's death; also called *obit.*

off-the-record   Describes material offered the reporter in confidence. If the reporter accepts the material with this understanding, it cannot be used except as general background in a later story. Some reporters never accept off-the-record material. Some reporters will accept the material with the provision that if they can obtain the information elsewhere, they will use it. Reporters who learn of off-the-record material from other than the original source can use it.

No public, official meeting can be off-the-record, and almost all official documents (court records, police information) are public information. Private groups can ask that their meetings be kept off-the-record, but reporters frequently ignore such requests when the meeting is public or large numbers of people are present.

op-ed page   Abbreviation for the page opposite the editorial page. The page usually is devoted to opinion columns and related illustrations.

P

play   Emphasis given to a news story or picture—size and place in the newspaper of the story; typeface and size of headline.

P.M.   Afternoon or evening newspaper.

pool   Arrangement whereby limited numbers of reporters and photographers are selected to represent all those assigned to the story. Pooling is adopted when a large number of people would overwhelm the event or alter its nature. Members of the pool share news and film with the rest of the press corps.

precede   Story written prior to an event; also, the section of a story preceding the lead, sometimes set in italic.

press release   Publicity handout, or a story given to the news media for publication.

proof   Reproduction of type on paper for the purpose of making corrections or alterations.

puff piece or **puffery**   Publicity story or a story that contains unwarranted superlatives.

Q

quotes   Quotation marks; also a part of a story in which someone is directly quoted.

R

rewrite   To write for a second time to strengthen a story or to condense it.

rewriteman   Person who takes the facts of stories over the telephone and then puts them together into a story and who may rewrite reporters' stories.

roundup   A story that joins two or more events with a common theme, such as traffic accidents, weather, police reports. When the events occur in different cities and are wrapped up in one story, the story is known as an *undated roundup.*

rowback   A story that attempts to correct a previous story without indicating that the prior story had been in error or without taking responsibility for the error.

running story   Event that develops and is covered over a period of time. For an event covered in subsequent editions of a newspaper or on a single cycle of a wire service, additional material is slugged as follows:

New lead—important new information; Adds and inserts—less important information; Sub—material that replaces dated material, which is removed.

S

sell   Presentation a reporter makes to impress the editor with the importance of his or her story; also, editors sell stories to their superiors at news conferences.

shirttail   Short, related story added to the end of a longer one.

short   Filler, generally of some current news value.

sidebar   Story that emphasizes and elaborates on one part of another nearby story.

situationer   Story that pulls together a continuing event for the reader who might not have kept track as it unfolded. The situationer is helpful with complex or technical developments or on stories with varied datelines and participants.

slant   To write a story so as to influence the reader's thinking. To editorialize: to color or misrepresent.

slug   Word placed on copy to identify the story, usually in top left of page.

source   Person, record, document or event that provides the information for the story.

sourcebook   Alphabetical listing, by name and by title, of the addresses and the office and home telephone numbers of people on the reporter's beat and some general numbers—FBI agent in charge in town, police and fire department spokesperson, hospital information, weather bureau.

split page   Front page of an inside section; also known as the *break page, second front page.*

stringer   Correspondent, not a regular staff member, who is paid by the story or by the number of words written.

style   Rules for capitalization, punctuation and spelling that standardize usage so that the material presented is uniform. The most frequently used stylebook is the common stylebook of the Associated Press. Also, the unique characteristics of a reporter's writing or news delivery.

stylebook   Specific listing of the conventions of spelling, abbreviation, punctuation and capitalization used by a particular newspaper or wire service.

sub   See **running story.**

subhead   One-line and sometimes two-line head (usually in boldface body type) inserted in a long story at intervals for emphasis or to break up a long column of type.

T

text   Verbatim report of a speech or public statement.

tight   Refers to a paper so crowded with ads that the news space must be reduced. It is the opposite of the *wide open paper.*

tip   Information passed to a reporter, often in confidence. The material usually requires further fact gathering. Occasionally, verification is impossible and the reporter must decide whether to go with the tip on the strength of the insider's knowledge.

trim   To reduce or condense copy carefully.

U

update   Story that brings the reader up-to-date on a situation or personality previously in the news. If the state legislature appropriated additional funds for five new criminal court judges to meet the increased number of cases in the courts, an update might be written some months later about how many more cases were handled after the judges went to work. An update usually has no hard news angle.

V

verification   Determination of the truth of the material the reporter gathers or is given. The assertions, sometimes even the actual observations, do not necessarily mean the information is accurate or true. Some of the basic tools of verification are the telephone book, for names and addresses; the city directory, for occupations. For verification of more complex material, the procedure of Thucydides, the Greek historian and author of the *History of the Peloponnesian War,* is good advice for the journalist:

"As to the deeds done in the war, I have not thought myself at liberty to record them on hearsay from the first informant or on arbitrary conjecture. My account rests either on personal knowledge or on the closest possible scrutiny of each statement made by others. The process of research was laborious, because the conflicting accounts were given by those who had witnessed the several events, as partiality swayed or memory served them."

W

wire services Synonym for *press associations,* the Associated Press and United Press International. There are foreign-owned press services to which some newspapers subscribe: Reuters, Agence France-Presse.

Broadcast Terms

A

actuality An on-the-scene report.

audio Sound.

C

close-up Shot of the face of the subject that dominates the frame so that little background is visible.

cover shot A long shot usually cut in at the beginning of a sequence to establish place or location.

cue A signal in script or by word or gesture to begin or to stop. Two types: incue and outcue.

cut Quick transition from one type of picture to another. Radio: A portion of an actuality on tape used on broadcast.

cutaway Transition shot—usually short—from one theme to another; used to avoid **jump cut.** Often, a shot of the interviewer listening.

D

dissolve Smooth fading of one picture for another. As the second shot becomes distinct, the first slowly disappears.

dolly Camera platform. Dolly-in: Move platform toward subject. Dolly-out: Move platform away.

dub The transfer of one videotape to another.

E

establishing shot Frequently a wide shot; used to give the viewer a sense of the scene of action.

F

FI or fade in A scene that begins without full brilliance and gradually assumes full brightness. **FO** or **fade out** is the opposite.

freeze frame A single frame that is frozen into position.

G

graphics All visual displays, such as artwork, maps, charts and still photos.

J

jump cut Transition from one subject to a different subject in an abrupt manner. Avoided with **cutaway** shot between the scenes.

L

lead-in Introductory statements to film or tape of actual event. The lead-in sets up the actuality by giving the context of the event.

lead-out Copy that comes immediately after tape or film of an actuality. The lead-out identifies the newsmaker again so listeners and viewers will know whom they just heard or saw. Used more often in radio. Also known as *tag lines.*

long shot Framing that takes in the scene of the event.

M

medium shot Framing of one person from head to waist or of a small group seated at a table. Known as *MS.*

mix Combining two or more sound elements into one.

montage   A series of brief shots of various subjects to give a single impression or communicate one idea.

O

O/C   On camera. A reporter delivering copy directly to the camera without covering pictures.

outtakes   Scenes that are discarded for the final story.

P

panning or **pan shot**   Moving the camera from left to right or right to left.

R

remote   A taped or live broadcast from a location outside the studio; also, the unit that originates such a broadcast.

S

segue   An uninterrupted transition from one sound to another; a sound dissolve. (Pronounced *seg-way.*)

SOF   Sound on film. Recorded simultaneously with the picture.

SOT   Sound on tape. Recorded simultaneously with picture on tape.

T

trim   To eliminate material.

V

V/O   Reporter's voice over pictures.

VTR   Videotape recording.

Z

zooming   Use of a variable focus lens to take close-ups and wide angle shots from a stationary position. By using a zoom lens, a camera operator can give the impression of moving closer to or farther from the subject.

Internet Terms

B

blurb   A summary of a story on a news Web page. It links to the full story.

C

chat   To talk in real time with others over the Internet or through a commercial service such as America Online.

content provider   Firm or organization that creates content, such as Salon or CNET.

D

deep Web   See **invisible Web.**

F

flaming   Hostile chat, commentary or e-mail.

H

hit   Request by a Web user to a server for an image or a file. Hits are used to measure the frequency or popularity of a site. Most sites now use *page views* as the more reliable measure of how many people visit a site.

home page   Online site or home for a multitude of information—about movie stars, athletes, pets or commercial messages. Can be in the form of text, graphics, sound, animation.

hotspot   A place that offers a Wi-Fi connection to the Internet. Also called an access point. See **Wi-Fi.**

HTML   Abbreviation for Hypertext Markup Language, the language used to create World Wide Web documents.

Hyperlink   Location on the Internet that takes the user to another site. Using the mouse, a user *clicks on* the link to be carried to the other document. Hyperlinks are indicated often by highlighting or boldface type.

Hypertext   System of coding text to link electronic documents with one another. Elements in a hypertext document are linked to elements in other documents.

I

instant message   Programs that allow users to send real-time messages across the Net. Popular versions are AOL's IM and icq.com.

Internet   Global network of computers communicating in a common language or protocol (TCP/IP, Transmission Control Protocol/Internet Protocol) over telephone lines or microwave links. Home to the World Wide Web, newsgroups and online forums. Always preceded by "the" unless used as a modifier. The "i" is always capped. Synonymous with the Net.

invisible Web   An online database, usually containing government records. Most search tools do not penetrate these databases. Also known as the **deep Web.**

L

listserv   Mail-handling software that allows people to subscribe to mailing lists. The lists consist of e-mail addresses. Subscribers receive the messages posted to the central mail-handling address.

log on   The process of identifying oneself on the computer to gain access to a network.

M

mailing list   Ongoing e-mail discussion devoted to a specific topic. Lists can be public or private, moderated or unmoderated. Also, a group of people (subscribers) with a common interest. The Internet has more than 30,000 mailing lists.

S

search engine   A tool to find information on the Internet by keyword(s) or concept. A search tool attempts to match your keyword(s) against a computerized index of words found on Web pages, in contrast to a Web directory. With Web access, most search engines are free.

snail mail   Postal mail.

spam   Electronic litter. Unwanted advertisements, junk postings. Similar to junk mail. Spamming is the act of sending spam.

U

Usenet newsgroups   Collection of informal forums, bulletin boards or newsgroups distributed over the Internet and devoted to a variety of interests and topics. More than 54,000 exist.

W

Web   Short for the World Wide Web, part of the Internet that allows users to access text, pictures, charts, documents, graphics, sounds and video.

Web directory   A list of Web sites by categories and sub-categories. It is used for finding a Web site about a particular subject. In contrast to a search engine, people—not computers—evaluate the sites and assign them a category in a Web directory.

Web site   Collection of pages on the Web that can be accessed through a main title or contents page, which is called a *front door*. A site can be likened to a TV network or a publishing house.

Wi-Fi   A popular way of connecting a computer wirelessly to the Internet. Wi-Fi refers to network connections that use a radio frequency of 802.11. Wi-Fi has a short range and usually serves a specific location, such as a building or park. However, some communities have established a system of overlapping Wi-Fi hotspots and created wireless networks that cover entire cities.

Appendixes

The following appendixes are included in *NRW Plus,* available online at www. mhhe.com/mencher11:

Stylebook

addresses Abbreviate *Avenue, Boulevard, Street* with specific address: *1314 Kentucky St.* Spell out without specific address: *construction on Fifth Avenue.*

Use figures for the address number: *3 Third Ave.; 45 Main St.* Spell out numbers under 10 as street names: *21 Fourth Ave.; 450 11th St.*

age Use figures. To express age as an adjective, use hyphens: *a 3-year-old girl.* Also use hyphens when age is expressed as a noun as in: *a 10-year-old.* Unless otherwise stated, the figure is presumed to indicate years: *a boy, 4, and his sister, 6 months.*

Infant: under one year of age; *child:* someone in the period between infancy and youth, ages 1 to 13; *girl, boy:* under 18; *youth:* 13–18; *man, woman:* over 18; *adult:* over 18, unless used in specific legal context for crimes such as drinking; *middle-aged:* 35–55; *elderly:* over 65. Avoid *elderly* when describing individuals.

a.m., p.m. Lowercase with periods.

amendment Capitalize when referring to specific amendments to the U.S. Constitution. Spell out for the first through ninth; use figures for 10th and above: *First Amendment, 10th Amendment.*

anti- Hyphenate all but words that have their own meanings: *antibiotic, antibody, anticlimax, antidote, antifreeze, antihistamine, antiknock, antimatter, antiparticle, antipasto, antiperspirant, antiseptic, antiserum, antithesis, antitoxin, antitrust.*

bi, semi When used with periods of time, the prefix *bi* means every other; *semi* means twice. A biennial conference meets every other year. A semiweekly newspaper comes out twice a week. No hyphens.

brand name A nonlegal term for a trademark. Do not use as generic terms or as verbs: make it *soft drink* instead of *Coke* or *coke; photocopy* instead of *Xerox.*

capitalization Generally, follow a down style.

Proper nouns: Use capitals for names of persons, places, trademarks; titles when used with names; nicknames of people, states, teams; titles of books, plays, movies.

century Lowercase, spelling out numbers less than 10, except when used in proper nouns—*the fifth century, 18th century,* but *20th Century-Fox* and *Nineteenth Century Society*—following the organization's practice.

chairman, chairwoman Use *chairman* or *chairwoman* instead of *chair* or *chairperson; spokesman* or *spokeswoman* instead of *spokesperson* and similar constructions unless the *-person* construction is a formal title.

The Standards

The stylebook contains guidelines to provide uniform presentation of the printed word, to assure consistency in spelling, capitalization, punctuation and abbreviation for those who write and edit the news.

Inconsistencies in addresses, dates and titles make readers wonder why it's 1280 St. John's Avenue in one paragraph and 1280 St. John's Ave. in another; January 25, 1977, in the lead and Jan. 25, 1977, three paragraphs later.

Because so many people write and edit a publication, a standard for style is essential. The stylebook fulfills that purpose. Different publications have different stylebooks, but most use a version of the *AP Stylebook,* which is the basis of this one.

Use *chairman* or *spokesman* when referring to the office in general. A neutral word such as *representative* often may be the best choice.

co- Use a hyphen when forming nouns, adjectives and verbs that indicate occupation or status: *co-star, co-written.* No hyphen for other constructions: *coeducation, coexist.*

Congress Capitalize when referring to the U.S. Senate and House of Representatives. The term is correctly used only in reference to the two legislative branches together. Capitalize also when referring to foreign governments that use the term or its equivalent.

Do not capitalize *congressional* unless it is part of a proper name.

Constitution, constitutional Capitalize when referring to the U.S. Constitution, with or without the *U.S.* modifier. When referring to other constitutions, capitalize only when preceded by the name of a nation or state. Lowercase *constitutional.*

court names Capitalize the full proper names of courts at all levels. Retain capitalization if *U.S.* or a state name is dropped.

dates *July 6, 1957, was her birth date.* (Use commas.) *She was born in July 1957.* (No comma between the month and year.)

Abbreviate the month with a specific date: *Feb. 19.* Spell out all months when standing alone. With dates, use abbreviations: *Jan., Feb., Aug., Sept., Oct., Nov., Dec.* Spell out *March, April, May, June, July.*

directions and regions Lowercase *north, south, northeast,* etc. when they indicate compass direction: *Police followed the car south on Route 22.*

Capitalize when they refer to regions: *Southern accent; Northeastern industry.*

With names of nations, lowercase except when they are part of a proper name or are used to designate a politically divided nation: *tourism in southern France,* but *South Korea* and *Northern Ireland.*

Lowercase compass points when they describe a section of a state or city except when they are part of a proper name (*South Dakota*) or when they refer to a widely known region (*Southern California; the East Side of New York*).

Capitalize them when combining them with a common noun to form a proper noun: *the Eastern Hemisphere; the North Woods.*

entitled Does not mean *titled. Citizens 18 and older are entitled to vote,* but *the book is titled "News Reporting and Writing."*

ex- No hyphen for words that use *ex* in the sense of *out of: excommunicate, expropriate.* Hyphenate when using in the sense of *former: ex-husband, ex-convict. Former* is preferred with titles: *Former President Gerald R. Ford.*

fireman Use *firefighter* because some women hold this job.

fractions Spell out amounts less than 1, using hyphens: *one-half, two-thirds.* Use figures for amounts larger than 1, converting to decimals whenever possible: *3.5* instead of *three and one-half or 3 1/2.*

Figures are preferred in tabular material and in stories about stocks.

gay Acceptable as a popular synonym for *homosexual.* May be used as a noun and an adjective.

handicapped, disabled, impaired Avoid describing an individual as *disabled* or *handicapped* unless it is essential to the story. If necessary to use, make clear what the handicap is and how it affects the person's mental or physical activity. *Disabled* refers to a condition that interferes with a person's ability to do something independently. *Handicap* should be avoided in describing a disability. *Blind* means complete loss of sight. For others, use *partially blind. Deaf* means complete loss of hearing. For others, use *partial hearing loss* or *partially deaf. Mute* refers to people who physically cannot speak. For others, use *speech impaired.* Do not use *wheelchair-bound* unless necessary, and then say why.

Do not identify someone as having a disability unless the disability is relevant, and the relevance is clear. People with disabilities should not be described as heroes or victims. Describe the symptoms or difficulties the person encounters and let the reader reach conclusions.

historical periods and events Capitalize widely recognized periods and events in anthropology, archaeology, geology and history: *the Bronze Age, the Ice Age, the Renaissance.*

Capitalize widely recognized popular names for eras and events: *the Glorious Revolution, the Roaring '20s.*

holidays and holy days Capitalize them. In federal law, the legal holidays are New Year's, Martin Luther King's Birthday, President's Day, Memorial Day, Independence Day, Labor Day, Columbus Day, Veterans Day, Thanksgiving and Christmas.

States are not required to follow the federal lead in designating holidays, except that federal employees must receive the day off or must be paid overtime if they work.

Jewish holy days: Hanukkah, Passover, Purim, Rosh Hashana, Shavuot, Sukkot and Yom Kippur.

in- No hyphen when it means *not: invalid; inaccurate.* Mostly used without the hyphen in other combinations, but there are a few exceptions: *in-house; in-depth.* Consult a dictionary when in doubt.

-in Always precede with a hyphen: *break-in; sit-in; write-in.*

initials Use periods and no space: *H.L. Mencken; C.S. Lewis.* This practice has been adopted to ensure that initials will be set on the same line.

like- Follow with a hyphen when used to mean *similar to: like-minded; like-natured.*

-like No hyphen unless the *l* would be tripled: *lifelike,* but *shell-like.*

mailman Use the term *letter carrier* or *mail carrier* because many women work for the Postal Service.

man, mankind *Humanity* is preferred for the plural form. Use *a person* or *an individual* in the singular. A phrase or sentence usually can be reconstructed to eliminate any awkwardness.

National Organization for Women. Not *National Organization of Women.*

nationalities and races Capitalize the proper names of nationalities, peoples, races, tribes, etc. Lowercase *black* and *white.* Lowercase derogatory terms such as *honky* and *nigger.* Use them only in direct quotations.

See **race** for guidelines on when racial identification is pertinent in a story.

nobility Capitalize *king, queen, duke* and other titles when they precede the individual's name. Lowercase when standing alone: *King Juan Carlos,* but *the king of Spain.*

non- In general, do not hyphenate if *not* could be used before the root word. Hyphenate before proper nouns or in awkward combinations: *non-nuclear.*

numerals Spell out *one* through *nine,* except when used to indicate age, votes, building numbers, scores. Use figures for *10* and above.

Spell out a number when it begins a sentence: *Fifteen members voted against the bill.* Use figures when a year begins a sentence: *1999 began auspiciously.*

Use figures for time, temperature, dimensions, percentages, percents and money: $5, but *a dollar.*

If a series has mixed numbers, use all numbers: *His table had scattered on it 6 magazines, 13 books and 11 newspapers.*

For amounts of $1 million and more, use the *$* sign and figures up to two decimal places with the *million, billion, trillion* spelled out: *$1.65 million.* Exact amounts are given in figures: *$1,650,398.*

When spelling out large numbers, separate numbers ending in *y* from the next number with a hyphen: *seventy-nine; one hundred seventy-nine.*

people, persons Use *person* when referring to an individual. *People* is preferred to *persons* in all plural uses.

People also is a collective noun that takes a plural verb when used to refer to a single race or nation: *The Philippine people are awaiting the president's decision on the offer of aid.* In this sense, *peoples* is the plural form: *The peoples of Western Europe do not always agree on East-West issues.*

percentages Use figures—decimals, not fractions—and the word *percent,* not the symbol: *2.5 percent; 10 percent.* For amounts less than 1 percent, place a zero before the decimal: *0.6 percent.*

When presenting a range, repeat *percent* after each figure: *2 percent to 5 percent.*

policeman Use *police officer* instead.

political parties and philosophies Capitalize the name of the party and the word *party* when it is used as part of the organization's proper name: *the Democratic Party.*

Capitalize *Communist, Conservative, Democrat, Liberal,* etc., when they refer to the activities of a specific party or to individual members.

Lowercase the name of a philosophy in noun and adjective forms unless it is derived from a proper name: *communism; fascist,* but *Marxism; Nazi.*

In general, avoid the terms *conservative, radical, leftist* and *rightist.* In casual and popular usage, the meanings of these terms vary, depending on the user and the situation being discussed. A more precise description of an individual's or a group's political views is preferred.

post office Should not be capitalized. The agency is the U.S. Postal Service.

prefixes See entries for specific prefixes. Generally, do not hyphenate when using a prefix with a word starting with a consonant.

Except for *cooperate* and *coordinate,* use a hyphen if the prefix ends in the same vowel that begins the following word: *re-elect,* not *reelect.*

Use a hyphen if the word that follows is capitalized: *pan-American; anti-Catholic.*

Use a hyphen to join doubled prefixes: *sub-subclause.*

presidency Always lowercase.

president Capitalized only as a title before an individual's name: *President George W. Bush,* but *the president said he would spend New Year's in Houston.*

presidential Lowercase unless part of a proper name: *presidential approval,* but *Presidential Medal of Freedom.*

race Race, religion and national origin are sometimes essential to a story but too often are injected when they are not pertinent. When in doubt about relevance, substitute descriptions such as *white, Baptist, French.* If one of these descriptions would be pertinent, use the original term.

religious references
DEITIES: Capitalize the proper names of monotheistic deities, pagan and mythological gods and goddesses: *Allah, the Father, Zeus.* Lowercase pronouns that refer to the deity: *he, him, thee, who,* etc.

Lowercase *gods* when referring to the deities of polytheistic religions. Lowercase such words as *god-awful, godlike, godsend.*

LIFE OF JESUS CHRIST: Capitalize the names of major events in the life of Jesus Christ in references that do not use his name: *the Last Supper; the Resurrection.* Lowercase when the words are used with his name: *the ascension of Christ.* Apply the same principle to events in the life of his mother, Mary.

RITES: Capitalize proper names for rites that commemorate the Last Supper or signify a belief in Jesus Christ's presence: *the Lord's Supper; Holy Eucharist.* Lowercase the names of other sacraments.

HOLY DAYS: Capitalize the names of holy days: *Hanukkah.*

OTHER WORDS: Lowercase *heaven, hell, devil, angel, cherub, apostle, priest,* etc.

rock 'n' roll Not *rock and roll.*

room numbers Use figures and capitalize *room:* The faculty met in Room 516. Capitalize the names of specially designated rooms: *Oval Office; Blue Room.*

saint Abbreviate as *St.* in the names of saints, cities and other places except *Saint John* (New Brunswick), to distinguish it from St. John's, Newfoundland, and *Sault Ste. Marie.*

seasons Lowercase *spring, summer, fall, winter* and their derivatives. Capitalize when part of a formal name: *St. Paul Winter Carnival; Summer Olympics.*

self- Always hyphenate: *self-motivated; self-taught.*

senate, senatorial Capitalize all references to specific legislative bodies, regardless of whether the name of the nation or state is used: *U.S. Senate; the state Senate.*

Lowercase plural uses: *the Iowa and Kansas state senates.* Lowercase references to nongovernmental bodies: *the student-faculty senate.*

Always lowercase *senatorial.*

sexism Avoid stereotyping women or men. Be conscious of equality in treatment of both sexes.

When writing of careers and jobs, avoid presuming that the wage earner is a man and that the woman is a homemaker: *the average family of five* instead of *the average worker with a wife and three children.*

Avoid physical descriptions of women or men when not absolutely relevant to the story.

Use parallel references to both sexes: *the men and the women,* not *the men and the ladies; husband and wife,* not *man and wife.*

Do not use nouns and pronouns to indicate sex unless the sex difference is basic to understanding or there is no suitable substitute. One way to avoid such subtle sexism is to change the noun to the plural, eliminating the masculine pronoun: *Drivers should carry their licenses,* not *Every driver should carry his license.*

Personal appearance and marital and family relationships should be used only when relevant to the story.

state names Spell out names of the 50 U.S. states when they stand alone in textual matter.

The names of eight states are never abbreviated: *Alaska, Hawaii, Idaho, Iowa, Maine, Ohio, Texas, Utah.*

Abbreviate other state names when used with a city, in a dateline or with party affiliation. Do not use Postal Service abbreviations.

Ala.	*Fla.*	*Md.*	*Neb.*	*N.D.*	*Tenn.*
Ariz.	*Ga.*	*Mass.*	*Nev.*	*Okla.*	*Vt.*
Ark.	*Ill.*	*Mich.*	*N.H.*	*Ore.*	*Va.*
Calif.	*Ind.*	*Minn.*	*N.J.*	*Pa.*	*Wash.*
Colo.	*Kan.*	*Miss.*	*N.M.*	*R.I.*	*W.Va*
Conn.	*Ky.*	*Mo.*	*N.Y.*	*S.C.*	*Wis.*
Del.	*La.*	*Mont.*	*N.C.*	*S.D.*	*Wyo.*

statehouse Capitalize all references to a specific statehouse, with or without the state name. But lowercase in all plural uses: *the New Mexico Statehouse; the Arizona and New Mexico statehouses.*

suspensive hyphenation Use as follows: *The 19- and 20-year-olds were not served alcoholic beverages.* Use in all similar cases.

Although the form looks somewhat awkward, it guides readers, who may otherwise expect a noun to follow the first figure.

syllabus, syllabuses Also: *memorandum, memorandums.*

teen, teen-ager (noun), **teen-age** (adjective) Do not use *teen-aged.*

telecast (noun), **televise** (verb)

temperatures Use figures for all except *zero.* Use the word *minus,* not a minus sign, to indicate temperatures below zero. *The day's high was 9; the day's low was minus 9.*

Temperatures are higher and lower and they rise and fall but they do not become warmer or cooler.

Third World The economically developing nations of Africa, Asia and Latin America.

time Exact times often are unnecessary. *Last night* and *this morning* are acceptable substitutes for *yesterday* and *today.* Use exact time when pertinent but avoid redundancies: *8 a.m. this morning* should be *8 a.m. today* or *8 o'clock this morning.*

Use figures except for *noon* and *midnight: 12 noon* is redundant.

Separate hours from minutes with a colon: *3:15 p.m.*

titles

ACADEMIC TITLES: Capitalize and spell out formal titles such as *professor, dean, president, chancellor* and *chairman* when they precede a name. Lowercase elsewhere. Do not abbreviate *Professor* as *Prof.*

Lowercase modifiers such as *journalism* in *journalism Professor John Rist* or *department* in *department chairwoman Kim Power,* unless the modifier is a proper name: *French Professor Jeannette Spear.*

COURTESY TITLES: Do not use the courtesy titles *Miss, Mr., Mrs.* or *Ms.* on first reference. Instead, use the person's first and last names. Do not use *Mr.* unless it is combined with *Mrs.: Kyle Scott Hotsenpiller; Mr. and Mrs. Kyle Scott Hotsenpiller.*

Courtesy titles may be used on second reference for women, according to the woman's preference and these guidelines:

- Married women: On first reference, identify a woman by her own first name and her husband's last name, if she uses it: *Betty Phillips.* Use *Mrs.* on first reference only if a woman requests that her husband's first name be used or her own first name cannot be determined: *Mrs. Steven A. Phillips.*

- On second reference, use *Mrs.* unless a woman initially identified by her own first name prefers *Ms.: Rachel Finch; Mrs. Finch; Ms. Finch.* Or use no title: *Finch; Rachel Finch.*

- If a married woman is known by her maiden name, precede it by *Miss* on second reference unless she prefers *Ms.: Sarah Wilson; Miss Wilson* or *Ms. Wilson.*

- Unmarried women: Use *Miss, Ms.* or no title on second reference, according to the woman's preference.

For divorced and widowed women, the normal practice is to use *Mrs.* or no title on second reference, according to the woman's preference. Use *Miss, Ms.* or no title, according to the woman's preference, if the woman returns to her maiden name.

If a woman prefers *Ms.* or no title, do not include her marital status in a story unless it is pertinent.

GOVERNMENTAL TITLES: Capitalize when used as a formal title in front of a person's name. It is not necessary to use a title on second reference: *Gov. Fred Florence; Florence.* For women who hold official positions, use the courtesy title on second reference, according to the guidelines for courtesy titles: *Gov. Ruth Arnold; Miss Arnold, Mrs. Arnold, Ms. Arnold, Arnold.* (Some newspapers do not use the courtesy title on second reference.)

Abbreviate *Governor* as *Gov., Lieutenant Governor* as *Lt. Gov.* when used as a formal title before a name.

Congressional titles: Before names, abbreviate *Senator* as *Sen.* and *Representative* as *Rep.* Add *U.S.* or *state* if necessary to avoid confusion.

Short form punctuation for party affiliation: Use abbreviations listed under **state names** and set them off from the person's name with commas: *Sen. Ron Wyden, D-Ore., and Rep. Barney Frank, D-Mass., attended the ceremony.*

Capitalize and spell out other formal government titles before a person's name. Do not use titles on second references: *Attorney General Jay Craven spoke. Craven said . . .*

Capitalize and spell out formal titles instead of abbreviating before the person's name in direct quotations only. Lowercase in all uses not mentioned already.

OCCUPATIONAL TITLES: They are always lowercase: *senior vice president Nancy Harden.* Avoid false titles: *bridge champion Helen P. George* should be: *Helen P. George, Sioux Falls bridge tourney winner.*

RELIGIOUS TITLES: The first reference to a clergyman, clergywoman or nun should include a capitalized title before the person's name.

On second reference: for men, use only a last name if he uses a surname. If a man is known only by a religious name, repeat the title: *Pope Paul VI* or *Pope Paul* on first reference; *the pope* or *the pontiff* on second reference. For women, use *Miss, Mrs., Ms.* or no title, according to the woman's preference.

Cardinals, archbishops, bishops: On first reference, use the title before the person's first and last name. On second reference, use the last name only or the title.

Ministers and priests: Use *the Rev.* before a name on first reference. Substitute *Monsignor* before the name of a Roman Catholic priest who has received this honor.

Rabbis: Use *Rabbi* before a name on first reference. On second reference, use only the last name of a man; use *Miss, Mrs., Ms.* or no title before a woman's last name, according to her preference.

Nuns: Always use *Sister* or *Mother: Sister Agnes Mary* in all references if the nun uses only a religious name; *Sister Ann Marie Graham* on first reference if she uses a surname. *Sister Graham* on second.

TITLES OF WORKS: For titles of books, movies, operas, plays, poems, songs, television programs and lectures, speeches and works of art, apply the following guidelines:

Capitalize the principal words, including prepositions and conjunctions of four or more letters.

Capitalize an article or word of fewer than four letters if it is the first or last word in a title.

Place quotation marks around the names of all such works except the Bible and books that are primarily catalogs of reference material, including almanacs, directories, dictionaries, encyclopedias, handbooks and similar publications.

Translate a foreign title into English unless a work is known to the American public by its foreign name.

Do not use quotation marks or italics with the names of newspapers and magazines.

TV Acceptable as an adjective but should not be used as a noun.

upstate, downstate Always lowercase.

venereal disease *VD* is acceptable on second reference.

versus Abbreviate as *vs.* in all uses.

vice Use two words, no hyphen.

vice president Follow the guidelines for **president.**

war Capitalize when part of the name for a particular conflict: *World War II; the Cold War.*

well- Hyphenate as part of a compound modifier: *a well-dressed man.*

wide- Usually hyphenated: *wide-eyed.* Exception: *widespread.*

words as words When italics are available, italicize them. Otherwise, place in quotation marks: *Rep. Ellen Jacobson asked journalists to address her as "congresswoman."*

years Use figures. Use an *s* without the apostrophe to indicate spans of centuries: *the 1800s.* Use an apostrophe to indicate omitted numerals and an *s* to indicate decades: the *'80s.*

Years are the only figures that may be placed at the start of a sentence: *1959 was a year of rapid city growth.*

Punctuation

Keep a good grammar book handy. No stylebook can adequately cover the complexities of the 13 punctuation marks: apostrophe, bracket, colon, comma, dash, ellipsis, exclamation point, hyphen, parenthesis, period, question mark, quotation mark, semicolon. The following is a guide to frequent problems and usages:

Apostrophe Use (1) for possessives, (2) to indicate omitted figures or letters and (3) to form some plurals.

1. **Possessives.** Add apostrophe and *s* (*'s*) to the end of singular and plural nouns or the indefinite pronoun unless it has an *s* or *z* sound.

   > *The woman's coat. The women's coats.*
   > *The child's toy. The children's toys.*
   > *Someone's pistol. One's hopes.*

   If the word is plural and ends in an *s* or *z* sound, add an apostrophe only:

   > *Boys' books. Joneses' farm.*

   For singular common nouns ending in *s,* add an apostrophe and *s* (*'s*) unless the next word begins with s:

   > *The witness's testimony. The witness' story.*

   For singular proper nouns, add only an apostrophe:

   > *Dickens' novels. James' hat.*

2. **Omitted figures or letters.** Use in contractions: *Don't, can't.* Put in place of omitted figures: *Class of '88.*

3. **To form some plurals.** When figures, letters, symbols and words are referred to as words, use the apostrophe and *s.*

   a. Figures: *He skated perfect 8's.*
   b. Letters: *She received all A's in her finals.*
   c. Symbols: *Journalists never use **&** to substitute for **and.***

Caution: The pronouns *ours, yours, theirs, his, hers, whose* do not take the apostrophe. *Its* is the possessive pronoun. *It's* is the contraction of *it is.*

Note: Compound words and nouns in joint possession use the possessive in the last word:

- Everybody else's homes.

- His sister-in-law's book.

- Clinton and Gore's party.

If there is separate possession, each noun takes the possessive form: *Clinton's and Bush's opinions differ.*

Brackets Check whether the newspaper can set them. Use to enclose a word or words within a quote that the writer inserts: *"Happiness [his note read] is a state of mind."* Try to avoid the need for such an insertion. Use for paragraphs within a story that refer to an event separate from the datelined material.

Colon The colon is usually used at the end of a sentence to call attention to what follows. It introduces lists, tabulations, texts and quotations of more than one sentence.

It also can be used to mark a full stop before a dramatic word or statement: *She had only one goal in life: work.* The colon is used in the time of day: *7:45 p.m.;* elapsed time of an event: *4:01.1;* in dialogue in question and answer, as from a trial.

Comma The best general guide for the use of the comma is the human voice as it pauses, stops and varies in tone. The comma marks the pause, the short stop:

1. He looked into the hospital room, but he was unable to find the patient.

2. Although he continued his search on the floor for another 20 minutes, he was unable to find anyone to help him.

3. He decided that he would go downstairs, ask at the desk and then telephone the police.

4. If that also failed, he thought to himself, he would have to give up the search.

Note that when reading these sentences aloud, the commas are natural resting points for pauses. The four sentences also illustrate the four principles governing the use of commas:

1. The comma is used to separate main clauses when they are joined by a coordinating conjunction. (The coordinating conjunctions are *for, nor, and, but, or*). The comma can be eliminated if the main clauses are short: *He looked into the room and he froze.*

2. Use the comma after an introductory element: a clause, long phrase, transitional expression or interjection.

3. Use the comma to separate words, phrases or clauses in a series. Also, use it in a series of coordinate adjectives: *He was wearing a long, full cape.*

4. Set off nonessential material in a sentence with comma(s). When the parenthetical or interrupting nonrestrictive clauses and phrases are in the middle of a sentence, two commas are needed: *The country, he was told, needed his assistance.*

Other uses of the comma:

- With full sentence quotes, not with partial quotes: *He asked, "Where are you going?" The man replied that he was "blindly groping" his way home.*

- To separate city and county, city and state. In place of the word *of* between a name and city: *Jimmy Carter, Plains, Ga.*

- To set off a person's age: *Orville Sterb, 19, of Fullerton, Calif.*

- In dates: *March 19, 1940, was the date he entered the army.*

- In party affiliations: *Arlen Speeter, R-Pa., spoke.*

Caution: The comma is frequently misused by placing it instead of the period or semicolon between two main clauses. This is called *comma splice:*

> WRONG: The computer was jammed, he could not write his assignment.
> RIGHT: The computer was jammed. He could not write his assignment.
>   The computer was jammed; he could not write his assignment.

Dash Use a dash (1) to indicate a sudden or dramatic shift in thought within a sentence, (2) to set off a series of words that contains commas and (3) to introduce sections of a list or a summary.

The dash is a call for a short pause, just as are the comma and the parentheses. The comma is the most often used and is the least dramatic of the separators. The parentheses set off unimportant elements. The dash tends to emphasize materials. It has this quality because it is used sparingly.

1. He stared at the picture—and he was startled to find himself thinking of her face. The man stood up—painfully and awkwardly—and extended his hand in greeting.

2. There were three people watching them—an elderly woman, a youth with a crutch at his side and a young woman in jeans holding a paperback—and he pulled her aside out of their view.

3. He gave her his reasons for being there:
   —He wanted to apologize;
   —He needed to give her some material;
   —He was leaving on a long trip.

Note: This third form should be used infrequently, usually when the listing will be followed by an elaboration.

The dash is also used in datelines.

Ellipsis Use the ellipsis to indicate material omitted from a quoted passage from a text, transcript, play, etc.: *The minutes stated that Breen had asked, "How many gallons of paint . . . were used in the project?* Put one space before and one space after each of the three periods. If the sentence preceding the omission ends with a period, use four periods, one to mark the end of the sentence (without space, as a regular period), three more for the ellipsis.

The ellipsis is also used by some columnists to separate short items in a paragraph.

Do not use to mark pauses or shifts in thought or for emphasis.

Exclamation point Much overused. There are reporters who have gone through a lifetime of writing and have never used the exclamation point, except when copying material in which it is used. The exclamation point is used to indicate powerful feelings, surprise, wonder. Most good writers prefer to let the material move the reader to provide his or her own exclamation.

When using, do not place a comma or period after the exclamation point. Place inside quotation marks if it is part of the quoted material.

Hyphen The hyphen is used (1) to join words to express a single idea or (2) to avoid confusion or ambiguity.

1. Use the hyphen to join two or more words that serve as a single adjective before a noun: *A well-known movie is on television tonight. He had a know-it-all expression.*

   Caution: Do not use the hyphen when the first word of the compound ends in *-ly* or when the words follow the noun: *She is an easily recognized person. His hair was blond black.*

2. Avoid (a) ambiguity or (b) an awkward joining of letters or syllables by putting a hyphen between prefixes or suffixes and the root word.

   a. He recovered the chair. He re-covered the chair.
   b. Re-enter, macro-economics, shell-like.

Parentheses Generally, avoid. It may be necessary for the insertion of background or to set off supplementary or illustrative material.

Use a period inside a closing parenthesis if the matter begins with a capital letter.

Period Use the period at the end of declarative sentences, indirect questions, most imperative sentences and most abbreviations. Place the period inside quotation marks.

Question mark The question mark is used for direct questions, not indirect questions.
DIRECT: Where are you going?
INDIRECT: He asked where she was going.

The question mark goes inside quotation marks if it applies to the quoted material: *He asked, "Have you seen the movie?"* Put it outside if it applies to the entire sentence: *Have you seen "Guys and Dolls"?*

Quotation marks Quotation marks set off (1) direct quotations, (2) some titles and nicknames and (3) words used in a special way.

1. Set off the exact words of the speaker: *"He walked like a duck," she said. He replied that he walked "more like an alley cat on the prowl."*

2. Use for titles of books, movies, short stories, poems, songs, articles from magazines and plays. Some nicknames take quotation marks. Do not use for nicknames of sports figures.

Terse
   "Our composing room has an unlimited supply of periods available to terminate short, simple sentences."
      —*Turner Catledge, managing editor,* The New York Times

3. For words used in a special sense: *"Indian giver" and similar phrases are considered to be ethnic slurs.*

Punctuation with quotation marks:

The comma: Use it outside the quotation marks when setting off the speaker at the beginning of a sentence: *He said, "You care too much for money."* Use inside the quotation marks when the speaker ends the sentence: *"I just want to be careful," he replied.*

The colon and semicolon: Always place outside the quotation marks: *She said she wanted no help from him: "I can handle the assignment myself." He mentioned her "incredible desire for work"; he meant her "insatiable desire for work."*

The dash, question mark and exclamation point: Place them inside when they apply to quoted matter only; outside when they refer to the whole sentence: *She asked, "How do you know so much?" Did she really wonder why he knew "so much"?*

For quotes within quotes, use a single quote mark for the inner quotation: *"Have you read 'War and Peace'?" he asked.* Note, no comma is used after the question mark.

Semicolon Usually overused by beginning reporters. Unless there is a special reason to use the semicolon, use the period.

Use the semicolon to separate a series of equal elements when the individual segments contain material that is set off by commas. This makes for clarity in the series: *She suggested that he spend his allowance on the new series at the opera, "Operas of the Present"; books of plays by Shaw, Ibsen and Aristophanes; and novels by Tolstoy, Dickens and F. Scott Fitzgerald.*

Classy

"I think one reason the critics have been slow, even up to this moment, in acknowledging me as a serious writer is that I don't use semi-colons. I never understood them. They don't really stand for anything. I think it's a way of just showing off you've been to college."

—*Kurt Vonnegut*

Credits

Name Index

Aaron, Hank, 449
ABC. *See* American Broadcasting
   Company
ABC News' *20/20*, 567
ABC's *World News Tonight,* 206
Abdul-Jabbar, Kareem, 453
"Above 125th Street: Curtis Haynes'
   New York," 265
Abrams, Judy, 166
ACLU. *See* American Civil Liberties
   Union
Acta Diurna, 61
Adams, George, 437–538
Adams, John Quincy, 161
Adams, Ruth, 437
The Adventures of Huckleberry
   Finn, 30–32, 503
Advertiser (Huntington, W. Va.), 537
Advisory Commission on
   Intergovernmental Relations, 492
The Advocate, 317
Agee, James, 266
Agnew, Spiro, 339
Akron Beacon Journal, 491
Alberts, James, 30
Alexander, Ames, 75
Alexander, Jack, 321
Alexander, Jan, 289
Ali, Muhammad, 426, 443
Alice's Adventures in Wonderland, 150
Allen, Everett, 139
Alliance Defense Fund, 481
Allman Brothers Band, 57
Almond, Steven, 267
Alterman, Eric, 571
AMA. *See* The American Medical
   Association
Ambrose, Stephen, 211, 487
American Bar Association, 90
American Broadcasting Company
   (ABC), 61, 525
American Center for Law and Justice, 481
American Civil Liberties Union
   (ACLU), 202
American Express, 541

American Family Association, 481, 543
American Farm Bureau Federation, 46
American Foundation for Suicide
   Prevention, 380
American Heritage Center, 192
The American Journal of Public
   Health, 132
American League, 433
The American Medical Association
   (AMA), 399
American Mercury, 270
The American Press and the Covering
   of the Holocaust, 256
American Public Media, 162
American Society of Newspaper Editors,
   256, 432, 531
Ames (Iowa) *Daily Tribune,* 324
"Among Women, the Talk is of
   Condoms," 538
Amsterdam News (New York), 65
Anderson, Gloria Brown, 508
Anderson, Jack, 306
Anderson, Paul Y., 342, 564
Anderson, Walter, 49
Andresen, Jack, 358
Andrews, Caesar, 37
Andrews, Edmund L., 242
Andrews, Peter, 436
Angell, Roger, 444
Angelou, Maya, 503
Annenberg School for
   Communications, 160
The Anniston (Ala.) *Star,* 75, 174,
   241, 488, 491
Anonymous, 168
Antonen, Mel, 315
AP. *See* Associated Press
Applewhite, Scott, 235
Arcaro, Eddie, 299
Argus Leader (Sioux Falls, S.D.), 9, 11,
   64–65, 74, 364, 388, 506, 507
Aristophanes, 173, 271
The Arizona Republic, 136
Arkansas Democrat-Gazette, 226
The Arkansas Gazette, 515

Armour, Stephanie, 137
Army Signal Corps, 167
Arnold, Benedict, 74
The Art of Scientific Investigation, 251
Asbury (N.J.) *Park Sunday Press,* 496
Ashbury (N.J.) *Park Press,* 427
Associated Press (AP), 6, 8, 9, 12, 13,
   14, 16, 23, 26, 27–28, 33, 41, 44, 50,
   81, 92, 118, 119, 136, 144, 147, 173,
   184, 190, 194, 197, 235, 243, 253,
   273, 283, 290, 298, 325, 359, 373,
   378, 408, 420, 436, 446, 458–459,
   521, 533, 534, 537, 545, 547
Associated Press v. Walker, 521
The Atlanta Business Chronicle, 67
Atlanta Constitution, 162, 290
Atlanta Journal, 537
The Atlanta Journal-Constitution,
   53, 80, 93, 225, 393, 459, 519
The Atlantic Monthly, 29, 280, 300, 320
AT&T, 339
Attention Deficit Disorder Forums
   Web site, 88
Atwood, Margaret, 326
Auburn Tigers, 433
Auden, W.H., 569
Austin (Tex.) *American-Statesman,*
   240, 487
Avery, Mark, 239
Ayers, H. Brandt, 75
azcentral.com, 4

Babel, Isaac, 163
Bacsik, Mike, 440
Bagdikian, Ben, 75
Bailey, Donovan, 320
Baker, Ray Stannard, 563–564
Baker, Russell, 73, 234, 280, 284, 441
The Bakersfield Californian, 546–547
Baldwin, James, 567
The Baltimore Sun, 147, 173, 318
Bandic, Darko, 545
Banks, Jack, 346
Baquet, Dean, 24
Barber, Red, 448
Barlett, Donald, 191, 289

599

Subject Index